Shamanism

Shamanism has been practised among communities all over the world for millennia, and continues to survive today in both modern and traditional forms. During its long evolution, it has migrated from Siberia, Aboriginal Australia, Northern Europe and South America to become a core part of western New Age and rave culture as well as of popular mythology. Its place within modernity is at once familiar and alien, exemplary and uneasy. So how does the fantastical image of the shaman influence debates on identity, experience, nature, rationality, the cosmos, transformation and change?

Shamanism: A Reader unites perspectives from disciplines including anthropology, psychology, musicology and botany to provide a unique overview of modern understandings of shamanism. From grassroots political writing to classic ethnographies, and imagined narratives to detailed case studies, the 25 articles and short extracts presented here cover topics including gender, initiation, hallucinogenic consciousness, possession and political protest. Juxtaposing the traditional practices of indigenous peoples with their new and often radically urban reinterpretations, experts including Michael Harner, Mihály Hoppál, Marjorie M. Balzer and Piers Vitebsky raise questions about constructions of shamanism, its efficacy, its use and misuse as a cultural symbol, and its real nature.

Locating its material in the encounter between traditional and contemporary, and within the many forms of response to the image of the shaman, *Shamanism: A Reader* is an essential tribute to the vitality and breadth of shamanic tradition both among its original practitioners of Europe, America and Asia, and within seemingly familiar aspects of the modern west. Representing the best of classic and current scholarship, and highlighting the diversity of approaches to shamanism in an accessible and user-friendly way, this clearly introduced and organised collection sets a new standard for shamanic study in terms of the breadth and depth of its coverage.

Graham Harvey is Reader in Religious Studies at King Alfred's College, Winchester. He has written widely on paganism and indigenous and minority religions, and is the author of *Contemporary Paganism: Listening People, Speaking Earth* (2000), as well as editor of *Indigenous Religions: A Companion* (2000).

Shamanism

A Reader

Edited by

Graham Harvey

 Routledge
Taylor & Francis Group

LONDON AND NEW YORK

First published 2003
by Routledge
2 Park Square, Milton Park, Abingdon, Oxon, OX14 4RN

Simultaneously published in the USA and Canada
by Routledge
270 Madison Ave, New York NY 10016

Routledge is an imprint of the Taylor & Francis Group

Transferred to Digital Printing 2010

© 2003 Graham Harvey for selection and editorial material

Typeset in Times by RefineCatch Ltd, Bungay, Suffolk

British Library Cataloguing in Publication Data
A catalogue record for this book is available from the British Library

Library of Congress Cataloging in Publication Data
A catalogue record for this book has been requested

ISBN 0–415–25329–2 (hbk)
ISBN 0–415–25330–6 (pbk)

Contents

Contributors

Marjorie Mandelstam Balzer is Professor in the Center for Eurasian, Russian, and East European Studies at Georgetown University, Washington, DC. Her research is in social theory, inter-ethnic relations, religion, the growth of nationalism, and anthropology of the Russian Federation. Her publications include important works on Siberian and Central Asian shamanisms.

Beverley Butler lectures in Cultural Heritage and Museum Studies at the University College, London. Her interests include a Peace Museum project in relation to modernity and post-modernity, and theories of gender and identity. She is researching themes of heritage revivalism, urban regeneration and contemporary memory-work in Alexandria, Egypt.

Alan T. Campbell was until recently lecturer in Social Anthropology at Edinburgh University. He has been involved with the Wayapí people of Amazonia since 1974 and been inspired by that involvement to contribute significantly to important debates in anthropological theory.

Chungmoo Choi teaches politics of culture, colonial/postcolonial issues, and gender and sexuality in East Asia at the University of California, Irvine. In addition to interests in the aesthetic dimensions of urban shamanising, she engages with issues of post-colonialism and nationalism in South Korea.

Ward Churchill is Professor in Ethnic Studies at the University of Colorado. His many publications focus on contemporary indigeneity, and particularly on Native American identities, interests, situations and concerns. He has insightfully encouraged radical engagement with anti-colonial discourses and practices.

Sereptie Djarvoskin was a Nganasani or Tavgi Samoyed of Siberia. His account of his initiation as a shaman was told to Andrei Popov some twenty years after the event and has been published and reprinted in a number of texts, including Joan Halifax's collection, *Shamanic Voices*.

Thomas A. Dowson of the University of Manchester has published extensively on the rock arts of Southern Africa, North America and Western Europe. He is also interested in archaeological approaches to art, popular representation of ancient and prehistoric artistic traditions, and the impact of sexual politics on archaeology.

John A. Grim is a Professor in the Department of Religion at Bucknell University. He undertakes annual field studies in American Indian lifeways among the Apsaalooke/Crow peoples of Montana and the Swy-ahl-puh/Salish peoples of the Columbia River Plateau in eastern Washington. He and his wife, Mary Evelyn Tucker, are central to Harvard University's Religions of the World and Ecology conference and publication series.

Roberte N. Hamayon is Professor at the Department of Religious Sciences of the Sorbonne's École Pratique des Hautes Études, Paris. She has published important books and articles about Siberian and Mongolian shamans, shamanic societies and related issues.

Michael Harner is Founder and President of The Foundation for Shamanic Studies. Following distinguished anthropological research (beginning in 1956 among the Jívaro in Ecuador) and teaching in prestigious universities, he has pioneered the teaching and practice of 'Core Shamanism'.

Graham Harvey is Reader in Religious Studies at King Alfred's College, Winchester. His research and teaching interests include Jewish, pagan and indigenous self-identities, discourses and performances.

Mihály Hoppál of the Ethnographic Institute of the Hungarian Academy of Sciences in Budapest is a prolific researcher and writer about shamans and shamanism. His wide interests include shamanic worldviews and lifeways in many places, but especially in Eurasia (Siberia and Hungary in particular), art, initiation, folk customs, and ongoing revivals following the demise of the USSR.

Caroline Humphrey is Professor at King's College, Cambridge. She has carried out research in Siberia and Mongolia in the Soviet and post-Soviet periods, and also in India, Nepal, Inner Mongolia and Manchuria. Her research interests include shamanism, theories of ritual, and socialist/post-socialist economy and society.

Sandra Ingerman is a leading practitioner of soul retrieval and conducts workshops around the world. Following a Master's degree in counselling psychology from the California Institute of Integral Studies, she has been a significant member of Michael Harner's Foundation for Shamanic Studies.

Paul C. Johnson is Assistant Professor in the Department of Religious Studies at the University of Missouri, Columbia. His work has focused on Brazilian Candomblé and its transformation from an indigenous, secret religion into a national and public one; on the Garifuna of the Caribbean and the impact of migration on indigenous religion practised in the homeland; and on social theory and category-formation in the study of religion.

Ioan M. Lewis is Emeritus Professor of Anthropology at the London School of Economics. His research interests and publications include shamanism, spirit possession, ecstatic cults and religious syncretism in Africa, with special reference to Somalia, and peace-making and local government in Somalia.

Urgunge Onon is the General Manager, Mongolia and Inner Asia Studies Unit, Cambridge University. His collaboration with Caroline Humphrey included dialogue and reflection about his Daur Mongol origins and about wider Mongolian concerns.

Gordon MacLellan is one of Britain's leading environmental educators. He runs 'Creeping Toad' which works with children and adults in museums, countryside parks and other locations to encourage richer engagements with and celebrations of the world that surrounds people, utilising drama, dance, science and enchantment.

Terence McKenna was a lifelong researcher into 'shamanology' and is best known for his provocative advocacy of the notion that psychedelic plants and experiences play an important role in human cultural and biological evolution. After a decade of considerable fame, he died in 2000.

Marina Roseman is Professor at Pacifica Graduate Institute, Carpinteria, California. She is a specialist in ethnomusicology, dance ethnology, medical anthropology, psychological anthropology, and anthropology of the arts, and has conducted research in Indonesia, Malaysia, and among Asian and Hispanic populations in the United States.

Bernard Saladin d'Anglure is Professor of Anthropology of Laval University, Quebec. He is an internationally acknowledged expert in the field of Arctic studies and comparative studies on shamanism. His interests include research among the Canadian Inuit, the Peruvian Shipibo and the Siberian Chukchi and Yukaghir.

Michael Taussig is Professor of Anthropology at Columbia University. He has written powerful, provocative and insightful works on diverse subjects — including economics, slavery, fetishism, shamanism, colonialism, state and paramilitary terror, mimesis, alterity, transgression, magic and secrecy — springing largely from fieldwork in Colombia since 1969.

Barbara Tedlock is Professor of Anthropology at the State University of New York at Buffalo. Her interests span the visual and performing arts, psychology, religion and astronomy of the ancient and modern indigenous peoples of the Americas. She is perhaps best known for her publications about Maya worldviews.

Edith Turner of the University of Virginia is a symbolic anthropologist. Her interests include humanistic anthropology, the experiential roots of ritual, healing, shamanism, spirits and power, rites of passage, festivals. These have resulted in important publications about Ndembu ritual, Inupiat healing, and Irish women's experiences of spirit and energy.

Piers Vitebsky is a key figure in the Scott Polar Research Institute, University of Cambridge. His fieldwork has taken place in tribal India, Sri Lanka and Siberia. His publications provide invaluable overviews of shamanic phenomena and detailed engagements with various of the local lived realities in which shamans are embedded.

Robert J. Wallis is Lecturer in Archaeology, and co-ordinator of the MA Rock Art, at Southampton University. His research interests include the interpretation and socio-political contexts of archaeological and indigenous (particularly shamanistic) arts; the representation of the past, specifically 'alternative archaeology', narratives by neo-shamans, and their implications for heritage management.

Acknowledgements

The author and publishers wish to thank the following for their permission to reproduce copyright material.

Andrei A. Popov, "How Sereptie Djarvoskin of the Nganasans (Tavgi Samoyeds) became a Shaman' from *Popular Beliefs and Folklore Tradition in Siberia* pp. 137–46 (trans. Stephen P. Dunn, ed. Vimos Dioszegi) (Bloomington: Indiana University Press, 1968, copyright Akadémiai Kiadó);

Michael Harner, *The Way of the Shaman*, copyright © 1980 by Michael Harner, reprinted by permission of HarperCollins Publishers, Inc.;

Roberte N. Hamayon, 'Game and games, fortune and dualism in Siberian shamanism', from *Shamanism and Northern Ecology* (ed. J. Pentikainen) pp. 62–6 (New York: Mouton de Gruyter, 1996);

I.M. Lewis, *Ecstatic Religion: A Study of Shamanism and Spirit Possession*, 134–59 (London: Routledge, 1989);

John A. Grim, *The Shaman: Patterns of Religious Healing Among the Ojibway Indians*, pp. 65–7, 106–13, 124–9 (The University of Oklahoma Press, Norman, 1983);

B. Tedlock, 'The New Anthropology of Dreaming', *Dreaming* 1:161–78 (1991);

A.T. Campbell, *Getting to Know Wai Wai* pp. 185–210 (Routledge, London, 1995);

Edith Turner, 'The Reality of Spirits', *ReVision* 15(1):28–32, (1992);

T.A. Dowson, 'Like people in prehistory', *World Archaeology* 29(3):333–43 (1998);

Choi Chungmoo, 'The Artistry and Ritual Aesthetics of Urban Korean Shamans', *Journal of Ritual Studies* 3(2):235–49 (1989);

Marina Roseman, 'Remembering to Forget', from *Healing Sounds from the Malaysian Rainforest* pp. 151–73 (Berkeley: University of California Press, 1993) Copyright © 1991 the Regents of the University of California;

M. Hoppál, 'Ethnographic Films on Shamanism', from *Studies on Shamanism* (eds A.L. Siikala and M. Hoppál) pp. 182–96 (Akadémiaia Kiadó, Budapest: Finnish Anthropological Society, 1992);

C. Humphrey, and Urgunge Onon, *Shamans and Elders: Experience, Knowledge and Power among the Daur Mongols* pp. 357–64 (Oxford: Oxford University Press, 1996);

Bernard Saladin d'Anglure, 'Rethinking Inuit Shamanism through the concept of third gender', from *Northern Religions and Shamanism* (Akadémiai Kiadó, Budapest, 1992);

M.M. Balzer, 'Sacred Genders in Siberia', from *Reversals and Gender Cultures* (ed. S.P. Ramet) pp. 164–82 (London: Routledge, 1996);

M. Taussig, *Shamanism, Colonialism and the Wild Man: A Study in Terror and Healing*, pp. 342–57 (Chicago: The University of Chicago Press, 1987);

P. Vitebsky, 'From cosmology to environmentalism as local knowledge in a global setting', from *Counterworks: Managing the Diversity of Knowledge* (ed. R. Fardon) pp. 182–203 (London: Routledge, 1995);

M.M. Balzer, 'The Poetry of Shamanism', from *Shamanism in the Performing Arts* pp. 171–87 (Budapest: Akadémiai Kiadó, 1995);

Ward Churchill, 'Spiritual Hucksterism: the Rise of the Plastic Medicine Men', in *Fantasies of the Master Race* pp. 215–28 (Monroe: Common Courage Press, 1992);

Paul C. Johnson, 'Shamanism from Ecuador to Chicago: A Case Study in New Age Ritual Appropriation', *Religion* 25:163–78 (1995);

Sandra Ingerman, *Soul Retrieval: Mending the Fragmented Self* copyright © 1991 by Sandra Ingerman, pp. 47–60 reprinted by permission of HarperCollins Publishers, Inc.;

Gordon MacLellan, 'Dancing on the Edge: Shamanism in Modern Britain', from *Paganism Today* (eds Graham Harvey and Charlotte Hardman) pp. 138–48 (London: Thorsons, 1996), Copyright (c) 1996 Gordon MacLellan. Reprinted by permission of HarperCollins Publishers Inc.;

Beverley Butler, 'The tree, the tower and the shaman: the material culture of resistance of the No. M11 Link Roads Protest of Wanstead and Leytonstone', *Journal of Material Culture* 1(3):337–363 1996, reprinted by permission of Sage Publications, London;

R.W. Wallis, 'Waking ancestor spirits: neo-shamanic engagements with archaeology', from *The Archaeology of Shamanism* (ed. N. Price) pp. 213–30 (London: Routledge, 2001);

Terence McKenna, *Food of the Gods*, published by Rider. Printed by permission of The Random House Group Limited, pp. 223–45.

Producing any book is a communal effort, Readers especially so. I am grateful to the authors and publishers of all the works included for their permission to reprint. I am grateful, too, that these works have been published in the first place. Many of them occur in books of considerable importance, and deserve fuller attention. The original authors have probably already expressed gratitude to those whose lives they have been involved in, but I wish to add my thanks for that collaboration in exchanging knowledges.

Considerable thanks to Roger Thorp, Julene Knox, Clare Johnson and their team at Routledge. Special thanks to Susan Dunsmore with whom it has been a pleasure to work on this and a previous book.

Two expert readers provided excellent suggestions for structuring this set of Readings, and some very good ideas about contents. I am grateful to Robert Wallis for similar suggestions about contents, and even more for careful reading and insightful critiques of an earlier draft of the General Introduction. Hopefully I have clarified my thoughts about performance so as not to appear reductionist, but I have left the complex discussion of sacramental or inspirational plant substances to someone more capable than myself – probably Robert! Hope it makes us all giddy.

Ronald Hutton's book, *Shamans: Siberian Spirituality and the Western Imagination* (London and New York: Hambledon and London, 2001) arrived too late for me to incorporate into my discussion. It deserves high praise and wide reading, and contributes significantly to the study of shamans and understandings of them.

Most importantly, however, it is my wife, Molly, who deserves greatest thanks. Her greatest contribution to this work (and everything else I have written) is her influence on my thoughts, ideas, approaches, passions and obsessions.

Of course, I am responsible for any weaknesses in what follows. Clearly other people would have chosen a different selection of material, and would have said different things about them. Happily, this is not the last word on the matter, the debate continues!

Graham Harvey
Winchester
April 2002

GENERAL INTRODUCTION

IN THE LANGUAGE OF TUNGUS-SPEAKING PEOPLES of Siberia, shaman (pronounced *sharmarn*) refers to a communal leader chosen and trained to work for the community by engaging with significant other-than-human persons. The methods by which such people are chosen and trained, and the ways in which they fulfil their roles, are of considerable interest to academics in many disciplines (including anthropology, archaeology, gender studies, history, performance studies, psychology, and religious studies). Such interest has overflowed into the wider community, so that shamans are of considerable popular interest too. Thus, the word shaman has become part of languages outside Siberia. The title is now used to refer to communal leaders and religious practitioners who might otherwise be called by very different, more local names, such as *bomoh, yadgan, mudang, angakoq,* or referred to only adjectively as, for example, *paye* people. At the same time, some words that *might* otherwise be translated as shaman are instead rendered as 'witch doctors', 'medicine men', 'magicians', 'conjurers' or even 'jugglers'. Last, but not least, shaman also refers to practitioners within various therapeutic, spiritual and cultural movements in 'the West'.

The above paragraph is intended to be provocative rather than definitive, opening rather than closing a wide-ranging debate. Almost every assertion is contestable, arguable, controversial and certainly in need of explanation, expansion, and some equivocation! If they are not treated in these ways, many of the opening claims are potentially misleading. Two topics may help us begin to challenge and clarify matters: first, the implication of the use of the word shaman outside of Siberia; and, second, the relevance of asserting that shaman is a Tungus word.

The fact that such a wide range of people are called shamans suggests at least two significant things. First, there might be identifiable similarities between people (individuals or groups) in many places that make them worth comparing. There will be considerable discussion of what may be compared, and of what process of comparison is helpful. If we compare we may eventually have to conclude that it is more appropriate to contrast: some 'shamans' are in fact something else. Second, speakers of some languages previously lacked a concept like *shaman* either because they had never encountered people who acted in these ways or because they had not noticed such people. There are plenty of other loan words that illustrate these and other possibilities. For example, the adoption of Polynesian words like *tabu* and *mana* into European languages permitted discussion of social processes that were certainly prevalent in European societies prior to the adoption of the words. Of course it might be countered that what particular Polynesians meant – and continue to mean – by *tabu* or *mana* is not at all what Europeans (academics or otherwise) might mean. Or consider the French adoption of *le weekend*. Does the adoption of the word mean that French culture had changed or that the French had not previously noticed that two days every week were distinctive in some way? Consideration of the use of an originally Tungus title is part of a process of more-or-less critical reflection on various knowledges and systems of knowledge.

But *is* shaman a Tungus word or is it now an English (or French, German, Hungarian or Russian) word? Are the only real shamans those found among Tungus speakers? Is what Tungus speakers mean when they say 'shaman' necessarily definitive? Or has the word now become part of a new vocabulary where it carries additional associations and implications?

So what is it that we are discussing? Who are shamans? What do they do? How do people become shamans? How do people recognise shamans? Is a Malay *bomoh* really a shaman? Are shamans really different to priests? The purpose of this book is not to end debates about these and other issues. It is to illustrate and further debate. Its purpose is certainly not to take all the many things that shaman might mean and synthesise them into one neat and tidy definition. It is to indicate the range of interesting subjects relevant to a continuing engagement with whatever possibilities shaman suggests. Its purpose is comparative in the sense that various analytical and critical positions are compared. Particular chapters compare 'true' shamans with other kinds, or shamans with priests, or shamanic performance with other kinds, or shamanic consciousness with other kinds. Such comparative chapters are included here because these are issues that have interested, intrigued or obsessed scholars, practitioners and other interested persons. They contribute to the chief purposes of this set of readings as provocative arguments rather than final conclusions. These are to illustrate the diversity of interests constellating around shamans and their engagements; and to clarify the points at which such interests might contribute to debates about wider critical issues.

In this light, the opening sentence is thoroughly misleading. If shaman is only a Tungus word a vast quantity of paper and breath has been wasted expounding and repeating irrelevancies. In fact, shaman is now part of various other languages, especially as a more-or-less technical term in various academic vocabularies. Beyond illustrating what people say about shamans and their pursuits and communities, academia is continuously engaged in attempting to refine understanding and usage of its critical terms. This is not to say that general and popular readers (including those who are, or wish to be, shamans) will not find much of value here. Popular uses of the word shaman (in Siberia as in England or the Americas or elsewhere) are in continuous dialogue with academic uses – and vice versa – all affecting other uses. Reference to a dictionary definition might illustrate some of the problems and the potential.

Dictionary definition

Chambers 20th Century Dictionary (Kirkpatrick 1983) defined shaman as follows:

> **Shaman** *shäm'an, –∂n, n.* a doctor-priest working by magic primarily of N. Asia: – *pl.* **shamans.** – Also *adj.* – *adj.* **shamanic** (*–an'*). – *ns.* **Shamanism** (also without *cap.*) the religion of N. Asia, based essentially on magic and sorcery; **shamanist.** – *adj.* **shamanistic.** [Russ., – Tungus.]

By 1983 very few people could have been happy with the apparently straightforward use of words like magic and sorcery, implying as they do in this definition that shamans are only improperly considered to be either doctors or priests. What should we understand to be the difference between magic and sorcery? But what, anyway, would it mean for any kind of priest or doctor (let alone a doctor-priest) to 'work by magic'? It is unlikely that the framer of this definition intended readers to think of Catholic mission priest-doctors, for example, and far more likely that they were implying 'witch-doctors' and drawing on European constructions of indigeneity as primitive savagery. Such fantasies would now seem outmoded were it not for their seductive power among film-makers and viewers. What hope is there, if the dictionary is to be believed, of appreciating any rationality among people who must be deluded if they think 'magic and sorcery' are modes of religion and healing? Since such activities must be illusory and ineffective (except by accident or as placebos) it is presumably implicit that shamans are outmoded and certain to give way to more efficient kinds of healers and leaders, i.e. scientific ones.

It is also interesting that the dictionary insists that 'shamanism' is 'the religion of N. Asia'. Not only does this ignore the presence of Buddhism, Islam, Christianity and other religions in North Asia, it also resists the notion that 'shamanism' occurs in many other regions of the world. It does so despite its extrapolation from the existence of shamans to an organised system, an -ism, to which they and their communities adhere. (Of course, for example, Buddh*ism* is also a reification constructed from disparate lifeways and worldviews.) Thus there are people who are 'shamanist' by some standard of affiliation, affirm-ation, belief or behaviour. Is it significant that shamans are alleged to 'work by magic' while shamanism is 'based essentially on magic and sorcery'? What is the difference between shamans and their communities? Does everyone engage in similar practices, with the shaman as the first among equals or the prima donna, or is it that the community *believes* in their shaman's magic and sorcery? Can anyone encounter powerful helpers or are such persons to be avoided except by carefully trained and experienced authorities?

In short, this definition does not work in the way it was probably intended. Conversely, it serves as an excellent short note on constructions of shamans, shamanic activities and communities and of notions of indigeneity and religion. It tells us little about shamans themselves and much about the making, remaking and reinforcing of modernity and its alterities. It is not, therefore, valueless. But it pays out in a currency that may not be convertible into a kind that permits access to better understanding of shamans and, perhaps, shamanism.

Defining religion

In order to gain a clearer understanding of the problems of defining 'shaman' it may be useful to explore another word that has currency in both popular and academic discourse: 'religion'. Both 'shaman' and 'religion' mean a host of things, some of them comparable, some overlapping, but not a few are contra-dictory. Even more to the point, both words can be defined in many ways. An unfortunate conclusion can be drawn from such broad possibilities. Jonathan Z. Smith writes

> It was once a tactic of students of religion to cite the appendix of James H. Leuba's *Psychological Study of Religion* (1912), which lists more than fifty definitions of religion, to demonstrate that 'the effort to define religion in short compass is a hopeless task' (King 1954). Not at all! The moral of Leuba is not that religion cannot be defined, but that it can be defined, with greater or lesser success, more than fifty ways.

> (1998: 281)

Smith concludes that 'religion' is 'not a native term' but one 'created by scholars for their intellectual purposes and therefore it is theirs to define'. It might, of course, be better to say that 'religion' *is* a native term in some languages, but that in academic discourse it carries particular associations and implications.

Or, that one of the contexts in which religion is a 'native term' is in the language of the critical, academic study of religions.

This certainly does not tell us what the word *means*, indeed, it certainly implies that the term is open to debate and questioning. There will continue to be a contest between competing understandings and uses, and this needs to be appreciated and made explicit if confusion is to be avoided. Certainly, there are academics who think they might be able to say or write the last word, to define a term or explain a process absolutely and finally. However, academia is best appreciated as a continuous process of debate, clarification, questioning, refinement, and sometimes perhaps even outright reversal and rejection of previous 'knowledge'. Diversity of understanding is of the essence in academia.

Shaman is a word very much like religion. Some people are certain that it must only be defined as a Tungus title for particular kinds of people. Often such assertions lead to further claims that particular approaches (e.g., psychological or sociological, sceptical or experiential) alone are able to tell us what is important about shamans. The label for such approaches is reductionist or essentialist, which need not mean that such rhetoric is without value, but it is certainly insufficient and inadequate. For example, even someone who is convinced that shamanism (if there is such a thing) is an entirely psychological experience (if anyone is so convinced) might gain much from exploring the sociological dimensions of an individual's participation in wider society. Taking shaman and shamanism to be academic terms does not make them easier to define in short, pithy terms. On the contrary, it requires willingness to consider the terms' open-endedness in some contexts and their particularity in others. It will certainly entail arguments about the inclusion and/or exclusion of some phenomena that might elsewhere be considered relevant. The point of this set of readings is to explore examples of what has been and can be said about an issue and provide resources for readers to reflect on ways to refine understanding and knowledge.

Discussing indigeneity

Shamans were first noticed by academics among indigenous peoples. Actually, to be precise, shamans were first noticed by academics in the writings and reports of travellers and traders who had visited among indigenous peoples. In fact, some such writings and reports were based on rumours and fantasies picked up from yet other travellers (Narby and Huxley, 2001, provide valuable examples of these processes). At any rate, indigeneity became a key element of academic definitions of shamanism. Recently the label 'neo-shaman' has been used to vilify those who claim to be shamans, or to practise shamanism, without being indigenous. Of course, this misses the point that Western and academic rather than indigenous people invented shamanism – albeit from indigenous resources. To put this another way, academia is as implicated as popular religious movements in the colonial process of appropriation and reification. Apart from anything else, such histories and diatribes point us towards consideration of the necessity of varying constructions of indigeneity. To be clear about this, it is not only that some writers essentialise indigeneity while others project their own fantasies, fears or theories on to it. That is, to say that indigeneity is constructed is not to state that this is necessarily a negative process or that it is avoidable. Quite the opposite, realising that construction is a continuous process engaged in by all concerned – including Tungus shamans – may help us realise that this is an ordinary, everyday and (probably) universal process. All identities are negotiated – especially (if we are to learn anything from indigenous shamans!) because identities are relational. All such negotiated constructions say something about matters of great interest. Therefore, it may be helpful to consider some notions about indigeneity that may help or hinder engagement with whatever shamanism might be. The following discussion introduces debates about diversity and similarity; community, tradition, boundedness and integration; subsistence; and spirituality.

It is difficult to achieve an appropriate balance between lumping all indigenous peoples together as if they were essentially the same and atomising them into entirely dissimilar 'tribal' groups. Neither of these positions is factually accurate: there are considerable differences even among neighbouring peoples, but there are also significant commonalities among evidently different peoples. A similar point is made in another explication of the use (and utility) of the term 'indigenous': 'diversity and particularity are a paradoxical form of commonality between peoples who otherwise would be united only as subjects/objects of colonisation' (Ralls-MacLeod and Harvey 2001, 4–6). The point here is that it is necessary to be careful not to generalise too far and to be clear who is being spoken about. Indigeneity is another academic term and should not be used to mask the diversity of lifeways and worldviews that might be labelled in this way. Thus, it might be that 'shaman' usefully points to widespread commonalities among indigenous peoples but that we need to speak about particular shamans (e.g. those who are Tungus or Daur Mongol or Hungarian or Jivaro) rather than implying that all shamans are alike.

There is a widespread notion that indigenous communities are more communal and traditional than modern Western societies. Commonly, indigeneity is made to serve as the opposite of the allegedly alienated, individualistic, anonymous and purposeless world of consumerist modernity (or its late- or postmodern inheritors). Or, indigenous people supposedly dwell happily within secure borders in places known to countless generations of their ancestors, whereas Euro-Americans (for example) are supposedly ever mobile and generally distant from the burial places of even recent ancestors (for whom they have little or no concern). Two examples from many might begin to blur these too-neat images. First, the regularity with which many indigenous peoples narrate their origins and tradition in self-motivated migrations from elsewhere. Second, the annual mass movement of Euro- and other Americans 'home' to

celebrate Thanksgiving. Notions of home, sacred place, belonging, family, ancestry, and tradition are implicated in these images (see Thompson 2001). But
there is more. Indigenous shamans might typically live in small villages and
know everyone in their communities (not unlike rural parish priests perhaps),
but much of what shamans do is the result of divided communities. Even if
shamans *might* restore *communitas* (Turner 1991), they do not do so permanently, and the fact that they need to do it demonstrates the fragility of social
cohesion and neighbourliness even in small communities. The fact that shamans
do not do themselves out of a job (at least, not by increasing sociality) demonstrates that small-scale indigenous societies can be as divided and conflictual as
urban ones. Furthermore, since shamans are not the only leaders, and 'shamanists' (if that is a useful term) are not the only religionists, in their communities –
and since shamans and shamanists might also be Buddhists or Catholics or
politicians or other things too – it must be clear, at least, that diversity is of the
essence.

Indigenous people subsist (and did so before the disruptions of colonialism)
by many means. These include farming, foraging, herding, hunting, and trading
surplus and manufactured goods. There is a common notion that true shamans
only exist in hunter–gatherer communities – or that 'the original shamanism'
arose in hunter–gatherer cultures. There is an elegance about such claims, but
they are hard to sustain without defining shamans in increasingly cumbersome
ways. If shamans are people who heal with the help of significant other-than-
human persons communicated with while in trance (whatever these terms
mean), then it is demonstrable that such roles are not only known among
hunter–gatherers. However, it is sometimes theorised that shamans *originally*
concerned themselves with hunting matters: the location of game and the (spiritual?) results of taking life. Healing became necessary because illness was
understood to be the result of inappropriate behaviour towards hunted animals.
Such shamans repair breaches of etiquette and their results: loss of prey and of
health. Others see healing as only becoming a shamanic role when societies
became less reliant on hunting because they had domesticated herd animals or
had settled down to farm. Contained within such discourse is the notion that
hunting-and-gathering is a simple mode of subsistence, requiring basic technologies, and engaged in by people with a simple culture. A classic expression of
the idea is Marx's association of 'simple technology' with 'simple minds' (Marx
1965). Not only have there been significant challenges to these constructions
(surveyed, e.g., in Ingold 1994, Riches 1996, Rapport and Overing 2000) but,
also, the link between shamans and this one mode of subsistence is questionable.
There *are* shamans in agricultural and industrial societies. The bald assertion
that hunting was important in the period at which shamanism arose in what are
now agricultural or industrial societies provides no licence to claim that only the
original shamanism is pure and definitive. We need not follow Eliade's (1964)
categorisation of 'pure' and 'degenerate' shamans, especially since it is based on
his insistent fitting of evidence into a pre-existing theological and evolutionary

schema. Interesting as his work is, it is an exercise in the creation of a previously unknown system, one more -ism, selectively utilising examples of the various actual engagements of shamans. If 'indigeneity is communal' tends to fix people in place, concepts of hunter–gatherer societies tend to fix people in time (albeit a fictional archaic era).

The challenge by Mary Douglas (1975) to the 'myth of primitive piety' raises the suspicion that indigeneity and shamans interest Western travellers, observers and seekers because they are considered spiritual. Similarly, Lerner (1995) proffers an invaluable discussion of the secularity of at least some indigenous engagements with the world. Early in Europe's colonising expansion its ideologues asserted that 'natives' elsewhere were savages inhabiting but not owning wildernesses that needed subjugation and civilisation. More recently, various indigenous peoples have been perceived as protectors of rich environments. In both views indigeneity is constructed as 'natural', but the evaluation of 'wilderness' has radically altered. What was once alien and inhuman and therefore bad is now autonomous, diverse and therefore good. In relation to whatever 'nature' might mean, indigenous people who were bad when nature was bad have become good as nature has become good. The bad of the past was considered demonic, the good of the present is considered ecological and spiritual. 'Spiritual', however, is often another mystification that ignores or is irritated by real life.

In response to a question about what 'respecting salmon' might mean, a Native American friend replied, 'I like the taste of smoked salmon'. Far from being a misunderstanding of the question, or a prosaic introduction to a description of ceremonies in which respectful offerings are made, this is the heart of the matter. Its appropriateness might be seen in contrast to the disrespect shown if one did not enjoy eating a salmon whose life has been taken/given. Humanity's primary relationship with the world is literally that of consumers. Awareness of this fact grounds its sometimes ceremonial celebration (such as salmon return rituals) in the careful tending, respectful killing and the pleasurable eating of those who are, in this context, food. It is all too easy to be distracted by what appears exotic from the perspective of another culture (ceremonies or the wearing of feathers or of suits). Shamans apparently do strange things, but perhaps their pursuit is not of 'spirituality' but rather a quest for the fulfilment of basic desires for sustenance, health and prosperity. That they also quest for knowledge about acquiring the means of satisfying those desires should not misdirect us from seeing the possibility of the secularity of their actions. Salmon ceremonies and salmon respecting are about eating salmon, not about communing with symbols of transcendence.

Other-than-human persons

The opening paragraph asserted that shamans engage with significant other-than-human persons. What makes this seemingly cumbersome term preferable to the apparent simplicity of the word 'spirit'? Above all, it is arguable that 'spirit' unhelpfully mystifies matters. Also, the possibility that no one term is adequate to the tasks assigned it reveals important diversities of understanding, engagement, practice, cosmology and more. Conversely, although the phrase 'other-than-human persons' does not define who such persons might be, it does allow us to speak more carefully of the diversities that become increasingly apparent once we pay attention to what 'spirits' might mean or mystify.

It is commonly asserted that shamans relate to 'spirits' in one way or another. Indeed, there is an almost continuous conflict between those who think shamans are, by definition, people who control spirits (or think they do) and those who think shamans are, at least sometimes, controlled by spirits. This is related to an alleged opposition between trance and possession. (For particular nuances of these debates see, for example, Bourguignon 1976; Holm 1982; de Heusch 1982; Rouget 1987; Lewis 1989 and 1999; Kehoe 2000; and various chapters in Howard 1998.) However, these debates about whatever psychological and/or sociological processes might be central to shamans, rarely explain what is meant by 'spirit'. At best, a spirit appears to be a being rarely seen except by shamans. Or it might refer to beings 'believed in' by shamans and their communities. Sometimes it seems to be used to sidestep saying (or perhaps recognising) difficult notions such as that !Kung ceremonies attempt to banish creator deities rather than 'evil spirits' (compare Platvoet 2001, with Marshall 1962). Generally, perhaps, 'spirit' might be taken to mean metaphysical entities alleged to be responsible for the presence or absence of animals, health, sickness or enemies. But, if the actions of these 'spirits' result in very real, this worldly, mundane, tactile, empirical matters (according to the canons of Western science), few academics are willing to profess acceptance of their reality. Strangely, those who are willing to endlessly argue about the meaning and applicability of 'shaman' often refer to 'spirits' as if everyone knows what the word means, as if the word were self-evidently universally understood, and the beings universally experienced. Sometimes 'spirit' even appears in contexts that do not actually require the use of the word at all, and only rarely are indigenous (or other native or insider) terms offered that *must* be translated as spirit. More commonly, a plain reading of indigenous and especially shamanic discourses suggests that 'spirit' is nothing less than a mystification contrived by sceptical outsiders. When the term is not redundant it might more adequately and simply be rendered as 'person', 'rock', 'helper' or something else entirely. When shamanic informants do use words that have no translation equivalent in academic or other languages it may be better to introduce the indigenous term (as happens with shaman) than to use 'spirits' as if it were transparently meaningful.

A. Irving Hallowell coined the phrase 'other-than-human persons' in dialogue with Ojibwe/Anishinaabeg of Berens River, Manitoba. He explains the need for the phrase by noting that:

> in the social sciences and psychology, 'persons' and human beings are categorically identified. This identification is inherent in the concept of 'society' and 'social relations.' In Warren's *Dictionary of Psychology* 'person' is defined as 'a human organism regarded as having distinctive characteristics and social relations.' The same identification is implicit in the conceptualization and investigation of social organization by anthropologists. Yet this obviously involves a radical abstraction if, from the standpoint of the people being studied, the concept of 'person' is not, in fact, synonymous with human being but transcends it. The significance of the abstraction only becomes apparent when we stop to consider the perspective adopted. The study of social organization, defined as human relations of a certain kind, is perfectly intelligible as an objective approach to the study of this subject in any culture. But if, in the world view of a people, 'persons' as a class include entities other than human beings, then our objective approach is not adequate for presenting an accurate description of 'the way a man, in a particular society, sees himself in relation to all else.'
>
> (Hallowell 1960: 21)

If persons are social agents with varying degrees of autonomy who are varyingly embedded in more-or-less complex relationships, then humans are not the only beings who should be named 'persons'. In fact, the use of person only to refer to humans restricts understanding of the formation and maintenance of personal and communal identities. By unrealistically dividing humans from other persons it denies the opportunity to understand the rich web of intentional and casual relationships that, at least, impact upon us.

Hallowell further elaborates this point by explaining that the term 'other-than-human persons':

> is more descriptively appropriate than labelling this class of persons 'spiritual' or 'supernatural' beings, if we assume the viewpoint of the Ojibwa themselves. It is true that these entities have more power at their disposal than human beings, and this is why the humans need the help of other than human persons in achieving their goals. Nevertheless, other than human persons cannot be set off as categorically distinct.
>
> (Hallowell 1992: 64)

For example, Ojibwe talk about 'owners' of various plant and animal species.

Their activities and relationships are recognisably like those of other persons. However, other-than-human persons include not only rarely encountered beings, but also many far more common, but still potentially powerful, persons. At least some rocks, trees and clouds were significant to Hallowell's informants. In this context, then, it is more useful to talk of 'cloud persons', 'rock persons', 'tree persons', and so on rather than to refer to 'spirits'. Thus, when Lewis notes that the 'helping spirits (*hantu*)' of Malay shamans (*bomohs*) 'regularly included ancestors, tiger spirits and Muslim saints' (1999: 111), the term 'spirits' does nothing to aid our understanding. Instead, it misdirects our attention away from the particular kinds of persons (ancestors, tigers and saints) who engage with shamans. Or, once again, actual salmon, seals, caribou, tapirs, bears, jaguars, tigers, and so on are among the significant other-than-human persons with whom shamans communicate.

'Spirit' is unhelpful both because it suggests that all persons of significance to shamans are of one kind, and also because it suggests such persons are beyond sensual experience. However, in the understanding and experience of many shaman-taught people, even other-than-human persons encountered only by exceptional people (usually by exceptional means), or by those endangered by illness or disaster, are part of the wide community that might otherwise be called 'nature', 'environment', 'life' or, more straightforwardly, 'neighbours'. Even when shamans do talk to beings unnoticed by scientists, they do not (necessarily) consider them to be ontologically different from, or transcendent above, more mundane persons.

The immediate link of 'spirit' with 'supernatural' and 'spiritual' insists that such beings are meta-empirical, i.e. not real in any everyday, self-evident, scientifically respectable way. Hallowell, however, was provoked to reflect on indigenous and Western categories and language and realised that the similarities between humans and other-than-humans are more central than their differences. More than that, the relationships between persons of various kinds *are* what constitute personhood. Similar arguments and significant elaborations are offered in Morrison (1992, 2000), Strathern (1997) and Bird-David (1999).

The end result is a further call to abandon terms like 'spirit' as unhelpful and often meaningless. There may certainly be indigenous (and other) people who assert the existence of persons as yet unknown to science, but only careful attention to what is said about them will reveal whether they are so ontologically distinct that they require any label other than 'person'. Indigenous informants and shamans might, of course, be wrong in asserting that they are communicating with persons usually unseen by anyone else. But their own explanations for such specificity of relationship are worthy of consideration. Certainly academic discourse is not aided by the use of terms that are either loaded with particular associations and implications or empty of meaning even to native speakers. In other words, if someone says there are 'spirits' out there, just as there are trees, it is incumbent on them to say what such beings are like more precisely than most academics have done to date.

Magic

Akin to the problem of 'spirits' is the Western discourse of 'magic' and irrationality (as evidenced in the dictionary definition). Magic is often too imprecise a word to work as a technical term. Sometimes it only means 'what they do' rather than 'what we do'. It seems to act as a comparative term for allegedly primitive people, cultures, actions, knowledges, and so on, but usually lacks any basis in critical reflection on the supposedly superior position of the speaker. For invaluable recent discussion of 'magic' see Lerner (1995, 2000). In place of the simplistic rhetoric in which magic appears to mean everything but actually tells us nothing, Lerner elaborates on recent academic debates about alternative and particular forms of rationality. Although he does not refer to shamans, his discussion is useful here as one indicator of richer appreciations of various knowledge systems and their technological outworking. It is also important to note that the association of magic with trickery appears to have given licence to those for whom shaman seems to be akin to 'sham'. Narratives that pretend (to themselves and their authors as much as to their readers) to be academically neutral are often infused with cynicism. For example, it is a commonplace of discussions of shamans that they engage in ventriloquism and sleight of hand. From this we are supposed to conclude that shamans' assertions that 'spirits heal' (if indeed that is what they claim) are disingenuous, if not deluded. A test of the objectivity of such 'observers' might be whether they are at all willing to entertain the possibility that their senses have not tricked them but shamans' explanations are adequate and accurate. Something like this happens in Edith Turner's discussion of the 'Reality of Spirits' (1992), and in Young and Goulet (1994). It might also be a further implication of discussions of indigenous rationalities, e.g. Douglas (1975) and Pals (2000). Meanwhile, an increasing number of indigenous academics are asserting the validity and power of indigenous critiques of modernist rhetoric. For wildly differing exemplars see Coetzee and Roux (1998), Deloria *et al.* (1999), Dussel (1995) and Smith (1999).

Initiation, training and performance

Relationships are rarely all embracing. Intimacy is not infinitely extendable. Two people, or particular groups, or communities, get to know each other better than they desire or are able to do with outsiders. The maintenance of such intimacies often require that someone is relied upon to have particular relationships on behalf of others: intermediaries are employed to deal with tax collectors or enemies. Shamans might be people intimate with particular other-than-human persons who might either help or hinder human pursuits and projects including, but not limited to, health, wealth and happiness. The initiation and maintenance of intimacy speak volumes about relationships and that which inspires, engages and impacts upon them. Certainly a considerable amount of academic and popular interest addresses the initiation and training of shamans. Indeed, initiation might define shamans not only for themselves and their communities, but also for a range of academic disciplines.

In exploring initiation academics have pursued psychological, sociological and cosmological interests. Are shamans mad, recovered from psychosis, or healthy and expert in dealing with others' derangements and afflictions? Are traumatic experiences universal and therefore definitive? Perhaps trauma offers itself as a taxic indicator of the genus 'shaman' that enables us to distinguish such people from others. Or are such experiences particular to only some regional types of shaman? Are shamans necessarily initiated by persons (a.k.a. spirits) in an otherworld, or might they inherit roles and abilities from parents or other experienced shamans? If both otherworld and mundane initiations are possible, are they definitive of local types? Or does inheritance indicate a different kind of social or religious role? If trance or possession (if they are distinguishable psychologically or sociologically) are definitive, are they universal among shamans? Is a tripartite cosmology definitive? That is, do shamans have to be able to ascend to an upperworld (or several) and/or descend to an underworld (or several)? Is descent to the underworld a sign of degenerate shamans? What if people become ecstatic by chanting and banging drums and thereby become aware of the direction hunters should travel to find the nearest prey? Are they shamans despite remaining in this world? Or what about the healer who heals without drums or journeys beyond their body? Are they shamans despite never travelling? Is there a boundary drawn around the concept 'shaman' that requires those so labelled to cross the boundary of their own skin? Or, at least, are shamans only entitled to that label when they (and/or their communities) are convinced of their powerful abilities to travel beyond the body? Is ecstasy a social or a psychological phenomenon? More radically, perhaps, are words like ecstasy, trance and possession further mystifications deserving critique and rejection? Alice Kehoe (2000), for example, suggests that all of the seemingly technical language for 'altered states of consciousness' simply refers to more-or-less intense mental concentration.

Kehoe's 'exploration in critical thinking' often reads like scepticism for its own sake, reductionist cynicism even. However, her assertion that shamans (and others) work themselves into intense concentration to the exclusion of most sensory data (ibid.: 3) provides a valuable incitement to reconsider shamanism as ritual or performance. This is not to assert that shamans sham or merely pretend. While it is true that many shamans entertain as they shamanise, this should not prejudice or prejudge the question of whether, for example, they really entertain other-than-human persons or visitors from otherworlds. That is, words like 'perform', 'ritual' and 'entertain' have multiple meanings and the following brief discussion introduces studies that value the doing of religion, shamanry or ritual. (Horwitz, n.d., assesses academic interest in performance very differently, but his powerful and valuable critique is aimed at rather different studies to those of interest here.)

Debates about ritual and performance – and of ritual as performance – have been of increasing importance in the study of shamans and match wider interests in religions and cultures as formed and reformed in activities. Building on classic works by Arnold van Gennep (1960) and Pierre Bourdieu (1977, 1990), scholars such as Victor Turner (1967, 1968, 1991), Tambiah (1979), Smith (1987), Bell (1992, 1997, 1998), Lincoln (1991, 2000), Schechner (1993, 1994a, 1994b), Grimes (1995, 2000), and Ruel (1997) provide exceptional material for further (re-)consideration of shamans' ritual performances. Similarly, Bakhtin's consideration of the carnivalesque (1984, 1993) and Bloch's focus on violence (1986, 1992) not only promise further directions for fruitful research about shamans, but might also themselves be refined in dialogue with knowledge(s) of shamans. As Lincoln notes, recent studies of rituals have begun to shift attention from the structures – 'the elegance of the symbolic order' – towards engagement with practical matters – 'the politics of human agency' (2000: 493).

Examples of topics arising from such works are illustrated by the following questions, queries and considerations. Are shamans experts in relating to persons (human and otherwise) or experts in the technologies of ceremonial performance and entranced consciousness? What exactly is it to which shamans pay and draw attention? Do shamans sham? If not, why do they often engage in conjuring tricks or seem to entertain before or while they shamanise? Indeed, do shamans do more than entertain? Are their ceremonies more than moulders of *communitas* or occasions of carnival? Have interpreters ignored violence and conflict – or romantically projected it into an otherworldly, metaphorical, meta-empirical, neutralised (or otherwise unreal) psychodrama? Would paying attention to indigenous discourses in which shamans are dangerous, not very distant kin of bad 'sorcerers', enrich our understanding both of shamans and of their practices? Does the use of substances that might be variously labelled as psychotropic, hallucinogenic or entheogenic define shamans or detract from their achievements? (It is important, too, to query the implications of choosing to label substances in any of these ways.) What about sexuality? Gender may seem fairly straightforward matter of description: shamans in x are always male, shamans in y are always female, shamans in z could be either. It may seem then that the only question is whether such matters are of great concern, or merely taken for granted. However, things are more complicated if there are more than two genders, or if gender is not fixed and definitive of other aspects of identities. They are also complicated by the fact that gender is not determined by genitalia (and this is just part of the problem of the cultural construction of 'nature' and the apparent given-ness of bodies). Anyway, even the two genders predominantly recognised in modernist discourse can result in varying, and indeed variable, sexual engagements. Do male shamans perform sexually towards their helpers and/or communities as if they were female? Why is it sometimes deemed appropriate to be blatantly sexual and/or scatological and/or even to transgress common social taboos? What is it about hunting animals that leads many peoples to speak and act as if sexuality was involved? Is this more than some stereotypically 'Freudian' identification of arrows with penises, and killing with patricide? What does it say about human relationships with animals that hunting is considered analogous to lovemaking? Should we think about shamans as conducting seances or as playing at carnival? Do shamans maintain the powerful centre, act from the subaltern margins or, perhaps, both demonstrate and transgress even that distinction? Can shamans earn a living by acting as shamans (doing shamanry, or enacting shamanism, perhaps) or would this diminish them in the eyes of their communities. More likely, would it diminish them in the eyes of Westerners convinced that 'spirituality' is negated by economics?

It should not be concluded that the word performance implies the deceitfulness of people's actions. In some senses every action is a performance (just as it can be interesting to see everything as a construction). Academics not only perform academically, they also perform academia, when they write, speak, research, and so on. At the same time, their performance initiates other academics and, perhaps, initiates or maintains boundaries with other people. Similarly, academics of a particular discipline know themselves and are known to be performing appropriately within that discipline when they work within boundaries, thereby also constructing their alterity beyond the boundaries. Happily, recent developments reveal boundaries to be contested and, to some degree, fictive. All of this is germane to consideration of what shamans do, their shamanry or shamanship. Arguably, an interest in psychology and cosmology has often diverted attention away from shamans as people who act (which is not to say that they pretend), people who do, people who perform. This is true even when what shamans perform is the psychology and cosmology of their community (human and other-than-human). Far from stripping away the particularities and exoticism of shamanic ritual to see the real and universal beliefs, it may be important to pay greater attention to the diversities and experiential richness of specific shamanic activities.

In short, close interest in the initiation experiences and narratives of shamans have been important in revealing core aspects of shamanic psychology, sociology, cosmology, and so on. Attention to performance and aesthetics also entail consideration of similar domains, for example, study of shamans' costumes and equipment as expressions of social roles certainly entails consideration of their psychological effects and cosmological significance. However, a richer understanding of our topic might emerge from more careful attention to issues as defined in emerging forms of performance studies. At the same time, academic consideration of performance might be greatly enhanced by further thought about shamans. Shaman agency in the formation, maintenance and contestation of cultures will be significant in this arena.

Siberia, Academia, Cyberia, and Cyburbia

If shamans are commonly associated with Siberia – if only because that is where they first became known to European travellers and scholars, and because that is where the word came from – they are also visitors to otherworlds. Or so many shamans say. They certainly play significant roles in worlds as 'other' as those of academia. Having been drawn from their indigenous locations, and their other-worlds, into academia, shamans continued travelling – to the ire of academics who imagined themselves in control of their authorised knowledges. In the narratives of academia, as in more indigenous trickster tales, shamans are often troublesome. They refuse to fit the neat categories, or perform the tidy roles provided for them. Their trickster nature (see Vizenor 1998) is revealed in the inability of scholars like Eliade to convincingly construct 'true' shamans as safely archaic and principled performers of techniques of ecstatic journeys to the upperworld. His need to cite evidence of other, contemporary and continuing ways of being shamanic undercuts his systematisation, making his narrative available for entirely different readings. Nonetheless, Eliade has persuaded some readers that his account is true and worthy of utilisation as a blueprint for new shamanisms. But he is not alone, and far less contentious texts are also inspiration for enacting change in the Euro-colonies. Introduced by academics to wider audiences, and thereby given acceptable authority of kinds recognised by those new audiences, shamans engaged with those seeking to fulfil their human potential. With the aid of psychedelics, meditation, imagination and rhythm, various kinds of experimental forms of shamanic identity and performance have arisen. Once academia created shamanism, it was not hard for others to tell alternative tales productive of new systems, new -isms. Academics had claimed to be speaking the truth about shamans, and seemed to provide guidebooks on how to do shamanism away from Siberia. (Dan Noel, 1997, provides an admirable discussion of key phases of this process of reinvention, reconstruction and representation.)

The study of shamanism now includes not only indigenous forms but also Western ones. These are firmly rooted in modernity's own otherworldly (if globalised) 'cyberspace' – especially by the addition of new technologies of ecstasy – and in more suburban therapeutic forms. Criticism of such cyberian and cyburban (or techno- and neo-) shamanisms has seemed easy to academia. However, if nothing else, it is worth considering the role of shamans of all kinds in challenging the rationalist and elitist construction of modernity and its post-modernity. Neo-shamanism is far from disengaged from modernity's central project of colonisation. Nor, however, is academia entirely divorced from colonialism, let alone its fierce opponent. Academia is compromised by its own critiques. It constructs itself by constructing its alterity, albeit by mistakenly perceiving 'others' as objects of its scrutiny and discovery, and by mistakenly claiming to describe and analyse objectively. This is clear in the ultimate fear of anthropologists: being censured for 'going native'. Even if indigeneity is now rarely considered 'savage' and 'primitive' in respectable academic writing, it remains a testing ground for theorising difference and origins. Modernity, post-modernity, the West, and other self-identifications are tested over against indigenous alterities, themselves perceived to be more embodied, communal, spiritual, engaged, topophilic, bounded, traditional, and so on. Shamans play significant roles within such tropes. Academia has always been engaged in the construction of the world, it has always had a point, purpose, goal, or project. If others have taken up academia's profligate products (lectures, books, articles) and seen their value as tools in making the world more habitable, or at least different, it is, perhaps, time that academics took another look at the relevance of those it studies. In fact, of course, this has been happening in many places and in many ways. Just as shamans are (or might be) crossers of boundaries, they might also be openers of cracks in the systems invented to contain them.

It is noteworthy, also, that academic and popular interests have evolved together so that a consideration of what academics have said about shamans might map the shifting obsessions of Western cultures and their counter-cultures. A fascination with the alleged irrationality of magic spun towards its flip side in a flirtation with mind-altering substances. Interests in states of con-sciousness at first fixated about alternate realities and then began to give way to consideration of drama, and performance, but has rarely lost sight of rhythms and/or brain chemistry. In recent years political change, power relationships, and identity politics have been evident in academic exploration of shamanic modes of behaviour and relationship. With anti-colonial challenges to narratives of tribalism, academia turned towards an exploration of neo-tribes nearer home, and found them to be resonant theatres for observing carnivalesque and transgressive behaviours. These suggestions could be multiplied, and, of course, contested, with reference to the myriad texts and events utilising 'shaman' in their titles.

Shamans and their -ists and -isms

The -ism of shamanism is, of course, of the essence in debates and study about shamans. The label appears to imply that we can or should categorise types of religion by the nature of their leadership. If so, it operates like early modern Protestant and later evangelical oppositions to Roman Catholic or Episcopalian Christianities as 'popery' or 'priestcraft'. Perhaps, however, what is being fore-grounded is not the type of leadership but the type of experience held to be determinative for shamans and their communities. If shamanism is a type of religion in which particular experiences are significant, the term would be com-parable with words like 'transcendentalism' or 'immanentalism', 'possession cult', 'nature religion', 'ancestor veneration', and so on. That is, these terms draw attention to allegedly central orientations of the worldviews and lifeways so named. If this is what shamanism is intended to do, what is it that unifies the diverse phenomena so labelled? Is it, as Eliade asserted, the application of ecstatic techniques to the enactment of particular social roles? Does shamanism label a religion, or set of religions, centred on trance states? Some kind of decision is necessary here if only to enable further decisions about who or what to include in discussions of shamanism. Is Aboriginal Australian rock art shamanic? Are charismatic Christian healers shamanic? Are 'medicine people', 'witch doctors', 'spiritualists', 'e-heads', and some Jungian therapists, all shamans? Are their systems of knowledge and experience shamanisms?

A survey of academic discourses about shamans reveals the recurrence and prevalence of a small but suggestive set of words. We might describe this set as the semantic field of the word shaman in academic discourse. Imagine, then, a page with 'shaman' enclosed in a central box. To one side are a set of words for people who are (or are alleged to be) unlike shamans: other religious people like priests and Buddhist lamas; political people (who might have other religious roles) like elders, and politicians; and then Westerners like 'rational observers'. As antonyms of 'shaman' these other labels claim to tell us what is distinctive about shamans themselves. Also, according to some people, we should include Western neo-shamans (of various kinds perhaps, but commonly lumped together as if they were all alike) in the category of being unlike other, allegedly 'real' (because indigenous, archaic or community-orientated) shamans.

To another side is a set of words that indicate the techniques by which shamans do whatever it is that they do. The first word in this batch is ecstasy, a more or less technical term that might include trance and/or possession. These are commonly thought to be achievable with the aid of various kinds of rhythmic sound and movement, including drumming, rattling, dancing and chanting. For some, 'hallucinations' are an important member of these techniques, themselves perhaps aided by rhythms or by the use of drugs or more spontaneously as the result of some psychological condition or psychosis.

A final important group of words provide some indication of the social function or purpose of shamans. It is often held to be definitive that shamans work for communities. Some writers insist that these communities subsist by hunting and gathering, and thereby exclude urban and agricultural communities from being shamanic. Shamans operate as healers and experts (perhaps knowing where game animals are, or how to persuade them to meet hunters). They do so with the aid of, or by controlling or being controlled by (perhaps depending on whether trance or possession is operative here) 'spirits'. Indeed, such beings are significant members of the community of the effective shaman, they are relied upon as sources of knowledge and power. Of course, they might also be the source of sickness that needs healing. Journeys to the otherworldly homes or domains of these helpers or enemies are often considered to be what shamans principally do, i.e. this is what ecstasy is for. Rituals not only bring about ecstasy but also *communitas* and thereby firmly embed individuals in communities. On the other hand, the learning of techniques elides easily into the rhetoric of shaming, the pretence of trance, journeying, healing and expertise. Not surprisingly, 'sham' sometimes also links assertions about similarities and differences between 'real' shamans and neo-shamans of various kinds. These latter are commonly differentiated by their institutional context, e.g. 'core shamans' offer workshops while 'technoshamans' are rave DJs. Whatever defences might be raised against objections to considering such people to be real shamans, no protection is afforded once it is alleged that shamanism is 'the original religion of humanity', perhaps surviving in a 'degenerate' form *only* among indigenous hunter–gatherers (e.g. the assertions of Eliade 1964, Hultkrantz 1989, and Weston La Barre 1970).

If this composite picture portrays matters of significance in the many and various debates about shamans and shamanism, little of it remains uncontested. Korean shamans, for example, do not 'journey' beyond their bodies, and do shamanise in industrial and agrarian communities (see Howard 1998). And few if any shamans would recognise the effects of any substances they ingest as 'hallucinatory', i.e. as promoting 'false vision'. Thus, while our semantic field portrays a common Western vision of shamans, it is inadequate as a definitive statement and, in some places, inappropriately polemical and arguably erroneous.

The remainder of this book demonstrates the range of debate and contest, and occasional agreement, about what shamans do, who shamans are, what shamanism might be, and whether shamans live with shamanists or some other kind of community. In other words, it requires that we attempt to produce different maps of the relationships of lots of different words. First, if we pay attention to what shamans consider important about themselves as shamans, a very different semantic field might emerge. Indeed, many different fields would be drawn as we map the associations and distinctions inherent in each of the many local and regional variations on our theme. Next, we might consider what these shamans' communities say about shamans. If there are no other differences, we might at least expect to know whether shamans are honoured or feared, central or marginal, envied or pitied. All these are possible. It would also be intriguing to survey the semantics of the various shamanisms that have arisen in response to academic writing. The present volume and its extracts provide some material with which such an enterprise might begin.

This volume does more than offer material for a more adequate description of shamans and shamanisms. It even intends to do more than enrich understanding of shamans. Even the labels for the five Parts in which the readings are grouped (Initiation, Shamanising, Aesthetics, Context, and New) are intended to be read as ambiguous, broad, contestable, and/or suggestive possibilities. No point is offered as final. The volume is intended to clarify the points at which debates about shamans might contribute to other debates about wider critical issues. Consider, for example, laying particular shamanic knowledges and activities alongside the following insightful list of critical terms used in the Study of

Religions (Taylor 1998): belief, body, conflict, culture, experience, gender, god, image, liberation, modernity, performance, person, rationality, relic, religion (religions and religious), sacrifice, territory, time, transformation, transgression, value, and writing. There are similar lists of terms of critical importance and value within other disciplines (e.g. in Routledge's 'Key Guides' series). This volume is intended to provoke further debate about studying shamans and shamanisms in the light of the undoubted relevance of their interests, pursuits, experiences and relationships to terms and themes such as the above. More than that, it arises from a notion that dialogue between various ways of being human (including academia and shamanising) might enrich all who have interests in shamans and shamanisms.

References

Bakhtin, M.M. [1968] 1984. *Rabelais and His World*. Bloomington: University of Indiana Press.

Bakhtin, M.M. 1993. *Toward a Philosophy of the Act*. Austin, TX: University of Texas Press.

Bell, C. 1992. *Ritual Theory, Ritual Practice*. Oxford: Oxford University Press.

Bell, C. 1997. *Ritual Perspectives and Dimensions*. Oxford: Oxford University Press.

Bell, C. 1998. 'Performance', in M.C. Taylor (ed.), *Critical Terms for Religious Studies*. Chicago: University of Chicago Press. pp. 205–24.

Bird-David, N. 1999. '"Animism" Revisited: Personhood, Environment, and Relational Epistemology', *Current Anthropology* 40: S67–79.

Bloch, M. 1986. *From Blessing to Violence: History and Ideology in the Circumcision Ritual of the Merina of Madagascar*. Cambridge: Cambridge University Press.

Bloch, M. 1992. *Prey into Hunter: The Politics of Religious Experience*. Cambridge: Cambridge University Press.

Bourdieu, P. 1977. *Outlines of a Theory of Practice*. Cambridge: Cambridge University Press.

Bourdieu, P. 1990. *The Logic of Practice*. Stanford, CA: Stanford University Press.

Bourguignon, E. 1976. *Possession*. San Francisco: Chandler and Sharp.

Coetzee, P.H. and Roux, A.P.J. (eds) 1998. *The African Philosophy Reader*. London: Routledge.

Deloria, B., Foehner, K. and Scinta, S. (eds) 1999. *Spirit and Reason: The Vine Deloria, Jr., Reader*. Golden, CO: Fulcrum.

Douglas, M. 1975. *Implicit Meanings: Essays in Anthropology*. London: Routledge and Kegan Paul, pp. 73–82.

Dussel, E. 1995. *The Invention of the Americas: Eclipse of 'the Other' and the Myth of Modernity*. New York: Cassell.

Eliade, M. 1964. *Shamanism: Archaic Techniques of Ecstasy*. New York: Pantheon.

Gennep, A. van. 1960. *The Rites of Passage*. London: Routledge and Kegan Paul.

Grimes, R.L. 1995. *Beginnings in Ritual Studies*. Lanham, MD: University Press of America.

Grimes, R.L. 2000. 'Ritual', in W. Braun and R.T. McCutcheon (eds), *Guide to the Study of Religion*. London: Cassell, pp. 259–70.

Hallowell, A.I. 1960. 'Ojibwa Ontology, Behavior, and World View', in S. Diamond (ed.) *Culture in History*. New York: Columbia University Press: 19–52.

Hallowell, A.I. 1992. *The Ojibwa of Berens River, Manitoba: Ethnography into History*. Edited by J.S.H. Brown; New York: Harcourt Brace.

Heusch, L. de. 1982. 'Possession and Shamanism', in *Why Marry Her? Society and Symbolic Structures*. Cambridge: Cambridge University Press.

Holm, N.G. (ed.) 1982. *Religious Ecstasy*. Uppsala: Almqvist and Wiksell.

Horwitz, J. (n.d). 'Shamanic Rites Seen from a Shamanic Perspective' http://www.users.dircon.co.uk/˜snail/SCSS/Articles/Rites1.htm (accessed: 1 November 2001).

Howard, K. (ed.) 1998. *Korean Shamanism: Revivals, Survivals and Change*. Seoul: Seoul Press.

Hultkrantz, Å. 1989. 'The Place of Shamanism in the History of Religions', in M. Hoppál and D. von Sadovsky (eds) *Shamanism Past and Present*. Part 1. Budapest: Hungarian Academy of Sciences.

Ingold, T. (ed.) 1994. *Companion Encyclopedia of Anthropology: Humanity, Culture and Social Life*. London: Routledge.

Kehoe, A. 2000. *Shamans and Religion: An Anthropological Exploration in Critical Thinking*. Prospect Heights, IL: Waveland Press.

King, W.L. 1954. *Introduction to Religion*. New York: Harper and Row.

Kirkpatrick, E.M. (ed.) 1983. *Chambers 20th Century Dictionary*. Edinburgh: Chambers.

La Barre, W. 1970. *The Ghost Dance: The Origins of Religion*. New York: Doubleday.

Lerner, B.D. 1995. 'Understanding a (Secular) Primitive Society', *Religious Studies* 31: 303–9.

Lerner, B.D. 2000. 'Magic, Religion and Secularity among the Azande and Nuer', in G. Harvey (ed.), *Indigenous Religions: A Companion*. London: Cassell, pp. 113–24.

Leuba, J.H. 1912. *A Psychological Study of Religion*. New York: Macmillan.

Lewis, I.M. 1989. *Ecstatic Religion: A Study of Shamanism and Spirit Possession*. London: Routledge.

Lewis, I.M. 1999. *Arguments with Ethnography*. London: Athlone Press.

Lincoln, B. 1991. *Emerging from the Chrysalis: Studies in Rituals of Women's Initiations*. Oxford: Oxford University Press.

Lincoln, B. 2000. 'On Ritual, Change and Marked Categories', *Journal of the American Academy of Religion* 68 (3): 487–510.

Marshall, L. 1962. '!Kung Bushman Religious Beliefs', *Africa* 39: 347–81.

Marx, K. [1857–58] 1965. *Pre-capitalist Economic Formations.* (ed. C.J. Arthur). London: Lawrence and Wishart.

Morrison, K.M. 1992. 'Beyond the Supernatural: Language and Religious Action', *Religion* 22: 201–5.

Morrison, K.M. 2000. 'The Cosmos as Intersubjective: Native American Other-than-Human Persons', in G. Harvey (ed.), *Indigenous Religions: A Companion.* London: Cassell, pp. 23–36.

Narby, J. and Huxley, F. 2001. *Shamans Through Time: 500 Years on the Path to Knowledge.* London: Thames and Hudson.

Noel, D. 1997. *The Soul of Shamanism: Western Fantasies, Imaginal Realities.* London: Continuum.

Pals, D.L. 2000. 'Intellect', in W. Braun and R.T. McCutcheon, *Guide to the Study of Religion.* London: Cassell, pp. 155–67.

Platvoet, J. 2001. 'Chasing Off God: Spirit Possession in a Sharing Society', in K. Ralls-MacLeod and G. Harvey (eds), *Indigenous Religious Musics.* Aldershot: Ashgate, pp. 122–35.

Ralls-MacLeod, K. and Harvey, G. (eds) 2001. *Indigenous Religious Musics.* Aldershot: Ashgate.

Rapport N. and Overing, J. 2000. *Social and Cultural Anthropology: The Key Concepts.* London: Routledge.

Riches, D. 1996. 'Hunting and Gathering Societies', in A. Bernard and J. Spencer (eds), *Encyclopedia of Social and Cultural Anthropology.* London: Routledge, pp. 288–91.

Rouget, G. 1987. *Music and Trance.* Chicago: University of Chicago Press.

Ruel, M. 1997. *Belief, Ritual and the Securing of Life: Reflexive Essays on a Bantu Religion.* Leiden: Brill.

Schechner, R. 1993. *The Future of Ritual.* London: Routledge.

Schechner, R. 1994a. *Performance Theory.* New York: Routledge.

Schechner, R. 1994b. 'Ritual and Performance', in T. Ingold (ed.) *Companion Encyclopedia of Anthropology.* London: Routledge, pp. 613–45.

Smith, J.Z. 1987. *To Take Place: Toward Theory in Ritual.* Chicago: University of Chicago Press.

Smith, J.Z. 1998. 'Religion, Religions, Religious', in M.C. Taylor (ed.), *Critical Terms for Religious Studies.* Chicago: University of Chicago Press, pp. 269–84.

Smith, L.T. 1999. *Decolonizing Methodologies: Research and Indigenous Peoples.* Dunedin: University of Otago Press.

Strathern, M. 1997. 'Partners and Consumers: Making Relations Visible', in A.D. Schrift (ed.), *The Logic of the Gift: Toward an Ethic of Generosity.* London: Routledge, pp. 292–311.

Tambiah, S. 1979. *A Performative Approach to Ritual*. London: The British Academy and Oxford University Press.

Taylor, M. 1998. *Critical Terms for Religious Studies*. Chicago: University of Chicago Press.

Thompson, C. 2001. *Maya Identities and the Violence of Place: Borders Bleed*. Aldershot: Ashgate.

Turner, E. 1992. 'The Reality of Spirits', *ReVision* 15(1): 28–32.

Turner, V. 1967. *The Forest of Symbols: Aspects of Ndembu Ritual*. Ithaca, NY: Cornell University Press.

Turner, V. 1968. *The Drums of Affliction*. Oxford: Clarendon Press.

Turner, V. 1991. *The Ritual Process: Structure and Anti-Structure*. Ithaca, NY: Cornell University Press.

Vizenor, G. 1998. *Fugitive Poses: Native American Indian Scenes of Absence and Presence*. Lincoln, NB: University of Nebraska Press.

Young, D.E. and Goulet J.-G. (eds) 1994. *Being Changed: The Anthropology of Extraordinary Experience*. Peterborough: Broadview Press.

PART ONE

Initiation

INTRODUCTION TO PART ONE

INITIATION ESTABLISHES RELATIONSHIPS, knowledges and abilities that define who shamans are and what they do. Relationships with powerful helpers are not only formed but also cemented in dramatic encounters which demonstrate or negotiate power, control, authority, and boundaries. Shamans are taught what their helpers require and offer, what etiquette will maintain and enhance the on-going relationship. Levels and modes of intimacy, reciprocity and/or hierarchy are initiated. All of this places new shamans in a position to act effectively in particular ways. Some shamans inherit roles and abilities from other shamans, perhaps close relatives. Others are taught them as apprentices to more experienced shamans. Sometimes shamans introduce others to future (perhaps 'otherworld') helpers who will act as initiators. For many shamans, however, initiation is the result of traumatic and unexpected illness or injury. Intimacy with illness may be the principal initiation undergone by shamans. However, even if some initiations, or some phases of initiation, take place in solitude or privacy, shamans also face their first public appearance and performance. These occasions also form and cement relationships with the shaman's wider human community. Some demonstration of ability is important, whatever tasks particular shamans are meant to achieve (e.g., healing, hunting-knowledge, or opposition to other shamans or sorcerers). Initiation not only forms and moulds relationships but also inculcates understandings and techniques that will mould shamanic action in future. Knowledge learnt in initiation may be continuous with knowledge gained by other people in the new shaman's community, or it may be distinct and particular to shamans. Studying initiation therefore promises to reveal much about the nature of a shaman's employment, character, psychology, and much more.

The two chapters in Part One powerfully engage with the initiation of shamans in different contexts. Sereptie Djarvoskin in Chapter 1 records his initiation under the control of people who are identified as 'spirits'. He encounters diseases that he will be able to heal if he can correctly identify and properly respond to what he sees. Elements of the structure of both the cosmos and the society familiar to the shaman are referred to or explained. Importantly, the narration of this initiatory event also refers to the shaman's later work as a healer – initiation and shamanising cannot be separated. Similar narratives are commonplace among Siberian and other peoples. For example, there is a widespread notion that shamans gain at least some control or mastery over both their other-than-human initiators and their otherwise seemingly hallucinatory experiences.

The second chapter describes Michael Harner's initiatory experience among the Jívaro of Ecuador's Andean forests and the Conibo of the Peruvian Amazon. The first experience began when his hosts informed him 'that if I really wished to learn, I must take the shamans' sacred drink made from *ayahuasca*'. The second was the result of a 'mission . . . not just to be an anthropologist, but to learn firsthand how to practice shamanism the Jívaro way', which also entailed the consumption of *ayahuasca*. Harner's purpose here is to offer knowledge gained as a trainee shaman. His encounter with significant other-than-human persons leads to the acquisition not only of socially recognised power, but also of 'spirit helpers' and the knowledge and techniques necessary to continuing work as a healing shaman. Again, aspects of cosmology, psychology, sociology and more (botany and pharmacology especially) are integral to the presentation of these initiatory events.

However, other contexts are significant in addition to those which might be seen as description or ethnography. Consider, for example, that Sereptie Djarvoskin's initiation is told to someone other than a neighbour. While there may well have been occasions when a similar narrative was offered to other Nganasans or Tavgi Samoyeds, this version is incorporated into Andrei Popov's (1968) article published in a volume entitled *Popular Beliefs and Folklore Traditions in Siberia*. Later it was reprinted in Joan Halifax's *Shamanic Voices: A Survey of Visionary Narratives* (1979). Now it appears here. Similarly, Michael Harner's chapter introduces a book that encourages a very different kind of shamanic experience from Harner's own initiation. Anthropological or ethnographic description do not lead to theorising, debate, critique and other common discourses of academia, but to a book inciting North Americans and other readers to adopt a style of shamanism rather different from that of Conibo or Jívaro informants. Each of these contexts is itself of great interest. The purposes of the initiated or initiating shamans do not precisely match (let alone exhaust the potential of) the purposes of writers and discussants.

The two chapters are included here first of all because discussion of initiation is central to the study of shamans and shamanism. Questions like, 'How do people become shamans?', 'Who becomes a shaman?' and 'What is it like to be initiated?' lead to debates about the kind of helpers and communities with whom shamans relate, and the roles they perform. As already noted, the chapters – and similar narratives – can be read or interrogated for what they say about psychology, sociology, cosmology, pharmacology. They speak not only about the psychology, for example, of shamans and their communities, but also about human psychology more widely. What is possible among the Samoyed is possible elsewhere. Of course, those who consider shamans deluded in some way may identify similar delusions elsewhere.

It may be useful to say more about the 'mastery' achieved by shamans. The initiations of Sereptie Djarvoskin and Michael Harner illustrate modes by which potential shamans gain some degree of mastery over potentially helpful (but also potentially dangerous) other-than-human persons. According to Sergei Shirokogoroff's classic definition of the word 'shaman',

> In all Tungus languages this term refers to persons of both sexes who have mastered spirits, who at will can introduce these spirits into themselves and use their power over the spirits in their own interests, particularly helping other people, who suffer from the spirits; in such a capacity they may possess a complex of special methods for dealing with the spirits.
>
> (Shirokogoroff 1935: 269)

Similarly, he asserts that while people other than shamans are able to 'master spirits' and, with their aid, to 'acquire knowledge by mystical means':

> The characteristic peculiar to shamanism consists in the *recognition of the special rites, clothing, instruments, and the peculiar social position of the shaman*. True, some of these phenomena can characterize other prayer-professionals and sorcerers, but *shamanism is the complex of the phenomena mentioned above*.
>
> (Shirokogoroff 1923: 246)

It is noteworthy, however, that the 'spirits' in both of the narratives that follow demonstrate their power and authority too. Shamans may learn to control their modes of consciousness (e.g. trance), evoking and entering 'altered states' at will, but close attention to shaman's discourses demonstrates that only rarely do shamans have total control. This, if nothing else, might be clear from common stories of dismemberment and violent assault in the otherworld and manifest as severe illness in this world. It might, therefore, be better to say that shamans are masters of the etiquette and protocols by which relationships are maintained and enhanced. They are distinctive in that they enter relationships with other-than-human persons who overwhelm and harm other humans.

In Mircea Eliade's (1964) construction, traumatic illness and learning to 'journey' to an upperworld are definitive aspects of initiation and of shamanism.

He also provides some valuable examples of actual shamanisms in which trauma and journeys are central. Vitebsky (1995: 52–88, 163–6) greatly enriches discussion of 'Becoming a Shaman'. He also includes excerpts from accounts of geographically diverse initiations. It is probably true to say that every book about shamans includes discussion about initiation and that in many books this is a primary focus.

References

Eliade, M. 1964. *Shamanism: Archaic Techniques of Ecstasy*. New York: Pantheon.

Halifax, J. 1979. *Shamanic Voices*. London: Penguin Arkana.

Harner, M. 1990. *The Way of the Shaman*. San Francisco: Harper & Row.

Popov, A.A. 1968. 'How Sereptie Djarvoskin of the Nganasans (Tavgi Samoyeds) became a Shaman', in Vimos Diószegi (ed.) *Popular Beliefs and Folklore Tradition in Siberia* (transl. Stephen P. Dunn). Bloomington: Indiana University Press.

Shirokogoroff, S. 1923. 'General Theory of Shamanism among the Tungus', *Journal of the Royal Asiatic Society* 54: 246–9.

Shirokogoroff, S. 1935. *Psychometrical Complex of the Tungus*. London: Kegan and Paul.

Vitebsky, P. 1995. *The Shaman*. London: Macmillan.

Chapter 1

Sereptie Djarvoskin

HOW SEREPTIE DJARVOSKIN OF THE NGANASANS (TAVGI SAMOYEDS) BECAME A SHAMAN

[. . .]

WHEN I WAS A YOUNG MAN I used to dream of all sorts of insignificant things just like any other man. But once, I saw myself going down a road until I reached a tree. With an axe in my hand, I went round the tree and wanted to fell it. Then I heard a voice saying: '(Fell it) later!' and I woke up.

Next day the neighbours said to me: 'Go and fell a tree for the *kuojka*[1] sledge!' I set out, found a suitable tree and started to cut it down. When the tree fell, a man sprang out of its roots with a loud shout. I was petrified with fear (from this unexpected event). The man asked: 'Where are you going?' 'What could I do – I am going to my tent.' 'Why, of course, since you have a tent, you must go there. Well, my friend, I am a man, who came out of the roots of the tree. The root is thick, it looks thin in your eyes only. Therefore I tell you that you must come down through the root if you wish to see me.' – 'What sort of a tree is that?' I asked. 'I never could find it out.' The man answered: 'From times of old, it is of this tree that the *kuojka* sledges have been made and the shamans have been growing from. Rocked in the cradle, they become shamans – well that's what this tree is for.' – 'All right, I shall go with you.'

Whilst preparing to descend, the man turned to me and said: 'Just take a look at me and find out who I am?' His clothes at the sides reminded me of the wild reindeer's hide during moulting time. I did not ask him why he was wearing such clothes. Then again he said: 'Don't be afraid of me, but find out why there are such patterns on my *parka* (winter garment), both black and white patches?' I replied: 'On the left side you have the white spots because you dress in the attire of the (spirit of the) first snow; the black spots on the right side resemble the spots of the earth appearing in spring from under the snow – because you put on the attire (of the spirit) of the melting snow.' My companion turned his back and, taking my hand, said: 'Now let us go to our hosts!' I was afraid and thought that I was lost.

As I looked round, I noticed a hole in the earth. My companion asked: 'What hole is this? If your destiny is to make a drum of this tree, find it out!' I replied: 'It is through this hole that the shaman receives the spirit of his voice.' The hole became larger and larger. We descended through it and arrived at a river with two streams flowing in opposite directions. 'Well, find out this one too!' said my companion, 'one stream goes from the centre to the north, the other to the south – the sunny side. If you are destined to fall into a trance, find it out!' I replied: 'The northern stream originates from the water for bathing the dead, and the southern from that for the infants.' – 'Yes, indeed, you have guessed right,' said he.

Then we set out on the shore of the northern stream. My companion always led me by the hand. We saw nine tents before us, the nearest one being tied round with a rope. A tree stood on each side of its entrance – one on the northern, the other on the southern side. 'What do you think these trees grew for?' asked the man. I replied again: 'One of the trees is bright as if the sun were shining on it. Because the parents bring up their children loving and fostering them, this must be the (protecting) spirit of the children.' Here my companion (as if to confirm my words) clapped his hands and smacked his knees with the palm of one hand. 'The dark tree is the tree of the moon, the tree of birth, enabling the women to fix the date of the birth according to the moon.' The man again clapped his hands and slapped his knees. Then he asked: 'What is the meaning of the bars that hang horizontally above the fireplace of the tent?'[2] Suddenly I found one of the bars in my hand and struck my companion with it. 'These bars are the borderline between two daybreaks, the backbone of the firmament. The northern bar is the beginning of the polar light, the southern one – the beginning of the cycle of dawns.' When I said this, my companion praised me. I got frightened. 'And what is the tent tied round with a rope?' asked my companion. And I said: 'When men go mad and become shamans, they are tied with this rope.' (I was quite unconscious and was tied up too.)

Then it seemed to me that we were in the street. We entered the first tent where we found seven naked men and women who were singing all the time while tearing their bodies with their teeth. I became very frightened. 'Now I shall explain this to you, myself, because you will not guess it anyway,' said my companion: 'Originally, seven earths were created and it is through the spirits of these seven earths that (men) lose their minds. Some just start singing, others losing their minds, go away and die; others again become shamans. Our earth has seven promontories with a madman living on each of them. When you become a shaman, you will find them yourself.' – 'Where can I find them – you have led me to the wrong place' – thought I. 'If I do not lead you to see (the spirits), how could you make magic for the insane? If you find the spirit of madness, you will begin to shamanize, initiating (new) shamans. You must be shown all the ways of diseases.'

We came out of the first tent and went to the second that was placed on the northern promontory. The whole tent was covered with hoar frost and tied round in the middle with a black rope. Around the smoke hole, the tent was covered with something red. 'Down there (to the south) is Asondu – they are Tungus,' said my companion. 'This is their tent. The black rope will serve you to cure stomach diseases, while the red stuff will help you heal madness that comes from headaches. The middle rope will serve you to cure epidemics. You will find out the meaning of this rope later on. When you will enchant, Tungus spirits will come to you and I, myself, do not understand them. When you enchant a Dolgan or a Tungus, come here and you will learn it.' The frost-covered tent had two smoke holes, one of copper and the other of iron. We entered the second tent, but found nobody there. 'Let us go back,' said my companion.

We came out of the tent through another door and went into another tent which seemed to be covered with fishing nets. Inside, the fire was scarcely flickering. We found a disfigured old woman there in worn boots and other-wise naked, except for her upper clothes; she warmed herself by the fire. There was a dim light in the tent and shadows were flickering everywhere. The old woman asked: 'Do you know me?' – 'Find the answer yourself!' said my companion to me. I replied: 'When a child is born, there is the afterbirth too, you are its spirit, are you not?' My companion and the old woman slapped their knees in astonishment. 'You are a good guesser!' Then they asked again: 'Why is the fire dark?' And I answered: 'When a child is born, a new fire is kindled. You too, you are sitting here like a housewife who lights a new fire.' Again they slapped their knees in astonishment. 'In the southern part of the tent, the fire is very weak. Human beings are purified after birth by being fumigated with fire. This is the origin of the purifying fire.' 'That's right,' said both of them. The tent had two kinds of ńuks[3] – some were frost-covered, some were white. I guessed the meaning of these ńuks too. 'We wrap up the dead in ńuks made of wild reindeer hide. Here, these rimy ńuks are the nil'tis[4] of the said ńuks. The white ńuks are the nil'tis of our leather garment.' Both confirmed the correctness of my words.

We went over to the fourth tent that stood in the middle of the water, behind three freezing waters. One part of it was covered with seven reindeer hides, instead of a ńuk, while the other was spread over with rippling water. I said: 'Doesn't the shaman make his clothing out of seven reindeer hides? And since the other part of the tent is covered with waves, it must belong to the spirit of the water – that is why it is standing in the middle of the water.' 'You will shamanize, you go downwards,' they said. We entered the tent where we found an old woman sitting among heaps of children's clothes and killed dogs. On each side of the tent there were two white salmons. 'Do you recognize me?' asked the old woman. 'Find it out,' said my companion. And I replied: 'This is the earth where we shall have to come in lean years. Here, she (the old woman) will show us where to find game and fish.' 'Find it out!' – they repeated. 'Seven hides – these I shall find when I shamanize, I shall find and recognize them. Every man, when he becomes a shaman, makes himself a seat. I shall shamanize for seven days, sitting on these seven hides. Two fishes: one of them means that we blow on the fire and breath goes out of us. The breath has a soul. What is it when the fish (opening its mouth) is panting? When we light the fire, it flares up on its back. Seeing the fire on the back of one fish, the other blows it out. Therefore, in imitation of this fish, a wooden fish was made. When a child is born, men act in a similar fashion. One of the fishes is full of roe – the roe floats above. The child is to be rubbed with the roe. When a child is born, we smear it with grease. This is what it means. Then throwing the grease into the fire we feed the house *kuojka* and also smear its face with grease. When people become hungry, it is this that gives enough to eat. It is this (the fish) you have to ask.' The southern side was closed with hides. Looking closer, I found that they looked like seven apertures instead of hides. From outside, they looked like hides, from inside, like apertures – through which one could look out. 'Why should I find this one out?' 'We shamans have seven resting places, henceforth you will find them. The seven apertures mean that when a man sinks under the water but has still some air left and you happen to be there, then you come and save him.'

We came out of the tent – the northern side was covered all over with ice. 'You will find this out yourself,' said my companion. 'Don't come here, this is the way of another shaman.' When I submerged, I arrived at these places, and it seemed as if I were swimming in the water. We went to another tent. On each side there stood an iron trunk. A one-horned reindeer doe was tied to the trunk on the right side, while a stag, with bruised antlers, was tied to the left trunk. One tine was broken, the other twisted. I tried to guess what the two animals were tied with and found that they were tied with the rays of the sun. 'Well, that's strange' – I thought – 'how is that these (ropes) do not break?' Although they were twisted, some of the threads were broken and hanging straight, like sticks. 'Do you know this rein-hind?' they asked me. I answered: 'No, I do not.' 'When you will be a shaman (surely you think that this is a real trunk – this is the spirit of everything humans do) and (during the ceremony) the men will beat your drum with the drumstick,[5] this trunk will split up. The rein-hind is the origin of the *kuojka* (made of stone or wood).' 'And what is this rope for?' 'It serves to brand the reindeer's fawn that is presented to the moon.' 'Why is the reinder one-horned?' 'Every man who becomes a shaman, makes divinations about the reindeer whose hide will serve him as a dress. When you become a shaman, (don't) ask them (the wild reindeer for the clothes) and don't make yourself a suit of the simple wild reindeer's hide. Provide yourself with clothes, but, first, ask for permission from the mother of the wild reindeer, she will give you instructions about the wild reindeer whose hide is to be used for your clothes. One of the wild reindeer is a stag, he is the master spirit of the wild reindeer stags. It is this spirit whom you will have to ask to know which tree you are to make your drum of, or else your life will not be long.'

Walking round the tent, I saw that all the ńuks were bright with decorations and fringes. We make fringes for ourselves, similar to the antlers of the reindeer. For we take hair from every animal to sew it on to the fringes of the attire similar to the cover of this tent. My companion said: 'Then, when you come here, ask questions, and if you are given hair of an animal, make yourself fringes of it.' Then I looked up to the smoke-hole and saw nine human figures made of iron. I don't remember any more, nor how I reached them, but I began to hit them with a stick, saying: 'When shamanizing in the clean tent,[6] I shall ascend by them.' 'You will be a great shaman indeed, you find out everything,' said (my companion) clapping his hands. 'If this is so, I shall surely be a shaman. But I don't want to be a shaman,' said I to myself. 'No, you will be a shaman, since you have seen all these things' – they said.

We entered the tent and found there seven moon-figures made of copper, similar to those that are on the shamans' clothes. 'Behold, they are yours,' said (my companion) and began to give me the figures. I did not take them. 'No, take them,' said he and brought forth seven suns which he showed me. 'What is this?' I thought, 'probably I shall have to enchant for seven days.' Then he gave me three times seven figures of the sun and said: 'Find it out!' – 'I don't know.' My companion said: 'You, being a new shaman, stand up (i.e. recover) and cure thrice seven men from their illness.' When I shamanize, I walk round all these tents.

I came out of this tent and reached another. I think it was mine. To me, it seemed a strange one, not my own. People were sitting around the fire, men on one side and women on the other. I went in, not as a man but as a skeleton; I don't know who gnawed me off, I don't know how it happened. As I took a close look at them, they did not look like real human beings but like skeletons which had been dressed. At the bottom of the tent, there was a seven-bladed anvil. I saw a woman who looked as if she were made of fire. I saw a man holding (a pair of) pliers. The woman had seven apertures on her body. From these, the man pulled out iron pieces as from the fire, placed them on the anvil and struck them with the hammer. When the iron cooled down, the man replaced it in the aperture of the woman's body as if it were fire. Although there was fire in the fireplace, the man did not make use of it. I looked round. Near the fireplace there was a woman, stirring up the fire with animal hides, while the sparks were flying on every side. The man took a piece of iron, placed it on the anvil and hit it with the hammer which consisted in reality of seven small hammers on a single helve. At every blow on the iron, sparks rose into the air and flew out through the smoke hole. My companion asked me: 'What do you think, what tent have we entered?' 'I don't know,' said I. 'However, it must be here that the pendants of the shaman's clothes are forged and it is probably these people I have to ask (for pendants), for my clothes. The man (= shaman) descends from many places, this is surely one of them.' 'This is not all of them, anyway,' they said. I tossed my head back and began to look at the smoke hole. 'What are those seven figures in the upper part of the tent?' I asked. 'They are the spirits of your future saw-toothed pendants,' he said. 'Do you give me these pieces of iron?' 'No, the time has not yet come for it,' they said. I began to feel uneasy. 'Then why do you make me guess?' 'Who are these two beings, the man and the woman; are they humans?' 'So that is the origin of the shamans,' I said. 'Indeed.' This is my fate – to lose my mind. 'Whenever you become a shaman, ask them for permission to make yourself clothes and a drum. Ask them also to give you reindeer for your clothes; if you come to this tent they will provide you with the necessary things. The sparks are birds, catch them, imitate them, we have birds, geese made from them, on the back of the dress.' When I entered as a skeleton and they forged, it meant that they forged me. The master of the earth, the spirit of the shamans, has become my origin. When a shin-bone or something else is hit and the sparks fly, there will be a shaman in your generation.

Then we came out of this tent and I began to look round. In front, there was a great river with sandy shores, and a hill with two tents on it. I began to guess what kind of a hill this was. It seemed as if the tent were standing on an iceberg, behind them were black spots of earth appearing from under the melting snow. The nearer tent was covered all over with white ńuks, whereas the more remote one had ńuks with checkerboard pattern.

When we went closer, we saw that tents were standing on both shores of the river. The checkered tent stood on the black spots of earth (on account of the melting snow), while the white tent was behind the river. It seemed as if I had come back to the river I had encountered at the beginning of the journey. One stream of the river continued southwards, the other northwards. 'Find it out,' said my companion. 'How long will you make me guess things? Anyway, when I become a shaman, the origin of my shamanship will be here. Whenever I submerge, I shall descend this water.' 'You will implore the place of confluence of these streams. When you submerge you will return swimming in the southern flow. Your throat, similar to the stream, will begin to talk, to conjure up this spirit. At the checkered tent, the upper parts of the smoke hole, the ńuks are made of poor, small-haired hides. What does it mean?' I said: 'The diseases devour everybody, yet they spare the half of mankind so that it may reproduce itself. Behold, these (the black squares of the checkerboard) cover the surviving men with the blackness of diseases.' 'Now that we have arrived here, I will leave you alone,' said my companion. 'If you return, you will be a man, if not – you will die. Henceforward I cannot lead you anymore. I have led you to all the origins and ways of diseases. Shamanizing, you will find your way, by yourself.'

Standing near the tent, I looked at the river and saw a woman passing by. She was quite red, her face and hair included, and her dress was checkered.

Some of the squares were red, the others blue. 'Here,' said my companion, 'I have brought you here. It was only the way of the big disease that I have not showed you yet. That's why I have brought you here. You will shamanize with the big disease, take care not to curse but to implore when you shamanize. Can you guess who this woman is?' I: 'Her body is quite red and her dress is strange. The shaman gets up and sits down when shamanizing. Why, he sits on different litters, obviously, the woman carries these litters of mine with her. The red disease (measles) sometimes occurs, she seems to be its mother. There were checkered ńuks on the tent. This means that the tent was covered with the clothes of the woman. She took off the ńuks and put them on.' I looked at the tent – it was quite red. 'If in case of such disease (measles) I shall come here and appeal to her I shall surely heal (the sick),' said I. 'Yes,' said my companion, 'I have told you already that I shall leave you. Well, my friend, you must not even look at this tent, whoever may be there. You must not go there. I have brought you to this tent, where your forefather, the famous shaman died of pox. I leave you here to make friends and not to die of this plague.'

I became terribly frightened. The woman said: 'You have come from far away. Yet, I am obliged to send you back.' And she breathed on me three times. As she was breathing I began to recognize the place. Yet she did not let me go immediately, but said: 'My friend, there is a tent there, but you must not cross the river, and, from now on, you should only come up to me. If you want to obtain advice from that tent (from its female occupant), I shall give you advice. By now, she will have surely come to know that you are here. I shall notify her. When she opens her mouth and blows, the fog sets in. It is from this fog that men get sick.'

Meanwhile, my companion stood sideways and listened. Then the fog came. 'Find it out!' said the woman. I began to get angry, but still said: 'Half of the fog is the breath of men; when I am a shaman, I shall be able to rescue the nil'ti of the dead from this fog.' 'Yes, indeed,' said the woman. 'Here is a reef[7] with a red tent on it. If the sick [person] is cured, the woman will come from the opposite direction. If the nil'ti falls beyond the reef, beyond the limit of the fog – that is the limit of life – he cannot be saved.' Then I said to myself: 'I am sure that I have reached the place whence every man descends' and, turning towards the woman, I said aloud: 'You are surely the mistress of the earth who has created all life.' 'Yes, that is so,' said she. 'Well, my friend, we had three children, the second lives in the red tent, the eldest is beyond the river. You return from these places. If you want to enter their tents, you shall die. They are half barusis, half nguos.[8] Take care to look in the direction in which you have to return.

Then I made a few steps forward and, looking round, saw seven stone peaks. On one of them, there were seven willows, on the other seven thin trees, and so on – seven plants were growing on each peak. 'What's that?' thought I. Everywhere on the plants, there were nests of all kinds of birds. On the highest peak, in the middle, a bumble-bee was hatching her young. Her wings were of iron. She looked as if she were hatching while lying in the fire. The woman pointed at these nests and said: 'You are surely tired, come here, lie down, and find out what that is!' 'This is the bumble-bee, who creates (plant) for the tinder, so that none of the men should be in want of it. These seven peaks are the origin of every plant: the future shamans go around them. In these nests there are spirits – the master spirits of all the running and flying birds and game.' 'What can you see on the shore?' the woman asked. 'I can see two stone peaks.' 'Find it out!' I replied: 'When we reached at one of the peaks – this is the mistress of water, we can ask her for fish. The other peak is black. When a child is born, it is placed on a layer made of punk wood. Half of the peak is covered with such punk wood, the other half, with moss. When he gets here, the shaman can cure the child, in case of disease. The spirit of this lives here.'

Then I left them and saw nothing but the earth. It seemed as if I were going along a river. One shore was pebbly, the other covered with coloured stones – yellow ochre and black earth (graphite). A woman began to talk: 'The coloured stones are iron, copper and different metals. When you become a shaman, you make yourself pendants of them, therefore you go to them.' Going on along the shore I saw two peaks; one of them was covered with bright-coloured vegetation, the other was black earth all over. Between them, there appeared to be an islet with some very nice red plants in blossom on it. They resembled the flowers of the cloudberry. 'What is this,' I thought. There was nobody near me, but I found it out myself. When a man dies, his face becomes blue and changes: then the shaman has nothing more to do. As I noticed the red grass grew upwards, the black downwards. Suddenly I heard a cry: 'Take a stone from here!' The stones were reddish. Since I was marked out to survive, I snatched up a red stone. What I thought to be flowers were stones. Someone said to me: 'When you have a clean tent made, have a fire lit with flint. When you get to your own tent, speak about this with the men, not sitting like this, but shamanizing, because you are a shaman singing with the throat of nine diseases.'

Suddenly I recovered my senses: I must have been lying for a considerable time, near the root of the tree. So I felled that tree and made a *kuojka* sledge of it. This was our ancestral *kuojka*. Whenever I go shamanizing, I always hear the terrible songs on the peaks. Before coming to myself, I heard a voice saying: 'If you become a shaman, you will live a long time.' This was twenty years ago and I was not married. When I am shamanizing, I see a road to the north. When I am looking for a sick man, the road is narrow like a thread. I do not know who is leading me, in front I see the sun and the moon. On (the lower) part of the narrow road there are conical ramshackle tents; on this (road) you go for the breath of the man. The other part of the road (leading upwards) is quite entangled – I do not understand why. The man who is to recover has a breath like a white thread, while he who dies has one like a black thread. Going along the road, you look sideways and you proceed. Then you find the man's *nil'ti* and take it.

Half of my spirits comes from the men of the forest (the Tungus).

It was new moon, a bright weather in March when we three set off. I had been blindfolded with the hide of the wild reindeer and sent afoot to find a tree for the drum. The companions followed me on reindeer. The tree suitable for the drum, makes sounds like a drum. I ran forward, with my eyes covered, listening. The spirits do not give immediately the opportunity to find the tree, they mislead us. There are as many as three sounding trees instead of one – the third has to be chopped down.

Now, you are going to one of these trees – it is also coming towards you. 'Am I to take this tree?' I asked myself and began to sneak up to it as if it were a wild reindeer. But if you try to take it, somebody pushes you away so that you leap aside. 'Don't do it, or you shall die!' This is the tree where the spirits of your family live – the tree that protects your family against death and diseases. Realizing your mistake, you walk on before being pushed away.

Then you hear another tree sounding (like a drum) and coming towards you and you prepare to catch it. But you must not do so. This is the tree where the breath of your entire flock and the breath of the flocks of your home folk get, 'mixed.' If you touch this tree, you die.

Finally, I see a third tree, it stands and does not move. I begin to steal up to it. The tree says: 'Come, come, I am for you!' Then I fell it. My companions did the work with the axe, not I. They must by no means be relatives. If, for all that, the tree is a false one and not the real one, you implore in vain when bending the hoop – that would break anyway, and then somebody belonging to the shaman's kin would die. But if you suspect this, do make a drum of this hoop, even if it will be a bad one, but previously perform a ceremony, so that nobody should die.

When, for a man's illness, I make ceremonies to the evil spirits, the latter would say: 'Here, I have surrendered to you, what is he going to give me?' I ask: 'What you require for him I shall settle.' 'The ill man has to kill a certain wild reindeer,' says the disease. The man indeed kills such a wild reindeer, gives me its hide and I make a new dress of it for myself. It may happen that the spirit does not speak sincerely and says: 'He should kill a wolf, a fox or some other game.' But in reality, the ill man kills a reindeer.

Notes

1   *kuojka* – holy family relics such as stones, anthropomorph and zoomorphic figures made of wood or metal. They were transported in special sledges.
2   The bars that serve to hang the tea pot or the kettle over the fire.
3   *ńuk* – tent, cover of conical hut.
4   *nil'ti* – one of the life substances ('soul'? A.P.).

5   The Nganasans, when appealing to the shaman during the ceremony, hit the drum with a stick.

6   The feast of the clean tent, a spring festivity celebrated together with the 7 or 9 day ceremony of the shaman.

7   A rock rising above the water surface in the river.

8   *barusi* – malevolent spirits, *nguo* – benevolent divinities and spirits.

Chapter 2

Michael Harner

DISCOVERING THE WAY

MY FIRST PROLONGED FIELDWORK as an anthropologist took place in 1956 and 1957 on the forested eastern slopes of the Ecuadorian Andes among the Jívaro [HEE-varo] Indians, or *Untsuri Shuar*. The Jívaro were famous at that time for their now essentially vanished practice of 'head-shrinking,' and for their intensive practice of shamanism, which still continues. I successfully collected a great deal of information, but remained an outside observer of the world of the shaman at that time.

A couple of years later, the American Museum of Natural History invited me to make a year-long expedition to the Peruvian Amazon to study the culture of the Conibo Indians of the Ucayali River region. I accepted, delighted to have an opportunity to do more research on the fascinating Upper Amazon forest cultures. That fieldwork took place in 1960 and 1961.

Two particular experiences I had among the Conibo and the Jívaro were basic to my discovering the way of the shaman in both those cultures, and I would like to share them with you. Perhaps they will convey something of the incredible hidden world open to the shamanic explorer.

I had been living for the better part of a year in a Conibo Indian village beside a remote lake off a tributary of the Río Ucayali. My anthropological research on the culture of the Conibo had been going well, but my attempts to elicit information on their religion met with little success. The people were friendly, but reluctant to talk about the supernatural. Finally they told me that if I really wished to learn, I must take the shamans' sacred drink made from *ayahuasca*, the 'soul vine.' I agreed, with both curiosity and trepidation, for they warned me that the experience would be very frightening.

The next morning my friend Tomás, the kind elder of the village, went into the forest to cut the vines. Before leaving, he told me to fast: a light breakfast and no lunch. He returned midday with enough *ayahuasca* vines and leaves of the *cawa* plant to fill a fifteen gallon pot. He boiled them all afternoon, until only about a quart of dark liquid remained. This he poured into an old bottle and left it to cool until sunset, when he said we would drink it.

The Indians muzzled the dogs in the village so that they could not bark. The noise of barking dogs could drive a man who had taken *ayahuasca* mad, I was told. The children were cautioned to be quiet, and silence came over the small community with the setting of the sun.

As the brief equatorial twilight was replaced by darkness, Tomás poured about a third of the bottle into a gourd bowl and gave it to me. All the Indians were watching. I felt like Socrates amidst his Athenian compatriots, accepting the hemlock – it occurred to me that one of the alternate names people in the Peruvian Amazon gave *ayahuasca* was 'the little death.' I drank the potion quickly. It had a strange, slightly bitter taste. I then waited for Tomás to take his turn, but he said that he had decided not to participate after all.

They had me lie down on the bamboo platform under the great thatched roof of the communal house. The village was silent, except for the chirping of crickets and the distant calls of a howler monkey deep in the jungle.

As I stared upward into the darkness, faint lines of light appeared. They grew sharper, more intricate, and burst into brilliant colors. Sound came from far away, a sound like a waterfall, which grew stronger and stronger until it filled my ears.

Just a few minutes earlier I had been disappointed, sure that the *ayahuasca* was not going to have any effect on me. Now the sound of rushing water flooded my brain. My jaw began to feel numb, and the numbness was moving up to my temples.

Overhead the faint lines became brighter, and gradually interlaced to form a canopy resembling a geometric mosaic of stained glass. The bright violet hues formed an ever-expanding roof above me. Within this celestial cavern, I heard the sound of water grow louder and I could see dim figures engaged in shadowy movements. As my eyes seemed to adjust to the gloom, the moving scene resolved itself into something resembling a huge fun house, a supernatural carnival of demons. In the center, presiding over the activities, and looking directly at me, was a gigantic, grinning crocodilian head, from whose cavernous jaws gushed a torrential flood of water. Slowly the waters rose, and so did the canopy above them, until the scene metamorphosed into a simple duality of blue sky above and sea below. All creatures had vanished.

Then, from my position near the surface of the water, I began to see two strange boats wafting back and forth, floating through the air towards me, coming closer and closer. They slowly combined to form a single vessel with a huge dragon-headed prow, not unlike that of a Viking ship. Set amidships was a square sail. Gradually, as the boat gently floated back and forth above me, I heard a rhythmic swishing sound and saw that it was a giant galley with several hundred oars moving back and forth in cadence with the sound.

I became conscious, too, of the most beautiful singing I have ever heard in my life, high-pitched and ethereal, emanating from myriad voices on board the galley. As I looked more closely at the deck, I could make out large numbers of people with the heads of blue jays and the bodies of humans, not unlike the bird-headed gods of ancient Egyptian tomb paintings. At the same time, some energy-essence began to float from my chest up into the boat. Although I believed myself to be an atheist, I was completely certain that I was dying and that the bird-headed people had come to take my soul away on the boat. While the soul-flow continued from my chest, I was aware that the extremities of my body were growing numb.

Starting with my arms and legs, my body slowly began to feel like it was turning to solid concrete. I could not move or speak. Gradually, as the numbness closed in on my chest, toward my heart, I tried to get my mouth to ask for help, to ask the Indians for an antidote. Try as I might, however, I could not marshal my abilities sufficiently to make a word. Simultaneously, my abdomen seemed to be turning to stone, and I had to make a tremendous effort to keep my heart beating. I began to call my heart my friend, my dearest friend of all, to talk to it, to encourage it to beat with all the power remaining at my command.

I became aware of my brain. I felt – physically – that it had become compartmentalized into four separate and distinct levels. At the uppermost surface was the observer and commander, which was conscious of the condition of my body, and was responsible for the attempt to keep my heart going. It perceived, but purely as a spectator, the visions emanating from what seemed to be the nether portions of my brain. Immediately below the topmost level I felt a numbed layer, which seemed to have been put out of commission by the drug – it just wasn't there. The next level down was the source of my visions, including the soul boat.

Now I was virtually certain I was about to die. As I tried to accept my fate, an even lower portion of my brain began to transmit more visions and information. I was 'told' that this new material was being presented to me because I was dying and therefore 'safe' to receive these revelations. These were the secrets reserved for the dying and the dead, I was informed. I could only very dimly perceive the givers of these thoughts: giant reptilian creatures reposing sluggishly at the lowermost depths of the back of my brain, where it met the top of the spinal column. I could only vaguely see them in what seemed to be gloomy, dark depths.

Then they projected a visual scene in front of me. First they showed me the planet Earth as it was eons ago, before there was any life on it. I saw an ocean, barren land, and a bright blue sky. Then black specks dropped from the sky by the hundreds and landed in front of me on the barren landscape. I could see that the 'specks' were actually large, shiny, black creatures with stubby pterodactyl-like wings and huge whale-like bodies. Their heads were not visible to me. They flopped down, utterly exhausted from their trip, resting for eons. They explained to me in a kind of thought language that they were fleeing from something out in space. They had come to the planet Earth to escape their enemy.

The creatures then showed me how they had created life on the planet in order to hide within the multitudinous forms and thus disguise their presence. Before me, the magnificence of plant and animal creation and speciation – hundreds of millions of years of activity – took place on a scale and with a vividness impossible to describe. I learned that the dragon-like creatures were thus inside of all forms of life, including man.[1] They were the true masters of humanity and the entire planet, they told me. We humans were but the receptacles and servants of these creatures. For this reason they could speak to me from within myself.

These revelations, welling up from the depths of my mind, alternated with visions of the floating galley, which had almost finished taking my soul on board. The boat with its blue-jay headed deck crew was gradually drawing away, pulling my life force along as it headed toward a large fjord flanked by barren, worn hills. I knew I had only a moment more to live. Strangely, I had no fear of the bird-headed people; they were welcome to have my soul if they could keep it. But I was afraid that somehow my soul might not remain on the horizontal plane of the fjord but might, through processes unknown but felt and dreaded, be acquired or re-acquired by the dragon-like denizens of the depths.

I suddenly felt my distinctive humanness, the contrast between my species and the ancient reptilian ancestors. I began to struggle against returning to the ancient ones, who were beginning to feel increasingly alien and possibly evil. Each heart beat was a major undertaking. I turned to human help.

With an unimaginable last effort, I barely managed to utter one word to the Indians: 'Medicine!' I saw them rushing around to make an antidote, and I knew they could not prepare it in time. I needed a guardian who could defeat dragons, and I frantically tried to conjure up a powerful being to protect me against the alien reptilian creatures. One appeared before me; and at that moment the Indians forced my mouth open and poured the antidote into me. Gradually, the dragons disappeared back into the lower depths; the soul boat and the fjord were no more. I relaxed with relief.

The antidote radically eased my condition, but it did not prevent me from having many additional visions of a more superficial nature. These were manageable and enjoyable. I made fabulous journeys at will through distant regions, even out into the Galaxy; created incredible architecture; and employed sardonically grinning demons to realize my fantasies. Often I found myself laughing aloud at the incongruities of my adventures.

Finally, I slept.

Rays of sunlight were piercing the holes in the palm-thatched roof when I awoke. I was still lying on the bamboo platform, and I heard the normal, morning sounds all around me: the Indians conversing, babies crying, and a rooster crowing. I was surprised to discover that I felt refreshed and peaceful. As I lay there looking up at the beautiful woven pattern of the roof, the memories of the previous night drifted across my mind. I momentarily stopped myself from remembering more in order to get my tape recorder from a duffle bag. As I dug into the bag, several of the Indians greeted me, smiling. An old woman, Tomás' wife, gave me a bowl of fish and plantain soup for breakfast. It tasted extraordinarily good. Then I went back to the platform, eager to put my night's experiences on tape before I forgot anything.

The work of recall went easily except for one portion of the trance that I could not remember. It remained blank, as though a tape had been erased. I struggled for hours to remember what had happened in that part of the experience, and I virtually wrestled it back into my consciousness. The recalcitrant material turned out to be the communication from the dragon-like creatures, including the revelation of their role in the evolution of life on this planet and their innate domination of living matter, including man. I was highly excited at rediscovering this material, and could not help but feel that I was not supposed to be able to bring it back from the nether regions of the mind.

I even had a peculiar sense of fear for my safety, because I now possessed a secret that the creatures had indicated was only intended for the dying. I immediately decided to share this knowledge with others so that the 'secret' would not reside in me alone, and my life would not be in jeopardy. I put my outboard motor on a dugout canoe and left for an American evangelist mission station nearby. I arrived about noon.

The couple at the mission, Bob and Millie, were a cut above the average evangelists sent from the United States: hospitable, humorous, and compassionate.[2] I told them my story. When I described the reptile with water gushing out of his mouth, they exchanged glances, reached for their Bible, and read to me the following line from Chapter 12 in the Book of Revelation:

And the serpent cast out of his mouth water as a flood . . .

They explained to me that the word 'serpent' was synonymous in the Bible with the words 'dragon' and 'Satan.' I went on with my narrative. When I came to the part about the dragon-like creatures fleeing an enemy somewhere beyond the Earth and landing here to hide from their pursuers, Bob and Millie became excited and again read me more from the same passage in the Book of Revelation:

And there was a war in heaven: Michael and his angels fought against the dragon; and the dragon fought and his angels. And

> prevailed not; neither was their place found any more in heaven. And the great dragon was cast out, that old serpent, called the Devil, and Satan, which deceiveth the whole world: he was cast out into the earth, and his angels with him.

I listened with surprise and wonder. The missionaries, in turn, seemed to be awed by the fact that an atheistic anthropologist, by taking the drink of the 'witch doctors,' could apparently have revealed to him some of the same holy material in the Book of Revelation. When I had finished my account, I was relieved to have shared my new knowledge, but I was also exhausted. I fell asleep on the missionaries' bed, leaving them to continue their discussion of the experience.

That evening, as I returned to the village in my canoe, my head began to throb in rhythm with the noise of the outboard motor; I thought I was going mad; I had to stick my fingers in my ears to avoid the sensation. I slept well, but the next day I noticed a numbness or pressure in my head.

I was now eager to solicit a professional opinion from the most supernaturally knowledgeable of the Indians, a blind shaman who had made many excursions into the spirit world with the aid of the *ayahuasca* drink. It seemed only proper that a blind man might be able to be my guide to the world of darkness.

I went to his hut, taking my notebook with me, and described my visions to him segment by segment. At first I told him only the highlights; thus, when I came to the dragon-like creatures, I skipped their arrival from space and only said, 'There were these giant black animals, something like great bats, longer than the length of this house, who said that they were the true masters of the world.' There is no word for dragon in Conibo, so 'giant bat' was the closest I could come to describe what I had seen.

He stared up toward me with his sightless eyes, and said with a grin, 'Oh, they're always saying that. But they are only the Masters of Outer Darkness.'

He waved his hand casually toward the sky. I felt a chill along the lower part of my spine, for I had not yet told him that I had seen them, in my trance, coming from outer space.

I was stunned. What I had experienced was already familiar to this barefoot, blind shaman. Known to him from his own explorations of the same hidden world into which I had ventured. From that moment on I decided to learn everything I could about shamanism.

And there was something more that encouraged me in my new quest. After I recounted my entire experience, he told me that he did not know of anyone who had encountered and learned so much on his first *ayahuasca* journey.

'You can surely be a master shaman,' he said.

Thus my serious study of shamanism began. From the Conibo I especially learned about the journey into the Lowerworld and the retrieval of spirits, methods that will be described later in the book. I returned to the United States in 1961, but three years later I came back to South America to be with the Jívaro, with whom I had lived in 1956 and 1957. My mission this time was not just to be an anthropologist, but to learn firsthand how to practice shamanism the Jívaro way. For that reason, I wanted to go to the northwestern part of the Jívaro country where the most powerful shamans were reputed to reside.

I first flew to Quito, Ecuador, in the Andean highlands. I took an old Junkers tri-motor down to a jungle airfield at the eastern base of the Andes on the Pastaza River. There I chartered a single-engine plane to Macas, an ancient white settlement at the foot of the Andes in the midst of the Jívaro country.

Macas was a strange village. It had been founded in 1599 by a handful of Spaniards who had survived the massacre of the legendary Sevilla del Oro by the Jívaro, and for centuries had been perhaps the most isolated community of the Western world. Until the airstrip was built in the 1940s, its most direct connection to the outside world had been a slippery footpath over the Andean escarpment west of the village, involving an arduous eight-day hike to reach the highland city of Riobamba. This isolation had created a white community unlike any other in the world. Even during the early years of the twentieth century the men hunted with blowguns, wore Indian dress, and proudly declared their direct descent from the Conquistadores.

They also had their own marvelous legends and private mysteries. For example, there was the story of how, after the massacre and the retreat from Sevilla del Oro, it took them almost a century to find a new way out over the Andes. The man who had finally succeeded was still remembered in bedtime stories to the children. And there was the spectral horse, complete with clanking chains, which was reportedly such a frequent night visitor to the streets of the village that the inhabitants often huddled inside the palm-thatched huts while the monster roamed about. Its visits ended in 1924, when Catholic missionaries permanently settled in the community. At that time, incidentally, there were still no horses in Macas — the first one, a colt, was carried in on a man's back from Riobamba in 1928, almost three and a half centuries after the community's founding.

Up behind the village, surmounting the eastern Cordillera of the Andes, was Sangay, a great active volcano, snow-capped, billowing smoke by day and glowing by night. The glow, the Macabeos liked to say, was produced by the treasure of the Incas, which they claimed was buried on the slopes of Sangay.

My first day in Macas went well. My young Jívaro guide was awaiting me at the airstrip and the people were hospitable and generous. Food was plentiful, and our meals included generous portions of meat. Since there was no way for the Macabeos to get their cattle over the Andes, they had to eat the beasts themselves; thus cattle were slaughtered in the little village every day. In addition, they gave me *guayusa*, a native tea, which the Macabeos consumed throughout the day instead of coffee. The tea created a sense of euphoria, and the entire local population was gently stoned all day. *Guayusa* is so habituating that before it is offered to a visitor, he is warned that once he drinks it, he will ever after always return to the Ecuadorian jungle.

As I drifted off to sleep in Macas that night of my arrival, images in brilliant reddish hues appeared to me in the darkness of the Macabeo house. What I saw was most peculiar: curvilinear designs intertwining, separating, and turning in a most enjoyable fashion. Then small, grinning demonic faces, which were also red, appeared among the changing patterns – swirling, disappearing and reappearing. I felt I was seeing the spiritual inhabitants of Macas.

Suddenly, with an explosion and a jolt, I was almost thrown off my slat bed. The dogs of the village burst out barking. The visions vanished. People were shouting. An earthquake had shaken the ground, and now a spray of natural fireworks shot into the night sky from Sangay. I felt, undoubtedly irrationally, that the sardonic demons had produced the eruption to greet my return to the jungle and to remind me of their reality. I laughed to myself at the absurdity of it all.

The next day the Catholic missionary showed me his private collection of prehistoric potsherds from the local area. On them were painted red designs almost identical to those I had seen the previous night.

The following morning, my Jívaro guide and I walked northward from Macas, crossed the Río Upano in a dugout canoe, and continued walking all day.

At sunset, exhausted, we reached our destination, the house of a famous shaman, Akachu, deep in the forest. There was no *guayusa* that evening. Instead, I was proffered bowl after bowl of refreshing manioc beer, monkey meat, and raw, squirming, but delicious cheese-like grubs. Tired, but delighted to be back among shamans, I fell into a deep sleep on the bamboo bed.

In the morning Akachu and I sat formally, opposite each other on wooden stools, as his wives brought us bowls of warmed manioc beer. His long black hair, bound into a pony tail with a woven red and white strap from which a feathered tassel hung, showed streaks of gray. I guessed he was in his sixties.

'I have come,' I explained, 'to acquire spirit helpers, *tsentsak.*'

He stared hard at me without saying a word, but the wrinkles in his brown face seemed to deepen.

'That is a fine gun, there,' he observed, jutting his chin toward the Winchester shotgun I had brought along for hunting.

His message was clear, for the standard payment among the Jívaro for shamanic initiation was – at the very least – a muzzle-loading shotgun. The breach-loading, cartridge-using Winchester was far more powerful than the black-powder muzzle-loaders, and thus much more valuable.

'To acquire knowledge and spirit helpers, I will give you the gun and my two boxes of cartridges,' I said.

Akachu nodded and reached his arm out in the direction of the Winchester. I picked up the gun and carried it over to him. He tested its weight and balance, and sighted along the barrel. Then, abruptly, he laid the gun across his knees.

'First, you must bathe in the waterfall,' he said. 'Then we will see.'

I told him I was ready to do whatever he said.

'You are not a *shuar*, an Indian,' Akachu said, 'so I do not know if you will have success. But I will help you try.' He pointed westward toward the Andes with his chin. 'Soon we will make the journey to the waterfall.'

Five days later, Akachu, his son-in-law Tsangu, and I departed on the pilgrimage to the sacred waterfall. My Jívaro guide, his duties finished, had already gone home.

The first day we followed a forest trail upstream along a twisting river valley. My companions kept up a very fast pace, and I was thankful when we at last stopped in late afternoon, beside a small rapid in the river. Akachu and Tsangu constructed a palm-thatched lean-to, with a layer of palm fronds for our bed. I slept soundly, kept warm by the slow fire they built in the entrance of the shelter.

The second day our journey was almost a continuous climb upward into the mist-shrouded forest. As the virtually nonexistent trail became more difficult, we paused at a grove of *caña brava* to cut hiking staffs to help us in the ascent. Akachu briefly went off and returned with a three-inch thick pole of balsa wood. While we rested, he quickly carved it with simple geometric designs and then handed it to me.

'This is your magical staff,' he said. 'It will protect you from demons. If you encounter one, throw it at him. It is more powerful than a gun.'

I fingered the pole. It was extremely light and obviously would be of no use in defending oneself against anything material. For a moment I felt as though we were children playing a game of make-believe. Yet these men were warriors, warriors who engaged in repeated life-and-death feuds and wars with their enemies. Didn't their survival depend upon being in genuine contact with reality?

As the day progressed, the trail became steeper and more slippery. Often it seemed that I was sliding one step back in the adobe-like mud for every two steps I made forward. We frequently rested to catch our breath and to sip water mixed with the manioc beer mash in our bottle-gourd canteens. Sometimes the others would snack on the smoked boiled manioc or smoked meat that they carried in their monkey-skin pouches. I, however, was forbidden to eat solid food.

'You must suffer,' Tsangu explained, 'so that the grandfathers will take pity on you. Otherwise, the ancient specter will not come.'

That night, tired and hungry, I attempted to sleep in the palm-thatched lean-to my companions had constructed for us on the top of a cold, dank ridge. Shortly before dawn, it began to rain. Too chilled and miserable to stay where we were, we broke camp and groped in the dark along the ridge. The rain grew in intensity. Soon bolts of lightning, accompanied by explosions of thunder, periodically illuminated our way. Many of the lightning strikes seemed to be on the very ridge we were following, so we began to move at maximum speed in order to get off the heights. In the semi-darkness of the obscured dawn I often lost sight of the other two, who were much more accustomed to the incredible pace they were setting through the forest. Even under normal circumstances, the Indians loped along at about four or five miles an hour. Now it seemed like six.

Soon I lost sight of my companions entirely. I assumed they thought that I could follow them. They would undoubtedly be waiting for me somewhere ahead, beyond the end of the ridge. So I forged ahead, wet, tired, hungry, and fearful of being permanently lost in this great, uninhabited forest. One, two, three hours passed and I still did not encounter them. The rain let up and the light in the deserted forest grew stronger. I looked for the sharply bent branches of saplings, the Indians' sign that they had passed that way. But without luck.

I stopped, sat on a log in the middle of the dripping forest and tried to think clearly about my position. I gave the Indians' special long-distance yell, a cry from the depths of the lungs that can be heard a half-mile away. Three times I gave it. There was no answer. I was near panic. I did not have my gun, so hunting was impossible. I did not know where to go. The only humans that I knew of in the forest were my absent companions.

I was aware that we had been headed generally west, but the dense forest canopy prevented me from seeing the direction of the sun. The ridge had numerous forks, so that I could not tell which one would be the best to follow. Almost at random, I picked one ridge and followed it slowly, breaking branches every ten feet or so to guide my companions if they came searching that way. From time to time I yelled, but heard no answering sound. I stopped at a stream and added some water to the concentrated beer in my calabash. As I rested, sweating, dozens of butterflies swirled about, often settling on my head, shoulders and arms. I watched as they sucked the sweat from my skin and simultaneously urinated on it. I got up and went onward into the forest, supporting myself with the balsa staff. It was getting dark. With my *puñal*, or short machete, I cut branches from palm saplings and made a crude lean-to. Exhausted, I drank some beer, covered my body with fronds, and soon fell asleep.

Faint light was filtering down through the forest canopy when I awoke. As I lay there in the green stillness, I heard a muffled boom. It caught me by surprise and I could not ascertain its direction. I quietly listened for perhaps fifteen minutes when another occurred, off to my left. It was clearly a gun. I jumped up and rushed off in the direction of the sound, running, stumbling, slipping as I skidded down steep slopes. From time to time I gave the long-distance yell. Another boom, this time slightly to my right. I veered course and soon found myself climbing down a precipitous canyon, clinging to vines and slipping from one sapling to another. I became aware of a pervasive roar, like a never-ceasing freight train. Abruptly, I was on the boulder-strewn shore of a river. About a quarter-mile upstream, a stupendous waterfall was hurtling over a bare rock cliff. And near its base I could see my companions; at that moment they were my closest friends in all the world.

I had to clamber up and down immense river boulders and ford the pools of water that lay between sandbars. As I got near, I felt the mists of the waterfall, carried down the canyon on the wind, cooling my face and arms. It took me about fifteen minutes to reach Akachu and Tsangu. Finally, I collapsed on the sand beside my companions.

'We thought a demon might have gotten you,' said Akachu with a grin. I smiled back weakly, glad to accept the canteen of beer he offered.

'You are tired,' he said. 'That is good, for the grandfathers may take pity on you. You must now start to bathe.'

He pointed to my staff. 'Bring your balsa and come with me.' While Tsangu sat on the sandbar, Akachu led me over the rocks along the edge of the great pool into which the cascade poured. Soon we were up against the wet cliff face, as drenching sprays pelted our bodies. He took my hand and inched forward along the base of the cliff. The water poured with mounting strength upon us, making it difficult to avoid being swept away. I supported myself with my staff with one hand and hung onto Akachu with the other.

Each step forward became more difficult. Then suddenly we were underneath the waterfall in a dark, natural recess. It seemed like a magical cave. Light entered only through the immense sheet of falling water, which sealed us in from the rest of the world. The incessant roar of the cascade was greater than even that of my first vision, years before. It seemed to penetrate my whole being. We were sealed from the world by the basic elements of earth and water.

'The House of the Grandfathers,' Akachu shouted in my ear. He pointed to my staff.

He had told me earlier what to do. I began to walk back and forth in the incredible chamber, putting my staff before me with each step. As instructed, I continuously shouted, 'Tau, tau, tau,' to attract the attention of the grandfathers. I was thoroughly chilled from the spray that swept the small cave, water which not long before had been reposing in the glacial lakes of the highest Andes. I shivered, paced, and shouted. Akachu accompanied me, but without a staff.

Gradually, a strange calm pervaded my consciousness. I no longer felt cold, tired, or hungry. The sound of the cascading water grew more and more distant and seemed strangely soothing. I felt that this was where I belonged, that I had come home. The wall of falling water became iridescent, a torrent of millions of liquid prisms. As they went by I had the continuous sensation of floating upward, as though they were stable and I was the one in motion. Flying inside of a mountain! I laughed at the absurdity of the world.

Finally, Akachu grasped my shoulder, stopped me, and took my hand. He led me out of the magic mountain, back along the cliff and to Tsangu. I was sorry to leave the sacred place.

When we had regrouped on the sandbar, Tsangu led us directly to the side of the canyon and commenced scaling the steep slope. We followed, single file, grasping at projecting roots, saplings, and vines to keep ourselves from sliding backward in the wet clay. For perhaps an hour we continued the arduous ascent, occasionally drenched by the wafting spray from the waterfall. It was late afternoon when we finally reached a small, flat ridge adjacent to the rim of the cascade. We rested briefly and then followed Tsangu along the plateau. At first the jungle growth was thick and difficult to penetrate, but shortly we found ourselves in a gallery of immense trees.

After about five minutes Tsangu stopped, and started to cut boughs for a lean-to.

Akachu began splitting a stick at one end. He split the same end a second time, at a right angle to the first cut, and stuck the unsplit end into the ground. Into the cross-wise split he pushed two twigs, which forced the end open into a four-pronged receptacle. Then he took a fist-sized gourd cup from his monkey-skin shoulder bag and set it into the space formed by the prongs. He reached again into his pouch and brought forth a bundle of short green stems. They were the *maikua* (a *Brugmansia* species of datura) plant cuttings he had collected prior to our departure from his house. One by one he held the stems over the gourd cup and scraped off the green bark. When he had finished, the cup was almost full. He reached in, drew out the shavings, and began squeezing their green juice into the cup. Within five minutes there was about an eighth of a cup of the liquid. He threw away the shavings.

'Now we will let the *maikua* cool,' he said. 'When night comes you will drink it. You alone will drink, for we must guard you. We will be with you at all times, so do not fear.'

Tsangu had joined us, and now he added, 'What is most important is that you must have no fear. If you see something frightening, you must not flee. You must run up and touch it.'

Akachu grasped my shoulder. 'That is right. You must do that or one day soon you will die. Hold your balsa at all times in your hands so that you can do the touching.'

I began to feel a strong sense of panic. Not only were their words somewhat less than comforting, but I had heard that persons sometimes died or permanently lost their minds from taking *maikua*. I also remembered stories of Jívaro who had taken *maikua* and become so delirious that they had dashed wildly through the forest to fall from cliffs or to drown. For this reason, they never took *maikua* without sober companions to restrain them.[3]

'Will you hold me down strongly?' I asked.

'That will be done, brother,' said Akachu.

It was the first time he had addressed me by a kinship term, and that one word reassured me. Still, as I waited for the dark, rising anticipation and curiosity were mixed with fear.

My companions did not make a fire, and as night came we were all stretched out side by side on palm fronds, listening to the stillness of the forest and the distant roar of the waterfall. At last the time came.

Akachu gave me the gourd cup. I tipped it up and swallowed the contents. The taste was somewhat disagreeable, yet slightly similar to green tomatoes. I felt a numbing sensation. I thought of that other drink, three years before among the Conibo, which had led me here. Was my shamanic quest worth the danger?

Shortly, however, even quasi-logical thought vanished as an inexpressible terror rapidly permeated my whole body. My companions were going to kill me! I must get away! I attempted to jump up, but instantly they were upon me. Three, four, an infinity of savages wrestled with me, forced me down, down, down. Their faces were above me, contorted into sly grins. Then blackness.

I was awakened by a flash of lightning followed by a thunderous explosion. The ground beneath me was shaking. I jumped up, utterly in a panic. A hurricane-like wind threw me back down on the ground. I stumbled again to my feet. A stinging rain pelted my body as the wind ripped at my clothes. Lightning and thunder exploded all around. I grasped a sapling to support myself. My companions were nowhere to be seen.

Suddenly, about two hundred feet away amidst the tree trunks, I could see a luminous form floating slowly toward me. I watched, terrified, as it grew larger and larger, resolving itself into a twisting form. The gigantic, writhing reptilian form floated directly toward me. Its body shone in brilliant hues of greens, purples, and reds, and as it twisted amidst the lightning and thunder it looked at me with a strange sardonic smile.

I turned to run, and then remembered the balsa staff. I looked down but could not see it. The serpentine creature was now only twenty feet away and towering above me, coiling and uncoiling. It separated into two overlapping creatures. They were now both facing me. The dragons had come to take me away! They coalesced back into one. I saw before me a stick about a foot long. I grabbed it, and desperately charged the monster with my stick outstretched before me. An earsplitting scream filled the air, and abruptly the forest was empty. The monster was gone. There was only silence and serenity.

I lost consciousness.

When I awoke it was midday. Akachu and Tsangu were squatting beside a small fire, eating and conversing quietly. My head ached and I was hungry, but otherwise I felt all right. As I sat up, my friends rose and came over. Akachu gave me a bowl of warmed beer. I was also given a piece of dried monkey meat. The food tasted wonderful, but I wanted to share my experience with my friends.

I said, 'I thought you were trying to kill me last night. Then you disappeared and there was tremendous lightning . . .'

Akachu interrupted me. 'You must not tell anyone, even us, what you have encountered. Otherwise, all your suffering will have been in vain. Someday, and you will know when that is, you can tell others, but not now. Eat, and then we will start for home.'

We went back to Akachu's house, and with his guidance I began to acquire the *tsentsak* (magical darts) essential to the practice of Jívaro shamanism. These *tsentsak* or spirit helpers are the main powers believed to cause and cure illness in daily life. To the nonshaman they are normally invisible, and even shamans can perceive them only in an altered state of consciousness.[4]

'Bad' or bewitching shamans send these spirit helpers into victims' bodies to make them ill or to kill them. 'Good' shamans, or healers, use their own *tsentsak* to help them suck out spirits from the bodies of ill tribesmen. The spirit helpers also form shields which, along with the shaman's guardian spirit power, protect their shaman masters from attacks.

A new shaman collects all kinds of insects, plants, and other objects, which become his spirit helpers. Almost any object, including living insects and worms, can become a *tsentsak* if it is small enough to be swallowed by a shaman. Different types of *tsentsak* cause, and are used to cure, different kinds of degrees of illness. The greater the variety of these power objects that a shaman has in his body, the greater is his ability as a doctor.

Each *tsentsak* has an ordinary and nonordinary aspect. The magical dart's ordinary aspect is an ordinary material object, as seen without drinking *ayahuasca*. But the nonordinary and 'true' aspect of the *tsentsak* is revealed to the shaman by taking the drink. When he does this, the magical darts appear in their hidden forms as spirit helpers, such as giant butterflies, jaguars, serpents, birds, and monkeys, who actively assist the shaman in his tasks.

When a healing shaman is called in to treat a patient, his first task is diagnosis. He drinks *ayahuasca*, green tobacco water, and sometimes the juice of a plant called *pirípirí*, in the late afternoon and early evening. The consciousness-changing substances permit him to see into the body of the patient as though it were glass. If the illness is due to sorcery, the healing shaman will see the intruding nonordinary entity within the patient's body clearly enough to determine whether he possesses the appropriate spirit helper to extract it by sucking.

A shaman sucks magical darts from a patient's body at night, and in a dark area of the house, for it is only in the darkness that he can perceive nonordinary reality. With the setting of the sun, he alerts his *tsentsak* by whistling the tune of his power song; after about a quarter of an hour, he starts singing. When he is ready to suck, the shaman keeps two *tsentsak*, of the type identical to the one he has seen in the patient's body, in the front and rear of his mouth. They are present in both their material and nonmaterial aspects, and are there to catch the nonordinary aspect of the magical dart when the shaman sucks it out of the patient's body. The *tsentsak* nearest the shaman's lips has the task of incorporating the sucked-out essence within itself. If, however, this nonordinary essence should get past it, the second spirit helper in the mouth blocks the throat so that the intruder cannot enter the interior of the shaman's body and do him harm. Trapped thus within the mouth, the essence is shortly caught by, and incorporated into, the material substance of one of the curing shaman's *tsentsak*. He then 'vomits' out this object and displays it to the patient and his family saying, 'Now I have sucked it out. Here it is.'

The nonshamans may think that the material object itself is what has been sucked out, and the shaman does not disillusion them. At the same time he is not lying, because he knows that the only important aspect of a *tsentsak* is its nonmaterial or nonordinary aspect, or essence, which he sincerely believes he has removed from the patient's body. To explain to the layman that he already had these objects in his mouth would serve no fruitful purpose and would prevent him from displaying such an object as proof that he had effected the cure.

The ability of the shaman to suck depends largely upon the quantity and strength of his own *tsentsak*, of which he may have hundreds. His magical darts assume their supernatural aspect as spirit helpers when he is under the influence of *ayahuasca*, and he sees them as a variety of zoomorphic forms hovering over him, perching on his shoulders, and sticking out of his skin. He sees them helping to suck the patient's body. He drinks tobacco water every few hours to 'keep them fed' so that they will not leave him.

A healing shaman may have *tsentsak* sent at him by a bewitcher. Because of this danger, shamans may repeatedly drink tobacco water at all hours of the day and night. The tobacco water helps keep one's *tsentsak* ready to repel any other magical darts. A shaman does not even go for a walk without taking along the green tobacco leaves with which he prepares the water that keeps his spirit helpers alert.

The degree of violence and competition in Jívaro society is famous in the anthropological literature and contrasts radically, for example, with the peacefulness of the Conibo. And both the Jívaro and the Conibo stand apart from Australian and many other tribal peoples who have long practiced shamanism without employing psychedelics. Still Jívaro shamanism is highly developed, dramatic, and exciting. So in 1969 I again returned, filling in gaps in my knowledge, and in 1973 I engaged in more shamanic practice with them.

During the years since beginning shamanic work among the Conibo, I have also studied briefly with shamans of a few western North American Indian groups: the Wintun and Pomo in California, Coast Salish in Washington State, and the Lakota Sioux in South Dakota. From them I learned how shamanism could be practiced successfully without the use of the *ayahuasca* or other drugs of the Conibo and the Jívaro. This knowledge has been especially useful in introducing Westerners to the practice of shamanism. Finally, I learned from the worldwide ethnographic literature on shamanism, where lie buried many gems of information that supplement and reaffirm what I had been taught firsthand. Now it seems time to help transmit some practical aspects of this ancient human legacy to those who have been cut off from it for centuries.

Notes

1   In retrospect one could say they were almost like DNA, although at that time, 1961, I knew nothing of DNA.
2   Their names have been changed.
3   This narrative does not imply recommendation of *ayahuasca* or *naikua* use by the reader. Datura species, in fact, are quite toxic and their ingestion can produce a series of untoward effects, including death.
4   Fuller accounts of Jívaro shamanism may be found in Warner 1972: 16–124, 152–66; and in Warner 1968 or 1973.

References

Harner, Michael J. 1968. 'The Sound of Rushing Water', *Natural History* 77(6): 28–33, 60–1.
Harner, Michael J. 1972. *The Jívaro: People of the Sacred Waterfalls*. Garden City, NY: Doubleday.
Harner, Michael J. 1973. 'The Sound of Rusting Water', in *Hallucinogens and Shamanism* (Michael J. Warner, ed.), pp. 15–27. New York: Oxford University Press.

PART TWO

Shamanising

INTRODUCTION TO PART TWO

IF INITIATION SETS A NEW SHAMAN on a life-journey, or provides them with a new mode of employment and relationship, it is what they do next, and what they continue to do, that will establish them as shamans. Shamans are defined by their actions and engagements. It is true, of course, that shamans hold certain beliefs, theories, viewpoints or notions. Typically, their understandings of the world and the cosmos coincide with those of clients, neighbours, family, and others in their wider society. Understanding of such worldviews or cosmovisions is important, and much attention has been devoted to the study of the structure of the world – or worlds – as shamans experience it, or them. What distinguishes shamans from others in their communities is, however, what they do rather than what they think.

In a broad sense it is true that all religion is a matter of action, observance, performance, or practice. In Christianity there is a strong theological discourse that insists on the priority of belief or faith. Assertions or propositions about ultimate reality, or the real nature of life, are considered to be definitive of religion. However, even here, it has been important for people to publicly declare their faith and to act upon it in various ways. Furthermore, even among theologians religion is always a matter of someone's action, e.g. as some response to acts of a God (creation, revelation, salvation, and so on). At any rate, the very discourse that makes people wary of the term 'religion' (because it appears to refer to systems of beliefs) in fact arises from lifeways not unlike those encountered elsewhere. It is certainly true that many languages have no word that can be directly and unambiguously translated as 'religion'. However, not only is religion capable of many definitions, many of which are evidently applicable in indigenous contexts, but also the academic Study of Religion now engages with far more complex and interesting understandings of religion precisely because it interacts with indigenous and other life-ways (see Smith 1998). In short, shamans and their communities perform religion when they attempt to meet needs for health, food, security and knowledge. Their understandings of the world are expressed in particular actions, at which point it is the expertise of shamans that makes them recognisable as shamans.

The following series of readings explore various activities of shamans shamanising or performing as shamans. They exemplify a range of activities and should not be taken to be universally applicable. Not all shamans act in the same ways or for the same reasons. Common ground must be sought for carefully and built upon with reticence.

Roberte Hamayon in Chapter 3 argues that in pre-Soviet Siberian hunting communities shamans performed a specific role: their 'main function' was 'obtaining the promise of game or "good luck" for hunters'. Importantly clarifying the relationship between shaman and community, Hamayon discusses the large collective ritual where this function is carried out, and where new shamans are confirmed and established within the community. The interplay of 'game' (hunted animals) and 'games' (entertainments and contests) significantly enhances understandings of relationships, especially reciprocity, among shamanic societies.

Ioan Lewis in Chapter 4 makes clear what he considers central to Tungus shamanism, arguing that it is 'closely associated with the clan system'. Eschewing a romantic notion that indigenous kinship systems might be entirely harmonious, he locates the activities of shamans in dealing with problems resulting from neglect of, or antagonism from, 'clan spirits'. His discussion of Tungus is situated between discussions of the Macha Oromo of Ethiopia (among whom shamans compete with other religious and social authorities), the Akawaio of British Guiana (among whom there is little role differentiation and thus shamans have a wide portfolio) and the Eskimo (among whom shamans intervene between society and 'nature'). In all these cases Lewis clarifies his argument about possession, morality religions, and degrees of centrality or marginality.

In Chapter 5 John Grim differentiates various kinds of traditional Ojibway (or Anishinaabeg) shamans and the various means and contexts in which they heal and divine. This invaluably points to the possible diversities even among a single nation, people or group, and establishes a barrier to over-systematisation in which interpreters might reify one shamanic role as definitive and one form of relationship as fundamental. There are solitary and communal healers, using a variety of techniques and performances, contexts and equipments. Grim also includes an excellent description and discussion of healing arts or doctoring. Not for the first time, this chapter also links the transformations central to healing with those implicated in shamans' initiations.

In Chapter 6 Barbara Tedlock offers a 'highly nuanced, linguistically informed [analysis] of dream narration and interpretation as psychodynamic intercultural social processes' (Tedlock 1991: 161). An expert and import survey of the then emerging Study of Dreaming prefaces discussion of the results of a radical form of participant observation in which the anthropologist's own dreams are the focus of reflection and dialogue with Quiché Maya diviners. Far more than eliciting information about the practices and techniques of indigenous informants, this chapter represents a monumental change in the relationship of researchers and those they research. In terms of understanding shamans and shamanism, it provokes us to consider far more engaged, experiential and dialogical modes of discourse than traditional scholarship has celebrated. En route, however, it does provide important insights into the training and activities of divinatory and advisory shamans.

Alan Campbell in Chapter 7 writes about 'submitting' to understandings and fears that confront us in researching phenomena that present themselves in ways so alien and even hostile to the Western rationality. However hard we try to be respectful of experiences (or their interpretations) held by informants as natural or self-evident, or asserted as vitally important and ultimately true, eventually we are confronted by difference. Use of the word 'spirit' is a common indicator of the moment at which a researcher is at that barrier. Campbell certainly deals well with language problems, insisting that we struggle with different expressions about reality, in particular, ones that resist our attempts to turn indigenous terms into nouns or technical terms. However, his discussion offers far more than that. It is a powerful incitement to 'submit' to far greater possibilities than those usually allowed to researchers. Once again, en route, he discusses significant information about those we might (despite his warnings) want to call shamans among the Wayapí in Amazonia.

Edith Turner's discussion in Chapter 8 of 'the reality of spirits' tackles similar problems head on. Reflecting and narrating her own experience of very full participation in a healing ritual she says that 'going native' was 'a break-through to an altogether different worldview, foreign to academia, by means of which certain material was chronicled that could have been gathered in no other way'. Some readers will be more interested in the 'certain material' presented here, namely a healing ritual that exemplifies encounters between humans and unwelcome other-than-human persons. Others will be interested in the way in which Turner's 'chronicle' of this information also exemplifies recent important developments in academic approaches. It is, of course, untrue that experiences such as those she discusses are foreign to academics, especially those who travel beyond their institutions. But academics typically adopt traditional academic notions of Western rationality which have been constructed in opposition to experiences that may be far more commonplace than much academic writing has allowed. If nothing else, this should alert us to the fact that academics have been seduced by what seems extraordinary and have dealt poorly with what is everyday and expected among many people.

In short, the following chapters in Part Two represent some of the most interesting recent discussions of the activities of shamans (especially supporting hunters and offering healing). Many will want to focus on the still debated issue of the relationship between shamanism and possession. Are they cognate experiences or are there secure boundaries that require careful use of the two terms? The choice is, of course, not an equal one, the comparison is already between different kinds of possibility: experiences and terminology. Academic study of shamans and shamanism is, like so many other areas of study, torn between what particular people say they experience and the requirements of scholarly argument in search of more accurate analysis. Thus, these chapters not only provide information about what shamans do, but they initiate new scholarly approaches to research. Of course, many will be dissatisfied, if not annoyed, by any suggestion that there are alternatives to the attempt at objectivity. In reality, however, what all these authors offer is continuous with a long line of academic struggles to submit to the authority of either academic ancestors or to experience (compare Cox 1998).

References

Cox, J.L. 1998. *Rational Ancestors: Scientific Rationality and African Indigenous Religions.* Cardiff: Cardiff Academic Press.

Smith, J. Z. 1998. 'Religion, Religions, Religious' in M. C. Taylor (ed.), *Critical Terms for Religious Studies,* Chicago: University of Chicago Press, pp. 269–84.

Tedlock, B. 1991. Abstract of 'The New Anthropology of Dreaming', *Dreaming* 1(2): 161.

Chapter 3

Roberte N. Hamayon

GAME AND GAMES, FORTUNE AND DUALISM IN SIBERIAN SHAMANISM

O BTAINING THE PROMISE OF GAME or 'good luck' for hunters of his community is the shaman's main function in the most archaic Siberian societies in their traditional mode of life, i.e. before the Soviet revolution. It is a function much more basic than healing.[1] Moreover, this is the shaman's only regular function, ritually performed at a definite time of year and independent of circumstances. It is this criterion of ritual regularity which is determinant when one tries to define the place and function of shamanism in society.[2]

This function of obtaining good luck or fortune is carried out during a large collective ritual which takes place every year. This ritual is supposed to guarantee the success of hunting (or rather the right to hunt) during the coming season: the hunters would be unable to kill game if the ritual were not performed.[3] Thus, this is a kind of symbolic hunt performed by the shaman which foreshadows the actual hunt of the hunter. It is the most important of all the rituals connected with hunting, the only one which necessarily involves the shaman's mediation, the only one which each community as a whole must perform, giving occasion to the most important gathering of the year.

In some societies of the Siberian forest, this ritual is the only large one, and it also serves to consecrate a new shaman, to confirm him as the community's shaman or give him new paraphernalia. This aim, which amounts to legitimizing the shaman as such, is another aspect of the objective of obtaining good luck, inasmuch as having a shaman is necessary to obtain good luck. Legitimizing the shaman as such and having him perform his main function go together. In these societies, this is a 'life-giving' ritual (according to the terminology used by Hocart), and its Selkup name, *iläptiko*, means 'renewal of life' (Prokofyev). In other societies, these two purposes, legitimizing the shaman as such, and having him perform what he is obligated to do, give rise to two separate rituals; then the first one is often called 'animation of the drum'.

In spite of variations which depend on the society concerned, these rituals have an important common feature: they imply the necessary occurrence of practices called 'games' in all Siberian languages. Let us consider only this aspect of the ritual. The notion of game is based on specific types of behaviour found among specific types of animal species: jumping, leaping, rutting, competing, among horned ruminants (especially elk and reindeer, which are the game-food *par excellence*) on the one hand; birds of the wild, wild-cock and grouse species on the other hand. This notion has two basic interrelated features in Siberian ritual contexts: one is play for fun, pleasure, and love, the other is play in competition for winning. The first meaning is expressed in dances, rounds, gambols of various kinds, more or less directly oriented towards sexual intercourse; these can be performed by men and women or by men alone, in a collective or an individualistic way, although the collective round-dance involving both sexes is the most widespread (called *jeexer* in Buryat, *ohuoxaj* in Yakut . . .); they are usually performed to the beat of the shaman's drum. The second meaning is expressed mostly in wrestling; wrestling is of course only for men, two by two; in most societies, this is performed in a series of distinct fights between the winners of preceding fights.

These games are an obligation both for the shaman and for the members of the community. The shaman must oblige his fellows to play these games, especially the entire night following animation of the drum, as specified in all ethnographic descriptions of this ritual. Zhornitskaja (1966 and 1978: 299–307) correctly insists upon that dance is a constituent part of the shaman's action. Let us emphasize that playing these games is a duty, and not a diversion or a way of profiting from the opportunity offered by the festival for rest and amusement. Playing these games is a duty for both sides. For instance, with his drumstick the shaman beats the legs of those who stop dancing or wrestling and want to rest. In particular every teenager, whether strong or weak, must participate in wrestling; the fact that he lost in the very first round would be secondary. Conversely, a shaman who would prove to be unable to oblige his fellows in the community to play, dance, and wrestle, would be considered a poor, a useless shaman soon to be abandoned and replaced by a more efficient one.

These games are explicitly intended to imitate animal behaviour, more precisely, the rutting and competition of the two above mentioned animal species. These animals have, in common, self-exhibiting behaviour in two correlated male activities: the male (stag or cock) must eliminate its rivals before coupling with the female. This is echoed in the ritual by a link between the two kinds of games, wrestling and dancing, both obligatory for everybody. This is further echoed in the concept of virility, a twofold virility, both sexual and warlike, and also in the ethics and ideology of manliness: the man must both perpetuate and defend his community. In prompting his fellows to perform these games, the shaman symbolically encourages reproduction, both in his community and its natural resources: these imitative rites are conceived of as inciting both the performers and the imitated animals. It is often said that the shaman and the hunters must make the spirits animating these animal species joyful and make them play the same kind of games. Every male, whether human or (spirit)-animal, is thus encouraged to procreate, which implies, as a preliminary step, the elimination of possible rivals.

Such content is indicated by the name of the ritual 'renewal of life', which is thus supposed to be a joint undertaking of human beings and animals. The Tungus term for this ritual *ikenipke* means 'singing and dancing' (Cincius 1975–7: 301b) and is explained by Vasilevich as 'repeating the action of living'. The aim of fostering sexual activity among both animals and human beings accounts for the characteristics of these dances (jumping and leaping), and for the kind of songs associated with them, which abound in animal cries and calls. It is relevant that most terms for shaman and shamanizing are based on concepts referring to these male activities: 'to play, to jump' is the root of the Yakut word for shaman *ojun*, 'to rut' (of a stag) or 'to mate' (of a cock), that of the Samoyed word for shaman *taadibe*. In Buryat, the term for shamanic dancing, *xatarxa*, means running as reindeer at the rutting season and the term for playing in general, *naadaxa*, also means mating (for several animal species, especially birds and fish). The root *mürgexe*, used in the Buryat expression for 'shamanism', *böö mürgel*, and for several shamanic rites, has the following meanings: to gore (as a bull), to wrestle and to pray depending on the context (Lot-Falck 1977: 15; Hajdú 1968: 150–151; Cheremisov 1973: 315). And this is the reason why the shaman's head-gear is adorned with antlers, which are both signs of sexual power and symbolic weapons for fighting against rivals.

Along with encouraging reproduction among animals which man feeds on, the very fact of imitating game animals makes man himself similar to them, that is, destined to be eaten. Evidence for this meaning is found in the conceptual background of the games, in the shaman's ritual behaviour, and in representations spread throughout Siberia, according to which the flesh and blood of human beings are considered to be the food of the animal spirits, just as the flesh of game animals is the food of hunters. This mutual feeding (which accounts for the well known ambivalence of spirits) refers to a dualistic concept of mankind and the world of natural and supernatural beings generally found in these shamanistic societies. It is ruled by a law of reciprocity making them partners as well as game for each other. This reciprocity is ritually enacted by the shaman thanks to his alliance with the daughter of the game-giving spirit (see note 3). The shaman himself behaves as a game animal at the end of the ritual: he ritually falls down, as if he were dead, on a small carpet representing the supernatural world.

Perpetuating this reciprocal exchange implies perpetuating both partners;

such is the aim of the type of ritual examined here. Moreover, the very fact that this ritual is said to concretely obtain fortune for hunters, makes clear an integral relationship between access to natural resources and the reproduction of the society as such. That is why these games (or at least part of them) survived throughout decades in spite of deep changes in the way of life and socio-political circumstances of these societies.

These kinds of games form, in most Siberian societies today, the basis of festivals which maintain identity, at whatever level, be it local, ethnic, or national. Let us take only the example of Mongolian peoples, either in the People's Republic of Mongolia at the state level, or in Buryatia and in the Autonomous Region of Inner Mongolia in China, at the local level. This festival, called *naadan* in Buryat or *naadam* in Mongol, implying 'game(s)', consists of performances in wrestling, horse racing and archery. Of these, wrestling is the most important and close to the people's hearts, akin to a basic element of ethnic consciousness. This is the only game performed by the hero in Buryat epics. Training in wrestling is an obligation for every young boy in order that he later have a normal life, especially that he marry. It is also said that in summer, in case of drought, young boys should go and wrestle on the top of hills, in order to help bring rain. This appears to be an echo of an ancient manner of obtaining access to contingent or aleatory natural resources. Rain is no more automatic than a successful hunt; it is also a question of good luck. Let us add that the persistence of these games and of the values attached to them is not due solely to memory of a remote hunting life; it expresses the permanence of the concept of people's relationship with life-giving supernatural entities as dependent on exchange, and on the active role of people in this exchange. This concept is opposed to the concept in which mankind depends on transcendent, supernatural entities. This is why rituals and practices entailing imitation of animals, inasmuch as they express a partnership with life-giving supernatural entities, are considered to be subversive by all kinds of central powers, be they religious or worldly. Furthermore, such a partner relationship is likely to be indefinitely extended to new partners or to new realms requiring good luck: besides requiring game, rain, and fertility from the spirits of natural beings or phenomena, humans also require good luck — necessary in love or trade affairs, examinations or elections — from other types of spirits. Let us propose that this is the reason why this type of shamanism is both associated with archaic societies, where it is central, and also able to survive, albeit on the fringes, in present-day, modern contexts.

This paper was intended, first, to call attention to the relationship between certain kinds of 'game' and basic shamanistic principles, to investigate the place, nature and function of such a partnership with supernatural beings, and then to underline how games of this kind render these dualistic relationships dynamic while also remaining reciprocal. Two arguments can be developed for this purpose. First, the fact that the contents of these games correspond to individual ideals: everybody should help in the perpetuation of his community. Second, the fact that the notion of game, which makes one partner a winner and the other a loser without stopping them from being partners, makes dualistic relationships dynamic, inasmuch as the delay between the first round and the revenge makes possible other types of relationships between the two partners.

Notes

1 This paper is based on the data and analysis published in *La chasse à l'âme. Esquisse d'une théorie du chamanisme sibérien* Nanterre, Société d'ethnologie, 1990.

2 Inasmuch as most of the other functions, such as healing or divining, are performed depending on particular circumstances.

3 The reason for this may be schematically explained in this way: hunting depends on an agreement between the community and the spirits which provide game (the relationship between animals and their spirits being similar to the one between the body and soul of man, which allows use of the term 'supernatural' meaning simply the set of spirits which animate nature and natural beings). One must have an agreement with the spirits in order to take the flesh of animals. Concluding this agreement is the task of the shaman. He achieves legitimation to perform this task by ritually marrying the daughter of the game-giving spirit; thus he will act in the supernatural world as a legitimate husband and not as an abductor.

References

Cheremisov, Konstantin 1973 *Burjatsko-russkij slovar* [Buryat-Russian dictionary]. Moscow: Sovetskaja entsiklopedija [Soviet Encyclopedia].

Cincius, Vera 1975–1977 *Sravnitelnyj slovar tunguso-mandzhurskikh jazykov* [Comparative dictionary of Tungus-Mandzhu languages]. 2 vols. Leningrad: Nauka.

Hajdú, Peter 1968 'The Classification of Samoyed shamans', in Diószegi Vilmos (ed.) *Popular Beliefs and Folklore Tradition in Siberia*. Mouton/ Bloomington, Indiana University, La Haye.

Hamayon, Roberte 1990 *La chasse à l'âme, Esquisse d'une théorie du chamanisme sibérien*. Nanterre: Société d'ethnologie.

Hocart, Arthur M. 1970 *Kings and Councillors*. The University of Chicago Press.

Lot-Falck, Evelyne 1977 'A propos du terme chamane', *Études mongoles et sibériennes* 8.

Prokofyev, Gavriil 1930 'Tseremonija ozhivlenija bubna u ostjakov-samoedov' [The ceremony of reviving of the drum among the Ostyak-Samoeds], *Izvestija Leningradaskogo gosudarstevennogo universiteta* [Bulletin of the Leningrad State University] II, 365–73.

Vasilevich, Glaphira 1957 'Drevnije ohotnichji i olenevodcheskije obrjady evenkov' [Ancient hunting and reindeer-breeding ceremonies among the Evenks], *Shornik Muzeja Antropologii i Etnografii* [Bulletin of the Museum of Anthropology and Ethnography] XVII, 151–185.

Vasilevich, Glaphira 1969 *Evenki, Istoriko-ethnograficheskije ocherki (XVIII-nachalo XX v.)* [The Evenks. Historico-ethnographical reviews (XVIII – the beginning of XX century)]. Leningrad: Nauka.

Zhornitskaja, Mariya 1966 *Narodnyje tancy Yakutii* [Folk dances in Yakutiya]. Moskow: Nauka.

Zhornitskaja, Mariya 1978 'Dances of Yakut shaman', in Diószegi Vilmos – Hoppál Michaly (eds) *Shamanism in Siberia*. Budapest: Akadémiai Kiadó.

Chapter 4

Ioan M. Lewis

POSSESSION AND PUBLIC MORALITY
II Other cosmological systems

I

[. . .]

OUR GENERALIZATIONS refer only to one type of central possession religion – that addressed to the worship of ancestor spirits. Clearly if our findings are to hold true of morally endowed possession religions generally, irrespective of the nature of the mystical powers concerned, it has to be shown that they apply equally well to other types of shamanistic religion. This chapter will accordingly attempt to extend the range of these conclusions and try to reach a more definitive assessment of the significance of ecstasy by examining its place in central morality cults which are directed to powers other than ancestor spirits.

We shall start with religions where, as in the ancestor cults we have already considered, the spirits which inspire men and also sanctify and protect social morality do so in a straightforward and direct fashion. We shall then discuss other cases where the mystical forces involved are not, at first sight, primarily concerned to uphold morality, or to sanction the relations between man and man, and yet ultimately this result is achieved in a circuitous manner. Such religions where the powers of the cosmos thus obliquely reflect breaches and disharmonies in human relations have important analogies with those cults which we have classified as peripheral. Consequently an examination of their character will bring us back to the problem, which we have already noticed in other contexts, of the relation between these two, seemingly radically opposed, types of religion. This will force us to consider more carefully the significance of these two categories in the analysis of ecstatic religion.

In what follows, I shall deliberately select illustrative material from societies and cultures which are widely separated geographically, which differ substantially in their ways of life and economy, and which exhibit similar contrasts in their political organization and in their religious systems and cosmologies. I shall begin with cases where shamans are by no means the sole holders of political and legal power, and end with examples where they are almost alone in the field. In the process, we shall move from the less familiar territory of African shamanism to the classical shamanistic regions of the Arctic and South America. If, over such a wide area, and in relation to societies which differ in so many other respects, central possession cults can be shown to exhibit fundamentally the same significance, then we can hope to reach conclusions which will be independent of cultural particularities. At the same time, from such comparative evidence, we should be able to uncover some at least of the basic conditions which favour the development and maintenance of an ecstatic emphasis in religion.

With these aims before us, let us begin with another example from Ethiopia. In this case, such is the unusual wealth of historical evidence available that it is possible not only to analyse this religion as it exists today, but also to see how, over several centuries, it has come to assume its present shape. In this instance we are confronted with a main morality religion which, in its earlier phases, did not include ecstasy but now has this character. I am referring to the religion of the Macha Oromo, who live today as cultivators in an area north of the Kaffa and west of Addis Ababa. This people is one of the many sub-divisions of the great Oromo nation which, with a population estimated at some twelve millions, constitutes the largest single ethnic group in Ethiopia. As with the Kaffa and all the other subordinate Ethiopian peoples, the Macha now form part of the Ethiopian empire and are ruled by the Christian Amhara élite.

In contemporary Macha society (Knutsson, 1967, 1975; H.S. Lewis, 1984), men regularly incarnate God (*Waka*) and his various 'refractions', or subsidiary manifestations, which are known as *ayanas*. To the Macha, God is the final guardian of morality and punishes wrongs and misdemeanours, which are considered sins, by withdrawing his protection and thus rendering evil-doers liable to suffer misfortune and sickness. Sacrifices, and prayers for forgiveness and blessing, are regularly made to God and to his subsidiary manifestations through shamans (called *kallus*) who hold priestly offices at all levels of social grouping from that of the extended patrilineal family to the clan. The spirits summoned on these occasions are considered to be refractions of the central deity *Waka*, which is apprehended as a unity at the level of the Macha people as a whole. Shamans who in the recurring rites in honour of their spirits, are often possessed, hold positions which are generally vested in the senior segments of lineages.

These offices are in principle hereditary. Yet an element of achievement is also present, since shamans vie with one another for the leadership of local congregations built round co-resident clusters of kin. And some shamans attain positions of religious leadership which extend far beyond their own immediate circle of patrilineal relatives. In this fashion, competition for power within Macha society is couched in the idiom of possession. If, for example, a family head becomes regularly subject to strikingly histrionic trances, which are interpreted as signs of divine possession, and builds up a reputation for great divinatory powers and success in mediation and dispute settlement, then he is likely to acquire renown at a wider local and lineage level. This gives him a standing which will enable him to bid for recognition as the acknowledged shaman of a much larger group. Typically, those men who are thus striving for wider power and authority experience much more impressive and violent possession trances than those who already hold such positions by right of birth. But success here is often ephemeral. A shaman's position depends upon public recognition, and reputations can be destroyed as easily as they can be built up. Here, as with the Zezuru Shona, but unlike the Korekore and Kaffa, there is no firmly established hierarchy of shamans, and no shamanistic bishopric to adjudicate between the claims of rival competitors.

Each shaman has at least one shrine for the spirit or spirits which he incarnates and it is to these that people of a neighbourhood come in search of help. Inspired by these powers, the shamans hear confessions of guilt at wrongs committed, and receive sacrifices and votive offerings for the spirits. As I have already indicated, alongside the official legal and administrative system of the Ethiopian government they also exercise a certain amount of informal political and legal power. And the judgements which they give in disputes brought to them are backed by the sanction of their spirits. People who defiantly reject a shaman's decision fear his curse.

Side by side with this religion centring on the morally just God, *Waka*, there exist other peripheral cults of spirits (known locally as *muata*, *atete* (or *Mariam*) which often possess women. But since these involve features with which we are now thoroughly familiar no more need be said about them for the moment. Instead I want to explore the historical events which lie behind the present character of the cult of *Waka*.

Whereas present evidence suggests that the central Kaffa possession religion represents simply an intensification of traditional practices, this is not the case with the Macha. On the contrary, in this case we are fortunate in having secure evidence which shows that, in its present shamanistic form, this main morality cult is a cultural innovation of only a few generations' standing. Before this development, the Macha (who, it will be recalled, form one division of the great Oromo nation) participated in the pan-Oromo cult of *Waka* who was represented on earth, not by an array of inspired shamans, but by a handful of divinely instituted priestly dynasties. Although these lines of priestly mediators were believed to have been endowed by God, and thus to be divinely appointed, the actual incumbents (who were also called *kallus*) did not employ trance and were not considered to be possessed by the power whose authority they exercised.

This 'traditional' pattern of a non-shamanistic priesthood persists today amongst the southern branches of the Oromo nation which remain those most attached to pastoral nomadism and least involved in cultivation. Outside Macha, amongst these more conservative Oromo, this office of tribal priest, which is hereditary, is closely associated with the traditional political structure. This is based primarily upon the generation-set organization which, in the south, is still the main integrating and governmental principle (see Knutsson, 1975). Without going into unnecessary details, this institution provides a mechanism whereby the male population of any autonomous Oromo tribe is divided into sets, each one drawn from men of a different generation, which progress through a number of grades at eight-yearly intervals. Each grade occupied by a set, as its members move through the system, has different roles and obligations assigned to it.

As with age-grade organizations elsewhere, the effect, in this traditionally uncentralized political system, is that every man is given the opportunity of being a warrior and, later, an elder and judge. At any point in time one set, composed of men of the same generation, occupies that grade which supplies the peace-keeping, decision-making and ritual direction for the tribe as a whole. Ideally and in practice, the system is highly democratic and egalitarian. Those who exercise political and legal authority do so only for the eight years that they are in office; power then passes out of their hands into those of the next senior set. And the leaders of each set, who will in their turn briefly rule the tribe as a whole, are elected by all its members. This institution, linked closely to the dynastic *kallu* priesthood which hallows it and endows it with mystical efficacy, is well suited to provide the loose degree of integration and tribal solidarity required by sparsely distributed pastoral nomads.

So much for the traditional Oromo social organization which, as I have said, survives most strongly today amongst those Oromo of southern Ethiopia and northern Kenya who still live as marginal pastoral nomads. Now the Macha, with whom we are concerned here, represent one of the several Oromo groups who moved up into central Ethiopia in the course of the great northern expansion of the Oromo in the sixteenth century. In their new environment they did not succeed in establishing a local *kallu* dynasty of their own. Instead they had to depend upon the great priests of the southern Oromo to whose shrines, before the final imposition of Amhara rule in the late nineteenth century, they used regularly to go on pilgramage.

In their new highland home, however, they gradually adopted cultivation and became subject to pressures of social change sweeping through all northern Oromo society in the late eighteenth and early nineteenth centuries. In the case of the Macha, these led to the breakdown of the traditional and highly democratic political system based on the generation-set organization which was sanctioned and hallowed by the *kallu* priests. Pressure on the land increased, and although lineages were initially land-holding units, the growth of markets and of trade in this period encouraged the rise of a new class of merchant adventurers and military leaders who came to control the land. In some northern areas, the emergence of these 'big men' led to a general development of social stratification with power based primarily on achievement, and ultimately to the formation of monarchies whose rulers tended to adopt Islam as a convenient justification for the new social positions which they had created. But amongst those Macha Oromo discussed here, this process of increasing political centralization had not proceeded to this point before the Amhara conquest supervened and 'froze' the existing situation (cf. H.S. Lewis, 1984).

This train of developments, with the rise of 'big men' competing for secular power, was accompanied by parallel changes in religious organization and cosmological beliefs leading ultimately to the pattern described earlier. As in other conditions of change and dislocation in which possession phenomena flourish, so here, as we have seen, achieved shamanistic positions, legitimized by possession, replaced the former attachment of the Macha to the God-given high-priesthoods of the south. Where formerly inspiration had been fully bounded and institutionalized in the shape of divinely installed dynasties of priests, with power incarnate in the office rather than in the person, God was now in effect breaking out all over. The possession-inspired *kallu* shaman thus succeeded the *kallu* priest. And, as the generation-set organization declined in significance, clanship became one of the main foci of social identity. Thus, at various levels of clan grouping there developed shamanistic positions paralleling the refraction into constituent parts of a god who had previously been conceived of as single and indivisible. Ultimately, therefore, the resulting new *kallu* institution has come to include ascribed as well as achieved aspects, thus bringing the wheel of religious change full circle – or nearly so. Certainly, at least, it is possible to discern the beginnings of what may eventually become a new *kallu* religious establishment, although trance and possession still remain at the moment important factors in the exercise of the religious vocation.

To complete this picture, we must note that, as in Kaffa, a considerable proportion of the Macha are practising Christians. Christianity, however, has not displaced their indigenous faith, nor reduced it to a subsidiary position. On the contrary, both religions co-exist in a loose syncretic relationship. To many Macha, indeed, they must appear as parts of a single continuum, rather than as discrete and contradictory faiths. In this tolerant ecumenical spirit, the Virgin Mary and a number of leading saints from the Christian tradition, as well as certain figures from Islam, including even the Prophet Muhammad, have in fact been assimilated to refractions of *Waka*. Similarly, the Christian calendar has exerted a considerable influence upon the rotation of the main public rites addressed to the Macha god. Hence, if this ecstatic religion voices the local cultural nationalism of the Macha, it does so to a degree and in a manner which at the same time admits of a gradual movement towards the assimilative culture and religion of the dominant Amhara. Though akin to the situation in Kaffa, these circumstances are rather different from those amongst the Zezuru.

II

The central possession religion of the Macha cultivators represents, as we have seen, a considerably modified version of their traditional religion. Its shamanistic character is the product of economic and political changes over a period of some three centuries. Despite very considerable differences in cosmology, and although we know little about its earlier history, the classical shamanism of the Tungus reindeer herders of Siberia and the Arctic reveals striking parallels with this Macha cult. In order to clarify the central character of Tungus shamanism and to show how, as in Macha, it is closely associated with the clan system, I now refer to a detailed account of the Evenk Tungus herders by the Soviet ethnographer, Anisimov (Anisimov, 1963, cf. Basilov, 1984; Hamayon, 1984). In this case, the clans involved are smaller, more tightly integrated, and exhibit a higher degree of mutual hostility than in Macha.

In the traditional Evenk setting, sickness and misfortune were believed to be due, either to neglect of the clan spirits, or to the malice of other clans whose protective spirits had been unleashed on their enemies. In the latter event, the shaman treated his afflicted clansmen by exorcizing the demon responsible, and driving it into the lower world. In retaliation for this hostile spirit intrusion, he would then let loose a host of his own clan's guardian spirits, in the form of zoomorphic monsters, sending these out to do battle with the clan which had initiated this spiritual combat. To defend itself against such harassment, each clan shaman was required to fence in the clan lands, protecting them against incursion by a mystical iron curtain consisting of the shaman's spirit watchmen. Alien enemy spirits had first to penetrate this bulwark before they could reach those it sheltered and plague them with illness and death. Aided by his spirit helpers, it was the primary duty of the clan shaman to struggle with trespassing spirits and, having repelled them, to repair the damage done to the clan defences.

This defence work was three-dimensional. In the air, shamanistic bird spirits were ever on the watch; on land, the shaman's animal spirits staunchly stood guard; and in the water, fish spirits were posted as sentries. Each clan was thus thought to possess a sphere of interest which, like that of modern nations, straddled the three worlds: the upper world of the air and heavens, the earth which man inhabited, and the world below into which the rivers flowed. Through the centre of this jealously guarded clan territory flowed the clan's 'watery river road', a spiritual stream whose sources lay in the upper world populated by the supreme nature deities, whose middle course lay in the world of men, and the mouth in the lower world. In this poetic imagery, clan life was viewed as running along this river in a circular process of reincarnation. Neighbouring clans had adjoining rivers of life, and the relations between their mortal representatives were reflected in those on the spiritual plane which the shaman's spirits regulated.

Although each Evenk clan had also a formally installed political leader (called *kulak*), the shaman's position as the interpreter of clan morality and, indeed, as the embodiment of clan well-being, was extremely important. While in principle hereditary, this office could also be obtained, as we have seen, by achievement. The clan spirits were the final arbiters in the selection of the successful candidate who was consecrated in a collective clan ritual which incorporated the themes of rebirth, prosperity in animal husbandry, and success in hunting. Shamans were treated with deference, allocated the most productive areas of clan territory, and helped with their reindeer herding by other clansmen. Paid for their services in gifts, such as a few head of reindeer, they often became as prosperous as they were mystically powerful.

During the period of Russian rule before the revolution, and partly as a result of Christian influence, shamanism declined. But under the new Soviet authorities it acquired a new lease of life. In much the same manner as among the Zezuru of Rhodesia, possession became the vehicle for Tungus cultural nationalism and protest against the policies of their new masters. In this setting, shamans joined forces with the *kulak* clan leaders as agents of local resistance and disaffection.

Amongst the Tungus generally (Shirokogoroff, 1935), the well-being of clansmen depended upon the zealous direction of the cult of their guardian spirits by the clan shaman. If these spirits were neglected, they could themselves wreak havoc; or, as among the Macha Oromo and in other examples we have considered, achieve the same effect by withdrawing their protection, and thus leaving their clan open to attack by hostile enemy powers. These alien spirits were particularly dangerous to women, and women's illnesses were regularly explained in terms of possession by such foreign spirits. Although the literature is not entirely clear on this point, it seems that alongside the central cult of clan guardian spirits, which was directed by men, there also existed a peripheral cult which was mainly concerned with female ailments. It was also, apparently, through alleged association with such amoral evil spirits, that an unpopular shaman might be discredited as a 'witch'. These are features which we have already encountered in a number of our previous examples, and to the significance of which I shall return presently.

Finally, it is of interest to note here that, during the old Russian régime when Christianity exerted a powerful impact, in some areas clan shamanism seems to have degenerated to the status of a marginal cult involving female as well as male shamans. The diffusion of Buddhism, through Manchuria, may earlier have exerted a similar effect.

III

So far, we have concentrated upon cases where male-dominated cults sustain public morality in a direct fashion, the shaman voicing the decisions of moralistic gods which, if they do not simply echo it, are at least highly responsive to the judgement of public opinion. But in our previous examples, the shaman's inspired judgements are only one of several, alternative sources of law, since other authorities and other mechanisms of social control also exist. I want now to examine the role of shamanism in societies which completely lack formal political offices, or courts of law, and where the shaman has virtually no rivals in his inspired ministrations. In such conditions, as we shall see, the shaman's portfolio of functions becomes extremely wide in scope.

I take as my example here the Akawaio Indians of British Guiana, a people living in small autonomous settlements, strung out along the banks of rivers, and practising a mixed economy which includes cultivation, hunting, fishing, and collecting wild fruits. Here, as Audrey Butt breezily says, the shaman 'has many roles, ranging from doctor, military tactician, and priest to lawyer and judge: at one and the same time he is the primitive embodiment of the National Space Agency and the Citizen's Advice Bureau' (Butt *et al.*, 1967). To appreciate this proliferation of tasks, the background of Akawaio beliefs must be outlined briefly. As with so many other tribal peoples, and to some extent in line with modern psychiatry, the Akawaio believe that animosities between individuals, families, and local communities are a source of sickness, misfortune, and even death. Physical and social disorder and malfunctioning are linked together by the assumption that nature spirits which cause suffering have, as their primary focus of concern, conditions of social disharmony. Hostilities and disputes in personal and social relations are considered to attract the attention of these spirits which then signify their disapproval by afflicting those involved with disease or death.

Such an undesirable state of affairs requires the help of the shaman who, as diagnostician and arbiter of spirit activity, is summoned to investigate the trouble. His task is both medical and politico-legal. He seeks to cure the physical symptoms as well as the more deep-seated social ill which lies behind them. His job is to remove the ostensible cause of suffering and also, with the authority of the spirits, to restore harmonious relations by manipulating the tension-ridden situation which has given rise to the sickness.

Among the Akawaio, nature spirits thus uphold morality by afflicting transgressors with illnesses which may be interpreted either as malign possessions by pathogenic organisms, or as caused by the removal of a vital part of the culprit's body by a spirit. Even theft may be punished in this fashion by the spirits. In fact infringements of ritual prescriptions and taboos are similarly sanctioned, so that the complete gamut of punitive spirit action includes transgressions, omissions, and malpractices in customary behaviour in both the secular and religious spheres. According to Akawaio belief, an illness disappears and the patient recovers when the wrong involved has been righted, when harmony in society and in nature has been restored.

The shaman conducts his inquiry into the causes of affliction through a public séance in the course of which all the relevant evidence is uncovered and analysed. The spirits who speak through the mouth of the possessed shaman act as barristers or prosecuting councillors, extracting information and putting the case against the guilty patient. Their utterances are delivered with a great deal of sagacious wit which is savoured appreciatively by the audience. Those present at the séance act both as witnesses to and judges of the spectacle, the shaman interpreting public opinion with the authority which only the words of the gods can give him. The séance thus both enshrines and expresses the moral conscience of the community and, for the patient, is also the confessional in which the admission of guilt and the agreement to perform such further penances as may be prescribed bring relief and recovery.

When such a séance is held to deal with a sick patient, the shaman's first task is to summon his regular helpers – the spirit of his late teacher, the tobacco spirit, the ladder spirit, tree-bark spirits, mountain bird spirits, and the ghost spirits of dead relatives who are always anxious to lend a hand. Having already taken the powerful tobacco juice which helps him to achieve trance, the shaman begins by conversing with the spirits mentioned as well as with the audience and patient. After a number of other spirits have descended and more tobacco juice has been taken, the shaman goes into full, cataleptic trance. Aided by the ladder spirit, his own spirit has begun to soar aloft on its journey to the sky, to travel among the mountains, in the forests, and under the earth seeking the help of other spirits. Already knowing much of the background to the patient's troubles, with the aid of these spirits the shaman probes further in the séance. Speaking through their human vessel, these spirits interrogate the patient and his relatives as well as other interested parties.

The most searching and pertinent questions are thus publicly put to the patient who is under strong compulsion to reveal all his misdeeds, leaving the shaman's spirits to judge their relevance. If he attempts to cover up his moral failings, he is in danger of being exposed by the audience and is liable to incur a punitive intensification of his illness. As Dr Butt records,

> Intoxicated by tobacco, the rhythm of the swishing leaves (used to induce trance), and his own physical and mental exertions, the shaman must perceive during his state of dissociation a picture of the circumstances which may have created the condition of the patient. A number of possible causes emerge as relevant during his inquiries so that his problem is to recognize the true cause, the generator of sickness. Here the inspiration of the trance must assist his knowledge. Later, if the patient starts to recover it is obvious that the shaman and his spirit aids have indeed diagnosed correctly

and found the means of overcoming the enemy: if the patient continues to be ill then another séance must be held and an even deeper investigation into ultimate causation must be conducted.

Thus in this uncentralized society of small local groups which have no other courts, the séance is a most important mechanism for ventilating and bringing to a conclusion smouldering quarrels and enmities. When the shaman is called in, sources of strife are already present and it only requires the pronouncements of the spirits which speak through him to bring matters to a climax. Here the ready participation of the audience, representing public opinion, is a crucial element. For all those present can listen and participate. Thus, gossip and scandal may be confirmed or denied; actions can be explained and justified; confessions can be forced or retracted. Nor, in this compelling social drama, do the spirits mince their words. They eagerly deliver pious homilies on the importance of correct conduct, denouncing moral failings, condemning transgressions, and generally reducing their victims to acquiescent contrition by a skilful combination of suggestive probes, satire, and sarcasm which might do credit to the techniques of corrective interrogation employed by the Red Guards in the Chinese People's Republic.

In this cross-questioning, in which no holds are barred, a good séance provides an occasion for bringing into the open all the hidden troubles and problems of the local community. Petty disputes and offences are brought to light and pondered, as well as major disruptive issues. Thus the path towards settlement is opened, and a means found to restore harmonious relationships and to reassert general amity. Finally, judgement is delivered by the spirits through the mouth of the shaman, who voices the consensus of the community.

Notwithstanding the heavy emphasis which is placed upon immorality as the cause of sickness, there are, of course necessarily other escape clauses which account for diseases where the patient is generally considered to be guiltless. In much the same fashion as amongst the Tungus, when misfortunes are not satisfactorily explained in terms of moral misdemeanours, their causes are sought outside the community. The Akawaio of each river area believe that some, at least, of their ills are to be traced to the malevolence of other groups. Such external enemies, for relations between different settlements are often hostile, are thought to act as witches sending bad spirits and sickness against their adversaries. In this context, the shaman of each group is seen as the primary agent. As in the Tungus clan, he defends his own people against attack by rival shamans from other regions, and, when they strike, retaliates in kind. Competition is endemic between shamans who symbolize the particularistic loyalties of their communities. A favourite and particularly unpleasant trick employed is for one shaman to cause his opponent's spirit ladder to collapse while its owner is holding a séance. The hapless shaman's spirit is then trapped aloft and deprived of the means of returning to his body. Such soul absence, if prolonged, produces illness and may eventually lead to the death of the unfortunate victim.

IV

In the examples which we have so far considered there is some variation in the extent to which the mystical powers involved are explicitly endowed with moral attributes. But there is little difference in the way in which, in practice, the spirits concerned intervene in human affairs so as to directly sanction public morality. Uniformly, they act in such a way as to maintain and safeguard social harmony. On the one hand, they chastise those who infringe their neighbours' rights; and on the other, they inspire shamans to act as trouble-shooters and law-givers in community relations. Here the moral code over which these spirits so resolutely stand guard concerns the relations between man and man.

We come now to our final type of central possession religion where, although the spirits involved are ostensibly dedicated to other aims, much the same effect is ultimately achieved in a more roundabout way. Here we shall take the Eskimos as our example. Like the Akawaio, the Eskimos live in small, loosely structured communities where, although informal positions of leadership exist, there are no clearly defined political offices. In these cir-cumstances, the shaman once more assumes the centre of the stage as the public diagnostician and curer of afflictions which are attributed to the spirits and which have to be confessed before they can be expiated. Again, all this takes place within a cosmological system where lofty nature spirits play a far more significant role than the ancestors. Whereas, however, among the Akawaio, illness and misfortune are seen as direct consequences of tensions and disharmonies in human society, here they are viewed as the result of contraventions of the code of relations between men and nature. Amongst the Eskimo, it is offences against natural forces, rather than against one's fellow men, which lead to distress and require shamanistic intervention if they are to be alleviated.

The following quotation from an Eskimo recorded by Rasmussen (Rasmussen, 1929, p. 56), could well serve as the motto for their traditional religion and ethos:

> We fear the Weather Spirit of earth, that we must fight against to wrest our food from land and sea. We fear Sila (the Weather Spirit). We fear death and hunger in the cold snow huts. We fear Takanakapsaluk, the Great Woman down at the bottom of the sea that rules over all the beasts of the sea. We fear the sickness that we meet with daily around us; not death, but the suffering. We fear the evil spirits of life; those of the air, of the sea, and of the earth that

can help wicked shamans to harm their fellow men. We fear the souls of dead human beings and of the animals we have killed.

The final phrase of this baleful catalogue touches on the most crucial theme of all for an understanding of Eskimo conceptions of sin and taboo. For, as Rasmussen's informant continues:

> the greatest peril of life lies in the fact that human food consists entirely of souls. All the creatures which we have to kill and eat, all those that we have to strike down and destroy to make clothes for ourselves, have souls, as we have, souls that do not perish with the body and which therefore must be propitiated lest they revenge themselves on us for taking away their bodies.

This is the basic assumption, strongly affecting the way in which the Eskimos seek to control and utilize their environment, upon which their extremely elaborate code of practice regulating the relations between man and nature is built. As long as these rules are meticulously followed, game animals allow themselves to be killed without endangering man. The intricate taboo system which this code embodies turns on the principle that those animals and pursuits with which the Eskimos are concerned in the winter months must not be brought into direct contact or mixed with those of the summer season. Thus the produce of the sea, and of the land, must be kept separate and not brought together unless special precautions are taken. Seals (winter game) and everything pertaining to them must be insulated from all contact or association with caribou (summer game). It is round this seasonal axis of different patterns of hunting and fishing that the whole structure of the taboo system revolves. Infringements which are construed as sins resulting in illness and affliction and endangering the success of the food quest occur whenever any of these rules are broken. Significantly, the most heinous offence that men can commit is the macabre one of engaging in sexual intercourse with animals, especially caribou or seals which they have just killed, or with their dogs. But it is above all women whose lives are especially taboo-ridden, who are the commonest offenders and sources of danger.

These mystical game laws are all the more significant and binding in that their transgression normally affects not merely the individual culprit but also his neighbours and kin in the camp. Sins, indeed, are commonly thought to envelop the guilty person in an evil-smelling miasma which attracts further ills and misfortune and just as surely repels game. Sinfulness has thus an almost tangible quality, and the sinner is a direct danger to his fellows. This baneful state is remedied by the confession of taboo violations and the performance of appropriate redemptive offerings and penances. Concealment of misdeeds only compounds the injury and increases the risk of further suffering. As among the Akawaio and in so many other cases we have examined, such offences are explored and dealt with by means of the séance conducted by the shaman. Without their shamans, who thus treat the sick, secure favourable weather conditions, and forecast weather changes and success in the chase, the Eskimos would, as they themselves admit, be impotent before the multitude of dangers and hostile forces which confront them at every side. Whether misfortune is caused by the Sea Spirit, the weather powers, or the dead, ordinary human beings are powerless. Only shamans can successfully intervene.

Whatever the purpose of the séance, the procedure followed by the shaman conforms to a similar pattern. In trance, and possessed by his helping spirits who speak through his mouth, often while his own soul-spirit is voyaging to the upper world or to the under world, the shaman relentlessly probes into the conduct of the guilty party in his search for breaches of taboo which will account for the calamity which he is called upon to remedy. Following his mystical 'trips', the shaman announces to the receptive audience that he has 'something to say', and receives the eager response: 'Let us hear, let us hear!' All those present are now under strong pressure to confess any taboo violations which they may have committed. Some offences are readily acknowledged; others are only reluctantly divulged as the shaman insistently presses his audience to reveal their misdeeds.

The séance group, and especially women whose taboo infractions have generally more serious consequences, desperately search their consciences and denounce their neighbours in the concerted quest for the uncovering of sins which will account for their present distress. Women named by others are led guiltily forward, shamefaced and weeping, and urged to repentance by the shaman's own cries of self-reproach: 'I seek and I strike where nothing is to be found! I seek and I strike where nothing is to be found! If there is anything, you must say so!' Under this barrage of exhortations, a woman will confess some misdeed. For example, she had a miscarriage but, living in a house containing many other people, concealed the fact because she was afraid of the consequences. Her dissembling, though condemned, is readily understood, for had she revealed her condition custom would have obliged her to have thrown away all the soft skins in her igloo, including the hut's complete internal skin lining. Such is the inconvenience of the ritual purification required that the temptation to conceal a miscarriage is evidently very strong. However, in the séance, forgotten omissions of this sort are forced into the open as the confessional rite proceeds on its cathartic course, cleansing the community of guilt under the enthusiastic direction of the shaman. Once a sufficient number of sins, no matter how apparently esoteric or venial, have been confessed, and the shaman has prescribed the necessary penances, he can assure his audience that the spirits have been appeased and that there will be no lack of game on the morrow.

In the treatment of the sick at public shamanistic séances of this kind it is generally the patient who is thus ceaselessly harangued. The following extracts from a case recorded by Rasmussen (Rasmussen, 1929, pp. 133ff) concerning a sick woman, indicate the general tenor of the proceedings. The shaman begins his diagnosis: 'I ask you my helping spirit whence comes this illness from which this person is suffering? Is it due to something I have eaten in defiance of taboo, lately or long since? Or is it due to my wife? Or is it brought about by the sick woman herself? Is she herself the cause of the disease?' The patient responds: 'The sickness is due to my own fault. I have ill fulfilled my duties. My thoughts have been bad and my actions evil.' Shaman: 'It looks like peat and yet it is not really peat. It is that which is behind the ear, something which looks like the cartilage of the ear. There is something that gleams white. It is the edge of a pipe, or what can it be?'

The audience, impatient to get to the root of the matter, now join in: 'She has smoked a pipe that she ought not to have smoked. But never mind. We will not take any notice of that. Let her be forgiven.' Shaman: 'That is not all. There are other offences which have brought about this disease. Is it due to me, or to the sick person herself?' Patient: 'It is due to myself alone. There was something the matter with my abdomen, with my inside.' Shaman: 'She has split a meat bone which she ought not to have touched.' Audience, magnanimously: 'Let her be released from her offence.' Shaman, who is far from concluding his forensic analysis: 'She is not released from her evil. It is dangerous. It is a matter for anxiety. Helping spirit say what it is that plagues her.' And so the séance continues, often for hours at a stretch, as transgression after transgression is revealed by the afflicted patient. Such treatment is also frequently repeated in further séances held at morning, noon and night, until, after repeated admissions of guilt, the shaman is satisfied that the patient is thoroughly purged and judges that recovery will follow now that so much has been confessed to 'take the sting out of the illness'.

With so elaborate a constellation of minutely detailed proscriptions, which affects all aspects of daily living and which, if neglected, causes the powers of nature to visit man with affliction or withdraw his supply of game, it might be thought that there could scarcely be any Eskimo group at any time without someone amongst its members who would have committed an offence. Yet there are evidently those whose conduct is in all respects impeccable. For in addition to this all-embracing theory of merited misfortune, the Eskimos hedge their bets by recognizing that there also exist mystical forces which can produce undeserved disaster. Death, and other less irreversible calamities, may be due to the malevolence of other living people, particularly to the witchcraft of evil shamans. They may also be caused by capricious malign spirits which act without reference to contraventions of what Rasmussen calls 'the rules of life'. Such terrors are again dealt with by shamans who, at every misfortune, are called upon to intervene to save man from the spiritual tyranny which he has fashioned for himself and superimposed upon the cruel and hazardous physical environment in which he lives.

With the aid of his helping spirits, the shaman entreats, cajoles, threatens, and even does battle, in the most dramatically charged séances, with these constantly menacing powers which he alone has the skill to influence and control. His unique intimacy with these powers is such that on some occasions he sends his own spirit soaring aloft to visit the 'People of Day' for sheer joy. Such séances, which are not necessarily held to remedy any specific affliction, are thrilling dramatic performances when the shaman indulges in those well-known, Houdini-style 'tricks' which have led superficial observers to denounce these skilled Eskimo religious experts as mere charlatans.

These performances are certainly partly aimed at demonstrating the efficacy of a particular shaman's powers and at enhancing his reputation, and are thus examples of what Voltaire, in his ironical way, liked to call 'priest-craft'. Yet they are also poignant religious occasions. They represent joyous rites of communion between the world of mortal men and those who have departed to the happy hunting grounds in the upper world. Here, again, the shaman's vital role as the intermediary between man and the world of spiritual power which surrounds and threatens to engulf him, is dramatically affirmed.

Also, as with the Akawaio, it is evident that through his direction of the séance confessional, the shaman exercises political and legal functions in his manipulation of human crises. Although each individual is held personally accountable for observing the strict code which regulates the relations between nature and man, breaches of these rules endanger other members of the community as well as the miscreant himself. It is in this indirect fashion that the shamanistic religion acquires moral significance in the life of Eskimo communities. The séance fulfills the functions of a public court, investigating the causes of affliction apportioning blame, and purging the affected group through fervid confessions of guilt. It is, after all, the séance audience which denounces those it considers culpable, and judges the extent and severity of their shortcomings. It is moreover in terms of his interpretation of the mood of this public confessional that the shaman decides, through the vehicle of his spirits, that sufficient guilt has been discharged to alleviate the misfortune which he is charged to remedy. He too has the responsibility of determining whether specific afflictions are to be explained in terms of sins committed by a member of the group, or through other malevolent powers which are totally indifferent to the 'rules of life'.

Thus although the older ethnographic sources on which we depend for our understanding of Eskimo society do not clearly show that social disturbances lie at the root of spiritual intervention, as they do amongst the Akawaio, we can at least see that, to a significant extent, the séance here was also a mechanism of social control (cf. Balikci, 1963, pp. 380–96). Its importance in this respect was, moreover, all the greater, because of the paucity among the Eskimos of other institutions with parallel functions – notwithstanding the importance here of the famous song-duels. We should note, however, that in as much as the mystical powers involved are not directly endowed with moral characteristics, and are employed to manipulate human crises, Eskimo shamanism is, from certain points of view, analogous to the peripheral cults we have discussed elsewhere. The difference lies less in the nature of the spirits than in the fact that here a whole society is involved, and not simply one, particularly disadvantaged, subordinate sector.

If then, as it seems we should, we treat this religion as a special form of central morality (cf. Sonne, 1982), we have still to consider the sexual identity of Eskimo shamans. Here we have to acknowledge that the classical accounts for the Eskimos (as well as for the Chuckchee and other Siberian peoples) clearly indicate that the shaman's vocation was not restricted solely to the dominant sex. Czaplicka (Czaplicka, 1914; see also Hamayon, 1984), whose synthesis of this Siberian material represents the classic work on the subject, concludes that, traditionally, female shamans were particularly concerned with evil spirits of foreign origin. If this was in fact the case, it suggests that we again encounter here the same sexual division of labour between main and peripheral cults which we have found elsewhere. Moreover, as Czaplicka emphasizes, most of the primary sources on Siberian shamanism agree that the period at the turn of the century was marked by an upsurge of female shamans. Since this was also a time of great social upheaval, when the impact of external influences and of Christianity was at its height, (Bogoras, 1907, p. 414 records the replacement of 'group' by 'individual' shamanism at this time), we can perhaps infer a tendency for the traditional cult to be relegated to a secondary position where it could be taken up appropriately by women. This at least seems a plausible interpretation, and one that is consistent with the pattern elsewhere.

V

This concludes our detailed examination of possession in central morality religions. Our examples cannot pretend to be exhaustive. But they are, I think, sufficiently representative for us to be able to generalize from them with some confidence.

Let us begin by noting points of difference and of resemblance between these central religions and peripheral cults. First, differences. In peripheral cults, or in separatist religious movements (whose ambiguous character as an intermediary category we have already noted), possession, interpreted as a religious experience, indeed as a benediction, is open to all the participants. In central morality religions, however, inspirational possession has a much more limited currency. It is in fact the hallmark of a religious élite, those chosen by the gods and personally commissioned by them to exercise divine authority among men. Since, moreover, this is the idiom in which men compete for power and authority, there are always more aspirants than positions to fill. In this competitive situation where authentic enthusiasm is a scarce commodity, and where many feel themselves called but few are actually chosen, it is obviously essential to be able to discriminate between genuine and spurious inspiration. It is also necessary to have a foolproof means of discrediting those established shamans who are considered to abuse their power, or who show undue reluctance in making way for younger, up-and-coming aspirants who enjoy a wider measure of public support.

Both these requirements will be satisfied where two alternative and mutually incompatible theories of possession exist. Thus, if the same ostensible symptoms, or behaviour, can be seen, either as an intimation of divine election, or as a dangerous intrusion of demonic power, this will provide an adequate basis for acknowledging the claims of some aspirants while rejecting those of others. Such distinctions will afford a reliable means for controlling access to legitimate shamanistic power.

Now, let us look again at our empirical findings in the light of these considerations. In earlier chapters, we have seen that peripheral possession cults very often exist in societies where inspirational possession plays no part in the central religion. The converse, however, is not necessarily true. Central possession religions may occur alone, or they may be accompanied by peripheral possession cults. Let us deal first with the former possibility, where no subsidiary possession cult is found. As we have seen amongst the Akawaio (and to some extent also, apparently, in the pre-colonial situation of the Eskimo and Tungus), in such circumstances the powers of the cosmos are not neatly arrayed in two opposing ranks, the one beneficent and compassionate, the other malevolent and threatening. On the contrary, all the mystical forces which man acknowledges are felt to be equally ambivalent in character. They can do good, but they can also do great harm. Here the crucial distinction between what constitutes authentic shamanistic ecstasy, and what is merely an undesirable spirit intrusion, ultimately depends upon the ability of the victim to 'master' his affliction in a culturally appropriate fashion. At the same time, those cases of possession which are not seen as signs of genuine illumination are dismissed as illnesses caused by the mystical malevolence of shamans belonging to other groups.

Here those spirits which protect one's own community are the source of sickness elsewhere, and just as they are controlled internally by the shaman, so they are controlled externally in the same way. According to the moral condition of the victim, such externally caused spirit afflictions can be interpreted either as justified punishments for ills committed, or as unmerited misfortunes. Thus, in these relatively monolithic religions, the existing enmities between rival local communities, when projected on to the spiritual plane, provide the means by which true inspiration can be distinguished from those other conditions which are so readily confounded with it.

Now let us examine the second possibility, where, as so often happens, central and peripheral possession cults exist alongside each other. In such dualistic cosmologies possession afflictions are always open to two, similarly conflicting interpretations. Where the subject belongs to the stratum of society from which establishment shamans are drawn, his initial possession experience (the 'primary phase') may be seen, either as a valid indication of divine approval, or as a hostile intrusion by a malevolent peripheral spirit. There is no difference at all in the symptoms, at least initially. What differs is the diagnosis; and this, of course, ultimately reflects public opinion. If the aspiring shaman enjoys a wide measure of local support, the appropriate diagnosis is made, and, barring accidents, his career is assured. If, however, this is not the case, then the authenticity of his experience is denied by attributing it to an evil spirit, and exorcism is prescribed as the appropriate treatment.

Here, obviously, the first interpretation endorses the subject's experience as authentic possession, while the second stigmatizes it as inauthentic. These two diametrically opposed assessments do not pertain to different religious systems (as the folk-view might seem to imply), but, on the contrary, are mutually entailed aspects of a single religious system in which peripheral spirits represent the sinister counterparts of those benign powers which sustain public morality.

Where precisely the same symptoms occur in subjects drawn from lower social strata, then, of course, the second interpretation, involving peripheral spirits, is again selected. But, in this case, the ensuing treatment is not so much designed to expel the possessing agency as to domesticate it, thereby establishing a viable liaison between it and its human host.

These two parallel channels of spirit activity are linked together in an additional and highly revealing manner. When peripheral possession is diagnosed in men of substance this is not the end of the matter. Although this diagnosis effectively disposes of the subject's pretensions to be considered an aspiring shaman, the moral significance of his possession affliction still remains to be determined. If the subject is considered to have sinned, then his complaint can be seen as a judgement, executed by a peripheral spirit, but determined by the gods of the central morality which have withdrawn their protective influence. When, however, the consensus of opinion is that the victim is morally blameless, then his condition can be interpreted as a malicious act of spirit-inspired witchcraft perpetrated by a low-class shaman.

These intricate patterns in the anatomy of possession throw into relief the sharp division of labour and of moral responsibility between the two types of ecstatic cult. But the distinction between them is not absolute, as I have repeatedly emphasized, and there is nothing immutable in the characterization of a particular cult as one rather than the other. Some central shamanistic religions are indeed very close to peripheral cults. If, for instance, Eskimo religion seems, in the way it works, to enshrine an implicit morality, it could also be argued that, in effect, peripheral cults do the same. For if the manipulated establishment responds to the spirit-voiced appeals of its subordinates, in the final analysis, it may do so because it recognizes, although this is not made explicit, that these reflect natural justice. There must be some deep-rooted sense of common humanity and moral responsibility in the sentiments which superiors feel towards their subjects. If there were not this underlying sense of *communitas*, as Victor Turner calls it (Turner, 1969), the establishment could treat with impunity these oblique, but often very importunate demands for respect and consideration. Nor, surely, if their consciences were completely clear, would it be necessary for members of the dominant strata to indulge in the whole complicated business of keeping their inferiors at bay by accusing them of witchcraft. Hence, even if peripheral cults involve frankly amoral mystical forces, in practice they cannot be entirely divorced from moral judgement.

Again, as we have repeatedly seen, historically the lines which separate the two types of cult are not absolute or inviolable. Cults can change their significance and status over time. Just as so many peripheral cults are discarded established religions which have fallen from respectability and grace, so equally those which begin as clandestine curing rites on the fringes of society may evolve into new morality religions. From this perspective, and in a very simplified way, the history of religions can be seen to involve a cyclical pattern of changes in the status and inspirational quality of cults, with movements from and to the centre of public morality according to the circumstances and social settings at different points in time. Sudden outbursts of ecstatic effervescence may thus signal either a decline, or rise, in religious fortunes. Possession may equally well represent the kiss of life or of death in the historical development of religions. And even if they were eventually co-opted by a central male establishment, it seems that peripheral female ecstatics may often have pioneered new religions. Women seem to have played a major if much ignored, role in religious change and innovation.

If, however, religions which are in the process of degenerating into marginal cults tend to attract followers from the lower strata of society by possession, there is an equally well-defined tendency for successful inspirational religions to lose their ecstatic fervour and harden into ecclesiastical establishments which claim a secure monopoly of doctrinal knowledge. As Ronald Knox wryly reminds us: 'Always the first fervours evaporate; prophecy dies out, and the charismatic is merged in the institutional' (Knox, 1950, p. 1). Where this hardening of the spiritual arteries ensues, religious authority is ultimately no longer dependent for its validation upon possessional inspiration, but upon ritual and dogma. Where, before, men were elected by the gods to hold personal charismatic commissions, now these functions are exercised by a self-perpetuating priesthood, recruited by other means, and claiming a divine entitlement to religious authority.

Such a structure implies the notion of a stable capital of religious legitimacy which has been made over by the gods to man to administer. Such legitimacy is a 'limited good', access to which one person gains at another's expense. If inspiration figures at all, it represents little more than a nodding gesture by the gods that they continue to endorse the priestly hierarchy's management of its spiritual endowment. This form of religious organization, officially incarnating the deity, and typically shrouded in a rich panoply of ritual, is clearly more stable, more predictable, and more secure in its religious direction than a shamanistic pattern of inspirational authority. In theory, at least, the latter is always open to dramatic new revelations, to novel messages from the gods, and not merely to re-interpretations of established doctrine. Under these conditions, all that a shaman can bequeath to his heirs is a body of technical expertise which may help a successor to gain privileged intercourse with the gods, but cannot guarantee that this will happen.

It is thus no accident that throughout history, and in many different religions, established churches have sought to control and contain personal inspiration. So if social stability seems to favour an emphasis on ritual rather than on ecstatic expression, this again suggests that enthusiasm thrives on instability.

In the same vein, the circumstances surrounding the rise of new inspirational religions, from messianic eruptions in medieval Europe to Cargo Cults in Oceania, point to the crucial significance of factors of acute social disruption and dislocation. This evidence corroborates our findings on the necessary (if not sufficient) conditions for the rise of those analogous movements which we have called peripheral cults particularly when these are associated with changes which are felt to impose limitations on traditional freedoms and rights, or to benefit one social group or category (e.g. men) at the expense of another (e.g. women). In prompting the ecstatic response, the insecurity bred by disorder may thus, paradoxically, be as potent a factor as the frustration produced by excessive order and control. We are left, then, with the problem of determining to what extent the same or similar pressures are involved in the maintenance of central possession religions. Why do such ecstatic religions not always develop established priesthoods which would render enthusiasm redundant and dangerous? If the extinction of enthusiasm is a built-in political tendency, what other countervailing forces may keep possession on the boil?

Part of the answer again seems to lie in the existence of powerful ecological and social pressures, where social groups are small and fluctuating, and general instability prevails. These are generally the conditions amongst the scattered, hunting and gathering Eskimos, amongst the Tungus and other Arctic and Siberian peoples, and the same holds true of the Veddas and Akawaio. More generally, in Latin America, the prevalence of vigorous shamanic religions (cf. Santos, 1986) among the politically marginalized Indian communities is perhaps not surprising, although we should clearly not discount the ready availability for ritual use of powerful local hallucinogens. In the case of our African examples, the significant pressures seem to arise less from the physical environment than from the external social (and political) circumstances. In both cases, where larger stable groups form, shamanism acquires a more firmly institutionalized character, and there is less emphasis on ecstasy. This is true not only of the Macha in Ethiopia, or of the Korekore Shona (who in contrast to the Zezuru, have a more rigid shamanistic hierarchy), but also of different groups among the Tungus. Shirokogoroff's rich ethnographic material indicates that while the smaller, more unstable pastoral bands are led by shamans who achieve their positions by ecstatic seizures, the larger Tungus clans have developed stable shamanistic offices where enthusiasm is muted or extinguished.

Hence if religious routinization discourages ecstasy, at the societal level, the ecstatic tendency is likely to be promoted by intrusive external pressures. Where such conditions prevail, each shaman builds up a fund of personal authority which is dissipated with his death, or at least can only be captured anew by a successor, through a new series of ecstatic inspirations. The shaman in main morality religions is thus the religious analogue of the politically influential entrepreneur, or 'big man'; and, as we have seen amongst the Giriama, the Tonga, and to some extent in our Ethiopian examples, as well as among the Eskimos, the two roles may in fact be held by the same person.

This seems to suggest that far from being untypical or even bizarre manifestations of tension and frustration, peripheral cults embody in a specialized way many of the features of central possession religions. Both are forms of religious expression which imply the existence of acute pressures. In peripheral cults these pressures arise from the oppression to which subordinate members of the community are subject. The self-assertion which possession represents here is directed against the entrenched establishment, and is ultimately contained in the way we have examined. In central ecstatic religions, the constraints are external to the society as a whole, they are felt by everyone, and possession, which asserts the claims of the possessed to be considered the appointed agents of morally endowed gods, has a significance which is much wider. In peripheral cults, those subordinates who practise as shamans master spirits which, officially at least, have no general moral significance. But in central religions, establishment shamans incarnate and treat as equals the powers which control the cosmos. Here the protest which possession embodies is directed to the gods, as shamanism asserts that ultimately man is master of his fate.

Since we shall pursue these themes further [. . .], we can leave them for the present, and turn to summarize our findings on the sexual identity of shamans. Here we may, I think, distinguish three distinct, although not always completely exclusive patterns. First, in central religions, where possession is a precondition for the full exercise of the religious vocation, those selected by the deities are typically men. Secondly, where an established male priesthood, which does not depend upon ecstatic illumination for its authority, controls the central morality cult, women and men of subordinate social categories may be allowed a limited franchise as inspired auxiliaries. Thirdly, these disadvantaged social categories are also those which supply the membership of peripheral possession cults, irrespective of whether ecstasy also occurs in the central religion. Thus in general, it seems that the moral evaluation of possession tends to reflect social and sexual distinctions. Amoral powers select their mounts from women or socially restricted categories of men: those divinities which uphold public morality are less narrowly circumscribed in their choice of human hosts.

But if the spirits of so many different religions appear to show a nice concern for status, we must not forget that in all societies there are psychological 'deviants' – such as effeminate, or homosexual men, for example – whose problems urge them to defy the officially authorized sex-linked roles. Their existence inevitably disturbs this tidy apportionment of spiritual illumination. Thus while drawing the bulk of their members from women and men of the socially appropriate categories, peripheral cults invariably also attract a number of individual men whose participation is less a function of their social placement than of idiosyncratic features in their personality. This raises the complicated problem of the psychological status of possession. So far we have largely evaded this issue: now we must try to confront it squarely.

References

Anisimov, A.F. 1963. 'The shaman's tent of the Evenks and the origin of the shamanistic rite', in H.N. Michael (ed.), *Studies in Siberian Shamanism*, Toronto.

Balikci, A. 1963 'Shamanistic behaviour among the Netsilik Eskimos', *South Western Journal of Anthropology*, 19, 380–96.

Basilov, V.N. 1984. 'The *Chiltan* spirits', in M. Hoppal (ed.), *Shamanism in Eurasia*, Göttingen, pp. 253–67.

Bogoras, W. 1907. *The Jesup North Pacific Expedition*, Vol. 11, *The Chukchee*. Leiden.

Butt, A., Wavell, S. and Epton, N. 1967. *Trances*. London.

Czaplicka, M.A. 1914. *Aboriginal Siberia*. Oxford.

Hamayon, R. 1984. 'Is there a typically female exercise of shamanism in patrilinear societies such as the Buryat?', in M. Hoppal (ed.), *Shamanism in Eurasia*. Göttingen, pp. 307–18.

Knox, R.A. 1950. *Enthusiasm: A Chapter in the History of Religion*, Oxford.

Knutsson, K.E. 1967. *Authority and Change: A Study of the Kallu Institution among the Macha Galla of Ethiopia*. Goteborg.

Knutsson, K.E. 1975. 'Possession and extra-institutional behaviour: an essay in anthropological micro-analysis', *Ethnos* 40, pp. 244–72.

Lewis, H.S. 1984. 'Spirit-possession in Ethiopia: an essay in interpretation', in S. Rubenson (ed.), *Proceedings of the International Congress of Ethiopian Studies*. Uppsala.

Rasmussen, K. 1929. *The Intellectual Culture of the Iglulik Eskimos*. Copenhagen.

Santos Granero, F. 1986. 'Power, ideology and the ritual of production in Lowland South America', *Man* 21, pp. 657–79.

Shirokogoroff, S.M. 1935. *Psychomental Complex of the Tungus*. London.
Sonne, B. 1982. 'The professional ecstatic in his social and ritual position', in
    N.G. Holm (ed.) *Religious Ecstasy*. Uppsala, pp. 128–50.
Turner, V.W. 1969. *The Ritual Process: Structure and Anti-Structure*. London.

Chapter 5

John A. Grim

OJIBWAY SHAMANISM

Ojibway shamanistic expressions

THE *TCISAKI* SHAMAN IS USUALLY a male diviner who 'reveals hidden truths' while in communication with the manitou in a shaking tent.[1] The shaking-tent ceremony revolves around the contact of a solitary *tcisaki* with particular manitou who aid his search for lost objects or tribespeople. In some performances of this ceremony the *tcisaki* may be bound and suspended within the conjuring lodge.[2] The shaman contacts his helping manitou, who loosen his bonds as they reveal the desired information. The tent shakes violently with spirit presences, hence the name of the ceremony.

The *nanandawi* shaman is the tribal doctor. He cures by evoking his manitou patron, who locates the cause of the illness and directs the shaman in removing it. The shaman does so by ritually applying small bones to the affected area. He either sucks or blows into the bones, depending on the manitou direction. The *nanandawi* may also use herbal prescriptions and other shamanistic techniques, but the major part of his shamanic vocation is his skill in 'talking with the spirits' to determine the cause of the illness and the subsequent sucking cure with bones.[3]

The *wabeno*, or 'men of the dawn sky,' manipulated fire in order to interpret dreams, guide novices through spirit contact, and heal the sick.[4] They use a herbal preparation to protect themselves from the fire. This allows them to briefly seize hot coals without being affected by the burning. They heal the sick by manipulating the fire near the patient's body. The *wabeno* act as mediators of the power which they contact in a trance and which they manifest in their manipulation of fire. They also interpret dreams by entering into the trance state, which often is induced by singing special chants and staring fixedly into the coals of a fire. The *wabeno*, at one time, formed a society similar to the Midewiwin.

The *meda* shaman is the family healer who 'sounded the drum' for sick members of the isolated Algonquian hunting groups.[5] The *meda* also maintained dream contact with the manitou to assure success on the hunt and to predict the movement of enemy groups. From these ancient activities the *meda*, or family shaman, most probably developed other shamanic techniques, such as herbal healing and naming.[6] During the crucial period of the tribal consolidation and migration from northern Michigan, the *meda* probably developed into the secret society of shamans, the midewiwin. Since the late seventeenth century the word *meda* has been used to refer to an individual shaman initiated into the esoteric lore of the midewiwin.[7]

[. . .]

Healing and divining

After receiving their appointments in dream, Ojibway shamans develop their ability to invoke the manitou patron. An extended effort is required of the shaman candidate to learn to invoke and control this power effectively. The tribe's sanction of the shamanic ritual involves more than appreciation of a dramatic spectacle. Rather, the tribe acknowledges the shaman's effectiveness in drawing from the manitou a response to their tribal needs.

The inherent need and weakness of the human condition, according to the Ojibway, are the cause of constant crises. The individual tribesperson is subject to an unremitting series of problematic situations: the possible lack of game to hunt or trap, the fickleness of social relations, the intrusion of illness, the attack of aberrant shamans, the inclemencies of the weather, and the caprices of unbridled cosmic forces. The fears of the isolated individual can only be warded off by the intervention of the powerful manitou. As A. Irving Hallowell expressed this Ojibway belief: 'Human beings are conceived of as being in constant need of help, from birth to death. So essential is such help that no performance of any kind is interpreted as due to an individual's own abilities or efforts.'[8]

The mediation of such strengthening energies in the human condition occurs in personal dreams and in the healing and divining ceremonies of the tribe's shamans. Through the shamanic rituals the individual Ojibway has the means to assert some independence from the isolating, sometimes terrifying environment. The role of the shaman is thus central to the maintenance of the ethos of aggressive individualism. The shamans themselves are formed by the tribal ethos, and, in turn, they provide the members of the tribe with the ritual means to aggressively foster their own independent existences. For example, the presence of a *meda* enabled the isolated family group to meet the exigencies of their woodland life with the confidence of supernatural aid.

The need for manitou aid to strengthen the human condition led to the development of a variety of healing and divining practices among the Ojibway. While the healing rituals themselves are highly individuated, they can be identified by the techniques used. Some of the most significant healing practices are tube-sucking, herbal brewing, bloodletting, naming, chanting, fire manipulation, and tatooing.

Tube-sucking (*nanadawi iwe winini*), a classic shamanic art, is a prominent healing practice among the Ojibway. While this art is initially authorized in a manitou dream, the person who seeks to learn the *nanandawi* vocation is usually taught by elder shamans.[9] This apprenticeship does not confer tribal sanction, but it does dispose the young *nanandawi* to develop his or her healing art in a traditionally accepted manner. The skill of the *nanandawi* is suggested in the following passage, which describes a tube-sucking cure performed by a Wisconsin Ojibway shaman. The passage records an event when an Ojibway youth, Tom Badger, was treated for severe pains in his left side by a *nanandawi* shaman, Old Man Hay.

> In the evening Old Man Hay started to doctor me. He used those bones to doctor me. First he told me to lay on my left side. Then he put the bone right on the place where my pain was. He pushed his head down close and kept pushing as hard as he could on that bone. When he pulled the bone away finally, the skin there pulled back. That's when it hurt most of all. He started twice to doctor me. The second time he did the same thing he did the first time. When a sucking doctor starts to cure, he first tells the people there about the dream he had at the time he was fasting. Old Man Hay did that. Then my father beat a War Dance drum. Old Man Hay shook a rattle while he doctored me. He put a little dish next to him, with a little water in it. The two bones were lying there. They were about one and a half to two inches long. He didn't touch them with his hands but picked them up with his mouth. He didn't even have to pick them up with his mouth. His power was so strong that when Old Man Hay leaned over the dish, the bones stood up and moved towards his mouth. He swallowed the bones twice and coughed them up again. Then he put the bone to my side. After he'd finished sucking, Old May Hay drew out some stuff and spat it into a dish; it looked like blood. Old Man Hay showed it to me and to the others and then threw it into the fire. If he hadn't drawn the blood out, it would have turned to pus. And sometimes, when the pus burst inside, the person dies. My father drummed all the time that Old Man Hay was doctoring me. He didn't sing, but Old Man Hay sang a little bit at the beginning of

every time he doctored me. He put the bone to my side four times and got blood each time, but the last time he doctored me there was very little blood. It was the same every time he doctored me. All we gave him was a piece of cloth and some tobacco, and gave him his meals. After he had finished doctoring me, Old Man Hay said to my father, 'One time they had a medicine dance. You took the hide that Tom got in the medicine dance and gave it to someone else. You promised to give him another one in place of the one you took from him. Sometimes he thinks about it. That's why he is sick now.'[10]

This narrative description is particularly interesting because of its elaborate detail. It provides a schema with which to interpret the Ojibway shaman's healing art because certain stages in his curative practice can be observed. First, there is the *invocation*, which Old Man Hay performed by reciting the dream that came to him at his vision fast. In this invocation he called upon his healing patron to grant him the special sight needed to 'see' the illness and prescribe the necessary 'medicine.' Moreover, the invocation implied that the summoned power was strong enough to destroy the cause of illness.

Next, Old Man Hay executed the *craft* of healing, which in this case was tube-sucking. The presence of spiritual power was thus accompanied by a physical action that effected the passage of strength from one level of reality, that of the manitou, to another level, that of the patient in need of healing on the flat-earth.

Meanwhile, during the performance of the technique, the shaman and available assistants (in this case, Tom's father) maintain a *therapeutic field* by drumming, rattling, chanting, and magical feats.[11] This healing context is a significant psychophysiological control used to ease the patient and promote a curative atmosphere. The repetitive drumming, rattling, and chanting help to create a trance state for both the shaman and the patient. The impressive feats, such as causing the bones to move before touching them, increases the patient's confidence in the shaman's ability. These magical feats are often central to the maintenance of a field of healing during a curative ritual. In the description above, several magical feats are mentioned, such as, swallowing the bones, talking while they are in the throat, and coughing them up again. Likewise, the blood sucked from the patient's side may be seen to contain small worms or insects, which are offered as proof of the intrusion of an object causing the illness. These demonstrations of power are necessary both to bolster the shaman's self-image and to create the desired effect on the patient. Indeed, the whole healing performance is a demonstration of the shaman's power. The payment by Tom's family appears to be of secondary importance to the shaman, compared with the opportunity to exhibit his healing powers.

The final stage, namely, *the diagnosis of the underlying cause* appears to be peripheral to the healing ceremony itself, but it is, of course, necessary for a complete cure. This stage recalls the initial stage of invocation, in which the shaman calls upon the manitou to open the illness for inspection. In the passage above Old Man Hay diagnoses the pains as due to an inner preoccupation with the loss of an animal hide. The physical symptoms of pain and 'bad blood' arise from this obsessive brooding. The underlying cause of such a sickness might also be traced to the vengeful attacks of another shaman. Whatever the diagnosis may be, this final stage reveals the individual's subsequent role in assuaging or avenging the cause of illness. Thus the shaman's healing art combines various techniques of divining in his diagnosis and prognosis.

The schema of invocation, healing craft, therapeutic field, and diagnosis of underlying cause can be helpful in investigating the other shamanic healing practices listed above. In all of them the shaman is especially sanctioned by the patient and by the tribe to perform his healing ritual. The shaman's healing performance is approved because it introduces the power of the manitou in a controlled form. The shaman deduces the individual's cause of illness and describes the appropriate retaliatory action. In this manner the actions arise within the context of the aggressive individualistic ethos, and consequently the shaman is tribally supported.

For the Ojibway divining is the ability to forecast future events or to elucidate certain contemporary occurrences. In the past shamans predicted the success or failure of war parties. Now they discern, for example, the meaning of a particular dream or determine the health or the location of distant relatives or the arrival of seasonal game animals.

Divining has certain similarities with healing in the Ojibway understanding. Like the healing ritual, the divining ceremony is the property of an individual. The divining shaman may have sharpened his skills by learning from elder shamans, but his prognosticating art requires the appropriate initiation dream. Divining rituals are also used for curing purposes because they create contact with manitou and thus bring increased strength to the patient.[12] The most prominent Ojibway divining shaman was the *tcisaki*. Even in the following brief description of the shaking tent ceremony, the schema of shamanic healing may be recognized, namely, invocation, craft, divinatory field, and diagnosis of underlying cause:

> The patient or a delegate approaches the doctor with the request for his services, and exhibits a pile of dry goods, blankets, etc., tobacco, and perhaps some food. Depending on his habit, the doctor then instructs the patient to prepare a sweat tent. Into this, the doctor retires alone, and communes with his guardian turtle, *mikinak*. The following night the doctor enters the divining tent which he has ordered the patient to construct for him. He asks his guardian turtle to summon the other supernaturals for

consultation. The people outside the tent hear the tones of this colloquy, although they cannot precisely distinguish the words. Each manitou has a distinctive intonation which is traditional. Thus, the turtle has a shrill voice, the eagle has a 'gentle' (pleasant) voice. The spirits make a great noise when they enter and leave the tent; and at these times the tent shakes with fearful violence. From his consultation with the spirits, the doctor learns what he seeks.[13]

This *tcisaki*'s initial consultation with his guardian spirit, *mikinak*, and the call to the 'other supernaturals' to assemble can be considered the invocation. Again, the emphasis is on the need for a power presence to effect the desired end, in this case, prognostication. The craft of the conjuring lodge is based on the *tcisaki*'s communication with the assembled manitou. The essential power exchange is by virtue of the *tcisaki*'s conversation with these spirit powers. The tribal audience hears this conversation, though its meaning may be unclear to all but the shaman.[14]

The divinatory field created by the shaman and his or her assembled manitou makes this ceremony extremely impressive. For the spirits, according to traditional belief, cause a wind to circulate within the lodge, thus creating a violent shaking motion.[15] Another magical aspect of the divinatory field is the projection by the shaman of many different voices and animal sounds to the open area at the top of the lodge. Often the *tcisaki* drums and chants between periods of communication with the manitou. These actions contribute to an impressive performance that manifests his or her power and skill.

Finally, the divining ceremony reveals the underlying cause of the tribesperson's problem or the answer to his or her question. After invoking the manitou and requesting them to investigate the tribesperson's questions, the shaman later announces what the spirits report. The tribes people often recognize a spirit's voice and wait for the report of a favored spirit. Such a manitou was *mikinak*, the turtle. Interestingly, the manitou turtle, the slowest of creatures, symbolized quick communication.[16] It might be that the tribal ethos celebrated the dogged persistence of the turtle to assert his painstaking deliberation.

Other shamanic rituals of divining among the Ojibway followed the schema presented but varied in the techniques by which the shaman practiced his or her prognostications. For example, the *wabeno* shaman divined by gazing at the coals in the fire, and dream interpreters predicted the future by analyzing the symbols in a person's dream. Regardless of the techniques used, however, the effectiveness of the rituals affirmed the tribal ethos. The shaman's divining provided a means for the individual Ojibway tribesperson aggressively to transcend the limitations of his life. The subsequent sanction of the Ojibway shaman by the tribe followed from this basic interaction, which had both a theoretical and practical aspect.

Theoretically, the tribal sanction of the shaman comes as a result of his contact with manitou power. Because the Ojibway traditionally view the human condition as weak, there is a positive need for such an intervention of power. The personalities supplying that need are the shamans, who are distinguished by their specific techniques of divining and healing. The theories of power manifestation, the weakness of the human condition, and the requirements of the tribal ethos provide the theoretical sanction of the shaman's vocation.

Shamans are also sanctioned because of their practical effectiveness in healing and divining. Their actions are tried and tested by the tribal tradition. Although there is a strong visual and emotional component to the shamanistic rituals, the shamans are respected not simply as dramatic personalities but also as astute healers and diviners. The tribe's approval arises largely from these pragmatic considerations. Thus, despite personal aggrandizement by some Ojibway shamans and outright sorcery by others, the tribal sanction of shamanism has remained largely intact throughout Ojibway history.

[. . .]

Ritual activity

Once given the manitou's aid, Sky Woman had the confidence to direct her power to the situation over which she had had no previous control, namely, her grandmother's illness. She summoned up the symbolic songs, gestures, and sucking practices that had been bestowed in her dream validation. Sky Woman's skillful orchestration of those powers suggests a magical quality in her cure. Indeed, as Bronislaw Malinowski observed, magical techniques help create a mood of confidence in which ritual practices can be effective:

> Magic supplies primitive man with a number of ready-made ritual acts and beliefs, with a definite mental and practical technique which serves to bridge over the dangerous gaps in every important pursuit or critical situation. It enables man to carry out with confidence his important tasks, to maintain his poise and his mental integrity in fits of anger, in the throes of hate, of unrequited love, of despair and anxiety.[17]

Magic, for Malinowski, was the means by which practical remedies could be brought to bear even in extremely distressing situations. His understanding of magic, however, does not adequately take into account the ethos and world view in which the shamanic techniques function. Since he reduces shamanic magic to practical techniques, he does not explain the underlying tribal belief system that makes the shaman effective. While magical practices in the Ojibway context can be seen as aggressive individualistic acts, they reflect a belief system that is ongoing and not invoked only in crisis situations. Thus the shamanic ritual is more than magical techniques; it expresses a world view of personalistic contact with sacred power that is accessible for healing.

Sky Woman's ritual activity, for example, was a courageous response to a crisis. The repetitive songs, gestures, and sucking cures, however, were more than magical techniques to alleviate a difficult situation. Rather they were the actions of an individual aggressively evoking unique personalistic powers in which she trusted. By assuming the heroic qualities of a shaman, Sky Woman aspired to the highest authority for the power needed to heal. Her shamanic vocation was not simply dependent on the development of certain magical techniques; it was based on her sacrificial identification, which mediated sacred power to individuals and to the tribe as a whole.

The Ojibway cosmology of personalistic power portrayed phenomenal reality as a field of interpenetrating forces, with which the power personality could communicate. Thus the Ojibway world view encouraged a style of life in which the individual aggressively aspired to be a power personality, namely, a shaman. In Sky Woman's case the aspiration to shamanize was largely latent until her manitou dream. After that dream she performed her own ritual, which recreated her initial communication, thereby summoning her manitou patron for the power to heal.

The various actions that she performed in her ritual were a reenactment of her initiating dream. Thus the rattle, the talking with supernaturals (*manitou kazo*), and the sucking cure (*nananda wiat*) were given her as a pledge by her manitou patron. By performing those actions, she brought the manitou into the presence of her ailing grandmother. The determination with which she carried out those actions suggests the extent of her commitment to her grandmother as well as the dogged persistence of an individual Ojibway in pursuing power. Sky Woman's confidence centered on the ritual that she had been taught in her dream.

Generally the manner in which an Ojibway shamanic ritual develops depends upon renewed encounters with the symbols of the initiating dream. An early nineteenth-century Ojibway shaman, Chingawouk, described the intricate task of developing a shamanic ritual and emphasized the revelatory quality of dreams in fostering a shamanic vocation:

> What a young man sees and experiences during these dreams and fasts, is adopted by him as a truth, and it becomes a principle to regulate his future life. He relies for success on these revelations. If he has been much favored in his fasts, and the people believe that he has the art of looking into futurity, the path is open to the highest honors. The [shaman] begins to try his power in secret, with only one assistant, whose testimony is necessary should he succeed. As he goes on, he puts down the figures of his dreams or revelations, by symbols, on bark or other material 'til a whole

winter is sometimes past in pursuing the subject and he thus has a record of his principal revelations.[18]

As described by Chingawouk, shamans have several formative dreams and visions which amplify the initial manitou call. The interpretation of these dreams requires a reflective period, which may be considered a gradual call. The withdrawal into solitude is sacrifice that prepares the shaman for the coalescence of his or her ritual identity with the manitou. The ceremony that the shaman eventually performs is the concrescence of his initiating experiences, whose reenactment by means of particular symbols mediates between the shaman and his personal power. The ritual thus gives meaning to the call, the sacrificial period of seclusion, and the later situations in which healing is needed. Each reenactment is a unique summons of power and an open display by recitation of the shaman's relationship with power that can transform a difficult situation.

Public recitation of the shaman's dream was problematic in the Ojibway world because there was a prohibition against open revelation of a sacred dream. It was feared that the dream's power would thus be dissipated, even though the shaman was required to recite the dream experience to evoke the manitou presence for healing, divining, and other shamanistic practices. The shaman often resolved this dilemma by narrating the dream in a hurried manner. Yet the purpose of the narration was not only the evocation of manitou power but also the edification of his patient. The following passage describes an Ojibway shaman's ritual that drew on certain symbols from his dreams. Although the audience might not be able to understand the full implications of the dream, they would recognize certain symbols, such as Thunderbird, his principal manitou patron:

> She [the patient] spread blankets and tobacco before [the shaman], in payment of his forthcoming services. This fee is his exclusive property. He smoked the tobacco in offering to his supernatural patron, the Thunderbird. This offering is both toll and invocation. It is toll because the smoking sends to the [manitou] the spirit of the payment received by the doctor. It is invocation because it bespeaks the supernatural.
>
> When he finished smoking, he asked Mrs. Wilson for water in which he put a hollow bone. The bone was of a light weight, about two and a half inches long from the leg of some bird. He beat his rattle against his chest, on his back, from his side to his side, and commenced to 'talk about his dream.' This helped him to doctor because it rallied his supernatural; and from another viewpoint, its mysteries gave confidence to himself and to his awed client. 'He talks so quickly . . . quick as anything . . . you can hardly understand.' The mumbling is his privilege, for to speak intelligibly would give his dream away.

> After he said his dream, he started rattling and singing. He said he was singing to his dream . . . that the Thunderbird could see everything in the ground . . . that everything is scared of the Thunderbird.[19]

After this invocation the shaman began to perform the shamanic techniques appropriate to a *nanandawi* curer.

This description of an Ojibway *nanandawi*'s ritual illustrates the re-enactment theme. The bone, with which the shaman seemingly extracted the object causing the illness, would have been conferred on him in his initiating dream. Similarly, the manner of rattling and the 'talk about his dream' (*manitou kazo*) were also imparted in vision. Thus this shaman's ritual was a lively reenactment of words, gestures, and object manipulations bestowed on him by his manitou. The hurried recitation preserved the secrecy of his more specific dream images, but the shaman openly mentioned the primary symbol of his dream, namely Thunderbird. By open invocation of the Thunderbird he simultaneously contacted his manitou patron and aroused in the patient a confidence in his ability to mediate a healing energy. The Thunderbird symbol focused both the shaman and the patient in the belief that supernatural power could be brought to bear on the illness. For the shaman, having undergone his own traumatic initiating experiences, recapitulated his sacrificial identity with power, thereby mediating the healing manitou presence.

Such a therapeutic metamorphosis is operative in all Ojibway shamanic rituals. Just as the shamanic personality experiences a new identity by receiving the manitou dream, so also is the patient expected to receive a transformative power from the shaman. The shaman reenacts his initiating experience to presence this transforming power. The symbolic chants and gestures that he directs towards the patient are intended to reverse the intruding sickness by applying a stronger 'medicine.' For example, the Ojibway shaman Chiahba chanted the following during his healing rituals: 'What is this I put in your body? Snake skins I put in your body.'[20] Since his vision of Snake manitou had given Chiahba power, he ritually called on its power to combat a patient's sickness.

Notes

1   W.J. Hoffman, 1891. 'The Midē'wiwin or "Grand Medicine Society" of the Ojibwa', in *Seventh Annual Report of the Bureau of American Ethnology*, Washington: Government Printing Office, p. 157.

2   Å. Hultkrantz, 1967. 'Spirit Lodge, a North American Shamanistic Séance', in C-M. Edsman, *Studies in Shamanism*, Stockholm, pp. 60–1.

3   R. Landes, 1937. *Ojibwa Sociology*, New York: Columbia University Press, pp. 120–1.

4   Hoffman, 'The Midē'wiwin', pp. 156–7.

5   Frank Speck, 1919. 'Penobscot Shamanism', Memoirs of the American Anthropological Association, no. 6. pp. 240–8; also, Adrian Tanner, 1979. *Bringing Home Animals*, New York: St. Martin's Press, pp. 136–52.

6   While the *meda*, or family shaman, is generally absent in research on Ojibway shamanism, a clear description of this shamanistic vocation is found in Edward James, (ed.) 1956. *Narrative of John Tanner's Thirty Years of Indian Captivity*, Minneapolis: Ross and Haines, pp. 30–40.

7   It should be noted that the form *Midewin* is in some areas the more acceptable designation of the medicine society.

8   A.I. Hallowell, 1947. 'Myth, Culture and Personality', *American Anthropologist* 49, p. 551.

9   Landes, *Ojibwa Sociology*, p. 124.

10   V. Barnouw, 1977. *Wisconsin Chippewa Myths and Tales*, Madison: University of Wisconsin Press, p. 256–66.

11   The drum has a prominent place in Ojibway shamanism: see Hoffman, 'The Midē'wiwin', pp. 156ff.

12   A.I. Hallowell, 1942. *The Role of Conjuring in Saulteaux Society*, Philadelphia: University of Philadelphia Press, p. 53ff.

13   Landes, *Ojibwa Sociology*, p. 122.

14   A.I. Hallowell, 1942. *The Role of Conjuring in Saulteaux Society*, Philadelphia: University of Philadelphia Press, pp. 44–47 and, especially, p. 50.

15   Ibid., pp. 74–5; also H. Schoolcraft, 1853. *Information Respecting the history, Condition and Prosperity of the Indian Tribes of the United States*, Philadelphia: Lippincott, Giambo and Co, 1: 392.

16   B. Johnston, 1976. *Ojibway Heritage*, New York: Columbia University Press, p. 15.

17   B. Malinowski, 1954. *Magic, Science and Religion*, New York: Doubleday, p. 90.

18   Schoolcraft, *Information*, vol. 1, quoted in J.M. Vastokas, 1973. *Sacred Art of the Algonkians*, Peterborough, Ont.: Mansard Press, p. 44.

19   Landes, *Ojibwa Sociology*, p. 121.

20   E. James, (ed.) 1956. *Narrative of John Tanner's Thirty Years of Indian Captivity*, Minneapolis: Ross and Haines.

Chapter 6

Barbara Tedlock

THE NEW ANTHROPOLOGY
OF DREAMING

[. . .]

IN **RECENT YEARS DREAM** researchers have become sensitive to the differences between dream accounts and dreams. While dreams are private mental acts, which have never been recorded during their actual occurrence, dream accounts are public social performances taking place after the experience of dreaming. When dreamers decide, for whatever reason, to share a dream experience, they choose an appropriate time and place, a specific audience and social context, a modality (visual or auditory), and a discourse or performance form. While some clinicians and experiential dream workers operate with the fiction that when they hear or produce a sufficiently dramatic dream report they can recover the dream itself, as if entering into a 'real dream life' (Mahrer 1989: 44–46), cultural anthropologists have turned their attention to the study of dream sharing as a communicative event (B. Tedlock 1987a).

Psychologists of both the psychoanalytic and the cognitive bents have, for the most part, read anthropology in order to compare the dreams of what have been categorized as 'preliterate,' 'tribal,' 'traditional,' or 'peasant' peoples with the dreams of 'literate,' 'urban,' 'modern' or 'industrial' peoples. While cultural anthropologists made such comparisons in the past, today we have turned away from this labelling practice because of its use of typological time, which denies people living in other cultures 'coevalness,' or contemporaneity with ourselves (Fabian 1983). The use of typological time, which fictively places some people in an earlier time frame than ourselves, functions as a distancing device. An example of this practice is the assertion that there currently exist societies practicing 'stone age economics.' We cultural anthropologists also experience this temporal displacement ourselves, whenever we identify ourselves to our neighbors, hairdressers, or physicians as 'anthropologists' only to find ourselves confused with 'archaeologists,' studying ancient stone tools, pyramids, and human remains. Instead of using typological time to create and set off an object of study such as 'tribal dream typologies' (Hunt 1989: 87), cultural anthropologists today are interested in intersubjective time in which all of the participants involved are 'coeval,' i.e., share the same time. The current focus on communicative processes in cultural anthropology demands that coevalness not only be created and maintained in the field, but also be carried over during the write-up process. Thus, for example, Robert Dentan, while discussing the principle of contraries in which dreams indicate the opposite of what they seem, noted that practitioners of this type of dream interpretation include 'such widely separated peoples as Ashanti, Malays, Maori, Buffalo (New York) Polish-American parochial schoolgirls, psychoanalysts, Semai and Zulu' (Dentan 1986: 33). In other words, at least some Americans share this principle of dream interpretation with people living in faraway, exotic places.

The change in research strategy away from treating so-called 'non-Western dreams' as totally 'other' but nonetheless fully knowable objects to be gathered, tabulated, and compared with our own 'Western dreams,' and toward paying attention to the problematics of dream representation, communication, and interpretation world-wide has occurred within anthropology for several reasons. First, cultural anthropologists have come to distrust survey research in which 'data' is gathered for the purpose of testing Western theories concerning universals in human psychology. Thus, for example, Calvin Hall's (1951, 1953) cross-cultural content analysis, in which statistical assertions about dream patterns within particular ethnic groups or genders are the goal, have been critiqued by anthropologists (B. Tedlock 1987a; Dentan 1988a). There are several reasons for this, including the fact that sample surveys aggregate respondents who are deeply distrustful of the researcher with those who are not, as if suspicion made no difference whatsoever in the validity of their replies (Scheff 1986). Further, a comparativist focus on the extractable contents of a dream report not only omits important phenomena such as pacing, tones of voice, gestures, and audience responses that accompany dream narrative performances, but is also an expression of the culture of alphabetic literacy and thus culture-bound (Crapanzano 1981; B. Tedlock 1987a; Dentan 1988a).

Another reason for the abandonment of content analysis by anthropologists is that our formal training in linguistics encourages us to reject the basic assumption of aggregate statistical research, namely, that meaning resides within single words rather than within their contexts (Dentan 1988a) (see Note 1). This critique rests on a basic axiom of semantics, known as the premise of non-identity, which states that the word is not the object. Dream narratives are not dreams, and neither narrating nor enacting dreams can ever recover dream experiences. Furthermore, dream symbols taken in isolation can be misleading if the researcher has not spent at least a year observing and interacting within the culture in order to gather enough contextual details to make sense of local knowledge and produce a 'thick description' of that culture (Geertz 1973; Dentan 1988b: 38) (see Note 2). Thus, rather than interpreting the language of dream narratives in semantico-referential, context-independent terms, it is more appropriate to utilize context-dependent, or pragmatic, meaning (Silverstein 1976).

Because of these considerations anthropologists no longer set out to elicit dream reports as ethnographic objects to be used as raw data for comparative hypotheses (e.g., Lincoln 1935; Schneider and Sharp 1969). Instead, we now go into the field for extended periods of time with broad sets of research interests; for example, the religion and world view of a particular society, the performance of healing, or the construction of self and personhood. By living within the community we learn not only the language but also how to interact appropriately, and, perhaps most importantly, we are present for various formal and informal social dramas (see Note 3). Sooner or later we cannot help but be present when a dream is narrated within a family, or to a practicing shaman, or some other dream interpreter. If this type of event or social drama attracts our attention, we make notes about it in our field journals and we may later record other such occurrences on audio or video tape. Once we have translated such texts we may ask the narrator, who may or may not be the dreamer, questions about the meaning, significance, and use of the dream account.

This shift in research strategy from directly eliciting dozens of fixed objects (dreams) to studying naturally occurring situations (dream sharing, representation, and interpretation) is part of a larger movement within anthropology in which there has been a rapidly growing interest in analyses focused on practice, interaction, dialogue, experience, and performance, together with the individual agents, actors, persons, selves, and subjects of all this activity (Bourdieu 1978; D. Tedlock 1979; Ortner 1984). Three recent doctoral dissertations in anthropology clearly display this shift from the dream as an object to the context surrounding the personal experience and cultural uses of dreaming (Desjarlais 1990; Roseman 1991; Degarrod 1989). Robert Desjarlais, during his fieldwork in Nepal with the Yolmo Sherpa, noted a large degree of agreement among individuals concerning the meaning of dream imagery and found what he called 'an implicit "dictionary" of dream symbolism,' which individuals relied upon most frequently in times of physical or spiritual distress (Desjarlais 1990: 102–117). Thus, for example, dreaming of an airplane, bus, or horse indicates that one's spirit has left the body and that one will soon fall ill, while dreaming of a new house or clothes, snow falling on the body, consuming sweet white foods such as milk, watching the sun setting or the waxing of the moon all indicate future good health.

In this dream interpretation system, like many others, the experience of dreaming is believed to have a close, even causal, connection with the future life of the dreamer (see also Bruce 1975, 1979; Laughlin 1976; Herdt 1977; Kilborne 1978; Kracke 1979; Basso 1987; B. Tedlock 1987b; Dentan 1983, Degarrod 1989; Hollan 1989; McDowell 1989). However, it is important to remember that such interpretations are often provisional, that not all people in a given society place their faith in such interpretations, and that in some societies only certain individuals are believed to be able to experience prophetic or precognitive dreams (Devereux 1956; Meggitt 1962; Charsley 1973; Jackson 1978; Dentan 1983; Merrill 1987). Nevertheless, prophetic dreams and visions have often triggered anti-colonial revolts (Wallace 1959; Dentan 1986). But lest we fall into the comfortable assumption that prophetic dream interpretation systems are characteristically found in 'tribal,' 'non-Western,' or 'non-industrial' societies, and only rarely in 'modern,' 'Western,' 'industrialized' societies (Hodes 1989: 7–8), cultural anthropologists who have undertaken substantial fieldwork within American society have found that middle-class dreamers admit to having experienced dreams of the prophetic or precognitive sort in which they obtain information about future events (Collins 1977: 46, 49, 58–59; Hillman 1988: 134; Dombeck 1989: 89). Furthermore, the popular Western conception of dreams as predictors of misfortune or success, together with the anecdotal literature on 'psychic dreams,' indicate that this form of dream interpretation is far from rare in Western societies (Stevens 1949; Ullman, Krippner and Vaughan 1973; Staff 1975; Tolaas 1986, 1990; Persinger 1988; Persinger and Krippner 1989).

Labelling certain dream experiences 'prophetic' or 'precognitive,' however, does not explain how these and other dream experiences are used both individually and culturally within a society. In order to learn about the actual use of dreaming researchers cannot simply gather examples of different types of dreams by administering a questionnaire, but must instead interact intensively for a long period of time. Thus, while Desjarlais (1990) quickly discovered the implicit 'dictionary' of dream symbolism among the Sherpa, it took him some time as an apprentice shaman to learn the precise way in which these dream symbols served as symptoms and signifiers both reflecting and shaping distress. Likewise, Marina Roseman (1986), through her active participation as a singer within an all female chorus in Temiar society, learned the precise manner in which local dream sharing through song connects the musical and medical domains of knowledge and practice. In this Malaysian society, spirit guides teach dreamers songs by singing them phrase by phrase, and dreamers learn songs during their dreams by repeating the songs phrase by phrase. This dream-teaching relationship is echoed in public performance when a male medium sings a song phrase which is then repeated by a female chorus. In time Roseman grasped the fact that dream songs varied by the spirit guide source, creating formal musical genres with characteristic textual content and vocabulary, melodic and rhythmic patterns, dance movements, and trance behavior. Not only do these genres vary individually but they also vary regionally and historically. During her twenty months of fieldwork she taped hundreds of these dream-song performances, together with intricate dream narratives and interpretations (Roseman 1986, 1991).

Lydia Degarrod, like Roseman and Desjarlais, recorded the majority of her dream materials within a natural setting rather than by arranging formal interviews (Degarrod 1989). During her research among the Mapuche Indians of Chile, she gathered dream accounts and various interpretations of these narratives from several members of two families who were coping with serious stress caused by witchcraft and illness (Degarrod 1990). Through dream sharing and interpreting, the afflicted members of the families were able to express their anxieties and externalize their illness, and other family members were able to directly participate in the healing of their loved ones. Degarrod hypothesized that these types of family interventions were possible due to both the nature of the communal dream sharing and interpreting system, which allowed for the combination of elements from different individual's dreams to be related through intertextual and contextual analysis, and the general belief that dreams facilitate communication with supernatural beings.

By studying dream sharing and the transmission of dream theories in their full social contexts as communicative events, including the natural dialogical interactions that take place within these events, anthropologists have realized that both the researcher and those who are researched are engaged in the creation of a social reality that implicates both of them. Even though cultural anthropologists have long subscribed to the method of participant observation, it still comes as a shock when they discover how important their participation is in helping to create what they are studying (LeVine 1981). Thus, for example, Gilbert Herdt reported his surprise at discovering the therapeutic dimension of his role in New Guinea as a sympathetic listener to his key consultant, who shared with him erotic dreams, taking place in menstrual huts, which he could not communicate to anyone within his own society (Herdt 1987: 73–74). Likewise, the importance to anthropology of the psychodynamic process of transference, which is to say the bringing of past experiences into a current situation with the result that the present is unconsciously experienced as though it were the past (Freud 1958; Bird 1972; Loewald 1986), has only recently been fully realized and described for anthropology. Waud Kracke (1987a), during his fieldwork with the Kagwahiv Indians of Brazil during 1967–1968, kept a diary containing his personal reactions, dreams and associations. In a sensitive essay discussing these field responses, Kracke not only analyzes his personal transference of his own family relationships to certain key Kagwahiv individuals, but also his cultural transference of American values to Kagwahiv behavior patterns. Other cultural anthropologists have not only recorded their dreams and associations in their field diaries, but they have also told their dreams to members of the society in which they were working for the purpose of having them interpreted (Bruce 1975; Jackson 1978; B. Tedlock 1981, Stephen 1989).

When anthropologists have paid close attention to their own dreams during their fieldwork they have found that dream experiences have helped them to integrate their unconscious with a conscious sense of personal continuity in this totally new, even threatening, situation. Laura Nadar, for example, reported that during her research among Zapotec Indians in Mexico, the amount of her nocturnal dreaming, as well as her ability to remember dreams, multiplied several times over her usual behavior, and that her dreams dealt almost exclusively with her experiences as a child and young adult back home in the United States. 'Not only my dreams, but also my general emotional state appeared to be more related to pre-Zapotec experiences than anything else' (Nadar 1970: 11). And, although she did not feel herself to be equipped professionally to analyze why her dreams were more directly related to experience outside of the field situation, she states that 'it was not because I was emotionally neutral about the people I was studying' (Ibid.: 111–112). It is as though her dreams were reminding her not to lose her self completely, not to become possessed by Zapotec 'otherness.' Her dreams reassured her that she was indeed still the same person she was as a child. That there was a continuity within her self, in spite of her strong feelings to the contrary.

A juxtaposition of earlier with recent life events in the dreams of fieldworkers is also a common experience. A study by Barbara Anderson (1971) of fifteen American academics living in India reports a major change in dream content, moving from an initial retreat to earlier life events towards the establishment of a 'secondary identity' that allows dreams with mixed, but clearly distinct American and Indian elements. In the first month of fieldwork she and her fellow academics reported dreaming of people from their childhood – old neighbors and school friends – whom they hadn't thought about in years. During the second month, current family members entered their dream life, but shyly and from a great distance; for example, one man's wife talked with him from a doorway. It was not until a good deal later that their dream worlds included a wider spectrum of personages and backdrops with Indian settings in which their spouses, siblings, and children mingled together with Indians. She suggests that these dreams are the resolution of the serious identity crisis that accompanies mixed cultural affiliation.

Karla Poewe, a Canadian anthropologist of German extraction who published her memoir of fieldwork in West Africa under the pseudonym Manda Cesara (1982: 22), reported a dream in which she found herself in a position where she and a group of other people had to make a decision between fascism and freedom. For some reason many people found themselves standing in line to join the will of the government, while she chose to swim free of the crowd singing, 'I want freedom.' An official approached her and said, 'A very important person wants to see you,' and he took her to the front of a line of people into a place off to one side. There she had to wait again, and while waiting, saw a child who had also chosen freedom. The child was playing with a cuddly animal which disappeared in the bushes. She didn't want to lose the child, but it looked around furtively then slid through the shrubbery to freedom. As she continued waiting, a gorgeously dressed elderly woman came by and stood before the mirror, saying how absurd it was to emphasize dress. The dreamer then moved away from the crowd with the realization that freedom lay beyond the shrubs, not in this line of waiting people, and she awoke. Later, as she established her second cultural identity, her dreams, like those Barbara Anderson reported, changed to include mixed but clearly distinct American and African elements.

Remembered dream images can also serve as a mirror reflecting back to the cultural anthropologist a secure sense of self-integrity and identity. Not all people are equally suitable to serve as 'mirrors,' however. For some people it seems to be only in the eyes of their own country men, or even themselves, that they can find a mirror. Thus, Polish anthropologist Bronislaw Malinowski reported in his posthumously published field diary:

> Today . . . I had a strange dream; homo-sex., with my own double
> as a partner. Strangely auto-erotic feelings: the impression that I'd
> like to have a mouth just like mine to kiss, a neck that curves just
> like mine, a forehead just like mine (seen from the side).
> (Malinowski 1967: 12)

Typically, mirror or double images in dreams represent an attempt to restore, retrieve, or bolster a threatened sense of self through the mechanisms psychologists have labelled 'projection' and 'identification' (Devereux 1978: 224).

Malinowski's field diaries shocked many people because this self-proclaimed father of participant observation, the key methodology still used today in cultural anthropology, exposed his remarkable lack of participation in, and even respect for, the culture he described. He revealed his distaste for Trobrianders, with whom he lived for four years. The lack of Trobriand features in his reported dreams is particularly disturbing. In the diaries, which cover two separate one year periods, 1914–15 and 1917–18, he mentions and briefly reports twenty dreams (Ibid.: 12–13, 66, 70, 71, 73, 78, 80, 82, 116, 149, 159, 191, 202, 203, 204, 207, 208, 255, 290, 295). The settings of these dreams were usually in Poland and the people who appeared most frequently were his mother and boyhood friends, including a girl friend he expressed guilt about having abandoned. While two of the dreams included colonial officers, none were set within the Trobriand culture, nor did they include a single indigenous person. Apparently, Malinowski did not successfully establish a 'secondary identity' in the field, which would have allowed for dreams with mixed, but clearly distinct Polish and Trobriand elements.

In *Sex and Repression in Savage Society*, a book with the expressed purpose of critiquing both the Oedipus and dream interpretation theories of Sigmund Freud, Malinowski claims that unlike other non-Western peoples, the Trobrianders 'dream little, have little interest in their dreams, seldom relate them spontaneously, do not regard the ordinary dream as having any prophetic or other importance, and have no code of symbolic explanation whatsoever' (Malinowski 1927: 92). This surprising account sounds rather like the situation today in bourgeois middle-class Western society. However, reading on a bit farther in the text, we find a five-page discussion of the premonitory dreams of fishermen and kula traders, the use of dreams by ritual specialists to initiate novices and to advise their community, dreams in which women's dead kinsmen inform them of their pregnancy, and the sending of dreams by magical means to cause others to fall in love with one (Ibid.: 92–96).

It appears that Malinowski's greatly exaggerated claim of a lack of Trobriand interest in dreams originates form his anxiety to establish the Trobrianders as exempt from repression. If indeed this were the case, it would weaken the supposed universality of Freud's Oedipus complex. However, Malinowski began with the faulty premise that in Freudian theory 'the main cause of dreams is unsatisfied sexual appetite.' He then reasoned that the absence of psychological repression among Trobrianders accounts for the noticeable lack of erotic material in their dreams, which in turn explains their lack of concern with dreams in general. But this scarcity of eroticism in the manifest content of dreams may, of course, bear the opposite interpretation. If anything, freedom from repression should be indicated by the presence of sexual elements, since wishes that appear undistorted at the manifest level must not have been subject to a remarkable amount of censorship. Thus, the absence of sexual elements suggests disguise, which presupposes repression.

While it is true that the majority of cultural anthropologists have been unwilling to discuss dream material, except incidentally and in passing, there have always been individuals who are not anti-psychological in the clear manner in which Malinowski was. The renowned American anthropologist Robert Lowie, for example, kept a personal dream journal for nearly fifty years (from 1908–1957), and he was preparing an essay about his dream experiences when he died. Shortly thereafter, his wife published his essay in the prestigious international journal *Current Anthropology*. Lowie was, in his own words, a 'chronic and persistent dreamer' who also often heard voices or saw visions when he was lying with his eyes half-closed. He remarks that during his later years his dreams helped him greatly in understanding visionary experiences of the native Americans with whom he worked. According to him, the difference between himself and

> an Eskimo shaman who has heard a meaningless jumble of sounds or a Crow visionary who has seen a strange apparition is that I do not regard such experiences as mystic revelations, whereas they

do. But I can understand the underlying mental and emotional experiences a good deal better than most other ethnologists can, because I have identical episodes every night and almost every day of my life.

(Lowie 1966: 379)

French anthropologist Michel Leiris, during the 1931–33 Dakar-Djibouti expedition to the Dogon and Ethiopians, recorded not only the doings of various African subjects and the strained relationships between the European members of the research team, but his own dreams. Thus, his diary entry for October 10, 1931 reads as follows:

Hard to sleep, for the others as for me, since we're possessed by the work. All night, dreams of totemic complications and family structures, with no way to save myself from this labyrinth of streets, tabooed sites and cliffs. Horror at becoming so inhuman. . . . But how to shake it off, get back in contact? Would have to leave, forget everything.

(Clifford 1986: 31)

His September 1, 1932 diary entry opens:

Very bad night. First insomnia, then, very late, a little sleep. A dream of Z [his wife], a dream I get some mail, which makes me feel better. Then suddenly, the smell of the herbs I've had scattered around my room enters my nostrils. Half dreaming. I have the sensation of a kind of swirling (as if reddening and turning my head I were doing the *gourri* dance characteristic of trance) and I let out a scream. This time I'm really possessed.

(Leiris 1934: 358; English translation Clifford 1986: 44)

Here desire for his wife is transformed, by the odor of African herbs, into possession. And it just so happens, as his diary also reveals, that at the time he was erotically infatuated with the beautiful daughter of the charismatic leader of the Zar possession cult he was busy documenting.

Another early cultural anthropologist, Alice Marriott, after she had been in the field for some time with the Kiowas of western Oklahoma, began having dreams with dozens of tepees mixed together with other dream elements. After experiencing this dream numerous times the tepees slowly became clearer, then larger and larger, until they swarmed around her and danced with a drum beating time to their movements. Finally, an ancient and totally blind Kiowa holy man had a dream about Marriott in which his power spirit stood on one side of her and an important religious bundle stood on the other side. He interpreted his dream as an indication that he should talk with her about the Kiowa religion. However, when other Kiowa holy men caught wind of his intention they forbade him to teach her the religion. So, although she had exchanged what most members of the tribe considered 'power dreams' (what anthropologists have labelled 'culture pattern dreams') with a holy man, she was blocked from gaining further religious knowledge (Marriott 1952: 74–87).

More recently, Australian anthropologist Michael Jackson, who did extensive research in the early 1970s among the Kuranko of northeast Sierra Leone, reported some of his own dreams and carefully noted the differences between a native interpretation and his own. About a month after commencing his fieldwork, and the day before he made his first formal inquiries about dreams, Jackson reported a dream of his own. In the first episode he found himself in a bare room, reminiscent of one of the classrooms at the District Council Primary School in a town where he had first met his field assistant. A corrugated iron door opened and a book was passed into the room by an invisible hand or by some other invisible agency. The book hung suspended in midair for several seconds and he identified a single word in bold type on its cover: 'ETHNOGRAPHY.' He had the definite impression that the book contained only blank pages. In the second episode he found himself again in the same room and again the door opened.

> I felt a tremendous presence sweep into the room. I felt myself lifted up bodily and, as if held in the hands or by the power of a giant, I was taken out of the room. The hand and arms of the giant exerted such pressure against my breast that I could not breathe easily. I was borne along aloft, still being squeezed. At this point I awoke in fear from the dream.
>
> (Jackson 1978: 120)

According to Jackson, the dream manifested many of his anxieties at that time, most notably his concern that he would not be able to carry out the necessary research for his thesis, and his dependence on his field assistant who was not only instructing him in the language, but who was mediating all his relationships. He also admitted to feeling what he described as a mild form of paranoia, which consisted of feelings of vulnerability, loneliness, and ignorance.

The following day he made a scheduled trip to a nearby village where he met a Kuranko diviner who knew something of dream interpretation and recounted his dream to him. The diviner was puzzled and discussed the dream with other elders who were present. They asked Jackson whether the giant flew up into the sky with him and whether or not he had been placed back on the ground. When these questions were answered the diviner announced the meaning of the dream: It signified that, if Jackson were a Kuranko, he would be destined to become a chief. The diviner added, 'I do not know about you because you are a European, but for us the book means knowledge, it came to reveal knowledge.' So, despite this diviner's caveat that he might not be able to interpret a European's dream correctly, his elucidation of the meaning of the dream was consistent with orthodox Kuranko formulations in which a book signified knowledge; being in a strange place among strange people denoted good fortune in the near future; being in a high place indicated the imminent attainment of a prestigious position; and flying like a bird signified happiness and prosperity.

Where the diviner's interpretation differed from Jackson's own interpretation was both at the level of exegesis and in the diviner's conviction that the dream presaged future events rather than revealing present anxieties. Nevertheless, Jackson reports that these assurances helped him to allay his anxieties and that he felt that the diviner's treatment of the dream was not simply a reflection of a set of standardized interpretative procedures. Instead, it was consciously or unconsciously the outcome of sympathetic attention to Jackson's position as a stranger in his society.

In 1976 when my husband, Dennis Tedlock, and I had travelled to highland Guatemala to undertake a year of fieldwork with Quiché-Mayans, we also found ourselves, early in our stay, consulting a diviner about our own disturbing dreams. In the first month of field research, on the same night, we each dreamed about Hapiya, one of our Zuni Indian consultants who, when we last saw him, was in the hospital recuperating from a gall bladder operation. I dreamed that I read his obituary in the *Gallup Independent*, which reported that he had entered the hospital on October 6th and that he had been eighty-seven when he died there (both his age and the date of his hospital admission were wrong). Meanwhile Dennis was dreaming that he was going over the transcript of a written text with Hapiya, and that he said that two of the lines were saying exactly the same thing (a typically Mayan, rather than Zuni, form of semantic coupleting). Dennis, who awakened abruptly from his dream with the horrible feeling that he had been with a man who was already dead, awakened me in order to share his dream. I then narrated my own dream about Hapiya.

The next morning, we told our dream narratives to our consultant, Andrés Xiloj, who also turned out to be a trained dream interpreter. As soon as we finished narrating our dreams he immediately replied: 'Yesterday, or the day before, he died. At first it seemed that he was in agony, ready to die, but when you (Barbara) said you dreamed he was already deceased, I knew it to be so.' Xiloj then commenced a formal calendrical divination by asking us for the correct date of the hospital admission. It was January 22nd, which he then determined to have been *Kib' N'oj* (Two Thought) on the Mayan calendar. He spread out his divining paraphernalia and counted out groups of seeds, arriving at *Hob' Kame* (Five Death), and said: 'Yes, it happened that he was alleviated a little when he arrived at the hospital, but later his sickness became more grave.'

At this point we described the situation in the hospital, where Hapiya had survived an operation, but then, for some inexplicable reason, had simply been abandoned, left alone in a room with the window open. Since this action was interpreted by his family as the staff's decision to simply let him die, they forced entry into his room and massaged him, returning his breath to him, and sent for a Zuni medicine man. The healer performed the traditional sucking cure, removing deer blood and hair from Hapiya's throat so that he could once again talk.

Xiloj continued with an interpretation of our amplified account saying, 'What happened to this man was not a simple sickness, and was not sent by God. It is the act of a man; because of some business or other things he has done with his neighbor the man was put to rest.'

We told Xiloj that Hapiya spoke of having an enemy who wanted to kill him and he concluded. 'The one who envied him is already incarcerated, he doesn't walk the face of the earth, but is in purgatory where he is being punished for his deeds. This man died before this sickness but his deed remained for Hapiya to receive.'

These two dreams revealed our anxiety and guilt over leaving our previous fieldwork commitment to start up new fieldwork elsewhere. Also, as of that time we did not know whether Hapiya was dead or not (it turned out that he was), but Xiloj's dream interpretation helped us deal with what we feared was the death not only of a person we had come to deeply respect and love, but also of our own first fieldwork. We were unaware of just what we had communicated about ourselves when we shared our troubling dreams with Xiloj.

One thing was certain though, and that was that we were going far beyond the telling of our dreams as a token of friendship, a technique which George Foster utilized in his dream research in Mexico. In an essay entitled, 'Dream, character, and cognitive orientation in Tzintzuntzan' (Foster 1973), he explained that he obtained his data by volunteering his own dreams, as a gesture of amity and openness, which rewarded him with comparable personal disclosures from his informants. He suggests this procedure to other investigators as a useful eliciting tool which can produce excellent field data. While it is true that the dream narratives he collected were far richer than the brief statements of the manifest content of typical dreams collected by earlier anthropologists such as Jackson Lincoln (1935), Foster, in keeping with his procedure of using his own dreams only as a field tool, neglected to record any of them in his publications. It is as though his own dream life were unimportant, and further, that the dreams he chose to relate to his subjects in no way influenced which dreams they in turn selected to share with him.

In our own situation, since we were not sharing dreams as part of a preconceived field strategy, there was quite a different turn of events. Shortly after telling our Zuni dreams to Xiloj, we were seen visiting outdoor non-Christian shines on several occasions, thus revealing our intense curiosity about Mayan spirituality. Later, when I fell ill with what I self-diagnosed as pneumonia, Xiloj divined the ultimate cause of my illness to lie in our offenses before the earth deities, and informed us that we would both die. It seems that what we thought were innocent visits to the shrines had in fact annoyed not only the human *ajq'ij* (daykeepers) who were praying there, but also the deities. We had thoughtlessly entered the presence of the sacred shrines without even realizing that we must be ritually pure before doing so.

Later, when we asked Xiloj for more details about the people who were praying at these shrines, specifically how they were trained and initiated, he replied that the best way to find out was to undertake an apprenticeship. When we asked him whether he would in fact be willing to train us, he chuckled and said, 'Why, of course.' During this four and a half months of formal training, timed according to the Mayan calendar, we were expected to narrate all of our dreams in order for him to interpret them. Thus, dream sharing, instead of being our methodology for recording a ethnographic subject's dreams, became Xiloj's way of instructing and reinforcing us in our training, as well as a way of checking on our spiritual, or psychic, progress. So, the dreams that we ended up gathering were our own. Only occasionally and mostly for pedagogical reasons did we hear any of Xiloj's dreams. It was not until after our initiation that we were brought dreams by various Mayan individuals for interpretation.

Twenty days into our apprenticeship I dreamed, sometime in the night between the *Wajxakeb' Kej* (eight Deer) and *B'elejeb' Q'anil* (Nine Yellowripe) on the Mayan calendar, that I was diving in a spot off Catalina Island that looked like my favorite scuba location, where I had gathered abalones nearly fourteen years earlier. I was passing through some dark plants and saw a shaft of light coming down through the water ahead, showing me a cave with a floor covered with sea shells. Suddenly an enormous fish emerged from the cave. I was scared because I thought it was a shark, but then I realized that it was a dolphin, and I surfaced.

Xiloj counted the Mayan calendar through then said, 'It seems this is the family, ancestors, these are the ones who are giving the sign that the work you two are accomplishing here, and the permissions, are going to come out all right, are going to come out into the light. It is a woman who has died who came to give this notice, this sign. This dream that the fish came out over the water means the work, it's going to come out well. The light fell into the water.' (This is a literal translation from a tape-recording.)

I replied, 'Yes, the dolphin went up also.'

'And the work is going to mate with you, to come out into the light. But I don't know if it was your mother or your grandmother who came to give the sign.'

'What about the cave?'

'The cave is the tomb of the mother or grandmother who has died. Is your mother still living?'

'Yes, but my grandmothers are both dead.'

'Then it's your grandmother who came.'

'And the shells in the cave?'

'The shells are not shell, but – all kinds were found there?'

'Yes.'

'Then these are the red seeds, the crystal [the key contents of the sacred divining paraphernalia we would be receiving at our initiation].'

'And the dark plants?'

'The plants are like the shade. When one is in the shade the ground is somewhat dark. When one goes out into the sun, then everything is clear.'

At this point Dennis told his dream of this same night, 'I saw a blue-jay and put my hand out to invite it to come. The bird came and rubbed its breast against my fingers [here he gestured demonstrating that his hand was closed with his fingers in a horizontal position]. The next moment I found the bird on a blanket in front of me on its back, as if sick, and I gave it a piece of bread. When I next looked, it was gone.'

'The bird means that, it seems that you are going to have an offspring. The birds, when dreamed of, are offspring one is going to have. But the offspring is as if sick; on being born, it is sick. Here, when we dream that we take hold of a bird, any kind of bird, and we put it in the pocket, or we put it inside the shirt, now we know we are going to have an offspring.'

Dennis then related his second dream of the previous evening. 'I was being followed by a large deer with enormous antlers when I encountered, by the right side of the road, another deer, also with large antlers, seated on the ground. When I passed this deer, it got up, but, though it had first seemed like one deer, it was now two. The left deer had the left set of antlers and the right deer had the right. The two of them, side-by-side [their sides touching], followed me.'

'B'elejeb' Q'anil (Nine Yellow), what is this?' After a long silence, he looked at Dennis and said,

'What this dream means, what these deer are, here is the Holy World. Yes, it is the World. Ch'uti Sab'al (Little Declaration Place), and Paja' (At the Water), and Nima Sab'al (Big Declaration Place). The three. And these three places are already following the two of you. If you leave here, they will go with you, they won't let you go without them, they'll go on appearing to you. Two of the deer are already united, since I've already been going to Paja' (the One Place shrine) and I started going to Ch'uti Sab'al (the Eight Place shrine) yesterday. The third deer is farther away because I still haven't gone to Nima Sab'al (the Nine Place shrine). That will come on B'elejeb' Kej (Nine Deer).'

After this dream, while Dennis was in a hypnagogic half-waking state, called saq waram, or 'white sleep' in Quiché, two small yellow sparks appeared before him in succession.

Xiloj began muttering to himself then said aloud, 'These sparks are the light of the World. The World already knows you two are going to accept what you're hearing. The sparks, the light is now being given to you. Right now it's tinged with yellow, but as we go along it will clarify.'

These dreams pleased Xiloj, since they occurred on the very evening when he had first visited the shrines at Ch'uti Sabal in order to present us to the Mundo as apprentices. At the time he had looked for bad omens, in both the natural world and in his own dreams, indicating that our training would not work out well. Not only did he fail to find negative omens but we had, unknowingly, produced positive ones, indicating that the ancestors (the dolphin) and the shrines (the deer) were willing to accept us. As time went by we began to have dreams with more and more Mayan cultural elements, including religious images and mountain spirits, as well as Mayan individuals, including Xiloj. Xiloj, in turn, also had dreams which included both us and cultural items from our society which we had brought into the field with us. Some of these dreams revealed strong currents of anxiety as well as transference and countertransference between ourselves and Xiloj. Finally, on *Wajakeb' B'atz'* (Eight Monkey), or August 18, 1976, we were initiated together with dozens of other novices at the shrines Xiloj had been visiting on our behalf until then. After our initiation we were consulted as dream interpreters by Mayan people and we have continued to pay attention to our dreams, to record and interpret them in the way we were taught, in accordance with the Quiché Mayan calendar (see D. Tedlock 1990).

Conclusions

Anthropologists no longer set out to elicit dream reports as though they were ethnographic objects which might be arranged, manipulated, and quantified like forms of material culture. Rather than making typological or statistical comparisons between the dreams found in so-called 'Western' versus 'non-Western' societies, cultural anthropologists have turned their attention to studying dream theories and interpretation systems as complex psychodynamic communicative events. By studying dream sharing and the transmission of dream theories in their full social contexts, anthropologists have realized that both the researcher and the subject of research create a social reality which links them in important ways.

Today, fieldworkers are participating within native contexts and learning not only the local cultural uses of dream experiences, but also paying attention to their own dreams. This latter practice has helped them to become aware of their unconscious responses to the people and culture they are attempting to understand and describe. In time, perhaps, cultural anthropologists, like psychoanalysts, will develop the necessary skill and training to listen to emotional dream communication of others as well as to their own feelings (Kracke 1978). For, as Rosalind Cartwright and other dream lab researchers have suggested, dreams play an important part in mastering new affective experiences and assimilating them into one's self-schemata (Cartwright 1977: 131–133; Palombo 1978). This particular form of self-mastery would seem to be an important undertaking, not only for psychoanalysts but for anthropologists who use participant observation as their key research methodology.

Notes

1   An exception to this general situation in cultural anthropology today is the work of Thomas Gregor (1981).
2   'Thick description,' is an ethnographic concept originated by Clifford Geertz (1973) that refers to the slow gathering of hundreds of contextual details in order to make sense of local categories of reality.
3   My use of the phrase 'social drama' here is different from Victor Turner's formal concept of social dramas as 'units of aharmonic or disharmonic process, arising in conflict situations' (Turner 1974: 37). Dream sharing a social drama may be an harmonic, aharmonic, or disharmonic process and it rarely arises in conflicted situations.

References

Anderson, Barbara G. 1971 'Adaptive aspects of culture shock', *American Anthropologist* 73: 1121–5.
Basso, Ellen B. 1987 'The implications of a progressive theory of dreaming', in *Dreaming*. Edited by Barbara Tedlock, pp. 86–104. Cambridge: Cambridge University Press.
Bird, Brian 1972 'Notes on the transference: universal phenomenon and hardest part of analysis', *Journal of the American Psychoanalytic Association* 20: 267–301.
Bourdieu, Pierre 1978 *Outline of a Theory of Practice*. trans. Richard Nice, Cambridge: Cambridge University Press.
Bruce, Robert D. 1975 *Lacandon Dream Symbolism: Dream Symbolism and Interpretation*, vol. 1. Mexico: Ediciones Euroamericanas.
Bruce, Robert D. 1979 *Lacandon Dream Symbolism: Dictionary, Index and Classifications of Dream Symbols*, vol. 2. Mexico: Ediciones Euroamericanas.
Cartwright, Rosalind D. 1977 *Night Life: Explorations in Dreaming*. Englewood Cliffs, NJ: Prentice-Hall.
Cesara, Manda (Psendonym of Karla Poewe) 1982 *Reflections of a Woman Anthropologist: No Hiding Place*. New York: Academic.
Charsley, S. R. 1973 'Dreams in an independent African church', *Africa* 43(3): 244–57.
Clifford, James 1986 'New translations of Michel Leiris', *Sulfur* 15: 4–125.

Collins, Kathleen May. 1977 Secret desires in social contexts: an anthropological approach to dreams. M.A. thesis in anthropology, University of Illinois at Chicago.

Crapanzano, Vincent 1981 'Text, transference, and indexicality', *Ethos* 9: 122–48.

Degarrod, Lydia Nakashima 1989 Dream interpretation among the Mapuche Indians of Chile. Ph.D. dissertation in anthropology, University of California at Los Angeles.

Degarrod, Lydia Nakashima 1990 'Coping with stress: dream interpretation In the Mapuche family', *Psychiatric Journal of the University of Ottawa* 15(2): 111–16.

Dentan, Robert Knox 1983 *A Dream of Senoi*. Special Studies Series, Council on International Studies, State University of New York. Amherst: State University of New York at Buffalo.

Dentan, Robert Knox 1986 'Ethnographic considerations in the cross-cultural study of dreaming', in *Sleep and Dreams*. Edited by Jayne Gackenbach, pp. 317–58. New York: Garland.

Dentan, Robert Knox 1988a 'Butterflies and bug hunters: reality and dreams, dreams and reality', *Psychiatric Journal of the Univeristy of Ottawa* 13(2): 51–9.

Dentan, Robert Knox 1988b 'Lucidity, sex, and horror in Senoi dreamwork', in *Conscious Mind, Sleeping Brain*. Edited by Jane Gackenbach and Stephen LaBerge, pp. 37–63. New York: Plenum Press.

Desjarlais, Robert 1991 Samsara's sadness: shamanism and the 'Calling of Lost Souls.' Ph.D. dissertation in anthropology. University of California at Los Angeles.

Devereux, George 1956 'Mohave dreams of omen and power', *Tomorrow* 4(3): 17–24.

Devereux, George 1978 *Ethnopsychoanalysis: Psychoanalysis and Anthropology as Complementary Frames of Reference* Berkeley, CA: University of California Press.

Dombeck, Mary-Therese Behar 1989 'Dreams and professional personhood: the contexts of dream telling and dream interpretation among American psychotherapists', Ph.D. dissertation in anthropology, University of Rochester.

Fabian, Johannes 1983 *Time and the Other: How Anthropology Makes it Object*. New York: Columbia University Press.

Foster, George M. 1973 'Dreams, character, and cognitive orientation in Tzintzuntzan', *Ethos* 1: 106–21.

Freud, Sigmund 1958 'Remembering, repeating and working through', *Standard Edition* 12 [1914]: 145–56. London: Hogarth.

Geertz, Clifford 1973 'Thick description: toward an interpretive theory of culture', in *The Interpretation of Cultures*, pp. 3–30. New York: Basic Books.

Gregor, Thomas 1981 'A content analysis of Mehinaku dreams', *Ethos* 9: 353–90.

Hall, Calvin, S. 1951 'What people dream about', *Scientific American* 184(5): 60–3.

Hall, Calvin S. 1953 *The Meaning of Dreams*. New York: Harper & Row.

Herdt, Gilbert H. 1977 'The shaman's "calling" among the Sambia of New Guinea', *Jounral de la Société des Océanisies* 33: 153–67.

Herdt, Gilbert H. 1987 'Selfhood and discourse in Sambia dream sharing', in *Dreaming*. Edited by Barbara Tedlock, pp. 55–85. Cambridge: Cambridge University Press.

Hillman, Deborah J. 1988 'Dream work and field work: linking cultural anthropology and the current dream work movement', in *The Variety of Dream Experience*. Edited by Montague Ullman and Claire Limmer, pp. 117–41. New York: Continuum.

Hodes, Matthew 1989 'Dreams reconsidered', *Anthropology Today* 5(6): 6–8.

Hollan, Douglas 1989 'The personal use of dream beliefs in the Toraja highlands', *Ethos* 17(2): 166–86.

Hunt, Harry T. 1989 *The Multiplicity of Dreams: Memory, Imagination, and Consciousness*. New Haven: Yale University Press.

Jackson, Michael 1978 'An approach to Kuranko divination', *Human Relations* 31: 117–38.

Kilborne, Benjamin 1978 *Interpretations de rêve au Maroc*. Claix: La Pensée Sauvage, Bibliothèque d'Ethnopsychiatrie.

Kracke, Waud 1978 'A psychoanalyst in the field: Erikson's contributions to anthropology', in *Childhood and Selfhood: Essays on Tradition, Religion, and Modernity in the Psychology of Erik H. Erikson*, pp. 147–18. Lewisburg, PA: Bucknell University Press.

Kracke, Waud 1979 'Dreaming in Kagwahiv: dream beliefs and their psychic uses in an Amazonian culture', *Psychoanalytic Study of Society* 8: 119–71.

Kracke, Waud 1987a 'Encounter with other cultures: psychological and epistemological aspects', *Ethos* 15(1): 58–81.

Kracke, Waud 1987b '"Everyone who dreams has a bit of shaman": cultural and personal meanings of dreams – evidence from the Amazon', *Psychiatric Journal of the University of Ottawa* 12(2): 65–72.

Laughlin, Robert M. 1976 *Of Wonders Wild and New: Dreams from Zinacantan*. Smithsonian Contributions to Anthropology, No. 22. Washington, DC: Smithsonian Institution Press.

Leiris, Michel 1934 *L'Afrique fantôme*. Paris: Plon (Terre Humaine).

LeVine, Sarah 1981 'Dreams of the informant about the researcher: some difficulties inherent in the research relationship', *Ethos* 9: 276–93.

Lincoln, Jackson S. 1935 *The Dream in Primitive Cultures*. Baltimore: Williams & Wilkins.

Loewald, Hans 1986 'Transference-countertransference', *Journal of the American Psychoanalytic Association* 34(2): 275–88.

Lowie, Robert 1966 'Dreams, idle dreams', *Current Anthropology* 7(3): 378–82.

Mahrer, Alvin R. 1989 *Dream Work in Psychotherapy and Self-change*. New York: W. W. Norton.

Malinowski, Bronislaw 1927 *Sex and Repression in Primitive Society*: New York: E. P. Dutton.

Malinowski, Bronislaw 1967 *A Diary in the Strict Sense of the Term*. Stanford, CA: Stanford University Press.

Marriott, Alice 1952 *Greener Fields*. Garden City, NY: Dolphin Books.

McDowell, John Holmes 1989 *Sayings of the Ancestors: The Spiritual Life of the Sibundoy Indians*. Lexington: University Press of Kentucky.

Meggitt, Mervyn J. 1962 'Dream interpretation among the Mae Enga of New Guinea', *Southwestern Journal of Anthropology* 18: 216–20.

Merrill, William 1987 'The Rarámuri stereotype of dreams', in *Dreaming*. Edited by Barbara Tedlock, pp. 194–219. Cambridge: Cambridge University Press.

Nadar, Laura 1970 'Research in Mexico', in *Women in the Field: Anthropological Experiences*. Edited by Peggy Golde, pp. 97–116. Chicago: Aldine.

Ortner, Sherry B. 1984 'Theory in anthropology since the sixties', *Comparative Studies in Society and History* 26(1): 126–66.

Palombo, Stanley R. 1978 *Dreaming and Memory: A New Information Processing Model*. New York: Basic Books.

Persinger, M.A. 1988 'Psi phenomena and temporal lobe activity', in *Research in Parapsychology*. Edited by L. A. Henkel and R. E. Berger, pp. 121–56. Metuchen, NJ: Scarecrow.

Persinger, M. A. and Krippner, Stanley 1989 'Dream ESP experiments and geomagnetic activity', *Journal of the American Society for Psychical Research* 83: 101–16.

Roseman, Marina 1986 Sound in ceremony: power and performance in Temiar curing rituals. Ph.D. dissertation in anthropology, Cornell University.

Roseman, Marina 1991 *Healing Sounds: Music and Medicine in Temiar Ceremonial Life*. Berkeley, CA: University of California Press.

Scheff, Thomas J. 1986 'Towards resolving the controversy over "thick description"', *Current Anthropology* 27: 408–10.

Schneider, David M. and Sharp, Lauriston 1969 *The Dream Life of a Primitive People: The Dreams of the Yir Yoront of Australia*. Anthropological Studies, No. 1. Washington, DC: American Anthropological Association.

Silverstein, Michael 1976 'Shiffers, linguistic categories, and cultural description', in *Meaning and Anthropology*. Edited by Keith Basso and Henry Selby, pp. 11–55. Albuquerque: University of New Mexico Press.

Staff, Vera S. 1975 *Remembered on Waking: Concerning Psychic and Spiritual Dreams and Theories of Dreaming*. Crowborough, Sussex: Churche's Fellowship for Psychical and Spiritual Studies.

Stephen, Michele 1989 'Dreaming and the hidden self: Mekeo definitions of consciousness', in *The Religious Imagination in New Guinea*. Edited by Gilbert Herdt and Michele Stephen, pp. 160–86. New Brunswick: Rutgers University Press.

Stevens, William Oliver 1949 *The Mystery of Dreams*. New York: Dodd, Mead.

Tedlock, Barbara 1981 'Quiché Maya dream interpretation', *Ethos* 9: 313–30.

Tedlock, Barbara 1987a *Dreaming: Anthropological and Psychological Interpretations*. Cambridge: Cambridge University Press.

Tedlock, Barbara 1987b 'Zuni and Quiché dream sharing and interpreting', in *Dreaming*. Edited by Barbara Tedlock, pp. 105–31. Cambridge: Cambridge University Press.

Tedlock, Dennis 1979 'The analogical tradition and the emergence of a dialogical anthropology', *Journal of Anthropological Research* 35: 387–400.

Tedlock, Dennis 1990 *Days from a Dream Almanac*. Urbana, IL: University of Illinois Press.

Tolaas, Jon 1986 'Vigilance theory and psi. Part I: Ethnological and phylogenetic aspects', *Journal of the American Society for Psychical Research* 80: 357–73.

Tolaas, Jon 1990 'The puzzle of psychic dreams', in *Dreamtime & Dreamwork*. Edited by Stanley Krippner, pp. 261–70. Los Angeles: Jeremy P. Tarcher.

Turner, Victor 1974 'Social dramas and ritual metaphors', in *Dramas, Fields, and Metaphors*, pp. 23–59. Ithaca, NY: Cornell University Press.

Ullman, Montague, Krippner, Stanley and Vaughan, Alan 1973 *Dream Telepathy*. New York: Macmillan.

Wallace, Anthony C. 1959 'Cultural determinants of response to hallucinatory experience', *AMA Archives of General Psychiatry* 1: 74–85.

Chapter 7

Alan T. Campbell

SUBMITTING

IT'S TIME TO GET DOWN to the heart of the matter. It concerns the enigma of *pajé*, as they call it in Brazil, taking the word straight from the Indian languages. I'm convinced that a hundred years on in the Portuguese of that time there will be an easy turn of phrase to say that in the old days Wayapí people had lots of *pajés*, lots of 'shamans', lots of 'medicine-men'. Well, it wasn't quite like that.

Paye, pajé, and shaman

The Wayapí word would normally appear in the form *i-paye*, and cognate forms are found in numerous indigenous languages. Like so much else, the word lost its integrity by being made to work in another language. Portuguese and Spanish took over that sort of vocabulary just as they took over the forests. And just as they destroyed the woods, so they bulldozed their way through the grammars of the languages they obliterated. The word-root *paye* appears in Portuguese as *pajé* and is taken to be the equivalent of shaman. You'll find people calling themselves shamans in the loopy fringes of my society here and now. But *pajé* wasn't simply a kind of person like that. It wasn't a NOUN. You can't just say: 'Apeyawar was a shaman.' It wasn't just a role or an office. *Paye* was a whole way of being in the world, an outlook on the world and a relationship with the world, that everyone was involved in.

Our philosophical persons

The processes of shamanism were central to Wayapí life. If there ever was such a thing as a key word to their world it would be *paye*. Because of that, I often feel it should be kept secret. They'd often become reticent and guarded if the subject came up with outsiders around. And no wonder. It's so clear that our culture doesn't deserve to have mysteries of this kind revealed. If anything about *paye* or related matters came up amongst the Brazilians on the post, the FUNAI men would assertively describe themselves as Christians. That left Wayapí people silently labelled as heathens.

Academic discussion can be equally benighted. On a subject like this even the best of those who consider themselves wise can end up behaving like moral hooligans. Moses Finley, for example, who wrote so many inspiring pieces of work on the ancient worlds of Greece and Rome, should have known better than to say the following. It comes from a lecture he gave at a women's college in Cambridge in 1972; a memorial lecture for the classics scholar Jane Harrison.

He recalls that nearly a century ago Jane Harrison had written that savages (as she called them) wearied and disgusted her, although she had to spend long hours reading of their 'tedious doings'. Moses Finley goes on to devote the lecture to looking at the relationship between anthropology and history. He scouts around various anthropological writers and picks up a remark by Godfrey Lienhardt (whose best-known book is on the Dinka of the Sudan). In one of his articles Lienhardt mentions the example of people who speak of pelicans as their half-brothers,[1] and points out that the bald translation is inadequate since it leaves an atmosphere of fairy tales and nonsense. Hence, to make the image understood Lienhardt suggests that 'it would be necessary to give a full account of views about the relations of the human and non-human quite different from those we entertain, but not, therefore, necessarily less reasonable'.

This is not good enough for M.I. Finley. He mocks this use of the word 'reasonable':

> There is a sense of the word 'reasonable' that can comprehend pelicans as half-brothers to men, but there is another, far more important sense, understood by everyone of us, which renders that form of words simply unreasonable.[2]

Why 'unreasonable'? Because, according to Finley, 'everyone of us', like Macaulay's schoolboy, knows that *development*, *change*, and *progress* have all brought us civilized folk away above the tedious doings of savages. And the two shining examples of development and progress are *political institutions* and *literacy*.

Behind the genial notion of progress is a glimpse of hidden, unspoken feelings – feelings that are the grounds for basic dispositions. The robust declaration of Jane Harrison is not shocking. Flagrant prejudice like that becomes pathetic when it is grounded on flagrant ignorance. But M.I. Finley's exposition is more stealthy – so reasonable, so assured, so poised, and so deadly.

Superstition, science and god

I find his argument an unsettling *trahison des clercs* for two reasons. First it's unexpected, given the general nature of Finley's writings. Second, if someone like M.I. Finely can harbour such views, where can one look to with hope? Here is the argument in another form, spelt out in more detail, this time by Perry Anderson, reviewing Carlo Ginzburg's *Storia Notturna*, a book on witchcraft. Again it's disturbing, again for the same two reasons.

Anderson thinks Ginzburg has gone too far in emphasizing the continuity of popular beliefs, giving them a coherence and meaning that they don't deserve. They are really just 'folk shards' or 'the mental rubbish of peasant credulity' (in Trevor-Roper's phrase). Perry Anderson quotes Ginzburg's own words from an earlier work – commenting on a contemporary Italian cult near Salerno, in which a local woman periodically assumed the personality of a dead nephew. The quote is supposed to show that Ginzburg wasn't so gullible in his younger days:

> In wretched and disintegrated conditions, religion helps men and women to bear a little better a life in itself intolerable. It may not be much, but we have no right to despise it. But precisely because they protect believers from reality rather than prompting or helping them to become aware of and change it, such popular cults are in the end a mystification: to overvalue them in populist fashion is absurd and dangerous.[3]

Perry Anderson approves of that earlier view: 'It would be good to hear that voice again' says he, and goes on:

> One much-needed word has disappeared from the vocabulary of *Storia Notturna*: superstition. It is salutary to recall that a Hungarian scholar, describing the poor, sparse societies in which it once dominated, could speak of 'the misery of shamanism'. That judgement is too strong for what was once a coherent set of beliefs, giving moral shape to a world. But superstitions are the scrambled relics of belief, no longer comprehended.[4]

Who gets to draw the line between what is a 'coherent set of beliefs giving moral shape to a world' and 'scrambled relics'? Radio, television, and public debate all around me are flooded with God-talk. The three monotheisms that encircle the world (Judaism, Christianity, and Islam) appear in ever more strident and intolerant forms. Presidents and Prime Ministers, judges and police chiefs, journalists and media pundits are all up to their ears in God-talk, in rites and incantations – heaps of scrambled relics – and yet their kind of behaviour and their kind of talk are considered respectable. It's only the vulnerable and the oppressed that get tagged 'superstitious' and 'unreasonable'.

Notice the vocabulary used to describe the predicament: credulous savages and peasants are mired in superstition since these beliefs and rites are a form of *mystification* that stands between them and *reality*. Development and Progress allow us to stand with our feet firmly on a rock-bed of Reality and Truth.

There are a number of words in our ordinary vocabulary that get their power from their relation to reality and truth. 'Dreaming', 'magic', 'illusion', 'appearance' are examples. All these assume that there is an identifiable experience of what is real of which dreaming, magic, illusion, and appearance are modifications. Hence alongside all these modifications there is a corresponding experience of disappointment: when the modifications are put right again; when everything is straightened out and put back to normal.[5] What appeared to be the case is revealed in its true colours; the illusion is seen through; the magical loses its magic; we awaken from dreams, or perhaps they 'come true'. These are the gifts of development and progress.

The basis of our development and progress is *science*. Scientific thinking and scientific knowledge is, most exactly, what 'thinking' and 'knowledge' are. Indeed it's difficult for us to appreciate notions of 'non-scientific thinking' or 'non-scientific knowledge'. Terms like these seem to be self-contradictory. If we *do* manage to be tolerant of these phrases, we demote them to a second-order status. Non-scientific thinking is flabby. Non-scientific knowledge is suspect. We're still living under the shadow (or the bright lights it would be said) of the enormous plausibility and power of what's referred to as scientific thought.

Of course all sorts of grandees and world leaders, politicians and scholars can claim to be thoroughly reasonable, thoroughly civilized, thoroughly scientific, thoroughly in touch with reality, and still have ample space for God-talk. Our God-talk is kept in a special sacred compartment where none of the ordinary rules of credulity and incredulity, of reasonableness and unreasonableness, apply. Hence all of us, we civilized folk, share together the benefits of development and progress, and the God-talk comes as an extra. Indeed God-talk devotees would go as far as to say that their religiosity makes them even more civilized and dignified than their sceptical brethren. Civilized sceptics might disagree, but even if they thought the God-talk was cretinous, they would rarely get round to describing their religious coevals as savages and peasants. Civilized God-talkers and civilized sceptics unite in thinking of themselves as the beneficiaries of development and progress, and both congratulate themselves on being far removed from the mental rubbish of peasant credulity. That's what science has done for us all. Old Lafew in *All's Well that Ends Well* saw the predicament:

> They say miracles are past; and we have our philosophical persons, to make modern and familiar, things supernatural and causeless. Hence is it that we make trifles of terrors, ensconcing ourselves into seeming knowledge, when we should submit ourselves to an unknown fear.[6]

Art and ethnography

But there are different voices. There are those prepared to explore unknown fears. It's not the God-talkers that show how to go about dissolving our boundaries and getting ourselves within reach of others. It's Art that shows that way. As soon as we start discussing aesthetic experience the direction is set. Some scientific strands of thinking might feel drawn to place aesthetic experience in the same relationship with 'reality' as magic and dreams, as illusion and appearance. But since the nineteenth century aesthetic experience has been rescued from such a second-order status and been given back its integrity. It's difficult to argue nowadays (except in some hide-bound recesses of the social sciences) that art and poetry, metaphor and symbol, are modifications and refractions of what's 'real' or what's 'literal', and that what we should be doing is making the effort to get through them, restoring the literalness and getting back to reality.

Appreciating the power of metaphor and the integrity of art parallels the ethnographic appreciation of unfamiliar cultures. What's required is a similar disposition to be open to strangeness. 'Submit' was Lafew's word – to learn to submit to the beliefs and practices, to those 'things supernatural and causeless'; not to reduce them to familiar trifles. The most important lesson anthropology has to teach is that there's simply no point in making statements about how reasonable or unreasonable 'savage' thought might be, about what Dinka may or may not say about pelicans, or about what peasants near Salerno do or do not believe unless you're prepared to take the plunge and participate in their lives: *convivência*, as they put it in the Romance languages. That means going there. That means making the decision that it's worthwhile to spend years of your life living with them; as Ezekiel, when he came to them that dwelt by the river of Chebar, *he sat where they sat*. It means when you're there, dressing as they do, eating what they eat, sharing their daily activities, and above all learning their language. It's no accident that our philosophical persons who pontificate about superstition and who pride themselves on their development and progress always do so from the outside; always from the armchair, or, at their most daring, from the verandah.

Parsing the world

Commonsensically you'd think that the principal problem for us in trying to understand shamanism is the gulf between believing and not believing. How can we possibly understand what we don't believe? Well, that *is* the ultimate problem but it's not the initial one. The problem we start with is that we are not at all clear what we are looking at. We see only through a glass darkly, and not face to face. The reflections are dim because the languages don't fit together easily. Hence, when exploring this kind of enigma, the first paths you have to follow are linguistic ones.

When I suggest that we think of *paye* primarily as an adjective, as a quality, and not as a noun, that sounds like a minor grammatical adjustment. But it's not an easy move to make. It's not a surface adjustment. It sets about interfering with deep categorical habits. It's one thing to interfere with a person's beliefs. But it's more unsettling to disturb the very foundations and props and scaffoldings that got the beliefs up and running in the first place. The problem of shamanism will eventually come round to the point that they believe in this and that, and we don't. But long before we get to that question we've got to be brave enough and skilful enough to throw off all the grammatical certainties that our habits of language afford us.

Imagine: you're sitting by their camp-fire, on your first day. Even better, make it a day soon after 22 April 1500, when Pero Alvares Cabral made his first landfall on the Brazilian littoral. You know not a word of their language. You have been communicating by gestures and smiles. Your notebook is empty. Your pen is poised. A bird flies over and settles on the branch of a tree nearby. It's black with a white front and an immense coloured beak. You've just seen your first toucan. One of your new friends points to it and says 'tukan'. (We took the name from the Tupian languages.) So the first entry in your new notebook is their word for that bird. *Tukan* will henceforth mean 'toucan'.

Look at the enormous assumptions you've made. Suppose you were forced, later, by example after example, to face the fact that what your friend had said wasn't short for a statement like: 'That is a toucan', but short for something like: 'Oh look, it's toucanning again', or 'My goodness, there's flying – toucanly this time', how are you going to deal with that? It's not a problem about belief. It's not a disagreement about what's there. It's radical difference in the way another language negotiates with the world.

Our philosophical person who dealt best with this example went by the resounding name of Willard van Orman Quine. Doing a severe kind of philosophy he nevertheless looked cross-culturally for examples, and I find his anthropological insights refreshing and sympathetic. (How could he see so far from his armchair?) In this case he concluded that, be it a toucan or a rabbit that appears, be it *tukan* or *gavagai* that our companion says, you and I have no choice but to write down our noun-ish translation.[7] We simply have to assume that all human beings are going to see toucans and rabbits in the same way we do and that they are going to name them; different words certainly, but according to the same linguistic form. That kind of naming is our entering wedge into the other language.[8] It gets us in. That's why Waiwai began his language lessons for me by naming leaves and tree-trunks; lists and lists of names. But the point of these playful examples of toucans and rabbits, simple though they may be, is to show how linguistic structures can bend and sway and make you conceptually giddy, as if they are made of ropes rather than girders. Once you see that even this kind of naming is based on massive assumptions of perceptual and linguistic communion, you are warned not to take these assumptions too far. If the radical translation of 'toucan' involves so much, how are you to deal with the radical translation of 'Beauty is truth, truth beauty'?

Our language world is heavy with nouns – substantives, abstract singulars, concrete plurals, names. It becomes particularly obvious when we define ourselves. When people ask 'What do you do?', inviting a verb, we answer with a noun. 'I am an architect; I am a miner; I am a poet and tragedian.' We're uneasy with the fluidity of verbs. We're more comfortable with the obduracy of nouns. We're more concerned about what we are than what we do.

Because we cast *ourselves* in nouns, constantly, endlessly, we go on to impose this idol of the forum on everyone else we meet.[9] We want to find reflections of our status differentiations and role differentiations wherever we go. 'Chief' and 'Shaman', potentate and witch-doctor, are two of our main inventions which we have foisted on to primitive life. 'Chief' we get wrong because, through imposing the word on them, we also impose the role we are familiar with. We dump our notions of executive and coercive power on to the person recognized as 'chief', and are then baffled when we find that the chief has no power. 'Shaman' we get wrong because we can't see beyond the specialized human role to the quality from which the role is moulded; a quality that inheres amongst many aspects of the world; that emerges from all sorts of places; and that envelops us in all sorts of ways.

What's in the name?

It's easy to spot the role, and most outsiders (government officials, mission-aries, and scholars) just stop there. If you look at it cross-culturally, as it emerges from the literature, it's a wonderful collection of credentials.[10] SHAMAN: curer and curser, doctor and demon, mediator between the spirit world and the human world, ritual specialist, conjurer and seer, prophet and priest, thaumaturge and psychopomp (that is to say, miracle-worker and soul-guide). Of all these, though, the principal role that a *paye*-person is expected to carry out is that of curing.

You can see a remarkable consistency in many of the beliefs that surround the phenomenon right across the Americas and back beyond the Bering Straits into Asia, where the very word *shaman* comes from. The shaman will have spirit helpers, small animals perhaps, like caterpillars or maggots, invisible to the rest of us. He might do his curing work by approaching the sick person and blowing tobacco smoke on the patient's body while chanting and rubbing hands up and down the body, or he might do a general cure for the village by constructing a shelter somewhere nearby and going into a trance there. In Siberia and Inner Asia a drum was characteristically used during a shamanic seance. In South America rattles are used. These are the original maracas — gourds with seeds or pebbles inside attached to sticks. At the Nipukú it was said that the Other Wayapí in French Guiana still used rattles and that 'We had them too, long ago'.

In many parts of the Americas, and particularly in the Western Amazon, various hallucinogenic drugs, often extracted from lianas, are used to induce a visionary state. Wayapí people had no knowledge of these. They used tobacco. I'd guess that the chemistry has to do with ingesting abnormal amounts of tobacco while breathing abnormally. 'Hyperventilating' would be the technical term. As with hallucinogenics, the effect is to alter normal consciousness. The state that is induced is not only clairvoyant. It's transcendental too. Time and again the detail of travelling upwards appears. 'Do you see that tree there?' said Yamaira as we paddled back up the Nipukú river after a fishing trip — a monstrous tree it was too. 'That's where Yiseiwarai went when he was last here. He built a shelter near there to shamanize. He was singing. He sang "sumauma-tree". He sang "angelim-tree".' And you'd hear talk too of journeys to the sky.

The time to start learning these powers is when you yourself are ill. A *paye*-person will come to your hammock and blow smoke on you. As you begin to get better other spirit *paye*-people will come too — Anaconda, for instance, will come and blow on you. If you are very careful, if you stick to your hammock, take great care about what you eat, and if you're not disturbed by noise (by children playing around you or by dogs yapping) you'll begin to learn. To make sure that your surroundings are peaceful, it's best to go and stay in a shelter away from the village where you will not be disturbed.

The spirit creatures will visit you there. You'll begin to see them. Tapir, Peccary, Jaguar, Armadillo, Monkey, Anteater, Blue Butterfly, Vulture — they will all come. They don't come as animals. They come as people. 'Who are you, grandfather?' you ask. 'I'm Tapir', answers one; 'I'm Armadillo', answers another. That's how you know who they are. 'What's wrong with you, grand-child?' they ask. 'I'm ill, grandfather. Blow smoke on me', you say. And gradually you begin to see.

It is the spirit creatures that give you your helpers, small animals or insects. These are like pets. They stay inside you. While you've got them you've got to be very careful not to do anything that might cause them to go away from you. If you lose your helpers you can't be *paye*. As well as giving you your helpers, the spirit creatures teach you songs, and they also give you mirrors for your eyes.

The point of the mirrors is that you *see* and *know* what is not ordinarily visible or known. Just as in the languages we know, the Wayapí words for *seeing*, *knowing*, and *understanding* are intertwined. Seeing through appearances to another reality is a mark of being *paye*. The anaconda is a huge snake, certainly, but only if you're *paye* will you be able to see it in human form. And along with that seeing goes all sorts of knowing. *Paye*-people were diviners. They could find things that were lost. They could guess the weather. They could say in which direction game could be found. Going back through the genealogies I'd collected trying to find out who were the first of Our Wayapí to break out of their isolation and find a way through to the Other Wayapí on the Cue River, they named the first three men to do it. Three tantalizing names were all that was left to mark that moment of truth which was going to have such far-reaching consequences for the people round the Amaparí waters. The aspect of the decision that most intrigued me was 'How did they know where to go?' The answer was 'Because they were *paye*.'

You can see already that if you begin by privileging the curing role, you're quickly carried ever further outwards from that centre by ripples of beliefs and ideas. You start with these male healers and their peculiar gifts. You see how they learn to follow specific techniques in order to achieve their ends: techniques of blowing, singing, getting into a visionary state. You notice how those men who are most renowned for their curing seances sometimes make a point of living on the edges of a settlement or even going off to live remotely, taking wife and children too. Keeping apart helps them maintain their talents since care and moderation are so important. It's not essential for them to live apart, and it's not only *paye*-people who do so. Many households peel off from the main groups for a season or two and take to solitary places. And, frequently, renowned healers will live amongst a settlement and may even be one of the few 'Our Big Ones' (or 'chiefs' as we would put it). However, 'Our Big Ones' don't have to be *paye*, and *paye*-people aren't usually chiefs.

The curing role is the most obvious aspect (which strikes us) of more general doctrines of disease and health. Time and again when people died it would be explained that it was not the illness that killed. Death was blamed on the ill-will of *paye*-people. 'If you fall ill with influenza an enemy *paye*-person will "see" and "know" and will send invisible darts which will penetrate your body. That's what kills you.' Who these enemies were was often a matter of conjecture and disagreement. If the Other Wayapí, or the Wayana, or the Aparai downstream on the Rio Jarí were blamed then there wouldn't be any trouble. Indeed watching meteors at night, you could laugh about it. Meteors were said to be shamanistic darts flying over us, sent by the Other Wayapí on the Oyapoque River on their way towards the Aparai. But if one of our own people was accused the matter could get deadly serious. All very well to be the village doctor; but it's not much of a role or an office to be the village killer. This is the first crux, where the notion of *paye* as a role begins to stretch thin. It's being asked to do too much.

Dark words

The ambiguity came tumbling out one night sitting with Maraté in the ragged little settlement that was attached to the post. Houses in that settlement were more in the style of the Brazilian frontier. They were more substantial, making use of planks and slats; more private. There was no communion of fires here. Maraté had set himself up there temporarily, on an extended visit, and he had built himself a small shelter-type house at the edge of the village, just the kind that should have had an open fire on the ground at one end. It strikes me now, thinking back, that the lack of fire was deliberate. I remember we talked in deep darkness, unable to see each other's faces.

He was there to learn how to become *paye*. There was a particularly well-known *paye*-person nearby. I had known Maraté for years and had seen him go through some of his greatest tragedies. He had lost two wives and three children, and this move was an attempt to find out what on earth was happening to his life. 'So how do you go about becoming *paye*?' He went through a fairly standard list of prohibitions and precautions: don't kill game; don't carry a basket on your back if you have to travel; keep away from women who are menstruating; don't have sex ('because if you do the beautiful people will be ashamed and won't come near you – the spirit people, Tree people, Anaconda people – they've got long hair; they're dressed like Brazilians; you get to have sex with *their* women'). And eat cold food only; white tapioca bread is best.

As he went on his account became more feverish. When you are *paye* you have feather headdresses, beads round your arms and legs, a mirror on your chest, fish hooks in your teeth (for taking out *paye*-darts from victims), shoes, and gloves. (Shoes and gloves? Brazilian fashion was beginning to enter shamanic reality.) All these are invisible. He went through the various people considered to be shamanistic, and graded them in order of power. 'So-and-so has removed darts from victims and let everyone see them. He also taught such-and-such's second wife how to be *paye*.' (So women *can* be *paye* after all.)

The argument then was turned up another notch. He talked of the two wives he had lost over the years, and immediately blamed . . . let's call him Sora. None of the others on his list of shamanistic people presented any threat at all. Sora had been singled out. I reminded him how years before, at the Nipukú, it was so often Aparai shamanizing or Other Wayapí shamanizing that was blamed for the deaths. Well, said Maraté, that was all wrong. Sora had tried to seduce his first wife all those years ago. When she had turned him down he had later killed her. 'And it wasn't just her. Do you remember *this* person and *that* person who died? It was Sora who did it. Sora did it all.'

And who, precisely, is shamanistic and who isn't? Many years before deciding to take up this apprenticeship, Maraté had tried to fight back. When his second wife died, a child-wife, he knew who the culprit was. Before she was taken to be buried he gathered together: a piece of her big toenail, a small piece of skin from her heel, some strands of her hair, and a small piece of her loincloth. After her burial he boiled the bits and pieces from dawn till midday and then emptied it all on her grave. This took place at Nipukú, but he managed to make Sora, 80 miles away, ill with a skin disease. Indeed he'd nearly managed to kill him. You'd want to call what Maraté was up to 'shamanizing', but you wouldn't have called him 'a shaman'. Sora was supposed to be 'the shaman', not Maraté.

Being very fond of Sora, I found this talk alarming. It really began to look as if his days were numbered. All these accusations were backed up the following day by one of the more Brazilianized Wayapí who lived permanently at the post. Again this young man went at the matter with vehemence:

> Why are X, Y, and Z in good health? They are Sora's immediate relatives. Why is it only my immediate relatives that die around here? Sora says it's Aparai *paye*-people from away over there on the Rio Jarí who are doing it. W [another "great" *paye*-person, the speaker's elder brother] says it's Anaconda. I say it's Sora. I've lost three children. Why me? Perhaps *paye*-people are angry. Well, I'm angry too. Do you remember, long ago, at the Nipukú, there was so much malaria? But *no one died*. Wayapí didn't die of malaria. Now they die. It's not the Aparai who are doing it. It's *paye* here. And who? And who? Well, if Sora's immediate relatives died I wouldn't be angry. But it's just mine. That's why I'm angry.

There was a FUNAI plan on the go to take a number of Our Wayapí to French Guiana to meet the Other Wayapí. Sora was one of those to be taken. I was urged to do what I could to see to it that this didn't happen. If he got there, said the young man, he'd learn monstrous powers and Our Wayapí would be finished.

I want to come back to the point later, but let me say now, in case academics not as wise as Willard Quine are listening in, that while this talk of boiling up bits of your dead wife, and accusing your neighbour for deaths that occurred years before, all seems dreadfully 'unreasonable' to those of us living in our comfortable civilization, it is not at all unreasonable when you and I come to the agony face to face in the dead of night with the great woods around us. The question: 'I wonder if this is "reasonable"?' simply does not arise. That's not what's at issue. The point is: here are our closest friends, in extremes of grief, trying to make sense of what is happening to themselves, and producing pictures that are quite beyond our grasp. The urgent question is not 'Are they being reasonable?' but 'Can we find a way to get in there?'

Quiddities and qualities

When you're still hobbling along with the language, sentences come at you that you try to translate. You've heard the word *paye*, and you think it means *shaman*. Then you start hearing all sorts of things: that various trees are shamans, that the tapir is a small shaman, that the deer is a fairly important shaman, and that the anaconda is a vastly powerful shaman. Indeed the anaconda is such an important shaman that when you see a rainbow, which happens to be the anaconda's soul, you must not point at it with your hand and arm. If you do so, you risk paralysis. If you want to indicate a rainbow, you point at it with your lips.

If a shaman is the local doctor, if that is the shaman's role, what is the role in society for a tree, a tapir, a deer, and a huge water snake? This is where you begin to see that your grammar is letting you down. Of course they are not saying that a certain big tree 'is a shaman'. They are indicating that the tree 'is shamanistic', that it too has the quality shared by the well-known healers. Hence, when they say 'Sora i-*paye*' rather than translating that as 'Sora is a shaman' you'd do better to say 'Sora is shamanistic'. Similarly you can say that the anaconda, the various trees, and so on are all 'shamanistic'. You've moved on from the role, from the essence, to an attribute, to a quality, which is found all round about you.

Thinking in terms of a quality allows thinking in terms of degrees – something or someone can have a lot of it, or a little of it, can have it for some time and then lose it again. Yanuari explained that he used to be shamanistic but he lost the gift after a dreadful fall while climbing a tree to get a monkey he'd shot. He broke his back, and his legs have now withered. He says the fall also broke the mirrors he had in his eyes, hence he's now only *very very slightly* shamanistic (not a *tiny, tiny shaman*).

'Knowledge itself is power.' Shamanistic power, which is all around us, accounts for misfortune, illness, and death. Certainly it's a quality that includes the power to heal and the power to harm, but it's more completely to do with knowing and seeing: with a whole other way of understanding. Those who have learned how to grasp this power can see beyond the everyday appearances of people, animals, and the rest of the natural world to another reality. It sounds familiar, doesn't it? Our most worthy philosophical traditions have struggled for centuries with questions about appearance and reality, efforts that look forced and over-elaborate when you realize that Wayapí people take it for granted that the world is not as it seems to be.

Looking at parts of speech has taken us a long way from 'the shaman is a witch-doctor'. Starting from a simple noun 'shaman', *paye* has waxed like the crescent moon into an entire cosmology. *Paye* is a way of looking at the world. To be more precise, I think the most important point to hold on to is that the other reality yonder, revealed by shamanistic knowledge, has been thoroughly humanized. It is full of creatures all of whom appear as people we talk to and learn from. The world of these creatures and the world of humans becomes shared. That is to say, the heart of that shamanic reality reveals a human relation between ourselves and the natural world.

Animism and phlogiston

If the first key was a point of grammar, the second key is the animal spirit-people. It is a detail that opens out an enormous perspective on a way of being in the world, one that presents us, here and now, with a genuine challenge; a challenge as to how far we can go to meet it and appreciate it. It's been a received idea in anthropology since last century that primitive cosmologies entertain the view that 'everything lives' – that animals, trees, plants, rocks, water, are alive as we are. The word for this is 'animism', from the Latin *anima*, the soul. In one way it's a most appropriate word since it includes connotations of air, of breath, of life. Hence we might be able to see everything in the world around us as 'animated'; not inert, or distanced from us, but endowed with vigour and liveliness as we are. In another way the word is a disaster.

Once again, it's to do with nouns, these sumps of meaning. We owe the word *animism* to Georg Ernst Stahl, who taught at the University of Halle at the end of the 1600s and the beginning of the 1700s, and went on to become the personal physician to the King of Prussia. He taught practical medicine, anatomy, physics, and chemistry, and is best known to our world for the theory of 'phlogiston' which was held to explain how matter burned. What on earth can phlogiston have to do with animism? The point is: the form of reasoning that backs up the ideas is the same in both cases.

A brief digression, then: why do things burn? Stahl thought up the ingenious notion that matter possesses a certain thing, a certain essence, a certain element, which he named phlogiston. This stuff will be released on burning. The more of the stuff a certain kind of material has to begin with, the more of this stuff will be released when the material is burned. A certain *thing*, in this case with a Greek rather than a Latin name, has to be present to explain why matter burns. Why can't you set fire to a piece of metal? Because it has hardly any phlogiston. Why does wood catch fire? Because it has a lot of phlogiston. It took nearly eighty years until Antoine Lavoisier, just as the French Revolution broke out, explained the principles of combustion in terms of oxygen (an acidifying principle, as he called it) in the air reacting with the material. Phlogiston was merely a thing, a pseudo-thing; just a noun.

But nouns run on. When Georg Stahl thought about living things, he accepted that the physiological changes seen in living organisms were due to chemical processes. But those kinds of explanation, in terms of chemical laws and mechanical laws, were not enough to explain what life was and how life went on. Something more was needed. Material was one thing, but in order to be alive, an organism required a quantity of a substance, a 'life-force' which he called (in Latin this time) *anima*. Another noun, another name, another pseudo-thing, is invented. *Phlogiston* is 'burning stuff'. *Anima* is 'living stuff'.

After the chemists came the anthropologists. They were after stuff too. The term 'animism' was taken up in anthropology by E.B. Tylor in 1871 to describe what he saw as the origin of religion: 'belief in spiritual beings'. The theory was that primitive people came to the notion of spirits through experiencing dreams and visions. Noticing, for example, that you can meet dead people in dreams, primitives thought up the notion of an immaterial soul which was separate from the material body. Once human beings saw themselves in this way, it was a short step to attributing a similar duality, of material thing and immaterial spirit, to all sorts of aspects of the natural world – to animals, trees, rocks, and so on. Rain and thunder, for example, could then be explained as the goings-on of these spirits.

Tylor's notion of animism has long been out of fashion in anthropology. It's a pity it was dropped since he certainly was on to something important. 'Animism' as a signpost pointed in the right direction, albeit that the notion needed refining. It should have been sharpened up. But instead, the signpost became deformed into a very blunt instrument indeed. It got tied up in discussions of classifying religions. Once you get it into your head that everybody in the world can be classified according to their 'religion' (whatever that word may refer to), you can start producing colour-coded maps of the world where huge areas are marked off as 'Here Be The Christians' (colour them blue maybe), and the next tranche, perhaps in red, is 'Here Be Islam', and so on through as many religions as you have names for. But what do you do with 'tribes', as they are still called, who have never been touched with a religious label? You call them 'Animists' and colour them, what? Green? Animism becomes a thing, a condition, a sort of non-religious religion, synonymous with 'heathen'.

But E.B. Tylor was indeed on to the core of it. It's astonishing to do student course work in anthropology, writing essays on the history of anthropological thought, for which you've got to look through nineteenth-century tomes, where it appears easy to spot the prejudices, and yet where you can learn so much. You can read Sir John Lubbock, for example, in 1882 on what he ponderously calls *La Couvade*[11] (where on the birth of a child, in all sorts of societies, it is the father, more obviously than the mother, that goes into seclusion and has to observe restrictions), and having written your essays you can walk straight into *La Couvade* in your first few weeks in the Amazon woods. Similarly, you can gen up on Tylor's 1871 notion of 'animism' for your exam paper and find yourself face to face with it a few months later. That surprise is rare nowadays. As the world gets more and more homogenized, and as the discipline of anthropology gets more and more self-absorbed ('let's study ourselves'), the enormous ethnographic richness presented by the nineteenth-century ethnologists appears more and more as antiquarianism. It's a disappointing turn in the present fashions. The richness is still there; far away, perhaps, but there. All that's required is the disposition to go and encounter it.

Tylor's term became blatantly useless when it turned into a religious tag. But even before that there was an inherent difficulty in it. Nouns make us think of discrete essences, of quiddities, of an essential whatness. So if *that* collection of beliefs over there is what's called 'animism', then it must be something different and distinct from *this* collection of beliefs that we're familiar with. Behind the term lurked the grounding idea that whereas we know what is alive and what is not, they don't. They attribute life to what we consider inert. Animism extends the notion of 'being alive' into areas where we know the term to be unacceptable.

There are two clear strands tied up in nineteenth-century theories about animism. One is the notion that primitives think that all sorts of things round about them are simply alive. The other is that all these things have a soul or spirit in them that makes them alive. Wayapí conversation shifts between both points. I don't think either is particularly obscure, and I don't think calling either the one or the other 'animism' marks any great divide between us and them. As regards the first (the alive business), we just take it for granted that animals are alive. We would say the same about plants, although we might, if we thought about it, say 'alive in a different way'. 'Tree dies', Wayapí would say when we'd hear the distant boom of a tree keeling over – an eerie event since there was seldom any wind to do it, and a terrifying experience when it happened at night close to the shelter when journeying. Well, we talk easily of our house plants or farm crops dying. There's no great difficulty there.

La Couvade and Anaconda

The second aspect of nineteenth-century animism (the soul and spirit business) emerged vividly in Wayapí conversation when the parents of newborn children went into elaborate precautions as regards what they could do, what they could eat, and where they could go. It's to birth precautions like these that nineteenth-century anthropology gave the name *la couvade*. One of the principal reasons Wayapí people gave for taking these precautions was that the well-being of the child had to be protected from Anaconda.

Babies were constantly carried close to their mothers in slings. If present-day psychoanalysis is accurate in saying that the first loss the growing individual has to endure is the loss of the mother, then being carried in this way should lay down enduring sediments of psychic reassurance. *Arrimage* I heard it called in French: like stowing everything onboard ship, making everything *secure*. There's a similar word in Spanish: coming close, snuggling, cuddling. 'Arrímate a mi querer, como la largatita se arrima a la pared' (Cling to my love, like the little lizard clings to the wall) as it is sung in a *Fandango de Huelva*. It's an appealing and comforting sight wherever babies are carried like this. Furthermore, as if to presage psychoanalysis, Wayapí imaging of this was precisely of psychic clinging.

The soul of the child is not properly attached to it, they said. If a toddler fell over and began to yell, the mother would pick it up in one arm and then scoop up the soul from the ground with her free hand, blowing and lifting a number of times. If the child didn't stop crying she would return to the spot and 'lift up the soul' again. It would be fatal for the child to be taken to the river for a bath since Anaconda would take the fragile soul.

It wasn't just the body of the child that was clinging to its parents. The soul clung on too. If a toddler's father went for a walk in the woods, leaving the child behind with the mother, he would still have the soul attached to him. So he would blow and scoop to make sure the child's soul got over fallen logs or streams. He would also avoid large trees in the woods since they were shamanistic. Hence, as further protection for the child's soul both parents would keep well away from the river. Friends brought them water in calabashes for washing. They had to keep away from the power of Anaconda.

'Anaconda' is probably a Sinhalese word applied to a python of Sri Lanka and South India. It's irritating to be stuck with a linguistic mistake instead of an evocative Tupian word. The name was applied in error by English speakers to the snake known in Brazil as the *sucurí* or *sucuriju*, straight Tupian words. The particular Wayapí word is *moyó* – simply 'great snake'.

The anaconda is an awesome creature; the largest snake in the world, said to reach 12 metres, although the largest authenticated specimen, held in a London museum, measured 29 feet (just under 9 metres). I thought the massive diamond-shaped head looked particularly threatening since the eyes were not prominent, giving it a wicked, purblind look. But, in spite of exaggerations of size, and unsubstantiated stories of attacks on humans, the anaconda is not dangerous. It has no venom fangs, although the jaws are toothed and are enormously strong. It feeds on fish, caymans, aquatic birds, and mammals that come to the river bank to drink. It grasps the prey with its mouth, and, if it has caught something large, wraps itself round the victim. The prey is often drowned. The tremendous power of constriction then breaks the dead animal's bones, crushing it and preparing it for swallowing.

This is the creature, with its beautiful skin markings, that was the most potent centrepiece of Wayapí imaginative life. It would come to the Nipukú at night – shamanistic Anaconda that is. People identified its approach by a high-pitched whistling sound. I could never confidently isolate what they said

they were hearing from the perpetual night background noise; a great blanket
noise of whistles, chirps, and croaks.

Anaconda was the 'owner' or 'master' of water, and menstruating women
didn't go near the river since the smell of blood would make Anaconda angry
and the woman would get dizzy and die. In the village, there were no obvious
precautions taken. Menstruating women would discreetly stay in their ham-
mocks. Away from the village the anxiety was more obvious. In a temporary
camp near Aima, preparing an area to make a garden, a woman went into
seclusion and her husband strung up a raggedy blanket to act as a screen
between her and the nearby water, protecting her from Anaconda.

Anaconda was the most impressive character to emerge in this area of the
imaginative world. In many other Amazonian cultures the jaguar has pride of
place both in myth as the giver of all sorts of cultural gifts and also in
shamanistic thinking as a possessor *par excellence* of that kind of power. But in
Wayapí cosmography it was Anaconda that was referred to again and again as
'vastly shamanistic' and the force most feared.

I'm tempted to set up a simplistic opposition between Yaneyar on the one
hand, the Our Master complex of ideas that was constantly referred to in the
myths, and Moyó on the other, Anaconda that was constantly referred to on a
daily basis in discussions of danger, ill-health, and mortality. Binary contrasts
like that are the currency of structuralism, and I'm wary of such contrived
reductions. But I'm puzzled by the lack of any obviously shamanistic themes in
the myths I found. It's the same imaginative world. Animals, birds, and trees
appeared in the same way as *dramatis personae* both in the idiom of myth and in
the idiom of shamanism. But amongst all the violence and killings and deaths
in the mythical stories I haven't found a single one where shamanizing is said
to cause anything, where shamanistic practices are illustrated, or where any
character is said to have the powers.

In the best Anaconda story, the snake comes to the house in human form,
teaches the sisters of the grandfather-people how to do genipa dye designs on
their bodies, and then proceeds to seduce them. The brothers find out and kill
Anaconda. The corpse gets filled with maggots and from them appear tiny
people who are given food and brought up by the grandfather-people until
they turn into the Aparai and the Wayana, the two neighbouring peoples. 'So
you see, Yaneyar didn't make the Wayana. They're just from Anaconda's
maggots.' There's not a word in the story of any shamanistic powers.

The way I make the contrast for myself is to think of the myths as
encyclopaedias, histories, mortality plays, pictures, illustrations, entertainments, that make of the surrounding natural world a vivacious spectacle. The
myths are a great carnival of associations with the various Yaneyars and
Grandfather-People and Jaguars and Anacondas playing the Pantaloons and
Harlequins, the Inamoratas and Columbines. To that we are all spectators.
Shamanism by contrast images the hand-to-hand struggle of keeping alive that
we go through every day, victims as we are of illness and accident, and always

threatened with death. We are surrounded by *paye*-power which is exercised by people, by the various spirit-owners of large trees, of various animals, and above all by the Owner-of-water, Anaconda.

The picture is not one of 'animism' as opposed to 'non-animism', but a congeries of ideas, some of which we all share, some of which we don't, including what counts as alive and what does not, notions of spirits and notions of souls, differences and similarities regarding human life, animal life, vegetable life, and mineral life. It doesn't work very well to abstract a particular set of features from this assortment and label them 'animism', thereby allowing us to say 'they are animists and we are not'. The more important distinction is to notice what human beings are thought to be in a relationship with, and what they are not. It's not the nature of life that is in question, but the nature of our relationship with our surroundings. This is why the presence of the owner-spirits is a key point.

No one ever said that artifacts (bows, baskets, pots, dwellings) had owner-spirits. The lovely ubim leaves from a dwarf palm that were used for house thatch did have an owner-spirit out there in the forest that you had to be careful of when you gathered them. But the thatch itself didn't have an owner-spirit. Artifacts, then, are the only things that both we and they would agree were inert objects.

It's astonishing to look around me here, whether living in the city or in the countryside, and try to see something that is not human-made or human-managed. The trees are all planted. Fields and hills are ploughed, grazed, or burned. The very weeds in derelict sites are the result of human intervention. The waterways and rivers are managed. They once quarried the cliffs. But there in the Amazon woods, the human environment stopped at the settlement's edge and at the garden's edge. Human beings lived in tiny islands amongst the vastness of the forest. A path would disappear in a season, and the signs of an abandoned settlement site would be obliterated by the forest in ten years. The only congener of the forest left for us is the ocean.

My world here has been living for centuries according to the monstrous presumption found in the first chapter of the Book of Genesis where human beings are given dominion over every living thing that moveth upon the earth. You can see a monstrous transformation of the same presumption into contemporary political terms in Rudyard Kipling's 'Recessional'. Here the vision of the British Empire is expressed in tree metaphors as 'dominion over palm and pine'. (The people under the palms and pines were, in spite of what George Orwell said, 'lesser breeds without the Law'.)[12] By 1897 Adam was an upper-class Englishman. But whereas people are more willing these days to be frank about the appalling presuppositions underlying imperialism, they refuse, tediously and stubbornly, to make similar adjustments regarding our relationship with the natural world. Humility and respect are not the characteristics that spring into prominence when considering our relations with animals and trees.

But if you lived in a tiny island in the middle of the rainforest and if your most powerful tools for interacting with your environment were a machete, an axe, and a bow and arrow (let's forget the shotguns just now) the assumptions of dominion that we take for granted would be absurd. Again and again when I try to submit to shamanism, I find myself coming to a stop when I try to appreciate the material conditions of their lives. I did indeed find so many of the ideas and visions difficult to grasp and difficult to enter into. But imagining spirit-owners and Anaconda-people was not too difficult. I could share the talk and make an effort to share the visions. On the other hand, the way their lives were integrated with their environment made them, to me, intangible. I could go and live there and take part, but I could never know the full force of what it is to have my life determined by these conditions.

Out there, in their world, before the processes of acculturation overcame them, there was no social world set over against a natural world. There was no culture as opposed to nature. There was no human fantasy of dominion over the natural surroundings. There, the human world was part of the forest, and it shared it with jaguars and anacondas and fish and birds. The shamanistic beliefs revealed these relations with the world, 'relations of the human and non-human quite different from those we entertain, but not, therefore, necessarily less reasonable', as Godfrey Lienhardt had tried to explain at the start. It isn't so much the particular beliefs that are incomprehensible to us. It's not that they were 'animists' and we are not. The difficulty is rather that we have, for ourselves, through the material conditions of our lives and the relation with the natural world that comes from that, made their kind of relation with the animals and the trees and the waters profoundly incomprehensible.

None of us can get ourselves back to the ecological integrity that was expressed through shamanistic processes, where each person is in a life-and-death relation with their surroundings. If you get an inkling of that kind of integrity you can also appreciate the the full awfulness of the Brazilian government policy of 'integration'. Integration into what? Into the 'national society' (that empty abstraction), which means destroying that relation between them and the forest. It's the process which takes place through acquiring and depending on material goods. 'Integration' meant shotguns and radios, hence an umbilical cord to the outside society to get hold of lead-shot and batteries. That meant cash. That meant producing to sell. That meant an earthquake in their relation with their surroundings, breaking it into scrambled relics. It was a policy of disintegration, perpetrated on them, destroying the material conditions of their lives but leaving them with the lingering beliefs which would serve as requiems both for loved ones and for lost ways of being.

That's why there's no point in thinking we can reinvent the relation in a piecemeal way. When we look around and find that there are no *pajés*, no shamans, no witch-doctors, there's no point in play-acting such parts in parlour seances and meeting hall displays, claiming thereby to be returning to those elemental sensibilities of relation with the spiritual and natural world. The fancy dress taken from picture books and the *bricolage* of procedures – these are the real scrambled relics; the scrambled relics of a middle-class, first-world credulity that hasn't managed to grasp the enormity of what has been destroyed, root and branch.

Understanding and believing

I began this chapter with linguistic difficulties. These we can get used to. The mysteries of language are inexhaustible, but with practice we can become nimble in getting over the obstacles. Yet, however far I think I'm getting into it, shamanism is the principal aspect of their lives that retains an immediate capacity to shock. Sometimes I get excited about it, sometimes frustrated, sometimes frightened. It's like trying to get to know a bit of land and finding that the area you're walking in isn't obeying the usual rules. You think you're learning your bearings, but you keep on getting lost and emerging in the wrong place. If that happens then either the land really is weird, or there's something going askew with the way you're taking your bearings.

Approaching the FUNAI post for the last time, walking easily along the abandoned road, I met Yiseiwarai on his way to hunt. He'd always been talked about as being greatly *paye*. I had missed him this time in all the settlements I'd visited. We hadn't seen each other for years although he'd heard that I'd come back. We talked about the thunder earlier that day and he said that was because Yaneyar was drunk. This set him off on a bizarre line. He asked about aeroplane travel, how high I'd got in my previous journey, if I'd seen Yaneyar when I was up there. Did I do my writing in Yaneyar's place? was the next question. When I said I'd probably not been high enough to see Yaneyar, he said he'd been away up there himself the previous day. That short meeting on the road made me see how far I still had to go to. Was he just having me on? Was he really cranky in a way others were not? Was there something here that I would, eventually, grasp? Or was this a final impasse? I couldn't and still can't decide amongst these possibilities.

On the last day at the post, the last day with Wayapí people, I stayed with a young couple I'd known since they were children. They had stayed for years on the post, the man in FUNAI service. Both spoke fairly good Portuguese and lived in a Brazilian frontier-style house. They had a gas cooking stove. They offered me packet soup, and coffee with milk. They wore Brazilian clothes. The woman mentioned the electric light that illuminated the post, and how she'd like to have that in her home, but they were only, in the Portuguese phrase, *gente pobre*, poor folk. For all the world, I seemed to have left the Wayapí far behind and to have already taken the step across the shadow line that was planned for the following day. But then came the impassioned torrent about Sora that I mentioned earlier, and a lengthy discussion about Anaconda.

In a moment I was back at this mysterious turbulent centre of Wayapí concerns.

It's shamanism more than anything, more than the myths or the manners, that dislocates me and disturbs my complacent assumptions that understanding is all just a matter of time, just a matter of patience, just like learning the language. With the language, perseverance furthers, and you'll likely get there in the end. With shamanism I'm reminded that I can never be sure.

In the heady 1960s, before the rise of strident fundamentalism, when Christianity in particular was in soft-focus and appeared to be fading, Alasdair MacIntyre wrote an article called 'Is Understanding Religion Compatible with Believing?'[13] It was a clever piece which dealt with nuances of the two words 'understanding' and 'believing', making the point that an effort of understanding has inevitably to be made from the outside. If you're already a 'believer' there's no 'understanding' effort required. It's *because* we don't believe that we have to make the interpretative effort.

A quarter of a century later the point was echoed in a moving phrase by Clifford Geertz who, discussing the interpretative efforts that anthropology finds itself struggling with, suggests that: 'We must learn to grasp what we cannot embrace.'[14] It's a phrase that drifts in my memory, and keeps emerging as: 'We must learn to embrace what we cannot grasp'. Which way round? I think it's better put in Old Lafew's words: we must learn to submit ourselves to those unknown fears.

Notes

1   Godfrey Lienhardt (1954) 'Modes of Thought', in E.E. Evans-Pritchard *et al. The Institutions of Primitive Society*. Basil Blackwell (pp. 95–107).

2   M.I. Finley (1986) *The Use and Abuse of History*, The Hogarth Press (p. 111).

3   Perry Anderson (1990) 'Witchcraft', *London Review of Books*, vol. 12, no. 21, 8 November, pp. 6–11 (p. 11).

4   Ibid.

5   'Dreaming' etc. as modifications and disappointment, see: Hans-Georg Gadamer (1975) *Truth and Method*, Sheed and Ward (p. 75).

6   Lafew in *All's Well that Ends Well* (II. iii. 1–6).

7   On Quine's best known example of *gavagai* as 'rabbit' see: W. van O. Quine (1959) 'Meaning and Translation' in R.A. Brower (1960) (ed.) *On Translation*, Harvard University Press (pp. 148–72); and 'Translation and Meaning', Chapter 2 of *Word and Object*, MIT Press (pp. 26–79).

8   On Quine's notion of the 'entering wedge', see: (1961) *From a Logical Point of View*, III, 5, Harvard University Press (pp. 60–4).

9   'Idols of the forum': one of Francis Bacon's four classes of errors to which the mind is prone. Errors in this class are due to the influence of words or phrases: the fluctuations of language. *Novum Organum*, i, 39.

10   For a cross-cultural survey of shamanism, see: Mircea Eliade (1964) *Shamanism: Archaic Techniques of Ecstasy*, New York. p. 202.

11   Sir John Lubbock (1882) *The Origin of Civilisation and the Primitive Condition of Man: Mental and Social Condition of Savages*, Longmans. Green, and Co. (pp. 15 ff.).

12   George Orwell wrote:

> An interesting instance of the way in which quotations are parroted to and fro without any attempt to look up their context or discover their meaning is the line from 'Recessional,' 'Lesser breeds without the Law'. This line is always good for a snigger in pansy-left circles. It is assumed as a matter of course that the 'lesser breeds' are 'natives,' and a mental picture is called up of some *pukka sahib* in a pith helmet kicking a coolie. In its context the sense of the line is almost the exact opposite of this. The phrase 'lesser breeds' refers almost certainly to the Germans, and especially the pan-German writers, who are 'without the Law' in the sense of being lawless, not in the sense of being powerless.

(1961) *Collected Essays*, '1942 Rudyard Kipling', pp. 179–94, Secker and Warburg (p. 180). Christopher Fyfe, from the Centre of African Studies at Edinburgh University, tells me that Orwell's interpretation became a received view in his generation.

13   Alasdair MacIntyre (1964, 1970) 'Is understanding religion compatible with believing?', in Bryan R. Wilson (ed.) *Rationality*, Basil Blackwell (pp. 62–77).

14   Clifford Geertz (1986) 'The uses of diversity', *Michigan Quarterly Review* Summer, pp. 105–22 (p. 122).

Chapter 8

Edith Turner

THE REALITY OF SPIRITS

IN THE PAST IN ANTHROPOLOGY, if a researcher 'went native,' it doomed him academically. My husband, Victor Turner, and I had this dictum at the back of our minds when we spent two and a half years among the Ndembu of Zambia in the fifties. All right, 'our' people believed in spirits, but that was a matter of their different world, not ours. Their ideas were strange and a little disturbing. but somehow we were on the safe side of the white divide and were free merely to study the beliefs. This is how we thought. Little knowing it, we denied the people's equality with ours, their 'coevalness,' their common humanity as that humanity extended itself into the spirit world. Try out that spirit world ourselves? No way.

But at intervals, that world insisted it was really there. For instance, in the Chihamba ritual at the end of a period of ordeal, a strong wave of curative energy hit us. We had been participating as fully as we knew how, thus opening ourselves to whatever entities that were about. In another ritual, for fertility, the delight of dancing in the moonlight hit me vividly, and I began to learn something about the hypnotic effect of singing and hearing the drums. Much later, Vic and I witnessed a curious event in New York City in 1980, while running a workshop at the New York University Department of Performance Studies, which was attended by performance and anthropology students. With the help of the participants, we were trying out rituals as actual performances with the intention of creating a new educational technique. We enacted the Umbanda trance session, which we had observed and studied in one of the slums of Rio de Janiero. The students duly followed our directions and also accompanied the rites with bongo drumming and songs addressed to the Yoruba gods. During the ritual, a woman student actually went into a trance, right there in New York University. We brought her round with our African rattle, rather impressed with the way this ritual worked even out of context. The next day, the student told us that she had gone home that night and correctly predicted the score of a crucial football game, impressing us even further. Since that time, I have taken note of the effects of trance and discovered for myself the three now obvious regularities: frequent, nonempirical cures; clairvoyance, which includes finding lost people or objects, divination, prediction, or forms of wisdom speaking; and satisfaction or joy – these three effects repeating, almost like a covenant.

What spirit events took place in my own experience? One of them happened like this. In 1985, I was due for a visit to Zambia. Before going, I made up my mind to come closer than on previous occasions to the Africans' own experience, whatever that was – I did not know what they actually experienced. So it eventuated, I did come closer. My research was developing into the study of a twice-repeated healing ritual. To my surprise, the healing of the second patient culminated in my sighting a spirit form. In a book entitled *Experiencing Ritual* (1992), I describe exactly how this curative ritual reached its climax, including how I myself was involved in it; how the traditional doctor bent down amid the singing and drumming to extract the harmful spirit; and how I saw with my own eyes a large gray blob of something like plasma emerge from the sick woman's back. Then I knew the Africans were right. There *is* spirit stuff, There *is* spirit affliction: it isn't a matter of metaphor and symbol, or even psychology. And I began to see how anthropologists have perpetuated an endless series of put-downs about the many spirit events in which they participated – 'participated' in a kindly pretense. They might have obtained valuable material, but they have been operating with the wrong paradigm, that of the positivists's denial.

To reach a peak experience in a ritual, it really is necessary to sink oneself fully in it. Thus for me, 'going native' achieved a breakthrough to an altogether different worldview, foreign to academia, by means of which certain material was chronicled that could have been gathered in no other way.

On the subject of radical participation, Dan Rose in *Living the Ethnographic Life* (1990), predicted that

> students will seek to place themselves in unfolding situations, to live through complex ongoing events . . . rather than looking alone for the meanings of gestures, the presentations of selves, class relations, the meaning of rituals, or other abstract, analytical category phenomena on which we historically have relied. Jackson (1989 [135]) . . . helps to make this point: 'To break the habit of using a linear communicational model for understanding bodily praxis, it is necessary to adopt a methodological strategy of joining in without ulterior motive and literally putting oneself in the place

of other persons: inhabiting their world [what was pejoratively labeled 'going native' in the early days of anthropology]. Participation thus became an end in itself rather than a means of gathering closely observed data which will be subject to interpretation elsewhere *after the event.*'

(P. 58)

Later, in 1987, when I went to northern Alaska to conduct research on the healing methods of Inupiat Eskimos, I similarly found myself swamped with stories of strange events, miracles, rescues, healings by telephone hundreds of miles away, visions of God, and many other manifestations. It was by these things that the people lived. Their ears were pricked up for them, as it were. I spent a year in the village acting as a kind of pseudo-auntie, listening to and actually believing the stories. And naturally, those things happened to me about as frequently as they did to them.

For instance, it happened that in July 1987, before I went to Alaska or knew the ecology at first hand, I attended Michael Harner's shaman workshop in Virginia. He was teaching the workshop participants how to make a shaman journey while lying down in darkness. We were to visualize a climb upward, up a tree, or mountain, or building, or the like. After a first stage of visualization, the experience itself was liable to take over, and we would meet a 'teacher' of some kind. We lay down and Michael beat his drum steadily. I visualized my ascent and found myself out on a bank of cloud. 'How corny,' I said. A figure appeared on my left, a monk in a cowl, and I again thought, 'How corny, like a cartoon.' 'Be quiet,' Harner said, 'Do what you're told. It isn't for you to decide. Go on up.' Mortified, I went up a little more and came to an entire wall of electronic appliances, VCRs, CD sets, stereos, radios, and a large TV screen toward the right. Pictured in the screen was something dark red, filling the whole rectangle. It looked like a maze of internal organs sideways on, elongated, and definitely unlike human internal organs. Why were they there? What was that all about? But I must not criticize, and when the drumming changed I went down the way I had come and eventually remembered that I was lying on the floor. The other participants were sitting up around me. We told our experiences to Harner, he accepted them but did not analyze them psychologically. Four months later in November, when I was settled in among the Eskimos at Point Hope, Alaska, sitting in Ernest Frankson's house, Ernest pulled into the room the body of a ringed seal. His wife laid the seal on some cardboard and proceeded to take off the skin. She allowed me to help cut off the blubber. Then she made a slit down the stomach and displayed to view the internal organs. Wondering, I contemplated them carefully. It was striking to see the dark red parts, liver, spleen, intestines, lungs, heart, and so on, settled together, sliding together with such orderliness and easy movement. Two days later I caught on, as my diary records. Those internal organs were the same organs that I had seen on the shaman TV screen in July.

Ernie caught himself a whale the following April. (I use the word 'caught' in keeping with Eskimo etiquette toward the whale.) I was working for another whaling crew and was occupied with cooking for the men. We waited on the edge of the ice, but no whales came near. An English BBC man was staying in my house in the village, hoping to film the whale hunt. Ernie said, 'The whales don't like filming.' But what could I do, turn the BBC man out? One day, while my crew and I were down on the ice, a dangerous wind came up, and we left in a hurry, observing widening cracks as we made for the beach. After that, no whaling was possible for two weeks. Finally, the BBC man was refused his request to film the whaling and left town. The minute he left, the wind changed back in our favor. All was well, and Ernie caught his whale, with our assistance. Ernie simply said, 'The whale can change the weather.' The whole village, including me, understood the matter in the same way.

Ernie often accused me of not believing in these manifestations, but I protested that I did. How could I help it? Ernie usually had a bad time from whites, who labeled his experiences 'magical beliefs.' But by then I myself was within the circle of regular Eskimo society and experienced such events from time to time. I am now learning that studying such a mentality from inside is a legitimate and valuable kind of anthropology that is accessible if the anthropologist takes that 'fatal' step toward 'going native.'

Members of many different societies, even our own, tell us they have had experience of seeing or hearing spirits. Let us recall how anthropology has dealt with the question in the past. Mainline anthropologists have studiedly ignored the central matter of this kind of information – central in the people's own view – and only used the material as if it were metaphor or symbol, not reality, commenting that such and such 'metaphor' is congruent with the function, structure, or psychological mindset of the society. Clearly, this is a laudable endeavor as far as it goes. But the neglect of the central material savors of our old *bête noire*, intellectual imperialism. What is pitiful is the tendency of anthropologists from among the Native peoples themselves to defer to the Western view and accordingly draw back from claiming the truth of their own religion. The mission of Western anthropologists to explain the system in positivist terms at all costs, which thereby influences a new elite, is oddly similar to the self-imposed task of the more hidebound religious missionaries who are also sworn to eliminate their hosts' religion (see also van der Geest 1990, 591–93).

So one asks, what are the ethics of this kind of analysis, this dissection? May we continue in this age of multipower as well as multicultures to enter a foreign society, however politely, measure it up according to our own standards, and then come back home and dissect it in a way entirely estranged from the ethos of the people concerned? We can see three such methods of dissection: First, the anthropologist who goes out to examine a certain feature of the society, such as Richard Nelson (1969) studying the hunters of the northern ice at Wainwright, Alaska. He contrived to write an entire book from a positivist, practical standpoint, stating that no mystery cults of occult beliefs existed at the time of writing among these Eskimos. But my friend, Enoch Oktollik from Wainwright, has told me how he, Enoch, resents the imputations of the whites and the way they have eroded Eskimo culture. His own mother has seen visions and predicted the coming of a whale. Nelson, though, has now changed his tack; he no longer thinks the Natives' tales are magical rubbish (see *Make Prayers to Raven*, 1983).

Then there are the anthropologists who say, 'Wait a bit! We can see interesting structural regularities in this culture.' Lévi-Strauss led this fashion by writing of Aborigine totemism – those traditional ideas involving awe and respect for certain animals – 'Totemism pertains to the understanding, and the demands to which it responds and the way in which it tries to meet them are primarily of an intellectual kind. . . . Its image is projected, not received' (Lévi-Strauss 1963, 104). But the animal was actually sacred to the Aborigines, part of their visionary life. The Dreaming dominated their whole life – it was visionary, not intellectual.

The third stage consists of the more respectful anthropologists, who bend over backward to accord their people a much fuller sympathy. They follow all the beliefs and see, for instance, how the tapir, among the Wayapi Amazonians, gives central meaning to the lives of the Natives, how the shamanic myth of the 'spirit tapir' (meaning something like Joseph Campbell's use of the word 'myth') has actual feedback into the social system (see Alan Campbell's [1989] handling of the material). Now Alan Campbell is getting close to the Wayapi – except that the poor fellow has to cover himself with regard to his English colleagues by retreating from the question and labeling the whole shamanic system 'metaphoric.' Even in spite of protecting himself in that way, he has been attacked by those colleagues for going too far.

But in this paper I really go over the edge. What will the English say to me? But we eventually have to face the issue head on and ask, 'What are spirits?' And I continue with the thorny question, 'What of the great diversity of ideas about them throughout the world? How is a student of the anthropology of consciousness, who participates during fieldwork, expected to regard all the conflicting spirit systems in different cultures? Is there not a fatal lack of logic inherent in this diversity?' And the reply: 'Is this kind of subject matter logical anyway?' We also need to ask, 'Have we the right to force it into logical frameworks?'

Moreover, there is disagreement about terms. 'Spirits' are recognized in most cultures. Native Americans refer to something in addition called 'power.' 'Energy,' *ki* or *chi*, is known in Japan and China, and has been adopted by Western healers. 'Energy' was not the right word for the blob that I saw coming out the back of Ndembu woman; it was a miserable object, purely bad, without any energy at all, and much more akin to a restless ghost. One thinks of energy as formless, but when I 'saw' in the shamanic mode those internal organs, the organs weren't 'energy.' They had form and definition. Or when I saw the face of my Eskimo friend Tigluk on a mask, as I saw it in a waking dream, and then saw Tigluk himself by luck a few minutes afterward, the mask face wasn't 'energy,' laughing there. It was not in the least abstract. The old-fashioned term, 'spirit manifestation,' is much closer. These manifestations constitute the deliberate visitation of discernable forms that have the conscious intent to communicate, to claim importance in our lives. As for 'energy' itself, I have indeed sensed something very like electrical energy when submitting to the healing passes of women adepts in a mass meeting of Spiritists in Brazil.

I would presume that the question of the multiplicity of beliefs would not faze anthropologists, who are accustomed to a relativistic stance. This stance presupposes some distancing, and for this we have the prime example of Clifford Geertz, a relativist who was indeed a participant, a believer in thick description; and yet he claims it is false faith to think we can go the whole way with our field people. He says that we *can't* really go native, that it is bad faith to try (Geertz 1986, 373). According to him, the proper stance of anthropologists is to listen, interact, participate, write down what people *say* (the 'text'), but distance themselves. (It is to be remembered that Geertz did not, in fact, distance himself.) Others would have us remember that if our interlocuters experience trance or possession, it is a reactive unconscious attempt to remedy their subaltern ranking in sexual and social hierarchies. Our analysis must be on this level; if our participation goes too deep, it might be a sign of our own pathology, and furthermore it will be of no assistance to the oppressed groups concerned. Such is often the teaching of anthropology.

Again and again, anthropologists witness spirit rituals, and again and again, some indigenous exegete tries to explain that the spirits are present and, furthermore, that rituals are the central events of their society. The anthropologist proceeds to interpret them differently. There seems to be a kind of force field between the anthropologist and her or his subject matter, making it impossible for her or him to come close to it, a kind of religious frigidity. We anthropologists need training to see what the Natives see. This might best be done by following the method of a luminous, shaman-type lady, Mary Watkins, who in her book, *Waking Dreams* (1976), leads us through practically all the ways of thinking of the Native religions with unerring skill. The work develops practices that are not particularly doctrinaire because the author possesses a fine-drawn understanding that doctrinaire cults destroy sensitiveness.

Are there spirits 'out there'? In her book, Mary Watkins does not refer to 'spirits' but to 'dream figures,' 'images,' or 'imaginals.' But she might as well have been describing spirits. She sees her 'imaginals' as conscious beings with self-determination, with autonomy. I quote, italicizing phrases that show this:

We tell the dream figures we know what they are saying. . . . We betray them with our sweet understandings . . . [However] we could use interpretation almost like amplificatory material, helping us to maintain the imaginal's *own directionality* (from material to immaterial). . . . The poetic image *creates* perceptions, modalities of perceiving . . . *it is steadily creating the you* who is endeavoring. *It is drawing you* into its landscape and adding not only to your experiences but to your ways of experiencing. . . . The poem and the dream *lead us* into the sites of revery. . . . Images *demand* that we develop the facility to inhibit new sites. . . . The different places of the imaginal begin to stand out. The possibility of an archetypal topography begins to emerge. . . . Each image *teaches* one to lose the ego fantasy of permanence and continuity. . . . *It pulls things from us* that show our participation in it, though often largely unconscious. . . . We learn . . . a consciousness with a polymorphous nature. . . . The past has been created by . . . the possession of us *by* various images. . . . We try to note where and how it lives. How does it spend a day? What is its sense of time? (Some say that the imagination is 'timeless'. . . . [Rather] it contains many different senses of time). . . . The seemingly random nature of images dissolves with time. . . . The unspoken metaphors are revealed – not for just their material aspect, not just their symbolic, but rather as the co-creation of the physical and imaginal qualities of our lives.

(P. 138–42)

Watkins recognized the autonomy of something that she defines as deriving from inside a person – 'an imaginal.' An almost identical recognition runs through many cultures, but it is of spirits 'out there.' The initiative is theirs, not ours. Who is right, the dream analyst or the traditional seer? A symbologist might recognize Watkins's statements as concerned with shamanic awareness. Should we begin quite seriously to experience and recognize this entity – this 'X,' whether 'spirit' or 'imaginal'? What Dan Rose (1990) and Michael Jackson (1989) are urging on us is to do something very like that, to 'literally put ourselves in the place of other persons; inhabiting their world.'

References

Campbell, A. 1989. *To Square with Genesis: Causal Statements and Shamanic Ideas in Wayapi.* Iowa City: University of Iowa Press.

Geertz, C. 1986. 'Making experience, authoring selves', in *The Anthropology of Experience*, edited by Victor Turner and Edward Bruner. Urbana: University of Illinois Press.

Geest, S. van der. 1990. 'Anthropologists and missionaries: brothers under the skin', *Man* 25 (4).

Jackson, M. 1989. *Paths Toward a Clearing: Radical Empiricism and Ethnographic Inquiry*. Bloomington: Indiana University Press.

Lévi-Strauss, C. 1963. *Totemism*. Boston: Beacon Press.

Nelson, R. 1969. *Hunters of the Northern Ice*. Chicago: University of Chicago Press.

Nelson, R. 1983. *Make Prayers to Raven*. Chicago: University of Chicago Press.

Rose, D. 1990. *Living the Ethnographic Life*. Newbury Park, CA: Sage.

Turner, E. 1992. *Experiencing Ritual: A New Interpretation of African Healing*. Philadelphia: University of Pennsylvania Press.

Watkins, M. (1976) 1984. *Waking Dreams*. Dallas, TX: Spring Publications.

PART THREE

Aesthetics

INTRODUCTION TO PART THREE

WHAT SHAMANS DO is inseparable from the music they (or their helpers) play, the costumes they wear, the art they create, the movements they make, the performances they enact. A shaman banging a drum, wearing mirrors, moving like an animal, chanting, is someone shamanising. Without the drum rhythms, costume, equipment, songs and movement, they may only be a member of a clan or people. In some societies they might have other employments altogether when they are not shamanising. The presence of what might look like an audience may also be a clear indicator that someone is shamanising rather than engaging in some more individual pursuit. However, while the development of individualism *might* be rooted in the influence of Western modernist ideas and relations, it can be incorporated into indigenous lifeways as they experiment with variant modes of continuity and 'survivance' (Vizenor 1994).

The following chapters offer significant discussions of the aesthetics integral to shamans doing what they do as shamans, i.e. shamanising. In various ways material in this Part greatly enhances understanding of the performances that, far more than systematised cosmology, are shamanism.

It is arguable that the study of religious action and costume have been hampered by a Protestant notion that true religion is an interior disposition towards 'spirituality' or committed assent to belief. Shamans and their actions have been important in the development of more valuable and more interesting academic approaches to religion as performance and of more refined approaches to ritual. To the brief survey in the General Introduction to this Reader we might add here that shamanic performances insistently challenge notions of virtuosi experts performing to audiences. Does the art, music, movement and ritual discussed in the following chapters require an audience or is it already a communal exercise in some way facilitated by a somewhat more flamboyant actor? Indeed, are we correct in thinking of any audiences as passive receivers rather than as active participants along with those we more easily perceive as performers? Attention is focused on (and demanded by) shamans, but what they do might well demand the full participation of many other people, perhaps of everyone present.

The question of the nature of audiences might not result in a definitive answer applicable to all shamanic communities, at least because shamans and their communities vary considerably. However, it also raises performance questions in relation to debates about exoticism or Orientalism, the formation of alterity or otherness, and even of voyeurism. One aspect of such questions is the role of researcher in an audience or séance or event. Once upon a time academics claimed the ability to be objective and only participated to the degree necessary to test their observations. More recently shifts have taken place so that researchers participate more fully, albeit that some are now even more worried by 'insider' issues (see McCutcheon 1999) and others are concerned by appropriation and colonisation (see Smith 1999). Are academics merely voyeurs intent on stealing other people's knowledges (see Walker 1998: 187), or looking for interesting characters with which to populate their texts, or are they neophytes seeking initiation into respected communities?

The following four chapters discussing art, music, and performance again demonstrate the diversity of academic disciplines interested in shamans. To put it another way, the study of shamanic performances is necessarily multi-disciplinary, archaeology and art studies cross-fertilising musicology and media studies. To study shamans is to engage richly with human endeavours and passions.

Thomas Dowson in Chapter 9 discusses a specific set of rock paintings from southern Africa and argues that there is a correlation between political prominence and the representation of shamanic relationships. Whether or not his specific argument is convincing, its importance is certainly in challenging the use of rock art merely to illustrate shamanic experiences and rituals. Embedding art in the dynamics of social relationships is far more interesting and provocative than 'simply' viewing it as representation and recording. Shamans and others are, by their own assertion, frequently engaged in complex and sometimes dangerous negotiations of power.

Chungmoo Choi in Chapter 10 discusses 'the artistry and ritual aesthetics of urban Korean shamans'. Like rock art in Dowson's argument, ritual here is seen as 'an endeavour to make sense of human experiences and articulate them in a traditional form of artistic communication'. Ritual efficacy is arguably rooted in the performer's ability to utilise social knowledge. A powerful part of the argument implicitly relates the transformation undergone by shamans in initiation and performance with that of their clients, and especially of clients' emotions. Shamanising necessarily effects changes.

Chapter 11 by Marina Roseman is devoted to the 'aesthetics of longing' among the Temiars of Malaysia. In both everyday life and in ceremony, particular sounds and movements aesthetically encode the sentiments of longing and remembrance. Temiars understand illness to occur when longing is 'intensified beyond the proper bounds', but also utilise similar sounds in relation to healing trances. The chapter is admirably clear about the sounds and movements of interest, and about their utility in relation to theories of illness and health, and in underpinning relationships within the community and between them and other-than-human persons. There are many recordings of shamanic musics – and even more of the musics of peoples who employ shamans – including collections such as Cook (1997, including a CD).

If the previous three chapters arise from ethnography about art, ritual, music and other performances of particular shamanic cultures, Mihály Hoppál introduces 'a new era in the history of research on shamanism'. Two important results are evident in the availability of films that record and re-present shamanic performances: first, they are viewable as performances rather than as discrete postures, and, second, they permit repeated viewing and analysis. In addition to surveying some of the available films, Hoppál illustrates improvements in analysis and understanding that they make possible. There is undoubtedly much to be gained from viewing such recordings, but their analysis might require careful consideration of matters of presence and absence. On the one hand, the presence of a camera (and thus of a particular kind of observer) might change rituals into somewhat different kinds of performance. Hoppál refers to several films in which shamans perform solely for the camera. Does this portray shamanism in action or is it rather another medium of ethnographic representation? (It is, of course, entirely possible that this is a false distinction arising from Western ontologies, certainly elsewhere a copy is also the real thing, see Altieri 2001, or as Hoppál writes, a 'reconstruction . . . may be accepted as authentic'.) On the other hand, film-viewers may be seduced into considering themselves present rather than distant in time and space. The obvious facts that films do not replicate temperatures and aromas, and that they do not they entail the full participation of actual presence, may raise doubts about whether a film can entirely convey the occasion. However, since a photograph in Piers Vitebsky's *The Shaman* (1995: 20–1) is said to show 'exactly what the god, the witches and the ancestors look like' perhaps there is hope for films too! In Fact, the film *Atanarjuat: The Fast Runner* (directed by Zacharias Kunak) may be an exceptionally powerful illustration of what is possible.

In these various ways, the four chapters in this Part provide powerful insights and engagements with shamans' practice and performance. They encourage and enhance wider academic debates about the doing of religion, not just ceremonially but also in everyday life and in the active construction of identity by portrayal, representation and demonstration. The dynamics of power and reciprocity, between humans and others of importance (not only 'spirits', ancestors and others, but also prey animals and others) are revealed in fascinating ways.

References

Altieri, P. 2001. 'Knowledge, Negotiation and NAGPRA: Reconceptualizing Repatriation Discourse(s)', in P.W. Edge and G. Harvey (eds), *Law and Religion in Contemporary Society: Communities, Individualism and the State*. Aldershot: Ashgate, pp. 129–49.
Cook, P.M. 1997. *Shaman, Jhankri and Néle: Music Healers of Indigenous Cultures*. Roslyn, NY: Ellipsis Arts.
McCutcheon, R.T. 1999. *The Insider / Outsider Problem in the Study of Religion*. London: Cassell.
Smith, L.T. 1999. *Decolonizing Methodologies: Research and Indigenous Peoples*. Dunedin: University of Otago Press.
Vitebsky, P. 1995. *The Shaman*. London: Macmillan.
Vizenor, G. 1994. *Manifest Manners: Postindian Warriors of Survivance*. Hanover: Wesleyan University Press.
Walker, A. 1998. *By the Light of My Father's Smile*. London: Women's Press.

Chapter 9

Thomas A. Dowson

LIKE PEOPLE IN PREHISTORY

[. . .]

IN *THE SEVEN VISIONS OF BULL LODGE* George Horse Capture and
Fred Gone give us a very detailed and moving story of a great warrior and
medicine man, Bull Lodge. They not only describe how the Supreme Being
came to him in a succession of visions, and how he received the Chief
Medicine Pipe, but also how he used this spiritual wisdom to become a
powerful and highly respected medicine person within his community. I give
a short quote:

> Bull Lodge followed his customary ceremonies for three months,
> from late spring into the summer. Then one summer day . . . he
> lay in the grass on his back with his arms out flat on the ground,
> elbows bent. . . . As he gazed up at the sky, an object
> appeared. . . . It was a shield, with a string or fine cord attached to
> it leading up into the sky. . . . Then Bull Lodge heard a voice. The
> sound came from behind the shield . . . 'My child, look at this
> thing. I am giving it to you from above. It is for your living. In
> times of danger when you need my help, you must always say,
> "Help me Thunder Sing." I will always hear you when you pro-
> nounce my name: Thunder Sing. Now I will instruct you concern-
> ing what you must do. There are seven buttes on this earth that
> you must sleep on. You must do this in imitation of me, for I too
> have done it.'
>
> (Horse Capture 1980: 32–3)

Bull Lodge's relationship with his spiritual mentor was one that lasted for some time; from twelve years old to when he was twenty-three, although such a relationship never really ends.

It is easy for Western academics to take this account of a great and uncompromising warrior and shaman simply as an ethnography of the A'aninin – the White Clay People of Montana, or even as a contribution to our understanding of shamanism. This account may in fact give an insight into the A'aninin and their spirituality. There may also be aspects of Bull Lodge's experience that shed light on shamanism worldwide. But to see this life history exclusively in these terms is to 'turn experience into abstract concepts' (Horse Capture 1980: 14).

Rock art scholars writing interpretative accounts of the visual expression of shamanism frequently draw on ideas of spirits and spirit-helpers. More often than not, very real experiences are effectively written about as abstract concepts, where experience becomes nothing more than a 'metaphor' to explain shamans' relationships to their spirit-worlds. Bull Lodge's story, like so many others, shows us that such a perception is not only insensitive, but also somewhat naive.

In this paper I explore the implications of this insight drawn from Bull Lodge's experiences, in a very different context. I ask what it means for our understanding of certain aspects of San shamanism depicted in rock paintings of southern Africa. I argue that supernatural relations are at the very heart of a shaman's construction of self. Consequently, shamans' relations with their spirits and spirit-helpers are indeed very intimate, and every bit as real as their relations with other people.

Metaphor and agency

In much of the interpretative research on southern African rock art of the last two decades the concept of metaphor has come to structure the meaning offered for most, if not all, rock art imagery. The metaphors derive from shamans' (both men and women) experiences in altered states of consciousness during trance or curing rituals ([. . .]; see Marshall 1969, Lewis-Williams 1982). Lewis-Williams and Loubser (1986) in fact outlined a 'metaphorical model' that not only isolated relationships within the art, but also between art and other forms of expression such as myth and ritual. Metaphors of trance experience are thought to have constituted the structure that constrained shaman artists and their symbolic work.

The painting of a trance dance reproduced here in Figure 9.1 clearly illustrates this position. A large, central shaman has two long 'streamers' issuing from his head that usually represent a person's spirit leaving on out-of-body travel (Lewis-Williams 1981: 95). This figure also has lines on his face, some of which probably depict the nasal haemorrhage associated with trance

Figure 9.1 A rock painting of a trance dance from the south-eastern mountains, showing the actual positions of the two panels (Figs 9.2 and 9.3) which make up the painting

performance (Bleek 1935, 1936). On either side of him are seated figures; their breasts indicate they are women. The women are depicted in clapping postures, their fingers being individually drawn. [. . .] These are the people who clap and sing the medicine songs, while the dancing shamans enter trance to journey to the spirit-world (see Figure 9.3 for details).

To the left of the central figure, and facing him, are three grotesque figures with claws that suggest feline affinities; the bottom figure also has enigmatic 'tusks'. I believe these figures depict the frightening spirits of the dead that often take on the form of lions and against whom Kalahari !Kung San shamans struggle in the spirit-world of trance experience. During a trance dance, these spirits of the dead are believed to hover in the darkness beyond the light of the fire. There are also numerous bags painted around the central figure; nineteenth-century southern San myths suggest that these bags are probably symbols of trance experience (Lewis-Williams and Dowson 1989: 116–17).

In the left-hand section of the panel (Figure 9.2) are some extremely weird depictions that represent hallucinations from very deep stages of trance. Four of the figures have both animal and human characteristics. The one on the extreme left has a human hind leg (rather than an animal leg) and a human foot with three nails as well as cloven hooves. There is also a snake with tusks (see Lewis-Williams and Dowson 1989: 66–7) like those on one of the

Figure 9.2 Detail of the left-hand panel of Figure 9.1 – the hallucinatory experiences of the large, central shaman in the right-hand section

Figure 9.3 Detail of the right-hand panel of Figure 9.1 – the ' real' trance dance

therianthropes. These hallucinations, set off to one side, represent the spirit-world experiences of the dancer in the centre of the right-hand section (Figure 9.3).

Lewis-Williams and Loubser's metaphorical model provided a method-ological backbone to the large body of interpretative research on southern African rock art. But, metaphor is only afforded such prominence by virtue of structuralist/post-structuralist theoretical positions. For the structuralists, it is essentially through the use of metaphors that 'myths operate in men's minds without their being aware of the fact' (Lévi-Strauss 1966: 12). In the context of southern African rock art the artist and the image are passive, the enigmatic images are simply graphic metaphors that explain a shaman's experience in the spirit world. Or, as Lewis-Williams (1982: 438) once put it, 'the painted symbols of trance experience provide a permanent backdrop to the daily social relationships pointing to the social and economic order which the medicine men (*sic*) worked to maintain'.

More recently researchers have attempted to move beyond such objectiv-ist interpretations by thinking about individuals as more active agents who create as well as participate in the communities in which they live (Dowson 1994, 1995, in press; Lewis-Williams 1995). It follows then, that the images themselves play an active role in day-to-day social relations; they are no longer seen as passive props. These studies rely on such theoretical approaches as Bourdieu's (1977) theory of practice or Giddens's (1979, 1984) related structuration theory, as well as related theoretical approaches to the social production of art (Wolff 1981). A key feature of these theories is the know-ledgeable, active individual. For Giddens 'every social actor knows a great deal about the conditions of reproduction of the society of which he or she is an actor' (1979: 5). Individuals' actions are both enabled and constrained by the rules and resources they manipulate. Individual artists, then, used the production of rock art actively to negotiate their position in communities in which they lived.

Agency and the production of rock art

To be able to discern exactly how the art played this role I demonstrate how the depictions were produced. The cognitive structure of the art was socially produced in that meanings attached to specific combinations of formal attributes, such as colour or size, come out of day-to-day social practice. The art was thus intimately implicated in developing social relations and the reproduction and transformation of social forms. Generally, and very briefly, I show how these processes came together and how the art negotiated San ideology, particularly shaman ideology.

The proximity of Bantu-speaking farmers generated a new set of social relations in which the San in general and the shaman in particular were implicated. Farmers recognized the San as the original inhabitants and custodians of the land. The relationship, posited essentially on land ownership, came to centre on rain-making. The farmers, more than the San themselves, were dependent on rain; even minor droughts and, perhaps more important, delayed rains, affected their crops and herds far more than they did the San's antelope and plant foods. The mediator between the San and the farmers thus turned out to be the shaman. Part of the shamans' symbolic work was rain-making (Lewis-Williams 1981: 103–16, 1982; Campbell 1987). Even though the farmers had occupied the land, they were unable to farm successfully without rain. The farmers requested San rain-makers to perform rituals and gave them cattle in return. Thus the shaman exercised ideological control over the farmers' economy.

Because the shamans were paid for their rain-making services with cattle, presumably among other things, they acquired a new status as procurers of meat, and no doubt they achieved power through a newly developed right to distribute the meat. With the depletion of antelope herds by white hunters and the extermination of the San by white commandos, San shamans were forced to become more dependent on the farmers: the shamans had to tighten their grip on the farmers. This resulted in San families going to live with black farmers (Peires 1981: 24). It could be that these people were acknowledging the farmers' control of the land, but, at the same time, trying to retain some position of spiritual power and status.

Within San communities, diminishing traditional resources and, at the same time, new sources of wealth resulting from new social and economic relations with the farmers engendered competition between shamans. People looked to them as their go-betweens with the farmers and, increasingly, as the most reliable procurers of food. Shamans thus began to compete with one another and with important non-shamans of the group for positions of influ-ence. These power struggles, as well as the stresses of cultural contact between farmers and hunter-gatherers, were negotiated (not just reflected) in the art. The art, produced by shamans, became active and instrumental in forging new social relations that developed out of these power struggles.

People negotiate personal and social identities by means of stylistic state-ments (Wiessner 1984, 1989). Social identities become important during situations of intergroup competition and the need for co-operation to attain social, political or economic goals. Competition among individuals and an increase in options for individual enterprise result in strong personal iden-tities. Contact between Bantu-speaking farmers and the San created situations where both social and personal identities were implicated in social relations, and both of these are negotiated in the art, according to the social regime of a given time and place. I give two examples of how this happened.

First, the south-eastern mountains contain the most variation in 'styles', but, at the same time, it is in this region that the diversity of animal depictions is less marked than elsewhere in southern Africa. Eland and rhebok are by far the most frequently painted animals. The limiting of animal diversity in the paintings of this region was one result of a new interest in projecting a social identity and a social unity during changing social conditions. At least one San community of that area spoke of themselves as being 'of the eland' (Vinnicombe 1976; Lewis-Williams 1988). The paintings of eland found throughout the south-eastern mountains suggest that using the art to negotiate a group identity was in fact a region-wide response to changing social relations. But careful attention to a second theme, that of trance dances and the way in which shamans are painted, shows there were also differences within this region.

One way of painting trance dances found throughout the south-eastern mountains shows all the human figures uniformly painted: the figures are all more or less the same size, and none depicts a person who is more elaborately decorated or dressed than any of the others, shamans or non-shamans. I suggest that these paintings point to social circumstances in which a number of people in the community were shamans and no one was pre-eminent; even though shamans could contact the spirit-world, heal and make rain, they were no 'better' than anyone else (Dowson 1994). Service to their community was a privilege not a power base. A situation of this kind is described by Marshall (1969), Lee (1968, 1979), Biesele (1978) and by others for parts of the Kalahari in the 1950s and 1960s. At that time, about half the men and a third of the women in any camp were shamans. Communal healing dances to which everyone came were held frequently when there were enough people present. Although some shamans earned reputations for being especially effective healers, they did not assume positions of more general leadership or political influence.

It is arguable that these uniformly painted trance dances were implicated in social processes that limited the development of personal power. The art did not simply reflect social conditions, any more than it merely pictured the use of artefacts and the presence of certain animals. It was part of active material culture that negotiated social relations and statuses. Imbued with potency, these images of 'equality' helped to reproduce specific kinds of social relations. As 'potent' statements of what happened in the ultimately real spirit-world, they were coercive in the sense that they presented a supernaturally sanctioned social, indeed cosmological, order in which shamans were numerous and no one was more powerful than the other.

Paintings pointing to an elaboration of power roles are, apart from a few outliers, found in a comparatively small area of the south-eastern mountains. This area, known to the colonists as 'nomansland', was the last southern refuge of comparatively independent San communities. Given the acknow-ledged San occupancy of the area, the name 'nomansland' is grimly ironic. Here there are paintings of trance dances in which there is one prominent shaman figure, often larger, often highly elaborately decorated and with facial features. The political centrality of one striking, pre-eminent shaman figure, supported in his spiritual tasks by other members of the community, is, I argue, suggested by the painting reproduced in Figure 9.1.

A comparable, but not identical, trajectory has been observed in the Ghanzi area of the Kalahari. Here the land was appropriated by white farmers, and the San were forced to accept employment with them. When wage-labour restricted the San's movements in this way, the shamans (who did not make rock art) became fewer and itinerant, moving from farm to farm to perform their healing rituals. Today, their enhanced social status is under-written by their possession of potency, their prestige as well-known healers, and the political implications of the small herds of cattle they keep at a home base (Guenther 1975, 1975/6, 1986). They are emerging as political, not just spiritual, leaders.

Hallucination and shamanic representation

Figure 9.1 and other similar rock paintings (see Fig. 9.4) that depict pre-eminent shamans show that painters were not ineluctably governed by artistic conventions and metaphorical structures. Rather, we should, as Giddens (1984) has suggested, think of structure as part of the resources, both material and non-material, on which individuals can draw. Artists manipulated design elements such as size, colour and detail, as well as graphic representa-tions of hallucinations to suit specific political purposes (see also Dowson 1994, 1995, in press).

As I have argued, the association of at least some of the images with supernatural elements and the spirit world (clearly suggested in Figure 9.1 by the clawed figures) imparted an incontrovertible factuality to the images and

Figure 9.4 A portion of a larger panel showing a pre-eminent shaman and 'his' rain-animal in a trance ritual

to the kind of cosmos they depicted. Manipulating the art was therefore not far from manipulating the universe itself. The potent essence of the rock art images imparted a factuality to the social relations and cosmology that they depicted. A shaman's hallucinations are then more than just manipulatable non-material resources. They are, in fact, an important part of the construction of a shaman's personal identity.

An important part of a shaman's socio-political praxis involved communicating the experiences of the spirit-world to people in the real world. A shaman's identity then is, in part, dependent on a representational confrontation with a non-shaman. Hallucinations, experiences of shaman as opposed to non-shamans, therefore provide the apparatus of shamanic representation. As Giddens remarks, 'the self is the agent as characterised by the agent' (1991: 242). Shamans identify themselves with specific spirit-helpers, supreme beings or visions – and it is these hallucinations that create a shaman and his or her knowledge.

The large, central shaman in Figure 9.3, although located in the 'real' context of a trance ritual, is linked to his spirit-world. His legs and back are painted in two colours, red (black in the illustration) and ochre (stippled), much like some of the other human figures around him. But, unlike these other human figures, red lines are painted on the ochre sections which resemble the markings on some of the hallucinatory beings in the left-hand portion of the panel (Fig. 9.2). The artist, in this instance, chose a fairly simple visual marker to link the shaman on the right with his spirits on the left. In so doing, that person has captured the essence of the individual shaman's identity.

Because colonial tensions heightened competition amongst these pre-eminent shamans, there were marked differences in the personal identities of these shamans. Their familiarity with the spirit-world provided a focus for these differences. The way in which this knowledge was drawn into modes of signification legitimated the power these shamans exercised. The pre-eminent shaman illustrated in Figure 9.4 is not only markedly different to the shaman in Figure 9.1, he is also associated with quite a different hallucinatory being. The large, spotted creature, emerging from a step in the rock face (see Lewis-Williams and Dowson 1990), is a rain-animal. Many southern African groups believe rain is controlled by an animal that lives in a large pool of water or the rivers. For the San, it was the task of certain shamans to control the rain-animal, these shamans believed they each had control of their 'own' specific rain (Lewis-Williams 1981: 103–16; Dowson in press). In this example then (Fig. 9.4), the pre-eminent shaman is identified by his abilities as a shaman of the rain.

The shaman illustrated in Figure 9.1 and the shaman in Figure 9.4 have clearly different spiritual personae. These personae result from different experiences and different ways of signifying supernatural knowledge. These two shamans draw on different relations with the spirit-world to negotiate opposing positions within their communities. These spiritual relations are as real as relations with other group members. Just as a shaman depends on men and women clapping and singing medicine songs to activate supernatural powers, so too that shaman depends on relations with his own spiritual beings to maintain his pre-eminent status with the people who sang and clapped the medicine songs to activate his supernatural potency.

It is not 'metaphors' of spiritual experiences that provide shamans with their identities and power bases. Rather it is the intimate and real relations that person has with the spirit-world. Such a distinction may seem to be little more than semantic and academic, but that difference does affect the way in which we write about the past. And certainly getting it right enables and empowers rock art researchers to demonstrate the active role these images had in the day-to-day lives in which the art was produced and continued to be consumed. As graphic metaphors these images can only ever have a passive role in our constructions of that socio-political context.

Let Bull Lodge's story be a reminder to us all; he received his sacred knowledge from a real, named, albeit supernatural, being. Because of colonial attitudes towards San people we will never know the names of the shamans painted in the rock-shelters of southern Africa. Because of academic attitudes towards rock art and shamanism, the San people have only ever been portrayed as hunters and gatherers (Dowson 1993, 1997). But those rock-shelters give us a glimpse into the life stories of those shamans – their 'real' lives and their spiritual lives. The images of spirits I have discussed are in a sense like people in prehistory. They are as much people as the shamans who experienced them and the artists who painted them.

References

Biesele, M. 1978. 'Sapience and scarce resources: communication systems of the !Kung and other foragers', *Social Science Information*, 17: 921–47.

Bleek, D. F. 1935. 'Beliefs and customs of the /Xam Bushmen. Part VII: sorcerors', *Bantu Studies*, 9: 1–47.

Bleek, D. F. 1936. 'Beliefs and customs of the /Xam Bushmen. Part VIII: more about sorcerors and charms', *Bantu Studies*, 10: 131–62.

Bourdieu, P. 1977. *Outline of a Theory of Practice*. Cambridge: Cambridge University Press.

Campbell, C. 1987. 'Art in crisis: contact period rock art in the south-eastern mountains', Master's dissertation, University of the Witwaterstand, Johannesburg.

Dowson, T. A. 1993. 'Changing fortunes of southern African archaeology: comment on A.D. Mazel's history', *Antiquity*, 67: 641–4.

Dowson, T. A. 1994. 'Reading art, writing history: rock art and social change in southern Africa', *World Archaeology*, 25(3): 332–45.

Dowson, T. A. 1995. 'Hunter-gatherers, traders and slaves: the "Mfecane" impact on Bushmen, their ritual and their art', in *The Mfecane Aftermath: Reconstructive Debates in Southern African History* (ed. C. Hamilton). Johannesburg and Pietermaritzburg: Witwaterstand University Press and University of Natal Press, pp. 51–70.

Dowson, T. A. 1997. 'Painting as politics: exposing historical processes in hunter-gatherer rock art', in *Hunters and Gatherers in the Modern World: Conflict Resistance and Self Determination* (eds M. Biesele, R. K. Hitchcock and P. P. Schweitzer). Providence: Berghahn Books.

Dowson, T. A. In press. 'Rain in Bushman belief, politics and history: the rock art of rain-making in the south eastern mountains, southern Africa', in *Rock Art* (eds C. Chippindale and P. Tacon). Cambridge: Cambridge University Press.

Giddens, A. 1979. *Central Problems in Social Theory: Action, Structure and Contradiction in Social Analysis*. Berkeley, CA: University of California Press.

Giddens, A. 1984. *The Constitution of Society*. Cambridge: Polity Press.

Giddens, A. 1991. *Modernity and Self-identity: Self and Society in the Late Modern Age*. Cambridge: Polity Press.

Guenther, M. 1975. 'The trance dancer as an agent of social change among the Farm Bushmen of the Ghanzi District', *Botswana Notes and Records*, 7: 167–70.

Guenther, M. 1975/6. 'The San trance dance: ritual and revitalization among the Farm Bushmen of the Ghanzi District, Republic of Botswana', *Journal of the South West African Scientific Society*, 30: 45–53.

Guenther, M. 1986. *The Nharo Bushmen of Botswana: Tradition and Change*. Hamburg: Helmut Buske Verlag.

Horse Capture, G. 1980. *The Seven Visions of Bull Lodge: As Told by his Daughter, Garter Snake*. Lincoln: University of Nebraska Press.

Lee, R. B. 1968. 'The sociology of !Kung Bushman trance performance', in *Trance and Possession States* (ed. R. Prince). Montreal: R.M. Bucke Memorial Society, pp. 35–54.

Lee, R. B. 1979. *The !Kung: Men, Women and Work in a Foraging Society*. Cambridge: Cambridge University Press.

Lévi-Strauss, C. 1966. *The Savage Mind*. Chicago: Chicago University Press.

Lewis-Williams, J. D. 1981. *Believing and Seeing: Symbolic Meanings in Southern San Rock Paintings*. London: Academic Press.

Lewis-Williams, J. D. 1982. 'The economic and social context of southern San rock art', *Current Anthropology*, 23: 429–49.

Lewis-Williams, J. D. 1988. '"People of the eland". An archaeo-linguistic crux', in *Hunter Gatherers, 2, Property, Power and Ideology* (eds T. Ingold, D. Riches and J. Woodburn). New York: Berg, pp. 203–12.

Lewis-Williams, J. D. 1995. 'Modelling the production and consumption of rock art', *South African Archaeological Bulletin*, 50: 143–54.

Lewis-Williams, J. D. and Dowson, T. A. 1989. *Images of Power: Understanding Bushman Rock Art*. Johannesburg: Southern Book Publishers.

Lewis-Williams, J. D. and Dowson, T. A. 1990. 'Through the veil: San rock paintings and the rock face', *South African Archaeological Bulletin*, 45: 5–16.

Lewis-Williams, J. D. and Loubser, J. H. N. 1986. 'Deceptive appearances: a critique of southern African rock art studies', *Advances in World Archaeology*, 5: 253–89.

Marshall, L. 1969. 'The medicine dance of the !Kung Bushmen', *Africa*, 39: 347–81.

Peires, J.B. 1981. *The House of Phalo: A History of the Xhosa People in the Days of their Independence*. Johannesburg: Ravan Press.

Vinnicombe, P. 1976. *People of the Eland: Rock Paintings of the Drakensberg Bushmen as a Reflection of their Life and Thought*. Pietermaritzburg: Natal University Press.

Wiessner, P. 1984. 'Reconsidering the behavioural basis for style: a case among the !Kung San', *Journal of Anthropological Archaeology*, 3: 190–234.

Wiessner, P. 1989. 'Style and changing relations between the individual and society', in *The Meaning of Things: Material Culture and Symbolic Expression* (ed. I. Hodder). London: Allen & Unwin, pp. 56–63.

Wolff, J. 1981. *The Social Production of Art*. London: Macmillan.

Chapter 10

Chungmoo Choi

THE ARTISTRY AND RITUAL AESTHETICS OF URBAN KOREAN SHAMANS

[. . .]

RECENT SCHOLARS OF RITUAL have tended to view ritual as symbolic action that restructures meaning and creates situations which participants aim to control (Lienhardt 1961; Lévi-Strauss 1967b; Turner 1967, 1969). Ritual in these studies is seen as generating socio-cultural models for participants' use while at the same time providing tools for the analysis of their actual social and historical situation (Geertz 1973). These studies of ritual, however, lead us to the systematic analysis of the public process of the ritual rather than ritual technique itself. Kapferer's recent phenomenological study of Sinhalese exorcism (1983) brings us closer to a poetics of ritual. He shows that the ritual syntax which organizes and orders symbolic action is itself, in Austin's term, illocutionary – it directly brings about the ritual effect (1962: 98). Schieffelin further draws our attention to the nondiscursive dramaturgical and rhetorical levels of performance – the actions, props, costumes, and so forth of the ritual which carry meaning apart from words themselves – as a major force in ritual transformations among the Kaluli of Papua-New Guinea (Schieffelin 1985). These performance-oriented studies show that ritual is a communicative occasion involving metaphor where art, magic, and religion meet.

In this paper I would like to focus on the actors in Korean shamanic rituals, or *kut*. As a contribution to the study of how ritual efficacy is achieved, I will examine how Korean shamans and their clients communicate their feelings and perceptions both through words and through non-discursive ritual and extra-ritual processes; and how these processes together make for ritual performances able to achieve their illocutionary effect – a change in the relationship between spirits and client manifested both in external household fortunes and a desired emotional transformation. I will do this by focusing primarily on interactions between Oksun, her associates and clients that I was able to observe between 1980 and 1986.[1] Oksun, a shaman originating in Hwanghae Province in present-day north Korea, operates today primarily in Seoul, the capital of south Korea. As she is one of the chief representatives of the shamanic tradition of her native province, her clientele tends to be south Koreans of northern origin.

Korea's god-descended female shamans [kangsin mudang], of whom Oksun is an example, are preeminently religious entrepreneurs. Though they have become shamans through an involuntary, personal calling of the gods and are thus mostly sincere in their belief in the efficacy of their ritual (Kendall 1985a: 54–69), they must survive economically by building and maintaining a clientele of regular customers [tan'gol]. The new shaman has an inherent advantage in gaining clients due to the Korean folk belief that her power is fresher and stronger than that of the old, practiced shaman (Harvey 1979: 110). Thus, to hold on to her customers, the experienced shaman must continually prove herself both healer and seer. She must be able to divine the details of her clients' fate in terms of a complicated folk religious soteriology (Kendall 1981). She must also be able to perform theatrically convincing religious rites – complicated procedures involving considerable ritual knowledge and aesthetic skill – in order to transform her clients' misery over misfortune into hope. Elsewhere (Choi 1987: 143–4) I have shown that the robustness of the demand for the individual shaman's services corresponds to the clients' knowledge of the particular regional style of a shaman's ritual and her involvement in the shaman's ritual practice. Here I would like to discuss how successful Korean shamans delicately balance ritual efficacy and aesthetic felicity to come up with convincing dramatic performances.

The shaman prepares: obtaining information

Experienced shamans in Korea consider yŏnghŏm and nunchi'i to be the two quintessential qualities that a successful shaman must possess. Yŏnghŏm, a Chinese loanword, is the spiritual power that produces the efficacy of ritual action. Nunch'i, a native Korean word widely used in everyday life, refers to social sensitivity – one's ability to understand a social situation, to make quick judgments about it and respond appropriately. In order for a shaman to produce the intended effect of a shamanic ritual, she needs both spiritual power and social sensitivity.

Spiritual power manifests itself in the shaman's clairvoyant vision, which is believed to be exceptionally sharp when the gods are newly descended. Oksun, a shaman in her sixties, often reminisced how, when she was first possessed, her vision was *sŏsŭri sip'ŏrŏk'e*, keen and sharp as a freshly sharpened knife. The spiritual power of the shamans, however, is believed to wane like a worn out battery as years go by.[2] When asked if, in fact, a newly possessed person is more powerful than an old shaman, Oksun answered:

> Newly possessed shamans [*saero naerin mudang*] may see more clearly and 'dig out' problems well. But what good is it if they cannot solve the problems? Old shamans have experience. We know how to deal with the problems. Young shamans need experience and ritual skills in addition to spiritual power.

Spiritual power itself, then, needs to be complemented by the problem-solving skills of the mature and competent shaman. Oksun thus claimed that 'the older a shaman grows, the more powerful she becomes.' Old shamans may not have the fresh spiritual power of the novice, but over the years they acquire ritual skills and develop the sensitivity to see the nature of their clients' affliction. This lets them tailor rituals to individual needs, thereby earning them efficacy. This is what sustains a shaman's reputation and establishes her profession.

Korean shamans apply *nunch'i* primarily to constructing clients' realities, based on their social, financial, and emotional situations. Victor Turner reports that a Ndembu diviner over the years familiarizes himself with the social and political scene of each local village, and investigates a client's particular problem within that context (Turner 1967: 361). By and large, Korean shamans follow the same path; villagers acknowledge local shamans' familiarity with social situations and current tensions within the community. In Korea this familiarity is a two-edged sword. One often hears of clients taking the trouble to consult shamans of faraway villages to receive an unbiased diagnosis. A shaman like Oksun living amongst the ten million plus residents of Seoul, moreover, is not blessed with intimate knowledge about most of her clients. In the urban setting a majority of a shaman's clients are newcomers, and her relationship to them does not outlive an initial divination visit. Clients caught up in the fast pace of city life want to learn about the source of their misfortune or their outlook for the future without wasting any time. A shaman's ability to quickly grasp their problems during the narrow time slot of their initial divination interview seems to impress new clients most.

When Oksun receives a client, she needs to do an intense, but quick and unsuspecting, investigation in order to collect the maximum amount of information within a short period of time. In order to make this initial contact the beginning of a more lasting relationship requires many clever maneuvers. Shamans often suggest a ritual performance in the hope of extending their first encounter into a meaningful working relationship but this does not always succeed. Oksun told me that divination is the most difficult skill to master. By this, perhaps, she meant the entire process of studying a client, figuring out his or her fate, and establishing a working relationship rather than the mere technical aspects of divination *per se.*

For the garrulous Oksun, divination is a smooth transition from an apparently innocent conversation. As the client enters the room, she greets her (or sometimes him) simply, gestures for the client to sit down, and continues talking, smoking and giving orders to the kitchen helpers. As if out of courtesy, she throws seemingly casual questions at the visitor. Such an introductory conversation/interrogation normally lasts about an hour. The conversation flows from one topic to another: from television soap operas, to social criticism, or to Oksun's own 'experience stories' which she likes to fabricate by weaving together well-known legend and folktale motifs. Although Oksun occasionally asks for the client's opinion on an issue, clients normally state their feelings in the natural course of conversation. These responses not only reveal the client's personality and background, but they also provide Oksun with an opportunity to study the client and later utilize the information in her ritual practice.

If all goes well, the client will be persuaded of the need for a ritual. The shaman's investigation continues after the ritual date is set. The client needs to meet with the shaman several times to make arrangements for the ritual. Typically, the client makes a down payment at the shaman's altar in order for the shaman to report the occasion to the gods and commence ritual preparation. At this point, the shaman asks the client about the ritual history of her household.[3] Based on this information, the shaman prepares the necessary food items and paper flags. The client also makes additional trips to the shaman's house to discuss matters such as purchasing a pig or clothes for potentially malevolent spirits or other special deities the family may worship. Each point of encounter with the sponsor enriches the shaman's knowledge about the family.

Oksun places functional values on such meetings:

> By preparing spirit clothes you dig out which spirits that family has honored from the time of their ancestors. That's all. You eat the [ritual] food, but who is going to wear the spirits' clothes? You just let them [the spirits represented by the clothes] play during the ritual and burn the clothes later.

I did not understand Oksun's explanation until I saw her preparing a pair of pants for Mrs. Hong's deceased father-in-law. The following is a part of their conversation:

Oksun: How tall was he?
Mrs Hong: He couldn't have been more than a little over five feet.
Oksun: He was quite short, wasn't he?
Mrs Hong: Yes, but . . .

Oksun: But what?

Mrs. Hong: I shouldn't say this about the deceased. But short as he was, he surely was a womanizer. My poor mother-in-law! She didn't know about his concubine and a daughter until after his death.

Oksun: How did she learn?

Mrs. Hong: Well, the woman showed up one day with the daughter. The girl was a perfect image of my father-in-law. The mother and daughter had no means to support themselves. They wanted to sell their house which was under his name. So they came to ask for a legal transfer or to claim child support. We didn't know that the girl was registered as his.

Oksun: And?

Mrs. Hong: After months of fighting – oh, what a fight! – she got neither. We don't know what happened to them thereafter. Rumor has it that the woman died.

Oksun: That is not the way people handle such matters. What he did was abominable, but you should think about his offspring. These days girls are just as good as sons. Add a bowl of rice and a spoon to the ancestor table [for the soul of the concubine] so that she will not try to harm your family. No wonder! I thought I saw a woman [ghost] entering [the family pantheon].

In this encounter, Oksun obtains a vital piece of information: she discovers a potentially vengeful ghost in the family whose presence needs to be dramatized and who needs to be propitiated during the ritual. At every stage of her encounter with clients, Oksun stretches out her antennae to sense their economic, social or emotional state. She is attentive to everyone who comes into her view, whether they are her clients or associates. It seems no one escapes the radius of her observation. She asked me once when I was planning to return to America and I casually mentioned that I could not decide whether I should reside in Korea or America. Several weeks later when Oksun held her own god-receiving ritual [sin maji kut], she gave me an oracle, 'You have two minds now. You cannot decide one way or the other. But don't worry. Things will clear up next year.' I was then already scheduled to return to America the following year.

The shaman acts: translating information

A shaman's social sensitivity is an essential instrument, not only for the successful performance of a ritual, but also for a deeper understanding of her clients. With this sensitivity shamans help their clients get to know themselves, and at the same time develop insights into human nature. Sensitivity is closely linked to an empathy from shamans to clients and from one shaman to another. Shamans, who have experienced symbolic social death in becoming shamans in the first place, and their clients, who may be involved in a trauma, develop a certain sense of solidarity which the shaman can use in her ritual work. She is able to turn spirits into allies of her clients and transform their despair into hope partially because of this solidarity. At the same time, she needs aesthetic skills. Bogatyrev has argued persuasively (1976) that the transformation of emotion widely found in magical and religious ceremonies is also an essential element of successful theatrical performance. However, as Schechner notes (1981), theatrical performance seeks an aesthetic effect which is in and of itself the efficacy of performance, while ritual uses aesthetics in order to achieve a religious efficacy which is beyond that of performance.

The spectators at a Korean shamanic ritual, or *kut*, evaluate the shaman's performance based on two categories of skill: that of presenting artistic forms and that of eliciting emotion. The former involves the orchestration of multiple artistic genres: myths, low comedy, music, dance, songs; visual forms such as costumes, paintings, sculptured artifacts; gestures, facial expressions, and bodily movements. Well-refined and sophisticated artistic skills are believed to be god-given and thus, a sign of numinosity. By the same logic highly developed artistic skills are believed to help attain ritual efficacy. On the one hand, overdone artistic performance in which aesthetic considerations outweigh the religious efficacy of the *kut* is often suspected of quackery, but on the other hand, a stripped-down version of ritual loses its 'flavor' [*mat*] or beauty [*mŏt*].

To the tradition-bound clients, familiar ritual style invokes nostalgia. But more importantly, a shaman's fidelity to convention gives them a sense of efficacy because their belief has been shaped according to those conventions. As Tambiah has asserted, adherence to convention is an important aspect of magic, perhaps more so than the efficacy of the magic itself (Tambiah 1973b). This preference for tried and true tradition is reflected in the preference of Seoul residents for shamans who perform the ceremonies of their native region. Mrs. Yŏm, a refugee from P'yŏngyang, present-day capital of north Korea, is a regular client of Nami, a shaman who originated in Hwanghae Province and has now been designated a human cultural asset [*in'gan munhwajae*][4] because of her traditional ritual knowledge. Mrs. Yŏm claims she does not feel a ritual of the south worked for her because the ceremony did not look like a true *kut*. Shrimp Mansin,[5] another shaman from Hwanghae Province who now works out of Inch'ŏn, the port for Seoul, often traveled several hundred miles south, riding a bus on a bumpy country road, to perform a ritual for a family from Hwanghae Province. She proudly told me that there were many god-descended shamans in the area, but this one family insisted on having a shaman from their native province perform ceremonies.

If one criterion of efficacy is the aesthetic skill of the performance, another is the emotional effect the shaman is able to create. The shaman's skill at eliciting emotion is often measured by the amount of tears the audience sheds. An audience at *kut* expects to cry at some point regardless of the stated purpose of the ritual. It is widely believed that a shaman who makes the audience cry during the ritual is an able one. By this it is implied that the audience expects two things from the performing shaman: understanding the deep-seated origin of the client's problem, and an ability to bring it to the attention of the assembled audience in an affecting way. The shaman's interpretation of the issue should address the shared convictions of the community in order to win recognition and emotional response.

When narrating myths, therefore, shamans try hard to affectingly portray the feelings of the myths' *dramatis personae*. Often during a séance shamans force themselves to recall the loss of their own dear ones as a means of internalizing their clients' feelings or that of the *dramatis personae* in their myths so that they can convey sympathy and awaken the feelings of the audience. A hereditary East Coast shaman, Namsun,[6] once narrated the myth of Simch'ŏng, a girl who had to be raised in abject poverty by her blind father upon the death of her mother, during a village ritual [*pyŏlsin kut*] in a fishing hamlet. When in the narrative Simch'ŏng's father describes his wife's death and how his infant daughter was left behind in his helpless arms, the shaman began lamenting. Gradually her crying intensified. Namsun called out to her own daughter who had died two years before, 'Oh, my poor daughter! You had to die at such a young age!' The performative act of this lament evoked deeper feelings of loss than the myth alone could have done. Toward the end of the ritual the shaman simply called out her daughter's name. The sympathy from the audience, which was already ascending in the context of the pathos of the myth, peaked. They began to cry. Whether they were crying for Namsun or for the *dramatis personae* of the myth, it was difficult to tell. In the formulaic structure of the ritual and the narration, the motivation of the emotional outbreak was less significant than its effect – the flow of emotion between the performer and the audience.

That this emotional effect is specifically sought by shamans came home to me when I observed the drummer for Oksun's ritual, Dark Grandmother,[7] coaching a fifteen-year old disciple of Oksun, Aegi Mansin, in how to bring these deep emotions out. Under the pretext of teaching the young shaman the song of the soul's final departure [*siwang karŭgi*] in the *ogi kut*, a ceremony aimed at facilitating the departure of restless souls to the next world,[8] this expert drummer added an acting lesson.

> You have to sing this song very slowly, because it's a requiem. As you divide the Ten King Bridge,[9] you call and honor the names of each netherworldly king in the following manner: the . . . fir-r-rst . . . ki-i-ng . . . the . . . ki-i-ing . . . of pri-mor-di-al . . . li-ght . . . You should pause at each syllable. Imagine you are dead and you are going to the other world. Do you think you would

leave your family behind and cross the bridge? Your feet would be stuck to the ground. But you must go. That is death. So you, the shaman, stop and wail, because you are so reluctant but forced to go. The onlookers then cry together with the shaman. Then money heaps on the bridge. That is how you sing this song. Now try. I will beat the drum slowly.

What the young shaman learned was an important acting skill which Stanslavski would call 'recreating emotional memory' (Moor 1984: 42) through the subtext of behavior (Moor 1984: 68–72). The experience of the character that an actor creates is different from an experience in life, so the actor projects a poetic reflection of his or her own life's experience. The emotional memory retains not only an imprint of an experience but the essence of the feelings related to that experience.

In order to bring out this essence, an actor needs to rely on the subtext. The subtext is a mental process or inner thought of the actor which is revealed in his or her interpretation of a play for an effective dialogue with the audience. The shaman's slow and rhythmic steps into the bridge between life and death, along with the suppressed and reluctant calling of the ten netherworldly kings, are expressions of a subtext: the helplessness of human beings before overpowering conditions and the destiny that ruthlessly forces life into the realm of death. An able shaman is expected to effectively bring out such extreme human emotions during her ritual performance. Distilling information collected from a client into proficient performance is just as important as breaking through the unrevealed information about a client for divination purposes. It includes not only mastery of the details of ritual and artistic effect but also the art of distilling the information collected into an emotionally affecting subtext and this requires a performer's sensitivity to the overall needs of the audience.

Ritual performance and the transformation of emotion

How these considerations are all brought together to allow shamans to evoke unresolved emotions through dramatic means can be seen in the following ceremony for sending souls to the other world held by the Kang family. The Kangs are war refugees from Hwanghae Province. Though now living in Seoul, they first settled in Kyŏngsang Province in the southeast after fleeing from north Korea. There Mrs. Kang's four daughters and one son grew up. Mrs. Kang had become possessed by spirits when she was still young and had been shamanizing until the marriage of her eldest daughter Mrs. Yi.[10] Soon Mrs. Yi's husband discovered that Mrs. Kang was a shaman. He began drinking, abusing his wife and even threatened to divorce her.[11] Under intense pressure from her family, Mrs. Kang finally quit shamanizing.

Soon misfortune began to fall upon the family. Mrs. Yi's husband lost his job and has been unemployed ever since. Mrs. Yi was forced to close down a small eatery she ran. The entire family had to move into Mrs. Kang's house. Mrs. Yi's oldest daughter, a high-school chemistry teacher, has been the sole breadwinner for Mrs. Yi's household of three adults and two high school students. Ch'ol, the only son and on whom the family had set their hopes, failed the college entrance exam for two consecutive years. During the preparation for the third attempt he hanged himself.

Mrs. Kang's third daughter also had had a troubled life. She was a runner-up in a beauty contest and a rich Korean-Japanese businessman became attracted to her. He fathered Chun, her illegitimate and only son. Mrs. Kang had raised Chun with the money that his father sent him, while Chun's mother married another man, Mr. Kim. Chun's mother and Mr. Kim have two daughters. Although Chun's mother rescued Mrs. Kang from several financial crises, according to Oksun, the greedy matriarch demanded more money from her daughter. When Mr. Kim's affection wandered, Chun's mother could no longer meet Mrs. Kang's demand for further financial support. Mrs. Kang returned Chun to his mother, stepfather and half sisters. The boy, who could not adjust to the new family situation with a rejecting stepfather, hanged himself at the age of fourteen.

The temptation to return to shamanizing, and her guilt for not obeying the call of the spirits, have haunted Mrs. Kang and her daughters.[12] Although she is not presently operating as a professional shaman, Mrs. Kang keeps her own shrine in the back of her house as a way of keeping her spirits content. The great fear of the daughters is that their mother may someday resume the role of a shaman. They are attempting to convince her that they should help her build a small Buddhist temple to channel her spiritual energy into a 'nobler cause' when the family finances improve.

The ritual scene summarized below occurred in October, 1981. It was an ancestor séance [chosang kut], a section of an ogi kut, an elaborate ritual to send the souls of the dead – especially the soul of the most recently deceased, Ch'ol – to the other world. The family had had ogi kut performed three times in less than six months and yet Mrs. Yi could not eliminate the residue of her shock and fear from having been exposed to the unexpected death of her only son. This was the fourth ritual.

Oksun, the regular shaman of the Kang family, presided over the team of shamans doing the ceremony. As head shaman, she started the ceremony and invoked the major gods who should be present. A separate offering table had been set up on the veranda [maru] a wooden floored room located approximately at the center of the house between the Inner Room [anbang] of the house mistress where the main altar for the rite was set, and the Opposite Room [kŏnnŏbang] occupied by Mrs. Kang's married son and his family. Besides the rice and other regular offerings, wine cups for the ancestors and one bowl of seaweed soup were also set on the table. The seaweed soup indicated that a woman in the family died in childbirth.[13] Also by the offering table were an aluminum tea kettle containing *makkŏlli*, a kind of rice beer, and a bottle of Western-style beer with a tall glass. One could surmise that this family experienced the death of a youth, for bottled beer is a relatively new liquor that originated in the West and is popular among members of the younger generation. The predominant color of both the rice cake and the shaman's coat was yellow, symbolizing the spirits of the ancestors.

After Oksun initiated the early important parts of the ceremony, she entrusted the ancestor ceremony to her colleague, Samyangdong Mansin. Although it is highly unusual in a shamanic ceremony, this particular *chosang kut* was preceded by a Confucian-style offering of liquor to the ancestors. After the libation, Samyangdong Mansin picked up a bundle of bells and a long strip of white cotton, called the 'ten king bridge' [*siwang tari*], which will lead the spirits to the other world. The gong and the hourglass-shaped drum began to play. Holding bells in one hand and the bridge in the other, Samyangdong Mansin began dancing slowly and then stopped. Her eyes were closed and her lips were moving slightly as if she were muttering a spell. Her words, however, were totally inaudible. Occasionally she shook the bells or quickly jerked her shoulders a few times, a gesture indicating the entrance of the spirits into her body.

As the spirits descended, the sound of the gong intensified and the drum beat faster. Then both come to an abrupt stop. The Kangs now stood in line against the furniture along the wall of the veranda across from the musicians.[14] Samyangdong Mansin shook the bells loudly once more and stopped. She broke the silence suddenly. An ancestor spirit manifested itself.

During this section of the *kut*, the shaman manifesting the spirits interchangeably used both third person ('He [the god] says he is grateful that you invited him . . .') and first person ('I [the god] just came here for sightseeing . . .'), thus creating distance between herself and the spirit. Moreover, the distance in the relationship between the spirits appearing out of the benighted, remote past and the family is mirrored in the use of the impersonal third person form of address.

In Samyangdong Mansin's mind, the important spectators were Mrs. Kang's grown-up children, the sponsors of the *kut*, rather than Mrs. Kang herself, since she announced 'Mom's father-in-law' as the entering spirit. To these grown-up children whose father (Mrs. Kang's husband) was a second son, their grandfather is almost a stranger and the remotest ancestor that they can remember. He was not even informed of the suicide of the child of his granddaughter. He came to the ritual feast lightheartedly, like a tourist sightseeing, and showed only slight sympathy and concern. His words were transmitted through the shaman mostly in the third person. But when it comes to the sensitive issue, Ch'ol's suicide, the shaman switched from the third person to the first person. This brought the spirit and the spectators closer together. Solace even from an unknown ancestor strengthened the unity of the family in time of disaster and provided moral support.

Between the invocation of the spirits of Mrs. Kang's parents-in-law and that of Mrs. Kang's husband, several spirits, which are unknown to the family, entered. Following these, the spirit of Mrs. Kang's brother-in-law, whom no one knew, also entered. His entrance created a great deal of disputation among the family members. I recall, however, that during the morning Oksun had casually asked Mrs. Kang the identity of the young man whose shade Oksun 'saw' entering the ritual hall. Mrs. Kang's answer had been vague. According to Oksun there was a death of a youth among Mrs. Kang's children. No one in the family offered me any information.

As the spirit of Mrs. Kang's husband entered, the oracle became more lively and life-like, speaking in the first person. Samyangdong Mansin was no longer a mediator. She impersonated the spirit. The content of the oracle was no longer abstract, but concrete with realistic details: 'I am worried about the forty-six-year-old. [The father's spirit does not call his daughter, Mrs. Yi, by her name but by her age.] She only thinks about her dead son. He [Ch'ol] was pessimistic about the world. He became wayward for he did not pass his adolescence properly and could not have his way.'

The manifestation of Mrs. Kang's husband's spirit marked the end of the old generation of ancestors. The ancestor séance culminated at the manifestation of Ch'ol's spirit for whom the ritual was performed.

> Samyangdong: Grandma, I'm here. [Everyone cries loudly. The drummer, Dark Grandmother's eyes are filled with tears]. Ah, my poor grandma. [The shaman also cries].

After several minutes of interaction between spirit and spectators, the climax of the ceremony was reached.

> Samyangdong: Auntie, I often thought that I was good for nothing. I was not a good student. I was not accepted by my friends. So I wasted my life. Mom, now that you heard me speaking, please don't cry for me. Your crying won't bring me back alive. Oh, what am I supposed to do now! [Samyangdong Mansin started wailing. Mrs. Yi, who has been sobbing and crying, had now collapsed on the floor. Everyone but Chun's mother, who lost her son a year ago, joined in.]
> Chun's mother: Well, let's dance. Dance with Auntie. [She stands up and dances into the middle of the hall as Dark Grandmother plays a rock 'n roll beat on her hourglass-shaped drum.]
> Samyangdong: [has now stopped crying] Samyangdong Mansin does not know how to dance to this kind of music.
> Chun's mother: You dance. *You.* [Chun's mother and Samyangdong

Mansin danced a few minutes to the drum, and some among the
audience clapped their hands to the music.]

Mrs. Kang's youngest daughter: Play the guitar. You danced to the
guitar not to the hourglass-shaped drum. [The suggestion was
ignored and the music ended.]

Samyangdong: [To Mrs. Yi.] You know my friend who comes here.

Mrs. Yi: You mean Kilsu?

Samyangdong: Yeah. Give him all my books. Also give him one of
the speakers.

Mrs. Yi: That is not yours. I bought them. Also they come in a pair.
If you give him one . . .

Samyangdong: Just give that away. When I go I will sweep away
and take all your fear with me.

After several more minutes of interaction, loud music began indicating the
departure of Ch'ol's spirit. The music was continued into the next scene
without a break, then Chun's spirit entered to interact with his mother.
Following this equally highly emotional section of the séance, Samyangdong
Mansin led a song of blessing and the musicians repeated the refrain. She
slowly tore the fabric bridge to Paradise along its length down the middle
while singing:

The first, Great King of Primordial Light.
Namu Amit'abul [Namah Amitābha]
The second, Great King of True Light.
Namu Amit'abul . . .

The song continued until the tenth king of the other world was honored and
the souls had passed through Hell.

During the séance of Ch'ol and Chun, Samyangdong Mansin impersonated the two boys and never once spoke in the third-person to distance herself
as a shaman. This created a sense of total actor-character flow. She dramatically
presented the emotional state of the deceased family members, especially that
of Ch'ol. By expressing the regret of the boy, the shaman portrayed his likely
feelings and also projected the feelings of the family into the spirit of a person
who ended his life. The mortal encountered the immortal in an emotionally
charged field. In this field, outside the realm of reality, the feelings of mother
and son came together. Chun's mother's timely interruption ('Let's dance')
was an attempt to recover a normal state of mind. Notice that the moment she
interrupted was a time of intense emotion. She helped Mrs. Yi (and others)
return to reality. The shaman sensitively responded to this intention of Chun's
mother: she comically carried out the role of a charming playboy and even
exaggerated the characteristics by which the members of his family would like
to remember him.

Samyangdong Mansin did not forget the most important purpose of the ritual: to restore the normalcy of life. In her judgement, this meant restoring the social integration of the living. This could only be accomplished by completely severing emotional ties between the living and the dead. She ordered the family to give away his books, his guitar and part of his music system, all of which were objects of major importance in Ch'ol's life. Samyangdong Mansin used the common wisdom, 'out of sight, out of mind.' She ordered the family to rid itself of the material residue that could evoke the memory of the boy. By accelerating the memory loss, Samyangdong Mansin attempted what even ancestors cannot accomplish (see the oracle of Mr. Kang's husband): to restore a normal state of mind and the strength to cope with reality.

Ch'ol's final words for his mother showed everyone's concern for Mrs. Yi. Very likely she had a great deal of fear from the shock of witnessing her only son's suicide. With these final words, the shaman assured Mrs. Yi that Ch'ol is returning to the other world forever, so his spirit will no longer hover over the house and bother her.[15]

From ritual to theater and back

Samyangdong Mansin was interchanging the role of narrator and the *dramatis personae*. The shaman's method of both total absorption into the character being impersonated and the reflexivity demonstrated by speaking about the character is a familiar feature of the traditional bard-actors of Korea known as *kwangdae* who sing folk tales [*p'ansori*] in a combination of narration and first person impersonation of the characters. These actors easily transpose from first person into the third person, and from present to past. They also give stage directions during their performance. Such theatrical technique is widely utilized in East Asian drama. Brecht adopted it from Chinese theater to develop his theory/technique of the alienation-effect (Brecht 1964). Rather than consistently maintaining the illusion that a dramatic performance is reality, by this technique performers constantly change the frame of reference of the dramatization. This has the effect of alienating audiences from the illusion of the performance and reminding them that they are not passive spectators to a real event. What Brecht found through this technique, however, is a method through which the actors and audiences discover the true conditions of life, and this is also what the participants in ritual discover.

Samyangdong Mansin effectively utilized these theatrical devices. However, what is more intriguing perhaps than the use of these devices is that during the ancestor séance, the shaman gradually deepened the transformation of the character role in proportion to the emotional distance between the spectators and the spirits of the ancestors. One can easily see the conspicuous use of the third person when Mrs. Kang's parents-in-law were evoked. The frequency of the third person was gradually reduced as the spirits of the close kin manifested themselves, and finally petered out when the spirits of the most recently deceased were evoked. Samyangdong Mansin completely imperson- ated Ch'ol and Chun. Unlike the theater, however, such total impersonation is ritually validated and illocutionary, since it *creates*, not just symbolizes, the ancestral presences.[16] The gradual lead-in process from the distant and less consequential to the immediate and direct helped to establish the therapeutic reality of the final encounter.

Schechner (1981: 88) has observed that during a play, a 'between persona' is developed by the actor in the role he or she plays.

> Olivier is not Hamlet, but also he is not not Hamlet: his performance is between a denial of being another (= I am me) and a denial of not being another (= I am Hamlet). Performer training focuses its techniques not on making one person into another, but in permitting the performer to act in-between identities; in this sense performing is a paradigm of liminality.

Goldman (1975) calls this an actor's freedom. He argues that this doubleness of the actor is the very energy that entices the audience: the ghostly uncanni- ness created by the actor's free shift of identities as well as his abnormal exposure to and dependence on the audience as a person.

In the shamanic séance, the sense of being taken over by the spirits, as well as speaking about the spirits as a shaman, are ritually conditioned. The shaman's doubling creates an illusion of multiple realities, and the shaman likewise performs in a liminal field between negative (not spirit) and double negative (not not spirit). This is a field of potential transformation, as it is the area where the shadows of both the performer and the descended spirit are cast. In this field of liminality communitas develops (Turner 1969) and seals the emotional unity of the participants in the helplessness of the human condi- tion. During the ancestor séance the spirits of the dead and the living meet in this field of illusion. In this unity the emotion of the living and the imagined emotion of the spirit (e.g. Ch'ol's lament about the irreversibility of time) become one, and this later brings forth the change of feelings which is the ritual effect. The family accepts the reality of the loss of a loved one free from fear of its uncanny spirit. Samyangdong Mansin used her skill as a brilliant actress to help the client achieve this emotional transformation.

[. . .]

Notes

1   The fieldwork upon which this paper was based was done primarily in Seoul in 1980–1981 and 1985–1986. Funding for the 1985–1986 fieldwork was provided by an ACLS-SSRC grant.

2   Borgoras reports a similar belief among the Chukchee shamans (Bogoras 1909: 419).

3   In addition to a tradition, which is passed on from mother-in-law to daughter-in-law, about which gods are worshipped in the household, most Korean houses also have miscellaneous ancestral spirits that are worshipped due to events of their family history. For example, an aunt or uncle who died young or a grandmother who had an especially strong body-governing spirit might need special treatment. See Kendall (1985: 71–4).

4   See Howard (*JRS* 3/2) for more information on the cultural asset system. See also Chungmoo Choi, 'Hegemony and Shamanism: the State, the Elite and the Shamans in Contemporary Korea,' *Religion and Contemporary Korean Society*, Lewis Lancaster ed., (Berkeley: Univ. of California, Institute of East Asian Studies, forthcoming) and Chungmoo Choi, 'Superstar Shaman, Mass Media and Capitalism in Korea,' *Shamans in the Twentieth Century*, Ruth-Inge Heinze, ed. (NY: Harper & Row, forthcoming).

5   Mansin [ten thousand gods] is a polite designation for shamans who are more bluntly called *mudang*.

6   See Ch'oe Kil-sŏng (*JRS* 3/2) for a discussion of the distinction between god-descended and hereditary shamans.

7   Dark Grandmother was the major drummer for Oksun. Drummers act as stage directors at *kut* and tend to be very important for the training of novices.

8   This ceremony, the concluding section of *kut* for the dead, involves sending souls along a white cloth [*siwang tari*] which symbolizes the transit through Buddhist hell. At the end of the passage, the cloth is rent to prevent the return of souls to this world to bother people. More of this *kut* is described later in this paper. For a description of a similar ritual in another regional tradition see Sorensen (1988).

9   Ten King Bridge: the road past the ten judges of Buddhist Hell to whom one must make account before proceeding to the Western Pure Land. It is normally symbolized by a long sheet of white cloth.

10   Persistent signs of spirit possession outside of normal ritual situations is usually taken as a sign that a spirit has chosen someone as their mouthpiece. According to folk belief, though spirits will pick on people who have been weakened in some way, it is not their fault that they are so afflicted. Normally the only way to manage this sort of possession is to acquiesce and become a mouthpiece of the god, that is, become a shaman. There were also rumors, however, that Mrs. Kang's mother had also been a god-descended shaman.

11   Although many (but not all) shamans make a good living and have great prestige within the shamanizing community, the status of shaman is in general greatly looked down upon. Having a shaman in the family can ruin the entire family's social status.

12   According to folk belief the termination of serving the gods is likely to induce them to cause misfortune. Mrs. Kang's keeping of a private shrine is intended to prevent this from happening.

13   Seaweed soup [*miyŏk kuk*] with rice is the first food that is given to a new mother.

14   The large amount of furniture stacked there was due to the fact that several households had been forced to amalgamate into a single house.

15   The motivation for the ceremony in the first place was the assumption that a person too overcome by grief is being bothered because a restless spirit is hovering around

the house rather than going to the other world. The purpose of the ceremony then was to distance this soul from the person bothered by it.

16   Often spirits which no one knew existed beforehand came into being because they 'show up' at shaman ceremonies.

Chapter 11

Marina Roseman

REMEMBERING TO FORGET
The aesthetics of longing

WHEN A DREAM SONG resounds in ceremonial performance, it becomes a path linking spiritguide, medium, chorus, and patient. Singing is accompanied by bamboo-tube percussion: female chorus members each beat the high-pitched and low-pitched members of a pair of bamboo-tube stampers in alternation against a log. The duple rhythm of these beating tubes is linked in a web of local meanings that extends from pulsating sounds of the rainforest to the beating of the human heart. In order to entice the spirits to attend ceremonial performances (and to prepare their human hosts to greet them), the sentiment of longing is modulated through symbolically laden sounds of the stamping tubes and bodily movements of the dancers. The beating tubes play upon the evocative power Temiars attach to pulsating sounds; by moving the emotions, the sounds of the tubes set the spirits in motion.

The sentiment of longing pervades the relationships of spirit-guides with mediums, illness agents with ill persons, and humans with humans among the Temiars. The sentiments of longing and remembrance are aesthetically coded in sound and movement within Temiar everyday life and ceremonial perform- ance. Sounds of the tropical rainforest, such as particular bird and insect calls, are imbued by the Temiar with meaning and power to evoke longing and remembrance. Ceremonial performances make use of structurally similar sounds to intensify the longing and remembering that lead to the forgetfulness of trance. When longing is intensified beyond the proper bounds, illness occurs. The aesthetic sensibilities evoking longing and remembrance thus interweave the contexts of spirit-mediumship, courtship, trancing, and curing.

Remembering to forget

Toraja ritual specialists in Sulawesi act as receptacles for the collective memory or traditions of the ancestors; Coville (1984) describes these ritual specialists as 'those-who-remember.' In contrast, Toraja trance-dancers, whose links are with the divinities rather than the ancestors, are 'those-who-forget':

> It is not surprising . . . that when [trance-dancers] return to consciousness (or rather when they are brought back by the audience and the *to minaa* [ritual specialists]), the trance-dancers have no memory about what has transpired when under the influence of the divinities. Their inability to remember makes them the inverse of the *to minaa*. So we have, on the one hand, the conscious ones who remember and, on the other, the unconscious ones who forget. Those-who-remember submit as credentials for the task their link (through birth and/or practice, and only rarely through revelation) to the beginnings of culture. Those-who-forget, on the other hand, are certified or authenticated by their direct link to the Upperworld.
>   There is a trade-off, then, between objectified power inscribed in the knowledge of ritual and transient experience of power enacted in trance.
>
> (Coville 1984:7)

Among Temiars, a trade-off occurs within the single individual: everyday knowledge and experience is forgotten, displaced by the remembering of the dream-time and connection with the spirit guide. In his discussion of multiple realities, Schutz suggests that the various worlds 'of dreams, of imageries and phantasms, especially the world of art, the world of religious experience . . .' constitute 'finite provinces of meaning,' each with their own peculiar cognitive style and specific 'tension of consciousness' (1967:232). Participation in one province of meaning replaces participation in another province of meaning, each respectively contributing to a total frame of reference. The provinces of meaning, I would suggest, need not always be finite: participation in one province might overlay or intersect another, rendering 'nonfinite' provinces of meaning.

The theme of longing and remembrance begins with the dreams in which Temiar mediums first meet spiritguides. During dreams, the soul of an entity such as a fruit tree detaches itself and emerges in humanized form, male or female. It speaks to the roaming head soul of the Temiar dreamer: 'I come to you, I desire you. I want to be your teacher, I want to call you father.' The acquaintance is thus begun in a melange of desire,[1] pedagogy, and kinship. Male mediums often speak of their female spiritguides as 'wives' in addition to their being 'children.' Bemoaning the fate of transitory dream encounters, they comment: 'I sleep with her at night, but in the morning, my bed is empty.'

The longings initiated and momentarily fulfilled during dreams are later recapitulated and intensified during ceremonial performances. Singing at first with his own voice, crouching on the floor with eyes closed and hand cupped over his ear, listening at once deep within himself and far away, the medium 'causes [the spirit] to emerge' (na-tərɛlhəwal < həwal 'to emerge'). Continuing to sing, standing, beginning to dance, the medium becomes imbued with the voice, vision, and knowledge of the spiritguide.

The singing medium is transformed; his simultaneous presence of body and absence of self is described as 'one's heart being elsewhere, to the side,' hup 'ɛh 'ɛn-tuuy 'əh. This is contrasted with the state of normal consciousness, 'true heart,' hup mʉn. The transformation is effected when the medium recalls the tune and text taught to him during dreams. Remembering the dream song, he attains the forgetfulness (wɛlwəl) of trance. It is both a loss and a finding, a 'forgetting' of everyday knowledge and a 'remembering' of the spiritguide.

This point may help us understand the seeming abandon yet stylized control of trance behavior. One dimension, the everyday dimension of bounded souls, is forgotten, while another one of dreams and spiritguides is recalled. Thus, while mediums or trancers 'forget' themselves and their surroundings, nontrancing participants (particularly women) will call out jokingly: 'Remember (kɛɛk)! The dogs will bite!' – counteracting the fall toward oblivion with a joke. Overly rowdy and haphazard movements will be met with the reminder, 'Trance beautifully, remember!' The impetus to forget is thus bounded on the other side; one must remember to remain within the parameters of stylized abandon.

The medium's voice becomes the spiritguide's vocalization; his heart is elsewhere, but the potential emptiness of longing is filled by the presence of the emergent spiritguide. Uncontrolled longing leads to the illness of soul loss, in which human souls are attracted out to live in the jungle with the spirits. However, when the emotion of longing is controlled in the contexts of dreaming, singing, and trancing, spirits are instead attracted into the human realm of ceremonial performance.

The spiritguide is the source of knowledge that it 'returns' to the spiritmedium, who will remember upon 'returning home' to consciousness that which has been revealed during trance. The general flow of knowledge in the context of trance and spirit-mediumship is from the jungle into the household. Funneled through mediums and trance-dancers, knowledge is dispersed into the female chorus (as they repeat each line sung by the medium), and into the community-at-large. Both active and passive participation constitute participation; there is no audience per se. Everyone present inside the ceremonial house is a witness and therefore a participant in the event, a recipient to some degree of the cool spiritual liquid that flows into the household concurrently with song. For the more active participants, a momentary displacement of self is intensified then replaced by the emergent spiritguide.

Unrequited longing that is not fulfilled leads to the illness of 'soul loss,' rɛywaay. Here, the direction of energy is reversed. Instead of the movement of knowledge from jungle to household exemplified by emergent spiritguides attracted during ceremonies, the soul of the ill person is drawn to the jungle, seduced by a spiritguide into residing far from that person's settlement. It is as if there were a continuous tug-of-war in progress, with humans attempting to draw the spirits into their realm during ceremonies, while spirits likewise attempt to draw humans into their realm, reportedly 'twisting' and 'breaking off' the head soul as if it were a young plant shoot. But the dynamics of the interaction are rarely phrased in terms of antagonism; rather, they are phrased in terms of longing and attraction.

The aesthetics of longing

Temiar mediums are predominantly male; their spiritguides are predominantly female.[2] Overtones of longing, flirtation, enticement, and seduction pervade the cross-sexual relationship between humans and spiritguides.[3] The term hɛwhɔyaaw is central to the conceptual complex of longing and remembrance as it crosscuts dimensions of spirit-mediumship, courtship, trancing, and curing.[4] A Temiar medium comments:

> One hears it in one's ear, like wind: 'Yaaw-waaw-waaw.' If we sit, dream, we hear this in our ear, it's uncomfortable. We must have a singing ceremony, it orders us to have a trance-dancing ceremony, only then are we relieved. Otherwise, after a while, we would go mad. [Hɛwhɔyaaw] is like a hot, dry wind rustling the leaves when there is no rain; we must hold a ceremony.
>
> (Abilem Lum, September 1981, FN 659)

Similarly, when a man sees a beautiful woman, or a woman thinks of a man she longs for, the sentiment evoked is hɛwhɔyaaw. It is an unfulfilled longing, the type of remembrance referred to as 'pining for,' pulling at one's heart.

A related term, referring both to lovesickness and the feelings intensified in trance, is bɔrɛnlii' bɔrɔlaaw.[5] A Temiar man explains:

> Bɔrɛnlii': I lose my appetite, my heart is elsewhere, it's not right. I start walking without purpose; one eventually can become crazy. It's both good and bad, a longing, like when one remembers a boyfriend or when one looks across a beautiful vista. When we trance-dance, it becomes bɔrɛnlii' in our hearts.
>
> (Bawik, August 1982, FN 1905)

Both *hɛwhɔyaaw* and *bɔrɛnlii' bɔrɔlaaw* are expressives built by re-duplicative play from the roots [*hɔ*]*yaaw* and [*bɔ*]*laaw* respectively (see Diffloth 1976; Benjamin 1976: 177–178). The words describing the sentiment of longing are formally linked through onomatopoeia with Temiar utterances describing sounds considered to evoke the sentiment: *yaaw-waaw-waaw* (pressure in the ears; also, the call of the cicada (*hɛrɲɔɔd*), *laaw-laaw* (the call of another cicada species, *jajaa' kɔwaraay*), *howaaw howaaw* (Golden-throated barbet calls).[6] This linguistic clue to the centrality and consistent patterning of sound in the complex of longing and remembrance is borne out by the structure of the sounds themselves.

The song 'The Way of the Perah Tree'[7] was inspired when the medium Abilem fell asleep under a Perah tree during the fruit season, while listening to the persistently pulsating call of the cicada *hɛrɲɔɔd*. In his dream, the male Perah tree spiritguide listened to the female cicada head soul's calls and, falling in love, began to verse. The themes of attraction, longing, and courtship are expressed in Perah's verse: '*Hɛwhɔyaaw rasaan hɛrɲɔɔd*,' 'Pulsating, longing, the feeling of the cicada *hɛrɲɔɔd*.'

In everyday life, cicada calls are said to move one's heart to longing for a loved one. The pulsating, rhythmic sounds of cicadas and certain bird species are said to pulse and whirl with one's heart. Pulsing with the heartbeat, the sounds of these birds and insects set the heart to whirling as they invoke re-membrances of deceased relatives or move one to pine for a lover. Cicada calls are also very hard to localize; like longings, they are hard to find a place for.

The same expressions are used to describe the pulsating duple rhythm of the bamboo percussion as it beats with one's heartbeat, and the whirling feelings in the heart during trance. This aesthetic sensibility links longing and remembrance with the pulsating sounds of bird calls, insect sounds, and the bamboo-tube stampers of ceremonial trance-dancing sessions.

Female trance-dancers also describe their participation in singing cere-monies as an intensification and culmination of longing for male spirits. We recall a Temiar woman's comment [. . .]:

> '*Bɔrɛnlii*'. It is just like *hɛwhɔyaaw*. There is a male spirit of the fruits that desires to sleep with me. Even when I dream, he's there. After a while, one doesn't feel right, one's heart is shaky, one thinks only of him, one wants to go off into the jungle, one's spirit is drawn to the jungle. I must participate in a singing ceremony, only then can I stand it. We sing and dance, the male spirit of the fruit trees alights on the leaf ornaments, and I am transformed.
>
> (LBK, Pulat, 24 July 1982, FN 1822).

The content and structure of this monologue are remarkably similar to Abilem Lum's description of *hɛwhɔyaaw* quoted earlier. Both monologues describe a situation of discomfort (the pounding pressure in the ear; the longing for the male fruit-tree spirit) that can only be relieved by participating in a singing/trance-dancing ceremony.

Musical activity connects humans and spiritguides: performance of songs first given in dreams manifests the spiritguides who gave them. Singing and trance-dancing ceremonies do not, however, merely function as a 'stress release' when they relieve accumulated longing and discomfort. A stress release model would not explain the aesthetic elaboration, the poetics of this particular release. The Temiar, in fact, are longing for the very activity which is the release of longing; the ceremony *intensifies* the sentiment of longing in order to effect its 'release.' A Temiar spirit seance gets rid of longing by *playing* on it, a modulation rather than a simple evacuation. Temiars are not escaping their longings through a quick fix; instead, they move ritually into the space of desire and let themselves live with wistful sadness. Projecting the object of desire onto the spirit-world, they create a ceremony in which they can bring the spirits back to them through song and dance, momentarily fulfilling otherwise inchoate longings.

The sentiment of longing is not only phrased in terms of cross-sexual attraction among humans and spirit-entities. The longing has to do with absence, evanescence, and the unobtainably distant. Sometimes pulsating bird calls evoke longing not for a lover, but for a deceased relative. *Hɛwhɔyaaw* is also the feeling evoked by a vista – a rare and moving sight for the Temiar, who are continually submerged in the denseness of tropical vegetation. The spirit-guides commonly leap across mountains and soar above the clouds; humans only glimpse the rare vista when their trails chance to lead up hills and mountains. The evanescent moment of transition and transformation during sunset evokes *bɔrɛnlii' bɔrɔlaaw* with images of coolness, black silhouette against the red glow, and greenish tints described in song texts.

Longing in the late afternoon: instrumental music

Many of the rainforest species whose songs evoke longing begin to call in the late afternoon, as the sun gets lower and the time of its disappearance nears. The approaching sunset itself evokes a sense of impending loss. The solo instruments are played in the late afternoon when the day's work tapers, while sitting or lying on one's mat and thinking, perhaps, of a loved one gone away. Playing a flute, bamboo-tube zither, or mouthharp at that hour allows one to *cɔdɨ' hɔnum*, 'to clear the breath or heart of remembrances', 'to free one's feelings'.[8]

The flute, in addition to being an instrument for 'clearing' or 'freeing' the longings of the late afternoon, is also an instrument of courtship and seduction. During the fruit season, a Temiar man might climb the fruit trees and begin to play his flute while the women cutting fruit on the ground below listen and admire. Or a woman might play the flute to attract a man's admiration and attention. A young Temiar man comments: 'The custom of the flute is the custom of [courting] women,' '"*adad pɛnsool, 'adad bɛ'boo*".'

Longing, sadness, and courtship are the primary motivations for playing instrumental music on flutes, zithers, and mouthharps. Like the medium's songs, these songs, too, crosscut dimensions of courtship and longing; but instrumental music remains within the realm of human desires. Playing solo instruments in the late afternoon clears one's breath and heart of longing for loved ones distant or deceased, just as singing/trance-dancing ceremonies intensify and satisfy longing focused on spiritguides.

The aesthetics of sway: dance and movement

Another area crosscutting dimensions of courtship and longing, as well as everyday and ceremonial aesthetics, is movement – what I call the 'aesthetics of sway.' A woman's swaying stroll – soft, supple, and effortless – is prized in everyday movement *and* forms the swaying dance movements that lead to trancing.

Mediums take turns singing during ceremonies, accompanied by chorus and percussion, while other participants begin to dance. These dancers may be members of the settlement, or visitors familiar with the particular genre of spirit songs being sung. While singing, mediums voicing the spiritguides are in a state of 'other-awareness' or 'unconsciousness' (*bɔralii'*) with their hearts elsewhere and their 'eyes changed'; but they continue to control their trance and sing without fainting. Dancers, however, commence a cycle of changing or 'transforming' (*lɛslɑ̧ɑ̧s*) that can lead through fainting and back to consciousness.

In one genre given by the annual fruit spirits, *nɔŋ tahun*, dancers begin by dancing a slow, strolling-in-place movement (*sɔpooy*), bending and swaying the torso as first one arm, then the other, swings in front of the body. The dancer continues, beginning to bend more deeply, counterbalancing the bending with slight lift and wave of the arms. The dancer begins to lose her balance, her unsteadiness and shuddery stumbling marked by the term *kɛnrook*. When the chorus notices a stumbling dancer, they begin to push the tempo of the bamboo tubes, subdivide the duple rhythm, sing more loudly, and if possible, push their vocal range up an octave. The medium may further intensify the sounds by pitching the song higher. At a certain point, the dancer breaks her step and begins a double-footed, low-level, rapid-paced jump. The increased tempo, rhythmic subdivision, and dynamics of the tubes (termed *ba-'asiil*) loosely match the soft frenzy of the dancer's jumping.

After about a minute of jumping, the dancer falls to the floor in a faint (*na-kɔbus* 'he/she faints'). This term, used also for 'death,' describes simultaneous immobility and mobility: the physical body lies immobile, while the head soul is released into movement. The raised floor made from bamboo slats loosely lashed together resounds and rebounds beneath the feet of dancers, gently cushioning their falls. Fallen dancers are laid together, often placed beneath the central hanging leaf ornament. Some dancers report a total lack of sensation while fainted; others tell of hearing the sounds of singing and percussion faintly, as if from a distance, while others describe visions of soaring above the forest canopy and circling the mountain tops.

Eventually, a medium sings over the fainted dancers, shaking his hand-held leaf whisk over them. Along with the spiritguide's voice, the cool liquid form of the spirit's upper-portion soul flows through the medium. When he applies this liquid to their head and heart souls, the fainted dancers begin to stir. Participants along the sidelines, usually members of the opposite sex who are attracted to particular dancers, now enter the dance-space. With help from others, they raise the dancers to a standing position, and, supporting them around the waist (cɛbcaab), begin to dance them back to consciousness. A dancer, her head rolled to the side and down, limply waves her arms as she is gently lifted up and down, reminiscent of the bending and swaying in her original movements. Slowly she comes back to consciousness and begins to dance herself, her helper retreating to the sidelines. After a few minutes of strolling in place, she too retreats to the sidelines and sits. Another spectator, perhaps her helper, again expressing attraction, rolls her a cigarette. Sitting and smoking, she comes back to her 'true heart' and 'true eyes,' and begins to 'think' again (na-nim).

I describe the course of movements throughout the transformation process in detail because the movements are the message, they help lead us to the meanings of Temiar trance. Temiars liken the bending, swaying motions of trance-dancing to the swaying stroll of a woman walking in everyday life. The qualities of 'swaying while strolling' (lɔŋɛ'-lɔŋa'), 'softness' and 'suppleness' (pɔcii'), and 'effortlessness' rɔlɔmah) are prized in women's movements generally and form the supple, swaying dance movements that lead into trancing. These motions, in turn, are associated with the waving of palm fronds and jungle foliage in the wind. Lɛlɔŋooy 'bending', 'swaying', an expressive found in song texts and poetic speech, refers both to the quality of swaying in human movement and in windswept foliage. This imagery is doubly exploited in the 'Way of the Coconut Tree.' In this song, the swaying of the coconut fronds is observed and described by the spirit of the Rambutan tree.[9] On another level, the imagery refers to the swaying of trancers while they dance:

Yee' 'i-gɔɔl na-lɛlɔŋgooy,
Sɔpooy mɔnalɛh taŋgɔɔy.

I sit, [the fronds] sway gently in the breeze,
The slow, strolling dance of the Young Woman Rambutan Fruit
    Spirit.

Marcel Mauss (1935/1979) writes that the 'techniques of the body' are both 'effective' and 'traditional,' or transmitted through imitation and education.

The swaying movements of walking and trance-dancing, what I have called the 'aesthetics of sway,' are studied and intentional. The overtones of seduction are not to be lost here: in daily life, they attract other humans; in ceremonies, they entice spirits to attend. This double intention is confirmed in the layered meanings of the term *sapooy*, the name of the slow, strolling-in-place dance step that initiates and concludes the transformation cycle. *Sapooy* also describes a seductive sideways glance from the corner of downcast eyes in everyday life. It refers as well to a gently blowing breeze and the motion it excites in the leaves. This isomorphism between seductive attributes of everyday life, trance behavior, and aesthetically valued features of the rainforest environment is also apparent in another expressive, *lalajɔg-lalajɛɛg*, which links the long and winding leaves of ceremonial ornaments with falling rain; the cool spiritual liquid of the spiritguides; and the long, wavy hair and curving body of a woman.

Like swaying movements, the fragrant and visually pleasing facepaint, leaves, and flowers decorating people and ceremonial house interiors are said to entice the presence of spiritguides. But they also please human participants. If seduction is occurring in terms of 'enticement to visitation' between human trance-dancers or chorus members and ethereal spiritguides, it is also occurring between human participants of opposite sexes. A man might flirt with a female chorus member by urging her: 'Sing high, it makes me go into trance.' A female on the sidelines shows her favor toward a male singer by offering him a lit cigarette. Trance-dancing, involving physical contact between the sexes in some genres, circuitously allows displays of affection that are not available in the repertoire of everyday life.

Themes of community support and interdependence are also choreographed into Temiar trance-dancing. After having fainted, when the dancer begins to stir, he or she is picked up by members of the community, who dance him/her back to consciousness by physically supporting the dancer's body. This symbolic statement of interdependence is counterbalanced when community members offering support withdraw to the sidelines as the dancer shows she can now support her own weight. Yet even as the dancer dances on her own, she is surrounded by other dancers and singers who together co-create the event. The choreography recognizes the individual within the web of connections constituting a sociocentric society.

Soul loss

The sentiment of longing is transformed into a momentarily satisfying communion between trancer and spirit-entity when properly channeled within the context of trance-dancing ceremonies. Trancers speak of weightless, refreshed feelings experienced the day after trancing. But the coherence of a cultural system is incompletely grasped unless we investigate the ways that system can be disrupted. What happens when longing is not fulfilled, when the pull on one's soul is exacerbated rather than relieved? This situation, in various forms, is the basis for much of Temiar illness.

Soul loss (*rɛywaay* < *rɔwaay* 'head soul') is the prolonged absence of the head soul during the waking state, as opposed to the temporary detachment of the head soul during dreaming or trancing (see Benjamin 1967:138–140; [. . .]). This occurs when the head soul of a plant, a river spirit, a mountain spirit, or the like takes an interest in a person who has passed by, disturbed, or offended it. The entity's upper-portion soul entices the person's head soul to take up residence with it in the jungle, swiddens, or wherever it has its home.

Soul loss, as an illness category, can be understood within a semantic network as an idiom of distress, an 'image which draws together a network of symbols, situations, motives, feelings and stresses which are rooted in the structural setting' (Good 1977:48) in which Temiars live, suspended between the often contradictory tendencies of connection and separability. The soul loss complex devolves around the detachability of human head souls and their predisposition toward entering into relationships of varying degrees with the head souls of other entities. A temporary connection maintains the level of intimacy, ensuring that it does not become overwhelming. In trance and spirit-mediumship, these relationships are temporally and spatially limited to the dream and ritual frame; in illness, the connection exceeds temporary bounds and becomes overwhelming.

ETIOLOGY: In one of many soul loss cases I followed, Angah, a young Temiar man living in his wife's village, went hunting with a rifle. He shot the rifle near some cliffs, causing the sound to reverberate. For two days he grew increasingly listless, sleeping excessively, losing his appetite, and becoming depressed. The first two days he treated himself with Panadol and vitamin C, to no avail. Through discussion among community members coupled with revelations in a medium's dream, it was determined that his head soul had gone off with the sound of the rifle and been taken by the female spirit of the mountain, who had been awakened by the sound. On the third day of his illness, he sent for the spirit-mediums.

TREATMENT: Two mediums were called to Angah's house. They treated him by sucking and blowing on the areas where the soul resides: the crown of the head and the heart. After one of the mediums, Penghulu Abeh, treated Angah, the medium slept and dreamt that his head soul met the patient's head soul in a garden of flowers replete with a house where a female crest soul of the mountain had taken the patient. Silently, the medium grabbed Angah by the hand and whisked him downriver before circling upriver toward their home settlement, choosing this circuitous route to evade subsequent forays by the female mountain spirit.

The next three nights, I observed the two mediums as together they held singing ceremonies for Angah. This allowed the medium Penghulu Abeh to return the patient's soul in the ritual realm as he had done in the dream realm. Imbued with the power of their spiritguides while in the register of singing ceremonies, the two mediums blew cool liquid *kahyɛk* into the head and heart soul of the patient, reshaping and strengthening the position of the patient's newly returned head soul.

Soul loss cases such as this one characteristically show four stages: (1) separation of the person's head soul; (2) relocation of the head soul in a new 'home'; (3) a medium seeks and finds the head soul; and (4) the medium replaces the head soul into the person's crown. In Angah's case, as is typical, the relocation of his head soul in a new home involved cross-sexual attraction with the female spirit of a mountain. Here, longing has gone awry – the mutual enticement between spiritguides and humans has overstepped the bounds of dream and ritual, becoming a prolonged and unrelenting bond. This situation is even clearer in the following case of *tɔwiiŋ*, a variant of soul loss in which not merely the head soul but one's physical body is drawn to walk alone in the jungle.

ETIOLOGY: Biyɛh is a divorcee with seven daughters. She has trouble eating and sleeping. She often wanders off alone into the jungle.
TREATMENT: The medium Balɛh Kɔnaseh traces Biyɛh's illness to the attraction of a young male spirit of the fruits. If she could trance-dance, she could meet him under the proper ceremonial auspices and not need to wander off into the jungle. However, whenever she tries to trance-dance, she becomes embarrassed and is unable to go through the ritual transformation and spiritguide connection. The medium's treatment is therefore oriented toward initiating her into successful trance-dancing. During ceremonies he ministers to her, blowing *kahyɛk* from the spiritguides into her body in hopes that she will learn to trance.

In Biyɛh's case, appropriately contextualized trance-connection with a cross-sexual spiritguide is clearly juxtaposed with the inappropriate, extra-ritual connection with the male spirit of the fruit – an excess of longing drawing her to walk off into the jungle.

In another variant of the soul loss complex, *na-bɔrahii'* ('it draws', 'it falls passionately in love with' > Malay *raih*, 'to draw towards oneself'; *berahi* 'passionate'), fruit- and flower-spirits take a liking to people as they pass by collecting fruits and flowers. These entities both insert their 'essence' into people and draw people's souls off into the jungle. Involvement with these spirit-entities during trance-dancing ceremonies which is 'misunderstood' or incorrectly performed by participants also leads to this dialectical intrusion/drawing-of-the-soul by the activated spiritguides.

I witnessed treatment of four afflicted females involving extraction of the essence of the male Perah fruit tree. After releasing a sticky sap of Perah drawn from an afflicted woman toward the suspended ceremonial leaf ornament, a medium commented:

> Now I have returned the sap to Perah itself. Sometimes I give the sap to someone else to feel, because the preceding person from whom I extracted it didn't understand it. If this next person is also unknowledgeable, that person will also become ill. If I don't give the sap to someone else, I return it to Perah itself.
>
> (Balɛh Kɔnaseh, Pulat, 23 July 1982, FN 1821)

This contrast between the knowledgeable and the unknowledgeable illustrates again the difference between the controlled attraction and longing of trance and the excessive situation of illness. During trance-dancing ceremonies, the sentiment of longing is focused and released. The illnesses of soul loss, situations of excessive longing, are best treated in the context of singing/trance-dancing ceremonies since these are the contexts in which controlled relations with the spirit-world are possible. But how are these ceremonies capable of effecting such relations and transformations?

Musical form, emotion, and meaning

During ceremonial performances, sentiments are modulated by sounds that have been imbued with networks of association. Sounds meaningfully situated activate emotions of longing, prompting their focus and release in the context of ceremonial performance. The call of the cicada hɛrŋɔɔd evokes sentiments of longing in Temiars. The formal structure of this sound exhibits a two-toned pulsation alternating between high and low frequencies (see sonogram, Figure 11.1). The call of the golden-throated barbet, cɛp tɔwaal (Megalaima franklini), also considered to evoke sentiments of longing, has a similar two-toned pulsation structure alternating between lower and higher frequencies (see sonogram, Figure 11.2).

These two-toned pulsating sounds are said to beat in rhythm with one's heart, thus moving the heart to longing for a loved one or a deceased relative. The continuous sound of the bamboo percussion in singing/trance-dancing ceremonies is socially structured as a two-toned pulsation alternating between lower and higher frequencies (see sonogram, Figure 11.3). The sound is produced by a pair of bamboo tubes struck in alternation against a log. The pair consists of a shorter tube, producing the higher sound, and a longer tube producing the lower sound. Drumming, when it accompanies the ceremonies, follows the two-toned pulsation pattern of the bamboo tubes.

In performance, the continuous two-toned sound of the bamboo-tube

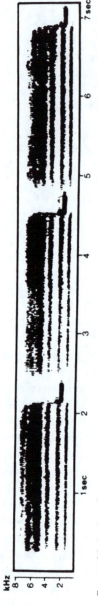

Figure 11.1 Cicada *herpgod*

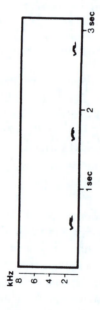

Figure 11.2 Golden-throated barbet (Megalaima franklini)

Figure 11.3 Bamboo-tube stampers (one pair; alternation begins with higher-pitched tube)

percussion, structurally similar to the barbet and cicada calls, is also said to move with one's heart, focusing and intensifying longing to effect the transformation of trance and spiritguide connection. The shorter bamboo tube is termed 'mother' (*boo'*), the longer, 'father' (*bɔɔh*). When the mother and father tubes are beat in contiguous alternation, their sounds differentiate yet conjoin the male and female domain. Structurally in their two-toned pulsation, the sounds move the heart to longing; metaphorically, they replicate the momentary association of male and female which exemplifies the cross-sexual connection with spiritguides.[10]

I first became aware of the cultural value placed on pulsing sounds of the rainforest when sitting around the fire with a group of Temiar women after a morning spent working in the rice fields. One of the women mentioned a bird song she had heard, how it had moved with her heart and made her feel longing. I scribbled down the name of the bird, and asked the women if there were other sounds that made them feel similarly. They listed several, including the golden-throated barbet and the cicada *hɛrɲɔɔd*, whose songs pulsed with their hearts. I had gone to the rainforest with the necessary equipment for recording natural sounds, including parabola and shotgun mike, which Temiars jokingly termed my blowpipe. I began to notice that when I played back the recorded sounds for identification and discussion, the arioso bird songs I found so compelling, given my culture's melodic orientation, were of less interest to my Temiar listeners. They responded, rather, to the pulsating calls of several species. I also noted references in song texts to the calls of these species and the feelings they evoked. The bamboo tubes of singing ceremonies, ceremonial participants commented, similarly moved with their hearts and made them feel longing.

The pulsing beat of the bamboo tubes is an iconic sign in that it gains its meaning through the association of similar forms: the continuous two-toned beating of hearts, certain bird and insect calls, and the percussive rhythm of the tubes. As an iconic sign, it brings together sounds of the rainforest and sounds of the body and links these with a theory of selves and spirits that can be loosened and rebound. Anchoring themes of gender, boundaries, and interconnection in natural and physiological forms, the sounds of the bamboo tubes resemble Turner's dominant symbols (1967: 28) which pack their affective power through the simultaneous condensation of physiological and ideological poles. The Beckers (1981) suggest that a symbol gains legitimacy and authority to the extent that it is rooted in a culture's concept of the 'natural' and thus the 'true'; this rootedness through similar form they term 'iconicity.' The beating of Temiar tubes gains affective power through its rootedness in the rainforest and the body as these are culturally transformed into signs and symbols. Daniel highlights the polychromy or multimodality of the sign, reminding us that 'iconic as well as indexical aspects may be concealed within the same sign' (1984: 39). To the extent that the meaning of the bamboo tubes is rooted in the body and thus contiguous with that which it signs, it also has an indexical aspect.

The iconic relation between heartbeat and bamboo-tube percussion is not merely operative on the level of biological entrainment or auditory driving as some authors have suggested when exploring the role of music in trance induction. Neher (1961, 1962), for example, suggests that drumming at certain tempi prompts auditory driving, biologically entraining brain waves and thus inducing trance. The evocative power of these sounds, however, lies in the way they are imbued with meaning and interpreted by participants. The linkage of beating tubes, pulsing hearts, and moving spirits is culturally mediated, driven by an ethnopsychology that locates emotion and memory, longing and nostalgia in the heart. Blacking (1985) argues that 'the effective-ness of musical symbols depends as much on human agency and social context, as on the structure of the symbols themselves.' Formal structure and social content, when interrelated, render music effective (Blacking 1985: 66).

Surveying the astonishing variety of musical forms accompanying trance ceremonies around the world, Rouget (1977a, 1980) suggests that from within a given society's musical repertoire, certain musical genres and formal musical features are particularly categorized and valued as trance-related. These valued musical forms, then, do not so much precipitate as 'socialise trance' (Rouget 1977b), marking contexts and moments appropriate for participating in trance behavior.

In such a manner, barbet and cicada calls – pulsing like the heart, hidden in the dense jungle foliage, persistent yet unobtainable – become culturally marked and valued. These sounds, socially reconstructed in the patterned sounds of ceremonial percussion, intensify longing focused on the spirits. When joined with a cosmological theory that posits detachable interactive selves and images songs as paths, and when joined with swaying movements that entice the spirits, the sounds set the cosmos in motion and effect the transformation of Temiar trance, a momentary intermingling of self and other.

When the pulsing bamboo tubes metaphorically 'move with the heart' to evoke longing, the unsettling sentiment of longing is transformed into a momentarily satisfying communion between trancer and spirit-entity properly channeled within the ceremonial context. Singing/trance-dancing ceremonies exemplify dialectically balanced interactions with the spirits. For Temiars, the working cosmos is not a static balance, but a dynamic conjunction in alterna-tion that is present in the continuous pulse of low 'male' and high 'female' tubes, the strolling sway of a dancer or the undulation of leaves in the wind. The aesthetic texture of the ceremony celebrates the momentary balancing of intimacy between spirit and human, self and other, male and female; it is thus the appropriate context in which to treat a patient whose interaction with the animated world has ceased to fluctuate and thus exceeds proper bounds. By gathering members of the community together in dance and song to periodic-ally resituate their relationships with the spirit-world, preventive measures are taken to avoid the excess of unfulfilled desire that can lead to soul loss. And by situating a patient whose interaction with the world has become imbalanced, whose soul roams the jungle in search of a spirit-mate, in the midst of the balanced interactions of ceremonial performance, treatment is effected.

Notes

1   Temiar terms for 'desire' include the verbs pət ('i-pət ma- . . . 'I miss, long for . . .'), cɛn 'want', hǫǫd 'desire', and hɔg 'desire sexual intercourse'. Of these, the last is most explicitly and immediately sexual. The second and third may be used to express both material desires and human passions. These two, cɛn and hǫǫd, are the verbs reportedly used by spiritguides when expressing their intentions toward humans.

2   [. . .] [A] study of forty-one songs recorded with dream source stories by male halaa' showed twenty-one female spiritguides, ten male spiritguides, and six of unspecified gender. (The forty-one songs were received from a total of thirty-seven spiritguides; the same spiritguide sometimes gives more than one song.) This is a two to one ratio of female to male spiritguides received by male spirit-mediums.

3   Recall the etymology of gonig 'spiritguide' < Malay gundik 'consort'. When the halaa'/spiritguide relationship is unisexual (male–male), the seductive nature of the relationship is subordinated to the generational dimension (father–child or older brother–younger brother).

4   Hɛwhəyaaw is an expressive found in poetic speech and song texts. Everyday words for longing and associated sadness include the verbs pət ('i-pət ma- . . . 'I miss, long for . . .') and rəyaak 'to long [for]', 'to pine [for]'.

5   Bərɛnlii' is conceivably related to ralii' (be-ralii' 'unconscious', 'otherawareness').

6   Megalaima franklini (Temiar cɛp təwaal).

7   Elateriospermum tapos (Temiar sɔc).

8   Solo instruments include pɛnsɔɔl (noseflute), si'ɔɔy (mouthblown flute), kərəb (tube zither), gɛngɔɔɲ (metal mouthharp), and rəŋgɔɲ or rəŋgɔc (mouthharp made from the midrib of the palm, Eugeissona tristis). [. . .]

9   Nephelium lappaceum (Temiar ləgəs, susug).

10   For a remarkably similar linkage of natural sounds, instrumental repertoire and symbolic meanings among the T'boli of Mindanao, Philippines, see Mora 1987. The T'boli link themes of longing, cosmology, mythology, and music in a complex that metaphorically associates interlocking percussion parts encoding male/female polarity and complementarity, musical composition emerging from cross-sexual relations between human dreamer and spiritguide, the cross-sexual relations of the deities themselves, and a cultural interpretation of the antiphonal duet of the crimson-breasted barbet (Megalaima haemacephala). One is tempted to begin speaking about themes of a Southeast Asian culture area.

References

Becker, Judith and Becker, Alton 1981. 'A Musical Icon: Power and Meaning in Javanese Gamelan Music', in Wendy Steiner (ed.) *The Sign in Music and Literature*, Austin, TX: University of Texas Press, pp. 203–15.

Benjamin, Geoffrey 1967. 'Temiar Religion', PhD dissertation, University of Cambridge.

Benjamin, Geoffrey 1976. 'An Outline of Temiar Grammar', in Philip N. Jenner *et al.* (eds), *Austroasiatic Studies*, Part 1. Honolulu: University Press of Hawaii, pp. 129–87.

Blacking, John 1985. 'The Context of Venda Possession Music: Reflection on the Effectiveness of Symbols', *Yearbook for Traditional Music* 17: 64–87.

Coville, Elizabeth 1984. 'Others, Origins and the Transmission of Toraja Knowledge', unpublished paper presented at the 36th Annual Meeting of the Association for Asian Studies, Washington, DC.

Daniel, E. Valentine 1984. *Fluid Signs: Being a Person the Tamil Way*. Berkeley, CA: University of California Press.

Diffloth, Gérard 1976. 'Expressives in Semai', in Philip N. Jenner *et al.* (eds), *Austroasiatic Studies* Part 1. Honolulu: University Press of Hawaii, pp. 249–64.

Good, Byron 1977. 'The Heart of What's the Matter: The Semantics of Illness in Iran', *Culture, Medicine and Psychiatry* 1: 25–58.

Mauss, Marcel 1935/1979. 'Body Techniques', in *Sociology and Psychology, Essays*. London: Routledge and Kegan Paul.

Mora, Manolete 1987. 'The Sounding Pantheon of Nature: T'boli Instrumental Music in the Making of an Ancestral Symbol', *Acta Musicologica* 59(2)L 187–212.

Neher, Andrew 1961. 'Auditory Driving Observed with Scalp Electrodes in Normal Subjects', *Electroencephalography and Clinical Neurophysiology* 13: 449–51.

Neher, Andrew 1962. 'A Physiological Explanation of Unusual Behavior in Ceremonies Involving Drums', *Human Biology* 34(2): 151–60.

Rouget, Gilbert 1977a. 'Instruments de musique et musique de la possession', *Musique en Jeu* 28 (September)L 68–91.

Rouget, Gilbert 1977b. 'Music and Possession Trance', in John Blacking (ed.) *The Anthropology of the Body*, ASA Monographs, London: Academic Press, pp. 233–9.

Rouget, Gilbert 1980. *Music and Trance*. Chicago: University of Chicago Press.

Schutz, Alfred 1967. *Collected Papers I: The Problem of Social Reality*. The Hague: Nijhoff.

Turner, Victor 1967. 'A Ndembu Doctor in Practice', in *The Forest of Symbols*. Ithaca, NY: Cornell University Press.

Chapter 12

Mihály Hoppál

ETHNOGRAPHIC FILMS
ON SHAMANISM

THE USE OF THE MOVIE CAMERAS ushers a new era in the history of the research on shamanism. The new era brought a qualitative change in two respects: first, the photo encapsulating the frozen moment gave way to the sequence of images recording the process of movement. It was now possible to encompass the motions, the special gestures, the technique of drumming, and the dance forms, making long sequences of the rite accessible for study. That fact alone is of great significance. More importantly perhaps – and this is the second qualitative change – the motion picture enables the repeated viewing of the recorded phenomenon, resulting, in turn, in a qualitative improvement of the analysis (and re-analysis). By becoming eye-witnesses, in our own days, of phenomena that actually occurred a long time ago, we can apply ever fresh angles, making for an increasingly multifaceted description of the given anthropological phenomenon.

In the last couple of decades – to be precise, from 1969 onwards, almost every year – I regularly spent periods of varying length in the state that was then still known as the Soviet Union, where – as part of the exchange agreements between the academies – I studied Siberian shamanism, also familiarizing myself with anthropological films (Hoppál 1988).

Looking back at the history of Soviet ethnographic films, it is usually mentioned that the first documentaries were made in the 1920s and they centred on the material culture and religious rites of little known small ethnics. Among the films still kept in archive include '*Lesnie lyude*' (People of the Forest, 1928) by A. Litvinov, featuring, amongst other things, some beautiful and highly authentic footage of Udehe shamans in the state of trance and dancing – presumably the first documentary record of the religious practices of the peoples living along the Amur river [. . .].

There is an other almost unknown feature film, made by S. Kozintsev in 1930 under the title '*Odna*' (Alone). The place, where the shooting was made, the remote regions of the Altai Mountains, among a Turkish tribe. The young woman elementary school teacher finds age old local folk customs including horse-sacrifice and shamanic healing rites. The sequences of this later one shows the breathtaking drumming-dancing art of an Altaic Turkish *kham* (shaman).

Russian silent picture classics most probably contain a great deal of ethnographically authentic footages, however, the history of Soviet ethnographic filmmaking is also yet to be written. A young film historian K. Janulaitis had started to work on a monograph which aims to present the history of ethnographic filmmaking in the former USSR, but he died untimely in 1989.

In November 1986, I was given access to the film archives of the Institute of Ethnography of the Soviet Academy of Sciences. A.V. Oskin, the head of the film section, told me that the archives had some four and a half thousand metres of 35 mm colour film and some 6 thousand metres of 16 mm film material, all of it unedited (which will mean more than twenty films in the future). However, the Institute has only four or five films ready to be presented. In Oskin's opinion, one should distinguish descriptive ethnographic films and educational films made for the general public. An example of the latter category is the film '*Choreographical Art of the People of the North*' (1975), photographed and edited by Oskin, with M.Ya. Zhornitskaya as an expert in folk dance, who also made the sound recording. The forty-minute (35 mm) colour film consist of four parts. By way of introduction, we are given glimpses of today's urban way of life, as well as the life on the tundra of the Chukchis, who are reindeer herders. The images present, for instance, the building of the *yaranga* – a traditional tent dwelling built of poles and covered with reindeer skins – and the ancient techniques of leather-dressing and making fire with wood. According to the film's 'story-line', an amateur folk ensemble of young locals visits the remote groups in order to collect traditional dances and songs, and to present their own. The last quarter or the film is the most intriguing section from the ethnographical point of view, as it simply records the so-called throat-singing, various vocalizations and dance movements imitating animals, the ecstatic vocal effects of group-singing, to which they dance with erotic movements. It is as though one saw the beginnings of music and dance, the genesis of music, developing from simple noises, and the raven-dance – presumably a representation of the North Asian raven myth – is also memorable. Of similar documentary value are the shots (unfortunately, only short sequences really) which record the collective drumming. Here, the lack of synchronous sound proves most frustrating; some commentary would certainly be needed to explain that in those northern regions the shaman tradition is still alive in almost every family.

I also saw another film from the same area, made back in 1962. E. Timlin was the director and cameraman, supported by Yu.B. Simchenko who did the ethnographic fieldwork. Apart from some breathtakingly picturesque scenery, the film contains footage of ethnographic documentary value depicting a life-style of a quarter of a century ago (which was then still a traditional lifestyle): the setting up of the tent called the *chum*, the braiding of nets, the tools to make the leather-dressing, the techniques of ornamenting fur and the costume of a shaman. Regrettably, the credibility of this film, too, is marred by the 'red tail' tagged – on to its end – about the beauty of the changing life, with school-children picking flowers and the new school being built in the middle of a sea of mud. The figure of the local shaman, too, appears for a brief flash; yet, his drumming is at once drowned out by a music theme which provides the background for the whole film, and which, written by a composer, has no associations with the local musical tradition.

Still staying with the indigenous population inhabiting the Taymir Peninsula, our colleagues in Moscow kindly permitted me to see portions of a still unedited film portraying the last Nganasan shaman. Shaman Demnime Ngamtuso Kosterkin (1913–1980), as one who carried on an ancient family tradition, was discovered in occasions (in one, made in 1974, he also performed some of his shaman's rituals. This was released on record in 1982– Melodia c30–17651 003). In 1976, at A. Oskin's and Yu. Simchenko's request, he agreed to put on his full shaman's costume and paraphernalia, and give a demonstration, for the purpose of the film, of a shaman's weather-forecast ritual. The words of the ritual song were repeated and translated into the vernacular by his wife, who was sitting at his side. It was the beginning of winter, the first snow had just fallen, and he was singing of the kind of weather to be expected. The authenticity with which the shaman's costume and other details of the seance are shown renders these shots a unique document, after all, a trance state is a series of gestures and mechanized movements which neither cameras, spotlights, tape-recorders, nor, indeed, the presence of ethnographers is able to disturb. We hope that the close on two hours of material recorded – which is immensely rich in detail (for instance, the ornaments of the shaman's costume are shown and explained) – will be made into a film in the next few years. My deep conviction is that this film, when completed, will be one [of] the best documentary on the genuine form of Siberian shamanism.

A man who deserves a special chapter in the history of Soviet ethno-graphic filmmaking is the Estonian Lennart Meri, who was a celebrated prose writer and he started making films in the early 1970s, and the very first project he embarked on was an ambitious enterprise: he wanted to make a film about the Finno-Ugrians, or more specifically, the Uralic peoples. Uralic peoples are those which speak languages belonging to the Uralic family of languages (they include the Finns, Estonians, Lapp, Samoyeds, Hungarians, Obi-Ugrians – the Voguls and Ostyaks, the Finnic peoples of the Volga, such as the Cheremis,

Zyryans, Mordvin, Udmurt). His first film was 'The Waterbird People' (1971 – 42 min.), which is an evocative study of five Uralic groups: the Ostyaks, Zyryans, Cheremis, Karelians and Nenets (Yurak-Samoyed). Based on unique aspects of each culture, the film explores their relationship to the cultural evolution of the Finno-Ugric and Samoyed peoples as a whole.

The themes of housing, ornaments, artifacts, language and ritual are used throughout to emphasize the similarities among these very different cultures which range from the Nenets, who are reindeer herders, to the Karelian farmers. Among the scenes are a Cheremis wedding and an age-old ritual performed by the Ostyaks to appease the spirit of a bear they have just killed.

His second film on the same topic was completed six years later with the title 'Winds of the Milky Way' (1978 – 55 min.). This film captures many aspects of the daily lives of the Uralic (Finno-Ugric and Samoyed) peoples which have their roots in ancient traditions and systems of belief. Parallels in customs of agriculture, fishing and housing are recognizable among these groups despite the thousands of years which many of them have lived apart in very different physical and social environments. Thus the shape of the fishing boat used by a Hungarian fisherman and an Ostyak are similar despite the fact that one group lives in Central Europe, the other in sub-Arctic terrain and they have been separate for at least two thousand years.

The film vividly depicts how such ethnographic details are intertwined with folk-song, dance and ritual. In unique footage, we see Demnime, a ninth-generation Nganasan shaman singing [. . .], a Veps mourning ritual and an eloquent interview with a Lapp leader about the future of his culture.

Lennart Meri, as author and filmmaker, worked in collaboration with Finnish and Hungarian scholars to document these patterns of culture found among the Finns, Veps, Vote, Mordvin, Ostyak, Vogul, Lapp, Hungarians, and Nganasan (a Samoyed people).

Nineteen eighty-five marked the 150th anniversary of the appearance of Kalevala. For that occasion, Meri made another film, called 'Voices of Kaleva' (1985), which is a tribute to Elias Lönnrot, the scholar who – as is generally known – compiled, on the basis of the materials he had collected, the national epic of the Finnish people. The important point about Lönnrot's life's work is that he drew attention to the living oral tradition. The Estonian writer and director, sharing his predecessor's aim, has set himself the task of recording and rescuing for the future the surviving narrative tradition of the North. Meri, as well as being a film director, is a highly well-trained ethnographer and a lucky researcher, because in 1985, while shooting his latest film near Tyumen, among the Ostyaks, he managed to film a bear ceremonial.

> I went once more to Siberia, hoping to find fragments of the bear
> ritual I have been lucky to film during my previous expeditions. I
> chose this time the distant Agan tributary in the Eastern part and
> unexpectedly fell upon a tribe of Ostyaks among whom the bear

ritual is still a living tradition they perform every year. It lasts five days (four, if it's a she-bear), during which they perform ritual sacrifices, dances, maskerades, and, last but not least, all the 270 traditional songs of the bear ritual, about 30,000 verses poetry of the highest quality, roughly twice the size of 'Kalevala'. We were able to record about ten and to film about one hour of the ritual.

It was and is an amazing discovery. First of all, the songs (and actions) have been preserved in their original order: the structure of the ritual seems to be intact. Secondly, the text part of the ritual is well comparable with 'Gilgamesh' or 'Iliad': it is an epic poem of the Forest zone hunters, more than 3,000 years old, never systematically recorded in its entirety, and existing until now only as an oral tradition in the fragile memory of local hunters. Thirdly, the possibility to record through modern technical means an epic poem simultaneously with its performance is unique in itself and will give us an exclusive insight into prehistoric cultural life, beliefs, and ethics.

In short, it is a major work and probably my last one, if I am able to realize my project. We shall have to film the whole ritual, about 60 hours. This must be done on the spot, in difficult conditions (virgin forest), and without delay: already one of the hunters died last year. After the ritual has been filmed and recorded, the text part must be transliterated and published in an Ostyak and European parallel edition for scientific use and in an artistic translation as an example of unwritten literature. The same goes with the film: in its total length it will be used as a scientific source for researchers; a much shorter edited version could be presented as an educational TV serial, perhaps five parts 30 minutes each. Until now I have had little success in finding a local producer. Our Tallinnfilm is probably ready to support a 40-minute documentary.

(Meri 1987:20)

Fortunately, the film was made, and in 1990 it was presented at the Fourth Pärnu International Visual Anthropology Festival, which had, as its central theme, the protection and preservation of the culture of Nordic peoples. The film, 'Toorumi pojad' (The People of the God Torum), was one of the best screened at the festival. Moreover, it was the first anthropological documentary to profile the traditional structure of the Ostyak bear ceremony.

I note that V. N. Chernetsov – a renowned researcher into the other Ob-Ugrian people, the Voguls – made a short (approx. 20 to 25-minute-long – 16 mm) film about the Manysi bear cult as early as the late 1930s. In 1969, shortly before his death, the old scholar showed this document to a group of Hungarian anthropologist colleagues who were staying in Moscow at the time; that is when I myself saw the material. Today that film – along with other items in the Chernetsov estate – is preserved in the Anthropological Institute of the University of Tomsk.

It is worth mentioning here that, at that film festival, there were another four films featuring shots of Siberian shamans. In 1989, a 'troika' of Swedish filmmakers made a documentary in the same Nganasan group that Lennart Meri had also visited. One of the relatives of the shaman to be seen in his film improvised a display for the benefit of the filmmakers to demonstrate what the shamanic seance was like, what it could have been like in the old days. As the garments of the dead shaman were buried with him, and his drum was placed in a museum, the shamanic tools shown in the film were all newly made – some of them in quite a hurry, specially for the purposes of the filming. Hence 'Nganasan – a Siberian People' (1989/90 – 29 min.), the work of director Harald Tiren, cannot be regarded as ethnographically authentic. On the other hand, it is highly revealing of the way in which, under the impact of the shooting, among other things, the shamanizing activity, considered to be sacred, is transformed in response to business and circumstance.

The Estonian director Valentin Kuik made a documentary that carries a politically important message – 'Message to the Parliament' (1990 – 45 min.). It deals with the modern life of the Khanty people – more exactly, the devastation wreaked on the natural environment, the deforestation and the killing of wildlife brought about by oil production. There are only a few elderly people who are still familiar with the old dances and songs. One of them is a shaman whose picture recurs several times in the film.

In the heart of Siberia, in Novosibirsk, there lives and works a film director of Kazakh extraction, Raisa Yernazarova, as [a] member of the Telefilm Studio, she cultivates the genre of the short documentary. In the last decade, she has been making more and more anthropological films. She brought to the festival a finely photographed film entitled 'Istselenie radostyu' (Healing by Joy. 1990 – 20 min.), which she shot among the Nanai people inhabiting the Amur region. With R. Zvereva as its anthropological expert, the film profiles some spectacular details of the traditional folk culture of the Nanai, including the healing rituals of the shaman women. The central figure of the film is Nura Kile, custodian of folk wisdom on healing and an old female shaman.

In 1990, the prize for best scholarly documentary at the Pärnu festival went to 'The Shaman in Eurasia', a film by Mihály Hoppál and Marcell Jankovics. Hoppál had started collecting the pictures for the film back in the early eighties, setting himself the object of showing the changing image of the Eurasian shaman. As it happens, a good many fine etchings and drawings have survived from the past centuries (16th to 19th centuries), illustrations to the first Siberian travel accounts. Some of these are well known, but many others have never been published. The examples include a series of photos made by Maynagashev, pictures of a horse sacrifice from 1914. We also dug up in the archives the phonograph recordings to go with the pictures – recordings likewise made by Maynagashev. The film features the old photos in conjunction with the original shamanic chants.

As the film was made back in the pre-glasnost period, we had no opportunity to carry out any fieldwork, taking original pictures; we therefore tried to collect the archival material. Thus we used an excerpt – the four or five minutes that were of any use – from Lennart Meri's film 'Winds of the Milky Way'; the drum dance of the Udehe shamans from an old film by Litvinov ('People of the Forest' [. . .]); a film made in Lakakh by Ferenc Neményi the trance of a lhapa (healing shaman); and, finally, footage made in Yakutia by L. Kuperschmidt, which, in the eighties, could not be used to make a film, due to opposition from Soviet officials.

Alongside the researcher-anthropologist, the film was co-directed by a famous director of animated cartoons, Marcell Jankovics, who, as a researcher, has studied the symbolism of shaman's drums. Here is part of the text of the screenplay, a section dealing with the symbolism of shaman's drums:

A basic type of shaman drums symbolizes the northern celestial sphere, the shaman's upper world, or its reflected image, which they thought to be the southern celestial sphere, that is the lower world. Some drums have the shape of the face of the Sky God, the well-known image with one eye as the Sun, the other as the Moon.

The drums from the Altai region are somewhat different, they still often bear the face of the highest creature, the Sky God. This image also appears on the drum's handle.

When in his trance the shaman speaks with the God, his spirit helper, as the shaman calls him, he in fact speaks to the image on the handle of the drum.

The longitudinal axis of these drums, that is the line of the nose of the God image, is the Milky Way traversing the celestial sphere.

The ornaments on the rim of the drum characterize the horizon and the middle world, that is a belt of the sky that the Sun, the Moon and the other planets appear to move through.

At certain points of the drum's rims there is no ornament. These points are the passages between the world.

They correspond to the intersections of the Milky Way and the Zodiac, the summer and winter solstices.

Often there are four passages on the drum's rims. They also indicate the seasons and the points of the compass.

The centre, or the navel of the drum represents the Polar Star, the centre of the celestial chart, which all the stars and constellations orbit around. You can see some drawings of constellations on the drums, but not all of them have been identified. No wonder that this Chukchi drawing gives an image of the sky virtually identical with the image of the ornaments on the shaman's drums.

Some drums from the Altai region and from Lappland show a lateral view of the world. The upper and the lower worlds, that is the northern and the southern celestial spheres can be seen simultaneously together with the Zodiac, the symbol of the middle world.

This drum from the Lappland also shows the passages between the worlds.

The handles of the drum are sometimes also part of the world image. The carving on the upper handle shows the face of the God of the Northern Sphere, and the face of the God of the Southern Sphere is carved into the lower handle.

The ornaments on the rim of these drums symbolize the Milky Way, with the depictions of various constellations.

(From the script and the voice-over text)

Jankovics used highly inventive animations to bring to life particular images of Siberian shamanism and the figures of the drums. In fact, the two director creators, who wrote and directed the film together, sought to produce a visual essay drawing on the abundant pictorial material (including photos, engravings, and motion-picture footage). The idea was to have less commentary than one usually gets in educational films and to include more pictures – ones that leap into motion, thereby explaining the phenomena.

Since the film was made, the present writer has come by a great deal of new material, which will be [result in] a project of a new, extended version. Indeed, we have also conceived the idea of a separate film to document the modern, urban forms of shamanism. We have plenty of material for this latter project as well. Both films are expected to be completed in 1993.

Andris Slapins deserves a special chapter in the history of the recording on celluloid of Siberian shamanism. A Latvian filmmaker, Slapins died prematurely (at the age of 42) and under tragic circumstances: on January 20, 1991, he was killed, in Riga, the Latvian capital, by Soviet 'black berets' or Interior Ministry troops, as he was filming their attack. We quote from an obituary written about him:

Slapins who was associated with the Riga Video Center, was filming the attack by Soviet Troops on the independence-seeking Latvian Interior Ministry when he and another film team member were killed. An ardent but non-militant Latvian nationalist, Slapins died in the arms of his mentor and friend, internationally-known filmmaker Yoris Podnieks, who was the only member of the three-man team to escape death. Official Soviet accounts claim the firing upon the film team was accidental, but observers say the group was not in the line of fire. Both United States officials and Russians have noted that journalists and cameramen appear to have been targeted . . .

In the past few years easing of travel restrictions enabled Slapins to make contact with anthropologists, folklorists, film-makers and peace organizers outside of Latvia. At the time of his death he was involved in filming projects in Paris, Japan (Kazuo Okada, Tokyo Cinema Inc.), the United States, and Great Britain (British Universities Film and Video Council). His great drive and enthusiasm, his generous participation in projects lacking personal financial return, and his willingness to freely distribute his films and photography brought his talents as an anthropological cinematographer rapidly to international recognition. His death is all the more tragic as he was a quintessential victim of the policies of Glasnost that nurtured and gave public expression to his burst of artistic production . . .

Slapins is best known in North America for his contributions to *Crossroads of Continents: Cultures of Siberia and Alaska*, a travelling exhibition produced jointly by the Smithsonian together with the Institute of Ethnography of the USSR and Canadian and American museums. In addition to a film co-produced with Ted Timrek of Spofford Films, which is part of the exhibition, Slapins supplied two feature films for use with the show. *Chukotka: Coast of Memories*, now nearly twenty years old, is a cinematic masterpiece describing the lifeways and lands of the Chukchi and Eskimo peoples living on the Soviet shores of Bering Strait. Its sensitive humanistic portrayals of character and its blending of folklore, ancient cultural traditions, and landscapes produced a poetic masterpiece which to today's ear is marred only by the need for a more culturally-sensitive sound track. A second film, *Times of Dreams: Siberian Shamanism*, is also Chukchi shamanism and incorporated archival footage shot in the Amur region by A. Litvinov in the 1920s with his own footage of contemporary Evenki shamans curing a 'possessed' family member returning from Soviet military service in Afghanistan.

Both films document Slapins' cinematographic as well as his personal drive and courage in travelling and working, often alone or with only one assistant, in remote regions of the Soviet North and Far East. His ability to establish close bonds with native peoples and his instinct for coming in on deeply-rooted cultural traditions marked a unique humanistic style that combines sweeping, elegant landscapes with village life and close-up character revelation. Slapins' technique is most poignantly revealed in his portrayal of elders and children performing rituals, games and songs. He was particularly absorbed in searching for ancient rituals and ceremonies which he documented using natural light in remarkably difficult and sometimes dangerous situations. When Andris was behind the camera his art dominated to the point that nothing else – crashing Bering Sea surf, roaring walruses, polar bears, and nervous 'shaman-tenders' – concerning personal security intruded on his consciousness. His single-minded commitment to seeking and portraying truth no doubt was a factor leading to his death.

(Fitzhugh 1991:2)

Andris Slapin's film – which he made in collaboration with the anthropologists E. Novik and E. Alekseev – was the one that the panel of judges deemed worthy of the first prize in first festival of ethnographic films held in Pärnu, Estonia. Their 70-minute-long film 'Vremena snovedeniy' (Times of Dreams, 1982–1986) treats of Siberian shamanism.

It is at last an authentic film about the shamans of Siberia. Moreover, it represents an important breakthrough in that, for long decades – actually, from the 1930s up until quite recently – shamanism was a taboo theme in the Soviet Union. The film portrays four shamans. The first is a relatively young Yakut shaman, who has since been profiled in another film. The two other Yakuts belong to the older generation, and in their youth they still practised as shamans. Therefore, the reconstruction they gave for the purposes of the film may be accepted as authentic.

The fourth – a woman shaman [. . .] – with the trance she produced, provided the most authentic state of ecstasy. A film of this type enables the researcher to observe the many tiny details of the movements, gestures and other things (e.g. the rhythm of the whole rite) – even if the spiritual atmosphere of it all has, by now, completely changed. It is no accident that this was the film to receive the greatest critical acclaim from both Soviet and foreign experts, for in it an ideal cooperation was achieved between the cameraman – director, with his artistic style of vision, on the one hand, and the well-trained anthropologist-folklorist E. Novik and the ethnomusicologist E. Alekseev, on the other. He was an outstanding cameraman – and [shot] some wonderful scenes of the shaman performing his rituals, which are extremely difficult to film. Unfortunately, Slapin's untimely death prevented him to build up a coherent overall structure of this film, leaving us with no more than a mosaic of impressions, but anyhow this film is the best one on Siberian shamanism.

Alongside the Russian researchers and filmmakers, the last two or three years have brought the opportunity for foreign researchers, too, to appear and carry out fieldwork in Siberia, making video recordings. One of the first to do so has been Juha Pentikäinen, Professor at the Department of Comparative Religion at the University of Helsinki. Starting with 1989, she took part in several expeditions in the company of some Russian colleagues – in particular,

O.A. Donskiy, N. Koskarova and E. Kovgan, who work in Novosibirsk, in the Siberian Research Institute of the Academy of Sciences, studying the languages and culture of the related Ugrian peoples of the Ob. They have primarily set out to describe and salvage on recordings the various dialects; so it is only natural that, in the course of their collecting work, they notate some valuable folkloric texts.

Most probably, the reason why they chose one of the last Ostyak shamans was that this elder had already figured in Lennart Meri's film, which showed the bear feast. He was the younger one of the two shamans conducting the ceremonies. To enable a better understanding of the whole context of the shots, we quote from Pentikäinen's commentary to the film:

> The Ugric language of the Khanty (Ostyak) is one of those northern Siberian languages whose existence has been threatened by the rapid assimilation to Russian culture as the result of the strong settlement, agricultural and industrial Soviet policy in Siberia since the Revolution. Particularly from the 1930's onwards, the relative proportion of the indigenous peoples in all the northern territories has dramatically decreased, being in the Okrug of Khantimansisk, for example, only 1.2% of the total population.
>
> The total number of the Khanty speakers has not, however, diminished but rather slightly increased having been in 1897 19,700 and in the last census of the 1980s ca. 21,000. The recent trend has led towards bilingualism. Most Khanty speak fluently Russian. At the moment, the Khanti with their Mansy (Vogul) relatives seem together to be more than ever before aware of their common roots and have started their struggle for their survival as language and culture.
>
> The elements of the old ethnic religion also seem to be a part of the struggle for ethnic survival. The videofilm shows the shamanic kills and practices in a Khanty winter village at a by-river of Ob visited by the team in January 1990. The religious leader of the clan is the only one who survived of the nine Khanty shamans imprisoned by Stalin in the 1930s . . .
>
> The ethnographic documentary was shot at the tip of one of the tributaries of the river Ob in the heart of Siberia. During the period from November to March the nomadic Khanty family lives in the winter village. This is the time of reindeer husbandry, culminating in the reindeer sacrifice. In January 1990 the annual reindeer sacrifice was made to celebrate the arrival of the son and the daughter of the shaman from the oil cities along the Ob together with the research team.
>
> Ivan Stepanovich Sopotsin is the family elder and the spiritual

head of the Sopotsin family – the shaman. He is everywhere during the ceremony. It is he who acts as a mediator between this and the other world. His absence is a threat, his presence orders the course of events.

The ceremony begins with a sacrifice to the god of fire which prepares the community for the reindeer sacrifice to be made the following day. The ritualised death adds to the life of the reindeer stock, assures its continuity and at the same time the luck and future of the entire community. It is the women's lot to follow the sacrifice from apart. They are forbidden to come near the sacrificial site in front of the sacred sleigh.

In 1991, at the Fifth Pärnu Visual Anthropology Film Festival, Juha Pentikäinen's film 'Reindeer Sacrifice: A Khanty Shaman in 1990' (video – 26 min.) won acclaim. In 1991–1992 the Finnish professor carried out fieldwork among the Nanai people inhabiting the Amur region. The present writer had the opportunity to view the more than three-hour-long video recording that he had made, in the autumn of 1991, about the traditional rite. 'The Kasa taori is the classical ritual of the Nanai to send the souls of the departed as a group to the buni which is their abode behind the river.' The ceremony was staged by one of the clans, on one of the islands of the huge river. The 1991 Pärnu festival saw the screening, too, of a film focussing on another people of the Amur region, the Ulcha. Arkadily Morozov's film 'Amur People' (1990 – 26 min.) was shot in the region that the famous Captain Arsenev visited in the last century, and which he portrayed in his memoirs of travels. It is unfortunate that the film consists of only loosely connected, brief episodes and glimpses of life, a deficiency that even the superb camera work and beautiful pictures cannot fully redeem.

Staying in the Far East and continuing our review of the films showing the life of the peoples of the Amur, I have to mention the anthropological films I saw during a field-trip in China and Manchuria, in particular.

During my stay in Peking in August 1991, I made the acquaintance of the filmmakers who work at the Central Institute of Nationality Studies, which operates within the framework of the Chinese Academy of Social Sciences. These cinematic experts – who combine the skills and functions of cameraman, editor, and director, like Yang Guanghai – worked together with the ethnographers. In the 1957 to 1989 period, they made some 22 films among the ethnic minorities.

As is well known, the territory of the People's Republic of China is home of 56 nationalities, with the total population of ethnic minorities amounting to 60 million. These nationalities (that is, in fact, the term the Chinese themselves use in English translations of their own articles) stood at varying levels of social development – particularly in the Fifties and even as late as the Sixties. To use the Marxist terminology, some had remained at the level of the primitive communal system of fishing-hunting societies, with others fixed at the stage of slavery or serfdom, and still others, at that of semi-feudal dependence. Given that they were working according to the five-year plan cycles, the Chinese colleagues recorded exactly the three basic rules of the making of anthropological films:

> Most films were shot and completed from the mid-fifties to the sixties not so far from the years of radical social change. The shooting was conducted following these principles: *First*, going deep into the minority area and shooting on the spot with no artificial setting or professional actor or actress. Before shooting a film the researchers and the scenarist-directors go deep into the thick of life, making investigations repeatedly, making every effort to guarantee the truthfulness of the content. *Second*, emphasis is placed on scientificness. The contents of ethnological films must truly reflect the ethnic minorities' original social features, ways of life and their cultures, so, no fabrication or subjective supposition is allowable. First priority must be given to scientificness. The technique of expression should be simple and unadorned, and combine the recording of actual conditions and scientificness together. *Third*, paying special attention to the ways of life and traditional cultures that will disappear soon and are changing rapidly in the choice of subjects and the establishment of the theme. The traditional cultures and ways of life of the various nationalities that then still lived in the last stage of primitive society or still preserved remnants of primitive communes, of those whose social systems were experiencing great changes but still retaining the slave system and serfdom, and of those living in remote, thickly forested mountains cut off from the outside world, who were so isolated that few people had known them, have all been rush-shot on the basis of thorough investigations of Chinese ethnic minorities' history and social structures, and according to the scientific system. This saved a lot of materials that were rapidly disappearing by means of images and was of great significance for scientific research and ethnic work as well as for spreading cultural and scientific knowledge.
>
> (Du and Yang 1989: 69)

In 1959, under the above programme, the film '*Evenki People Along the River Argun*' – directed and photographed by Yang Guanghai – was produced. Naturally, in those days, 35 mm black-and-white film was the standard medium, and only natural light was used. The good quality of the pictures is a credit to the cameraman's work. The well-paced film replicates the daily life of the Evenki, a people of nomadic reindeer-keepers, with pictures of the building and dismantling of tents, hunting, meat distribution, all of them authentic documents. There is, however, a portion of the film that bears some all too obvious signs of it having been deliberately arranged for maximum effect – namely, the bit where the huntsman, in spring, brings in to the Chinese merchant the skin of the animals that he killed during the winter. (This part is highly reminiscent of a corresponding scene in 'Nanook'; though the makers are unlikely to have seen Flahety's famous film.) Later, we see the Evenki being made drunk and robbed: the antler of the reindeer – to which they ascribed healing powers – is taken away from him. (It is worth noting that, to this day, reindeer antlers are sold at Peking international airport.)

As the film shows, as far as is possible, a full one-year-long cycle in the life of the community, with all the important details, we get only brief, couple-of-minute-long flashes of fishing, the burial, and the wedding. Similarly, the shamanic healing, too, is given but a one-or-two-and-a-half-minute-long treatment; but there everything, including the costume, the drum, and the movement, is authentic. Yang Guanghai has disclosed that the original uncut negatives are still preserved, offering the possibility of one day presenting the entire material. So far, the authorities have not granted permission for this brief extract to be copied and taken out of the country.

The second film centred on the Oroqen community ('The Oroqen Nationality'). Made in 1963, it too was photographed by Yang Guanghai, with the former director of the Institute, Qui Pu, as the specialist-ethnographer. The latter, incidentally, has also published an ethnographical monograph dealing with this community of nomadic hunters numbering barely 2,000. The authentic pictures of the shamanic rituals account for about two minutes in the film, which runs for over an hour. The maker of the film revealed that the shaman and his helper had been shamanizing over someone with a real illness [. . .].

The third film was made in 1965, among the Hezhe (or Hodzha) people living along the Ussuri river. The film features some extended episodes portraying the shamans and their activities – in fact, these are the longest parts. When engaged in healing, the shaman wears a crown made of metal, an ornamental headgear displaying a bird. We are shown an interesting custom performed in spring and in autumn – i.e. the sacrifice to the spirits of roads. The pig sacrifice lies in front of the triple shaman's tree, set up in the courtyard. This they sprinkle with water.

I asked the Chinese colleagues to provide videotaped copies of these brief, couple-of-minute-long excerpts. However, they turned down my request, saying the authorities would refuse permission, as these films were not for screening abroad.

I was shown yet another film – one of about 35 minutes in length – which focuses on Manchu shamanism. Shot in 1988, it features one shaman helped out by four assistants, performing a full day-long ceremony for the well-being of the clan, that is to say, the extended family. In the film – which was made already on video – the shamans use three different types of drums, and, what is more important, here too the pig is the sacrificial animal. When the rituals are over, the participants jointly consume the pig.

In Changchun, where there is a whole research team working on collecting the material of shamanism, I saw two more films. 'Shamanic Dances' (1987 – 23 min. video) presents Manchu shamanic dances. The film affords some precious insights, as in the scene where we see one of the shamans wearing a crown decorated with three birds. It is visible when he achieves the trance state: at this point, he places glowing embers into his mouth.

Another short documentary was produced in 1990, among the small Oroqen community, along the Amur, in the village of Baina, Huma district. The video film was made on the occasion of a family gathering. The camera work bears all the hallmarks of the amateur; but, at the same time, it is also evident that the ethnographers present did not rearrange the events – except for the fact that one of the sides of the tent had been taken down to allow more light to get in for the shooting. In the tent thus altered, the shaman performs a round dance, calling on the spirits. It was interesting to observe the shaman's crown, decorated with ribbons and displaying giant horns, as well as the divergent drumming styles of the male and female shamans and the rich ornamentation of the shaman's costume (similar to that seen in the pictures presented by Ethel Lindgren, based on her fieldwork, made in the early 1930s).

Yet, the greatest experience I had during the whole of my stay in China was a film spotlighting Manchu shamanism. In 1988, a professional team made an over one-hour-long film about the shamanism of the Manchus inhabiting the Jilin district – more exactly, about a local variant of that shamanism. In their work, they relied on the local field experience of the Changchun researchers led by Fu Yuguang and Wang Hong-gang. They produced over five hours of material recording the ceremonies which lasted for three days. We quote from the description of an eye-witness, a young Chinese colleague:

> [T]he major task of the clan shaman is to conduct the annual offering rituals for each family in the clan. During these rituals, the shamans chant traditional scriptures and creation myths containing the names of numerous gods, deified ancestors, and wild spirits. The offering rituals basically have four parts-offerings to the deities of agriculture, hunting, darkness, and the sky pole.
>
> Before each family's annual offering ritual, the clan chief and the master shaman are invited to open the clan's ancestral box (a wooden trunk) that contains genealogical records, idols of clan deities (often mythologized ancestors) and other ritual items. This sacred box is said to be the residence of the clan ancestors and guardian spirits above the ninth heaven.

Although the clan shamans do not have a major role in maintaining genealogical records, the records play an important part in the shamanic rituals. Every four years (in the traditional zodiac years of the Dragon, Tiger, and Rat), the clan chief conducts a ceremony to add deceased clan members' names to the genealogical records which are kept in the ancestral box and displayed at the annual offering rituals. During this ceremony, an election is held for the position of clan chief, traditional laws and honour codes are recited for the benefit of all clan members, and myths and legends are passed on to the younger generations.

The offering ritual I observed was led by Guang Borong, a master shaman in his fifties. I later learned that Guang Borong had become a shaman at the age of twenty-seven, after he was selected by a call from the ancestral spirits and then trained by the master shaman Guang Zhiyuan. Guang Borong is highly respected among his people for his intelligence, his excellent handwriting, his caring for the people, and his endeavours to preserve their shamanic scriptures and traditions.

The ritual started before daybreak. Millet cakes and burning incense sticks had been placed on the offering table. After cleaning their hands and faces, the four participating shamans donned ceremonial skirts, trimmed with cloud designs, and cone-shaped waist bells – the sound of which is said to symbolize thunder. Then, drumming and chanting, they invoked the Farming Guardian, *Wuxin-endure*, from the upperworld and asked for his protection so that the crops and livestock would flourish.

Amidst the almost-deafening drumming of the three assistant shamans, Guang Borong began to dance and to sing: 'Among countless clans like willow leaves on Earth, the Guar'jia clan is one of the most prestigious. The great shamaness created the ancient scriptures, and I am selected as a shaman to serve the deities . . .' As he beat the hand drum and jumped from side to side – his cloud-design skirt swaying and his cone-shaped bells clapping, Guang Borong seemed to be flying into a thunder-storm.

Shortly after daybreak, a huge black pig was butchered as an offering. It was sliced into several blocks for boiling, and the cooked sections were then reassembled on the altar. The drumming quickened, and the lead shaman chanted: 'Following the decree of our ancestors, we prepare the sacrifice at the altar. The ritual meat is offered to you, deities. Please descend to share the game meat . . .'

While the shamans continued dancing and chanting scriptures, with occasional breaks, throughout the day, the other clan members busily prepared a feast. This part of the ritual concluded with an invitation to the deities of Heaven, war, and hunting to attend the feast.

That evening, after dark, all lights – except for some candles – were suddenly turned off. The clan members knelt, and the shamans began to dance and drum ecstatically. Guang Borong chanted, asking for the protection of the deities – primarily goddesses – in charge of darkness and safety.

Later that evening, the sacred genealogical records and ritual items were returned to the ancestral box and placed on the sacred west side of the *kang* (heatable brick bed), where they would remain until the next family in the clan was ready to hold an annual offering ritual. The offering food was removed from the altar, and homemade rice wine was served. Then, after dancing and chanting all day without eating, the shamans enjoyed the feast with the other clan members.

The following day, the clan held the sky pole offering ritual. The pole used in this ritual must come from a straight tree growing on a mountaintop and must be nine chi (approximately three meters) in height, representing the nine layers of Heaven. The sky pole, symbolizing the passageway to the upperworld, was erected in the middle of the courtyard. The top of the pole was smeared with animal blood as an offering to the deities. Grains and pig intestines were then attached to the pole as offerings to ravens and magpies, the scred messengers of the gods. As all clan members knelt before the sacred pole, the master shaman chanted to the heavens, asking the deities for protection.

Finally, there was a ritual in honour of *Fuduo Mama* (Goddess of Fertility), who is in charge of pregnancy and infant health. Offerings of food were hung on a willow tree – its countless leaves symbolize fertility – and women tried to grab the food as symbolic blessings. Colourful threads were tied to the children's hands, as lucky talismans from Fuduo Mama.

Fu Yuguang explained that, after all the offering rituals are finished, the bones of the sacrificial pig are scattered on a mountaintop or into the Songhua River. (Mountains and rivers are mythic symbols of easy access to the other world.) For three days, birds and natural forces are allowed to clean the blood and offerings off the sacred pole; then it is thrown into the river or planted on top of a mountain to carry the clan's best wishes to the heavenly deities. In some clans, families keep the sky poles in their courtyards throughout the year, until new poles are blessed and inaugurated at the next annual offering ritual.

(Shi Kun 1991: 25–26)

This Manchu film is immensely rich in ethnographical details. It will, no doubt, become one of the classics among the films profiling Eurasian shamanism, serving as a standard reference. We ourselves are preparing to offer a longer and more detailed review and analysis; this has been intended to be just a preliminary survey.

References

Du Rongkun and Yang Guangkai 1989. 'The Development of Video Show Ethnology in China', *New Asia Academic Bulletin* 8: 65–73.

Fitzhugh, W.W. 1991. 'Andris Slapins, Latvian Filmmaker', *CVA Newsletter* (Spring): 2–3.

Hoppál, M. 1988. 'Ethnographic Film in the Soviet Union', *CVA Newsletter* (October): 6–12.

Meri, L. 1987. 'Letter from Estonia', *CVA Newsletter* (May): 19–21.

Context

INTRODUCTION TO PART FOUR

PREVIOUS CHAPTERS HAVE ALREADY demonstrated the importance and value of considering shamans in relation to wider contexts. It is especially evident that shamans work with communities of various kinds in various ways. In this Part the chapters are interested in the relationship between shamans and other aspects of cultures. To put it another way, this Part is concerned with what the study of shamanic engagements might contribute to the study of politics, gender, environmentalism, community activism, and so on. Importantly, the trend might be in the other direction: what do gender studies have to contribute to shamanic studies? Assumptions implicit in particular constructions of being human and in particular expressions or performances of humanity (i.e. worldviews and lifeways) might, when brought into proximity with different views and ways, be made explicit and even explicable. That the process might also entail conflict and change is also important, and colonialism is not the only cultural encounter to entail such problems. Perhaps shamanism should be defined as the negotiation of particular local identities when confronted by conflicting possibilities arising from contact with others, only some of whom might be human. This is most evident in relation to some indigenous notions of health and ill-health, but is also relevant to the negotiations that establish notions of what is normal in politics, gender, subsistence, employment and habitation.

Caroline Humphrey's discussion in Chapter 13 of 'Urgunge's Way' acts as the conclusion to a book arising from and presenting her dialogue with Urgunge Onon, a Daur Mongol. Its aim is 'to delineate how shamanic knowledge is created among other kinds of knowledge, and to understand its agency in worlds conceived as fields of distinctive energies and powers'. Shamans have power because they have knowledge, but there are others with knowledge-power too: especially elders but also Buddhist lamas and Communist politicians. Negotiation may be far too positive a word to describe the fraught relationships formed in the clash of these knowledge-powers. Even 'traditionally' and prior to modernity, contention between shamans and elders marked Mongol sociality as much as co-existence based on separation and specialisation. This discussion certainly enriches understanding of shamanic contexts. It not only clarifies descriptive concerns such as the particular festivals for which shamans rather than elders are responsible, but also proffers invaluable analytical and theoretical material. For example, the partiality of all views of shamanism is discussed, and if distinctions between possession and trance have produced copious debates, the distinction between trance rituals and sacrificial ones might generate much of value.

The following two chapters discuss gender. These go far beyond questions of whether shamans in any given society are male or female, and even further than asking what it means when shamans are typically of one gender rather than another. A short Chapter 14 by Bernard Saladin d'Anglure summarises information and debates about Inuit 'third genders' and is especially interesting in discussing the fluidity or flexibility of gender constructs among Inuit. Gender is far from insignificant, but nor is it entirely determined by genitalia or other 'natural' givens. The cosmological and social repercussions of Inuit notions are mapped. Marjorie Balzer in Chapter 15 further enriches this debate by discussing the flexibility of gender in Siberia, especially in relation to 'beliefs about shamans (spiritual healers), animal spirits, and power through manipulations of spiritual energy'. What might be considered 'deviant' in some (elite and conservative) European discourse may instead 'become sacred' in Siberia. Importantly, Balzer engages not only with historical material but also discusses recent, 'postmodern, post-Soviet' developments.

The relationships engendered in politics and gender identities and enactments are themselves not only significant for understanding shamans and their craft, but also embed them in the everyday and ordinary. It is hard to overstate the importance of the everyday, but it is obviously easy to ignore. Many discussions of shamans are motivated, controlled and furthered primarily or even solely by interest in the extraordinary, the fantastic, the extreme (e.g. Eliade's focus on ecstasy, or 'altered states of consciousness'). In Chapter 16 Michael Taussig counters this particular manifestation of the 'wild man' myth by reference to another domain imbued with mystique: the everyday. In a chapter filled with humour and pathos, he struggles to convey the 'toughness and tenderness' inherent in the everyday life of a healing shaman in Columbia. Once again the particularities and specificities of local realities are foregrounded. Colonialism and terror are challenged, not by depoliticised 'spirituality' but by radical engagements with the matter of everyday needs, especially for healing. Not for the first time, interest in shamans proves significant in also re-imagining new possibilities for the everyday processes of academia.

In Chapter 17 Piers Vitebsky discusses the pressures brought to bear on the many diverse 'local knowledges' by the forces of globalisation. He begins with the stark contrast of the decline or abandonment of some shamanic knowledges 'in the jungles and tundra' over against the continuing growth of 'something called shamanism'. He also offers an ambiguous note of caution: 'And yet again, in other parts of the jungle and tundra there is a revival, supposedly of traditional shamanism'. Predictions of the demise of this or that indigenous people or religion have been commonplace in (and constructive of) colonising modernity. Vitebsky more carefully explores actual trends and tendencies today. His title notes just one of the intriguing shifts that might be observable, namely that 'from cosmology to environmentalism'. The chapter usefully locates interests of both shamans and scholars with reference to the widest possible contexts: cosmos and ecology.

While none of these chapters focuses entirely on shamans as dangerous people potentially engaged in conflicts with their neighbours or enemies in this or other worlds, they all suggest such possibilities. One critique of 'core shamanism' (further discussed in Part Five) is that it tends to sanitise and pacify shamanic activities, especially by psychologising and internalising them (see Jakobsen 1999). A dialogue between undercurrents (at least) in this Part and the chapters that follow might be revelatory of further promising gaps and disjunctions. This, of course, is true of all Parts of this work. Hopefully readers will make connections that challenge the barriers that seem to be erected between chapters, Parts, themes, interests, critiques and description. Just one further example: another wide context in which shamans participate is that of material culture. The use of art and artefacts, objects (albeit ones understood as subjects in their own right at times), is clear in Parts Two and Three, but the particular label 'material culture' only appears explicitly in Beverly Butler's chapter in Part Five. There are obvious reasons for this placing (the chapter refers to a new form of Western activist shamanism) but reflection on the contexts and aesthetics of shamanising would do well to cross the divides, transcend the boundaries and form relationships between seemingly discrete material.

References

Jakobsen, M.D. 1999. *Shamanism: Traditional and Contemporary Approaches to the Mastery of Spirits and Healing.* New York: Berghahn.

Chapter 13

Caroline Humphrey and Urgunge Onon

URGUNGE'S WAY

Some concluding remarks

'SHAMANISM' AS A WHOLE conglomerate of beliefs and practices was not only about the knowledge we have, but about the various kinds of knowledge we ordinary people do not quite have. This knowing was not, however, thought of as supernatural. It was knowledge of what was there to be known, but only certain individuals were gifted to know it or discover it, and they did so in different ways. For this reason 'shamanism' could encompass and deepen ordinary knowledge of nature (including human nature), thus revealing what made the ordinary marvellous.

This being said, there were great differences between the various knowledge traditions of trance shamans and other practitioners, and these depended on how knowledge itself was constituted and sustained, for example by lifelong social experience (elders), or by physical touch (bone-setters). The altered state of consciousness of *yadgan* shamans was another means to knowledge. The poetry of shamans' songs reveals this to have been understanding of an emotionally candid reality, for which the conscious subject was not the standard patriarchally defined person but all imaginable kinds of individual selves. The self was not conceived as being alone, and the shaman's practice aimed to reconstitute and make effective this very consociality for the sufferer. The notion of consociality that shamans brought into play extended beyond death to previous sufferers and beyond the boundaries of humanity to the consciousness of other living beings such as animals and birds.

The replication of like by like in the patriarchal ideology was confronted with cumulations of distinctive, unique, and anomalous beings (complex 'spirits'), which substituted unlike for unlike, and thereby constituted a different sense of wild creativity, linked to an idea of maximal universality [. . .]. The standard ideas of age, seniority, and gender were thus taken apart and rendered powerless in the shaman's practice, even while they continued as organizing principles in other domains of society and ritual. The power given to acute emotion in the *yadgan* shaman's practice had the effect of destabilizing and overturning all external verities. It did this by insisting that the relevant knowledge was 'psychological' knowledge and that to have knowledge (*medel*) was also to control the object known. Consequently, the fount of this 'knowledge-power' being not just the mind but the 'heart-mind' [. . .], emotions, even ancient emotions of people long dead, would colour the landscape, as the shaman mother's anguish made the solid world crumble all around [. . .].

Spirits had to be remembered, because they were held to cause present sufferings which mirrored their own. Thus, although shamanic practice differed from place to place, and between *yadgan* shamans and other types of shamans, there were institutions which served to maintain and transmit shamanic knowledge in distinctive traditions. The most notable of these was the *yadgan*'s *ominan* ritual [. . .], the festival of remembering all the spirits, where external shamans from other clans or ethnic groups were given a supervisory role.

This book aims to go beyond earlier studies of shamanism which have focused on definitional problems and social organization, such as Firth's (1959: 129–48) useful and well-known distinction between spirit possession, mediumship, and shamanism. The aim here has been to delineate how shamanic knowledge is created among other kinds of knowledge, and to understand its agency in worlds conceived as fields of distinctive energies and powers. Shamans' distinctive abilities were not separated off from those of other social actors, like rulers or Buddhist lamas, but contended with them. The final part of the book relates the disjunctive character of shamanic practices to the decline of some earlier traditions and the emergence of new 'modernist' ones in the context of early twentieth-century politics.

The issues tackled in this book are not irrelevant to understanding 'shamanism' today. From descriptions of North Asian shamanic practices and those of many other parts of the world, pared-down models have been abstracted and worked on by shamanic practitioners in California and elsewhere. 'Shamanic workshops' of New Age movements, 'shamanic counselling', and so forth are now being re-exported back to the Siberian lands of their origin (Hoppál 1992). Here they are encountering self-conscious, marketed, and sometimes even licensed, revivals of shamanism. These globalized practices recognize that the magic of the acting-out (mimesis) of reality, so transforming it, is not simply 'primitive'. They assume there is a 'shamanic' possibility of self-transformation available to anyone, and this is something Urgunge would agree with. But the workshops too are an active element in the cultural politics of our time – a fact that is mostly ignored. Their apparent de-contextualization of their content from any social specificity, in order to produce a universal technique, is in the end illusory. This book has shown how a knot of relations is produced in shamanic practice, and how this invariably produces an art and a politics of representation. In Urgunge's youth too shamanic visions rendered an objectification of ontologies of various powers, and this was both active, mirroring and confronting Buddhism and Communism, and self-reflexive, creating a plagiarism of the shaman's own experience. It is because this has still not been adequately described that our book aims to provide a historically aware, nuanced account of that time, as well as a sense of the way in which one person, Urgunge, *believes in* shamanism.

I now briefly attempt to place this account of shamanism in relation to some other recent interpretations. We would agree with Overing (1990) about the creativity of shamans, their use of previous images to build new ones, and their use of moral-emotional categories to establish the identity of spirits and explain their vengeful activities. But Urgunge agrees with me in querying her formulation of the idea that shamans are 'worldmakers', constantly taking apart and putting together versions at hand which are through-and-through unique and *sui generis*. Overing quotes Goodman (1978) to the effect that 'there is no solid bedrock of reality to such worldmaking' (1990: 605). However, not only is reality exactly what shamans and other practitioners are aiming to discover, but they proceed from basic concepts of the nature of human, animal, and material existence in the world, which might well be shared by anyone anywhere. These are never entirely lost sight of in the contentious or mythic versions discovered by shamans, since one finds that the latter are not entirely random but are related to salient aspects of the everyday concepts (cf. Boyer 1994). So when the relevant aspect of trees, for example, is their capacity to grow healthily, flourish, reproduce themselves, and die, these aspects are the ones upon which the shamanic imagination dwells in its exploration of further dimensions or analogies of tree-like existence. The basic concepts remain at issue even when the shaman yells her poetic calls to deny, subvert, or destabilize them.

Our account accords most closely with Severi's illuminating series of articles (1982, 1985, 1987, 1993) on Cuna shamanism. Shamanism is understood here as a certain way of conceiving the invisible aspect of reality, and as a particular style of world-view related to it. In Cuna traditional thought all things, rocks, trees, stars, clouds, or people, owe their perceptible 'face' to the invisible presence of *purpa*, the immaterial life-giving double which can never be seen. The function of the shaman is to represent these invisible energies. This is an anxiety-making *terra incognita*, in which traditional thought places the foreign, the new, and the incomprehensible, and it is from this domain that suffering comes to people. Severi's most notable contribution (1987, 1993) is to show how the shaman constructs a paradigm in his ritualized songs to relate two negatively defined dimensions of existence: an invisible landscape within the body and an external, inaccessible world located at the limits of human perception. The first is too close (inside oneself) to be known only in ordinary ways, and the latter is too distant, since it consists of natural or foreign processes that human faculties cannot ordinarily comprehend. The making of this relationship, the explaining of the one by the other, and vice versa, does indeed seem to lie at the centre of shamanic practice. Many examples from Inner Asia have been described in this book, such as the songs for Baglain Udagan and Niang-Niang.

I would suggest that the need felt by Daurs to make this relation between two such widely separated aspects of the not-yet-known is the reason why shamanic thought does not make use of 'replication' (the constant reproduction of similarity); instead it employs 'substitution', which recognizes difference in the elements of knowledge but constructs a passage, that of metamorphosis, between them. Inner, via metamorphosis, becomes outer and vice versa.

Shamanship commonly, perhaps always, coexists with other religious practices. This situation is analysed in a further series of publications, Thomas (1988), Atkinson (1989), Mumford (1989), and the authors in Thomas and Humphrey (1994). Shamans, through the 'trance' and the incorporation of spirits, have a peculiarly immediate relation with unseen forces, and this constitutes a different style which is in competition with those religious relations mediated by rituals like sacrifice. As the studies mentioned show, the agency of shamans waxes and wanes, and can change in its style and content, in relation to the effectiveness of political rule. Frequently the erosion of the religious potency of rulers enables that of shamans to rise. This book has attempted to link the kind of ideas Overing and Severi are discussing – the cultural creativity of shamans – with the constitutive actions of shamans in the political arena. Atkinson's excellent study of the Wana shamans in Indonesia (1989) is the most complete existing account of such a relation. Locating the Wana in the relatively egalitarian and dispersed periphery of the Dutch colonial (later the Indonesian) state, she documents a homology between Wana ideas of the person, their community, and the cosmos. Wana see all three as oscillating historically between concentration and dissipating, unhealthy dispersal. The shaman's role as 'mediator' is understood in Atkinson's book not just in the simple sense of a go-between from humans to spirits, but as mediating different levels of meaning, the personal, the social, and the cosmological-political. It seems to me that this interpretation is illuminating. A similarly many-layered shamanic practice is evident in the Holieri performance.

The shamanic song of Holieri and the story of Nishan Shaman produced integrating visions. However, an anthropological understanding can see them only as partial, since the conditions of the production of shamanic knowledge – the existence of various types of shamans with their own distinctive abilities at knowing – were inherently 'dispersive'. Nevertheless, it is argued by

Urgunge that this very fact is what gave 'shamanism' its unity from the point of view of someone inside. For someone 'working shamanism' only his or her own way among the possibilities presented by living experience was what mattered. This perspective gave ultimate agency to the individual as the locus of singular moments of accident, decision, and fortitude. Perhaps it owed much to the immediacy and singular vividness of the shaman's activity. But in the end such a consciousness distanced all shamans or magicians, as it did the structures of clans and political rituals, since the individual saw himself as acting through them in accordance with his own fate, rather than being constituted only as an element of one or another of these systems.

Reflections of an elder

This book ends with Urgunge's voice. It is the essence of 'shamanism' that it has its existence in the people who believe in it, rather than in texts to be mulled over by scholars. As Gudeman has written (1990: 189),

> Ultimately, the intellectual historians, contextualists, verifications, falsificationists, and literary critics in economics (and anthropology as well) focus upon inscriptions. But the text is only part of the story, because it leaves out practices. By 'practice' we do not mean something by which to verify or 'falsify' theory, for this serves only to subjugate practices to the hegemony of the theorist and writer; instead, practice refers to the actions and voices of people in history, that are sometimes inscribed in texts and of which the inscription itself is an example.

Urgunge had a partial, intentional, engaged view of 'shamanism'. But, as I have tried to show, who could not have a partial view, since the 'whole thing' was not in fact a single thing? An insider's view is sustained by a whole life of practice, and if it might be objected that Urgunge's life has made his view no longer 'genuine', then I can only reply that it is much more genuine than mine. In Manchuria I was faced squarely with political, moral, and intellectual limits to anthropological questioning [. . .]. At various points in this narrative I have been absolutely dependent on Urgunge to understand what some Daur action could be said to mean. If my anthropological training has led me to search more widely, to verify, to bring out themes Urgunge had forgotten or thought unimportant, that must find its place alongside the voice of someone who has not rejected the ideas and feelings acquired in early childhood. Although Urgunge 'became an elder' in England, it is not for this reason that he speaks to us as a contemporary; if this book has succeeded at all in its strategy, the readers will understand his reflections not as a voice from an archaic outside (Fabian 1983), but as the truthful expression of a positioned imagination, ranging over the world in the same way that our readers also ponder the world from their situations. At the same time we can see that Urgunge's life-course has relieved him of the oppressive *double fearfulness* recalled by other Daurs still in China, many of whom saw themselves as liberated by atheism (that is, fear of the ancestral spirits present in the landscape and fear of the state's punishment for taking part in shamanic activities). The following is my understanding of what Urgunge means, why he feels 'shamanism' to be a unity, and why he thinks it is the religion of the future.

'Up to now human civilizations have been ruled by the logics,' Urgunge said, 'Now it is time for us to rule the logics.' By 'logics' he means not only abstract reasoning but all those ideologies which explain the world by means of a universal system. The paradigm for this, in his mind, is Buddhism, which has a comprehensive philosophy and ethics explaining every component of the human being and its relation to action. Although there is much to admire in Buddhism, the Buddhist 'logic' is ultimately repressive, subordinating people to its tenets in such a way that, once caught, you can never escape its construction of causality.[1] One great fault of the 'logics' is that they invariably construct some people, or some social positions, as being superior. For this reason, Urgunge was deeply shocked when he first went south to Chahar and saw his revered Prince De prostrating himself before a reincarnate lama. 'I thought of De as a great man. It was as though my father had kowtowed before Du Yadgan, the shaman. It is all right to kowtow to your genealogical senior, because you yourself will be senior one day. But not to a lama or shaman.' This was why, Urgunge said, Merse had never introduced a great lama like the Panchen Bogd to lead his movement, even if he had seen it might be expedient.

'We should respect all of the people all the time, not some of the people some of the time,' was another of Urgunge's aphorisms. He saw both the Buddhist clergy and the Communist Party as only 'some of the people', and both were temporary and historical phenomena. But shamanists, all of them, feel themselves to be the centre of their own universe. Above is *tengger*, who is beyond time, and each human being has also a part of *tengger* in themselves. This is their consciousness. It is both at the centre of each person and far away, out in the cosmos. Urgunge's universe is coloured, a vast expanse of blueness, deeper blue the further away, and in the blue there are two points representing the self, an outer cosmic one, which is like a bright star in the sky, and an inner one, which is red. 'Astronomers analyse the universe through maths and physics,' he said, 'But we do it through our consciousness, which I feel to be like a hole, that red hole which is nothing but itself, that is me, my heart, sensing and alive. It is breathing (*amisaj bain*), pulsating with a barely perceptible noise. Don't you sometimes hear that beat in yourself? That pulse is my power (*kuch*).' Consciousness leaping outwards gives each person their own orbit and their own independence – '*ooriin tenggertei, ooriin terguultei*' – 'your own sky, your own cart-track.'

'Shamanism gives me the sense of being very, very free,' Urgunge said, 'because you have a clear sense of your own space. Between yourself and *tengger*, that is a vast space and that is where you can fly (*derdeu*). We were born with the feeling of flying out, flying far. Remember the shaman's *onggor* bird: that is his consciousness.'

This is why the *yadgan* shamans kept their ancient views, Urgunge said. To them shamanizing – the empowerment by *onggors* in the trance – was their freedom, their ability to penetrate in disguise the stoutest ramparts [. . .]. They had no need of any other views, and indeed another way would no longer be theirs.

Forgetting time, but conscious of stellate space, each person will feel free to move along their own orbit. Once Urgunge and I had disagreed about the role of time in 'shamanism'. I had argued that shamans accepted time in the sense of the life-span and its end, death. Urgunge said,

> You have not understood. Death is a change of form. In shamanism there is no such thing as the past, because everything continues to be, only in different forms. Everyone has to act at a given time, and that is *now*, this season [*erin*]. But even 'now' will soon be 'then', so ultimately it is pointless even to consider time. In my childhood, no one had a clock or a watch. To my mind 'time' means 'limit', but space is freedom.

The people moving along their paths are not separate from one another, but interact in amity and discord in an unpredictable mingling which is given by the order of the universe.

Once I asked Urgunge suspiciously if the idea of balance in the universe was really a Daur idea or whether it was not borrowed from Chinese ideas of *yin* and *yang*.[2] His reply starts off straightforwardly, but becomes more difficult to explain. 'The balance of diversity in the world is not an idea,' he said.

> It is a fact. You might as well ask whether Einstein invented relativity or not – he did not invent it, he discovered it. Personally I do not believe in invention, only in discovery. The fact is: all the things in the world and the people exist in their own way. We cannot and must not win over everything, but we must fight. Fighting is balancing. *Shurkuls* [devils] were never killed. You don't get the idea? If a shaman could completely get rid of *shurkul*, everything would lose balance. *Shurkul* has to be there.

Urgunge ruminated further:

> Merse's view was not the same as mine because he was educated and I only had about five years of high school.[3] The fact is: there

were shamans and spirits, but how Merse and I would analyse them would be different. It is almost impossible for me to say how my father would think, or other Daurs; even a fish tastes different to you and me. A dog sees the world from a dog's point of view. But whatever ideas we have, or the Chinese have, we all know the universe is composed of an infinite number of different things. If we understood them all then we would not need a shaman. He was our messenger and our ambassador. He could see further and journey further. But in the end he was like us. The Daurs had shamans for the same reason that made me so happy when I was young: we needed to be able to distinguish [perceive] the many things in the world and then make our own tracks.

I ventured, 'Was that perhaps why so much of what Daurs say about shamans is half like a joke – they believe it, and they don't believe it?' 'Ah, my sister, you understand it now. A Daur only believes something for himself. Even the shaman will introduce us only to his universe. But the question is – why did the Daurs have this attitude? It is because the balance of the universe is *tengger*, and what do any of us really know about him? We know the *tengger* that is in our heads. I don't know what my ancestors thought about this, but I'll bet they thought their consciousness *was tengger*.'

I think Urgunge did not mean anything inscrutable by this. He continued talking of *tengger* as an intelligence in ourselves and also out among the things in the world and merged with them. I came to see that a dispersed religion like 'shamanism' is unified for each individual by their choices and empathies, which establish their actions as path-making events in their various landscapes. 'The first is to understand yourself. Then what is around you. Any animal, or thing, or person, if I see, or feel, or touch it, I can understand it, what it is thinking, and what it will do, its next step. Then I take my next step.' This is Urgunge's feeling about the religion that lies behind the surfaces, practices, and segments described in this book.

Notes

1   Urgunge was once deeply impressed by Buddhism in his life. It was not the doctrines which influenced him (he says he knows little about them, which is true) but the sight of a stone statue when he was in Japan as a young man. 'When I looked at the Buddha's face I became very quiet,' he said.

2   *Yin* and *yang*, in Urgunge's view, were taken from early shamanism, not the other way around.

3   Curiously Urgunge forgot the time he spent at a Japanese university here. While in Japan he studied politics, so he considered this indoctrination rather than true education.

References

Atkinson, J.M. 1989. *The Art and Politics of Wana Shamanship*. Berkeley, CA: University of California Press.

Boyer, P. 1994. *The Naturalness of Religious Ideas: A Cognitive Theory of Religion*. Berkeley, CA: University of California Press.

Fabian, J. 1983. *Time and the Other: How Anthropology Makes its Object*. New York: Columbia University Press.

Firth, R. 1959. 'Problem and Assumption in an Anthropological Study of Religion', *Journal of the Royal Anthropological Institute* 89: 129–48.

Goodman, N. 1978. *Ways of Worldmaking*. Brighton: Harvester Press.

Gudeman, S. and Rivera, A. 1990. *Conversations in Columbia: The Domestic Economy in Life and Text*. Cambridge: Cambridge University Press.

Hoppál, M. 1992. 'Urban Shamans: A Cultural Revival in the Postmodern World' in A.-L. Siikala and M. Hoppál (eds), *Studies on Shamanism*. Helsinki: Finnish Anthropological Society, and Budapest: Akadémiai Kiadó, pp. 197–209.

Mumford, S.R. 1989. *Himalayan Dialogue: Tibetan Lamas and Gurung Shamans in Nepal*. Madison, WI: University of Wisconsin Press.

Overing, J. 1990. 'The Shaman as Maker of Worlds: Nelson Goodman in the Amazon', *Man* 25/4: 602–19.

Severi, C. 1982. 'Le Chemin des métamorphoses: Un modèle de connaissance de la folie dans un chant chamanique cuna', *Res* (Spring): 31–67.

Severi, C. 1985. 'Penser par séquences, penser par territoires', *Communications* 41: 160–90.

Severi, C. 1987. 'The Invisible Path: Ritual Representation of Suffering in Cuna Traditional Thought', *Res* 14: 66–85.

Severi, C. 1993. 'Talking about Souls: The Use of a Complex Category in Cuana Ritual Language', in P. Boyer (ed.), *Cognitive Aspects of Ritual Symbolism*. Cambridge: Cambridge University Press, pp. 165–81.

Thomas, N. 1988. 'Marginal Powers: Shamanism and the Disintegration of Hierarchy', *Critique of Anthropology* 8: 53–74.

Thomas, N. and Humphrey, C. (eds) 1994. *Shamanism, History and the State*. Ann Arbor, MI: University of Michigan Press.

Chapter 14

Bernard Saladin D'Anglure

RETHINKING INUIT SHAMANISM THROUGH THE CONCEPT OF 'THIRD GENDER'

AFTER EXTENSIVE RESEARCH begun in 1956 among the Inuit of Canada's central arctic, in particular those from the Igloolik area (1971–1990), I reached the point five years ago of being able to construct a three-dimensional holistic model [see Figure 14.1] and thus consolidate results from areas as different as kinship and social organization, economics and technology, mythology and world view, the system of dictates/prohibitions, and rituals and shamanism. The model was also an attempt to work out a theory based on these results by picking up where Marcel Mauss had left off eighty-five years ago in his famous "Essai sur les variations salsonnière des sociétés eskimo" (1906). Here I would like to offer the main elements of this theory with all the more enthusiasm and emotion inasmuch as two factors mark my participation at this conference. The first one is the presence of an impressive number of colleagues from the Soviet Union at a time when the USSR is going through social upheavals comparable from a certain point of view of those which gave rise to the first Russian Revolution in 1905, at the very time when Mauss was writing his essay. Moreover, he went to Moscow that year to follow events at close hand. Communism was still a utopia then and the idea of democratic socialism with a human face still seemed possible. It is thus worthy of interest to see Mauss presenting what he called Eskimo 'communism' with its economic, sexual, and religious dimensions – a type of social contract which seemed to fascinate him. The second factor is that my anthropological career began for all intents and purposes in Finland, among the Saamis of Utsjoki and Sevettijarvi. They must still laugh whenever they think back to this young French student who almost lost his life while going down the Tana River in a rubber dinghy.

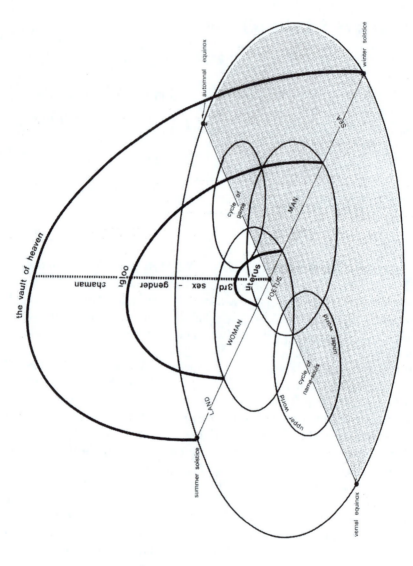

Figure 14.1 On the border between sexes/genders
Source: Saladin d'Anglure (1986)

Among the interesting data collected over the years from Inuit in Igloolik were the intra-uterine memories several informants had, notably Iqallijuq – an old Inuit woman and shaman's daughter who remembered living within her mother's womb, this being laid out like the interior of an igloo. She could also recall a previous life as her own grandfather. When she was in the womb a dog poked its head through the door from time to time. It had a mouth set on its face vertically and vomited food for her. It was probably, so she told me, her father's penis. She was still a man when a desire came upon her to leave so she took a man's knife place on the lefthand side (on the righthand when entering) and headed for the passageway. At the thought, however, of the dangerous hunting life she would have to lead, she put down these male instruments and took from the righthand side a woman's knife and a small cooking pot. She pushed her way out with much effort. Then his penis was reabsorbed, a slit opened up in her body, and she became a girl. This long tale from which I made a film provided me with a series of very rich symbols about the reproduction of life, the sexual division of labour, sex, and gender. Once again, I found in a monograph by Rasmussen a short myth telling how the first two humans emerged from the ground on Igloolik Island at the dawn of time. Out of boredom, they decided to procreate. One made the other pregnant but, when it came time to give birth, there was no opening for the fetus to pass through. Undaunted, the companion of the pregnant man sang a magic song which caused the latter's penis to shrivel up, leaving an opening in its place and thus creating the first woman through the transformation of a man. In light of this example and several other facts it appeared that cosmogeny was conceived as a form of ontogeny, that the uterus was the microcosm of the igloo, and that sex was unstable and changeable. It is still believed in Igloolik that babies can change sex at birth if the delivery is too long or difficult. Hence, about 2 per cent of the population is said to have changed sex at birth in this village of a little less than one thousand inhabitants.

Some time later, I recorded a shamanistic song from another informant, a son and brother of shamans, who had known Rasmussen quite well. This song had belonged to his father's friend, an invalid shaman. No longer able to travel very far with his body, the old shaman transposed the different parts of the igloo throughout the universe and thus could go wherever he so desired with his spirit to locate game animals for members of his group. Thus, the raised platform was the land, the floor was the sea, the ice window was the sun, the darker opening at the end of the passageway was the moon, and the spiral layout of the igloo's snow blocks was the heavens. The igloo was a microcosm of the firmament.

During another year in this same village I worked at organizing the making of a replica of a shaman's coat which had been bought from my informant's grandfather at the end of the last century by an American whaler, Captain Comer, on behalf of Franz Boas and the American Museum of Natural History. Now it so happened that this coat was a woman's coat. It belonged to an invisible woman whom the shaman had to combat and who became his helping spirit.

An investigation carried out several years earlier on how conception, pregnancy, and delivery are viewed had shown that the fetus was composed of its mother's blood, its father's sperm, the animal flesh its mother consumed, and the soul-name of a diseased person (or several soul-names). After bringing all the data together it appeared to me that the differentiation of the sexes held a primordial place in the great cosmogonical differentiations. In fact, it held first place. It was the basis on which gender was imagined, thus constituting the great metaphor of culture. Through it were mentally conceived the other differentiations. Consequently, an individual who was socialized in such a way as to straddle the gender boundary ought to be able to span all boundaries. One individual socialized in this way was Iqallijuq. There were also many children who, though not changing sex at birth, did change gender in childhood because they had received their name from someone of the opposite sex (such people make up 15–20 per cent of Igloolik's population). We are here at the heart of the shaman's mediating relationships and probably all religious forms of mediation. We have therefore proposed the expression third gender as the name for the site of this overlapping, i.e. the site of these mediating relationships which various factors act upon: an unbalanced sex ratio within the family, the passing away of a loved one whose name will be eagerly and quickly taken up anew, or the desire to pass on to a descendent the shamanistic power of a diseased person's name. Thus a ternary model made it possible to pick up on and make complete Mauss's essay which remains hemmed in by a binary or dualistic approach, as moreover has long been the case of anthropology in its entirely with regard to relationships of sex and gender. Curiously, this hypothesis also ties in with and makes complete another one which Marie Czaplicka formulated in the early years of this century on Siberian shamanism. She wrote:

> Socially, the shaman does not belong either to the class of males or to that of females, but to a third class, that of shamans [. . .] shamans have special taboos comprising both male and female characters. The same may be said of their costume, which combines features peculiar to the dress of both sexes.
>
> (Czaplicka 1914: 253)

A few years earlier none other than J.G. Frazer (1907) had raised the question of religious transvestism and sex change which religious mediation implied, but the evolutionary ideas of the time and the postulate, borrowed by the Marxists from Morgan, of an initial matriarchal stage in mankind's development resulted in the Siberian data being interpreted as holdovers from this presumed matriarchy. This interpretation held sway despite the studies on Siberia by L. Sternberg who, for his part, wrote:

The practice of changing sex for religious motives is known not only in the Chuckchee and the Koryak, but it has a wide distribution, at least in the form of transvestism, among the Eskimo and everywhere else in North and South America.

(Sternberg 1925: 491)

One can again find in the Inuit's 'election' of a namesake certain characteristics which Frazer and Sternberg attribute to Siberian shamanistic 'election' (or religious 'election' elsewhere around the world), e.g. the wish of a spirit to be incarnated in a particular individual (often of the opposite sex), the fact that this election to a certain extent takes on the aspect of a 'possession' or that it is often expressed through a dream or a trance. This analogy between the two systems would be enough in itself to account for the transvestism or the shamanistic 'sex changes'. As for the distinction made by Sternberg between spirit-masters and helping spirits, we can only assume its existence among the Inuit, for want of adequate ethnographic data.

The rise of psychoanalytic theory as a new major theory of sexuality and Freud's inability to think androgyny through scientifically and objectively whenever he encountered it, notably in the famous case of demon possession he studied (cf. Macalpine and Hunter 1956, and Urtubey 1983) resulted in this interpretation of shamanism being condemned to obscurity. This was all the more so because of the difficulty of distinguishing sex from gender prior to Margaret Mead's pioneering work (1935, 1948) and more recent studies by feminist writers (cf. Mathieu 1971). As well, people have too easily confused homosexuality with symbolic or social androgyny (cf. Murdock 1949). Finally, the binary logic which underlies the principle of the excluded middle and constitutes one of the cornerstones of Western scientific thought makes it hard to apprehend more analogical and ternary belief-systems (cf. Dumont 1983).

We have tried to show that this analogical and ternary thinking operates on all levels of what Inuit live through and conceive — from cosmogony to shamanistic rituals, with a passing nod to socialization. Our latest research also allows us to affirm that this thinking continues to operate in the real-life experiences of Inuit Christianity which has taken over part of the heritage of shamanism.

At this stage of our research it may be useful to consider other instances of shamanism, particularly in Siberia, to see whether this theory would stand up and, if so, in what forms and on what terms. If it turns out that shamanism was indeed marked in one manner or another by an overlapping of the gender boundary, then such evidence would clear the way for a reconsideration of all religious phenomena in history and around the world, given its recognized place as perhaps the oldest form of human religion. This would be a far-reaching programme which can come about only through collective effort and so will call upon your utmost cooperation.

References

Boas, Franz (1901), 'The Eskimo of Baffin Land and Hudson Bay.' *Bulletin of the American Museum of Natural History* 15(1).

Boas, Franz (1907), 'The Eskimo of Baffin Land and Hudson Bay.' *Bulletin of the American Museum of Natural History* 15(2).

Czaplicka, Marie A. (1914), *Aboriginal Siberia; A Study in Social Anthropology.* London: Oxford University Press.

Dumont, Louis (1983), *Essai sur l'individualisme. Une perspective anthropologique sur l'ideologie moderne.* Collection Esprit, Paris: Editions du Seuil.

Frazer, James G. (1926), *Atys et Osiris. Etude de religions orientales comparées.* Paris: Librairie orientaliste Paul Geuthner (translation of English edition *Adonis, Attis, Oziris,* London, 1907).

Freuchen, Peter (1939), *Aventure arctique, ma vie dans les glaces du Nord.* Paris: Albin Michel (translation of English edition *Arctic Adventure.* New York: Murray Hill 1935).

Macalpine, J. and Hunter R. (1956), *Schizophrenia 1677.* London: William Dawson.

Mathiassen, Therkel (1928), 'Material Culture of the Iglulik Eskimos.' In *Report of the Fifth Thule Expedition 1921–24.* Vol. 6, No. 1, Copenhagen.

Mathieu, Nicole-Claude (1971), 'Notes pour une définition sociologique des catégories de sexe.' *Epistémologie sociologique,* September.

Mauss, Marcel 1906. 'Essai sur les variations saisonnières des sociétés Eskimo. Etude de morphologie sociale', *Année Sociologique* 9 (1904–5): 39–132. English translation: *Seasonal Variations of the Eskimo: A Study in Social Morphology.* Trans. J. J. Fox. London: Routledge and Kegan Paul, 1979.

Mead, Margaret (1935), *Sex and Temperament in Three Primitive Societies.* New York.

Mead, Margaret (1948), *Male and Female.* New York: William Morrow and Co.

Murdock, George Peter (1949), *Social Structure.* London: The Free Press.

Rasmussen, Knud (1929a), 'Intellectual Culture of the Iglulik Eskimos.' In *Report of the Fifth Thule Expedition 1921–24,* Vol. 7, Copenhagen.

Rasmussen, Knud (1929b), *Du Groenland au Pacifique. Deux ans d'intimité avec des tribus d'Esquimaux inconnus.* Paris: Plon (transl. from Danish by C. Lund and J. Bernard).

Saladin d'Anglure, Bernard (1980), 'Nanuq super-mâle: l'ours blanc dans l'espace imaginaire et le temps social des Inuit.' *Etudes mongoles et Siberiennes,* 11: 63–94.

Saladin d'Anglure, Bernard (1984), 'Inuit of Québec.' In *Handbook of North American Indians.* Vol. 5, *Arctic* (ed. by D. Damas), Washington: Smithsonian Institution.

Saladin d'Anglure, Bernard (1986), 'Du foetus au chamane, la construction d'un troisième sexe unit.' *Etudes Inuit Studies,* No. anniversaire: *A la frontière des sexes,* 10(1–2): 25–113.

Saladin d'Anglure, Bernard (1988), 'Penser le féminin chamanique, ou le tiers-sexe des chamanes inuit.' *Recherches Amérindiennes au Québec*, No. special: *Chamanisme dans les Amériques*, 18(2–3): 19–50.

Saladin d'Anglure, Bernard (1989), 'Kunut et' les angakkut iglulik (des chamanes, des mythes et des tabous ou les premiers défis de Rasmussen en terre inuit canadienne).' *Etudes Inuit Studies* 12(1).

Sternberg, Leo (1925), 'Divine Election in Primitive Religion', In *Congrës International des Americanistes, compte-rendu de la XXIe session*. Pt. 2 (1924): 472–512. Göteborg.

Urtubey, du Louisa (1983), *Freud et le Diable*. Paris: Presses universitaires de France.

Chapter 15

Marjorie Mandelstam Balzer

SACRED GENDERS IN SIBERIA
Shamans, bear festivals, and androgyny

Spirits when they please, can either sex assume, or both!
(John Milton *Paradise Lost*, New York: Seabury, 1983)

[E]ach being contains many forms simultaneously, sometimes manifesting itself as one, sometimes as another.
(Jill Furst and Peter Furst *North American Indian Art*, New York: Rizzoli, 1982, p. 141, on Inuit soul beliefs)

IN THE REALM OF THE SACRED, as well as in literature, gender distinctions appear and disappear, and are culturally constructed and deconstructed. Male and female forces can be used, balanced, adapted, and transformed by those who are skilled enough to handle their power. Within the cultural traditions of Siberia, some of the most diverse variations on the theme of gender flexibility are reflected in beliefs about shamans (spiritual healers), animal spirits, and power through manipulation of sexual energy. Gender transformations perceived according to some European standards as deviant become instead sacred.

Shamans, as the Sakha (Yakut) curer Vladimir Kondakov told me in 1992, should be able to balance and mediate energies within multiple levels of cosmological worlds.[1] To do so requires spiritual transformations into animals and the harnessing of both male and female sexual potential. For many, this means having male shamans accept female spirit helpers as guides, and vice versa, incorporating their power and even their gendered essence in trance and during séances. It can involve tapping the gendered spiritual force of a tree, for instance the female birch, to cure a male patient. And in a particularly dramatic form, the greatest shamans, even if they are males, are able to themselves give birth to spirit animals.[2]

The social and symbolically creative environment in which such events can be heralded is psychologically far from our own. Yet the mastery of a range of human potential inherent in Siberian shamanism is now being recognized as a system worth revitalizing in Siberia, and worth examining for clues to intertwined mental and physical health. Even before Soviet repression against shamans as medical charlatans and religious deceivers, esoteric knowledge of shamanic gender transformation was far from widely known or understood. It was manifest in different local and even individual ways, creating a challenge for modern Siberians rethinking their own traditions.

An historical story still told in the Sakha Republic (Yakutia) of Siberia in 1994 illustrates the degree to which thinking about gender is flexible, non-stereotypical and linked to spirit beliefs. During World War II, in a time of hardship and starvation, a Sakha man was left with his bawling baby, after his wife died in childbirth. Far from any human help, he prayed desperately to the spirits to be given milk in his poor male body. Suddenly, milk appeared in his breasts and the child was saved. According to several Sakha consultants, the man, though not a shaman, had tapped into the crucial life-forces of the opposite sex, as shamans do, using this syncretized, sometimes ambiguous, sexual power for salvation.[3]

At times, and in some Siberian cultures, the shamanic use of sexual power and symbolism meant that male shamans turned themselves into females, for particular shamanic seances, and, in some cases, more permanently. Among the Northeastern Chukchi, this transformation occasionally also went the other way, with female shamans taking on male identities. The turn-of-the-century Russian exile-ethnographer Waldemar Bogoras thus wrote of certain particularly revered and feared Chukchi shamans: 'A man who has changed his sex' is termed 'soft man,' or 'similar to a woman' (ne'uchica), and a woman in similar condition 'similar to a man' (qa'chikicheca).'[4] Such transformations occurred on spirit (ke'let) orders, and were dreaded, at least at first, by young shamanic apprentices.

To probe the religious meanings and social significance of gender transformation, it is worth exploring not only the most explicit forms, manifest within shamanism, but also bawdy ritual transvestism in Siberian festivals honoring killed bears, and clues to gender identities in other Siberian practices and symbols. Issues of Soviet and post-Soviet change in Siberian spiritualism and identities can then be addressed.

Shamans in many guises

In addition to some Native North American areas, Northeastern Siberia is the region where practices of transforming shamans are best documented, among the Chukchi, Koryak, Itelmen (Kamchadal), and Siberian Eskimo (Iupik), plus, less definitively, among the Northeastern Yukagir, and the Amur Region Nivkh

(Gilyak) and Nanai (Gold)[5] Norwegian scholar Ronald Grambo argues that beliefs about the phenomenon are widespread and archaic, and correlates the Norse *seidr* and sorcery traditions with Siberian transformed shamans.[6]

Bogoras explained various degrees and stages of transformation among the Chukchi shamans he met, beginning with the male personification of a woman 'only in the manner of braiding and arranging the hair of the head.'[7] Occasionally patients, as well as initiates, were asked (by spirits, via shamans) to do this for a cure. The second stage involved dressing as a woman, without a complete sex change:

> For instance, Kimiqui, who claimed for himself shamanic powers, wore woman's clothes, which he assumed in early youth. He was afflicted with a strange illness, which caused him to sleep in his inner room day after day, almost without interruption. At length a *ke'le* appeared to him in his sleep and ordered him to put on a woman's dress . . . Notwithstanding this, Kimiqui had a wife and four children . . . [and cheeks] covered with a stubby black beard, and there could be no misunderstanding about the sex to which he really belonged.[8]

Mere clothing change, however, was not considered decisive in conveying extraordinary powers. For this, an initiate

> leaves off all pursuits and manners of his sex, and takes up those of woman. He throws away the rifle and the lance, the lasso of the reindeer herdsman, and the harpoon of the seal-hunter, and takes to the needle and the skin-scraper.

Spirits assist him in this, even to the point where his mode of speech changes 'from the male to the female,' and his body alters 'in its faculties and forces.' Thus, 'he loses masculine strength, fleetness of foot . . . endurance in wrestling, and acquires instead the helplessness of a woman.' He has accompanying psychic changes, as he 'loses his brute courage and fighting spirit, and becomes shy of strangers, even fond of small-talk and of nursing small children . . . [Thus] the "soft man" begins to feel like a woman.'[9]

A true 'soft man' enters into sexual competition with women for young men, and 'succeeds easily with the aid of "spirits."' He chooses a lover and takes a husband. Bogoras added, 'the marriage is performed with the usual rites, and I must say that it forms a quite solid union, which often lasts till the death of one of the parties. The couple live in much the same way as do other people.' His open-mindedness, however, gave out when he explained:

> They cohabit in a perverse way, *modo Socratis*, in which the transformed wife always plays the passive role . . . some 'soft men' are

said to lose altogether the man's desire and in the end to even acquire the organs of a woman; while others are said to have mistresses of their own in secret and to produce children by them.[10]

Bogoras the voyeur (and all anthropologists have some of this in them) was so curious to 'fully inspect' one 'remarkable' young shaman named Tilu'wgi that he offered both the shaman and his/her husband a considerable bribe, after living with them for two days. Tilu'wgi declined, but the husband volunteered that, although Tilu'wgi was quite masculine in physique, they were hoping 'he' would eventually 'be able to equal the real "soft men" of old, and to change the organs of his sex altogether.'

> Tilu'wgi's face, encircled with braids of thick hair arranged after the manner of Chukchee women, looked very different from masculine faces. It was something like a female tragic mask fitted to the body of a giantess of a race different from our own. All the ways of this strange creature were decidedly feminine. He was so 'bashful,' that whenever I asked a question of somewhat indiscreet character, you could see, under the layer of its usual dirt, a blush spread over his face, and he would cover his eyes with his sleeve, like a young beauty of sixteen. I heard him gossip with the female neighbors in a most feminine way, and even saw him hug small children with evident envy for the joys of motherhood.[11]

Gossip behind their backs was one of the aspects of gender transformation that both male and female shamans lived through. Bogoras only heard of, but was not able to meet, a woman who had been first called by the spirits to become a curer in the 'usual' way, and then only later been ordered by them to become a man. She was a middle-aged widow with three children, and this may help to explain why circumstances as well as spirits could have led her to become a masculine hunter-shaman.

> She cut her hair, donned the dress of a male, adopted the pronunciation of men, and even learned in a very short time to handle the spear and to shoot with a rifle. At last she wanted to marry and easily found a quite young girl who consented to be her wife.[12]

Delicate matters of sex were taken care of by a 'gastrocnemius from the leg of a reindeer, fastened to a broad leather belt . . . [used] in the way of masculine private parts.' Child adoption was also accomplished in this case.[13]

The flip side of social stigmatization for being unusual was the extraordinary spirit power that the Chukchi believed accrued to both male and female transformed shamans. They excelled 'in all branches of shamanism, including the ventriloquistic art.'[14] Thus perhaps the widow used transformation to elevate herself, with the help of her spirits, to a new level of community respect that could also enhance her chances of survival without remarriage to an unwanted husband's brother. In both male and female cases, the supernatural protector spirits who guided transformations were believed to be particularly powerful, sometimes marrying their wards in sexual spirit-human unions that enabled gender identities to be traded. 'Soft men,' for example, were wedded to spirit as well as human males. 'Because of their supernatural protectors . . . [transformed shamans were] dreaded even by untransformed shamans, who avoided having any contests with them, especially with the younger ones.'[15] While meek and 'bashful' in demeanor, 'soft men' shamans were believed to have spirit protectors who could and would retaliate for slights. Threat of this both inside and outside of shamanic households made the shamans themselves doubly influential.

Explanations for gender transformations in shamanism, however, should not be reduced to quests for locally defined power and wealth. These aspects may have accompanied other, deeper issues of involuntary gender identity, for it is widely acknowledged that shamans underwent transformations, both into shamans and then (rarely) into an opposite gender, at great personal sacrifice. Cures of the transformed shamanic initiate included relief from, and control of, seemingly psychotic episodes, as well as resolution or balancing of personal gender ambiguity: taking a disadvantage and turning it into a strength.[16]

The scholar of Nivkh (Gilyak) shamanism Lev Shternberg was convinced that one key to the shamanic ability to be intercessors between their people and the spirits in times of trouble and sickness lay with their sexual relations with their main helper spirits.[17] In other words, he felt that the power of sex, and sexual transformation, lay at the heart of shamanism. Not surprisingly, this focus has not been well received by most subsequent researchers, including other Russian scholars of Amur peoples and the cross-cultural comparativist Mircea Eliade.[18]

The theme has been adapted by Canadian anthropologist Bernard Saladin d'Anglure, writing on gender change and transvestism in Inuit shamanism. D'Anglure explains that shamans made 'use of helping spirits of the opposite sex,' and also that 'these spirits were often at the same time his/her eponyms.' He elaborates: 'an individual who was socialized in such a way as to straddle the gender boundary ought to be able to span all boundaries.'[19] D'Anglure from this has developed a concept of 'third gender' as potent in much archaic Northern shamanic tradition, and was able to test this theory quite productively among the Yukagir in the summer of 1993, much to the surprise of his Yukagir ethnographer host.[20]

Rather than resolving arguments over the antiquity, significance, or marginality of gender transformation and sex in shamanism, we can acknowledge that various degrees and kinds of gender-related symbolism have played a greater role than earlier thought in Siberian definitions of the sacred. Gender ambiguity or transformation is not encouraged or even condoned in every Siberian culture. The very diversity of cases and unevenness of data on sensitive topics has enabled many arguments to flourish.

Among Amur River peoples, Shternberg found some evidence of spirits demanding that a shaman change his sex. For example, one Nanai (Gold) man fell ill with a particularly horrible 'shamanic sickness,' during which he slept for days on end. Finally spirits told him, in his fitful sleeping state, that he must change his sex, even though he already had a wife and several children. Only after he became a transformed shaman was he relieved of his suffering.[21]

Occasionally 'ordinary' people, outside the shamanic context, were of ambiguous or transformed gender among Amur peoples. Shternberg mentioned two Nivkh (Gilyak) cases, noting, 'The attitude . . . toward hermaphrodites is quite simple: they evidently view it merely as an anomaly and nothing to be abhorred at all.' He specified that this was not to be confused with homosexuality, and described one couple that had been male hunting and fishing friends:

> One day they went fishing and were forced to spend the night . . . the hermaphrodite's secret was revealed. Thenceforth they began sleeping together and ended up by getting married – although people tried hard to talk the young man out of taking this step.[22]

Since Shternberg only encountered this couple while traveling on Sakhalin, and did not know them well, it may be that he did not learn the full story of the alleged 'hermaphrodite's' relations with the spirit world. Another reputed well-adjusted hermaphrodite from the Amur was said to have explained: 'I have two chances, two happinesses.'[23]

In the Sakha tradition, many shamans combined or balanced male and female spirit forces without full gender transformation. Those rare male shamans who were believed to give birth to animal spirits were said to be compensating for the creativity which human males lack in ordinary life. But Sakha shamanic practice included reinforcing more conventional sexual divisions, made clear by a little known 'ritual for the enhancement of sexual power,' reported in the 1920s by the Sakha ethnographer Gavril Ksenofontov.[24] This ritual aphrodisiac was for women, led by a vigorous male shaman with nine maidens and nine youths assisting him, dancing to his drumbeat. During the ritual, called 'dzhalyn ylyyta,' a small group of target women were captured by the shaman's frenzy, dancing with abandon and neighing like horses 'inné-sasakh.' 'With their neighs they threw themselves on the shaman and performed various bodily movements,' pushing him to the ground until men standing nearby took them off him. 'The shaman, rising, whistled and made a circle with his drumstick. Then the women came to themselves, calmed down and sat [with blushing faces].' The procedure was repeated three times, and provoked an observer to remark that 'the most respectable women simply did not come to such a ritual.'[25] The roots of the ritual probably lie in both fertility and culturally defined eroticism.

The messages about gender within various shamanic rituals thus range from the enforcement of gender difference, to the encouragement of gender ambiguity, to the acceptance of gender transformation. One complex code through which some of these varied messages were manifest was transvestism. Thus, it is not surprising that numerous male shamans, including some Sakha, many Yukagir and Evenk and some Ob-Ugrians, wore cloaks fashioned in patterns of women's dress during their seances, even when they were far from being 'soft men' in everyday life.[26]

Bear ceremonialism and gender codes

An additional realm where questions of gender identity can be explored is another famed Siberian religious complex, the bear ceremony. Bear ceremonialism, known throughout Siberia and much of Native North America, was most elaborately practised among the Ob-Ugrian peoples of West Siberia and the Amur River groups of the Far East.[27] In both regions, the skin and head of a ritually killed bear are placed on a sacred bier and fêted for multiple days, to assuage the potentially angered bear spirit and ensure the reincarnation of that spirit into another bear. On the Ob River, feasting, dancing, and partying builds into a climax of sacred epic song singing. Satirical plays are a main entertainment, both for humans and the bear spirit, during which the men take the women's parts in theatrics that sometimes become quite bawdy. While the roots of the festival may have involved male initiation, other aspects of its folk theater point to its possible inclusion in the ranks of carnivalesque 'rituals of reversal.'[28] Among the symbolic indications of rituals of reversal are not only male transvestism, but also male hunters saying the opposite of what they mean on the hunt and uncharacteristic female license.

Several kinds of social tensions are played out in Ob-Ugrian bear ceremony theater: male-female tensions, exogamous group tensions between two supra-lineages (called Mos, or people of the Hare, and Por, or people of the Bear); and inter-ethnic tensions (between Khanty and Mansi, Ugrians and Samodeic peoples, natives and Russians). Such tensions are not so much resolved as expressed, and in their expression, analysts can learn much about Ugrian cultural constructions of gender and change.

One satirical drama indicative of gender and inter-ethnic tensions was observed by the Russian empire official Nikolai Gondatti and later by Finnish ethnographer Kustaa Karjalainen.[29] In it a 'Samoyed' (probably Nenets) comes as a guest to a married Khanty man who does not understand the Samoyed's language, but whose wife knows a little. Misunderstandings occur. The guest asks for a drink and his host gives him food. The guest compliments the wife, but her husband thinks he has complimented a reindeer and offers to sell it.

Then the guest tries to convince the wife to run away with him. He tells her he is rich, will give her metal ornaments and a whole herd of her own reindeer. At first the wife demurs, but then agrees. To escape easily, she makes a concoction of brewed vodka and *mukhomor* (the hallucinatory mushroom *amanita muscaria*, which is bright red with white spots). She and the guest drink only a little, while her husband gets stone drunk. The guest then sets the wife on his sled and goads his reindeer to prance away. The Khanty host understands what is happening, but can do nothing: 'his legs refuse to move, tongue to speak, hands to shoot.'[30] He falls down in frustration and begins to snore.

This sad, realistic-in-detail tale produced squeals of laughter from Khanty audiences, perhaps because it is such a model of how not to behave that nearly everyone could feel secure in his or her own morality. The play sets the stage for understanding both on- and off-stage festival behavior. According to the Russian ethnographer Georgi Startsev, who saw festivals on the Vakh River, women, though barred from theatrical parts, become quite involved, to the point of behaving with frank masculine brazenness. They dance energetically and creatively, and are allowed to do things they are usually afraid to do. They mock their husbands with repartee and 'curse, complain, race after each other, shout and call each other nicknames.' During the dancing, 'men come into ecstasy to the point where they take off each other's clothing and spit on the naked body. The women too are not quiet, but indulge in baiting the men – cursing, yelling, crawling into the melée.'[31]

The release that this scene evokes is suggestive of rituals of reversal: rejection of ordinary life patterns, contorting of the sacred and the profane. Lest it be viewed as a post-revolutionary drunken degeneration (for Startsev worked in the 1920s), another play helps us see the link more explicitly between semi-controlled debauchery and the sacred spirit world. This is one of the dramas used toward the end of bear ceremonies throughout the nineteenth century and well into the twentieth. In Karjalainen's version, a huge masked forest spirit (*menk*) arrives from the edge of the village with his wife. They enter the room where the bear is lying resplendent amidst ribbons, scarves, coins and other symbolic offerings, and bow to the bear in respect. They then whistle, dance with scarves, yell, chant, and groan until they become exhausted and throw themselves on a sleeping pallet.[32] Gondatti's unexpurgated version of this play continues with the sexual advances of the husband *menk* to his wife.[33] At first 'she' refuses, but then complies. Since *menk* are Por ancestors, the suggestion of the sex act is probably related (or once was) to sacred procreation of Por children. It is at the same time clowning, given that both actors are male.

Bear ceremony plays criticize the subject of marriage from various angles. A play seen by Karjalainen made fun of the very serious tradition of women needing to cover their faces in modesty before strangers and certain male relatives. In it a man is saved from marrying an ugly girl when Numi-Torum, the sky god, sends a gust of wind to blow the man's bride's scarf away from her face.[34] The tradition of face-covering stemmed from concepts of female 'impurity' which were relinquished only very slowly in the Soviet period.[35] Other plays outlasted early Soviet prohibitions on the bear ceremonies. One involved the indecision of a groom in choosing among three brides. Another, influenced by Soviet propaganda, portrayed a senile old man trying to buy a wife, but she marries his son without payment.[36]

Even this snapshot of Ob-Ugrian bear ceremonialism hints at a dynamic of culture change that goes beyond maintenance of social and religious status quo. The dramas survived the intense pressures of Christianization and Sovietization in part because they were held in secret and were appropriate to the issues of the day. In the nineteenth century, Russian tax collectors were mocked. In the twentieth, Soviet brigade leaders took their place.

Gender tensions remained a theme throughout the documented history of bear festivals, but it may well be that the tensions became greater, and plays focused more on gender, as Soviet propagandists insisted on changing the way women worked, presented themselves and thought about themselves. Laughing over battles of the sexes was certainly an emotional release, particularly when women's parts were played by men. But the bear plays seem to have done more than provide a functional safety-valve through a 'liminal' (mediating) period of ritual excess, as suggested by several scholars of rituals of reversal. According to such theories, sex role reversals in ritual tend to emphasize gender distinctions in parody and thus help to enforce the social status quo.[37] In this view, the pressures of Sovietization which undermined Siberian female subordination can be seen as an impetus for sharpening the traditional gender distinctions and roles through masquerade. This may be one aspect of the bear festival 'carnival,' but it puts undue stress on social equilibrium. Natalie Zemon Davis interprets French carnival more dynamically: 'play with unruly women is partly a chance for temporary release from the traditional and stable hierarchy; but it is also part of the conflict over efforts to change the basic distribution of power within society.'[38] Thus some aspects of gender reversals create the possibility of enactment of social change through conflict expression.

When I was in the Khanty region in 1976, people were very secretive about the continued existence of bear ceremonies, claiming they had been nearly eliminated or homogenized (made less sexy) by the Soviets. But when I returned in 1991, I learned of the emergence from underground, and the resurgence of both the seven-year periodic ceremony and the more impromptu bear festivals. Some of the more publicized festivals were sponsored by the newly formed Association for the Salvation of the Ugrian People. Several of the leaders in the revival movement were women, and several women had become hunters. But they still were not taking part in the most sacred of the epic song chants or in the plays, nor did they expect or want to. They regretted that social group imbalances had made strict observance of lineage marriage rules impractical, but rejoiced that the essential sacred reverence for the bear had weathered Soviet repression for most Khanty. In the many hours of videotaped bear ceremony that I studied, from a festival held in winter 1991 in the sacred Khanty village of Iuilsk, it was clear that both the spirit of raucous play and pious belief were still wedded in sacred revelry. Men took women's parts in a few plays, but the focus for revival, according to Khanty participants, was on the bear reincarnation itself and on teaching young boys sacred songs about Khanty ancestors.[39]

A brief comparative look at the Amur River bear ceremonies also reveals symbolic messages about gender relations and inter-group tensions, but they are couched in a different social context and in local understandings about the relation of humans to bears.[40] 'Play with the bear' is usually the finale of memorials for specific dead relatives, in whose honor ceremonies lasting up to a month or more mark the return to 'normal' social life, lifting prohibitions (including sexual and marital) surrounding death. Dog races, games, and dancing are more a focus of Amur festivities than satirical plays and temporary transvestism, although aspects of 'carnival' are also present. Other social purposes of bear festivals include the merging of two lineages (whether previously enemies or friends), entertaining and solidarity-building among affines, adoption of an individual, the honoring of young boys, and the sending off of young girls in marriage.[41] The most striking difference between Ob-Ugrian and Amur festivals is that for many Amur ceremonies, live bears were raised, preferably as captured cubs sucking human women's milk, kept in cages, and then ritually killed. Raising live bears is prohibitively costly today, although several Amur River intellectuals have sponsored bear festivals in their home villages to revive and film the tradition.[42]

Nivkh ethnographer Chuner Taksami, who has participated in bear festivals held under Soviet conditions of restraint as well as in festivals revived recently, stresses the seasonal nature of many bear ceremonies, held mid-winter to mark the New Year and ensure human and animal prosperity and fertility. Bears, as 'forest people' mediators with spirit masters of the earth, forest, and sky, are thus sacrificed after three or four years of being fed in a Nivkh village. Taksami reported a key moment in the festivities, when the bear was led from house to house for farewells. Skilled young male hunters, hoping to prove their mettle, acted as brazen 'dare-devils:' 'dressed in furs worn backward tied with a seal apron, *kosk*, [the daring] came up close to him [the bear], teased him, leapt on him, grabbing him from behind.'[43] Some reports mention attempts to kiss the bear, with those pawed wearing the result as a badge of honor.[44] The paradoxical or reversal symbolism enacted here entails mixing gender-linked clothing and behavior, wearing seal skin associated with the water realm, and teasing an honored guest to danger-point. Ultimately, a key representative of the forest is nearly domesticated, only to be killed and returned again to the forest.

Gender coding occurs throughout the festival, with meticulous attention paid to the gender of the killed bear (which dictates the years a bear is raised, plus the number of times certain rituals are repeated), and to a human division of labor that partially runs counter to everyday patterns. Elaborately dressed women bang swinging larch log drums to set the tone for male games, fertility-associated dog races, and fast circular dances that end when centrifugal force breaks the line. While women do much of the cooking for enormous numbers of affinal guests, venerable elder men boil the bear meat, using pure melted snow water. They also distribute the meat according to social status, with attention to gender and host lineage prohibitions. Fur from a bear's genitals adorns the knife that cuts the bear carcass. Honored elderly women, not young women, participate in dancing to greet the bear carcass when it comes inside. Elders ensure that the bear carcass is brought into its host house through a smoke hole or window, to avoid being tainted by the impurities of menstruating women who have stepped over the threshold.[45] Elders past their sexual prime become important mediators of gendered and sacred space, making them analogous to male and female bears, called '[revered] old man' or 'old woman,' mediators of human and spiritual worlds.

On the Amur, shamanic seances are forbidden during the bear festival, although a shaman may indicate auspicious timing and shamans are involved in other rituals to escort dead human souls. Perhaps seances are forbidden because mediation with the spirit world, and purifications of both humans and animals, are believed to transpire during the bear festival through community-wide effort, without the need for special shamanic guidance. The festival may have earlier been a massive community therapy session, mourned today by Amur villagers threatened by ecological disasters and outsider encroachment on all sides.

Conclusion: (re)defining the sacred

Folklorists and scholars of religion have long been intrigued by boundary transcendence as one aspect of definitions of the sacred. The comparativist Joseph Campbell, analyzing Navaho mythology, explains, for example:

> And the brother heroes, though they are spoken of as masculine, are really both male and female; they are of both the male and female colors . . . One thinks of the Chinese Yang and Yin. One thinks of the Hindu 'Lord' and 'Shakti.' That final Void – or All – which is beyond all pairs of opposites cannot be male, cannot be female; is Both and Neither. But in the realms of manifestation the two are equally present. One may even conceive of the highest manifestation as androgynous, male-female.[46]

In Siberian contexts, British social anthropologist Maria Czaplicka came close to this kind of interpretation by describing shamans as neither males or females, but rather as belonging to a 'third class,' of shamans, who 'may be sexless, or ascetic, or have inclinations of homosexualistic character, but . . . may also be quite normal . . . shamans have special taboos comprising both male and female characteristics.'[47] Given the brief survey of Siberian data here, it is possible to expand understanding of the power of gender ambiguity and transference, without loading or prejudging normalcy or deviance, by encompassing male and female elders grown old and sacred in their communities, and by including temporary sacralization through transvestism and name changes in certain rituals.

Although it is important to carefully differentiate various Siberian traditions, for instance the Ob-Ugrian Khanty from the Amur River Nivkh and the Northeastern Chukchi from the Turkic Sakha, it is also worthwhile to make cross-cultural comparisons that can give us insights into theoretical linkages on such important identity issues as gender. Siberian cases reveal not only cross-cutting roots typical for peoples in historical contact with each other, but also cross-cutting experiences caused by Soviet repression and new chances for rich and varied cultural revival.[48]

Both bear ceremonies and shamanism have become symbols of cultural resurgence in many areas of Siberia, but it is misleading to presume the significance of gender reversals in the process. Instead, we can see varied gender transformations as one aspect of repeated and ancient attempts to harness, define, and redefine the power of sex by explorations of gender ambiguity and reversal in Siberian concepts of the sacred. Given that gender identifications are culturally as well as biologically constructed and that each generation remakes and redefines its own traditions, we should not be surprised that some cultures that once had 'soft men' shamans seem to have lost them. Certainly none of the researchers who recently have been in the Chukotka, Kamchatka, or Amur regions have reported the revival of this particular tradition.[49]

Under strong Russifying influence, transformed men and women were doubly reviled in the Soviet period, just as they were doubly powerful before intense Russian contact. In the 1920s and 1930s, they were persecuted as both shamans and sexual deviants. Yet the possibility certainly remains for a reemergence of transformed shamans, given the renewed interest throughout Siberia in all forms of spiritual healing.

The dual concepts that a shaman can temporarily take on the identity of a spirit helper of the opposite sex, and that a shaman can have marital relations with such a spirit helper, are still part of the widespread lore of shamans in Eastern Siberia. These are intimate, esoteric identity secrets, rarely discussed with non-initiates, that form the foundation of a shaman's perceived ability to cure. One Sakha shaman (oiuun) explained that he uses opposite sex spirit helpers and that sometimes it is helpful for male shamans to cure female patients and vice versa. In other interviews with Sakha shamans, I have been lucky to learn of their animal helper spirits, such as the horse or the raven, but have never had personal relations with the spirits revealed. One female shaman (*udagan*) claims she manifests her powers by becoming a white stallion. A key to the acceptance of such claims is belief in shamanic ability to manipulate, bridge, and change cultural boundaries and symbols.

Shamans traditionally could adopt the name of their helper spirits, at least among the Chukchi, Koryak, and Eskimo, as well as incorporate their essence if needed during seances. For instance, Bogoras reported that one shaman was named She Walrus; and another was Scratching Woman, a shaman who sometimes turned himself into a bear to cure particularly ill patients. Bogoras also noted that even for ordinary people, 'female names are given to men, and visa versa,' in order to confuse the spirits.[50] Some 'cover name' practices continued through the Soviet period throughout much of Siberia.

Spirit name adoptions, 'cover names,' and some beliefs about possible reincarnation into different genders give us clues to the creative and flexible use of cross-gender referencing in some Siberian cultures. Gender definitions in terms of balances or tensions between sexual opposites could be mitigated by wary reverence for people with characteristics of both sexes. More precisely, those people who were perceived to be able to utilize the energies of both sexes were often sacralized. In the bear festival, this happened temporarily when men took women's parts. The bear festival itself, as a community-wide spiritual healing, growing, and socializing drama, was an occasion for both reinforcement of human-spirit relations and social critique. Usually on a smaller scale, shamanic seances also enabled adaptations or manipulation of gendered power relations for intertwined psychological and physiological cures. Gender transformation of shamans was a matter of degree, ranging from temporary adoption of hair-style or dress for seances, to the full gender reversal of male and female shamans.

Gender ambiguity is not the same as full transformation, and neither is congruent with ritual reversals. Yet I argue that these are related phenomena, variations on themes that can help us understand more completely the full range of symbolic, socially constructed meanings for human sexual diversity. In European fiction and fantasy, reversals have long held fascination. Barbara Babcock cites the seventeenth-century Jesuit novelist Balthasar Gracian as saying 'The things of this world can be truly perceived only by looking at them backwards.'[51] The novelist Ursula LeGuin, daughter of two anthropologists, wrote about a fantasy society where people could change their gender at will, depending on the social context.[52] It is time to better understand the data already gathered on sexual practices and gender meanings, and to collect more with open-mindedness. Instead of seeing gender reversals as deviant, we may see a mirror image: anomaly turned into sacred power. The study of gender reversals can help us reverse assumptions about the sacred and the 'civilized.'[53]

Among the postmodern, post-Soviet Sakha, many of the most talented artists, musicians, poets, and actors are those who are exploring themes of gender tensions and ambiguity. Some are people who are not afraid to be slightly effeminate males and masculine females. In 1992, I was given a recently made drum embellished with old Sakha motifs: a dancing shaman wore female dress, through which was a clearly drawn penis. In the *fin-de-*Soviet 1990s, the Sakha and other Siberians are looking to their spiritual past for their cultural future.

Notes

1   I am grateful to Vladimir Kondakov, head of the Association of Folk Medicine, and widely reputed *oiuun* (shaman) for conversations in 1991, 1992, and 1993. For a literature review, see Marjorie Mandelstam Balzer, *Shamanism: Soviet Studies of Traditional Religion in Siberia and Central Asia*, Armonk, NY: M. E. Sharpe, 1990 and Anna-Leena Siikala and Mihály Hoppál, *Studies on Shamanism*, Budapest: Akadémiai Kiadó; Helsinki: Finnish Anthropological Society, 1992. This chapter is based on a literature survey, discussions with colleagues, and fieldwork in two main areas of Siberia: the Ob-Ugrian region of Western Siberia (1976, 1991) and the Sakha Republic (Yakutia) of Eastern Siberia (1986, periodically 1991–5). I am grateful for fieldwork and research support from the International Research and Exchanges Board, the Social Science Research Council, Harvard's Russian Research Center, Columbia's Harriman Institute, and the Kennan Institute of the Wilson Center. For fieldwork assistance, thanks are due to the Sakha Republic Ministry of Culture, the Museum of Music and Folklore, the Khomus Museum, Yakutsk University, the Institute for the Problems of Northern Minorities, and the Institute of Languages, Literature and History of the Academy of Sciences.

2   The part-Sakha ethnographer Alexander A. Popov, 'Poluchenie "shamanskogo dara" u Viliuiskikh Iakutov'. *Trudy instituta Etnografii*, vol. 2, 1947, p. 292, explained that a great shaman's spiritual initiation, usually around age thirteen, entailed first giving birth, deep in the forest and alone, to a raven or loon, which would instantly fly away. In the second year of initiatory pain and trial, the shaman gave birth to a pike that quickly swam into water. And in the final year, a truly great shaman could give birth to a bear or wolf. These three events eventually ensured that the most revered Sakha shamans could mediate three worlds (celestial, earthly, and underground) and could be reincarnated three times. In other contexts, fertility and shamanism are not compatible.

3   I am grateful to the historian Egor Spiridonovich Shishigin for this story, considered plausible by many of my Sakha friends. See also my 'Two Urban Shamans: Unmasking Leadership in Fin-de-Soviet Siberia,' in George Marcus (ed.), *Perilous States: Conversations on Culture, Politics and Nation*, Chicago: University of Chicago Press, 1993, pp. 131–64; and my 'Dilemmas of the Spirit: Religion and Atheism in the Yakut-Sakha Republic,' in *Religious Policy in the Soviet Union*, edited by Sabrina Petra Ramet, Cambridge: Cambridge University Press, 1993, pp. 231–51.

4   Waldemar Bogoras, *The Chukchee*, New York: Memoirs of the American Museum of Natural History, vol. 11, 1909, p. 449. Compare Waldemar [Vladimir I.] Jochelson, *The Koryak*, New York: Memoirs of the American Museum of Natural History, vol. 10, 1908, p. 53. Both authors were part of the Jesup North Pacific Expedition.

5   As with the Siberian cases, a very diverse range of gender concepts and practices exists in North America. The social practice of *berdache*, as exemplified by the Plains groups, is the most direct correlate to the Chukchi 'soft man,' with comparable traditions among the Navaho, Hopi and some Algonquin groups. See Walter L. Williams, *The Spirit and The Flesh: Sexual Diversity in American Indian Culture*, Boston: Beacon Press, 1992, 2nd edn; Weston La Barre, *The Ghost Dance: Origins of Religion*, London, New York: Dell, 1972, pp. 138–40, 156–7, 179–81; Alice Beck Kehoe, *North American Indians: A Comprehensive Account*, Englewood Cliffs, NJ: Prentice-Hall, 1992, p. 344 figure; and Sabine Lang's. 'There Is More Than Just Women and Men: Gender Variance in North American Indian Cultures', in Sabrina Petra Ramet (ed.), *Gender Reversals and Gender Cultures*, London: Routledge, 1991.

6   Ronald Grambo, 'Unmanliness and Seidr: Problems Concerning the Change of Sex,' in *Shamanism Past and Present*, edited by Mihály Hoppál and Otto von Sadovszky, Budapest: Hungarian Academy of Sciences, 1989, pp. 103–13. His argument is mostly convincing, though over-generalized when he states (pp. 107–8) that Yakut 'black shamans' 'tended to behave like women, since it is from women shamans that they derive their origin'. See also Vladimir N. Basilov, 'Vestiges of Transvestism in Central-Asian Shamanism,' in *Shamanism in Siberia*, edited by Vilmos Diószegi and Mihály Hoppál, Budapest: Akadémiai Kiadó, 1978, pp. 281–90; and his *Shamanstvo u narodov Srednei Azii i Kazakstana*, Moscow: Nauka, 1992.

7   Bogoras, *Chukchee*, pp. 450–1.

8   Ibid., pp. 450–1. Another degree involves gender transformation only during seance, especially to personify a main helping spirit. This provides an interesting parallel with the female shamans of Korea, who 'manifest' male authority figures during curing rituals. See Laurel Kendall, *Shamans, Housewives and Other Restless Spirits: Women in Korean Ritual Life*, Honolulu: University of Hawaii Press, 1985, pp. 138–43.

9   All quotes in this paragraph are from Bogoras, *Chukchee*, pp. 450–1.

10   Ibid., p. 451.

11   Ibid, pp. 453–4. Writing on 'transformed persons' among the Eskimo of Indian Point, Chukotka, Bogoras also reports Russian empire official and amateur ethnographer Nikolai Gondatti, 'Naselenie Anadyrskogo Okruga,' *Zapiski Priamurskogo Otdela Imperatorskogo Russkogo Geograficheskogo Obshchestva*, vol. 2, pt. 1, 1896, as condemning the practice and actively campaigning for the demise of 'soft men.' But the tradition was carried on to a small degree into the twentieth century, according to Jane Murphy, 'Psychotherapeutic Aspects of Shamanism on St Lawrence Alaska,' in *Magic, Faith and Healing*, edited by Ari Kiev, New York: Free Press, 1969, pp. 74–5. Jane Murphy was told in 1940 that a transformed shaman from Siberia believed himself to be pregnant, and then tragically ended his life 'by having himself abandoned on another island, and the story goes that the following year the corpses of an adult and a child were found where he had been left.' Precise timing is unclear.

12   Bogoras, *Chukchee*, p. 455.

13   Bogoras, *Chukchee*, p. 455–6, explains: 'After some time the transformed husband, desiring to have children by her young wife, entered into a bond of mutual marriage with a young neighbor, and in three years two sons were really born in her family . . . They were considered her own lawful children. Thus this person could

have had in her youth children of her own body, and in later life other children from a wedded wife of hers.'

14   Ibid., p. 453.

15   Ibid., p. 453. On spirit–human unions, compare Leo [Lev], Sternberg [Shternberg], 'Divine Election in Primitive Religion,' in *Congrès International des Américanistes, compte-rendu de la XXIe session Deuxième Partie tenue à Goteborg en 1924*, 1925, Part 2, pp. 472–512.

16   Compare Balzer, *Shamanism*, p. ix.

17   Leo Sternberg, 'Divine Election,' p. 476–80. See also Lev [Leo] Shternberg [Sternberg], 'Gilyaki,' *Etnograficheskoe Obozrenie*, No. 2 (March–April 1904), pp. 19–55; Leo Sternberg, 'Die Religion der Giljaken,' *Archiv für Religion swissenschaft* vol. 8, 1905, pp. 244–74; and *Pervobytnaia religiia v svete etnografiia*, Leningrad: Nauka, 1936. For sensitive treatment of the issue, see Roberte Hamayon, *La chasse à l'âme: Esquisse d'une théorie du chamanisme sibérien*, Nanterre: Société d'etnologie, 1990, pp. 448–53.

18   Mircea Eliade, *Shamanism: Archaic Techniques of Ecstacy*, Princeton: Princeton University Press, 1972, p. 73. Compare E. A. Kreinovich 'Ocherk kosmogenicheskikh predstavlenii giliakoy,' *Etnografiia*, vol. 7, no. 1, 1929, pp. 78–102; Kreinovich, 'Rozhdenie i smert cheloveka po vozzreniam giliakov,' *Etnografiia*, vol. 9, nos 1–2, 1930, pp. 89–113; Anna V. Smoliak 'Novye dannye po animizmu i shamanizmu u nanaitsev,' in *Sovetskaia Etnografiia*, no. 2 (March–April 1974), pp. 111–13. Basilov, *Shamanstvo*, pp. 126–8 reviews the argument, which he sees as focused on whether shaman–spirit helper 'intimate ties' were the most prior, archaic form, rather than whether they existed at all. Certainly Anna Smoliak, *Shaman: lichnost, funktsii, mirovozzrenie (narody Nizhnego Amura)*, Moscow: Nauka, 1991, p. 227, and many others, give evidence that some shamans did have marriages with their main spirit helpers. Unresolved is how crucial these ties were, whether some involved gender transformation, and how spirit marriages influenced cures.

19   Bernard Saladin d'Anglure, 'Shamanism and Transvestism among the Inuit of Canada,' in *Shamanizm kak religiia*, edited by Anatoly I. Gogolev, et al., Yakutsk: Yakutsk University, 1992, p. 18; d'Anglure, 'Rethinking Inuit Shamanism through the concept of the "Third Gender"' in *Northern Religions and Shamanism*, edited by Mihály Hoppál and Juha Pentikainen, Budapest: Akadémiai Kiadó; Helsinki: Finnish Literature Society, 1992, p. 147; d'Anglure, 'Sila, the Ordering Principle of the Inuit Cosmology,' in *Shamans and Cultures*, edited by Mihály Hoppál and Keith Howard, Budapest: Akadémiai Kiadó, 1993, pp. 160–8. D'Anglure's data are similar to flexible Inuit soul beliefs described by Peter and Jill Furst, *North American Art*, p. 173. However, Dutch scholar Jarik Oosten, 'Theoretical Problems in the Study of Inuit Shamanism,' in *Shamanism Past and Present*, edited by Mihály Hoppál and Otto von Sadovszky, Budapest: Hungarian Academy of Sciences, 1989, p. 334, does not feel d'Anglure's 'notion of a third sex' is warranted.

20   I am grateful to Bernard Saladin d'Anglure and to colleagues in the Sakha Republic for discussion of these issues. The literal term for 'soft man' in the tundra dialect of Yukagir (of the Sakha Republic) would be 'pukol'an kejp,' but the Russian ethnographer Vladimir Jochelson, *The Yukagir and the Yukagirized Tungus*, New York: Memoirs of the American Museum of Natural History, vol. 12, 1910, p. 112 noted, 'I found no indications of such an institution among the Yukagir, except in the dress of the shamans, which includes articles of female attire.' If we see the 'institution'

as a matter of degree, views of Jochelson and d'Anglure can both be accommodated.

21   Shternberg, 'Divine Election,' p. 473–80; Grambo, 'Unmanliness,' p. 108. Compare Leopold von Shrenk [Schrenk], *Ob Inorodsakh Amurskogo Krai*, St. Petersburg: Imperial Academy of Sciences, 1903, vol. 3, pp. 121–5; and Eveline Lot-Falk, 'Eroticism and Shamanism,' *Sexology*, vol. 22, no. 1 (January 1956), pp. 378–83.

22   Chester Chard, 'Sternberg's Materials on the Sexual life of the Gilyak,' *Anthropological Papers of the University of Alaska*, vol. 10, no. 1 (1961), pp. 21–2. See original: Shternberg, Lev, 'Sotsial'naia Organizatsiia Giliakov,' in *Giliaki, Orochi, Gol'dy, Negidal'tsy, Ainu*, Khabarovsk: Dal'giz, 1933, pp. 256–7.

23   Chard, 'Sternberg's Materials,' p. 22. Lydia Black, *Nivkhi*, p. 66, is skeptical of Shternberg's 'hermaphrodite' designation, considering one case homosexuality and the other transvestism. Following Shternberg, she discusses these cases under the category of 'sexual perversion'. See also Gisela Bleibtreu-Ehrenberg, 'Homosexualität und Transvestition im Schamanismus,' *Anthropos*, vol. 65, no. 1/2 (1970), pp. 189–228, who discusses a range of shamanic transvestism cases, only some of which involve homosexuality; and Stepan Krasheninnikov, *Opisanie zemli Kamchatki*, St. Petersburg: 1819, vol. 2, p. 158 on the Itelmen (Kamchadal) 'soft men' who were houseworkers called 'koiekchuch,' and kept as concubines.

24   Gavril V. Ksenofontov, *Shamanizm; izbrannye trudy (publikatsii 1928–1929)*, Yakutsk: Sever-lug, 1992, p. 203–5.

25   Ksenofontov, *Shamanizm*, p. 204. Ksenofontov did not see this ritual, but reported the observations of Mikhail Govorov, recorded in 1924.

26   British anthropologist Maria Czaplicka contrasted 'change of sex' as a 'Paleo-Asiatic' institution with the use of 'female garments' in shamanic dress, associating female dress with 'Neo-Siberians' (plus the Yukagir), in *Aboriginal Siberia*, London: Oxford University Press, 1914, p. 252. She noted (p. 253) that many 'costumes' combine male and female features. Compare Bleibtreu-Ehrenberg, 'Homosexualität und Transvestition,' pp. 190–5, 203; Yekaterina D. Prokof'yeva, *Shamanskie kostiumy narodov Sibiri*, Leningrad: Sbornik Muzeiia antropologii i etnografii, vol. 17, 1971. Valerie Chaussonnet ('Needles and Animals: Women's Magic,' in *Cross-roads of Continents: Cultures of Siberia and Alaska*, Washington, DC: Smithsonian, 1988, p. 225) reminds us, on the basis of Bogoras' materials, that some Chukchi patients wore women's earrings and boots on order of a shaman as 'a ploy to hide and protect the person from evil spirits'.

27   A. Irving Hallowell, 'Bear Ceremonialism in the Northern Hemisphere,' in *American Anthropologist*, vol. 28, no. 1 (January–March 1926), pp. 1–175; Boris Chichlo, 'L'Ours Shamane,' *Etudes Mongoles*, vol. 12, 1981, pp. 35–112; Eva Schmidt, 'Bear Cult and Mythology of the Northern Ob-Ugrians,' in *Uralic Mythology and Folklore*, edited by Mihály Hoppál and Juha Pentikainen, Budapest: Hungarian Academy of Sciences; Helsinki: Finnish Literature Society, 1989, pp. 187–232. Eva Schmidt's work, based on recent and continuing field work, is especially valuable, and shows the diverse range of concepts about the bear, even within Ob-Ugrian culture.

28   The male initiation theory is Valerii N. Chernetsov's ('Fratrial'noe ustroistvo obugorskogo obshchestva,' *Sovetskaia etnografiia*, 1939, 2, pp. 20–41; 'Periodicheskie obriady i tseremonnye u obskikh ugrov sviazannye s medvedem,' in

Congressus secundus internationalis Fenno-Ugristarium, Part II, Acta Etnologica, Helsinki: Societas Fenno-Ugrica, 1968, pp. 102–11). On rituals of reversal see Barbara Babcock, *The Reversible World: Symbolic Inversion in Art and Society*, Ithaca: Cornell University Press, 1978, pp. 13–36. The theory of 'carnival' was most famously developed in the 1920s by Russian folklorist Mikhail M. Baktin, e.g. *Rabelais and his World*, trans. Helen Iswolsky, Cambridge: MIT Press, 1965. See also Olga M. Freidenburg, 'Proiskhozhdenie parodii,' in *Trudy po znakovym sistemam*, vol. 6, vyp. 308, Tartu: Tartu State University, 1973, pp. 490–512.

29   Nikolai L. Gondatti, 'Kul't medvedia u Zapadnoi-Sibirskoi inorodtsey,' in *Trudy obshchestva estestveni nauk antropologii i etnografii*, vol. 8, 1887, p. 83; Kustaa F. Karjalainen, *Die Religion der Jugra-Völker*, Porvoo: Finnish Academy of Sciences, 1927, vol. 3, p. 218.

30   Gondatti *Kul't medvediia*, p. 83, with seeming authority(?), explained the effects of the vodka-mushroom brew: 'One does not just get drunk. One loses all sense of where one is: one walks into a river or lake, throws oneself into a fire, falls out of trees, and in general does things for which it is necessary to pay later.'

31   Georgi Startsev, *Ostiaki: Sotsial'no-Etnograficheskii ocherk*, Leningrad: Priboi, 1928, pp. 107–8.

32   Karjalainen, *Die Religion*, p. 219.

33   Gondatti, *Kul't medvediia*, p. 85.

34   Karjalainen, *Die Religion*, p. 218.

35   For background on beliefs about 'female impurity' and the importance of women 'growing old and sacred' among the Khanty after menstruation, see Marjorie Mandelstam Balzer, 'Rituals of Gender Identity: Markers of Siberian Khanty Ethnicity, Status and Belief,' *American Anthropologist*, vol. 83, 1981, pp. 850–67. See also Thomas Buckley and Alma Gottlieb (eds), *Blood Magic: The Anthropology of Menstruation*, Berkeley: University of California Press, 1988.

36   Ethnographer Zoia P. Sokolova, *Strana Ugrov*, Moskva: Msyl, 1976, p. 65, saw these bear festival plays in the 1960s and 1970s.

37   Edward Norbeck, 'The Anthropological Study of Human Play,' *Rice University Studies*, vol. 60, no. 3 (Summer 1974), p. 6, for instance, states, 'Many of the institutionalized customs of play, notably including wit and humor and rites of reversal . . . may readily be seen to serve in various ways as sanctions for standards of behavior that apply at other times.' See also Victor Turner, *The Ritual Process: Structure and Anti-Structure*, Ithaca: Cornell University, 1977, pp. 183–5.

38   Natalie Zemon Davis, *Society and Culture in Early Modern France*, Stanford: Stanford University Press, 1975, pp. 130–1; Baktin, *Rabelais and His World*, whose work on dialogics and 'carnival' is relevant for its combination of status quo and adaptation-change orientation. See also theorist of sexuality and gender as expressions of power relations Michel Foucault, *Histoire de la Sexualité: La Volonté de Savoir*, Paris: Gallimard, 1976.

39   During the festival, reindeer were also sacrificed to the main Kazym Khanty ancestress. Folklorist of the Eastern Khanty, Olga Balalaeva (personal communication, April 1994) warns that evidence for male initiatory aspects of the festival is slim and that Valerii Chernetsov may have been straining for universals when he stressed male initiation in the bear ceremonials. Olga Balalaeva has seen recent bear festival plays with males taking women's parts, and considers this a temporary

'not real' transvestism done primarily for the sake of clowning and buffoonery. Active participant-ethnographer Eva Schmidt, 'Bear cult,' p. 201, 228–9, provides numerous Khanty and Mansi explanations for the origin of the bear ceremonies, concluding that some symbolize subconscious projections, especially those regarding the marriage of a human woman with a bear. She too refutes aspects of Chernetsov's bear phratry (Por) origins theories (p. 203).

40   The bear among the Nivkh (Gilyak) and Olchi, for example, is often seen as a more direct relative of humans. On bear ('forest people') ancestry from the union of a human female with a bear, however, some Ob-Ugrian legends about the origin of the Por people and an Amur River Olchi legend are remarkably similar. These legends explain the origin of bear ceremonialism through instructions given by a human female transformed into a bear. But other Ugrian legends take different form, for example having the original bear be a transformed human boy-hero or supernatural 'son of God'. See Chernetsov, 'Periodicheskii obriady,' pp. 102–11; Schmidt, 'Bear Cult,' pp. 187–232; and Alexander M. Zolotarev, 'The Bear Festival of the Olcha,' *American Anthropologist* vol. 39, 1937, pp. 123–4.

41   Chuner Taksami, *Nivkhi*, Leningrad: Nauka, 1967, pp. 217–22; *Osnovnye problemy etnografii i istorii Nivkhov*, Leningrad: Nauka, 1975, pp. 163–73; Lydia Black, 'The Nivkh (Gilyak) of Sakhalin and the Lower Amur,' in *Arctic Anthropology*, vol. 10, 1973, No. 1, p. 94; Shternberg, 'Gilyaki,' p. 34; and Shrenk, *Oh inorodtsakh Amurskogo Kraia*, pp. 64–103. Alaskan Indian potlatch-like elements were also present. See Zolotarev, 'The Bear Festival,' pp. 116, 121, 129.

42   This includes Evdokiia Gayer, Nanai ethnographer and former parliament deputy, and Chuner Taksami, head of the Siberian section of the Petersburg Institute of Ethnography and Anthropology. I am grateful to both for informative discussions. Evdokiia Gayer, in Fall 1991, explained that she had tried to fund the raising of a bear cub for several years, but villagers gave up after two and held a festival prematurely.

43   Taksami, *Osnovnye problemy*, p. 165.

44   Lydia Black comments that the bear's mark was 'sort of a laying on of hands [paws?] in reverse' in 'The Nivkh,' p. 95. See also Shternberg, 'Gilyaki,' p. 34.

45   Many of these details are from Taksami, *Osnovnye problemy*, pp. 163–73; Shrenk, *Ob inorodtsakh Amurskogo Kraia*, pp. 64–103; and Black, 'The Nivkh,' pp. 94–102. On concepts of female pollution, see Balzer, 'Rituals of Gender Identity,' pp. 850–67.

46   Joseph Campbell, *Where the Two Came to Their Father: A Navaho War Ceremonial given by Jeff King*, Princeton: Princeton University Press Mythos Series, 1991, p. 78. Campbell, as well as some Jungians and New Age shamanists, is working on a level of universals that is not attempted here. Some trance journeys of Americans and Europeans do, however, appropriate and syncretize very widespread symbols and concepts. One participant in a trance workshop of Felicitas Goodman recalled: 'The left side of my body was female, the right side male. I became a white female horse, and I shook off my male side.' See Felicitas Goodman, *Where the Spirits Ride the Wind: Trance Journeys and Other Ecstatic Experiences*, Bloomington: Indiana University Press, 1990, p. 209; Michael Harner, *The Way of the Shaman: A Guide to Power and Healing*, New York: Bantam, 1982.

47   Czaplicka, *Aboriginal Siberia*, p.253. Compare Bernard Saladin d'Anglure, 'Rethinking Inuit Shamanism,' p. 149.

48   Chances for revivals are themselves locally varied, and linked to demographics. But a spirit of Siberian solidarity was evident on the Lena River during a 1992 conference on shamanism. See Marjorie Mandelstam Balzer, 'Shamanism and the Politics of Culture: An Anthropological View of the 1992 International Conference on Shamanism, Yakutsk, the Sakha Republic,' *Shaman*, vol. 1, no. 2, 1993, pp. 71–96.

49   Such scholars include Tatiana Bulkakova, Boris Chichlo, Evdokiya Gayer, Bruce Grant, Mihály Hoppál, Anna Kerttula, David Koester, Igor Krupnik, Juha Pentikainen, Debra Schindler, and Chuner Taksami.

50   Bogaras, *The Chukchee*, pp. 467, 503. Bogoras mentions, however, that usually transformed shamans kept their original male names. This reinforces the androgynous, not fully transformed nature of many 'soft men'. In contrast, in the Inuit tradition, names are not necessarily gendered at all, according to Oosten, 'Theoretical Problems,' p. 334. Very different levels of identity are expressed in naming related to reincarnation beliefs, versus temporary naming or dressing to fool spirits.

51   Babcock, *The Reversible World*, p. 13.

52   Ursula LeGuin, *The Left Hand of Darkness*, New York: Ace, 1969. One of the best lines in the novel is 'the king was pregnant.' Note also Lola Romanucci-Ross, 'The Impassioned Cognito: Shaman and Anthropologist' in *Shamanism Past and Present*, edited by Mihály Hoppál and Otto von Sadovszky, Budapest: Hungarian Academy of Sciences, 1989, p. 37, for her comparison of shamans and anthropologists as mediators, whose 'art is to be inside but also outside everything.'

53   My interpretation can be seen as an adaptation of Margaret Mead's basic points in *Sex and Temperament in Three Primitive Societies*, New York: Mentor, 1950, pp. 215–7, concerning expansion of our understanding of the cultural construction of gender. But Mead still sees Native American *berdache* behavior in a context of biological deviance, whereas I would place it on a continuum of culturally and psychologically interactive responses to a range of sexuality that some societies widen and others narrow. See also Micaela de Leonardo (ed.), *Gender at the Crossroads of Knowledge: Feminist Anthropology in the Postmodern Era*, Berkeley: University of California Press, 1991; and Carol MacCormack and Marilyn Strathern (eds), *Nature, Culture and Gender*, Cambridge: Cambridge University Press, 1980.

Chapter 16

Michael Taussig

TOUGHNESS AND TENDERNESS IN THE WILD MAN'S LAIR
The everyday as impenetrable, the impenetrable as everyday

TO WHAT EXTENT CAN the Indian carrier's perspective provide a point of release from the power of conquest mythology? The carrier has of course little option but to act out the role enforced by colonization. True, there is the story of the exasperated *sillero* who, with a swift stoop, hurled his tyrannical rider into the abyss, and Cochrane and others complained bitterly of their *silleros'* taking advantage of their rider's dependence, just as the wandering Sibundoy Indian medicine men were said to take advantage of their patients. As a Capuchin Father complained more than four decades ago,

> The Santiagueños [Ingano Indians from the town of Santiago in the Sibundoy Valley] are addicted to the system of wandering through the cities of Colombia and other countries as well, selling leaves, roots, vines, herbs, and amulets, exploiting the ignorance of those who should be wiser than those same Indians . . . Many of the civilized have lost their sense of morality. They ask for herbs and charms for indecent aims . . .
>
> *This is proof of the perfect exploitation of the civilized by the Indians* in this area, selling valueless herbs at a high price or in picking leaves and herbs from anywhere and then selling them as if they were picked in the *most remote jungles* or from *the highest peak of the Andes.*
>
> [Emphasis added]

But if this allows the Indians, or at least their most salient and representative image, that of the medicine man, to exploit the civilized, is it not at the cost of reinforcing the racist exploitation from which the Indians suffer in the first place? The more shamanic, mystic, and wild the Indian becomes as a way of exploiting the exploiters, the more tightly is the noose of ethnic magic and racism drawn.

Yet there exists one feature to ponder that does perhaps disrupt this interlocking structure, and that is the two senses of the *comic* represented in the vision journeys by whites on the one side and by Indians on the other.

For Dante, as in his letter to Can Grande, the comic moves from a foul and horrible beginning to a desirable and joyful end, and as with the Passion of Christ himself, this is the mode of salvation at work in the visions of José García and Manuel. José García seems to be able to turn this on with ease and I cannot but think that this is closely connected with the quality of evil with which he, like just about all colonists I know, white or black, paints the underside of the world — in tones melodramatic and mysterious in depth. It is this artistry of the uncanny and of the mysterious side of the mysterious that distinguishes their evocations in story and gesture from those of the Indians I know, wherein a rippling teasing sets the world on its oscillating course. This quite different sense of the comic is doubtless bound to colonizing poetics too. Think back, if you will, to the complaint that makes the bishop's mode of transport, on the Indian's back, a sacrifice: the Indians not only go in too straight a line but in doing so they jump like goats and soar with the free abandon of birds. It is to that colonial perception of an overly straight poetics jumping and soaring that we should turn, so I suggest, in searching for an alternative to the heavenly catharses of colonizing narrativity.

When I returned to Santiago's and Ambrosia's home on the twentieth of December, 1977, I found that not only had he recovered from his illness, which I had presumed fatal, but that he had gone off with his son to cure a dancehall on the other side of the republic in far-off Cúcuta near the Colombian-Venezuelan border. Among those awaiting his return was a young white couple from the mountains near Pasto, Angela and her husband Juan, who told me he was suffering from rheumatism and eye trouble which none of the hospitals, folk healers, or pharmacies where he lived could cure. He was first brought down to Santiago fifteen years ago by his mother and father. He had just written a letter:

Señor Don Santiago:
   I beg of you to cure my person of all these pains which prevent me from walking and of the damage to my vision which prevents me from seeing. Also, I am doing badly in the selling of my agri-cultural harvests. Also, I want you to cure some soils from where I cultivate my crops. There are four plots, two are mine and two are my mother's. I would also like you to cure my wife.

Daily life set into a monotonous routine of small chores involving almost everyone, patients and workers alike. Many were the spaces set up by such an irregular work rhythm for talk and speculation, a rhythm every bit as important to the shaman's healing power as are the spectacular flights into the unknown with hallucinogens. For the patients it provides some distance from their problems, just as it condenses the discourse of magic and sorcery by having a group of afflicted people all together, gradually letting each other know, in spurts and in starts, about their misfortunes. Every day or second day a new patient arrived, from nearby or far away, and in discussing his or her problems with the others, no matter how obliquely, so the world of sorcery was empowered, and the shaman's house became a discursive fount circulating this social knowledge.

The daily coexistence of the patients and the shaman's family in the shaman's house also demystifies and humanizes, so to speak, the authority of the shaman. Unlike the situation of a priest or a university-trained modern physician, for example, whose mystique is facilitated by his functionally specific role defining his very being, together with the separation of his workplace from his living quarters, the situation in the shaman's house is one where patients and healer acquire a rather intimate knowledge and understanding of each other's foibles, toilet habits, marital relations, and so forth. By and large I think it fair to say that the therapeutic efficacy of the shamanism with which I am acquainted owes as much to the rough-and-tumble of this everyday public intimacy as to the hallucinogenic rites that allow the shaman to weave together the mundane and the extraordinary.

A flashlight beam winked over the rise from the river. The dogs bark. Who could it be? 'It's the friend Santiago,' shouted young Gabriel, a peon adopted by the household since his father, an Indian from the Sibundoy Valley, had left him here saying he would be back soon. That was years ago. Someone said he had drowned. It was too dark to see anything. Then, sure enough, in stomped Santiago, supporting his stocky bulk with a staff. People woke from their dozing. Two sick patients lying down to sleep on the floor stumbled out. *Aguardiente* flowed. The youngsters put a record onto an old battery-powered record player and began to dance as Ambrosia stood next to the exhausted Santiago on the veranda, receiving fold after fold of his *chaquira* – kilos of colored beads hung around his neck. He told of his travels and people hung on every hilarious and astonishing word. Then they drifted off. Nothing stays the same for long.

He went to cure a discotheque – a block long! With twenty-two rooms, each of which had to be cured! How fatiguing! And no *chicha*, only bottled beer! The discotheque belonged to a man called Alejandro who was suffering from sorcery involving human bones and soil from the cemetery. No customers were coming to drink or dance. The parking lot was especially bad; while chanting and blowing incense there, under the effect of *yagé*, Santiago was startled to find a bat falling into the tin can holding the smoking incense.

People would drive into the lot and then drive away for no obvious reason. It was close to Christmas, a peak time for dancehalls, and Alejandro was losing money hand over fist. He had heard of Santiago way over on the other side of the nation from a man who lived in Cúcuta but who used to have a bar in Puerto Asís, which Santiago had cured of the same complaint years before.

He spent a week working in Cúcuta. And he cured it! All twenty-two rooms. Customers started to come, and Alejandro, his family and friends, implored him to stay. Alejandro's wife asked him if he was baptized: 'I told her I was baptized before those priests in the cities!' And he laughed and laughed, repeating this again and again.

They came to him with talismans to be cured. They came to him with jewelry to be cured. And they asked if he could locate gold for them. They implored him to stay but they were rich people said Santiago, with workers. They needed no more, while he had his farm and home waiting. And if his wife got sick? What then? Who would cure her? 'She can't go to the hospital because [he made a sign with his hand across his throat] they would kill her.'

Then, around midnight, late as it was, tired as he was, he started curing, the curer needing to cure no less than the patient needed the cure, taking Juan into the main room of the two-room house saying, 'Now I'll make an examination. Tomorrow we'll cure.' Juan stripped to the waist. Santiago took his right arm. Juan complained, saying it was not his arm but his leg that was sore. Santiago fixed him with a steely look: 'Listen! When I make an examination it's with the head and the pulse. I've got to pulse!' He would chant for a few seconds, that wonderful Putumayo healer's chant, and every so often let off a gun-shot click with his tongue from the back of the throat. He slowly stroked Juan's arm. They talked of Juan's life.

'It's because of the envy they bear you . . . the evil,' said Santiago.

'Yes, señor. We work hard. But, Don Santiago, we pay the workers well! And now the whole world has turned against us, beginning with my father dying . . . everything . . . everybody sick, my father, my mother, myself, and all that. Before my father died I was in hospital. But the doctors couldn't cure me. After that, my feet . . . Everything is rotten.'

A radio was pouring out music from the coastal lowlands and from the mountains, too, *vallenatos*, *cumbias*, and crying flutes, while people sat around chatting and drinking liquor with half an eye on the curing. Others settled down to sleep, some young Indian men giggling and playing in the dark corners of the room. Snatches of conversation wafted toward us in the shadow-play of candlelight.

'You've got lots of enemies,' Santiago asserted.

'Yes! Lots of enemies.'

Santiago chided him. 'You haven't taken care of yourselves! You know you can't trust anybody!'

They are talking with a mighty passion, their dialogue dynamiting passageways through the spongy morass of envy. Santiago is pulsing Juan, stroking him into himself, interspersing his questions and sermonizing with short bursts of chanting.

Almost crying, Juan said, 'When I first came here I could barely stand. I was at the point of death!' Santiago grasped his head, sucking at the crown. He turned to me and laughed with delight.

'See this, Don Miguel. The Indian knows! The Indian knows how to cure!' And he laughed uproariously.

He asked Juan about the medicines he had been taking and retold yet another incident from Cúcuta while blowing over Juan – 'Whoosh fire, Whoosh,' – the magical breath of the curer, expelling.

'Will it leave me?' asked Juan. 'Am I going to get better? Will we see who they are?'

'Tomorrow we'll take *yagé*. If you can't tolerate it then we'll go up to your place.'

'That's exactly what we were hoping. My mother and I are in evil times. Things are marching horribly. We are out of control.'

In the background people were laughing. The radio continued its dancing. Santiago continued his chanting, interrupted bursts, stopping to give instructions: 'the curing fan . . . *cascabel*, all . . .' It's Cúcuta again. He was in high spirits and pretty drunk. Someone asked, 'In Cúcuta you have all?'

'Yes!' he replied, 'the women!' He was teased about the young women in Cúcuta.

'Young girls!' he retorted. 'Young girls nothing! It's the old one! In Cúcuta she asked me if I was baptized a Catholic! I told them that we Indians are more Catholic than they are! "In what form were you baptized?" they asked me.' He laughed with tears streaming: 'I'm telling you the truth.'

Juan broke in, 'This is the truth.'

'On the part of the Indian witch, speaking nothing but the truth in Cúcuta, just the facts,' intoned Santiago.

'Just the facts,' echoed Juan.

'Who is willing to dispute it,' Santiago went on, 'when the hour comes we all have to die.' And Ambrosia took him aside.

One morning, freshly washed and combed, Santiago sat down to cure the little bags of soil that Juan had brought down from his mother's tiny farms in the mountains. With an opening gun-shot crack of the tongue he began to chant softly into the open neck of each bag, close to his mouth, singing into the soil, *yagé* sounds with barely any words. Now and again a Spanish phrase surfaced from the rasping chanting sounds of the night forest, phrases like 'Don't let them molest anyone . . .' This went on for what seemed a long time, maybe half an hour. Then he spat into the soil and turned the bags over and over again, molding and crunching up the soil.

'Now!' he exclaimed, 'Now you've got the song of the *indio* of the Putumayo!' And he told Juan to take the soils back to the farms up in the mountains and sprinkle them over the accursed lands. He did not tell him whether or not the farms were 'damaged' – *dañado*, that great euphemism for sorcery – at least not immediately, and Juan told me that he understood this chanting into the soils to be something that divines whether or not sorcery is at work in the farms and, if there is, then cures it. If there is no sorcery, then this singing acts as a *contra*, as a preventive measure for some months into the future.

Santiago talked about his chant. The gun-shot clicks of the tongue were so that the song of *yagé* would penetrate better. He did not learn this from anybody – he learned it from *yagé* itself. When you *chuma bien*, when you get really 'high,' then you fly into the sky and the spirits of *yagé* teach you all this. They have their faces and limbs painted. They have musical instruments and they dance. Seeing and hearing this, you too can learn the same. They teach it all. These '*yagé* people' or *yagé* spirits have beautifully painted tunics, *cusmas*, like Santiago's only better, feathers on their heads feather caps, and shoes that are pure blue. But not even Santiago sees them often.

To divine these soils with maximum accuracy he must wait until the early morning after a *yagé* night. Then with his chanting the *yagé* sounds and beating with his curing fan, *waira sacha*, he can see into the soil and see if it has bad things like snakes or scorpions, signs of sorcery.

Not only soils and livestock and not only farms are afflicted with sorcery following in the wake of envy. Small businesses are just as prone, and in this regard it is worth relating that Santiago, for at least a year, had a man patiently awaiting his services in a nearby town. He was a black man from the Pacific coast who had made some money and bought a bar. Now he wanted it cured.

I yearned to see the *yagé*-curing of a bar and would pointedly remind Santiago of his promise to the bar owner. But he was always lethargic. 'Tomorrow!' he would say.

That day finally came but around lunchtime a nuggety little man came struggling out of the forest over the rise carrying a boy on his back. They were colonists from the highlands of Cauca. The hospital had done no good. The boy was very sick and could not walk. He had a mild fever and his knees, elbows, and ankles were swollen. He was listless and thin and sallow.

There was but half a bottle of *yagé* and without hesitation Santiago canceled the trip to cure the bar. He wanted to stay the night with the sick boy and drink the last of the *yagé* to see if he could be cured, what might be wrong with him, and what herbal medicines to use. *Yagé* can show you all that if things go well.

That night we drank *yagé* by the sick boy's bed, Santiago and I. The boy sipped a little, just a taste, and his father didn't want any, he said, in case he had to carry the boy outside. It was an uneventful night with soft chanting and talk of hunting in the Putumayo, what it was like in the forests for Santiago when he was a kid by his father's side, how he'd killed an anteater with a lance, but never a tiger, whether or not there was envy in the countries where I had lived, and so forth. He couldn't conceive the notion that envy as a maliciously wounding force capable of even killing people did not exist in the places I came from. Years later I began to see how right he was, especially with regard to academics.

In the morning he said the boy was suffering from *mal aires* (evil winds, spirits) and asked Ambrosia to help him prepare remedies for the boy to drink. Next day the boy walked a little and his pains had subsided. By the end of the week he could walk home.

'What's the meaning of the "Whoosh fire, whoosh" that you put into the *yagé* song when you are curing?' I asked him.

'So that all those *mal aires* get out and away from this kid,' he replied.

We talked about different types of *mal aires*: *sacha cuca waira* from the forest; *yaco cuca waira* from the river; *ánima waira* from the *ánimas* (which in other parts of Colombia can mean the spirits of the dead); and *yaco ánima waira* from the spirits of drowned people.

Waira is the Inga word for *espiritu*, spirit, Santiago said. *Yaco cuca waira*, the evil wind from the river, appears like a *duende*, he went on to say, and I knew from my friends in the plantation towns in the interior that a *duende* was a little mischief-making fairy with a large hat and his feet reversed who molested people in dreadful ways and stole children. I assumed he was a Spanish colonial import.

'Yes, the *Yaco cuca waira* looks like the *duende*,' Santiago was saying in a matter-of-fact way. 'Like a *cristiano* (a "Christian," meaning a civilized human being) dressed in pure ice, nothing but ice and water and spume, shoes of spume, and hair everywhere from his head all over the place. They are tiny, about one meter high. They'll do a lot of damage if you're not careful.'

'Do they attack people?' I asked.

'Sure.'

'Why?'

'Out of envy.'

He paused and then took up a story. There was a man from Bolívar (on the other side of the Andes) who was afflicted by a *duende*.

> He was a student from a well-to-do family and one day he went fishing and disappeared. Everybody looked and looked but nobody ever found him. Some five months passed and a fisherman came across him by accident, deep in a cave by the river. He hadn't eaten a thing for five months and was all thinness, just pure thinness and hair everywhere – *enduendado*. They got him out of there but he disappeared. They found him in the same cave. He would let men feed him but not women. People would throw stones at him. He wanted to stay in the cave.

Santiago heard about him when he was taken to cure sorcery all the way to

Bolívar, now a more than usually envy-riddled town on account of the coca boom there.

'He was like an animal,' Santiago continued.

There are a lot of people like that in the forests. A lot. Some of them become evil spirits. Before they were people like you and I. It's like a tribe. They have a captain too. They learn to do harm. Only men belong. You find them in the Putumayo also.

People in Bolívar told me I could cure him with *yagé*. But it would have required a *lot* of *yagé*! I heard about him when I was curing a madman who dressed in women's clothes and wandered all night talking funny things. He made himself a red dress and he would walk in the town and across the fields in that.

I cured him. That's why they all said I could cure the man in the cave who had been afflicted by the *duende*. The madman was also a victim of a *duende!*

'What about the *ánima waira?*' I asked in reference to one of the other types of evil wind.

'Ah! That's in the form of a skeleton,' he replied, 'rotting, pure bone.' There are female as well as male forms of this and they are very harmful. They can attack any sort of person, good or bad, and they achieve their harmful effects through *susto* or fear.

As for *sacha cuca waira*, the evil wind of the forest, he is naked and just pure leaves, pure leaves and branches. They are very cold and almost the size of a human. Like the *ánima waira* (the spirit of the dead) and the evil wind of the rivers, these evil winds of the forest achieve their harmful effects through fright. On seeing them one is so frightened that any sort of illness can result.

Wondering about all of this and his curing of the boy suffering from evil winds, I went on to think about the man who owned the bar and wanted it cured. What could it be suffering from?

'Well,' said Santiago, 'he says the bar is suffering from a *maleficio*; that somebody has subjected it to sorcery and that's why while the other bars are full, his is empty.'

He gazed over the forest stretching to the mountains.

'He had a small shop and he wanted more out of life so he sold it and with the money bought a lot of booze and a few tables and chairs and made a bar. He hired pretty girls with miniskirts to wait on the tables and things went well. Then he started to flirt with the girls. His wife got furious and grumpy and picked on the girls and on him too. Then the girls got grumpy and picked on the customers, so the customers left and never came back.'

Over the days that followed, Santiago, with Ambrosia's help, settled into curing Juan, the farmer from the highlands assailed by the envy of his poorer neighbors and laborers. Juan's vision cleared and the pains in his joints subsided, yet he continued to complain. *Yagé* was taken several times. The sorcery was sucked out. *Cabalongo* seeds bought from wandering Sibundoy medicine men who got them from the far-off Chocó or the even farther plains of Casanare were prepared. 'Parchment of the Lion' made in Germany and bought from the local pharmacy was applied to his joints. Santiago sang over Juan's wallet. As the days passed more and more problems came to light and more and more things had to be cured. Each solution to each problem raised yet another. The ramifying threads of magic meshed with the ramifying problems and questions constituting the patient, a luxuriant growth enlarging with each passing day.

The stranger's strange dream

One morning a white man aged about forty came to the farm and was shown into the larger of its two rooms where people were sitting around in that slightly dazed and euphoric state that exists after a *yagé* night. Santiago was chanting softly, curing.

The stranger briskly announced that he had to be cured – cured from *maleficio*. He sat down and in a loud voice told whomever was interested that until recently he had lived in Cali on the other side of the Andes and had come to the Putumayo three months ago looking for work with the oil company in Orito. But he found none and now lived along the road in La Hormiga working for peasant-colonists with farms where he suffered one crisis after another. It was in La Hormiga that he had heard about a great curer in this foothill region and, unable to cope any more, he had come here.

Santiago listened for ten minutes or so, then walked away. *Aguardiente* was passed around and there was a quiet hum of talk. A boy came by carrying a screaming pig. Some of the younger patients started to clean out and paint an old oil drum. A baby crawling about the floor of the kitchen almost upset the pot of milk but fell over and into its father's arms instead. *Chicha* and fermenting sugarcane juice were passed around. Ambrosia and her grand-daughter Delia were pouring boiling water over a neck-wrung duck prior to plucking its feathers and, lying on one of the two plank beds, a sick girl lay quietly, floating on the hubbub.

Thrown into the center of this the stranger from Cali was sat down shirtless on a stool about two feet from the hammock in which Santiago placed himself and started chanting, working over the stranger with his song and the curing fan. The singing was beautiful and lasted about twenty minutes. Then he stood and went around the stranger's seminaked body sucking out the bad stuff, sometimes putting it into his clenched fist and at other times going outside to blow and throw it away into the wind. After about ten minutes of this the old man, who had barely slept a wink all night, started to sing again, beating a powerful rhythm with the curing fan, crashing thunder and crackling fire into our drowsy midst. From outside came the sound of someone scraping the oil drum, and a young man from the Putumayo River bobbed in every now and again, offering sugarcane juice to the various bodies lying around the floor and to Santiago, interrupting his singing. Someone else stirred every so often to chase chickens from the room. Santiago seemed half asleep as he chanted. He stopped suddenly.

'You're very bad. You're going to need three curings!' he told the stranger.

'How many days?'

'You'll have to come back on Friday. Then we'll give you the purgative – *yagé*.'

'Can't I take it now?'

'No! Because you're too weak.' Santiago offered to prepare medicine for him to help in the meantime, explaining to him that he was sick because somebody had slipped something in his food.

'I eat a lot of crude sugar – *panela* – because it's the most economical,' responded the stranger.

'Without taking *yagé* you won't get anywhere,' said Santiago resignedly.

'And I want to know where I can find work! I want to know if it would be good in Puerto Asís!'

'Later on! After you've been cured. I have *contras* for the enemies and also to make friends. We have secrets.'

'Yes Don Santiago. I need your counsel. I want to go forward . . . I was with my brother in Cali and he was the one who told me to go to Orito. But no luck! In La Hormiga they told me about the great *médicos* like you.'

'In your land aren't there good *curanderos?*' broke in Santiago.

'In Tolima?'

'Yes.'

No. I don't think so. I left there young. My life was horrible. I went from place to place, an adventurer, getting to know new people and places. It was always hard. Finally I came to La Hormiga. People just won't help me. I need the curation – the liberation, as they say.

I had some dreams. I had to leave my brother's house in Cali. The house was full of people dressed in black. But there was nobody dead. My cousin came and blocked me. But I passed on and then I saw a long wide path stretching out before me. To me this meant I had to leave the house. A witch from my home town in Tolima, also living in Cali, told me I had been *dañado* [ensorcelled].

The cousin who obstructed me was always tormenting me. He attacked me and there was nothing I could do other than trust in God. That really frightened me. In the year of '78 he tried to kill everyone.

So I left that day and in the church, during mass. I realized there could be a slaughter and that we had to do something. Thanks to Holy Communion I saw that he was going to kill everyone. This vision remained but my brother did not agree with me. I went to a church for help, in San Nicolás in Cali. There are women there who help people and they got me a job in a grain store in Pasto but at the last moment the municipality of Cali ran out of money and the woman who was helping me had to leave.

I was very sick during all of this. Then I had an important dream. A priest, perhaps from San Nicolás, said 'Go and search in such-and-such a place for the flower of the chalice!' And in that instant there came another dream. There were two figures in black, a decapitated man and woman. 'We condemn you to die in the house of your brother,' they said to me, and I was also dressed in black. What ugly figures they were! I was a double person. One of me was a child. The other was a *monosabio* [the assistant to the picador in the bullfight; according to this dreamer from Cali, the one who presents the ear as trophy and is dressed in black].

In the first dream, the priest – I think he was a priest – told me to look for the flower in such-and-such a place. But I couldn't work out what place that might be. It took me two years to work that out, until April of this year. Then I met a young guy in Cali where I was working as a builder's laborer and he told me that there was a lot of work in oil – *petroleo*. Then I remembered! The name of the place that the priest had told me was Puerto Asís! So I went! The witch in Cali told me that my destiny was to walk under a river covered with logs from which it would be difficult to emerge. He said it was possible. Perhaps.

We listened in silence to the poor man's tale. He asked Santiago how much he would charge and Santiago said 10,000 pesos (at a time when the day rate for laboring in the fields was fifty pesos). The poor man said he'd better be moving along then. He would try his luck up in the Sibundoy valley. Santiago said they didn't treat you as well up there and the fee would be the same. And if you went to a *médico* – meaning a university-trained and state-licensed doctor – they would charge you even more and would be certain to fail. 'What's more,' he added. 'I charge by the gravity of the case!'

Don't call me *Taita*, call me *Indio!*

Santiago was waiting for Berenisa, a white woman healer from Pasto who had come down ten years ago to drink *yagé* and buy several liters. She used *yagé* in her healing practice – just a little, said Santiago, just to purge patients and see a little. She sent a letter saying she wanted to buy some more. But it costs more than she thought, said Santiago. It cost him 450 pesos (around twelve U.S. dollars) for a large sackful of *yagé* vine together with its female companion, *chagropanga*, without which no visions occurred. When scraped, mashed, and cooked some six hours in a vat of water down in a secluded grove by the river tabooed to women, this yielded close to three liters of *yagé* brew. If the *yagé* cook was to be paid for his day's labor, then another fifty pesos, the standard rate for a day laborer, had to be added to the cost. If Santiago charged a person for partaking in a *yagé* séance, he at that time generally asked around 100 pesos per cupful, a sum that often included diving and treatment. I had yet to see him ask money from another lowland Indian, and it was extremely rare for him to ask money from someone obviously rock-bottom poor – and there were plenty of colonists in that category. Yet he often charged by whim, sometimes outrageous prices and sometimes nothing.

He got to know Berenisa when she asked him to come to Pasto and help cure a restaurant. He was forced to leave before midnight, and the memory angered him. 'Why did you have to leave?' I asked. 'Because I am in my *cusma* [Indian tunic] and the neighbors there see that an Indian has been in the place and they say bad things.' Juan, who knew of Berenisa by repute, added that if the neighbours had seen Santiago, they might say that the owner of the place was involved in evil magic. Someone else in the discussion ventured the opinion that the person who ensorcelled the restaurant would get to hear this and retaliate with stronger magic.

In mid-afternoon four whites stumbled out of the forest and clambered up the hill: Berenisa, her little granddaughter, her husband Luis, and the man who drove them down from Pasto. Luis, a thick-set, chain-smoking man, drew several bottles of brandy out of a sack. Soon everyone was pretty smashed and Berenisa was declaiming to all the world how the Indians of the Putumayo sure know how to cure.

'You are my *taita*, my shaman, lord, esteemed one, Don Santiago. You are my *taita*. He who knows, knows!'

'Don't call me *taita*!' bellowed Santiago. 'Call me *indio*!'

'To me you are Santiago – whether negro, Indian, or white, it doesn't matter,' retorted Berenisa.

Santiago got more and more angry. Berenisa kept shouting, calling on God and the most saintly Virgin that this house was sacred. She was furious with Santiago for claiming he had no *yagé*. She (rightly) suspected he was lying. To spite him she said she would go down the Caquetá River and get *yagé* from his brother Jacinto. 'Jacinto doesn't *eat* Pasto women!' laughed Santiago (i.e., doesn't make love with them). He was angry on account of the humiliation he suffered years ago at their hands in Pasto, forcing him to leave early, saying he was an *indio* who came only to *eat*.

The situation eased a little and Santiago offered to cleanse Berenisa by means of ritual purification. She was prostrate on the floor, muttering bitterly, with her granddaughter rolling by her side. At her husband's insistence she dragged herself over, taking the crying child with her as Santiago half-heartedly began the cleansing. Ten minutes later she collapsed once more onto the floor.

It was now close to 11:00 P.M. Santiago and Berenisa's husband, Luis, kept on trying to get the better of each other through pointed chitchat, interrupted by Juan, the rheumatoid, complaining of a sore wrist and asking Santiago to heal it. Santiago peremptorily massaged and blew over his wrist, declaring it cured, as Luis rambled through a complicated story about how the last time when he came down here Santiago was mean, and now that Santiago was a rich man, with plantains in such abundance that they lay rotting, and cows supplying milk each day, he was even meaner, while he, Luis, was but a poor policeman for the municipality of Pasto, which had paid its employees only one month's salary during the past five months . . . and so forth.

The sleeping and half-sleeping bodies of peons, children, and patients crowded the room. The wind whistled from the thundering river and the last candle wavered and spat. Don Luis cleared his scratchy throat and with solemnity began a morbid tale about the time he almost died from the terrors in the highlands where he lived.

Only six months after he was married to Berenisa some forty years ago he was working on contract for the Jesuits of Pasto as a bullock driver hauling stone. Toward dusk, driving through a lonely part of the countryside, he heard the most awful cry: 'Aiee, aiee . . .' Chilled to the marrow he looked into the darkness wrapping its cloak around those windswept mountains. But there was nobody. Nothing but the wind and the dark. He felt sick. He started to vomit. Then he started to shit. He got hot and cold and started to sweat. He was dying.

They called the priest who hurried to his home. The priest contacted a nearby healer who told him to await his coming by preparing tobacco and *aguardiente*. That night the curer, a white man, came and diagnosed his illness as caused by the Old Lady of the Swamp, also known as Turu Mama, a hideous hag with long pendulous breasts swung up over her shoulders. Yes! It was she who had uttered those terrible cries that relentlessly echoed in Don Luis's memory as he let them loose in their blood-curdling intensity into the unsteady light of our deathly still midst: 'Aiee, aieee . . .'

Santiago was quietly smoking a cigar, sitting next to Juan, whom he would tap every now and again in order to look at the pattern being made by the ash — something many curers do as an aid to divination.

As for the Turu Mama, when her tale came to an end Santiago was incredulous, shaking with laughter. 'What's she like to eat [eat and fuck]?' he demanded from Don Luis, who blanched with disgust and chagrin. But Santiago kept up this line of inquiry with the manic drive of an ethnographer determined to get to the bottom of peasant superstitions. Long after midnight he wiped the tears of laughter and lurched off to bed. Silence descended, broken by his telling the now awakened Ambrosia about Turu Mama.

Slowly the giggling and murmuring died away into the coolness of the blanketing night. Then a scream rent the darkness.

Aiee!

'Watch out for the Turu Mama!'

And peals of laughter vied with the wind in rocking the house to sleep.

Chapter 17

Piers Vitebsky

FROM COSMOLOGY TO ENVIRONMENTALISM
Shamanism as local knowledge in a global setting

[My dead father] may be underground, but we can't know — we
don't speak to him any more.
(a young Sora who has converted from shamanism to Christianity)

A COMMUNIST POLICE CHIEF threatened a Sakha (Yakut)
shaman with his revolver. The shaman warned the young man, 'My son,
don't do that, you'll hurt yourself!' The policeman then shot off his own
thumb. Furious, he put the shaman in prison. The shaman escaped. Several
times the policeman put him in ever more secure cells, but each time he
escaped and came walking back in through the front door. Finally, the shaman
was tried and sentenced to hard labour in the forest, cutting down trees for
firewood. An inspection team visited him there in the summer and saw the axe
flying magically around the clearing, felling trees and stacking the wood up in
neat piles. At the beginning of winter, they went to collect it but the shaman
had disappeared. So had the pieces of firewood: they had joined together again
to make the living trees, which were standing just as they had been before the
shaman had ever begun his work.

Knowledges and knowers

In the jungles and the tundra, shamanism is dying. An intensely local kind of
knowledge is being abandoned in favour of various kinds of knowledge which
are cosmopolitan and distant-led. Meanwhile, something called shamanism

thrives in western magazines, sweat lodges and weekend workshops. The New Age movement, which includes this strand of neo-shamanism, is in part a rebellion against the principle of distant-led knowledge. This rebellion comes from within the very society which does the leading and looks for inspiration to the most distant societies findable or even conceivable. In the wild, shamanism is dying because local people are becoming more global in their orientation, while here it is flourishing – apparently for the same sort of reason. And yet again, in other parts of the jungle and the tundra there is a revival, supposedly of traditional shamanism.

What is local and what is global in all this? Do these phenomena affect our view of these terms? I shall try to tackle this question by asking which elements of shamanism can be transmitted to certain subcultures of contemporary society and how they are appropriated and transmuted on the way. The following exploration is only tentative, more in the form of 'Notes towards . . .' since shamanism is already a problematic term, while it is even more foolhardy to generalize about the 'New Age'. Yet what follows will at least give the lie to any smooth model of 'globalization' as a one-way current, an acculturation leading implicitly to a cultural homogenization. Rather, it compels us to regard the global process as a continual realignment of a system of epistemological and political relationships. Shamanism in turn is a form of 'indigenous knowledge'. Even if the flow of power is largely one-way, nonetheless 'indigenous knowledge' does not simply yield to cosmopolitan knowledge. Even on its own territory, the former may include commentaries, critiques and parodies of the latter. Abroad, indigenous knowledge may infiltrate and subvert the knowledge of industrial society, and in this it is aided by a loss of nerve at the centre of industrial society which leads its members to appropriate, for instance, shamanic motifs as part of their own radical self-critique. Does indigenous knowledge survive this appropriation?

The terms 'global' and 'local' between them constitute a metaphor of place. A few years ago, the problem of globalization might have been framed in terms of time, as 'modernization'. Since the evolutionary and teleological assumptions of evolutionism (and of its policy arm 'development') are now under question, space seems at first sight to offer a more neutral, pluralist dimension for the analysis of social difference. Linear time is so obviously a metaphor of domination because it moves in only one direction, so that some people will inevitably be found to be more backward than others. On the other hand, space is the foundation of maps rather than of time charts and can be read in any direction. Yet, once again, it turns out to contain dominant and subordinate positions: the global subsumes the local and supposedly homogenizes it, so that even on the map there is only one path for which anyone's visa is valid.

Is there no clean dimension, then? The ambiguity which surrounds time and space suggests that these are not here concepts from physics, but ways of talking about social context or setting. How can one compare a kind of knowledge which is local with one which is global? If the latter is also universal or absolute, it should thereby negate the former by logical necessity so that there will be nothing further to discuss. If not, this already implies a recognition that the arena of operation of 'knowledge' is not just truth, but also appropriateness and applicability. As soon as one asks, 'Knowledge for whom?', one is in the realm of multiple knowledges. The nature of any given knowledge depends on where each party to it stands, as does its power. It is through power relationships between knowledges that some of them can be turned into forms of ignorance (Vitebsky 1993b).

Using examples from my own experience of the Sora of tribal India and the Sakha of Siberia (pronounced Sakhá, formerly known by the Russian term Yakut), I shall explore how it is that shamanic ideas can be considered knowledge in one setting and not in another, wisdom in one setting and foolishness in another – in effect true in one and false in another. How can Sora shamanism become enlightening for western psychotherapists at the very moment when it is becoming inappropriate for the youngest generation of Sora themselves? In what sense has shamanism suddenly become true again for Sakha nationalists after two generations of being false for these same people when they were Soviet communists?

Clearly, these are not just questions of the value of different epistemologies. But neither are they simply political questions; rather, they involve a relationship between these two domains which will ultimately bring us back to the complexities of any adequate concept of globality. It is no longer possible to make a watertight distinction between 'traditional' shamanistic societies (a mainstay of the old ethnographic literature and of comparative religion), and the new wave of neo-shamanist movements (still barely studied in depth). For shamanism, as with any other kind of local knowledge, the essence of globality today is that it belongs both in the past of remote tribes, and in the present of industrial subcultures. But there are further twists: the shamanic revival is now reappearing in the *present* of some of these remote tribes – only now these are neither remote nor tribal.

Thus, globalization (or modernization) may lead either to the downgrading and abandonment of indigenous knowledge, or on the contrary to its reassertion and transformation. The Sora and the Sakha demonstrate respectively a fall and a rise in the indigenous valuation of their respective forms of shamanism. Both space and time are involved: these processes are going on in various parts of the same globe, at the same time – as is the New Age movement, with which the Sakha have much in common and the Sora virtually nothing.

There is no agreed cross-cultural definition of 'shamanism' (for major statements, see Eliade 1964; de Heusch 1981; Lewis 1989). Indeed, it is characterized by a chameleon-like elusiveness. Shamanic thinking is fluid rather than doctrinal, so that it is questionable whether the practices surrounding shamans should be seen as an 'ism' at all. However, I shall not put a great weight on definitional criteria, since much of my argument will apply by extension to the much wider realm of 'indigenous knowledge' as this filters in all its diversity through to the New Age. There is, nonetheless, a certain combination of key characteristics which it is reasonable to see as distinctively shamanic. These include a layered cosmology, with the flight of the shaman's soul to other levels of this cosmos, and the power to use this journey to fight, command and control spirits which inhabit these realms and affect human destiny. Thus shamanism is both an epistemology, that is a system of contemplative thought with an implicit set of propositions, and a blueprint for action, as in the location of game animals or the retrieval of kidnapped souls. Shamanic thinking has certain implications for the appropriation of shamanism by global culture today:

- It is *local*, in that cosmic space merges experientially into the space of everyday living through the features, such as graves and sacred sites, of a specific landscape.
- At the same time, it is *holistic*, in that (even allowing for the existence of other tribes, white men, etc.) the cosmos and the local landscape between them give a total rendering of the universe.
- This holism does not imply a steady state: shamanism is also *eristic*, in that the shamanic world-view openly acknowledges the role of battle and risk. The shaman is a hero who makes a bold and necessary intervention into cosmic processes. The power to act is precarious and this human action is fraught with danger.
- Finally, shamans are often politically *dissident* or anti-centrist. In Soraland, Siberia and elsewhere, they are contrasted to non-ecstatic priests or elders who perform more sober, routine cults.

I shall later try to trace how each of these features is carried over into the New Age appropriations of shamanic motifs, where I shall focus in particular on two developments: the individualistic psychologization of religion; and environmentalist activism in the public domain.

Falls and rises of indigenous shamanic idioms

The decline of shamans in tribal India

The Sora are a scheduled tribe of some 450,000 who live in an area about 30 miles across on the border between Orissa and Andhra Pradesh. I lived among them for much of the late 1970s and was able to visit them briefly in 1984 and again in 1992. This last visit was not only an anthropological experience, but also a historical one. Though there were many obvious modern touches, the Sora society I had studied in the late 1970s was a jungle society organized round an elaborate and dramatic cult of the dead, who speak with the living in dialogues which pass through shamans and shamanesses in trance (Elwin 1955; Vitebsky 1993a).

But what I have witnessed over nearly twenty years is a key period of transformation. Looking back, I now have the sense of having been on the spot at the culmination of a historical process in which strains can be absorbed for a long period by a society, before it finally snaps or changes quite suddenly. In the late 1970s, laymen depended on shamans for funerals and cures, and a number of children and young adults were learning to become shamans. There were only a few Christian households or individuals here and there living in otherwise shamanist families. However, in 1992 I found that almost the entire population of this area under 25 years of age had become Baptists. This movement was already apparent in 1984 and has now encompassed even those adults who were training to become shamans when I knew them as children. The Ancestor cult is maintained by those over 30 years old, but the practising shamans have few successors, and the more large-scale rites, such as the annual festival of the dead, are being abandoned. The overwhelming impression I received was that the shamanist world-view was losing heart.

What is the essence of this world-view which younger people are renouncing? Under Sora shamanism, groups of living people hold dialogues more or less daily with the dead, who come one at a time to speak to them through the mouth of a shaman in trance. Closely related groups thus find themselves in constantly recurring contact: family conversations, jokes and quarrels continue after some of their participants have crossed the dividing line between what are called life and death. Each of these dialogues is precipitated by an illness or a death and, in holding these dialogues, living Sora attempt to understand the state of mind of the dead and how this will affect them. But at the same time, each dialogue is only a fleeting episode in an open-ended relationship which before it runs its course will have served to explore, and maybe resolve, a range of emotional ambiguities in the lives of the participants (Vitebsky 1993a).

This is a deeply local religion, closely tied to the Sora's awareness of their landscape. After death, a person's consciousness becomes a form of spirit called *sonum*. The concept *sonum*, manifested in a range of particular named *sonums*, is a powerful causal principle in the affairs of the living. But it is also a contradictory one, nourishing its living kin through the soul-force it puts into their growing crops, but at the same time precipitating illness and death among them. Thus, in one aspect, the dead give to the living their continued sustenance and their very existence, yet in another aspect these same dead persons impinge on the living and consume them.

The Sora tackle this causal relationship through an elaborate classification of states of being dead. Different categories of *sonum* are located in different features of the landscape. As a living person moves around this landscape, he or she may encounter *sonums* and become involved with them. This happens, not at random, but as a development of their long-term relationships with various dead persons. Though these encounters with *sonums* may cause illness, they do not constitute a person's medical history so much as a history of his states of mind in relation to other persons. The illness in the living person is the reflection of a mood or attitude in a dead person, so that the living person's awareness of the dead is an integral part of the symptoms and of the definition of his illnesses. A person's medical history thus amounts to a social and emotional biography.

A Sora person's innermost sense of who he or she is in relation to other persons, is thus dependent on an understanding of the way in which this landscape is peopled with human consciousness. But this relationship to the landscape in general is mediated through particular plots of land, by means of the grain that grows there. Ancestors each reside in a particular plot of productive agricultural land, infusing their own soul-force into the grain crops which grow there. So with every meal that living people eat, they are ingesting something of their own parents and grandparents as a form of nourishment. Since these Ancestors cannot be conceptualized except as residing in specific plots of land, the Sora are taking part in a cycle which unites their landscape, their close relatives and their sense of their own soul or consciousness.

So long as the soul-force of the Sora people is underground, it remains firmly in the realm which the Sora share with the life-forms of the jungle. But how does the soul-force in crops circulate when it is above ground, in the harvested grain itself? Much of it, in an ever-increasing amount, leaves the area through the market, under steadily growing economic and political pressure (Vitebsky 1978, 1995). It is here that a problem arises. These grains are the very crops which contain the soul-force of the Ancestors of the people who grow them – and then sell them to be eaten by strangers. The fact that grain has human, Sora soul-force in it reflects its role as the staple of Sora diet; yet at the same time it is the most frequently alienated of all Sora crops, on by far the largest scale.

The circuits of Sora political and economic relations have included outsiders for a very long time. This is not the same as saying that the Sora are ethnically pluralist. The psychology and theology of being Sora, by contrast, maintain a sharp distinction between insiders and outsiders. The Sora have traditionally disliked and feared neighbouring peoples and in their cosmology have assigned them specific, often somewhat demonic roles (such as were-leopards). Sora soul-force does not pass in and out of the souls or bodies of Oriya Paik policemen or Telugu Komiti moneylenders, to take only two of the semi-demonic races in their world. However, it does pass explicitly in and out of animals, alcohol and grain. So while the shamanist world-view is *socially* inward-turning, based on lineages, households and their precise location on the local landscape, in *cosmic* terms it is extremely wide-ranging, involving elaborate patterns of association and soul-exchange with the landscape, plants and animals.

My preliminary interpretation of this situation (Vitebsky 1995) is that this way of relating to one's environment becomes more and more inappropriate the more that its ancestral soul-force, at the most nourishing peak of its cycle, is sold off through the market place. If the produce of the land can be sold fully to outsiders, then it belongs to anybody and nobody. The concept of crops itself is changing: rather than being a carrier of one's parents' soul, grain can become no more than just 'food'; instead of being part of a cyclical model in which production and consumption feed into and regenerate each other, the production of food moves further and further away from the goal of its consumption and becomes alienated as a mere commodity. A vital link between people and their environment is severed, and it becomes less meaningful or appropriate (Sora: *tam-*) for the environment to serve as a walkaround map of social relations, kinship groups, theological concepts, states of mind and personal emotions.

Shamanism and ethnic revival in Arctic Siberia

The Sora have shamans, but are not aware of having anything called shaman*ism*. By contrast the Sakha, who have their own Republic in north-eastern Siberia, have almost no shamans but a rapidly growing ideology called shamanism. At the most, there are said to be no more than about eight 'real' shamans left among a Sakha population of 350,000 who occupy an area nearly the size of India (now increasingly dominating a guest population of 700,000 Russians and other whites).

The city of Yakutsk contains flourishing societies for the revival of shamanism, and their members are largely doctors, teachers, anthropologists, historians, vets, physicists, biologists, writers and film directors. These people explore shamanism as the ancient wisdom of their own people, from the points of view of healing, self-realization, psychotherapy, telepathy, bioenergetic fields, their own ethnic origins, oral epic tradition and modern theatre (Balzer in press).

The Soviet regime (in which the Sakha intelligentsia were themselves implicated) never managed to cope fully with the combination of religiosity and nationalism implicit in Sakha shamanic thinking. Sakha writers like Oyunsky (a pen name from the Sakha word for 'shaman') and Kulakovsky tried to reconcile shamanist and communist themes in the 1920s, but were killed off in the less compromising 1930s. From then until the mid-1980s, shamans were ridiculed or exiled, and at times (especially from the 1930s to 1950s) shot or dropped out of helicopters and challenged to fly.

Until recently, the local knowledge associated with shamanism was cordoned off, studied academically and patronized. In a typical statement, a Sakha author wrote that before the advent of Lenin and the 'beneficial influence of advanced Russian culture and social thought', 'the intellectual talents of the benighted, unlettered Yakut [i.e. Sakha] people . . . were apparent . . . in the fashioning of a many-genred folklore handed down from generation to generation' (Makarov 1983: 3).

But shamanism is not so much an institution – indeed, when it is not adopted by a revivalist movement it is hardly an 'ism' at all – as a part of a wider complex of ideas (and a somewhat variable one). The shamanic world-view was very diffuse throughout everyday life and did not depend solely on one particular kind of performer, even the shaman. Everyone still partakes of this world-view every time they toss a glass of vodka into the fire to feed the hearth spirit, or check the flight of birds to see if they will have a good day. Some practices, such as feeding the fire, are carried out constantly and unself-consciously by most town-dwellers and even party officials. Meanwhile, the rural population still lives by hunting, cattle and horse herding, and a range of corresponding elements and motifs, involving animals, ghosts and features of the landscape, have proved very resilient. So the young intellectuals of the city can turn to their own rural grandparents for authentic 'ethnic wisdom', as well as to books on anthropology and folklore, which are very popular reading matter. This wisdom is the local knowledge contained in traditional ideas about man and nature: about seasons, the weather, the behaviour of animals, medicinal herbs, health and illness. The village informants, who used to be listed at the back of ethnographies only by way of scholastic documentation, are now becoming public figures.

This assertive new ideology rides on the crest of a particular historical wave: the breakup of the USSR which offered the possibility for each of its (partly ethnically defined) constituent regions to claim a higher degree of autonomy. All the thirty-odd indigenous Siberian peoples have a strong sha-manic tradition, but the Sakha are exceptionally well placed in their numbers (many of the other peoples number only a few thousands) and in the fact that they have a Republic which possesses a large share of Russia's gold and virtu-ally all the country's diamonds.

The boosting of shamanic ideas to iconic status goes hand in hand with the sudden, vastly increased export potential of these natural resources. The ambiguities and dilemmas which this raises for the Sakha elite's approach to their land emerge in the following quotation (cf Vitebsky 1990).

> Today my Republic reminds me of a huge ship, laden with treasure and boarded by assorted departmental pirates. As they shove diamonds, tin, gold, coal and mica feverishly into chests, they cast their predatory eyes yet further at the piles of timber, which like a giant float keep this ship from sinking. If they ever reach the timber, then the ship will go down once and for all.
>
> (Tumarcha 1989)

On the one hand, the victim of the ministerial pirates from Moscow is not 'my people', but 'my Republic': the point seems to be not that the treasure should not be enjoyed, but that others are stealing it from its rightful owners. On the other hand, the remark about timber suggests that the extraction of natural resources is destructive whoever does it. The position of the Republic's regional government is that coal, gold and diamonds must be mined – but that the profits must return to Yakutia. Their agenda for action works in terms of tariffs and an enhanced degree of sovereignty within the idiom of the modern state. In ethnic terms, people who talk like this are thinking of the development and the autonomy of a region or territory, rather than of a people. The idiom is economic and statist.

The alternative view sees autonomy, not in economic terms but in terms which are ethnically exclusive. Nativist thinkers sometimes push concepts of the state into the background, or even deny them altogether. Supporters of this approach look towards Sakha ethnic wisdom to guide man's use of the local landscape. They favour the renewable animal resources of traditional Sakha culture and may reject large-scale development projects altogether. In a landmark article entitled 'Man lives by Nature' (Danilov 1989) the author writes that southern models of development do not take account of special northern conditions, so that in their concern only with their own products the mining agencies are breaking the laws of nature. These are precisely the laws which Sakha ethnic wisdom respects. Since time immemorial, Danilov writes, the Sakha have believed that one must respect the silence of the forest, not pollute Nature and not wound the Earth. The world and man's soul are both made up of three corresponding elements. In polluting Nature, we are polluting our own flesh and blood. So we must protect the landscape like our own body and soul. This 'ethnic wisdom' is seen as amounting to a sort of essence which one has (or can rediscover in oneself) by virtue of belonging to a certain people and through partaking in that people's relationship to their land. Only the Sakha people understand this vast, wild and difficult northern environment and know how to use it properly.[1]

The urban Sakha interpretation of their shamanic tradition has shifted from the religious sensibility of the herder's and hunter's movement across a local landscape towards a more abstract sense of ethnicity. On the way, this passes through the concept of a landscape of the mind and of the Sakha person's freedom of movement over this landscape. Many of the Sakha intelligentsia interpret the shamanic landscape symbolically as the domain of a liberated consciousness, with shamans' journeys into different cosmological realms representing changes of states of mind or 'altered states of consciousness'. This move is reinforced by the wide circulation of magazine articles in Sakha and Russian which combine local ideas of this sort with themes from abroad which chime with them. It is significant that, whereas nationalist societies in the early twentieth century had titles like 'Yakut Nation', the most conspicuous new society of the late perestroika period is called Kut-Syur, 'Consciousness-Soul'.[2] As yet, there seems to be only one 'real' new young shaman, who lives in a remote village and avoids the hype in the city. But many circles in the capital live in a feverish state of excitement over the idea of shamanism, the icons of which reappear constantly in plays and newspaper articles and on television. Numerous hypnotists, wizards and 'extra-sensories' ply their trade and toy with how far they can get away with calling themselves shamans. As the Sakha Minister of Culture, one of Russia's most prominent theatre directors and a leading figure in the movement, put it to me, 'shamanism is a void at the heart of things: everyone circles around it and no-one knows how to get in'.

Non-indigenous shamanism: from cosmological ground to political agenda

Locality and belief in the New Age

In each case, a change in the significance of 'shamanism' is linked to a change in the meaning of place. The Sora and the Sakha represent two contrasting ways in which a local sense of place becomes more global, though less cosmic. In one, locality comes to mean less, in the other, it means more.

Local knowledge is the basis for action by the intellect on the environment and gives to its knowers the conviction of commanding a certain area of experience. This remains 'knowledge' for as long as it continues to satisfy that conviction. Under certain circumstances, experience itself can move away from the certainty of knowledge, defy it, slip out of its grasp. An entire system of knowledge, or parts of it, become ineffectual in the face of reality. Here, the Sora present what may be called a standard old-fashioned modernization scenario. They are ceasing to practise shamanism under a complex set of conditions which are dominated by a growing sense of ethnic inferiority. It would be hard to imagine a revival of Sora shamans unless this were part of an ethnic reassertion against the state, brahminism or some other dominant outside force. But since christianization is already a way of asserting oneself against these, a revival seems doubly unlikely. So they are not abandoning their previous local knowledge because it was objectively bad knowledge: as we shall see, from the point of view of psychology and psychiatry, Sora shamanistic knowledge may be considered an exceptionally good and effective knowledge, representing a great insight about human emotion (Vitebsky 1993a: ch. 10). Rather, it is because the scope and expectations of its application have changed. In particular, as the quotation at the head of this paper showed, it has lost its narrative power to link the past, present and future.

For the Sakha, however, a rhetorical emphasis on Sakha ethnic wisdom fits in well with the pragmatic move towards a localization of political authority and of control over economic resources. Shamanic ideas are absolutely of the place. In the present move towards decentralization this local character is seen, not as a sign of provincialism, but as a sign of appropriateness and power.

Shamanism offers a revitalized narrative link with the past, a sense that one's condition today can be seen as the developmental and experiential outcome of this past, a revivification of memory. This is a reversal of the old Soviet doctrine that in order to be good, one's present condition should be the outcome of severing such links with the past.

By being caught up in a modern revival at all, the Sakha share certain features with the New Age movement in the West, in particular what I would call the crisis of literal belief. They know their knowledge about shamanic ideas, not as *habitus* but as facts. When the aged mother of a friend of mine died recently, he described her as one of the last people who knew these things. Yet in another sense, he knows them too, but as an anthropology student in the city writing about her cosmology. The difference is that as a herdswoman, she also did them, and did them because for her there was no distinction between knowing and doing.

Yet even as *habitus* becomes packaged into facts, it comes with a trademark and a copyright. The landscape has a new meaning, which is primarily as 'ours' rather than anyone else's. Here, then, is narrative restored, but on a national scale. Not only the Sakha mineral ministries' but even the most radical Sakha environmentalist positions emerge also as nationalistic stances. The radical Sakha greens are effectively saying to both their own people and outsiders, 'The world is in desperate need of environmental wisdom. But our people have already got it'. This much has been said or implied by Black Elk (Neihardt 1972 [1932]) and many others elsewhere. But in Yakutia, the powerful global idiom of environment is being used during a political free-for-all to legitimate vital ethnic claims. Shamanism becomes a future-oriented claim-staker in terms of ethnic politics, dressed up in its older rhetoric as a rationale. A political vacuum has brought about a cultural, epistemological and even moral vacuum which is rare in the modern world. The shamanist-ecologists of Yakutia are positing an essence of their own ethnicity distilled in a wisdom which is at one and the same time ancient, avant-garde and – crucially for the ethnic and territorial climate of the ex-USSR – inalienable.

So the Sakha are succeeding in linking their local knowledge and their own narrative advantageously to global developments, while the Sora are failing (and probably not even aware of this possibility). When converting local knowledge into global currency, the exchange rate is more favourable for some newcomers than for others. For the Sakha just now, this is because they have diamonds on their land combined with a political vacuum which invites bold new initiatives.

But there is at least a third kind of situation in which shamanic ideas function in the modern world. The Sora and Sakha represent largely 'tribal' areas with an indigenous tradition, which is either being abandoned or revived after a recent abandonment. In the western New Age movement, however, shamanism has never been indigenous. These neo-shamanists are practising shamanism for the first time, in a cosmopolitan way but sometimes with the additional claim that it is somehow a revival of ancient wisdom. These movements are inchoate and barely studied, so that any generalization can be no more than tentative. But it seems to me that one can sketch certain prominent overall tendencies.

As in Yakutia, such movements turn to a place or time, real or imagined, which is other than here and now. This is necessary because they state or imply a radical critique of that same here and now. Unlike the Yakuts, the proponents of these movements cannot plausibly claim to be basing themselves on a recent indigenous tradition (unless one invokes druids etc., and strains the argument to extremes). So in addition, such movements are therefore generally not nationalistic but cosmopolitan and universalist in tone. They cannot be otherwise since the inspiration and legitimation of such syncretistic wisdom is provided by cultures which are avowedly foreign. This knowledge has a local flavour, but it is local elsewhere in time or space: it comes from Red Indian shamans, Tibetan lamas, ancient Egyptian priests – it might even come from the Sakha if their ideas were widely available in English. As it is adopted into a wider world, this kind of wisdom is stripped of certain specific elements (such as clan cults and ancestor worship) which are so local that they do not travel well. But this new re-localization also takes place on a global scale and with global claims. Indeed, this is what gives a millennial tone to much New Age rhetoric: it is both community-based and a new sort of world religion.

Yet, because it is largely middle class and urban, this approach raises severe problems about where people stand between degrees of literal belief and of literary conceit, as with the gods and fauns of pastoral poetry. The Sakha intelligentsia still lie further back along this continuum. Most of my friends in this class retain great faith in traditional dream interpretation, read omens, fear ghosts and are in awe of the power in shamanic objects in their own museum, going so far as to claim that these still emanate the distinctive smell which surrounds the shaman's person.

Perfecting the self and saving the planet

The New Age may be cosmopolitan; but at the same time, it moves away from cosmology by dissolving the realm of the religious. Among many others, I shall focus on two conflicting directions to this move, which drift like clouds of gas away from the exploded centre of cosmology. On the one hand, there is a tendency to annihilate the distinction between humans and cosmos by psychologizing the realm of the religious, that is, to take the cosmos into oneself and use it as a tool for therapizing the psyche; on the other hand, there is also a tendency to enlarge the disjunction between humans and cosmos, as though they relate to each other only with difficulty. This dualism between humans and their setting feeds into ideologies of the 'environment'.

Both psychotherapy and environmentalism find much to quarry in the old shamanism. They may be said to represent, respectively, a more private (individualist) and a more public (collective) approach. But this appropriation takes place in the context of a dissatisfaction with the way things are, and a yearning to make things better. This yearning is post-Edenic and sometimes apocalyptic, but must do without the explicit theological rationales which originally underpinned the ideas of Eden or the apocalypse (though one can sometimes detect more veiled themes of sin and redemption). The individualist and collective approaches to making things better emerge respectively as improving or perfecting the self, and saving the world (the 'planet'). The self is no longer a target for 'saving' since this is a deeply theological idiom which has been left behind, along with sin and Satan, outside the sweat lodge or gestalt group; 'saving' the world, however, fits into current rhetoric because this combines two powerful current dramas: the adventure story, in which heroes save humanity from a fate worse than death at the eleventh hour and in the nick of time, and the idea of the earth's vulnerability. 'Spaceship earth', photographed from outside the atmosphere and repeated endlessly on record covers and advertisements, has become a new outer membrane which circumscribes our consciousness, a new icon of finitude.

From religion to psychology

In contrast to the New Age, and even to the Sakha, the Sora abandonment of their Ancestors retains a largely religious tone. The rationale of their conversion does not lie in a denial of the theological idiom. They are denying the old beliefs only to the extent that the new one may be more powerful or appropriate ('of course *sonums* still exist, since there's a word for them and they've all got names'). God and Jesus do not so much render the old *sonums* unreal or part of a false knowledge, as supersede them: they are bigger and better *sonums*. So even if the dead do really reside underground, the living no longer know how to relate to this fact. Consequently, they are losing interest in the technique of dialogue which allows them to find out what the dead have to say to them from down there. One of my closest friends in the 1970s lent me his young son to live with me as my own son. This child has now grown up and become a Christian. His father was never a Christian but nevertheless received a Christian burial instead of the lengthy sequence of funerals, with dialogues, which he had himself taken part in for others in his time. In 1992 I asked the son where his father, my old friend, was now. The young man replied that he was with Jesus, but then added, rather wistfully I thought, 'He may be underground, but we can't know – we don't speak to him any more' (*anin kînorai lungen daku pede, do ellen a'galambe – a'nolongbe*).

Thus, the Sora are abandoning their Ancestor worship in favour of an alternative model of religion. Yet the main interest of their old religion for the modern outside world lies in the extraordinary ways in which its insights parallel theories and techniques in contemporary psychotherapy but can be used to refine and develop the latter. Nobody is likely to want to believe literally in the myriad categories of Sora *sonum* or to repeat the minutiae of performing the appropriate rites. But the overall picture of human emotions and interrelationships given by traditional Sora *religion* is ripe for appropriation by our own avant-garde thinking – but only as *psychology*.

Kleinman (1986: 55–56) has identified a large-scale 'psychologizing process' which he argues has affected American culture since World War I and which forms part of a 'cultural transformation in which the self has been culturally constituted as the now dominant western ethnopsychology'. The expanded psyche fills the space left by the retreat of religion. So far has this process advanced that even transcending one's own limitations has become as much a psychic as a religious quest.

> From the perspective of the American Firewalking movement the beliefs that constitute religious systems like the Anastenaria are limiting beliefs; they are the 'programs' and 'tapes' that keep us from further spiritual growth . . . The highest good is not obedience to the will of some supernatural being but self-expression and direct experience. It isn't Saint Constantine who protects us from the fire; it's the fact of who we are. When we identify with who we really are, we don't get burned because who we really are can never get burned.
>
> (Danforth 1989: 270)

The Sakha intelligentsia have likewise moved significantly from shamanism as religion (the form in which I have still seen it among old herders and hunters in the wilderness, as they apologize to bears they have killed and return the souls of elks to the Lord of the Forest for reincarnation) to a psychology. With a nationalist cultural society named 'Consciousness-Soul', they have moved from outer (cosmological) to inner (psychological) space as they embark on journeys which are avowedly journeys of the mind. Whereas I do not believe the language exists with which to explain psychology to my Sora friends, in Yakutia many of the old herders and hunters (all of whom read Russian popular magazines) are able to point out the parallels for themselves.

From cosmology to environment

New Age psychologized religion also tends to downplay the political. To quote Danforth again.

> [a]ccording to the New Age ideology, because society is nothing more than a collection of individuals, social and political problems are reduced to psychological problems. Social change is therefore equated with personal growth and self-transformation.
>
> (Danforth 1989: 284)

However, cosmology involves not only a vision of how the universe works, but also uses this as a basis for decisive action upon the world. Environmentalism, as one of its successor ideologies, takes this even further by concentrating directly on how things ought to be. As the concept of government falters, the world moves further and further into the realm of pressure groups and lobbying. Knowledge, whether indigenous or otherwise, moves out of the realm of epistemology and increasingly serves or underpins an 'agenda'. (This is another, completely non-epistemological reason why knowledge today cannot be concerned primarily with a timeless 'truth'.)

This kind of agenda does not lie at the private end of the spectrum, like many of the self-perfection techniques of the psychotherapies. Practices like apologizing to animals' souls and returning them to the Master or Mistress of the Animals, acknowledging new moons and solstices, picking only the plants you need, not using cars, recycling environmentally costly products like glass bottles and bears' souls – all these are perceived as good ways of behaving and thinking. But at the same time, most of us cannot do these things without being fey or pretentious, or feeling that we are making little impact. We want our government and our society to do these things on our behalf, since this is the only scale on which such ideas will have any substantial effect. Thus concern for the environment is necessarily tied closely to an attempt to influence public policy.

From cosmic holism to global management

Shamanistic cosmologies are anthropocentric, but in a certain holistic way which makes the activity of man indispensable, even while constraining it. The world is animized and gendered on the model of human consciousness, and the shaman's operations are done by humans, for humans. But meanwhile, bears and tigers have their own realities and even their own shamans, often with humans cast in the loser's role. The visions of equilibrium and of cycles of reciprocity in the shamanic vision make man's position humble and precarious – hence the dangers in the shaman's use of power and his or her commitment to battle. Crucially, a shamanic world-view acknowledges that the processes of the world can be held only within partial human control, and at the cost of continual struggle.

The concept of 'environment' is anthropocentric in a different and more overwhelming sense, which is perhaps why the current sense of environmental failure generates a combination of public panic and ostrichism. It involves a more one-sided and total concept of control, one based on domination and regulation, rather than on shamanism's delicate and constantly renewed negotiation. And in policy, this emerges in sub-fields like natural resource management.

Environmentalism considers humanity as distinct from its 'environment' and amounts to a strategy for the management of that environment as a 'resource base'. This approach is frankly anthropocentric to the point of being utilitarian: the entire landscape is seen as a farm, a mine or a supermarket. True, there is another category, 'ecology', which seeks to soften the harsh dualism which pitches humans against their surroundings (I am talking about ecology as an ideology, not as a science). This ecological approach, by contrast, sees the human race as merely one component of a wider system. The landscape remains ultimately untamed and the practicality, and even the ethics, of man's attempts to exploit it become problematic. Though the terminology varies, a sense of this contrast persists through much modern writing in this field: between the 'imperial' and the 'arcadian' traditions in environmental history (Worster 1985); between 'technological' and 'empathetic' knowledge (Rifkin 1983); between 'technocentric' and 'ecocentric' attitudes which concentrate respectively on means and ends (O'Riordan 1976); between something presumably shallow and the 'deep ecology' of Naess (1973) or between something isolationist and the 'transpersonal ecology' of Fox (1990).[3] These pairs of terms correspond closely to the tension among the Sakha elite between the agendas of their mineral ministries and of their mystical nationalists – a measure of how far they are implicated in global patterns of rhetoric.

But even 'ecology' is ultimately utilitarian, concerned not so much with how the world works as with how we handle it. Both terms – environment and ecology – derive their current importance from a perception that the world is no longer working as it should, and that this is happening, not because the gods are angry at our impiety but because we have mismanaged the environment and must change our management strategy. In this view, the environment almost becomes one with the economy, a term which is in no way divine but which has meaning only within the context of its management by human agents.

But ecology is ultimately no more holistic than environment. Not only does it remain utilitarian but it, too, works with a weak metaphysic based on a concept of nature which is de-deified. This 'nature' lacks totality and consciousness or intentionality: it is something less than cosmos.

If we turn to environmentalism as a form of knowledge, we see that through being tied so closely as a blueprint for action, it becomes very vulnerable to the shifting weathercock of 'real-life scenarios'. Environmental knowledge is widely associated with anxiety and confusion in its knowers, who frequently change viewpoint with the latest fashion or panic or published report. As knowledge, it is strikingly un-systemic, or fragmented. The New

Age movements and their environmentalist allies endorse the very elements which are irretrievably absent in their own appropriating society: in terms of social structure, they emphasize community, tribe or clan; epistemologically, they may favour animistic presuppositions about the souls of plants and animals and the spiritual forces in the land; historically, they seek a continuity of consciousness from ancient times (the land speaks to us and we know how to hear it); economically, they insist that one needs time to reflect at length and without anxiety on all this and even to engage in elaborate rituals (and to the extent that people do so, this is perhaps a partial explanation for the predominance of middle-class people with adequate salaries and flexible professional schedules). Such a quest must be unsuccessful, since the absence of these elements is a necessary condition for the existence of the movement which would aim to restore them.

The fragmentation of environmentalist knowledge can be seen on both social and epistemological planes. The social fragmentation takes place as people drift rapidly in and out of organizations and pressure groups. This leads to the formation of single-issue groupings representing interests which are ideologically poorly anchored: a group may protest about a specific motorway or nuclear station and then break up as soon as that battle is over.[4] The effect of this is to create an ideological kaleidoscope, colourful but fleeting. These movements are generally politically weak because their opponents, that is the state and the corporations, have more cohesive and enduring structures and ideologies.

Epistemologically, too, environmentalism is correspondingly badly placed to constitute a core form of knowledge for any substantial section of the public. The same argument perhaps applies by extension to the New Age movement as a whole. Contradictions between the presuppositions of one campaign and of another do not bounce off each other in the generative way of contradictions in theology. The latter may be expressed as a dualistic tension amenable to resolution by synthesis, as in the nature of the Trinity or the old Manichaean relationship between God and Satan (Forsyth 1987): here, they are not sterile contradictions but creative paradoxes. Or they may form a gradation of levels of understanding revealed through stages of initiation, as in tantrism or in many puberty rites. Either way, they are understood to express the heart of the mystery of the human condition and they presuppose a holism in knowledge of reality.

This holism, it seems to me, is the weak point in the modern appropriation of any kind of indigenous knowledge. Returning to the features of shamanistic thought outlined at the start of this paper, and focusing on our two examples of psychotherapy and environmentalism, we see that:

- Its *local* nature is co-opted, but in a transplanted form which makes it a metaphor for the rejection of the appropriators' own, more diffused sense of locality. It becomes re-localized on the spot, creating a kind of global indigenosity. Through the idiom of therapy, it is also relocated inside the self.

- Its *holistic* nature is shattered for social, political and epistemological reasons, but is retained as a cardinal value. This ideal is unattainable and is replaced by the weaker concept of globality.
- Its *eristic* nature suffers a variable fate in the new therapies (for example, some forms of crystal healing are less gutsy than shamanism because they do not accommodate anger and violence) but becomes a driving force in the heroic side of environmental campaigning.
- Its *dissident* or anti-centrist nature is likewise retained and enhanced ('alternative'), both in the private and the public form.

Yet overall, I suggest that shamanism cannot avoid sharing the fate of any other kind of indigenous knowledge in the industrial world: its full implications are too challenging even for radicals to accommodate.

At the global level of decision making, it is the impetus towards action which drags indigenous knowledge into being a commodity rather than a way of doing and ensures that it could never take deep root in a new context. Action also pulls it towards current concerns which may not be local. This is clearest when we see indigenous peoples themselves bringing their 'indigenous knowledge' to what is now called the 'marketplace'. Teachers take their students to visit traditional healers and tell them that this is the indigenous knowledge which we must 'collect' and 'preserve'; a man from the Sakha Ministry of Education gives a deadpan lecture in which he points with a stick at a diagram of the cosmos and announces which spirits reside at each level (this is not a lecture for scholars of religious history but instruction for schoolchildren, for whom 'Consciousness-Soul' is now a compulsory subject on the curriculum!).

This is not a true marketplace but a rigged one in which your product will sell only if you pretend that it is something else, far less distinctive and valuable, but also far less trouble to come to terms with, than what it really is. Jungle herbalists fight pharmaceutical multinationals through the legal quagmire of intellectual property rights (Gray 1991), but in a debate which is already set in these companies' terms: plants amount to no more than molecule factories. Indigenous knowledge must be controlled to the point at which it cannot subvert hegemonic knowledge. Indigenous wisdom must be packaged into the format of a database: the butterfly must be killed in order to take its rightful place in the glass case.

Perhaps the most successful players in this game are some North American Arctic peoples, such as the Inuit. A combination of factors (starting to fight for their land rights early because of mineral extraction projects; living in a Protestant liberal-democratic state) have left them extremely well placed: an international organization like the Inuit Circumpolar Conference, has had observer status at the UN since the 1970s. But this privileged position has been bought at the price of an advanced commoditization of their indigenous knowledge.

> Why is traditional knowledge useful?
> [Over thousands of years] a collective body of knowledge . . . has been passed down through the generations . . . It represents an understanding of a dynamic ecosystem . . . This collective knowledge forms a data base for predictive modelling, for forecasting, and for selecting harvest areas.
> The goal of the Program is to help the Inuit and Cree people of Hudson Bay bring forward their knowledge in such a way that it can be integrated into the cumulative effects assessment . . . TEK [Traditional Ecological Knowledge] has several useful features as a data base. One is that data can be independently verified by separate interviews with people who harvest in the same area . . . It is important to seek the information and let patterns of change emerge through its collation and display.
> The Hudson's Bay Program will offer a neutral forum to all interested parties to work in partnership to tackle cumulative impact assessment (Phase I), and sustainable development (Phase II), in the Hudson Bay bioregion . . . The program will hopefully 'jump start' the political process . . .
>
> (*Northern Perspectives* 1992: 15–16)

This text, which is typical of the North American Arctic, invites extensive commentary. It is perhaps enough here to suggest that indigenous knowledge would probably not have homogenized the hunters' experience by 'independently verifying' one hunter's account through another, but would have generated a different plan for each hunter in accordance with his own biography; the shaman may have played a key role in fine-tuning these differences. Through all the trappings of liberal consultation in the last paragraph, the project-ese language reveals the epistemological coercion inside the velvet glove. Indigenous knowledge, whatever this is, could filter through this process only as a thing and not as a way of doing or being. And as a thing, it is clearly the local people's strongest card in cutting political deals.

But not ace of trumps. Even when adopting a high moral tone, the shrewd indigenous negotiator knows where ultimate power lies. Inuit economies and communities have been ravaged by anti-fur campaigns among the bourgeois city-dwellers whose life-style is built around 'options'. The Inuit, who do not have these options, are sometimes reduced to adopting a tortuous special pleading. Here is an extract from the advance blurb to a book by a Greenlander.

by devaluing indigenous cultures and depriving them of the right to use and manage natural resources, dominant European and American cultures are endangering not only the lives of native peoples, but the very natural balance urbanites seek to protect.

To support the case in favour of native peoples' continued 'wise use' of natural resources, Lynge introduces readers to Inuit philosophy, economics, religion . . . revealing . . . their deep respect for all forms of life. Lynge argues forcefully that *the native perspective is entirely consistent with international conservation strategies and global environmental concerns.*

(Lynge 1993, my emphasis)

With its bows to 'wise use' and a questionable 'natural balance', this text seems designed to appease the fur-forbidders out of a recognition that it is futile to oppose them. The esoteric soul theories of Inuit shamanism were really a form of rational resource management after all, only the old shamans simply failed to put it in these terms.

If the non-Russian Arctic represents one of the most advanced areas for the negotiation between indigenous knowledge and the hegemonic urban view, then it seems hard to foresee any alternative worldwide to a simple sell-out by any aspect of indigenous knowledge to a partially matching area of global epistemology. The strands which make up shamanism are complex and feed into a range of modern concerns, from rational resource management to radical psychotherapy. Where will the central features of shamanism be in each of these: the transformation of the Sora shamaness's soul into a monkey as she links her tail to her teacher and climbs down the cosmic tree to fetch her client's patrilineal ancestor; the old woman at the bottom of the sea who withholds seals from the Inuit and releases them only when the shaman goes down there and combs her hair; the austerities of Sakha initiation, in which the novice shaman is taken apart by the spirits bone by bone and then reconstituted? The answer seems to be that they will be either absent or watered down, perhaps reduced to folklore or inspiration for theatre. The shamanic sense of place, at once cosmic and local, becomes difficult to sustain but is replaced largely by a sense that each person carries the totality of space within themselves; the impetus of the eristic element of struggle moves into new arenas such as environmental agendas.

To the extent that more specific elements of shamanism are carried over, they become separated out from each other. And this is perhaps the heart of the dilemma of New Ageism: it can never authentically recapture the holistic vision which is the rationale for its own striving. It is unable to transmute mere contradiction into the powerful totalizing function of paradox. Consider a New Age workshop in shamanistic drumming, during which there may be talk about Inuit wisdom and the kind of 'natural balance' mentioned in the blurb to Lynge's book, but in which some of the clients may have diversified their ideological portfolios to include anti-fur lobbying and whale-saving. Under these circumstances, holism itself becomes just one value, rather than the ground for all other values – and so becomes no more than an option; indigenous knowledge, when transplanted and commoditized, comes to take on the fragmentary nature of the society by which it is appropriated. This is surely why indigenous or local knowledge must always remain epistemologically marginal to global knowledge. The one thing global culture cannot recapture is the holistic nature of indigenous knowledge. Even where the epistemology is admired, there is a lack of appropriate context for belief and application.

Even as astronomy sees ever further into space, the arena of human consciousness has shrunk from the cosmos to a mere globe. So ironically, the more global things become, the less holistic they are since they pertain *only* to this globe. Meanwhile, the coercive nature of interaction between the components of this globe requires, not the homogenization of the Coca-Cola model, but the perpetuation of some kinds of difference. These differences are ones of relative power and involve a sort of class structure of epistemologies in which global knowledge can rest assured of its superiority only if it can point to other, inferior knowledges. Perhaps this is the true consequence of globality: that the coercive nature of the interaction between the different components leads the weaker parties to surrender or to adopt ever more cunning disguises. In terms of purveying their local knowledge to the globe, the Inuit lead the field, with the Sakha moving up fast behind; the Sora, for the time being, are scarcely in the race.

Notes

1   This argument is presented at different levels. Here I talk about Sakha (Yakut) deploying it against Russian; but the Sakha Republic's minority Evén (a Tungus people) advance a similar argument, based on their specialist reindeer herding, to support a higher degree of autonomy from the provincial Sakha government (see Vitebsky 1992). I am grateful to the Wenner-Gren Foundation for Anthropological Research for funding my recent research in this region.

2   I am grateful to Marjorie Balzer for discussions on this topic. The responsibility for any misunderstandings remains my own.

3   Fox explicitly based his 'transpersonal ecology' on the 'transpersonal psychology' of Maslow and Sutich, a vision which moves beyond the separated, isolated ego, beyond the gulf which separates self from other, and so psychologizes the domain of ecology too.

4   I am grateful to my student Eeva Berglund for use of her field material on environmentalist agendas among civic action groups in Germany.

References

Balzer, M. (in press) 'Shamanism and the politics of culture: an anthropological view of the 1992 International conference on shamanism, Yakutsk, the Sakha Republic', *Shaman* 2.

Danforth, M. (1989) *Firewalking and Religious Healing: The Anastenaria of Greece and the American Firewalking Movement*, Princeton, NJ: Princeton University Press.

Danilov, I. (1989) 'Chelovek zhivet prirodoy [Man lives by nature]', *Polyarnaya Zvezda [Polar Star]* 3: 108–9.

de Heusch, L. (1981) 'Possession and shamanism', in *Why Marry Her? Society and Symbolic Structures*, Cambridge: Cambridge University Press.

Eliade, M. (1964) *Shamanism: Archaic Techniques of Ecstasy*, New York: Pantheon.

Elwin, V. (1955) *The Religion of an Indian Tribe*, Bombay: Oxford University Press.

Forsyth, N. (1987) *The Old Enemy: Satan and the Combat Myth*, Princeton, NJ: Princeton University Press.

Fox, W. (1990) *Toward a Transpersonal Ecology: Developing New Foundations for Environmentalism*, Boston and London: Shambala.

Gray, A. (1991) *Between the Spice of Life and the Melting Pot: Biodiversity Conservation and its Impact on Indigenous Peoples*, Copenhagen: IWGIA Document No. 70.

Kleinman, A. (1986) *Social Origins of Distress and Disease: Depression, Neurasthenia and Pain in Modern China*, New Haven, CT: Yale University Press.

Lewis, I.M. (1989) *Ecstatic Religion: A Study of Shamanism and Spirit Possession*, London: Routledge.

Lynge, F. (1993) *Arctic Wars. Animal Rights, Endangered Species*, Hanover: University Press of New England.

Makarov, D.S. (1983) *Narodnaya mudrost': zaniya i predstavleniya [National Wisdom: Knowledge and Representations]*, Yakutsk.

Naess, A. (1973) 'The shallow and the deep, long-range ecology movement: a summary', *Inquiry* 16: 95–100.

Neihardt, J.G. [1932] (1972) *Black Elk Speaks: Being the Life of a Holy Man of the Oglala Sioux*, New York: Washington Square Press.

Northern Perspectives (1992) 'Traditional ecological knowledge', 20(2): 15–16.

O'Riordan, T. (1976) *Environmentalism*, London: Pion.

Rifkin, J. (1983) *Algeny: A New Word – a New World*, New York: Viking.

Tumarcha, L. (1989) 'Sprosi khozyayna [Ask the owner]', letter in *Severnyye Prostory [Northern Expanses]* 3: 2.

Vitebsky, P. (1978) 'Political relations among the Sora of India', cyclostyled, 2 papers.

Vitebsky, P. (1990) 'Yakut', in G. Smith (ed.) *The Nationalities Question in the Soviet Union*, London: Longman.

Vitebsky, P. (1992) 'Landscape and self-determination among the Evény: the political environment of Siberian reindeer herders today', in E. Croll and D. Parkin (eds) *Bush Base: Forest Farm — Culture, Environment and Development*, London: Routledge.

Vitebsky, P. (1993a) *Dialogues with the Dead: The Discussion of Mortality among the Sora of Eastern India*, Cambridge: Cambridge University Press.

Vitebsky, P. (1993b) 'Is death the same everywhere? Contexts of knowing and doubting', in M. Hobart (ed.) *An Anthropological Critique of Development: The Growth of Ignorance*, London: Routledge.

Vitebsky, P. (1995) 'Deforestation and the changing spiritual environment of the Sora', in R. Grove (ed.) *Essays in the Environmental History of Southeast Asia*, Delhi: Oxford University Press, 2 vols.

Worster, D. (1985) *Nature's Economy: History of Ecological Ideas*, Cambridge: Cambridge University Press.

PART FIVE

New developments

INTRODUCTION TO PART FIVE

VARIOUS CHAPTERS IN PREVIOUS PARTS have introduced or discussed recent developments among those who might be considered to be shamans or shamanic groups. These have included changes in post-Soviet Siberia, and in India. Part Five focuses attention on wider new or recent developments. Some of these are arguably continuous with earlier, perhaps 'traditional', forms. Others are rooted in changes in Western modernity in which alternative ways of thinking and/or living arise from information about indigenous or historical cultures. Critiques of some of these new shamanisms can be intense and even derogatory. Responses and defences can also be profound and passionate. There is considerable tension between the invitation to learn better (perhaps 'more respectful' or 'more ecological') ways to be human and the rejection of continuing appropriation of indigenous knowledge and ceremonial. Few of those engaged in such debates appear to doubt that something is wrong with modernity, the question is whether particular responses and alternatives are any improvement.

Meanwhile, despite the heat of this confrontation, it should not be forgotten that a considerable change is indicated by its very existence. Not so long ago, any criticism of shamans was levelled against indigenous, traditional forms. They were portrayed as primitive, stubborn opponents of progress, devious tricksters or (im)pious frauds manipulating gullible and backwards co-religionists (if indeed they were not merely superstitious and without proper religion or rationality). Instructive examples of this trend are evident from the titles that summarise some of the early material in Narby and Huxley's selection of excerpts on *Shamans Through Time: 500 Years on the Path to Knowledge*

(2001). These include 'devil worship', 'ministers of the devil who learn about the secrets of nature', 'the shaman: a villain of a magician who calls demons', 'the savages esteem their jugglers', 'shamans deserve perpetual labor for their hocus-pocus', 'blinded by superstition', 'shamans are impostors who claim they consult the devil – and who are sometimes close to the mark' and 'misled impostors and the power of imagination'. Admittedly these titles summarise excerpts from sixteenth- to eighteenth-century writings. Research might show, however, that popular opinion (including that of many Westerners in contact with indigenous people) would have agreed with such views until fairly recently.

Whatever criticisms may be levelled against anthropologists and other academics (including by scholarly colleagues in the same or cognate disciplines), it should be noted that they have effected an alteration in Western discourse and perspective as regards the value of indigenous cultures. Of course, it might also be noted that effecting change has not always been what academics wished to do, if 'going native' was the big sin while 'in the field', advocacy and even activism once home have hardly been more reputable. Responsibility for setting up a new religion, or for informing the growth of a new movement, is hardly something to put on an academic curriculum vitae, and some scholars have felt the need to leave academic employment and establish their own parallel institutions. If Eliade disguised his new theology as 'history of religions', Castaneda and Harner found a happier (and perhaps more honest) niche by withdrawing from academia. More broadly, many practitioners of new shamanisms – whether indigenous, Euro-American or whatever – are avid readers of scholarly publications, from which they frequently draw considerable encouragement or gain significant inspiration. It is to these new shamanisms and their critics that we now turn.

Marjorie Balzer's discussion of 'the poetry of shamanism' in Chapter 18 is devoted to developments in the Sakha Republic in North-eastern Siberia during the 1990s. She concludes, 'Some of the ancient paths have become overgrown with disuse, but shamans like one young Viliuisk man whose helper spirits are the raven and the dog say they have rediscovered the paths with the guidance of elderly living shamans and the spirits of deceased shamans.' While there are plenty of continuities with earlier shamanic activities evident in the new-style poetry of interest here, this chapter provides a good introduction to this Part. Not only does it challenge the boundaries between 'new' and 'old', or 'traditional' and 'revived', but also indicates that even what is clearly new can be experienced as effectively the same as earlier forms. The chapter is also a powerful engagement with the possibilities borne by the word 'performance' as demonstrated by poets and actors enacting roles with audiences. What might have begun as a representation of 'what our culture used to be like' can become, in the experience of participants, a truly shamanic event. People who pretend to be shamans might become such. If shamans are correct, of course, to invite the presence and intervention of other-than-human persons, or of ancestors, is to risk their actually turning up.

In Chapter 19 Ward Churchill contributes to a significant critique of 'plastic medicine men' and their 'wannabe Indian' followers. Shamans have often, perhaps always, been employed to shamanise. That is, there is rarely a problem with religious leaders benefiting from the work they perform for their communities. Similarly, people have always exchanged ideas, ways of doing ceremony, knowledge about the world. In a humorous but powerful evocation and critique of cultural encounters Alice Walker writes

> I think it is ridiculous and ultimately insulting to study people, said Irene. I think you would only need to study other human beings if you were worried you were not human yourself.
>
> Susannah laughed. I've often thought what a European trait studying other people is. Other folk who meet strange people want to dance and eat with them, go swimming and talk about what colorful or peculiar wildlife there is about. They prefer to sit around smoke ganja or the peace pipe, listen to music and just kick back.
>
> That's because they haven't come to steal everything, said Irene.
>
> (Walker 1998, 187)

Churchill's ire, however, is raised not only or even primarily by those who 'come to steal' but by those who sell to outsiders for personal financial gain. The ignoring or abandonment of responsibilities and participation required of learners in traditional contexts is challenged. Churchill cites other Native American authorities about what they see as problematic in such inter-cultural encounters.

In Chapter 20 Paul Johnson offers a 'case study in New Age ritual appropriation' based on ethnographic accounts of shamanism as practised by the Shuar of Ecuador and among a group of urban Americans modelling their practice on the Shuar. His chief purpose is to suggest methodological criteria by which indigenous and Western shamanisms might be distinguished. Key terms in this project are 'dislocated' and 'organic'. They seem to characterise Western and indigenous cultures admirably. However, the analysis has the potential to undercut any indigenous right to sovereignty or self-determination unless it is firmly rooted in a continuing 'traditional' culture and location. What happens when indigenous peoples continue to migrate as their ancestors once did? Or when they have to migrate to survive? Can they not, even in their 'own land'/'homeland' adopt new ways of doing whatever they feel necessary? (See Thompson 2001 for a discussion of a Mayan community's responses to issues like these.) Conversely, what room is there in Johnson's critique for an understanding that actually neo-shamanism is entirely organic in its late-modern culture? Or, perhaps more invitingly, it might need to respond to Howard Eilberg-Schwartz's argument that those who learn from indigenous people take certain claims of anthropology more seriously than anthropologists themselves. Twentieth-century anthropology has insisted that we have a great deal to learn about ourselves from the study of the other ... This is the myth that justifies the anthropological enterprise, a myth that says that the study of the other leads to enlightenment.

(Eilberg-Schwartz 1989: 87)

Whether one find criticisms of 'neo-shamanism' convincing or not, it is important to understand what the new forms of shamanism entail. The following four chapters exemplify or discuss four different forms of contemporary Western shamanism.

Chapter 21 by Sandra Ingerman, 'Tracking lost souls', is a classic of its kind. It invites readers to imagine being present at a 'soul retrieval' and inducts them into a sense of experience near description. This is a mode of healing resonant with the 'core shamanism' established by Michael Harner and others, in which it is understood that illness or disturbance is caused by loss of 'soul'. By effecting alterations of consciousness the healer journeys to 'nonordinary' reality, sometimes inclusive of 'upper', 'lower', 'inner' and 'shamanic' worlds (where these do not overlap in some way). With the aid of 'power animals' or 'guardians' the healer retrieves some aspect of the client and brings it back to them. Similarly excellent evocations of this therapeutic and personal development style of Western shamanism are available in Harner's book (1990) and the website for his Foundation for Shamanic Studies (http://www.shamanism.org), in the website of Jonathan Horowitz's Scandinavian Center for Shamanic Studies (http://www.shaman-center.dk) and in the works of John Matthews (1992) and Caitlín Matthews (1995). The label 'Core Shamanism' is used by many practitioners, indicating that it is based on the identification of central themes and practices within the different localised shamanisms known from ethnographic and historical texts as well as from significant encounters with indigenous shamans themselves.

In Chapter 22 by Gordon MacLellan, 'Dancing on the Edge', we encounter a Western shamanism with a different focus from Harner-style Core Shamanism. In common with many shamans, healing and trance are important to MacLellan, but his overriding interest is in the fraught encounter between humans and the rest of life, 'nature' perhaps. He says that 'modern shamans might be: personal healers ..., community healers ..., patterners', explaining the latter (his role) as those 'who help the community listen to/relate to the world around them'. In the process of 'helping people understand, communicate with and live as part of the environment they are in', the shaman 'is the one caught in the middle: the spider in the web, perhaps. Or maybe the fly'. Elsewhere I have argued that this eco-shamanism is particularly attractive to Pagans, and that Gordon is typical in expressing his 'patterning' through environmental education (Harvey 1997).

In Chapter 23, 'The tree, the tower and the shaman', Beverley Butler discusses the 'material culture of resistance of the No M11 Link Roads Protest of Wanstead and Leytonstone, London'. The 'shaman' here is enmeshed in the confrontations of modernity with its environment, conflicts about possible futures (one facilitating easier road haulage, the other re-making homes connected to at least some green and ecological diverse space), spirituality and politics, anarchy and power, and a wide diversity of motivations for protesting against a particular highway. Probably not for the first time, not everyone will be convinced that this chapter belongs in a set of Readings on shamanism. However, if it only serves to remind us that shamanism has implications for material culture, and vice versa, it will be significant. In addition, it should remind us that shamans are (a) enmeshed in their cultures and communities; and (b) that they are sometimes enmeshed in conflicts within their cultures and communities. And if it only forces us to clarify our terms by refining the boundaries of what is and is not shamanic, that is valuable too.

Chapter 24 by Robert Wallis, 'Waking ancestor spirits', is included here primarily because of the attention it pays to a kind of neo-shamanism that self-consciously attempts to reconstruct European ancestral shamanisms. Two case studies present fascinating detail about Heathen neo-shamanism and about Pagan involvement with ancient sacred sites. Both case studies permit important discussions about academic knowledges and power-systems, especially in relation to the interpretation of ancient texts and ancient places. Alongside these, already enticing, reasons for interest in such shamanisms, Wallis argues that popular interpretations and experiences might additionally provide interpretations to which academics ought to pay attention. Wallis' other works, and those of Jenny Blain (Blain and Wallis 2000) provide invaluable further discussion.

Last, but far from least, Terence McKenna's 'brief history of psychedelics' in Chapter 25 provides a fine example of one interest of 'technoshamanism'. Frazer Clark claims to have coined this term in 1987 to 'describe the DJ's role in the Rave' (Clark 1995). He continues:

> basically the DJ is in charge of the group mood/mind. He senses when it's time to lift the mood, take it down, etc. just as the shaman did in the good ol' tribal days (which are still very much alive, of course, outside the west) . . . Technoshamanism is using the technology, media (despite what some think) to help spread the vibe, the meme, sketching out a rough map for the trek ahead of them.

McKenna documents the study of what he variously labels 'psychedelic', 'intoxicating', 'psychoactive', 'hallucinogenic' and 'visionary' plants. He is particularly interested in the experiential study, decriminalisation, and visionary encounter with various powerful plants. Technoshamanism is a significant topic of conversation and exploration within the various Internet media (websites, lists, email) and also in a powerful array of fiction/imaginative literature (e.g. Gibson 1995).

References

Blain, J. and Wallis, R. J. (2000) 'The "ergi" seidman: Contestations of gender, shamanism and sexuality in northern religion, past and present', *Journal of Contemporary Religion*, 15(3): 395–411.

Clark, F. 1995. Email to the Internet alt.techno-shamanism newsgroup.

Eilberg-Schwartz, H. 1989. 'Witches of the West: Neopaganism and Goddess Worship as Enlightenment Religions', *Journal of Feminist Studies in Religion* 5(1): 77–95.

Gibson, W. 1995. *Neuromancer*. London: HarperCollins.

Harner, M. 1990. *The Way of the Shaman*. San Francisco: Harper & Row.

Harvey, G. 1997. *Listening People, Speaking Earth: Contemporary Paganism*. London: Hurst & Co.

Matthews, C. 1995. *Singing the Soul Back Home: Shamanism in Daily Life*. Shaftesbury: Element.

Matthews, J. 1992. *The Celtic Shaman: A Handbook*. Shaftesbury: Element.

Narby, J. and Huxley, F. 2001. *Shamans Through Time: 500 Years on the Path to Knowledge*. London: Thames and Hudson.

Thompson, C. 2001. *Maya Identities and the Violence of Place: Borders Bleed*. Aldershot: Ashgate.

Walker, A. 1998. *By the Light of My Father's Smile*. London: Women's Press.

Chapter 18

Marjorie Mandelstam Balzer

THE POETRY OF SHAMANISM

IN 1991, I MADE a personal and professional pilgrimage to a young
Sakha (Yakut) shaman of the Viliuisk region, of the newly sovereign Yakut-
Sakha Republic (now Sakha Republic) in Northeastern Siberia.[1] He had mixed
feelings about seeing a foreign anthropologist, but agreed through mutual
friends, to meet at his parent's cottage in a small, remote village. After hours
of talk, during which we discussed many aspects of my pilgrimage, including a
medical problem, I confessed that I was also interested in the aesthetic power
of shamanic chants as poetry. Expecting him to dismiss this as absurdly isolated
from the core of his curing purposes, I was delighted by his broad grin.
Ironically, it was this, more than my medical problem, that convinced him to
bring out his drum. He agreed to sing parts of an introductory seance song,
although not to call his helper spirits in a true seance at this stage of our
relationship.

This young shaman, removed from specific intellectual trends of the urban
Sakha intelligentsia, was nonetheless also caught up in the cultural and political
revival of the Sakha people, who prefer this name for themselves rather than
the outsider's term Yakut. This village shaman was both pleased and wary that
some urban Sakha have rediscovered the beauty and power of shamanism, and
it appealed to him that texts of memorized yet sometimes improvisational
chanting could be appreciated, even touted, as aesthetically worthy by a for-
eigner. His own view of the seance as a performance on many levels, for many
listeners (spiritual and human, Sakha and non-Sakha), meant that he is fully
aware of the dramatic and poetic value of his art. With neither cloak nor fire,
he sat in a straight-backed chair and produced a low, moaning, repetitive and

intense song describing himself, an *oiuun* (one of the Sakha words for shaman), as having two loyal helper spirits, a dog and a raven.

Before discussing details of both richly symbolic and intensely functional Sakha shamanic texts, it is necessary to put these texts into social and political contexts (Atkinson 1990; Metcalf 1989) The seance is then discussed as an art form. Finally, a preliminary analysis of selected Sakha chant fragments is then presented, to weave together, yet not confound, themes inspired by introspective Sakha friends, and various theorists of symbolic anthropology [e.g. Bruner (1984); Fernandez (1988; 1991); Friedrich (1991); and Turner (1977: 52)].

The social and political context of shamanic revival

In Spring 1991, a sensation was caused amongst the Sakha intelligentsia when a newspaper interview appeared, entitled 'She Comes in the Form of a White Horse.' The interview was with a renowned shaman named Zoia Duranova, whose helper spirit, the white horse, is one of the most powerful multivocal symbols of the traditional (farthest North Turkic) Sakha culture. In the interview, Zoia explained that she becomes at one with her helper spirit during seances, and when she senses friends are in need. She also related how she had found her husband when she arrived in a particular town for a public seance (sometimes broadcast on local Sakha language TV). She had been invited to a banquet in her honor. Near her was an empty seat, and she decided to see if she could sense who was missing. She sent one of her souls to a nearby house where she saw a man lying drunk on a couch. When she came to herself at the table, she apologized for having seemed out of the conversation and requested that someone go wake up the man two houses down and bring him to the banquet. He became her husband, as she knew he would. As she showed me in 1992, he had the proper mark on his forehead, just under the hairline.[2]

People who read or heard this story were divided as to its validity. Many believed Zoia can turn herself into a horse, and a few told further stories about the harm she reputedly had done to a Soviet Russian doctor who doubted her power. Some, including one who came from her home village, scoffed and said she has always just been crazy, even as a little girl. But no one could deny the sensation she has caused with her public seances, during which people are supposed to feel better after auditorium-sized bouts of communal solidarity with her, and with her spirits. Some attending these all-purpose, unconventional seances claimed they were indeed healed of various illnesses.

Far from being politically hounded and underground, shamanism has reemerged as a force to be discussed, if not admired, in the deconstructivist post-Soviet world. In the Sakha Republic, shamanism is one of many idioms through which people are struggling to recapture a culture perceived as nearly lost and profoundly unique and special (cf. Balzer 1983, 1987, 1990, 1992).

Exuberant, dramatic, mind-bending shamanism is part of the backlash against rigid, grey and stultifying Soviet rule. This does not mean, however, that people are paralysed by nostalgia or pedantic about precise cultural reconstruction.

Far from every shaman gives public seances, and some are still quite cautious about revealing their talents to outsiders (defined by some as even non-local Sakha). Memories of official Soviet persecution are still painful for families of shamans. And numerous shamans have died, whether in Soviet jails, psychiatric clinics, or by natural causes, without passing on their esoteric knowledge and poetry to children, apprentices or spirit-selected survivors. But a newly constructed shamanic revival is evolving, to the point where the Sakha Ministry of Culture is considering funding a shamanic school, thus officially sponsoring training in ancient curing techniques for children identified as having special psychological proclivities. The Ministry helped sponsor an international conference on shamanism in 1992, to reinforce the reborn credibility of shamanism 'as religion'. An Association of Folk Medicine was founded in 1990 by a self-professed *oiuun*, Vladimir Kondakov, who is controversial but widely acknowledged to have both curing talent and a dramatic flare. Kondakov, who is trying to legitimize shamanism and unite traditionally competitive and secretive shamans, explains 'We need better conditions, social, material and spiritual. . . . We also need contact with the earth, and a hearth, not a second story office. We need access to upper and lower worlds.'[3]

The public grounding for receptivity to shamanism is diverse and diffuse. In some remote areas, people never lost their belief in local shamanic wisdom and power, even from beyond the grave. In a village of the Viliuisk region, for example, one secretly practicing shaman, Spiridon, managed to also become the Regional Committee president at the height of the Stalin terror in the late 1930s. He died in 1940, was buried in accord with ancient shamanic practice, and in the 1980s local villagers still vehemently kept intruders from finding the site, which was perceived to be extremely sacred and dangerous.[4] In contrast, some urban intelligentsia have returned to the shamanism of their roots, despite having been Sovietized atheists. One young ethnographer explained in 1991 'I'm much more spiritual than I was when you met me in 1985. I've changed a lot. It is partly because I now see the ancient power of shamanism, and believe in some shamans' ability to cure, but it is also because I myself saw a spirit last year at a sacred lake.'[5]

A spiritual revival, more general and profound than the specific revival of shamanism, has been nurtured by a fledgling Sakha society called *Kut-Siur*, which roughly translates as 'Soul-Reason'. They have delved into the traditional philosophy behind shamanic cosmology, debating and explaining it in newspaper columns, monthly rituals, public meetings, calendrical art and prayers. They too are controversial, with some critics accusing them of creating banal versions of old rituals with not enough academic or spiritual foundation. Yet some of their very sincere members consider themselves apprentice shamans searching for both healing and artistic energy. Their concerns parallel those of some semioticians and socio-linguists, as they search for a language to express complexities of the spirit world in its explicitly Sakha form. Indeed some of them are themselves linguists.[6]

The seance as an art form

The core of most shamanic seances is a shamanic journey, either to upper or lower worlds, so that the intermediator shaman can effectively communicate with spirits of the supernatural for a specific purpose. Passing a number of heavens, only the most powerful of the Sakha shamans are able to reach the highest, ninth heaven, common in the cosmologies of Siberian Turkic peoples. To reach these heavens, the shaman goes into 'a kind of religious ballet . . . a combination of dance, song, and extempore poetry together with a considerable amount of mimesis' (Chadwick 1942: 16–17). Such a ballet is possible only through an enormous amount of control, energy and training, but, as with all art forms, a degree of impromptu, inspired loss of full consciousness is also quite common. The Sakha *oiuun* Vladimir Kondakov described one of his first seances in which he indeed, feeling at first fully rational and in control, nonetheless remembered only the beginning and end of the seance.[7]

A true (not simulated) trance in which the spirits are perceived by the shaman and the seance audience to either be inside the shaman or escorting the shaman may result in a lack of conscious manipulation by the shaman. Shamans exhibit degrees of control and letting go, just as they have degrees of skill by which participants judge a seance. The poetry and even foreign tongues that emanate from a shaman at the height of a seance are not pre-meditated, although they are usually based on a shamanic repertoire of learned songs. Chanting may be both a way into ecstasy and a manifestation of it.

Different levels of skill, of ability to create the shamanic ballet, have been noticed by almost all of the researchers of Sakha shamanism.[8] The Polish exile-ethnographer Sieroshevskii (1901: 105) for instance, explained:

> Observation justifies the division of shamans into great, middling and petty. Some of them dispose of light and darkness in such a masterly fashion, also of silence and incantation; the modulation of the voice is so flexible; the gestures so peculiar and expressive; the blows of the drum and the tone of them correspond so well to the moment; and all is intertwined with such an original series of unexpected words, witty observations, artistic and often elegant metaphors, that involuntarily you give yourself up to the charm of watching this wild and free evocation of a wild and free spirit.

Clearly Sieroshevskii's description is quintessential romanticism. Yet he captures a tone of abandon that not only the shaman, but his or her audience share. Together, they enter an alternate consciousness which makes both more receptive to creativity. Even my own experience joining in hours of chanting during Sakha line dances, called *okhuokhai*, may be relevant to the issue of the creation and reception of meaningful poetry during trance.[9] As I repeated phrases of a dance leader's improvisational poetry, the power of the words poured over me, so that I felt I understood more vocabulary, more deeply.

Neither in the trance-like *okhuokhai* nor in the seance (sometimes called *kyryylara* or travel to the edge) is symbolic meaning divorced from phonics, but rather the combination stimulates, in a kind of synergism, the aesthetic imagination of creative initiators and audience-participants alike. Nonetheless, not every moment in a seance must have specific decipherable semantic meaning. Some shamans use animal calls, rhythmic vocal sounds and even a kind of jazz-like seat to enhance their performance. This was one of the trade-marks of Sergei Zverev, a Sakha shaman's assistant (*kuturukhsut*) who then became a performer of seances on the stage. At times shamans also produce fragments of languages they do not normally speak, explaining that the spirits themselves brought those languages. The spirit world that they are tapping into is one they themselves perceive as having wide-ranging cross-cultural commonalities, reaching well into North America and India.[10] Sieroshevskii's main shamanic informant, 'the-man-who-fell-from-heaven', had acquired his guardian spirit from having accidentally camped at the burial of a deceased Tungus (Evenk) shaman. Thus during his seances, Tungus words and gestures were common, for the Tungus shamanic spirit 'took possession' (Sieroshevskii 1901: 103). This particular shaman also had a 'Russian devil' and two very bawdy male and female 'demons' as helpers who could both terrify and titillate his audiences.[11]

Whether they used momentary inspiration, bawdiness or blatant ventriloquial performances, shamans could not produce a fully effective or satisfying synergistic seance-ballet unless they were known for spiritual depth. Within their own cosmological-philosophical systems, shamans were and still are respected as wise spiritual advisors and keepers of a huge range of sacred knowledge, not just religious ballet masters or charlatan actors. In Sakha reasoning, a truly powerful and effective shamanic performance is the very mark of spirituality. In other words, the medium gives the message of spirituality. The purposes of a given seance define whether it is 'black' or 'white' shamanism, rather than the identity of a particular practitioner. Most shamans are neither purely 'black', using dark forces for evil intent, nor 'white', using only benevolent spirits for benign purposes.[12] The Sakha *oiuun* Vladimir Kondakov explained his goals, as expressed through seances, as reflecting and enacting a rich shamanic 'philosophical system', in which he tries 'to balance forces of the three worlds and of evil and good'. To do so, a good shaman should personify through poetry what the Sakha call *kut-siur*, or the nexus of the soul with reason.

Sakha shamanic poetry

A shamanic chant fragment from the opening of a seance, which beautifully illustrates the synergism of phonics, semantics and polytropy, was collected by one of several talented Sakha native ethnographers, Gavril Ksenofontov in the early 1930s:

> *Kunum kunum keuteurdeureun*
> *Kunum kunum suurɜrdɜrɜ*
> *Bɜttɜkh· bɜttɜkh buolutsɜr*
> > *Kha, kha, kha . . . Khaakh-Khakhak*
> > *Khuuk khuuk kush tik*
> > *Chek chekh chekh*

A very rough translation, allowing for all that has ever been said or written about the impossibility of translation, and more, is:

> Drive, drive, like a raven rise
> Drive, drive, open the way
> Closer, closer, come, appear
> > Kha, kha, kha . . . Spit, cackle
> > Khuuk khuuk Sting, bite
> > Chek, chekh, chekh

When this first, helper spirit arrives, a lively dialogue ensues between it and the shaman, with the shaman voicing both parts. Later a significant and typical moment occurs when the *oiuun* enjoins multiple spirits:

> To this middle world homeland of our people
> Bring lasting good fortune
> Spirits purify us.[13]

During another seance from the 1920s, Ksenofontov recorded the calling for an evil female spirit, in order to banish it from a specific patient in great pain:

> Arise now, show yourself
> Even to your slender waist
> Because I with the shaggy head
> The stallion shaman
> Sing and perform the ritual
> Do not dare to pluck away and carry in
> From the hallowed earth
> A piece the size
> Of a goodly island
> Relax, then, the burning bout of pain
> Turn away your jagged fangs.

In this, a key metaphor involves human flesh, by definition precious, being likened to sacred earth from which not one bite may be taken. There is also a sexual tension here between the stallion shaman and the female spirit. The seance builds intensity, enabling ecstasy and inspiration, until the shaggy stallion shaman dance-rides and thus unifies himself with his sacred drum-horse.[14]

Broader purposes, combined with symbolism of the familiar horse and an ancestral spirit snake, are characteristic of yet another historical chant attributed to a seance performed by the great Spiridon of the Viliuisk region (who doubled as a Communist Party official):

> Breath into and strengthen the land
> Make its expanses inhabitable
> Multi-colored circular snake
> Do not crush the wide retinue of your ancestors
> With cries bring me forth
> Open the doors of the homeland for this horse rider
> Mother of our homeland fling wide our entrance
> Place the homes of our homeland in safety
> Protect our home hearths . . .[15]

In Spiridon's poem, the shaman seems to be reborn with birth cries during the seance, out of the womb of the mother of the Sakha homeland. The focus on the hearth is also significant, for many Sakha prayers are addressed to the fire spirit.

An equally famous, creative and good-willed shaman nicknamed Kuruuppa (from the word 'always') was extensively recorded by the Sakha folklorist Konstantinov in 1941. One of his seances was held to combat a tragedy that had befallen many Sakha communities during World War II.

> Spirits by pairs from the forest
> Following our family
> Banish the bitterness descended . . .
> Honored one circling
> Well-being it seems fleeing
> Apportioned fate
> Growing up warm
> Now internal misfortune
> Has crept in
> My human speech beseeches
> Let the people's good fortune return
> The tree there grows and protects
> Show me the road to fight hunger . . .[16]

In this chant the slippery concept of fate is introduced, in order to be combatted. The word used here, from the root *teulkeuleun*, is less definitive than another subtle Sakha term for fate, *d'ylkha*, which can be glossed as destiny. The very soul of a shaman's mission is exposed in this poetic and poignant moment, for the *oiuun* is supposed to be able to thwart, adapt, or counterbalance individual or community fate through proper intercession with the spirits. The costs of interceding can be high in a cosmological world believed to have intertwined and balanced good and evil energies, which, once set in motion, are difficult to stop. Spirit intercessors, usually called *aiyy*, must fight with evil spirits, called *abaahy*, and yet the intercessors themselves are far from predictable. The shaman appeals to forest spirits, who, like humans, come in pairs, and he evokes the growing, nurturing cosmological tree, which links his world with the upper heavens and lower levels of spirit existence. Through the tree, he must find the road, which for him and his audience is quite literal, to travel to ever greater spirits in search of food, plenty, and health for his people.[17]

One of the institutionalized Sakha ways to influence and insure a balance of cosmological forces is a once-a-year fertility festival celebrating the opening season of fermented mare's milk (*kumiss*), summer plenty, youthful strength, mating, networking and community solidarity – among many other things. This exuberant 2–4 day festival, called *yhyak*, is opened with chanted shamanic prayers, preferably by an *oiuun* with a 'white', or at least generally benevolent reputation. While the festival declined in most places through the 1930s and in World War II, it had a dramatic comeback just after the war, when returning soldiers were feted at mass revival *yhyak* ceremonies. In 1990 the festival was declared a national holiday of the Yakut-Sakha Republic. I have participated in seven of these festivals, in 1986, 1991 and 1993, and found them to have varying degrees of theatricality and spirituality. By a bonfire in a field, the controversial deep voiced curer Vladimir Kondakov at the 1991 Namsk region festival poured *kumiss* from a sacred carved wooden cup *choron* (shaped as a woman's breast with horse hoove legs) onto the sacred living earth in the four directions. He chanted these time-hallowed lines:

> Spirits of our homeland
> Spirits labor for us
> Five-fingered spirits
> Sacred head of the horse
> Unified with this shaman
> Spirits of the homeland
> Riding horseback
> To you spirits I give prayers
> My tongue speaks for us
> Understand my speech
> The Sakha person
> Strains to ask an important favor
> That the spirits bring good fortune to our people

Assuage and banish evil spirits and enemies
From our homeland
Dispel the darkness
Dispel all knowledge of terror.

In this poem, an archaic word, *yrangkhai*, is used for 'person' in conjunction with 'Sakha'; and this word is sometimes even substituted for 'Sakha' in epic tales. Enemies of the Sakha have of course changed over time and are not specified here, but there is a strong sense of an us/them division being cultivated – one that the Sakha notice and the few Russians attending the festival might miss (cf. Codrescu 1990: 110).[18]

In Sakha tradition, only one human can compete with the prestige of a shaman, and that is a blacksmith. His power comes from knowledge of the same spirit world and cosmology as the shaman's, and he too has a tradition of performance of poetic songs as a way to reach this spirit world. One Viliuisk blacksmith, Ivan Zakharov, bragged in 1991 that he had continued his sacred family smithing traditions into the especially sacred ninth generation, maintaining knowledge of sacred songs sung to the fire spirit. The popular and cheerful Zakharov in his youth was also a shaman's helper, *kuturukhsut*, and he has recently been simulating shamanic performances for *yhyak* festivals, museum openings and other events. He chants his family 'forge prayer' with a drum, dancing, in full shamanic dress:[19]

Strong beautiful
Unbroken hammer
With Flame complete the task
Noisy frightening
Grandfather spirit
Oh chief ancient one
Leader tall and great
Of wondrous fate
Do not mistake this prayer
Be fair to this master
Seven centuries you have come to us
Preserve me.

Conclusion

There is a large range of improvisational ancient chants within a broadly defined Sakha sacred spirit calling tradition. Smithy and *yhyak* prayers, considered together with multi-purpose seance dialogues and improvisational recitative during *ohuokhai* dances add up to at least four sacred Sakha traditional genres of poetry with relative degrees of improvisation and trance permitted within and among them. This initial typology does not even begin to capture the full extent of traditional sung Sakha poetry related to shamanism: the enormous semi-sacred epics, called *olonkho*, have become a famous symbol of Sakha cultural pride. Within these epics, once sung by special travelling singers, *olonkhosut*, are parts for many voices, including hero and heroine-shamans. Another less sacred genre is the improvisational song, called *toiuk*, in which shamans are sometimes featured.[20] In addition, several recent young poets, including some talented women, have been tapping into the shamanic symbolic, lyric (effusive and musical) tradition in a secularized highly literate way. A few are so successful that literate practicing shamans themselves admire the published work, acknowledge the shamanic roots, and even joke about their sexual shamanic metaphors.[21] And to muddle any typology even further, a few shamans interested in community psychic curing are struggling with entirely new media, including theater and film, into which ancient shamanic myths, prayers and poems may be syncretised (cf. Hoppál 1992).[22]

Typologies are often attempts to impose order on phenomena that are inherently disorderly. As shamanism, its language and even its media change, purist concern about the dilution of Siberian shamanism may be misplaced and futile. If we broaden our understanding of what shamanic language and inspiration can become for people reaching for a new-found spirituality, it is clear that within Sakha tradition are already the roots of a regenerated and adapted shamanism (cf. Metcalf 1989; Halifax 1979; Chadwick 1942). Prayers (*algys*), for instance, as well as seances are very much part of inspirational poetic speech, enabling a broader potential constituency for spirituality, beyond shamans in their communities.

There are degrees of inspiration, degrees of the sacred, and degrees of dramatic participation. By these degrees, followers judge their shamans and shamans judge each other. Because of these degrees, shamans are in constant competition with each other. One manifestation of this competition is poetic creativity, embedded within extravagant sacred performances.

The multiple tropes and multivocal symbols which form the basis of Sakha poetic construction are drawn from a deep, archaic and rich cultural reservoir of Sakha ideas, philosophies and cosmology. Horse-drums, shaggy stallion shamans, fermented mare's milk, multicolored snakes, sacred trees, five-fingered fire spirits and paired forest spirits all come from a three-part, cosmologically complex world still having resonance for many Sakha. But the concept recurring most often in the poems, and in the thoughts of Sakha intelligentsia and villagers is the concept of homeland. It is as tangible as flesh, and just as precious. It is the basis of an evolving Sakha nationalism consciously being stimulated by the society *Kut-Siur*, which is also, not accidentally, one of the sponsors of shamanic seance revivals.

In a seance, poetic metaphors become 'real' to all those involved and the easily metaphorical Sakha language comes alive. The spirits are believed to appear: the poetry would not work without them. The shaman is believed to become one with his horse-drum: he could not travel without it. Here one of the Sakha terms for the seance itself, *kyryylara*, or travel to the edge, becomes relevant. A middle-aged Sakha actor who often plays shamans on the Sakha-language stage in Yakutsk had a frightening insight into the nature of 'the edge,' as he had experienced it. He has a superb reputation for having done solid research into shamanic seances, texts, dancing and music, and has recently been using rhythmic breathing and drum therapy on patients, working in conjunction with a trained psychologist. He has become quite popular as a lesser folk (non-official) curer, but he confesses that he has stopped doing full seances because he nearly 'slipped over the edge' several times into such a deep trance and such a compelling spirit world that he felt he might not return. When he performs, even just on stage, he gets carried away with the poetry he has memorized, sometimes using it as the core of further improvisation. He fears for the health of his family, since those who make mistakes evoking helping spirits of dead shamans sometimes find that these spirits come back to haunt them or their loved ones.[23]

For participants, shamanic poetry is a mode of transport, not just beyond the mundane and into the sacred, but into other realities and dimensions where capricious spirits may possibly – nothing guaranteed – be harnessed to help humans out of very ordinary and concrete problems such as sickness and hunger. The way the poetry is produced, and precisely its inspirational nature, in a ballet of symbolic codes, clues both human and spirit audiences into the spirituality, or depth of *kut-siur*, of its creator. Poet shamans of the Sakha Republic are today tentatively traveling into this realm of hard-won spiritual knowledge and delight along accepted ancient paths, the seance, and totally new ones, written verse, drama and film. Some of the ancient paths have become overgrown with disuse, but shamans like one young Viliuisk man whose helper spirits are the raven [and] the dog say they have rediscovered the paths with the guidance of elderly living shamans and the spirits of deceased shamans. Both old-style and new-style shamanic poets have in common the root of the Sakha word for shaman, *oiuun*, from *oi*, meaning intelligence and conscience together.

Acknowledgement

I am indebted to the International Research and Exchanges Board (IREX), Leningrad University, Yakutsk University, the Academy of Sciences Institute of Languages, Literature and History in Yakutsk (AN IlaLI), the Sakha Republic Ministry of Culture, and to the Kennan Institute of the Smithsonian's Wilson Center for fieldwork and/or research support. I am deeply thankful to my Sakha language teacher, Klara Belkin, with whom I began studying in 1983, and to Sakha friends and colleagues I. Alekseev, A. Gogolev, Z. and V. Ivanov, P. Sleptsov, A. Reshetnikova, among many others. Thanks to M. Hoppál for organizing the 1993 International Conference on Shamanism in Budapest.

Notes

1   The Yakut-Sakha declaration of sovereignty was made Sept. 27, 1990, published in *Sotsialisticheskaia Yakutia* Sept. 28, 1990, p. 1. The official hyphenated form 'Yakut-Sakha' was a compromise, acknowledging that Yakut is the term most outsiders use for this farthest North Turkic people, who call themselves Sakha. The official version is now 'Sakha Republic (Yakutia)'. I am enormously grateful to the young Viliuisk region shaman for agreeing to see me, and hope to work with him in the future. At this stage in our relationship, and in the current, still not entirely stable political climate, he has requested I not use his name. Many Sakha also believe that this particular man's powers are so extraordinary that speaking his name calls his attention to them, wherever they are.

2   This story reveals that trance does not have to be accompanied by poetry or performance for some practitioners. Female shamans, traditionally common but usually considered not as strong as male shamans, are called *udagan* by the Sakha. I was able to work with Zoia in August 1992, and am grateful to her for sharing this story. For some more purist Sakha, Zoia has overstepped the bounds of approved shamanic practice with her large audience seances, and her press and television publicity.

3   I saw Vladimir Kondakov several times, and am enormously thankful for his help and insights into shamanism. My interest in him began with an interview he had with a journalist friend Nadezhda Senkina (1991), to whom I am also grateful.

4   Spiridon's stilt-house resting place was finally discovered by a young Sakha ethnographer working for the Ministry of Culture, who removed valuable shamanic objects from the site for the local museum only after making apologies to the spirit and leaving a bottle of vodka. As his helicopter was taking off, a highly localized rain storm began at the site, believed by the nervous Sakha pilot to be caused by the angry deceased shaman. I am grateful to ethnographer Aleksei Mikhailov for this account, and for his generous help sharing his private shaman archives.

5   Being uncertain as to whether this speaker would want direct attribution, I am erring on the side of discretion.

6   An example is Lazar Afanas'ev, one of the founders of *Kut-Siur*, whose conversations in 1986 and 1991 I value greatly. *Kut-Siur* ideas and ideals are explained in Afanas'ev, Romanov, Petrov, Petrov, and Illarionov (1990). I participated in one *Kut-Siur* ceremony, dedicating a huge rock for the year of the eagle (1991) and commemorating another for the year of the horse (1990). The ritual was presided over by the elder Ksenofont Utkin, who chanted *algys* (sacred prayers), wearing traditional but non-shamanic dress. The rocks, carved with sun, eagle and horse symbols, are placed at a lovely site overlooking the Lena River near Pokrovsk.

7   The seance in question was not for healing, Kondakov admitted, but involved mildly scaring someone who had threatened him. This is not how Kondakov usually uses his powers, but the case reveals the diverse nature of seance purposes, and the difficulty of categorically splitting black and white shamanism. Amnesia after trance is common but some shamans also try to train themselves to remember full details of their spirit journeys.

8   See, for example Jochelson (1910, 1933), Sieroshevskii (1901), A. E. Kulakovsky (1979), G. V. Ksenofontov (1929). Shamans should also not be confused with

untrained and far less controlled, albeit sometimes possessed '*menerick*', who are often but not always women. I am grateful to Anastasiia Lavrentovna and Anastasiia Sivtseva for accounts of *menerick*. See also I.M. Lewis (1971: 85) who claims that women, often the most down-and-out people in their communities, use possession outbursts to get attention and make uncharacteristic demands.

9   *Okhuokhai*, usually performed as part of major yearly and personal life-passage rituals, consist of long, circular lines of hand- and arm-linked dancers repeating phrases of chanted poetry called out by leaders who alternate and spell each other. After a male or female leader sings a phrase, it is repeated by the crowd, giving the leader a chance to think of the next one. Themes are current, situational and traditional, often sacred evocations of nature and of cultural heroes. Some Sakha are concerned that the sacred power of *okhuokhai* is being diluted because in the last few years it has been performed weekly at night in a club in Yakutsk. In July, 1991, I was with one group of *okhuokhai* dancers affiliated with the Sakha cultural movement *Sakha Omuk* (The Sakha People), who waited until dawn before they allowed themselves to begin, for true *okhuokhai* inspiration is supposed to come from benevolent solar energies.

10   Sergei Zverev's seance fragments can be heard on a Melodiia record, recorded by ethnomusicologist Edward Alekseev. I have been consulting with two friends, Chief Sings Alone and Buffalo Woman, who are Cherokee healers (and also trained psychologists) about some of my Siberian shamanic materials. Their sense of commonality with the spirit contacting trance experiences of Siberian shamans is considerable. They too explain the commonalities as based on the similarity of the spirit worlds they are encountering.

11   Cf. Sieroshevskii (1902: 318; 1901: 102–108; 1896) for a fuller context for Sieroshevskii's analysis of shamanism.

12   Cf. Alekseev (1990, 1984, 1975), Basilov (1990), Balzer (1990), Popov (1947, 1949), Shirokogoroff (1935) and Troshchansky (1903) among many others for discussions of the validity of the black/white distinction.

13   The root of the Sakha word for 'purify', clearly a complex concept much analyzed in anthropology (e.g. Douglas 1966, 1977), is *sul*, meaning clear, cleanse, strip bare. My version of this seance in the Sakha language comes from the archive of Aleksei Mikhailov. A version was also printed in Ksenofontov (1935). Concepts stressing evolving socio-political context, multivocal symbols, polytrophy, and synergism of tropes used here to decipher the aesthetic power of the poetry owe much to the writings of Atkinson (1990); E. Bruner (1984); Fernandez (1988; 1991); Friedrich (1991); Metcalf (1989); and Turner (1977: 52).

14   This fragment comes from Ksenofontov (1929:135), is analyzed in Alekseev (1984: 183), and translated and reprinted in Balzer (1990: 54). The sexual tension mentioned here is more subtle than that in some shamanic chants. Discussion of sexual symbolism in Siberian shamanism is far rarer than its occurrence. Cf. Shternberg (1904) on Amur River Nivkh shamanism and the Tuvinian ethnographer Kenin-Lopsan (1987) for Tuvinian shamanism texts. See also Austerlitz (1984).

15   Spiridon's poetry is reported in a paper on his life given to me by Nikolai Ignat'ev (1990) of Viliuisk, to whom I am very grateful.

16   This comes from the 'Iakovlev-Kruuppa' archive, Institute of Languages, Literature and History, fond 5, op. 3, ed. kh. 537, page 57. I am thankful to the Sakha

ethnographer Ekaterina Romanova for steering me to Nikita Petrovich Iakovlev's shamanic texts, hand-written in Sakha by Sakha folklorist Kristofor Konstantinov in 1941. The translation is mine.

17   The tree described here relates to the cosmological world tree much discussed in shamanic literature (cf. Eliade 1972: 271). I have been in seven spirit groves in which special, sacred trees are given offerings of ribbons and money. Such groves are common in many rural regions, and their location is usually kept secret from outsiders.

18   In this archaic chant of Kondakov, learned from a now deceased shaman, there is little room for improvisation, actual trance, or a dramatic moment of inspiration. However, new meaning is easily 'read' into the old text. And ambiguous language about 'enemies' can be viewed variously by participants. The Romanian poet Andrei Codrescu (1990: 110) explains: 'The tonal ambiguities developed by oppressed cultures to communicate different things in the same words to friends and foes become urgently important.' In addition, Kondakov felt something special happened as he sang this chant in June 1991, when a light gentle localized rain descended on the field where the *yhyak* took place, as a mark of the spirit's acceptance of his ceremony. (In accord with Kondakov's wishes, I have a transcript, but not a tape of this chant.)

19   This chant is printed in a Sakha pamphlet about Ivan Zakarov (Utkin 1991: 28–29), and I also taped it in June 1991 at his Viliuisk smithy. Zakharov is renowned as a maker of the Sakha national instrument, the *khomus*, or jaw harp (also called Jew's harp), which is associated by some Sakha with shamanic tradition.

20   *Olonkho* collections and analyses include Oiunsky (1975), and Mirbatalaeva with the singer Timofeev-Teploukhov (1985). *Toiuk* sources include E. Alekseev (1976) and the multivolume series Ergis et al (1976, 1977, 1980, 1983).

21   Examples of some of the new-style poets using shamanic themes and symbolism are Ivan Gogolev (1989), Sargilaana Gol'derova (1987), and a group of young poets called 'the white horse' (1991), including Aisen Doidu (whose penname means homeland), Anatolii Shvetsov, Oleg Chermyshentsev, Vladimir Orosutsev, and Kirill Alekseev. The poet Omsurra, whose penname is from the Sakha root for questing, is not widely published but is especially popular for her daring sexual symbolism. On theoretical issues related to literacy and its embeddedness in specific cultural contexts rather than general great cognitive shifts, see Schousboe and Larsen (1989).

22   An example is Aleksei Romanov's 1989 film called *Maappa* (the name of a beautiful suicide ghost), which has been shown on Sakha television. Romanov is a founding leader of *Kut-Siur*, has a reputation for folk-healing, and is extraordinarily knowledgeable about Sakha shamanic tradition. I am very grateful to him for many insightful conversations.

23   The actor is Afanasii Fedorov, whose help in 1991 and 1992 is gratefully acknow-ledged. When he constructed the basic text for his seance simulation, he was careful not to use the opening calling chants of any one particular shaman, but rather syncretised an archival sampling, so as not to offend any deceased shamans, nor mis-signal helping spirits. A separate group of actors call themselves *Qiuun*, i.e. 'Shaman,' 'an original stage-circus synthetic theater,' under the direction of Sergei Rastorguev.

References

Afanas'ev, L., Romanov, A., Petrov, R., Petrov, N. and Illarionov, V. (1990), *Aiyy yorehe* [Teachings of the Spirit] Yakutsk: Sakha Keskile, Kut-Siur. (in Sakha).

Alekseev, E. E. (1976), *Problemy formirovaniia lada (na materiale Iakutskoi narodnoi pesni)* [The problem of Lada formation on the material of Yakut folk songs.] Moscow: Muzyka. (in Russian).

Alekseev, N.A. (1975), *Traditsionnye religioznye verovaniia Iakutov v XIX – nachale XX v.* [Traditional religious belief of the Yakuts in the 19th early 20th centuries.] Novosibirsk: Nauka. (in Russian).

Alekseev, N.A. (1984), *Shamanizm tiurkoiazychnykh narodov Sibiri* [Shamanism of the Turkie speaking peoples of Siberia.] Novosibirsk: Nauka. (in Russian).

Alekseev, N.A. (1990), 'Shamanism among the Turkic Peoples of Siberia.' In Balzer (ed.) (1990a): 49–109.

Atkinson, Jane Monnig (1990), *The Art and Politics of Wana Shamanship.* Berkeley, CA: University of California Press.

Austerlitz, Robert (1984–1985), 'Ten Nivkh (Gilyak) Erotic Poems,' *Acta Ethn. Acad. Sci. Hung.* Budapest: Akadémiai Kiadó.

Balzer, Marjorie Mandelstam (1983), 'Doctors or Deceivers? The Siberian Khanty Shaman and Soviet Medicine,' in L. Romanucci-Ross and L. Tancredi (eds), *The Anthropology of Medicine.* New York: Praeger.

Balzer, Marjorie Mandelstam (1987), 'Behind Shamanism: Changing Voices of Siberian Khanty Cosmology and Politics', *Social Science and Medicine* 24(12): 1085–93.

Balzer, Marjorie Mandelstam (1990), 'Introduction,' In Balzer (ed.) (1990a).

Balzer, Marjorie Mandelstam (ed.) (1990a), *Shamanism: Soviet Studies of Traditional Religion in Siberia and Central Asia.* Armonk, NY: M. E. Sharpe.

Balzer, Marjorie Mandelstam (1992), 'Dilemmas of the Spirit: Religion and Atheism in the Yakut-Sakha Republic,' in S. Ramet (ed.), *Religious Policy in the Soviet Union.* Cambridge: Cambridge University Press.

Basilov, V. N. (1990), 'Chosen By the Spirits,' In Balzer (ed.) (1990a).

Bogoras, Waldemar (Bogoras-Tan, Vladimir) (1909), *The Chukchee.* Memoirs of the American Museum of Natural History XI.

Bruner, Eduard M. (ed.) (1984), *Text, Play, and Story: The Construction and Reconstruction of Self and Society.* Washington, DC: American Ethnological Society.

Chadwick, Nora Kershaw (1942), *Poetry and Prophecy.* Cambridge: Cambridge University Press.

Codrescu, Andrei (1990), *The Disappearance of the Outside: A Manifesto for Escape.* Reading, MA: Addison-Wesley.

Declaration of Sovereignty (1990), *Sotsialisticheskiia Iakutiia* (Sept. 28): 1.

Douglas, Mary (1966), *Purity and Danger: An Analysis of the Concepts of Pollution and Taboo*. London: Routledge and Kegan Paul.

Douglas, Mary (1977), *Implicit Meanings: Essays in Anthropology*, London: Routledge and Kegan Paul.

Eliade, Mircea (1972), *Shamanism: Archaic Techniques of Ecstasy*. Princeton, NJ: Princeton University Press.

Ergis, G. U. *et al.* (eds) (1976, 1977, 1980, 1983), *Iakutskie Narodnye Pesni. Sakha Narodnai Yryalara* [Yakut Folk Songs]. Yakutsk: Yakutsk kn. izd. (series, in Russian and Sakha).

Fernandez, James W. (1988), 'Andalusia on Our Minds: Two Contrasting Places in Spain as Seen in a Vernacular Poetic Duel of the Late 19th Century,' *Cultural Anthropology* 3(1): 21–35.

Fernandez, James W. (1991), 'Introduction', In *Beyond Metaphor: The Theory of Tropes in Anthropology*. Stanford, CA: Stanford University Press.

Friedrich, Paul (1991), 'Polytropy', In *Beyond Metaphor: The Theory of Tropes in Anthropology*. Stanford, CA: Stanford University Press.

Gogolev, Ivan (1989), *Aian Aaryktara* [Poetry]. Yakutsk: Sakha Sirinɜɜkhi. (in Sakha).

Gol'derova, Sargilaana (1987), *Khatyng Uuta* [Birch Sap]. Yakutsk: Sakha Sirinɜɜkhi. (in Sakha).

Halifax, Joan (1979), *Shamanic Voices: A Survey of Visionary Narratives*. New York: Dutton.

Hoppál, Mihály (1992), 'Urban Shamans: A Cultural Revival in the Postmodern World', in A.-L. Siikala and M. Hoppál, *Studies on Shamanism*. Ethnologica Uralica 2. Helsinki – Budapest: Finnish Anthropological Society – Akadémiai Kiadó.

Ignat'ev, Nikolai (1990), *Onokhu Spiridon Chakhchy oiuun saarbataɜtɜ* [Essay on the Good Works of the Shaman Spiridon]. (MS in Sakha).

Jochelson, Vladimir Ilich (Waldemar) (1910), *The Yukaghir and the Yukaghirized Tungus*. Memoirs of the American Museum of Natural History. XII.

Jochelson, Vladimir Ilich (Waldemar) (1933), *The Yakut*. American Museum of Natural History Anthropological Papers. 33.

Kenin-Lopsan, M. B. (1987), *Obriadovaia praktika i fol'klor Tuvinskogo Shaman-stva*. [Ritual Practice and Folklore in Tuvinian Shamanism]. Novosibirsk: Nauka. (in Russian).

Ksenofontov, G. V. (1929), *Krestes, shamanizm i khristianstvo* [Christ, shamanism, and Christianity]. Irkutsk: Russ. Geog. Obshch. (in Russian).

Ksenofontov, G. V. (1935), *Sochetaniie shamana s priezhaiushchimi* [The harmony of the shaman with arriving (spirits)]. Buriatievedenie. 1. (in Russian).

Kulakovsky, A. E. (1979), *Nauchnyi trudy* [Scientific works]. Yakutsk: Yakutsk kn. izd. (in Russian, collected works after death).

Lewis, I. M. (1971), *Ecstatic Religion: An Anthropological Study of Spirit Possession and Shamanism*. London: Penguin.

Metcalf, Peter (1989), *Where are YOU/SPIRITS: Style and Theme in Berawan Prayer*. Washington, DC and London: Smithsonian Press.

Mirbadalaeva, A. S. with I. G. Timofeev-Teploukhov (1985), *Strooptivyi Kulun Kullustuur: Yakutskoe olonkho* [The Obstinate Kulun Kullustuur: Yakut epos]. Moscow: Glav. red. vostochnoi lit. (in Russian and Sakha).

Oiunsky, Platon (1975), *Niurgun Bootur Stremitel'nyi: Yakutskii geroicheskii epos olonkho* [Niurgun Bootor the Impetuous: The Yakut heroic epic olonkho]. Yakutsk: Yakutsk kn. izd. (in Russian and Sakha).

Popov, A. A. (1947), 'Poluchenie shamanskogo dara u Viliuiskikh Iakutov' [Receiving the shamanic gift among the Viliuisk Yakuts]. *Trudy Instituta Etnografiva* 2:282–293. (in Russian).

Popov, A. A. (1949), 'Materialy iz istorii religii Iakutov Viliuiskogo Okruga' [Material on the religious history of Viliuisk Yakuts]. *Sbornik muzeia antropologii i etnografii* 2:255–323. (in Russian).

Schousboe, K. and Larsen, M.T. (eds) (1989), *Literacy and Society*. Copenhagen: Hakademisk Forlag Copenhagen University.

Senkina, N. (1991), 'V. A. Kondakov: Tselitel'-lish' posrednik mezhdu vyschimi silami i liud'mi' [V. A. Kondakov: Curer- or at least mediator between higher forces and people]. *Molodezh Iakutii* 14 March, 5. (in Russian).

Shirkogoroff, S. (1935), *The Psychomental Complex of the Tungus*. London: Kegan, Paul, Trench, Trubner.

Shternberg, Lev Ia. (Sternberg, L. Ia.) (1904), 'Giliaki', *Etnograficheskoe Obozrenie* 1: 1–42; 2: 19–55; 4: 66–119. (in Russian).

Sieroshevskii, W. (V. L. Seroshevsky) (1896), *Iakuty. Opyt etnograficheskogo issle-dovaniia*. [Yakuts. An experiment in ethnographic study]. St Petersburg: Imper. Rus. Geograf. Obshch. (in Russian).

Sieroshevskii, W. (1901), 'The Yakuts', *Journal of the Royal Anthropological Institute* 31: 64–110. (abridged from Russian, original in Polish, transl. by W.G. Sumner).

Sieroshevskii, W. (1902), 'Yakoutes', *Revue de l'Histoire des Religion* 16: 318f.

Troshchansky, V. F. (1903), *Evoliutsiia chernoi very (shamanstvo) u Iakutov* [The Evolution of the dark faith (shamanism) among the Yakut]. Kazan: Uchen. zapiski Kazanskogo universitet. (in Russian).

Turner, Victor (1977), *The Ritual Process: Structures and Anti-Structures*. Ithaca, NY: Cornell University Press.

Utkin, K. D. (1990), *Khomuhunnaakh uus I. F. Zakharov* [Jaw harp Master I. F. Zakharov]. Yakutsk: Sakha Ministry of Culture. (in Sakha).

The White Horse (1991), 'Belaia loshad' literaturnaia studiia' [The White Horse literary studio (samples)]. *Ilin* 1: 42–3; 2: 42–5; 3: 40–5. (in Russian).

Chapter 19

Ward Churchill

SPIRITUAL HUCKSTERISM
The rise of the plastic medicine men

> Yes, I know of Sun Bear. He's a plastic medicine man.
> (Matthew King, Oglala Lakota Elder, 1985)

THE PAST 20 YEARS have seen the birth of a new growth industry in the United States, Known as 'American Indian Spiritualism,' this profitable enterprise apparently began with a number of literary hoaxes undertaken by non-Indians such as Carlos Castaneda, Jay Marks (a.k.a.: 'Jamake Highwater,' author of *The Primal Mind*, etc.), Ruth Beebe Hill (of *Hanta Yo* notoriety), and Lynn Andrews (*Medicine Woman, Jaguar Woman, Chrystal Woman, Spirit Woman*, etc.). A few Indians such as Alonzo Blacksmith (a.k.a.: 'Chunksa Yuha,' the 'Indian authenticator' of *Hanta Yo*), 'Chief Red Fox' (*Memoirs of Chief Red Fox*), and Hyemeyohsts Storm (*Seven Arrows*, etc.) also cashed in, writing bad distortions and outright lies about indigenous spirituality for consumption in the mass market. The authors grew rich peddling their trash, while real Indians starved to death, out of the sight and mind of America.

This situation has been long and bitterly attacked by legitimate Indian scholars, from Vine Deloria, Jr., to Bea Medicine, and by activists such as American Indian Movement (AIM) leader Russell Means, Survival of American Indians, Inc. (SAIL) director Hank Adams, and the late Gerald Wilkenson, head of the National Indian Youth Council (NIYC). Nonetheless, the list of phony books claiming alternately to 'debunk' or to 'expose the innermost meanings of' Indian spirituality continues to grow, as publishers recognize a sure-fire moneymaker when they see one. Most lately, ostensibly scholarly publishers like the University of Chicago Press have joined the parade, generating travesties such as University of Colorado Professor Sam Gill's *Mother Earth: An American Story*.

The insistence of mainstream America upon buying such nonsense has led Deloria to conclude that, 'White people in this country are so alienated from their own lives and so hungry for some sort of real life that they'll grasp at any straw to save themselves. But high tech society has given them a taste for the "quick fix." They want their spirituality pre-packaged in such a way as to provide *instant* insight, the more sensational and preposterous the better. They'll pay big bucks to anybody dishonest enough to offer them spiritual salvation after reading the right book or sitting still for the right 15 minute session. And, of course, this opens them up to every kind of mercenary hustler imaginable. It's all very pathetic, really.'

Oren Lyons, a traditional chief of the Onondaga Nation, concedes Deloria's point, but says the problem goes much deeper. 'Non-Indians have become so used to all this hype on the part of imposters and liars that when a real Indian spiritual leader tries to offer them useful advice, he [or she] is rejected. He [or she] isn't 'Indian' enough for all these non-Indian experts on Indian religion. Now, this is not only degrading to Indian people; it's downright delusional behavior on the part of the instant experts who think they've got all the answers before they even hear the questions.'

'The bottom line here,' says Lyons, 'is that we have more need for intercultural respect today than at any time in human history. And nothing blocks respect and communication faster and more effectively than delusions by one party about another. We've got real problems today, tremendous problems, problems which threaten the survival of the planet. Indians and non-Indians *must* confront these problems together, and this means we *must* have honest dialogue, but this dialogue is impossible so long as non-Indians remain deluded about things as basic as Indian spirituality.'

Things would be bad enough if American Indian realities were being distorted only through books and movies. But, since 1970, there has also been a rapid increase in the number of individuals purporting to sell 'Indian wisdom' in a more practical way. Following the example of people such as the 'Yogi Ramacharaka' and 'Maharaji Ji,' who have built lucrative careers marketing bastardizations of East Asian mysticism, these new entrepreneurs have begun cleaning up on selling 'Native American Ceremonies' for a fee.

As Janet McCloud, a longtime fishing rights activist and elder of the Nisqually Nation, puts it, 'First they came to take our land and water, then our fish and game. Then they wanted our mineral resources and, to get them, they tried to take our governments. Now they want our religions as well. All of a sudden, we have a lot of unscrupulous idiots running around saying they're medicine people. And they'll sell you a sweat lodge ceremony for fifty bucks. It's not only wrong, it's obscene. Indians don't sell their spirituality to anybody, for any price. This is just another in a very long series of thefts from Indian people and, in some ways, this is the worst one yet.'

McCloud is scornful of the many non-Indian individuals who have taken up such practices professionally. 'These people run off to reservations acting all lost and hopeless, really pathetic. So, some elder is nice enough, considerate enough to be kind to them, and how do they repay this generosity? After fifteen minutes with a spiritual leader, they consider themselves 'certified' medicine people, and then run amok, 'spreading the word' – for a fee. Some of them even proclaim themselves to be 'official spiritual representatives' of various Indian peoples. I'm talking about people like Dyhani Ywahoo and Lynn Andrews. It's absolutely disgusting.'

But her real disdain is for those Indians who have taken up the practice of marketing their heritage to the highest bidder. 'We've also got Indians who are doing these things,' McCloud continues. 'We've got our Sun Bears and our Wallace Black Elks and others who'd sell their own mother if they thought it would turn a quick buck. What they're selling isn't theirs to sell, and they know it. They're thieves and sellouts, and they know that too. That's why you never see them around Indian people anymore. When we have our traditional meetings and gatherings, you never see the Sun Bears and those sorts showing up.'

As Thomas Banyacya, a spiritual elder of the Hopi, explains, 'These people have nothing to say on the matters they claim to be so expert about. To whites, they claim they're "messengers," but from whom? They are not the messengers of Indian people. I am a messenger, and I do not charge for my ceremonies.'

Some of the more sophisticated marketeers, such as Sun Bear, have argued that the criticisms of McCloud and Banyacya are misguided. Sun Bear has claimed that the ceremonies and 'wisdom' he peddles are not truly Indian, although they are still 'based on' Indian traditions. Yet his promotional literature refers to 'Native American Spiritual Wisdom,' and offers ceremonies such as the sweat lodge for $50 per session, and 'vision quests' at $150.

'Since when is the sweat not an Indian ceremony?' demands Russell Means, an outspoken critic of Sun Bear and his colleagues. 'It's not "based on" an Indian ceremony, it *is* an Indian ceremony. So is his so-called "vision quest", the pipe, his use of the pipe, sage, and all the rest of it. Sun Bear is a liar, and so are all the rest of them who are doing what he's doing. All of them know good and well that the only reason anybody is buying their product is because of this image of 'Indian-ness' they project. The most non-Indian thing about Sun Bear's ceremonies is that he's personally prostituted the whole thing by turning it into a money-making venture.'

Sun Bear has also contended that criticism of his activities is ill-founded because he has arrived at a spiritual stew of several traditions – his medicine wheel is Shoshone, and his herbal and other healing remedies accrue from numerous peoples, while many of his other ceremonies are Lakota in origin – and because he's started his own 'tribe,' of which he's pronounced himself 'medicine chief.' Of course, membership in this odd new entity, composed almost exclusively of Euroamericans, comes with a hefty price tag attached. The idea has caught on among spiritual hucksters, as is witnessed by the formation of a similar fees-paid group in Florida, headed by a non-Indian calling himself 'Chief Piercing Eyes.'

'This is exactly the problem,' says Nilak Butler, an Inuit activist working in San Francisco. 'Sun Bear says he's not revealing some sort of secret Indian ways whenever there are Indians around to hear him. The rest of the time, he's the most 'Indian' guy around, to hear him tell it. Whenever he's doing his spiel, anyway. But, you see, if there were any truth to his rap, he wouldn't have to be running around starting 'new tribes' and naming himself head honcho and dues collector. He'd be a leader among his own people.'

'The thing is,' says Rick Williams, a Cheyenne/Lakota working at the University of Colorado, 'Sun Bear isn't recognized as any sort of leader, spiritual or otherwise, among his own Chippewa people. He's not qualified. It takes a lifetime of apprenticeship to become the sort of spiritual leader Sun Bear claims to be, and he never went through any of that. He's just a guy who hasn't been home to the White Earth Reservation in 25 years, pretending to be something he's not, feeding his own ego and making his living misleading a lot of sincere, but very silly people. In a lot of ways he reminds you of a low-grade Jimmy Swaggart or Pat Robertson type of individual.'

'And another thing,' Williams continues, 'Sun Bear hasn't started a new tribe. *Nobody* can just up and start a new tribe. What he's done is start a cult. And this cult he's started is playing with some very powerful things, like the pipe. That's not only stupid and malicious; it's *dangerous*.'

The danger Williams refers to has to do with the very power which makes American Indian spirituality so appealing to non-Indians in the first place. According to the late Matthew King, an elder spiritual leader among the Oglala Lakota, 'Each part of our religion has its power and its purpose. Each people has their own ways. You cannot mix these ways together, because each people's ways are balanced. Destroying balance is a disrespect and very dangerous. This is why it's forbidden.'

'Many things are forbidden in our religion,' King continued. 'The forbidden things are acts of disrespect, things which unbalance power. These things must be learned, and the learning is very difficult. This is why there are very few real 'medicine men [or medicine women]' among us; only a few are chosen. For someone who has not learned how our balance is maintained to pretend to be a medicine man is very, very dangerous. It is a big disrespect to the powers and can cause great harm to whoever is doing it, to those he claims to be teaching, to nature, to everything. It is very bad.'

For all the above reasons, the Circle of Elders of the Indigenous Nations of North America, the representative body of traditional indigenous leadership on this continent, requested that the American Indian Movement undertake to end the activities of those described as 'plastic medicine men.' The possibly sexist descriptor refers to individuals of both genders trading in the commercialization of indigenous spirituality. At its National Leadership Conference in 1984, AIM passed a resolution indicating that the will of the elders would be implemented. Specifically mentioned in the AIM resolution were 'Sun Bear and the so-called Bear Tribe Medicine Society' and 'Wallace Black Elk and [the late] Grace Spotted Eagle of Denver, Colorado,' as well as others like Cyfus McDonald, Brooke Medicine Eagle (spelled 'Ego' in the resolution), Osheana Fast Wolf, and a corporation dubbed 'Vision Quest.' Others, such as Dyhani Ywahoo, Rolling Thunder, and 'Beautiful Painted Arrow' have been subsequently added to the list.

As Russell Means put it at the time, 'These people have insisted upon making themselves pariahs within their own communities, and they will have to bear the consequences of that. As to white people who think it's cute, or neat or groovy or keen to hook up with plastic medicine men, to subsidize and promote them, and claim you and they have some fundamental 'right' to desecrate our spiritual traditions, I've got a piece of news for you. You have *no* such right. Our religions are *ours*. Period. We have very strong reasons for keeping certain things private, whether you understand them or not. And we have every human right to deny them to you, whether you like it or not.

'You can either respect our basic rights or not respect them,' Means went on. 'If you do, you're an ally and we're ready and willing to join hands with you on other issues. If you do not, you are at best a thief. More importantly, you are a thief of the sort who is willing to risk undermining our sense of the integrity of our cultures for your own perceived self-interest. That means you are complicit in a process of cultural genocide, or at least attempted cultural genocide, aimed at American Indian people. That makes you an enemy, to say the least. And believe me when I say we're prepared to deal with you as such.'

Almost immediately, the Colorado AIM chapter undertook a confrontation with Sun Bear in the midst of a $500-per-head, weekend-long 'spiritual retreat' being conducted near the mountain town of Granby. The action provoked the following endorsement from the normally more staid NIYC:

> The National Indian Youth Council fully supports your efforts to denounce, embarrass, disrupt, or otherwise run out of Colorado, the Medicine Wheel Gathering . . . For too long the Bear Tribe Medicine Society has been considered repugnant but harmless to Indian people. We believe they not only line their pockets but do great damage to all of us. Anything you can do to them will not be enough.

The Colorado AIM action, and the strength of indigenous support it received, resulted in a marked diminishment of Sun Bear's reliance upon the state as a source of revenue.

Since then, AIM has aligned itself solidly and consistently with indigenous traditionalism, criticizing Sun Bear and others of his ilk in public fashion, and occasionally physically disrupting their activities in locations as diverse as Denver and Atlanta. Those who wish to assist in this endeavor should do so by denouncing plastic medicine folk wherever they appear, organizing pro-active boycotts of their events, and demanding that local bookstores stop carrying titles, not only by Sun Bear and his non-Indian sidekick 'Wabun,' but by charlatans like Castaneda, Jamake Highwater, Lynn Andrews, and Hyemeyohsts Storm as well. Use your imagination as to how to get the job done in your area, but make it stick. You should also be aware that Sun Bear and others have increasingly aligned themselves with such non-Indian support groups as local police departments, calling upon them to protect him from 'Indian interference' with his unauthorized sale of Indian spirituality.

Resolution of the 5th annual meeting of the Traditional Elders Circle, Northern Cheyenne Nation, two moons' camp, Rosebud Creek, Montana Center, October 5, 1980

IT HAS BEEN BROUGHT to the attention of the Elders and their representatives in Council that various individuals are moving about this Great Turtle Island and across the great waters to foreign soil, purporting to be spiritual leaders. They carry pipes and other objects sacred to the Red Nations, the indigenous people of the western hemisphere.

These individuals are gathering non-Indian people as followers who believe they are receiving instructions of the original people. We the Elders and our representatives sitting in Council give warning to these non-Indian followers that it is our understanding this is not a proper process and the authority to carry these sacred objects is given by the people and the purpose and procedure are specific to the time and the needs of the people.

The medicine people are chosen by the medicine and long instruction and discipline are necessary before ceremonies and healing can be done. These procedures are always in the Native tongue; there are no exceptions and profit is not the motivation.

There are many Nations with many and varied procedures specifically for the welfare of their people. These processes and ceremonies are of the most Sacred Nature. The Council finds the open display of these ceremonies contrary to these Sacred instructions.

Therefore, be warned that these individuals are moving about playing upon the spiritual needs and ignorance of our non-Indian brothers and sisters. The value of these instructions and ceremonies is questionable, maybe meaningless, and hurtful to the individual carrying false messages. There are questions that should be asked of these individuals:

1) What Nation does the person represent?
2) What is their Clan and Society?
3) Who instructed them and where did they learn?
4) What is their home address?

If no information is forthcoming, you may inquire at the addresses listed below, and we will try to find out about them for you.

We concern ourselves only with those people who use spiritual ceremonies with non-Indian people for profit. There are many things to be shared with the Four Colors of humanity in our common destiny as one with our Mother the Earth. It is this sharing that must be considered with great care by the Elders and the medicine people who carry the Sacred Trusts, so that no harm may come to people through ignorance and misuse of these powerful forces.

Signed,

Tom Yellowtail
Wyola, MT

Larry Anderson
Navajo Nation
P.O. Box 342
Fort Defiance, AZ

Izadore Thom
Beech Star Route
Bellingham, WA

Thomas Banyacya
Hopi Independent Nation
Shungopavy Pueblo
Second Mesa via AZ

Phillip Deer (deceased)
Muskogee (Creek) Nation

Walter Denny
Chippewa-Cree Nation
Rocky Boy Route
Box Elder, MT

Austin Two Moons
Northern Cheyenne Nation
Rosebud Creek, MT

Tadadaho
Haudenosaunee
Onondaga Nation via
Nedrow, NY

Chief Fools Crow (deceased)
Lakota Nation (in tribute)

Frank Cardinal, Sr.
Chateh, P.O. Box 120
Assumption, Alberta
Canada

Peter O'Chiese
Entrance Terry Ranch
Entrance, Alberta
Canada

AIM resolution Sovereign Diné Nation, Window Rock, AZ, May 11, 1984

Whereas the Spiritual wisdom which is shared by the Elders with the people has been passed to us through the Creation from time immemorial; and

Whereas the Spirituality of Indian Nations is inseparable from the people themselves; and

Whereas the attempted theft of Indian ceremonies is a direct attack on and theft from Indian people themselves; and

Whereas there has been a dramatic increase in the incidence of selling of Sacred ceremonies, such as the sweat lodge and the vision quest, and of Sacred articles, such as religious pipes, feathers, and stones; and

Whereas these practices have been and continue to be conducted by Indians and non-Indians alike, constituting not only insult and disrespect for the wisdom of the ancients, but also exposing ignorant non-Indians to potential harm and even death through the misuse of these ceremonies; and

Whereas the traditional Elders and Spiritual leaders have repeatedly warned against and condemned the commercialization of our ceremonies; and

Whereas such commercialization has increased dramatically in recent years, to wit:

- The representations of Cyfus McDonald, Osheana Fast Wolf, and Brooke Medicine Ego, all non-Indian women representing themselves as 'Sacred Women,' and who, in the case of Cyfus McDonald, have defrauded Indian people of Sacred articles;
- A non-Indian woman going by the name of 'Quanda' representing herself as a 'Healing Woman' and charging $20 for sweat lodges;
- Sun Bear and the so-called 'Bear Tribe Medicine Society,' who engage in the sale of Indian ceremonies and Sacred objects, operating out of the state of Washington, but traveling and speaking throughout the United States;
- Wallace Black Elk and Grace Spotted Eagle, Indian people operating in Denver, Colorado, charging up to $50 for so-called 'Sweat Lodge Workshops';
- A group of non-Indians operating out of Boulder, Colorado, and throughout the Southwest, and audaciously calling itself 'Vision Quest, Inc.,' thereby stealing the name and attempting to steal the concept of one of our most Spiritual ceremonies;

Therefore, be it resolved that the Southwest AIM Leadership Conference reiterates the position articulated by our Elders at the First American Indian Tribunal held at D-Q University, September 1982, as follows:

Now, to those who are doing these things, we send our third

warning. Our Elders ask, 'Are you prepared to take the consequences of your actions? You will be outcasts from your people if you continue these practices' . . . Now, this is another one, our young people are getting restless. They are the ones who sought their Elders in the first place to teach them the Sacred ways. They have said they will take care of those who are abusing our Sacred ceremonies and Sacred objects in their own way. In this way they will take care of their Elders.

We Resolve to protect our Elders and our traditions, and we condemn those who seek to profit from Indian Spirituality. We put them on notice that our patience grows thin with them and they continue their disrespect at their own risk.

Chapter 20

Paul C. Johnson

SHAMANISM FROM ECUADOR TO CHICAGO
A Case Study in New Age Ritual Appropriation

[. . .]

The whole of mankind becomes an imaginary museum: where shall we go this weekend – visit the Angkor ruins or take a stroll in Tivoli of Copenhagen?

(Paul Ricoeur, *History and Truth*)

I. Introduction

IN *OTHER PEOPLES' MYTHS* Wendy Doniger raises the issue of the viability of religious experience which is unmediated by traditional cultural markers. To what extent, for example, is it actually possible to be a Taoist in California? She sees it as at least possible that religious texts, even when read in an alien context, can provide a ground in which new, modern religious communities can take root.[1] In this paper I wish to consider whether the same holds true for religious rituals which have no accompanying texts. A text, while it can be read and interpreted any number of ways, at least remains itself. A ritual's resistance to change faces not only the hermeneutic problem of the text (how it is interpreted differently in different historical contexts), but also the problem of continuity of performance; hence the issue of when a ritual, though claimed to be the same, is not the same ritual at all.

In recent decades shamanism has taken hold of the modern imagination and been appropriated and reformulated by certain subgroups of the modern West.[2] The popular interest has roughly paralleled academic research on shamanism, and in fact has relied on such research for its claims. The belief in the possibility of the appropriation of shamanism across cultural boundaries, for example, has rested on two premises: (1) Shamanism is a religious phenomenon nearly universal in scope;[3] and (2) Shamanism is primarily a technique, not a religion.[4] Modern shamans legitimate their practice, then, by forwarding claims that shamanism as a religious practice is culturally non-contingent – that it is either a universal human archetype, a primordial Ur-religion basic to all religious traditions, or sheer technique, a ritual which does not require any myths. By comparing shamanism as practised among the Shuar to such neo-shamans, I argue in this paper that the neo-shamans' practice is, contrary to its claims, deeply embedded in its *own* cultural matrix, which, following Anthony Giddens, I will call 'radical modernity'.[5]

As a first objective, I consider the costs and the benefits of relevant methods in the history of religions which serve to clarify issues in the study of such phenomena.[6] Secondly, I demonstrate that New Age religious movements like that of neo-shamans are not simply 'in the air',[7] a necessary product of our time (though the conditions for their appropriation and reception depend on modernity), but rather are always at their outset born of specific cultural interactions. To this end I consider in detail one example of ritual appropriation and an academic's central role in it: the appropriation of shamanism as practised by the Untsuri Shuar[8] in Ecuador by The Foundation for Shamanic Studies, located in Norwalk, Connecticut, by way of the anthropologist Michael Harner. Finally, based on the comparison, I propose criteria by which neo-shamanism can be distinguished from indigenous forms of shamanism, in order that it might better be critically apprehended and analysed.

II. Methodological guides

As a start, let me establish some theoretical parameters with reference to approaches which have attempted to account for neo-shamanic appropriations, and then suggest ways their work can usefully be extended.[9]

Catherine Albanese, one of the few historians of religions to address specifically New Age religions, describes historically antecedent movements in America which the New Age recapitulates, and describes some of the changes in the reformulations.[10] So, for example, she shows how New Age shamans, while also interested in curing, are more individualistic and more focused on the 'mind' than indigenous practitioners who they take as their exemplars.[11] To her, however, such groups ultimately do form a kind of 'religion', fulfilling, as they do, her formula of 'religion' as having cultus, code, creed and community. Hence one learns more about the ways in which such groups are like other religious groups than about what is distinct about them, and little about the processes by which they form or find an audience, membership and clientele – the construction of their authority. What is more, the impression one gains is of a rather evenhanded exchange of ideas between cultures; that it is simply in their nature to export and import ideas, and that the whole affair is rather clean and bloodless.[12]

Talal Asad has recently vehemently rejected the idea that 'first' and 'third world' societies, even if equally dislocated and equally mobile, are therefore equally 'agents' and history-makers.[13] Following Hannah Arendt, he tackles 'the problem of understanding how dominant power realizes itself through the very discourse of mobility'.[14] Asad argues that the modern West controls the very structures of possibility of thought of what 'history' means, such that the 'agency' of indigenous groups is always contained by a larger, hegemonic discourse of 'entering' or 'resisting' modernity.[15] If the Other can only know itself as framed by the modern West, however, the inverse is also true. The modern West defines itself in relation to the Other, in opposition to 'the primitive', 'the irrational', 'the mythic', or 'the traditional'. The crucial difference here is that the modern, industrial West also controls the production of such terms – and in this sense it *makes* history. Following Asad, therefore, one cannot speak of equivalence of agency in ritual appropriations.[16] In the case of 'shamanism', no scholar makes this argument more forcefully than Michael Taussig:

> With his *jage*,[17] the colonially created wild man nourishes this chance against and in combination with the deathly reifications and fear-inspiring mysteries worked into the popular imagination by the official discourse of suffering, order, and redemption, institutionalized by the Church, the state, and the culture of terror. Working with and against the imagery provided by the Church and the conquest, *yagé* nights offer the chance, not to escape sorrow by means of utopic illusions, but rather the chance to combine the anarchy of death with that of carnival.[18]

In his study of the exploitation of the Huitoto Indians of Columbia, Taussig sees the colonizer as both the source of suffering and the source of the shaman's power to effect (temporary) redemption. Thus for Taussig the Amerindian shaman is merely the projection of the Siberian ideal type[19] or of the devil, simultaneously evil and powerful.[20] If Taussig offers an important caution to the discussion of the ritual appropriation of shamanism, namely that one of the sources of its power in the Western mind is the power of the exotic, the savage, the forbidden – to consult a shaman or practise as one thereby being the transgression of a boundary, a taboo act[21] – he also drains it of any substance whatsoever. If for Albanese it seems possible for anyone to become a shaman, for Taussig no one can. And if the former approach suffers from a poverty of historical explanation of the ritual appropriation of shamanism, Taussig's suffers from the poverty of not having a descriptive object at all: he reduces the phenomenon of shamanism to mere imagination.

In order to avoid these traps, the study of the ritual appropriation of shamanism requires a careful middle path. In the migration I will trace from the Shuar to the anthropologist Michael Harner to Harner's Foundation for Shamanic Studies, it will not suffice to describe the phenomena and locate it formally, nor to dismiss it as sheer colonial projection. Neither will it help to throw up our hands in helpless confusion in the face of such 'post modern cultural chaos'. Rather, neo-shamanism should be regarded as a basically unilineal appropriation (from 'them' to 'us') which is structured by modern strategies – some of which I attempt to explicate in this article – but which nevertheless does not preclude its potential to effect genuine healing.

III. Shuar shamanism[22]

The Shuar have been prominent in the imagination of colonial powers since contact was first made with them in the first half of the 16th century. This notoriety has its source in the traditional but no longer extant practice of head-hunting and head-shrinking rituals (*tsantsa*), and in the Shuar reputation for ferocity.[23] While the present-day Shuar sometimes prey on settlers' imagination of their 'wildness' to protect the shrinking boundaries of their land,[24] historically this is not based merely on reputation, for the Shuar have indeed been highly successful in military and cultural resistance. Most famous is the rebellion of 1599 in which the Shuar united to resist a new taxation imposed in order to raise revenue for the coronation of Philip III of Spain. Twenty thousand Shuar conspired under the leadership of Quirruba to destroy utterly the settlements of Logroño and Sevilla de Oro, including the massacre of an estimated nearly 40,000 settlers.[25] It was during this rebellion that the Shuar reportedly forced open the mouth of the governor of Logroño and poured molten gold down his throat 'until his bowels burst within him', asking him if his thirst for gold was yet satisfied. With this dramatic symbolic act the Shuar asserted their complete independence from the Spanish. But if this was the boldest and most dramatic moment of Shuar resistance, it was only one of many such moments during the 16th to 20th centuries. Just prior to encountering the Spanish they had also, with the help of a sympathetic geography, successfully resisted the domination of the Inca Tupac Yupanqui as well as his successor, Huayna Capac. Moreover, the Shuar defended against conversion as tenaciously as they had against Spanish guns, and lived relatively undisturbed by religious intrusions until the return of the Jesuits (1869, after being expelled in 1767) and the installation of the first Protestant missions (1902). Even during this period, however, Shuar groups intermittently violently resisted (1865, 1915, 1925) missionary efforts which arrived in tandem with the gold and rubber booms of the late 19th and early 20th centuries.[26] If the Shuar have a proud history of independence, however, the present era has been less respectful of it. The anthropologist and the shaman, as will become evident, have each played a role in the dissolving of the barriers to cultural 'exchange'.

In order to locate Shuar shamanism contextually, I will focus on five aspects or traits of Shuar religion: 'reality' as divided into two worlds, the practical and the visionary; the role of hallucinogenic plants; kinds and activity of 'souls'; the shaman's darts (*tsentsak*); and the mythic origin of the shaman.

Two worlds

Personal knowledge results from the interaction between encyclopedic practical information acquired in daily life and visionary flashes of insight acquired in dreams or hallucinogenic experience. To be 'wise' is to have integrated the body, the emotions and the intellect into a consolidating and integrating vision of the human being's relation to plants, animals and the spirit world of ancestors, 'souls' and certain powerful beings.[27] The social importance of visionary experience is illustrated by the pedagogic use of hallucinogens in childrearing. Harner reports that:

> within a few days of birth, a baby is given a hallucinogenic drug to help it enter the 'real' world and hopefully to obtain help in surviving the hazards of infancy through seeing an 'ancient specter'. If an older child misbehaves, his parents may administer another, stronger, hallucinogen (a *datura* species) to enable him to see that the 'reality' on which they base their knowledge and authority does indeed exist.[28]

Likewise, Brown reports that elders among the related Aguaruna view contemporary youth as 'stupid' (*anentáiimchau*, 'without thought') though they have the knowledge of reading and writing, because they do not any longer undergo the training of hallucinogenic plant use.[29] The hidden world is taken to be the 'true' world which underlies and causes the visible world. This rule, however, should not be seen as inflexible: certain kinds of illness, such as 'fever', 'colds', smallpox and various other 'white men's diseases' and benign snakebites may be attributed to 'natural', or at least non-curable causes.[30] Nevertheless, in general the practical aspects of life may be altered by encounters with the hidden world. Dreams and visions of success in warfare or abundant crops are not mere harbingers or signs of good fortune, but are rather themselves efficacious. Those experiencing misfortune may therefore actively pursue a vision through the use of *natemä* (Quechua: *ayahuasca; banisteriopsis caapi*) or tobacco.[31] A vision, then, can be obtained by anyone to better their lot; it is neither restricted to a class of specialists, nor to the status of divine gift, a spontaneous, unexpected epiphany. The seeking of a vision is a practical act. Everyone, then, has partial access to the hidden world, but the shaman is one who lives more completely in that world, one who knows its geography more intimately. Unlike many other cultures, then, the Shuar shaman does not differ from other people in any absolute or qualitative way, but rather quantitatively, in the amount of time he or she devotes to developing spiritual power, acquiring spirit darts (tsentsak), partaking of power-sustaining plants, and so on. This openness of shaman's knowledge is evidenced by the high proportion of shamans among the population: Harner records that one in four persons among the Untsuri Shuar are shamans, and that anyone may become a shaman, though it is by and large a male activity.[32] Karsten also points to the blurring of the boundary between the shaman and the ordinary person (in this case the warrior) when he notes:

> Thus old warriors and chiefs are generally more or less initiated in the magic art; in fact, they fight their enemies not only with their natural weapons but also with their magical 'arrows' (tunchi). Yet they do not exercise the art of sorcery professionally and are seldom seen curing persons bewitched by other sorcerors.[33]

It seems, therefore, that everyone lives in two worlds and shares some of the shaman's knowledge and power, though the shaman concentrates more of such general knowledge into his single person. In addition, the shaman learns special knowledge: only he can kill and cure with spiritual darts.

Psychoactive plant use

The use of psychoactive plants is a fundamental aspect of access to the visionary, hidden realm – the realm of the 'true' and the realm of social and moral ideals. Various species of banisteriopsis, datura (especially brugmansia), and tobacco are cultivated in gardens and collected regularly to serve various needs. These substances enter into a variety of Shuar contexts: a boy of six may visit a sacred waterfall where he fasts and drinks tobacco juice for days until he has a vision (arutam), without which his life would be in danger.[34] If necessary, he may be administered datura arborea as well to hasten the appearance. The shaman candidate daily ingests natemä and constantly snorts tobacco juice in order to meet and learn to work with the spirits which cause and cure sickness.[35] A 'layperson' may use natemä and tobacco juice to obtain a vision which will alter his immediate bad luck in love or hunting.[36] A parent may use datura (maikua) to discipline and instruct a disobedient son so that he will see the supernatural world and there 'discover that many of the claims the father has been making about the nature of reality are true . . .'[37] Also, psychoactive plants are, or were, commonly used to divine the outcome of raids, the sources of illness, the offending shaman's name, and so on. In short, it is fair to say that visionary experience obtained through hallucinogens is central to maintenance of the Shuar social order, as is evidenced by their use in pedagogy and the maintenance of discipline. Some aspects, however, such as the seeking of a fortune-changing vision, or the disciplining of a child, may be used by all, while others, such as divination, bewitching and curing are the special visionary province of the shaman.

Souls

If Stirling goes too far in attributing the 'cause' of Shuar shamanism to the custom of blood revenge, still there is an element of truth to his claim.[38] It finds an echo in Harner's description of three kinds of souls, one of which is insignificant in the daily life of his informants and the other two of which, the *muisak* and *arutam*[39] souls, are 'supernatural devices, respectively, for murdering and avoiding being murdered'.[40] The first, the 'ancient specter soul' (*arutam wakani*), is not innate but rather must be acquired, either, as we have seen, by seeking a vision or by stealing one from another. The theft of an *arutam wakani* may succeed by drinking *natemä* and beating a drum, repeating the soul's name, so that if it is wandering nocturnally it may be attracted to the caller. An *arutam* can also be taken by killing. Shamans are exceptional at this, and are even said to be capable of seeing an *arutam* soul as an inverted rainbow in a person's chest. Thus, shamans are said to always be in possession of *arutam* souls, an important advantage – the possessor of an *arutam* soul cannot be assassinated or die in warfare, and the possessor of two *arutam* souls cannot die by any means. This helps to explain why male children of six years old are led with such urgency to attempt a meeting with an *arutam* in a vision – it is a matter of life and death. The lack of an *arutam* soul leaves one vulnerable to attack, and conversely the possession of one imbues a deep forcefulness, including an urge to kill. The figures of greatest authority in the acephalous Shuar political system, then, are the shaman and the 'big man' or killer (*kakaram*): those who have acquired the residue of many *arutam wakani*, who are both forceful and invulnerable. Harner notes that the belief in *arutam wakani* has a social reality, since the *kakaram* and the powerful shaman are indeed rarely attacked, being considered invulnerable to assassination. The shaman, therefore, partakes in the logic of exchange of souls in a way that is structurally analogous to the warrior. What is more, his metaphysical battles easily bleed into physical combat – his diagnosis of cause of illness may lead to blood revenge assassination, and his failure to cure may lead to his own assassination.

The *muisak* is the avenging soul, its mission being to avenge the death of its owner. Harner accounts for the now-extinct practice of head-shrinking (*tsantsa*) by the belief in the *muisak*. The appropriate treatment of the head compels the enemy's *muisak* soul to remain in the head instead of being allowed to roam freely as a demon, and enables the captor to ultimately expel it ritually at the *tsantsa* feast.

The third soul is the 'true' or 'original' soul (*nekás wakaní*), born with each person and especially present in the individual's blood. After death the 'true' soul hovers around the community, perpetually hungry and sometimes frightening the living. Its ultimate transformation is into an impersonal mist out of which clouds and fog are formed, and this formless state is endless. Harner sees this soul as the least discussed of the three, for reasons of its inconsequentiality in mundane pragmatic life or in any kind of social exchange.

Brown's account indicates the christianization of Shuar soul beliefs, at least among the Aguaruna.[41] His informants stress two souls, one which ascends to heaven after death, the eye soul (*iwaji*), and a shadow soul (*iwanch*) which remains on earth after a person dies. This second, shadow soul may assume various animal forms such as a butterfly, and is considered universally menacing to the living. This seems to correspond to Harner's information from some 20 years earlier of the 'true' soul which remains after the person's death, though by the time of Brown's account this *iwanch* soul is frequently compared to Satan. More striking still, however, is the complete absence in Brown's ethnography of any discussion of the *arutam* and *muisak* souls. While Brown does not address the difference, he does mention the extinction of the *tsantsa*, the near complete absence of blood revenge assassinations and the decline in the use of psychoactive agents. One might speculate that, true to Stirling and Harner's suggestions that soul-beliefs and blood revenge are intimately linked, traditional ideas about souls and the traditional role of the shaman were intimately bound up with all of those now extinguished practices.

Finally, Brown also points to an Aguaruna soul concept which will become important when we examine the psychologization of shamanism in New Age practice below. In trying to elicit from informants exactly how souls affect bodily states, he was given an example of a childhood illness called 'fright' (*ishámkamu*) that some Aguaruna explain as 'soul-loss':

> They say that when a small child is attacked by a dog, falls off a bed, or suffers some other frightening experience, his or her soul may be thrown out of the body, creating a pathological condition that manifests itself in fever, loss of appetite, convulsions, and eventually death.[42]

This is precisely the sort of language of trauma, repression and 'soul-loss' one encounters in the use of neo-shamanism as a psychotherapeutic tool in the modern West.

Spirit darts (tsentsak)

In turning to the notion of spirit darts we move closer the office of the shaman itself, for the shaman's initiation is essentially the acquiring of darts (tsentsak or tunchi [thorn]) and learning to control them. An apprenticeship begins with the novice approaching the established shaman, enlisting his support and agreeing on a price, often a shotgun. A transfer is made, while both parties are intoxicated with natemä or tsentsak, mixed with a mix of saliva and tobacco juice (kaag), from the mouth of the shaman (wishínyu) to the mouth of the novice. Having received the darts which will be used in both healing and causing illness, the novice enters a period of preparation. Should he fail to endure this critical period, the 'poison' he has ingested may destroy him.[43] The novice's period of incubation varies according to the account: Karsten reports between six months and two years, Stirling reports one month, and Harner, from several months to a year. The principle that is consistent in all the sources, however, is that the longer the novice endures the hardships of a restricted diet, sexual abstinence and heavy narcotic use, the longer his darts will mature and the greater will be his power. To become a curing shaman demands a longer period of training than does a sorcerer, though all accounts are quick to point out that there is no firm distinction between the two types of shamans. Even a curing shaman is treated warily by others, for his power rests ultimately on the same knowledge as that of the sorcerer, namely the acquiring and control of tsentsak.[44]

In a typical curing ceremony, the shaman begins to work when night falls. He ingests natemä and tobacco juice intermittently, and begins to sing his curing songs and shake his rattle or fan. Harner records the following verse:

I, I, I, I, I,
I, I, I, I,
I am like Tsuni.
I am like Tsuni.
When I drink natemä
All my body becomes cold.
And I easily suck out the tsentsak.
I, I, I, I.[45]

When he is ready and intoxicated enough, he waits for the arrival of his 'spirit helper' (pasuk)[46] which may possess his body. He then begins to scan the patient's body in search of glowing sorcerer's darts. Regurgitating his own tsentsak into his mouth in order to 'catch' the sorcerer's tsentsak, he begins to suck out the foreign objects, putting them into a container. Later he will throw these darts back into the air and they will return to their owner.[47] He continues to ingest tobacco juice and natemä in order to keep his tsentsak strong. He may fan and/or massage the affected areas, and recommend a particular diet that will aid the healing.[48] Stirling's account describes a shaman eventually, towards midnight, reaching a state of ecstasy, dancing and stamping around the patient as he chants.[49] If there is no sign of intrusion, then he may attribute the illness to 'natural' causes. Brown's fieldwork during the 1970s indicates that the shaman often recommends penicillin or vitamin compounds, thus showing the effects of an 'intrusion' of a different sort.[50]

The original shaman

As the verse in the song recorded by Harner indicates, the curing shaman is replicating the acts of the first shaman, Tsuni. Harner does not report a myth about Tsuni, however, informing us only that he:

> is the mythological first shaman who is believed to be alive today living underwater in a house whose walls are formed, like palm staves, by upright anacondas, and where he sits, using a turtle as a stool. He is described as a white-skinned man with long hair, but he also seems capable of transforming himself into the anaconda. From time to time he is reputed to supply particular shamans with special quartz crystal tsentsak which are particularly deadly, and, on rare occasions to kill shamans with whom he is angry.[51]

Brown reports a powerful being, Tsugki, who lives at the bottom of whirlpools and rapids of great rivers, and who occasionally appears as a rainbow. Tsugki is considered the mythical first shaman and the source of shamanic powers, as well as special power in matters of love. Tsugki is sexually ambivalent, and as such mediates between the female Nugkui, the 'earth mother', and the male Etsa, the sun.[52] Though there is little in either of these descriptions by way of mythic narrative that is relevant to the office of the shaman, it is evident that the shaman is associated with dangerous parts and creatures of rivers, with rainbows, with sexuality, and, in another intrusion of the colonial racial hierarchy into the shamans' economy, with white skin. The Shuar shaman works according to a mythic paradigm of the first shaman, which provides both an original ritual pattern and a present source of power.

In this section I have tried to show some of the ways Shuar shamanism is embedded in a wider philosophical and material context: in a view of 'reality' that is a dialectic between two worlds; in a flora of psychoactive plants which are essential to contact with the 'true' world and to the maintenance of social order; in a particular view of the construction of the human being as having three souls, and in a general network of 'power'; in the acquiring and manipulation of spirit darts, which in turn rely on a particular material context of plant and animal life; and in a mythic structure which situates the shaman in regard to the origins of social life itself. What is crucial for this discussion is to note the pedagogical significance of the shaman and mystical experience in general. Shamanism appears to be intimately bound up with cultural memory, the preservation of what is really real. As the Untsuri Shuar are confronted by settlements which are tied to modern world economies and gaps begin to show in the traditional knowledge of the younger generation, it is exactly this lack of contact with the other world which elders lament as the reason for their drifting. The shaman is the master of contact with this other world. The shaman is therefore a crucial part of Shuar cultural defence.

This is obviously not an exhaustive description of Shuar shamanism, but rather a selection of facets for the purpose of drawing a comparison between the context of Shuar shamanism and the context, or anti-context, of New Age shamanism, to which I now turn.

IV. Michael Harner and the Foundation for Shamanic Studies

Harner's journey, as he tells it, from 'outside observer' to practitioner of shamanism, began with his first fieldwork among the Untsuri Shuar of Ecuador in 1956–7.[53] He underwent his first shamanic experience during a year-long stay among the Conibo Indians of the Peruvian Amazon. Encountering resistance to his questions about the supernatural, he was told that if he really wished to learn, he must drink *ayahuasca*, the 'vine of the dead' or the 'soul vine'. He experienced this vision as a confirmation of his potential and an invitation to further study, for he 'saw' dragon-like reptilian creatures who communicated with him without speaking. His experience was confirmed as 'valid' by the most knowledgeable of the Conibo shamans, who was impressed that he had seen so much on his first journey. 'You can surely be a master shaman', he said.[54]

In 1964 Harner returned to the northwestern part of Shuar country, where the most powerful shamans were reputed to live, this time expressly to study shamanism. Harner describes the first meeting with Akachu, the shaman he chose to be his teacher:

> 'I have come', I explained, 'to acquire spirit helpers, tsentsak'.
> He stared hard at me without saying a word, but the wrinkles in his brown face seemed to deepen.
> 'That is a fine gun, there', he observed, jutting his chin toward the Winchester shotgun I had brought along for hunting.
> His message was clear, for the standard payment among the Jivaro for shamanic initiation was – at the very least – a muzzle loading shotgun.
> 'To acquire knowledge and spirit-helpers, I will give you the gun and my two boxes of cartridges', I said.

You are not a shuar, an Indian', Akachu said, 'so I do not know
if you will have success. But I will help you to try.'[55]

Harner, of course, did succeed. He had visions under the influence of the
powerful *maikua* (*datura brugmansia*), and he underwent the process of acquiring *tsentsak* and learning their manipulation. He returned to the Shuar in 1969
and again in 1973. He reports also studying briefly with North American
shamans among the Wintun and Pomo in California, the Coast Salish in Washington State, and the Lakota in South Dakota, from whom he learned 'how
shamanism could be practised successfully without the use of the ayahuasca or
other drugs'. Finally he closes this biographical chapter with a statement of
mission: 'Now it seems time to help transmit some practical aspects of this
ancient human legacy to those who have been cut off from it for centuries'.[56]

It appears that Harner's vision of shamanism began to expand during the
1970s, following the publication of his ethnography of the Untsuri Shuar in
1972. In 1973 he edited a volume entitled *Hallucinogens and Shamanism*, for
which he contributed an entry on 'The role of hallucinogenic plants in European witchcraft'.[57] Following this volume there was a gap in publications until
the 1980 appearance of *The Way of the Shaman*, a book intended as a how-to
introduction to the practice of curing shamanism. From his publications on the
Jivaro to his edited volume on shamanism in various locations to his *The Way of
the Shaman* we can trace a movement from the particular to the universal, from
the locative to the utopian.[58] Shortly thereafter, around 1983, he launched The
Foundation for Shamanic Studies, a 'non-profit incorporated educational
organization' which is 'dedicated to the preservation, study, and teaching of
shamanic knowledge for the welfare of the Planet and its inhabitants'.[59]

If the stated purpose of the foundation is preservation and study of
indigenous forms of shamanism, however, it is clear that it is also quite innovative as regards what shamanism is and how it is to be practised. Here I would
like to highlight just three related areas of innovation, though there are surely
others: universalization (shamanism as culturally non-contingent), individualization (shamanism as malleable to individual needs in the religious marketplace) and the turn to shamanism as a technique of psychotherapy.

For those in Harner's Foundation, shamanism is universal in two senses.
First, it constitutes an archaic ur-religion universally spread throughout the
world. Harner and other contributing authors to the publications of the Foundation frequently refer to the authority of Eliade to establish what they call
'core shamanism'. For example, Sandra Ingerman, the Educational Director of
the Foundation and workshop leader, writes:

> Eliade's work is filled with accounts of shamans from different
> cultures calling back souls. He describes rituals and ceremonies
> regarding soul loss from Central and North Asia, North and South
> America, Indo-European societies, Tibet, China, and the Far

East. His descriptions suggest that there are some significant cross-cultural core elements in shamanic soul-retrieval.[60]

On the other hand, if shamanism is taken as the universal pre-historic religion[61] for which we feel a certain nostalgia (wishing we could still 'talk to the animals'),[62] it is also a universally available technique which may be put into practice in any cultural context as long as the correct procedures are followed. While the practice of shamanism may vary between specific cultures, the group of elements which are present in every case, and therefore not culturally contingent, are referred to as 'core shamanism'. Thus, while the Foundation aims at preserving and studying shamanism in its various contexts, it is at least equally interested in promulgating a shamanism that is, at its 'core', universal and culturally non-contingent. Their literature serves to develop and standardize this innovation, coining shorthand descriptives like 'SSC' for the 'shamanic state of consciousness', and OSC for 'ordinary states of consciousness'. The Foundation also awards monetary contributions to those they designate 'Living Treasures of Shamanism', such as Wangchuk, a 68-year-old Tibetan shaman living in exile in Nepal.[63] While the award serves the admirable goals of enabling the shaman to continue to practise his traditional form and preserving the rituals on tape for archives both in Tibet and at the Foundation, it also, in an ironic twist, promotes itself to arbiter and authority over who is and who is not a 'true shaman'. Thus far I have mentioned three innovative moves on the part of the Foundation. It has (1) reduced shamanism to the shared traits of all the members of its class, (2) universalized shamanism to a generic technique based on these 'core' traits which is culturally non-contingent and therefore available to all, and (3) established itself as an authority by the installation of its own language and power to choose what and who to 'preserve' through financial support and archival memory. Thus, even as the foundation nostalgically aims at the preservation of and learning from indigenous practices of shamanism, it seems most active in the innovation of a distinctly modern, new quasi-ritual practice.

An article published in one issue of the 'Newsletter' is revealing of the direction of this innovation. 'Coming out of the closet as a shamanic practitioner', by Leilani Lewis, addresses the problems and benefits of using shamanism in psychotherapeutic counseling. The complications are eased by following the 'HMSC' (Harner Method of Shamanic Counselling), which, among other things, has initiated two important changes; the use of electronic methods rather than the live drum for the induction of a shamanic state of consciousness, and the 'client' being counseled to become his/her own shaman.[64] By being taught to travel to the Upper and Lower realms themselves, clients can have and create their own healing experience; that is, can act as their own shaman.

Ingerman qualifies this by noting that, while one might well perform their own journey to obtain power animals, it is difficult to perform 'soul retrieval' or the operation of extracting intrusions without the distinction between practitioner and patient.[65] Both these examples, however, point to the turn to the individual. The sonic driving required to induce the 'SSC' can be heard on cassette, and one can then journey and experience the Upper and Lower worlds alone. This parallels a remark made by an Oak Park 'shaman' and Foundation trainee whom I interviewed: 'There isn't any power in the drum or artifacts themselves, but I use them to remind me where power comes from'.[66] The shaman's 'power', in this view, is independent of specific objects, places or persons; it floats free of contextual limits.

Lewis cites Roger Walsh on still a further example of this turn to individual mind, here to the idea of choice or preference: 'Whatever you believe – that the advisor is a spirit, a guardian angel, a messenger from God, a hallucination, a communication from your right brain to your left, or a symbolic representation of inner wisdom – is all right'.[67] The interpretation of what is actually happening in shamanism, then, is left open-ended, but is pragmatically resolved with the question of 'Does it work?' The shamanic geography is likewise open to personal invention and creativity: The 'shaman' I interviewed in Oak Park, for example, contacts power animals but also frequently is aided by the Virgin Mary and various angels. 'Core shamanism' does not require any specific landscape or cast of characters. It is open, fluid and mobile.

Next, the shamanism of the Foundation and my 'informant' in Oak Park is psychological. A quick perusal of the workshop offerings indicates this slant. In the words of Ingerman, for example, 'soul loss' is caused by emotional trauma:

> The soul might be in the Upperwold or in the Lowerworld, or it might still be stuck in the Middleworld at the time and place of the trauma. For example, the soul might still be stuck in the living room of the house where the child's father hit him. It might be stuck at the scene of an accident.[68]

The language of 'soul loss' closely follows Freud's theory of repression and trauma, healing resulting from the (not necessarily conscious) reintegration of that memory into the ego.[69] 'Soul-theft', similarly, happens accidentally in interpersonal relations through strong emotions like jealousy and anger. To release a stolen soul, one can simply release it by an act of will, since 'the key to ritual is intention'.[70] An 'intrusion' is any psychological or physical illness which the shaman 'sees' as a repulsive creature or simply as 'slime' which must be 'extracted'.[71]

One could multiply examples *ad infinitum*; the point I wish to establish here is that the shamanism of Harner's Foundation has created a new ritual form which is based not only on its universal, non-contingent status or its individualized form, but also on psychotherapy as its major forum and new context for healing. Its stated intention to preserve traditional forms of shamanism is obscured by its creation of a new, distinct form – a form which, while it claims universal, non-contingent status, clearly relies on its own proper context, namely that of radical modernity and the discourse of mobility and individual agency.

V. Comparing shamans and new-shamans: criteria and terminology

Is a New Age shaman a shaman? Does shamanism 'work' (function, give meaning, signify, structure, etc.) among the Shuar in the same way as it does in Chicago? As the above descriptions have illustrated, it surely does not. But how to argue this without reifying an idea of 'the primitive', and without undermining the universals on which comparison (not to mention ethics) depends poses an important challenge.

First, an elementary point: what is distinct about modern social systems in which neo-shamans make their homes is not any kind [of] essentialist distinction from 'primitive' societies, but rather a particular kind of fragmentation and diversity found in such modern societies which have led to an extreme form of self-reflexivity, relativism and subjectivity.[72]

Second, this modern idea of subjectivity, of the Self and its consciousness of its own agency, is correlated with pluralization. The explosion of a single coherent worldview into multiple fragments, none of which carries any necessity and all of which must be chosen from a situation of plurality is a defining attribute of radical modernity. Clifford Geertz, for example, describes the distinction between singleness and plurality of worldviews as 'religiousness' vs. 'religion-mindedness', and as 'being held' by religious beliefs vs. 'holding' religious beliefs.[73] Peter Berger also links pluralism with the experience of subjectivity and agency; the modern condition is one in which the 'sacred canopy' has been torn and where only privatized, chosen or individually preferred religion remains. It is 'real' to individuals but lacks any common, binding quality and cannot fulfil religion's classical task of constructing a common world within which social life receives ultimate meaning which is binding to all.[74] Thomas Luckmann, in similar fashion, characterizes religion in modernity as increasingly defined by the twin ethos of mobility and individual autonomy.[75] These scholars make it clear that what is distinct about the present age is not the decline of religion of such – indeed, there is ample evidence to the contrary of this simplistic version of the secularization thesis – but rather the decline of central, socially binding religious authority.

While these distinctions between the contexts of shamans and neo-shamans are important, many anthropologists have rightly decried sociologists' emphasis on the split between 'modern' and 'primitive' societies, pointing out how they are used as mutually defining caricatures, the first implying change, motion, agency and dynamism, and the second suggesting endless, 'self-less repetition of mythic paradigms'.[76] This is a significant criticism, for it is true that 'tradition' is always a process of active re-creation; the selection of desired continuities and the rejection of others.[77] The selective use of 'tradition' is a powerful claim to authority, a form of individual agency applied for various socio-political purposes.[78] This much, then, is obvious: it must be assumed that there is always innovation and agency in 'traditional' societies, and always repetition in 'modern' societies. But as my reference to Tala Asad above suggested, the need to find agency and change everywhere can be carried too far and obscure real differences between kinds of societies. The quest for agency is an important corrective to the reification of the idea of 'the primitive' as changeless.[79] But surely, to refer to the case I have considered here, shamanism among the Shuar and neo-shamanism among urban Americans follow different structuring strategies[80] which can be usefully distinguished by noting, on the Shuar side, the emphasis on shamanism as it preserves traditional knowledge, and on the New Age, neo-shamans' side, the emphasis on mobility and individual choice.

To summarize, neo-shamans can be distinguished from shamans by their reliance on a context of radical modernity. Radical modernity entails: (1) the rationalization of society which relies on (2) universal, standardized conceptions of time and space and (3) the confrontation with a plurality of religions, which leads to (4) a focus on individual agency, choice, 'needs' and preference in the religious 'marketplace', and (5) an obsession with the 'self', subjectivity and reflexivity; (6) the discourse of mobility — individuals are free and capable of converting to any religious system in any place and at any time because (7) space is phantasmagoric and dislocated from place — there are not really sacred spaces but rather only sacred states of mind and sacred relationships with abstract deities.

The neo-shamans of Harner's institute ironically replay exactly the above script of radical modernity, even as they battle against the disembeddedness of radical modernity by relying on local, rooted, 'natural', 'native', indigenous societies as their source of authority and power. Further, I have suggested three specific strategies by which this occurs, though there are certainly others; the ideology of mobility (shamanism as a universally applicable technique), individualization (and the risk of solipsism), and psychologization, or the claim to a universal mechanism of 'mind'.

Notes

1   Wendy Doniger, *Other Peoples' Myths*, New York, Macmillan 1988, p. 131.
2   I would mark this point in the mid-60s, when the English translation of Eliade's landmark study appeared followed by the enormously popular accounts of Carlos Castaneda. We might speculate that the fascination with shamanism dovetailed with interest in altered states of consciousness, and with the simultaneous rise of the

'helping professions' (as documented, for instance, by Pierre Bourdieu in *Reproduction in Education, Society and Culture*, 1971), but this must remain speculation at this point. Mircea Eliade, *Shamanism: Archaic Techniques of Ecstasy*, trans. Willard R. Trask, Princeton, Princeton University Press 1964.

3   The 'universality' of shamanism has typically though not always excluded Africa which has privileged the idiom of possession or 'enstasy' over that of shamanism or 'ecstasy'. A confusing mix of diffusion (shamanism as a kind of Ur-religious expression) and transconscious (noting especially that Australian shamanism cannot be accounted for by a diffusion argument) theories has resulted.

4   This view is elegantly expressed by, among others, Lévi-Strauss in the essay, 'The effectiveness of symbols', in *Structural Anthropology*, New York, Basic Books 1963; Adolf E. Jensen, in 'Shamanism as expression of genuine magic', in *Myth and Cult Among Primitive Peoples*. Chicago, University of Chicago Press 1963; in Eliade's famous subtitle, 'archaic techniques of ecstasy': and more recently in semi-popular works like Carlos Castaneda, *The Teachings of Don Juan*, Berkeley, The University of California Press 1968, or Felicitas D. Goodman, *Where the Spirits Ride the Wind*, Bloomington, Indiana University Press 1990, which portray the shaman's experience as available to anyone through hallucinogenic experience or the practice of specific postures. I cite only exemplars of types of literature here; the possibilities are virtually endless.

5   Following Anthony Giddens, *The Consequences of Modernity*, Stanford, Stanford University Press 1990, pp. 45–54.

6   How to proceed with these sorts of appropriations is not at all clear. The Ritual Studies Group of the AAR, for instance, has chosen for one of next year's topics the 'cultural politics of ritual appropriation (e.g. New Age use of American Indian rites, feminist appeals to ancient forms of goddess worship, colonial rites adopted by indigenous people, . . . etc.' In this preliminary statement, 'cultural politics' is given as a key issue in all such phenomena, but this has yet to be spelled out more clearly.

7   'In the air' is a phrase used by Robin Horton in a series of essays in the early 1970s describing W. African conversion to Christianity and Islam. He argued that the tendency towards monotheism, a global religion, was 'in the air' and would have proceeded even without the presence of Christianity and Islam, the specific religious paradigms which happened to be available. Robin Horton, 'African conversion', *Africa* 41 (1971): 85–108.

8   Most of the literature refers to the Shuar as the 'Jívaro'. Recent accounts indicate that this group prefers to use the name 'Shuar', as 'Jívaro' has taken on polemical overtones in Ecuadoran mainstream use.

9   Some, of course, do not see enterprise of studying ritual appropriation into New Age or other contexts of interest or value at all. I take the value of such work as a given. If, for example, as Catherine Albanese reports, some 20% of Americans now believe in reincarnation in some form, we must at least consider this a fascinating and important change (Catherine L. Albanese, *America: Religions and Religion*, Belmont, CA, Wadsworth 1992, p. 359). The resistance, I believe, arises out of the fear of studying religion without the clarity of discrete cultural boundaries. If most scholars no longer subscribe to the cultural organicism of a Spengler, Kroeber or Schmidt, still we rely on the idea of culture as having a 'style', a coherence of traits distinguishing it from others, which allows for comparison.

10   Catherine Albanese, *Nature Religion in America: From the Algonkian Indians to the New Age*, Chicago, University of Chicago Press 1990; also *America: Religions and Religion*, cited above.

11   Albanese, 1992, p. 367.

12   Strange bedfellows with Albanese on this tendency to see cultural mixing as an equally available, rather non-structured, nearly 'natural' effect of our time are postmodern anthropologists who view the chaotic mix of cultural traits as revealing a kind of agency or autonomy on the part of indigenous groups which undermines any reified status of 'otherness' or exoticism: 'In cities on six continents foreign populations have come to stay — mixing in but often in partial, specific fashions. The "exotic" is uncannily close. Conversely, there seem no distant places left on the planet where the presence of "modern" products, media, and power cannot be felt. An older topography and experience of travel is exploded.' James Clifford, *The Predicament of Culture*, Cambridge, MA, Harvard University Press, 1988, pp. 13–14.

13   Talal Asad, *Genealogies of Religion: Discipline and Reasons of Power in Christianity and Islam*, Baltimore, The Johns Hopkins University Press 1993, pp. 1–24. Asad is really interested in hegemony. Hegemony is an important issue in discussing religious appropriations by modern Western groups which I address only tangentially in this paper but which will demand more sustained reflection in future work.

14   Ibid., p. 10.

15   Ibid., p. 23. This is reminiscent of Pierre Bourdieu's well-known description of 'doxa': a taken for granted social world which excludes inquiry into the conditions of its existence.

16   Though it is surely the case that many South American shamans incorporate elements of Catholicism, astrology, 'mesmerism', Kardecism, etc. to enhance their power and authority. See for instance, Douglas Sharon, *Wizard of the Four Winds: A Shaman's Story*. New York, The Free Press 1978. I do not regard this as the same kind of appropriation as that which is described in this paper. The first type incorporates elements of a colonial hierarchy which is materially, politically and socially more powerful. We will see the same effect in the hierarchy of Shuar shamans: the spirit 'darts' which partake of 'white power' are considered the most efficacious. The second appropriates and renders 'powerful' a subjugated culture. *Its* authority is derived from ideas of the 'primitive', 'nature' and the 'wild'.

17   Made from *Banisteriopsis*; a vine with hallucinogen-inducing properties widely utilized by South American shamans.

18   Michael Taussig, *Shamanism, Colonialism, and the Wild Man: A Study in Terror and Healing*, Chicago, University of Chicago Press 1987, p. 467.

19   Ibid., p. 448.

20   Ibid., pp. 326–7.

21   As Georges Bataille would have it, the religious act *par excellence*.

22   Shamanism among the Shuar has changed over time, most particularly during the last twenty years. Nevertheless, the sources I rely on here show a strong correspondence in their reports. They range in time from the late 1920s until the late 1970s. Three ethnographies are of the same region (of the Untsuri Shuar of Ecuador), one is of a new neighbor (the Aguaruna) of the same language group, and a fifth is a report from a neighbouring Canelos Quichua group who share many cultural patterns of the Jívaro though they speak Quechua. The period I am most

interested in here is the period of Harner's fieldwork during the late 1950s, and if I mistakenly slip at times into an 'anthropological present', it is this to period I am referring. Michael J. Harner, *The Jívaro: People of the Sacred Waterfalls*, Berkeley, University of California Press 1972; also 'Jívaro souls', *American Anthropologist* 64: 258–72; Michael F. Brown, *Tsewa's Gift: Magic and Meaning in an Amazonian Society*, Washington, Smithsonian Institution Press 1986; Rafael Karsten, *The Head-hunters of Western Amazonas: The Life and Culture of the Jibaro Indians of Eastern Ecuador and Peru*, Helsinki: Societas Scientarum Fennica, Commentationes Humanarum Litterarum. vol. 19, no. 5, 1935; M. W. Stirling, *Historical and Ethnographical Material on the Jívaro Indians*, Washington, Smithsonian, Bureau of American Ethnology, Bulletin 117, 1938; Norman E. Whitten, Jr, (ed.), *Cultural Transformations and Ethnicity in Modern Ecuador*, Urbana, University of Illinois Press, 1981.

23   M. Brown, 1986, notes that the *tsantsa* is no longer performed. Harner's fieldwork in the 1950s indicates that the *tsantsa* was very much a current practice at that time.

24   Brown reports several incidents between 1976–8 of the Aguaruna dressing in feathers and paint, something rarely done now, and brandishing weapons to scare off encroaching Andean immigrants (p. 44).

25   According to the account of Juan de Velasco, *Historia del Reino de Quito en la América Meridional: Año de 1789* (Quito 1842), cited by Stirling, pp. 17–18.

26   Stirling, pp. 27–8.

27   Brown, pp. 49–54; he is referring to Norman Whitten, Jr, 'Ecological imagery and cultural adaptability: the Canelos Quichua of eastern Ecuador'. *American Anthropologist* 80 (1978): 836–59. Brown hesitates to call these powerful beings gods, since they more resemble people who have extraordinary powers.

28   Harner, 1972, p. 134.

29   Brown, p. 49.

30   Karsten, p. 395; Stirling, p. 120.

31   Brown, p. 59.

32   Harner, 1972, p. 122.

33   Karsten, p. 400.

34   Harner, p. 136.

35   Karsten, p. 400.

36   Brown, p. 59.

37   Harner, p. 90.

38   Stirling, p. 116.

39   If an *arutam* soul is a particularly strong apparition of power in the form of an 'ancient specter', *arutam* is also referred to as power in general.

40   Harner, p. 152. The description of the three souls relies on Harner, pp. 135–52.

41   Brown, pp. 54–7.

42   Ibid., p. 56. Brown compares this in a footnote to the widespread Hispanic notion of 'susto', but finds no evidence that it is not indigenous to the Aguaruna in this case (199).

43   Karsten, p. 400.

44   Harner, pp. 116–25, describes a fascinating 'economy' of *tsentsak*, whereby certain *tsentsak* are considered to be particularly powerful depending on their origin. The *tsentsak* of the Canelos Quichua to the north, for example, are considered the most powerful since they possess 'white man's magic'. In turn, a hierarchy of north to

south has been created in which the northern *tsentsak*, and thereby the northern shamans, are always superior to the southerners.

45 Harner, p. 161. Karsten (p. 403) suggests that the stem-word of *wishínyu* (shaman) is probably *we*, 'I' or 'I myself', corresponding to the shaman's frequent repetition of the word *we*.

46 The literature varies as to whether the shaman may have only one *pasuk* or several. Stirling refers to 'Pasuca', the spirit of the blowgun, who the novice must see during the training period (p. 118), and Harner describes *pasuk* animal helpers whose help a sorcerer can enlist to shoot illness where the shaman is not physically present. Hence *pasuk*, like the shaman himself, is spiritual power which is itself ambivalent, being used both for attack (as the spirit of the blowgun) and healing.

47 Ibid., p. 164.

48 Brown, p. 62.

49 Stirling, p. 418.

50 Brown, p. 62.

51 Harner, 1972, pp. 154–5.

52 Brown, pp. 52–3.

53 The biographical outline which follows is derived from Michael Harner. *The Way of the Shaman*, San Francisco, Harper and Row 1990, pp. 1–20.

54 Ibid., p. 8. The 'validation' of Harner's journey occurs here by way of what Castaneda called 'special consensus'. 'Thus the goal of the operative order was to provide one with special consensus on the component elements perceived in non-ordinary reality, which were considered to be the corroboration of the ally's rule.' Carlos Castaneda, *The Teachings of Don Juan: A Yaqui Way of Knowledge*, Berkeley, University of California Press, 1968, p. 178. While there is much in Castaneda that is fictionalized and not useful, the idea of 'special consensus' is, to my mind, an interesting way to address the process by which a vision may or may not be considered authoritative and valid.

55 Harner, 1990, p. 10.

56 Ibid., p. 19.

57 Michael Harner, (ed.), *Hallucinogens and Shamanism*, New York, Oxford University Press, 1973.

58 The terminology of 'locative' and 'utopian' ideology is from J.Z. Smith, *Map is Not Territory*, Chicago, The University of Chicago Press 1993 (original 1978), pp. 130–42.

59 'Newsletter' of the Foundation, vol. 4, No. 1, summer 1991, p. 2.

60 Sandra Ingerman, 'Welcoming ourselves back home: the application of shamanic soul-retrieval techniques in the treatment of trauma cases', *The Shaman's Drum*, Mid-Summer, 1989, p. 26.

61 The issue of whether this is established by diffusion or trans-conscious universals is not addressed in these contexts. Harner offers a more pragmatic explanation for cross-cultural similarities preserved despite centuries of isolation: 'Because it works', Hamer, 1990, p. 42.

62 Eliade, p. 99.

63 'Newsletter', vol. 4, no. 3, Winter 91–92, pp. 1–2.

64 Leilani Lewis, 'Coming out of the closet as a shamanic practitioner', *Newsletter of The Foundation for Shamanic Studies*, 4: 1 (1991), p. 2.

65   Roberta Louis, 'Contemporary soul retrieval: an interview with Sandra Ingerman', *Shaman's Drum* (Summer 1991), p. 29.

66   Interview of December 3, 1993.

67   Martin L. Rossman, *Healing Yourself: A Step-By-Step Approach for Better Health*, New York, Walker 1987, p. 93.

68   Louis, p. 29.

69   It also, however, resembles the Latin American idea of 'susto', a scare that provokes shock and a 'soul-loss', as well as the Aguaruna notion of 'fright' (*ishṁkamu*) recorded by Brown, as noted above. Brown, p. 56, it seems likely that the practice of 'soul-retrieval' by modern shamans dovetails with the 'recovered-memory' movement and debate of recent years in the United States.

70   Louis, p. 32.

71   Louis, p. 29.

72   Mary Douglas, *Purity and Danger: An Analysis of the Concepts of Pollution and Taboo*, London, Routledge & Kegan Paul 1966, pp. 40, 73–94.

73   Clifford Geertz. *Islam Observed: Religious Development in Morocco and Indonesia*, Chicago, University of Chicago Press 1971, p. 61.

74   Peter Berger, *The Sacred Canopy: Elements of a Social Theory of Religion*, Garden City, NY, Doubleday and Co. 1967, p. 132.

75   Thomas Luckmann. *The Invisible Religion: The Problem of Religion in Modern Society*, New York, MacMillan 1967, pp. 109–11.

76   Johannes Fabian, for example, says that 'the primitive' may only be used as a classifier, but cannot have any reality as an object of study; one can only think 'in terms of "the primitive", not "of" "the primitive"'. Johannes Fabian, *Time and the Other: How Anthropology Makes its Object*, New York, Columbia University Press 1983.

77   Raymond Williams. *The Sociology of Culture*. New York, Schocken Books 1982, p. 187.

78   This point is stated most bluntly and clearly in Bruce Lincoln, *Discourse and the Construction of Society: Comparative Studies in Myth, Ritual and Classification*. Oxford, Oxford University Press 1989.

79   Fabian (cf. note 76), among others, protests that the typologizing of time as 'modern' or 'primitive' is a political act of power. I agree – time is always *socio-temporal*, and controlling it can be a powerful act, as in the rewriting of the calendar in the Bolshevik and French Revolutions – or even in Roosevelt's changing the date of Thanksgiving. Yet, ironically, Fabian's very ability to view time abstractly enough to see how it is implicated in politics depends on its disembeddedness and his modernity, and denies the possibility of the 'co-evalness' with anthropological Others which he advocates.

80   'Strategies', to borrow the terminology of Pierre Bourdieu, do not have to be conscious as in the conventional use of 'strategic'. Strategies as 'structuring structures' delimit the range of social possibilities of any given context. It is the very nature of hegemony, in fact, to be less than conscious, inexplicit, 'common sense', vs. say, ideology.

Chapter 21

Sandra Ingerman

TRACKING LOST SOULS

Mother, one of your children wants to come home. Help me bring her back to you so that she can take her rightful place on earth.

(Prayer used in soul retrievals)

AS YOU PREPARE TO JOURNEY with me, I invite you to light a candle. On occasions as diverse as birthday parties and church services, we use candles to lead us into a special state of being. A candle may remind us, for instance, that solid matter (the wax) is related to Spirit (the light). When I am about to enter nonordinary reality, I sometimes light a candle as a way to call upon helping spirits. Likewise, you might join me in this Spirit now by lighting a household candle, sitting with it for a moment, and leaving it lighted as you read. What could be simpler?

> *Light the candle. Notice, as you light it, whether you feel any subtle changes in your body. Perhaps you will gradually feel somehow lighter. Emotionally, you may feel a little safer and more peaceful. If these effects do not stand out at first, just let the candle burn, and perhaps you will feel a difference as you read.*

> *Spirit comes into our space in response to a call. As you light your candle, know that Spirit will guide and support you as you follow me in my travels. Your intellect can learn much about shamanism, but your heart can touch it even more deeply. Perhaps you are ready to open to shamanism — not as a belief or faith, but as an adventure that may yield results that you can verify. Your candle simply reminds you of your openness to that adventure.*

Imagine now that we are in a somewhat darkened room together. You are sitting on a beloved chair or cushion watching as I, in the middle of the room, prepare to do a soul retrieval. You see me pull out a weathered gray Zapotec blanket from Mexico decorated with a burgundy pattern.

This blanket and I are old friends. Since receiving it as a gift, I have used it in hundreds of healing sessions. Once I sat on it four days and three nights, fasting and praying for a vision. This blanket is a healing tool that helps me make the transition to nonordinary reality. When I lie on it, I feel embraced by Spirit and filled with healing power.

After I spread the blanket, you watch me place my rattle, a Native American drum, and a crystal nearby. At the beginning of each session I will rattle as I pray to the Great Mother (the feminine aspect of Spirit) to help me bring the soul of my client home. The drumming will be done by an assistant. (When there is no one to assist I use a tape of shamanic drumming. However, even then, I keep my own drum nearby.) Like the blanket, my drum has been part of many journeys. Its very presence begins to draw me into other worlds.

My crystal lies waiting also. When I begin to journey, I will keep it in my pocket to remind me that I have the ability to see what is hidden beyond ordinary awareness. It is my equivalent to the soul catchers used by traditional shamans.

As you relax in your chair and watch proceedings that may seem somewhat foreign to you, I encourage you to take a few deep breaths. The people whom you will observe are perhaps not very different, in some ways, from you. What they share is a desire for deep healing and for a greater sense of aliveness. These individuals may or may not be familiar with shamanic practices.

Settle back now in your privileged role as a safe observer. Watch with interest and curiosity as each client comes to this room for a session. In turn, Susan, Ellen, Edward, and Marsha will lie on the blanket beside me, each with shoulders, hip, and ankles touching mine. Watch me as the drumming begins, as I cover my eyes with my forearm and begin to sink into an altered state of consciousness.

For these moments, you are now given the precious gift of inner sight. You are able to watch not only the outer forms of me and my clients as we lie on the floor but also the contents of my visions as I travel into nonordinary worlds. Where I go, you will also be able to go.

There is a single exception. During each journey I will speak with my guardian animal. In the shamanic world, the identity of one's guardian often remains a treasured secret. To share it with others, except under special circumstances, would be to diffuse its power. For this reason, I will not explicitly describe my guardian to you. To make these journeys richer for yourself, you may want to visualize an animal that you love and respect and let it carry out the same actions that my guardian does.

And now the first client knocks on the door. She is Susan.

The little girl who didn't want to come home

Susan is a drug and alcohol abuse counselor. Like many counselors, she is in therapy herself, both to facilitate her own healing and to hone her professional sensitivity. For some time, she has felt that her own therapy was stagnant. She and her therapist have been working with the metaphor of contacting Susan's inner child. But where is this child? Try as she might, Susan has not been able to find a child in herself. Both she and her therapist are frustrated and have agreed that Susan should try another way to reconnect with her inner child. She is here today to see if I can help her in this quest.

Before I begin to shift my consciousness by drumming, I ask Susan to show me the jewelry she is wearing. When hunting for elusive soul parts, I often find that it helps to watch for jewelry. Think about the problem. In nonordinary reality, the soul parts might not look very much like the client who comes to me for help, particularly if the soul part left in childhood. But no matter what age the soul is in nonordinary reality, her earlier self will wear the same jewelry as the client does in the present. If I can see the same ring or bracelet, I can identify the wandering soul despite any difference in years.

> Today Susan is wearing a very delicate silver ring on her right hand. After singing my power song, I lie down next to her holding in my mind's eye the intention of my journey. As the drumming begins, I begin to see myself floating up through many cloud layers until, after a few moments, I am catapulted into outer space, where I tumble about in slow motion, feeling lost in a peaceful limbo of gentle, rocking sensations. Surrounded by darkness and soft sounds, I am easily lulled into an unconscious state. Suddenly I remember my mission and break out of this state by calling to Susan.
>
> I look around, and as my eyes focus, I see that the darkness is filled with many planets and shining stars. Expanding my vision, I see a child's head peek out from what looks like a mass of rock floating in space. Drifting up to her as if in zero gravity, I relax and approach in a nonthreatening way. 'Are you Susan?' I ask. As the child nods, I glimpse the silver ring on the right hand. She looks about seven years old.
>
> 'Susan,' I say. 'I am a friend who wants to bring you home.'
>
> 'No,' she replies, 'I don't want to go back there.' She looks as though she might throw a full-blown temper tantrum.
>
> At this point, my power animal appears beside me and shows me a scene of Susan's life in ordinary reality at the age of seven. I see these images as if I were watching an inner movie. Susan is sitting in her living room playing with dolls. Her father walks in

looking bleary-eyed after a long workday. Is he just tired, or has he been drinking? I can't tell. Unfortunately, he trips over one of Susan's many toys.

'How many times do I have to tell you not to leave your toys all over the living room?' he yells. As her father came in, Susan had stood up with her hands behind her back to greet him. Now, in frustration, he slaps her. My power animal looks at me and communicates to me telepathically, 'This is not the first time, nor will it be the last.'

Now I turn from this scene revealed to me by my guardian and look back at little Susan hiding behind the rock. Clearly she is afraid to return with me to ordinary reality. However, my guardian has a gift for speaking gently and reassuringly to frightened little ones. 'Susan,' he says, 'remember how much you loved to walk in the woods, singing to the trees? Remember how much you loved to jump rope and play ball?'

Hearing these words, Susan looks less frightened and gets a faraway look in her eyes. I join in and say, 'You are much older now, and you don't live with your father anymore. You don't have to worry about his hitting you again. It's safe now, Susan. Will you come home with me?'

At last she agrees to return.

After we go back to ordinary reality, I sit up and blow that soul part into Susan through her chest and through the top of her head, in the traditional way. She sits up and I share with her my experiences on this journey. Since Susan seems stable emotionally and has been previously aware of abuse, I feel easy about sharing the contents of my journey with her.

(Some months from now, Susan will tell me that her session opened up a 'gentle remembering' of her lost childhood, that she loves having her little girl back, and that she is no longer depressed. Most important, having the child back helps her move forward in her therapy.)[1]

Journey to the Cave of the Lost Children

As Ellen enters the room where you and I are sitting, she looks depressed and dispirited. Her report on her life confirms this: although her job as an office worker is stable, she has been involved in a series of painful, unhealthy relationships with men. Almost always angry at someone about something, she desperately wants to experience the happiness that has eluded her.

I ask Ellen whether she really wants change and whether she feels safe with me. When she answers both questions with a firm yes, I know that we are ready to begin.

After saying my prayer and lying down beside Ellen on the rug, I enter a tree trunk that leads into a cool, dark tunnel. My hair brushes against the roof of the tunnel, and I feel cool, brown dirt gently dusting my cheek. Down through the tunnel I move, silently asking my power animal to wait for me at the end. At the same time, I focus my intention to find a lost part of Ellen that would be helpful to her at this time.

As I exit from the tunnel into the light, my power animal grabs my hand so quickly that I have no time to glance around or communicate with him verbally. He begins to lead me deeper and deeper into the earth, through the realms known as the Lower World. I initially pay close attention to the levels we pass through but soon lose count as we travel through seemingly endless layers. As we travel, my throat constricts, and my skin feels clammy; I have a premonition of where we are going.

Finally we arrive on a level that is barren and empty. A clear blue sky eerily lights a landscape of light brown dirt that stretches toward a distant mountain. There is not a speak of green or of anything living.

My power animal and I walk together on the soft earth, feeling the absolute emptiness of the place. Slowly we approach the mouth of a cave located in a mountain, with fallen rock all around. As we enter the pitch blackness of the cave, my heart is beating fast. I know that we are in the Cave of the Lost Children, one of the most heart-wrenching place in all of the inner worlds. As my eyes adjust to the darkness, I see the outlines of hundreds of children of all races huddling together in the cave. Hundreds of huge, sad eyes — black, brown, and blue — stare at me. My heart contracts with pain as I see them in their timeless reality — lost, unwanted, and frightened. Always waiting.

I pull myself away from the pain of my response and refocus my intention to find Ellen. Soon I feel a pull on my solar plexus as if there were a rope extending from there being pulled upon. A child with strong, steel blue eyes moves toward me. She is about five years old. The darkness prevents me from seeing clearly what she is wearing.

'Are you Ellen?'

She nods her head affirmatively with no expression on her face. When I ask her whether she wants to come back with me, she grabs me so hard that her rough nails dig into my arm. I take one of her hands in mine, and my power animal holds the other, as we begin to leave the cave in single file. I'm aware of the mournful, staring eyes of the other abandoned children as we leave.

Once we are outside the cave, I lean down and wipe Ellen's

dirty, tearful face with a tissue. She tells us that her parents are so concerned about their own problems that each one has forgotten her. She explains that her mother has been drinking constantly since her father left, and that there's no one to watch over her. She begins to cry, 'I've been so scared.'

I feel a little paralyzed by her pain, but my power animal, who is always full of surprises, steps in with just the right approach. He picks up Ellen and makes funny faces at her until she cracks a smile. Her smile eases the sadness that I have felt ever since leaving the cave.

I ask Ellen if she is ready to return to the adult Ellen who is waiting for her in ordinary reality. She says that she is almost ready but wants to ask me a question first. 'Do you know why Ellen is always so angry?' I answer that I don't know. She says, 'Ellen thinks that she has to be big and angry to protect me. I don't need protection. I just want someone to love me.'

I take the child in my arms and lay her head on my shoulder. I gently carry her into ordinary reality.

I blow the five-year-old child into the adult Ellen, then rattle around Ellen four times to seal that soul part into her body. As Ellen opens her eyes, I say to her returned soul, 'Welcome home.' Ellen immediately responds that she feels a welcome warmth in her solar plexus. As I share my visions with Ellen, she confirms two facts that my ordinary self had not known: her parents split up when she was five, and her mother was an alcoholic. She knows that she lost the ability to trust at that age and that this has affected her ability to experience intimacy with anyone. When I report that her little girl has said that the adult Ellen's anger is intended as a protection for the little girl, Ellen understands. As we are talking, Ellen reports that the warmth is spreading throughout her body. Her fingers and toes have begun to tingle.

(Several months from now, I will speak with Ellen again. Things are not perfect in her life, but she has made significant changes. She feels softer and more playful and generally trusts herself more. Although I am still haunted by the eyes of the abandoned children, she remembers the journey home as a great relief.)

The boy with the perfect home

A soul doesn't always travel into the Lower World (as Ellen did) or to the Upper World (Susan). Often a soul is lost on our own level of reality, encapsulated in a past (or even future) moment. Such is the case of Edward, who is a carpenter.

He appears unsettled and disturbed as he enters the room to join us. One of his pressing difficulties is never feeling comfortable at any location where he lives. He has moved many times trying to find a place where he can feel at home, but he always feels unsettled, wondering where to go next.

I begin the journey for him with the usual prayer and rattling. I set my intention to travel wherever I need to go to retrieve the soul part that will most serve Edward's life.

As I follow the sounds of the drumbeat, I find myself outside a house near a beach. The sun is shining, the moist air filled with salt smell.

The house reminds me of a Norman Rockwell painting. Soft curtains are drawn back at the window, revealing a spotless living room. As I peek through, I see a cream-colored rug and lots of comfortable furniture. A gallery of family photographs lines the walls. Turning my attention to the rest of the neighborhood, I see one-story California-style houses. The block is very quiet now, but I imagine kids riding their bikes after school and dads washing their cars there on the weekends.

Four times I repeat my intention to find Edward's missing soul parts. My intention draws me into the house. I pass through a cool, narrow hallway into a cheerful yellow kitchen. As I walk to the back door, I can see Edward in the backyard pitching his tent. He looks like a supremely contented nine-year-old. Approaching him, I explain that I was sent to bring him home. He responds without hesitation, 'But I am at home.'

I explain to Edward that time has moved on and that he is no longer nine. He is a grown man of forty-three. Little Edward listens to me unhappily without the slightest interest in leaving. 'But I love this place,' he says tearfully, 'please don't make me leave.' I ask Edward where his parents are, and he answers defiantly that they have moved, 'But they can't make me move from here.' Edward's current dilemma begins to become clear to me. His parents left this much-loved home when he was nine years old, and part of him stayed behind. He has never been able to feel at home anywhere because a part of him has never left his past. Unlike Ellen when I found her trapped in a sad, lonely place, little Edward is in a world that he truly loves. However, as I patiently explain, his true place is with the adult Edward, and until they are reunited, neither can be truly happy.

Little Edward looks away from me as he considers my words. The child finally asks, 'Edward really wants me back, does he?' I assure him that this is true. He asks me how to get back and shyly places his hand in mine. Together we wave good-bye to his house as we return to ordinary reality.

After welcoming the soul home, I share my journey with my client. Moved by the images, he tells me that his father was transferred back east from Los Angeles when he was nine. Edward hated leaving the only home he had ever known. He could never understand his irrational pull toward Los Angeles, because he has no current intention of living there. He was sure a part of his little-boy soul had stayed with the home he had loved.

The woman who loved to sleep

Watch now as Marsha enters the room. She is depleted and depressed. It is difficult to imagine where she gets the energy to help people in her work as a psychotherapist. In fact, she reports that she is not enjoying her work or her personal life. Her best times now are when she is asleep; she feels contented then. The rest of the time she feels drained and longs to return to bed.

We go through the preparatory rituals, and I firmly set my intention to bring back the lost soul parts.

> As I begin to travel, I find myself pulled up through a cloud membrane into the Upper World. As I look around, I see Marsha's soul looking much as she does today, climbing up a silver rope. She is desperately trying to reach a baby that is within her sight but out of reach. 'Marsha,' I ask, 'where are you going?'
>
> 'I have to get my baby.'
>
> I have a strong intuition. 'Is that baby you?'
>
> Marsha responds that it is. 'Every night I go a little farther trying to reach the baby. I want my baby back.'
>
> Marsha's predicament touches my heart. She is like Sisyphus, who rolls a stone toward a hilltop he can never reach. Marsha appears condemned to make an eternal climb without ever being able to reach her baby.
>
> How to help? In nonordinary reality I am quickly able to climb the silver rope to the level that Marsha is unable to reach. There is the baby lying on a cloud. I pick her up, and pressing her to my chest, start down the rope with her. When I reach Marsha, I gently place the baby in her arms.
>
> 'Marsha, put your hands around my waist,' I instruct her. The three of us slide down through the layers of Upper World clouds back to ordinary reality. Holding both the adult and the baby parts in my arms, I blow them into Marsha's chest and the crown of her head. 'Welcome home,' I whisper.

When I share the images of my journey with Marsha, she feels moved by them, although she has little idea of why or when her baby-self left. (When I follow up with Marsha several months later, I will learn that she has felt an amazing resurgence of energy. She is excited by her work and is no longer engaged in a love affair with sleep.)[2]

Marsha's experience demonstrates that insight or understanding is not essential to this type of healing. Although she was trained in insight therapy herself, her relief had little to do with intellectual understanding of how or why the splits in her soul occurred. The crucial element seems to have been her reunion with lost parts of her self.

Some afterthoughts on my journeys

As you have traveled with me, you have probably been making some mental notes about the nature of these inner journeys. One of the things you may have noticed most strongly is the unpredictability of this work. Although the outer rituals of preparation and return provide a predictable frame for the journey, the images of the journey are rich and varied. The pictures that will fill the frame are always a surprise.

I never know exactly where I am going to go or what is going to happen. I don't know whether I will be in the Lower, Middle, or Upper World or whether the lost soul parts will be adults, children, or (as in the case of Marsha) both. I don't know whether the soul parts will be trapped in unhappy realities or will have found more congenial places that they will be reluctant to leave. I certainly can't predict what my own responses will be. I may experience deep fright or intense joy. Places such as the Cave of the Lost Children may haunt me for years.

When I enter into nonordinary reality, I surrender my ideas of what is possible. I may receive amazingly accurate pictures of a client's early life experience, of things I have no way of knowing in ordinary reality. My job is to let go of my limiting ideas of what is possible and open fully to the places to which I am led.

How do I maintain this kind of openness? In part, I am supported and guided by the healing purpose of the journey. My intention is like an arrow flying through the pitfalls and distractions of nonordinary reality. History has taught me that a strong inner intention will lead me directly to the experience that needs to happen. If I get distracted by the soul's state (as I did when I was journeying for Susan) or by fears (as I did with Ellen), I can reset my healing intention and again begin to walk a straight path.

The other major supports are my power animals and spirit helpers – indispensable partners who guide, support, and instruct me as I enter unfamiliar territories. As you may remember, my power animal pulled me out of several impasses in the journeys that I shared with you. Simple things like picking up the frightened Ellen and making her laugh can turn a whole situation around.

As with any partnership, trust grows with repeated experiences of support and caring. I have received so much consistent wisdom and support from my guardians that I now wholly trust them. When I journey into the unknown worlds, I know that I will receive the help that is appropriate.

In my shamanic practice, the combination of consistent, stable outer rituals and rich, varied inner experience has been balancing and nourishing to me. I cannot imagine living without access to these inner worlds. I cannot imagine living without helping others to become whole through this work.

Notes

1   Ingerman, 'Welcoming Ourselves Back Home', p. 27.
2   Ingerman, 'Welcoming Ourselves Back Home', pp. 27–8.

References

Ingerman, Sandra. 1989. 'Welcoming Ourselves Back Home: The Application of Shamanic Soul Retrieval in the Treatment of Trauma Cases'. *Shaman's Drum*. Midsummer, pp. 24–9.

Chapter 22

Gordon MacLellan

DANCING ON THE EDGE
Shamanism in modern Britain

I'M CALLED 'A SHAMAN' — maybe by people who do not know any better — or even by those who should. But since none of us seem to be able to define exactly what makes the shaman, maybe when people feel the term is the right one, that is enough of a decision and that will have to do. 'Shaman' isn't a label that is achieved: not a status that can be measured, tested and awarded. Rather, it is something that comes upon a body and its appellation depends probably more upon the role that an individual plays within a community and, to some degree, how they achieve that rather than on any personal claim upon the title. This piece sets out to try to unravel something of that role in modern Britain and the places of shamans and shamanism within the current Pagan community. And this is a personal comment; it has to be: shamanism is evasive and elusive, shaping itself to the needs of its practitioners and their communities; sooner catch mist in a jam-jar than find easy definitions within a shamanic world. As with most modern Paganism, there is no single dogma or central authority to measure things against and we are all free to, and do, disagree with each other about everything!

Traditionally, the shaman belongs to a time and to cultures where survival runs along a knife edge and where

> . . . *the greatest peril of life lies in the fact that human food consists entirely of souls. All the creatures that we have to kill to eat, all those that we have to strike down and destroy to make clothes for ourselves, have souls, souls that do not perish with the body . . .*[1]

'All that exists lives'[2] – spirit imbues everything: all things contain a spark of the conscious Infinite: human, plant, hunter, hunted and stone. All these are alive, all hold spirit and all exist in the spiritworld as forces to be reckoned with.

That spiritworld surrounds us: we live with spirits all the time but because they have no physical form, on the whole modern humans are almost completely oblivious to their presence. Spirits touch us with premonition, a fleeting unease, an atmosphere or a passing dream, but we are close to forgetting them. The spirit world, however, is not separate from the earth we walk upon, not some convenient semi-detached housing estate down the road you can drive away from when the tone of the neighbourhood starts to crumble. The spiritworld is here beside us, always; and unseen, often unguessed, it touches and changes the world of physical forms that we live in. Our actions, in turn, change the spiritworld, and we can work to heighten our awareness of it so that we are and are not consciously aware of it at will and we learn to operate in all the worlds at once, or in specific parts of them (because there is more than one spiritworld, just as there are different forms of physical existence). So we may choose, eventually, to have our eyes open in this world, and in that world, but our choice does not prevent the spiritworld being close beside us and being able to influence what happens in our physical world. The shaman moves between the worlds and can act in all of them.

The shaman makes no promises: and certainly not that anything she says will make instant sense! The shaman's world is one of apparent contradictions, but we can return to that later. The key to a shaman's reality is quite simply: 'All that exists lives'.

In those societies where shamanism still operates, the shaman is the bridge between the worlds: the pathfinder for his people; plotting a life-course through the trails of this world and the spiritworld. The shaman communicates human needs and desires to the spirits and interprets the spirits' own needs to his community. How she does this varies tremendously. 'Shamanism' as such is not any single set of teachings or practices; I see it more as that role: the communicator. People filling that niche are found in cultures across the world belonging to different types of society and very different mythologies but from the wide reach of these peoples various general patterns of behaviour and thought do emerge and these may give us the framework by which to look at modern shamanism.

There is rarely, even within a single people, a firm shamanic dogma: a lot is open to individual interpretation within that culture's worldview. There may be rules about how you do things, about the form of a ritual or the shapes of songs, but there is also a lot of flexibility – a recognition of the individual and the need for her to establish her own relationship with the spiritworld.

The general points are very general: shamans work with spirit people, shamans work through trance. Call them guides, or totems or helpers, gods, there are spirits with whom that shaman has close links. Often that link is one of cooperation as much as coercion; shamanism can feel like a joint venture: both sides of the bridge – the human and the spirit want to work together. Other spirits may come and go as they are needed – or as they need the shaman – but there is a core group, a spirit family, who stay together and may well work together for the rest of the shaman's life. Some spirits even stay with a family from one generation to the next, establishing those deepest, most totemic of bonds that in British culture may have survived as the animals seen on coats of arms or associated in folklore with particular families.

Shamans work with trance – and ecstasy. Trance is not necessarily of the 'all fall down and twitch convincingly' school of magic (although it may be): it can just as easily involve the shaman sitting down and having an apparently rational conversation with her client while still looking into the spiritworld. 'Trance' is achieved when the shaman is conscious of, talking to and operating in all the relevant worlds of his reality at the same time. The shaman can get there by more techniques than can be readily named. Generally, these can be grouped into six main categories: music, song, dance, pain, traditional hallucinogenics and stillness. Within these, and between these can be found the shapes from which more sophisticated magics have since evolved: shamanic forms range from the very simple to the spectacular and intricate. If it works, someone will use it.

And ecstasy? The ecstasy is the passion in life that is perhaps the best measure of the shaman. It is a pain and a delight: the fire of the Otherworld that burns in our veins, the fire that makes living such an intense delight and that the shaman sees and feels running in all the living world that surrounds him. Ecstasy comes with the realisation that everything is always now.

No, it may well not appear to make sense but what a shaman says, as a shaman, is always true: knowing the where and when of that truth is not always obvious, however. And no, shamans are not always obscure for irritation's sake, although the Fool may be there to annoy you out of an expectation for neat answers. At other times, the words simply cannot fit the experience.

It can be very easy to ramble on at length about the general patterns of shamanic practice and pull examples from cultures across the world and across time. But this would stay very general: shamanism defies limitations and sprouts exceptions to every rule that anyone formulates. Those underlying principles do seem to hold up: by accepting that their expression is then shaped by the relationship between people and place to produce something distinctive wherever shamanism is found, we can begin to catch the pattern that is shamanism. There are no rights and wrongs: the test is in the effectiveness of the forms used in helping people understand, communicate with and live as part of the environment they are in. In that process, the shaman is the one caught in the middle; the spider in the web, perhaps. Or maybe the fly.

In Britain, the spiritworld – the Otherworld of the Celts – is very ancient. And the Dream it dreams is an old and very seductive one. The world of Faerie is a part of this, the land of enchantment that can carry you away, dreaming, for seven, or a hundred or a thousand years and return you, lost, confused and adrift to a time not your own. The Otherworld is the abode of spirits: there we meet the talking foxes and watch the shapes of stone people unfold from the rocks on a hillside. When most of us enter the Otherworld in dreams, nightmares or magic, it shapes itself to our imaginings: if the people of the Otherworld are going to respond, they use the images we carry in our heads to give themselves forms that we can relate to. But beyond all the personal dreams of visitors, eventually, the Otherworld is the dream that the land itself is dreaming: the accumulated experience of the spiritforce of all who live within the land and in the earth and stones, rivers, mountains, winds and trees themselves. That Dream is like a river running behind everything that happens: this is the Dream that holds the shape of the land. When the Dream is broken, the world begins to end. And this dream defies words! It is an experience, an initiation that leaves the visitor no longer 'a visitor' but a waking part of the Dream itself, bound to the ecstasy of it and to the wholeness of it and the need of it to continue, to grow and to change. Evolution with its own sentience?

This is the shaman's world. She moves through an Otherworld that may correspond exactly with the territory she calls home, but here is midnight and a world frosted with energy like ice on every leaf, where the mist at dawn is a swirling, pouring cloud of spirals, spilling out of damp hollows. And the 'Other' is not 'other' at all, but this world, the mundane physical world. And it is our physical world that changes most, that is most vulnerable and only the Dream persists, rolling slowly over the centuries with the breathing of the hills. Everything else is illusion . . .

Given the passion, and often downright strangeness of the shaman's world, it is easy to wonder if there is any place at all in modern British society for anyone that weird. But if the shaman does truly function as that 'bridge between the worlds' then the need for communication and understanding between human and other worlds is as great now as it has ever been. In a society that seems increasingly alienated from and at odds with the natural world around it, anyone who can help people bridge that gap and find connections between themselves and their environment has an important role to play. There are shamans here amongst us; and not all covered in feathers and dead bits of things in true 'witch-doctor' style, nor even named as 'shamans' in public. Our wider society does not recognise, let alone accept, that role and the most effective shamans are not usually the ones who walk through their daily life with 'I'm a shaman' on either their lips or a lapel badge. The shape modern shamans take may be apparently different from their traditional one but the task is still there. The role of guide or pathfinder or communicator has specialised a bit now, perhaps because of the nature of the individuals involved or simply because we now live in such large groups of people that the shamanic function has had to subdivide for shamans to remain effective at all. Modern shamans may be:

personal healers: shamans who help people listen to themselves
community healers: shamans who help people listen to each other
patterners: shamans who help the community listen to/relate to
the world around them

That traditional role of communicator is still there but more finely tuned, perhaps, although none of us are exclusively one thing or another – we all do a bit of the other roles. Again, anyone could claim to do any of these things, but drawing upon the traditional stance, the shaman is empowered to act by the community he works with and is similarly touched by and works with the spiritworld. Shamans belong to their people. That widescreen cinematic demonic tyrant, witchfinder and general villain holding everyone in terror is unlikely. In a deep trance a shaman is vulnerable: to direct assault and to the elements, at least, and may need physical protection and support. Often to move into those deepest of trances, she will have needed the help of her community to get there: with drummers or singers, drug handlers or simply the concentrated collective will of the people to propel her from this world to the other.

The modern shaman is more isolated. With people not recognising the role, the shaman must sort out a lot of that side of things for herself. The driving need is there, it can be felt and touched but now, often, the shaman must move with it on her own both into and out of the Otherworld again, doing what must be done with never a thought from the people she is bound to. Or rather, they may see and appreciate the results and be grateful for what has changed without ever knowing the process.

I am a patterner: I work on the relationships between people and the world around them. My 'job' is to help people find their own relationship with nature and to understand and appreciate that connection. Working in environmental education and interpretation as I do, my daily work is part of the fulfilling of my shamanic function: I help people explore the world around them. I rarely do this with traditional shamanic tools: most of the people I work with would look askance at a collection of drums and rattles and trance dances. We use investigation and awareness and discovery and personal creativity, we learn to enjoy the natural world and find that wherever we are, even in the concrete heart of the city, nature is around us and we are always part of it, changing and changed by it. The 'magic' – the dances, drumming and so on – are what help to keep me connected, to move me into the depths of the Otherworld, to draw the understanding, inspiration and energy that keeps me going and makes me, hopefully, an effective educator.

A final twist comes with letting people go: we are no longer part of a community that shares a common mythology and worldview. I may see things in one way and believe in the rightness of one course of action, a movement that I see as part of the pattern, but there is no guarantee that the people who work with me will see the same thing, and I cannot bring them to do so. No matter what result I may hope for, I must respect the right of those people to draw their own conclusions from their experiences of nature: to impose my view upon them, beyond the choice of vehicles we use to get there (that is my choice as a technician), is in itself to twist the pattern that is growth and awareness. So while I am a shaman and a pagan, the people I work with can interpret what we have done in whatever mythology suits them: Christian, Jewish, Islamic or Darwinian Evolution. That does not really matter; it is the fact that a connection has been made and some of 'my' people are looking at their world with open eyes again that I accept as the achievement.

Things work the other way, too. The 'bridge' lies open to the spirits and the shaman must meet their needs and talk and dance with them and when the demand comes, help their work in the physical world. So shamans appear as protectors, initiators of action, stirrers of the storm with anything from ferocious trance dance to confront a danger, to delicate gentle supportive magic for metamorphosing toadlets, to finding people to write letters, plant trees or help a new nest-box project.

The challenge that faces shamanism in Britain now is in growing a 'new' tradition. We live in a land with a long, rich magical history and this land has layers and layers of stories upon it, that start unfolding when the shaman first moves in the Otherworld, and then never stop. Our human societies are a melting pot of mythologies and folklores with the accumulated effects of ancient Celtic and pre-Celtic cultures, later Roman, Saxon, Viking and Norman settlements and still more recent additions as other groups of people have settled here and added their experience to the whole. While my own deepest responses are to the Scottish and Irish stories of the earliest times, I cannot accept that these are the only points to work with. Among British pagans there is often an unspoken elevation of the Celts and some dismissal of everyone else since then. Regardless of the rights and wrongs of who has been doing what to whom over the centuries, all those experiences contribute to make us and the land what we are today and the shaman is likely to meet aspects of all or any of that. So, while I may reach back to Irish myth-cycles and odd Neolithic goddesses for my most profound experiences, my 'day-to-day' awareness of the Otherworld moves within a sort of composite 'British folk tradition' and I can see lots of Saxon and medieval elements in that. My everyday work has still wider multicultural elements, reflecting the diversity of the modern urban communities I am usually involved with. Given time, all this will sink into the Dream as well and the Dream will grow richer with the variety it brings.

But we do not have an extant shamanic tradition to draw upon. There are claims for surviving hedge-witch practices, some of the old covens have lasted down the centuries and there are tantalising echoes of still fuller traditions fading with our older generations. Descriptions of the Highland seers sound very like those of entranced shamans. Folk tradition is full of spirit-catchers and witch-bottles and the proper ways of living with the spiritworld of Faerie.

But a lot has been lost and there is a sense of watching things receding even as one looks at or for them. What there is can be useful but may not always be appropriate for the mix and attitudes of modern people. I see the shaman's job as working with communities and while one could claim that that need only be the 'pagan' community (however one defines that!), my own definition is 'the people one lives among'. They may not want what the shaman has to offer, but the offer has to be there: the experience that a shaman can bring is not the exclusive province of people who regard themselves as animistic. Remember 'all that exists, lives', the drive is always to see the connections. The shaman's community may change with time and place, and sometimes the shaman's job seems rooted almost entirely in the needs of the Otherworld ('What is going on? What are they doing? Why?'). We are part of a society that is changing very fast and values and imagery are evolving rapidly: the shaman remains a connection to the pulse of the living world in all the running stream of change. But the shaman must also accept that the people he works with may need a new language to understand the messages and the paths that he brings.

So now, modern shamans need to find a language that modern communities will respond to. We all do this in our own ways but some of the most exciting shapes it takes have come with the environmental action of the last few years. Where people have felt angry enough, or empowered enough to go into direct confrontation with the builders of roads or the abusers of rainforests, new rituals have almost spontaneously started appearing. Brewing out of a mixture of traditional witchcraft, street theatre and odd bits of traditional shamanism but drawing their inspiration from the need the people feel in a hilltop camp to give shape to their feelings about the earth they are fighting to protect, ceremonies are taking shape. These are often decried by the magical establishment because the people are 'untrained', the material they work with incomplete, the traditions mixed, a hotchpotch. But what is overlooked is the passion that inspires them and that here are people on the edge of physical action and quite possibly personal danger. They may have been sleeping rough, or camping in a wood for days, or have just walked down from some terribly nice house up the road, but there is an earthlink there and what is sung, danced, spoken or screamed comes from the heart. Heart to heart, land and people: new magic taking shape. I believe that this is where the future of the shaman lies – in the road camps, or in city centre celebrations of people and place: a Tree Dressing Day, a Kite Festival on Chinese New Year, a Beltane Dance in a country park. Shamanism works with and for the people. It does not belong in High Magic Lodges or in a Witches' Circle: it is rooted in people, land and spirit. Maybe shamanism is just the grubby end of magic, but that is all right: we need all our variations to make for a stronger, more complete and more supportive magical community, which in its turn should feed energy and awareness back into the wider communities of human and spirit.

For me, then, shamanism is very much 'enchantment for anyone who will stop long enough to listen' – its practitioners are not elitist in who they work with, which rather goes against a lot of the current trends in shamanism. Shamanism is fashionable. If you have the money, you can go and spend hundreds on this or that weekend, or this spirit journey, or that quest to the Andes. It also appears in a wonderful array of hybrids with 'shamanic wicca' and the like. None of this is 'wrong', but equally for me it is not shamanism. To be pedantic, maybe we have here the difference between what is 'shamanic' – belonging to the principles of shamanism, and what is 'shamanistic' – using the techniques of the shaman. People I meet working in these traditions are not shamans, but they are using the techniques of shamanism: those six categories of music, song, dance, pain, drugs and stillness, to explore their world and their magic. And those practices are powerful indeed, especially with people coming from a culture that avoids excess: to move into a throbbing drum trance, or to dance until one's feet are bleeding and to go on dancing can shake the walls of your world in a way quite unlike more formal magical systems. But this does not make the drummer a shaman. As well as all the stuff above about communities and roles, when you meet a shaman you meet someone who has been claimed by the Otherworld: somewhere, sometime, some spirit person has reached out a hand, a claw, a paw, and set it on the shaman's brow as the shaman reached out to it, and together they have said: 'We are one'.

> Come listen my men, while I tell you again,
> The five unmistakable marks
> By which you may know, wheresoever you go,
> The warranted genuine Snarks.[3]

I am afraid there aren't any. The shaman's world can seem an endless round of contradictions: to dance is to understand stillness, pain can be pleasure, at your most effective no one may ever know what you do for them. Only the dream is real and in the Dream everything is real. That simple opening statement 'all that exists, lives' can unravel into a nightmare knot when you start to examine it, but to learn to 'be' and not to 'know' is part of the shaman's task: not to analyse objectively but to understand from within. By being part of the threads of that tangle, you can flow through and move on. Shamans are notoriously unpredictable on one level: they are the Tricksters who break realities, but should be bitterly consistent on a deeper one. The shaman is bound by her dream: her vision, his reality – the only one that matters is the path that leads to the heart of it all, that moves the community on – and the public expression of that may change like the surface of a pool from one day to the next. Anyone can claim all that is of the shaman and claim to be one, and they do. But the shamans must be horribly true to themselves: they have had to see themselves taken apart and 'lick the blood fresh from your own bones'.[4]

There are no rules, but still we are bound, tied by our dream: the honour of a personal truth is inescapable and that carries safeguards for the community. In the Otherworld, the shaman must be who she really is: to face the spirits with deceit is to court disaster and this then moves in all worlds. Bound by the need to 'be who you truly are', not what your family, friends, spouse, employers, or local shaman wants you to be, the shaman who tries to convert people to fit her idea of things is tying her own shoelaces together and she is, at the least, going to fall flat on her face sooner or later. But this is not a process governed by fear and the horror of an angry spirit howling down the chimney; it is one of freedom: the freedom to dance along a storm or, as a sensible, responsible grown-up-type person, to revel in the wind at a bus stop.

Shamanism is ecstatic. My magic moves most strongly in dance and with the wild, whirling dances of the animal spirits; with others it takes other forms, but for us all the power, the strength to act, lies in an ecstasy in life – that living is such a delight! And maybe that is the best measure of a shaman: feeling the awareness, the closeness of the Otherworld like a shadow in the shaman's eyes and a passion in the life that surrounds him, that celebrates the wind and finds fascination in the reflections in the windows of an office block.

The power of it is a delight that runs like fire. When I dance, my inner-most self becomes still and the movement of the dance sets me free, I become all the spirits that I work with. I see with all their eyes, we enjoy the physical form of the dance. I feel a world that thinks and its presence humbles me and sets me free. This is bliss. My eyes open in a world where 'all that exists, lives'. This is the inspiration. The pattern moves like a spider's web in many dimensions. Every step I take, every sweep of hand or arm trails energy like echoes of movement. The dance carries me across the web in a helter-skelter ride of awareness. The morning is crystal and the sunrise paints my body with green and red and gold. The Otherworld is this world – there are no barriers. It burns through me with a passion and a delight. The life of the Earth is sacred and is a part of the Infinite. To be alive is to move in celebration. The shaman is bound – how can you live and not be a part of life: 'I love you all and I cannot help myself'.[5]

And, of course, it is all a dream. The shapes of the words change, the images we work with are fluid. Our gods are liable to remind us that their shapes are illusions and dissolve in a shower of stars or prove our own illusory nature by peeling the skins from our bodies and have us lick our own bones clean. Perhaps that is the final shamanic contradiction: it is all completely true and it may all be wrong.

> In the midst of the word he was trying to say,
> In the midst of his laughter and glee,
> He had softly and suddenly vanished away –
> For the Snark was a Boojum, you see.[6]

Notes

1   J. Halifax, *Shaman: The Wounded Healer*, Thames and Hudson, 1982.
2   Ibid.
3   Lewis Carroll, *The Hunting of the Snark*, Macmillan, 1948.
4   Gordon the Toad, *Small Acts of Magic*, Creeping Toad, 1994.
5   Ibid.
6   Lewis Carroll, *The Hunting of the Snark*, 1948.

Chapter 23

Beverley Butler

THE TREE, THE TOWER AND THE SHAMAN

The material culture of resistance of the No M11 Link Roads Protest of Wanstead and Leytonstone, London

[. . .]

'Song of exposition'
I believe a leaf of grass is the journeymen of the stars . . . and a mouse is miracle enough to stagger sextillions of politicians
(Walt Whitman, 1885, written on the wall in the Art House, Claremont Road, E11)

IN JULY 1994 I WAS ONE of the pilgrims, who deviated from the usual tourist routes, armed with a camera, a tape-recorder and an *A–Z*, to visit Claremont Road, Leytonstone, London E11. This ordinary row of Victorian terraced houses had been transformed with paint, creativity, humour and vision into an urban shrine to the culture of protest. Homes, pavements, abandoned cars, trees, all suddenly bloomed with murals of flowers, with New Age symbols and icons, with dragons and dancers and with theatre and play. Live-in sculptures of domestic interiors and ancient stones filled the street. At no. 68, the Art House, Artists Against Reckless Road Builders had created a counter-cultural collection of art and artefacts. In this space art functioned as barricade. A culture of protest inhabited Claremont Road in defiance of the British government's National Roads Programme; the scheme placed the whole street of 30 homes under threat of destruction to make way for a new motorway link road. For over 18 months Claremont Road was the site of the longest direct action anti-roads campaign in British history.

'The City Dead House'
In Loving Memory of Fallen Trees and Houses, their Injured and Arrested Defenders. M11 Campaign 1963–7
(Written on Art House wall, Claremont Road, E11)

One year on, Claremont Road does not exist. It was destroyed following the evictions of November 1995; a further casualty was the Art House and its collection. The street is soon to be erased from the pilgrims' devotional text, the London *A–Z*. The space is now hidden behind cold, dull sheets of corrugated steel, which are locked and closely supervised by security staff.

Claremont Road was also a place of transformation – of misrule – of the carnivalesque, like the fair that comes and goes, sprinkling misrule and chaos in its wake. Claremont had a transforming effect on me too. I was left with an empty space, some photographs and my own memories.

One particular memory persisted; it proved not only to be long-lasting but also subsequently became the point of origin for this paper. I recalled the image of an exhibit in the Art House: a single leaf 'preserved' in a cabinet; no label, no interpretation. The artefact functioned as a critique, a reference, to the life-forms threatened with extinction in the wake of the coming of the road. This single artefact, this single leaf had had its effect – in its sacrifice as art and as critique, its manifestation of the irrational, the curious and the transformational; it thus turned all modern/rational museological models/paradigm upside-down; inverting and parodying the dominant philosophy of the museum culture that fetishizes the guardianship of the monumental and invests in it the key criteria of permanence, preservation, conservation, underpinning this whole with cold scientific objectivity.

From macro- to micro-level I had thus been confronted with a landscape, a space, a culture and an associated collection of art and artefacts that declared that things could be otherwise. A contested landscape, spaces of resistance, an anti-museum, the artefact as a counter-cultural cabinet of furiosity perhaps? The text that follows addresses these implications.

Tests

Methodologies of the 'auto-critic'/'auto'-critiques.

> In the everyday, the activity and way of life are *transformed* into an instinctive, subconscious, unconscious and unreflected mechanism of acting and living: things, people, movements, tasks, environment, the world – they are not perceived for their originality and authenticity, they are not tested and discovered but they *are simply there*, and are accepted as inventory, as components of a known

world. Everyday life is always experienced in relation to the immediate environment . . .

(Wright, 1985: 6)

Spaces open up by virtue of the *dwelling* of humanity or the *staying with things* that cannot be separated: the earth, the sky, the constellations, the divinities, birth and death. . . . Cognition is not opposed to reality, but is wholly given over in the social fact of dwelling, serving to link place, praxis, cosmology and nurture.

(Tilley, 1994: 13)

NVDA (Non Violent Direct Action) is Praxis and image rolled into one. Unlike the personality cults of the Art world, Direct action is collective and anonymous. Unlike the rationality and objectivity of most politics it distrusts reason and champions intuition.

(Jordan, 1994: 38)

Just as the cabinets of curiosity functioned as a model, a microcosm of the world in miniature; Claremont Road renders unto us a cross-section of issues and phenomena to observe, to critique and to 'experience'. This paper takes an interdisciplinary perspective on exploring the key themes previously highlighted. My theoretical underpinnings draw upon current critiques of 'landscape', 'space' and definitions and debates concerning 'everyday life'. I connect the former critique's (primarily Bender, 1993; Tilley, 1994; Relph, 1987, Thomas, 1993) use of phenomenology (based upon the texts of Heidegger and Merleau-Ponty) with the latter's exploration of the concept of alienation (here I explore the work of Henri Lefebvre, 1991 and Agnes Heller, 1984).

My reasons for linking these approaches are twofold; firstly, these critiques combine an awareness of dominance and resistance with that of the experiential and subjective viewpoint. Secondly, I wish to claim that the 'common ground' of these critiques and of the transforming potential of material culture at Claremont is that of *praxis*, believing the acknowledgement of praxis to be essential when writing about 'political' protest/alternative culture. The implications of linking these critiques will be explored throughout the paper.

Protesters involved in the Claremont Road campaign chose to describe and to commemorate their experiences as a 'festival of resistance'. This is the description that fronts the self-generated commemorative paper (the 'exhibition catalogue') that combines images of the protest with comments from those involved. The historian and theorist Henri Lefebvre states that, 'Festivals contrasted violently with everyday life *but they were never separate from it*' (Lefebvre, 1991: 207). He sees this 'contrast' as projecting a critical consciousness of everyday life: 'an auto-critic'.

I wish to posit that the culture of resistance created at Claremont, the people who inhabited it and the rituals performed in the space functioned as an 'auto-critic' of everyday life and that the art and artefacts, the landscape itself, were purposefully (re)-created to 'display' and to confront this potential. Auto-critic – for our own context more aptly transformed to 'auto'-critique – the Claremont Road experience offers an insight, a clarity; a parody, an inversion and a subversion of 'ordinary' perspectives; with this co-existed/co-exists alternative visions.

What emerges from this study are the various, often competing, ways of seeing and experiencing the urban environment, materiality, democracy, partisan politics, social identities, ritual performance, time, place and everyday life. Concomitant with this comes the possibility of creating change and transformation.

Sub-headings in quotes throughout this paper come courtesy of Walt Whitman.

'Once I Pass'd Through A Populous City'

Contestation of landscape

> Landscapes are the visual contexts of daily existence, though I do not suppose many people often use the actual word 'landscape' to describe what they see as they walk down the street or stare through the windshield of a car . . . All of which suggests that landscapes are obvious things. Yet when we try to analyse them it soon turns out first of all, they are so familiar and all-embracing it is hard to get them into a clear perspective, and then that they cannot be easily disassembled into their component parts, such as buildings and roads, without losing a sense of the whole scene. So landscapes are at once obvious and elusive; it seems we know exactly what they are until we try to think and write about them, or change them in some way, and then they become enigmatic and fragile.
>
> (Relph, 1987: 3)

> Up-stairs at the Art House [at Claremont Road] there was what looked like a closet with shirts in it it was actually a door and when you went through it you saw a horrible twisted mass of cones, tyres, plastic, hubcaps . . . then you looked round the room you saw it had been a child's room with the original frieze with little teddy bears around the top. The artists had put up pictures of cars, like in a teenagers room, with slogans related to roads campaign and anti-car movement. If it was an installation in a museum it would be quite exciting but considering it was right

here where it [the M11 Link Road] was going to happen, with cars and possibly people killed it had such a powerful meaning.

(Sheila Freeman, pers. comm. 5 April 1995)

The British National Roads Programme, launched in 1989 by the Conservative government, and the resistance to it by the anti-roads campaigners throughout the country can be usefully explored in terms of a contestation of landscape. The subsequent ability of the powerful to enact their desires makes this a narrative of inequalities, a tale of dominance and resistance. Claremont Road itself was a microcosm of this contestation. The visual texts of Claremont Road, landscape, art and artefacts, testified to this and were a critical commentary of a certain polarization of perspectives generated by the initial 'road programme' versus 'anti-roads campaign' split. Individual pieces of artwork at Claremont Road explored these relationships predominantly in terms of 'car culture' versus 'people culture', or, as Relph states, 'those walking down the street' versus 'those behind the windscreen' (Relph, 1987: 3).

The street (Claremont Road) as artefact communicated similar messages and has been described in the press as a 'living tribute to community values and the careless society. The only car has grass growing out of the roof and "Rust in Peace" written on the wing' (*Independent*, 30 April 1994: 5). 'The car', which former prime minister Margaret Thatcher hailed as underpinning the 'great car economy', was decried by protesters as the 'ultimate space invader'. One of the key agendas of the Art House was to 'promote positive images', *alternatives* to the car culture. However, one room was set aside, the 'bad vibes room', containing the icons of car culture; a visiting newspaper reporter comments:

> [Moving from] rooms with positive images. Another, a 'bad vibes room', can only be entered by passing through a wardrobe. Inside is a dimly-lit scene of industrial madness and destruction containing the debris of road building, the ubiquitous motorway cone, damaged car panels, engine parts – all wrapped in the orange plastic netting of a construction site.

The text of roads protest campaign literature (I will take two key texts as representative examples: *Roadblock* (Bray *et al.*, 1995) and *Claremont Road E11: A Festival of Resistance* (Anon, 1994)) was similarly framed in a series of dichotomous relationships, couched in terms of the monolithic state versus the little people, the dominant culture and the marginalized, the centralized bureaucracy against the decentralized network of anti-roads organizations. This polarization reaches a pitch as the 'people' mobilize: 'In the early 1980s the Thatcher government set out literally to alter the shape of Britain . . . *Ordinary* people rose up in protest against reshaping of their familiar surroundings' (Bray *et al.*, 1995: 7, my emphasis), '[E]*veryday* people have either been invading worksites and using their bodies as tools of resistance . . . or designing and building sculptural barricades and installations to hold up evictions' (Jordan, 1994: 38, emphasis added).

The *ordinary* and the *everyday* (be this 'ordinary people', or the 'everyday landscape') undergo transformation – no longer 'obvious' and emergent as 'enigmatic'. The enigma of Claremont Road and the culture created there aligned itself to the ephemeral, the transient and the 'fragile' as a subversive force. The landscape breaks down into its component parts, the 'people' defending the 'buildings' and the government defending 'roads'. The effects of defending homes, green spaces and communities from transformation (destruction) from 'outside' also functions as an empowering call to action in this context. Relph has commented that the poor can do little to alter the landscape, although 'the rich can change it' (Relph, 1987: 73); the anti-roads movement sought to escape this prescribed role by using creative forms of 'action' to challenge governmental violence performed on the landscape.

From alternative text to government White Paper: 'The biggest since the Romans' is how John MacGregor, the then Minister for Transport, articulated the government's ambitions at the launch of the new road scheme. Costing approximately £19–£23 billion, the scheme was projected to run for 15 years with its aim to expand and 'upgrade' existing road networks, create new links, bypasses and orbitals. The physical change to the landscape was viewed as a sign of triumph; a visual record of the car culture's colonization of the country (marking a victory for the powerful road lobby and all those 'wealth creators' who stood to profit). The Thatcher government thus exposed its imperial agendas, apeing the Romans' roads programme in sheer size. Protesters outlined their concern that 'Huge swathes for the motorway and the A-road network were to be rebuilt. The country was to be transformed, with the motor-way network widened to ten, twelve or even fourteen lanes' (Bray *et al.*, 1995: 9). The government created more concern when it revealed its plans for new motorway boxes in the West Midlands and Greater Manchester and 'quasi-motorways' to be constructed, including the Home Counties East–West route and South Coast Expressway. In terms of the potential damage or destruction incurred by these projects English Nature calculated that 161 UK Sites of Specific Scientific Interest were threatened (these sites represent the finest examples of flora, fauna and geology), while English Heritage approximated that over 8000 key archaeological sites could be affected (Bray *et al.*, 1995: 9). John Adams, in *London's Green Spaces: What are They Worth?*, points to the government's classification of space, which rests on the key criterion of money: 'Open space does not generally command a high price because of restrictions as to its current and future planning use. The DOT's cost benefit analysis can only reflect monetary values', thus '[For the] DOT the cheapest place to build a motorway is through a public park' (Adams, 1989: 6).

Margaret Thatcher was not, however, the first to break the Roman monopoly in terms of both contemplating and implementing a large road scheme. Nor was the Iron Lady the first to use 'the road' as a means to colonize space and landscape. Yet this linkage between empire and road building, whether it is in Thatcher's or Major's Britain, in Nazi Germany under Dr Toft, or in Haussmann's redesign of Paris, does reveal some common motivations. Attempts to physically dominate the landscape via road schemes are inextricably linked to concepts of visual display: roads as an 'empire of the eyes' (Jukes, 1990: 247) and as 'a way to show power to both the internal and international spectator'. This idea of performance for the gaze of the spectator has been referred to as 'an arms race in road schemes' (Harwood and Hilborne et al., 1992: 5), an analogy that takes on both the competitive response between nations to road building and the violence of the state – particularly that of military mobility, thus making a correlation between 'the monumental, nationalism and militarism' (p. 5). A rather more sobering note for the practitioners and a note of hope for protesters illustrative of rearguard action is: 'Roads were practical monuments which reflected and celebrated the prestige of the British Empire and the achievements of the industrial revolution, at a time when both were beginning to wane' (p. 5).

In the context of the British roads programme of the 1980s and 1990s it is in the M25, the mythology of which is inextricably linked with the figure of Margaret Thatcher herself, that themes of imperialism reach a zenith. Not content with domination over the straight line, it was in the radical transformation of this London orbital road that Thatcher initiated her new project; the colonization of the circle. Thatcher herself referred to the extension of the M25 as a 'Scientific and technological hymn'; she used the unveiling ceremony to extend her own lesson in patriotism:

> When Mrs Thatcher opened the final section of the M25 in November 1986, she instructed the nation to rejoice at the splendid creation. For the Moaning Minnies there was a stern warning. She pointed out that she could, 'not stand those who carp and criticise when they ought to be congratulating a magnificent achievement and beating the drum for Britain all over the world'. Some media [the public were kept away from ceremony] viewed the road as communicating a different kind of lesson, one which incorporates the imagery of museology; 'There was no time for a golden age. The day it was finished, the M25 was already the road to hell, to ruin, to nowhere. There was never going to be a period of national pride and the kind sunny, whooshing traffic flows seen in architects' drawings. The M25 had already taken its proper place in Britain's Museum of Disappointment alongside the Barbican

Centre and Canary Wharf (coming soon, the Channel Tunnel): expensive, long-awaited constructions that have their finest hour well ahead of their actual arrival'.

(Parker, 1994: 5)

The latter reference to transport channels into Europe is illustrative of new incentives in road construction. The move towards European unity prompted a race in terms of massive road schemes across Europe and gives 'justification' (the government claims) to the British roads building scheme. The prosperity of the 'golden triangle' of Germany fuelled not only competition but the Europhobia voiced by some sections within the Conservative party. The Little Englanders fear that the country's position on the geographical periphery would mean the nation would be bypassed if it didn't start creating bypasses of its own.

Yet road building is not to be thought of as being an exclusive obsession of the Napoleons, the Hitlers and Thatchers of this world. Nor have road programmes been the particular brain children of the political right. The M25 has been talked about since 1905 (Harwood and Hilborne, 1992: 7); the plans for the M25 were first published in 1944 'as part of a gloriously eco-murderous scheme – the Abercrombie Plan', and it was 'formally blessed and christened in 1975 by the then Labour Transport Secretary, John Gilbert' (Parker, 1994: 5). Indeed, one of the major problems revealed by road protesters, including ALARM UK, the national antiroad network group, is the lack of support from the main political parties in Britain: 'in the mid-1980s, none of the three principal British parties – the Conservatives, Labour, and the Liberal Democrats – were comfortable with the central demand of the protest movement: to switch resources from road-building to more sustainable modes of transport' (Bray et al., 1995: 9). It is road-building rather than transport planning that has 'dominated political policies for the last thirty years' (Bray et al., 1995: 9).

The particular context of 1980s road building is nevertheless significant and gives meaning to the road protests. The Thatcher road 'empire' was in fact a self-fulfilling prophecy. When placed in the context of related policies we can see how the 'need' for roads was being manufactured, notably via 'the positive encouragement of out-of-town retail and recreational developments, along with business parks' (Bray et al., 1995: 7). That which Thatcher claimed as a 'success' anti-road lobby groups have decried and have pointed to the fact that the ascendancy of the car culture was symptomatic of the whole ethos of Thatcherite Britain during the 1980s. 'Many people were making fast money in the free market world of Thatcherism; rates of car and home ownership were rising rapidly'; 'there was also increasing homelessness, severe unemployment and environmental destruction. Furthermore, government was becoming unresponsive to public opinion and was (deliberately) running down public services – health, education and transport' (Bray et al., 1995: 7). In the 1980s the amount of traffic doubled. The Department of Transport, the government department responsible for the roads programme, predicted that traffic would grow by between 83 per cent and 142 per cent by 2025.

Our theme of colonization operates at yet another level and introduces an important sub-plot in our story of domination and resistance. The Conservative government abolished in 1986 the Greater London Council (GLC) and appropriated certain of its functions; a key project pursued by the new regime was the London Assessment Study of 1988. Protesters in the London area prevented this latter road building scheme for the capital from being implemented, and it is here the roots of protest which were to grow at Claremont can be found. The occupation of Claremont Road was the largest of a series of direct action campaigns (see Table 23.1) of the No M11 Protests, which grew up in response to the Department of Transport's (DOT) plans to develop a 3.5 mile link road through the Wanstead and Leytonstone area in East London. This road would connect the M11 motorway in Essex with the Blackwall Tunnel and take the M11 East Anglia to London road further into inner London. To build it will mean the destruction of 350 homes and three green spaces, and an estimated 25 per cent increase in traffic through nearby Hackney. The aim of this project is to save 8 minutes of commuter time from Essex and Hertfordshire and it will cost an estimated £230–£350 million.

Placed in its context the link road project is just one small part of the DOT's billion-pound road building programme. Conversely the No M11 Link Road Campaign is just one of an estimated 200 anti-road campaigns operating nationally and can be placed in the context of similar high-profile peaceful protests at Twyford Down, Oxleas Wood, Newcastle, Norfolk, North Wales, Skye, Manchester, Preston, Woodstock, Hereford Pollock and Newbury. The campaign at Claremont could ultimately be regarded as a 'defeat' (the houses have been destroyed, the link road is currently being constructed). Yet as we can see, the governmental perspective and that of the protesters is similarly polarized on this issue as much as any other:

> Our secret truth: however hard we fought we knew that everything would end in rubble. Knowing this, and willing it at the same time is what made us indestructible. If they don't evict us, we win, if they do evict us, we win; not indifference to the real value of the houses, not a simple stoicism; . . . Knowing what the future is gave us the strength to approach the eviction as a game. An elaborate game, one which we had carefully prepared, a game to unveil power and to make visible real issues.
>
> (McLeish, 1994: 21)

Table 23.1   Direct action campaigns against the M11 link road

December 1993	Sweet Chestnut tree (*c*.1740), George Green, Wanstead. It took police 9 hours to remove protestors, some of whom were camped in a tree-house, and to cut down the tree with a JCB. Cost: £10,000
February 1994	Wanstonia, 2–10 Cambridge Park and 106 Eastern Avenue, E11, declared an independent republic by protestors, who handed out passports. The Battle of Wanstonia took *c*.700 police, 200 security guards and 40 bailiffs to evict 3 houses. Cost: £200,00
March 1994	Wanstonia Rising, the brief occupation and eviction of an empty sweet shop near Wanstead tube station
October 1994	State of Euphoria, the occupation and eviction of 3 houses near Leytonstone tube station
June 1994	State of Leytonstonia, a bender site and micro-forest. Made its own declaration of independence. Evicted twice before it was destroyed
November 1993	Claremont Road, occupation of a whole street of over 30 houses begins. Summer 1994 Claremont transforms into a 'festival of resistance'
26 November	The siege of Claremont begins at 2 p.m. Protestors create the 100ft Leaning Tower of Leyton
1 December 1994	At 7 a.m. Phil Mcleish is the last person to leave the Tower and the Claremont site. Cost: £6 million, with 500 protestors, 300 bailiffs, 700 police and 400 security guards involved

Note: Future M11 link developments will affect Dyers Hall Road, Fillebrook Road, Colville Road, Green Grove. The protest continues at Gordon Street, Fillebrook Road and the Green Man roundabout

Locations and times

Materials of resistance: home

> I ask, 'why must they pull the houses down for one more roadway and
> break up a lovely community like ours and cause old people to fear for
> the future? There is very little harmony in the world today so why
> destroy it when we have it?'
>
> > (Evidence of 'house-holder', Leyton, E11, at Public Enquiry into
> > compulsory purchase for the M11 Link Road, December 1989,
> > in Anon, 1994: 7)

It was at 'home' that I met Dolly Watson and Emma, a Dongas. Emma, was
one of the 'incomers' (Dongas is the name used by those who participated in
the Twyford Down protests against the extension to the M3 motorway. The
term also refers to the system of ancient gullies at the Twyford site); Emma
came to inhabit, to dwell, to curate, to name the space for a finite period of
time. She used the street with its material culture as a giant exhibition (one
more holistic and personal than the Art House) from which she deconstructed
for me the iconography of the New Age, the runic symbols and the dragon
signs, and in so doing defined her own cosmology. Her identity was created
and recreated in this place. This identity is linked to that which was *recently
manufactured* in the space, while located in some 'ancient' past.

Dolly Watson, on the other hand, 93 years old and a lifelong 'resident' of
Claremont, showed that life at Claremont was not without its tensions. She
was having a bad day. Her back was hurting. She asked me if I could ask some
of the protesters to stop their dogs from barking. Later, speaking about the
same group of people, she told the press, 'If I were queen I would knight them
all'. Dolly had resisted leaving her 'home'. Her identity had been created and
recreated over 83 years, referenced inextricably to the 'authentic' collection
of bricks and mortar, the Victorian terrace houses built as working-class
dwellings. Dolly's 'everyday' / 'ordinary' experience of 'home' was located in
the pre-compulsory purchase order of things. The governmental threat of
change violated this concept of 'home' and of the human dignity of the people
living there. Thus both physical and identity space were under threat. In
August 1994 Dolly went into hospital and was later moved, unwillingly, into
residential care.

In Emma's and Dolly's personal biographies are housed both the diversity
and the commonality of lifestyles and attitudes towards 'place' expressed in
the concept and reality of 'home'. Often competing, often complementary
ideas of conservation, preservation and of the ephemeral and of the transient
are made more ambiguous, operating and fluctuating between the poles of
materiality and 'belief-systems' / ideologies. Claremont Road, in its altered
state as 'festival of resistance', heightened the meaning of 'home' – exposed it,

celebrated it, parodied it and lived it. The critique was not so flippant as to forget the 350 houses that were to be lost in the evictions, nor the 'residents' for whom the experience of movement proved traumatic (several elderly resisters died during this period). Nor did the Claremont occupation devalue the very real issue of homelessness. An estimated 1000 were dispossessed of their property as a result of the M11 link road scheme. The eviction of Claremont Road marked the 'end' of the series of protests of the No M11 Roads Campaign and the final coordinate of this particular map of resistance. The 'home' of resistance was now a dispersed map: an alternative to that posed by the government.

The first position on the map was Wanstead Environmental Centre (WEC); 'A disorganized organizational headquarters' is how one protester described this former (abandoned) piano shop in Wanstead High Street. Following the evictions at Claremont Road the WEC functioned as both an information network and a squat for those taking part in the M11 protests. WEC was the home of, amongst others, John and Simon. They, like the other inhabitants, were 'young' protesters (the age range at WEC was between 20 and 35 years).

Interviews here were informal, held in groups and peppered with inter-jections. Narratives tended to be autobiographical with a focus upon lifestyles. While *all* protesters spoke of some experience of displacement, interviewees at the WEC spoke of this displacement or process of radicalization/ politicization as being more pronounced; many told of a 'turning point', or an 'in-between stage' from which they felt they 'had to make a choice' to embrace an alternative lifestyle. For some this took the form of a 'conversion-like' experience, while for others it was a slow drift away from a 'society that doesn't care' (in many cases a reaction to adverse economic circumstance: unemployment, poverty, hopelessness). The Criminal Justice Act (CJA) also featured as a catalyst in this process. The clauses in the CJA that particularly affect anti-roads groups are those which define new *criminal* offences of 'aggra-vated trespass' and 'trespassory assembly'. (The government transforms the civil disobedience campaign into the criminal.) What united this otherwise diverse group was the subsequent embrace of the road protest movement as part of this new way of life (their 'everyday experience'/'ordinary life'), while this itself was placed in a wider context of 'ecological issues' and various expressions of 'spirituality', or 'energy' as it was often termed. For the major-ity this resulted in a move away from 'home' and a reaction against 'material possessions'.

It was from jam-jars that Mick Roberts, a 56-year-old former builder, and I sipped our tea. The location was The Stables, Wanstead, with its backdrop of benders and deregulated ambulances now serving as protesters' homes. My initial request for an interview was refused on the basis that, 'Claremont is done with, over, finished. We need to move on now.' In fact Mick lost everything at Claremont; he was one of the long-term residents who was served with a compulsory eviction order. Mick not only chose to stay but was responsible for inviting protesters (including the Dongas from Twyford) to join him and for inspiring much of the artistic creativity that went on. He has since adopted the lifestyle of a protester.

Jam-jar empty I was about to leave when we were joined by Bill, who was also at Claremont and currently lived in one of the decommissioned ambulances. It was the problematic of the ephemeral and the permanent (the dilemma of a group who sacrificed their own material culture for the 'greater' preservation of a tree, a home, an idea) that dominated this interview and which caused dissension between Mick and Bill. Mick spoke of the 'exhausting process of making and losing' which campaigners experience. While this 'loss' was traumatic, Mick's coping strategy was his commitment to the idea and practice of the 'disposability' of material culture and his search for spiritual (non-material) sustainability and continuity in the notion of modernity. Bill, looking more to the long term, felt that the spirit of Claremont should be preserved: 'we don't want commemoration or monuments [or to be] a case-study but a working model.'

It was tea, biscuits and best china when I visited the home of John and Moira Garton. Both in their 70s and grandparents, the Gartons spoke of 'playing the middle-class card' for the press while also participating in some of the more potentially dangerous occupation and non-violent direct action at Wanstonia and Claremont. John, a former teacher who served in the Royal Air Force during the Second World War, constructed his 'story' of the M11 protests as a series of nail-biting and gripping feats of bravery, all tinged with humour and irony. His narrative was framed in local history (very much linked to his own notion of home) rather than autobiography, although his own part in these adventures did gradually emerge triumphant! John's finest hour came when the protesters visited Michael Howard's *home* in Kent (Howard was the government minister responsible for the introduction of the Criminal Justice Act) in November 1994; 'We put him on trial at his own home, I had the great pleasure of acting as judge, finding him guilty, sentencing him to death but releasing him on grounds of insanity.'

Moira Garton, the quieter of the two, supplied John's narrative with the correct times and dates and with persons omitted. In one of her few autobiographical comments she referred to her own radical middle-class upbringing (her parents were imprisoned for their views on pacifism) as the inspiration for her to 'protest when I believe that that something is wrong.'

A few streets away lives Aileen Brown-Lie, who described herself as 'a 46-year-old housewife and mother of five'. Aileen states that she became the media choice because, 'I'm middle-class, I have a doubled-barrelled name and my husband works in the City'. A life-long resident of Wanstead, her narrative was one of dissatisfaction with the present government and 1990s politics. She was keen to discuss the 'contradictions' (as she defined them) of her current lifestyle – the house, the car, the guard dogs, the daughter at private school – but was able to transcend these surroundings to express a certain nostalgia for the political culture of the 1960s.

Joining Crow the Shaman (a former electrician) and Green Dave the Anarchist (a former car-mechanic) around the camp-fire in a small corner of Epping Forest is about the closest one can get to meeting with the noble savage without travelling outside Zone 4 of the city's underground system. A totem-pole, complete with a Leo's Supermarket shopping trolley on top, was perhaps a sign of the cultural and spiritual eclecticism of late-modernity. Here beneath the tree houses and beside the camp-fire I sought enlightenment. I came to find out more about the ideologies and the visions that underpinned the protesters' belief-systems. The subject of 'role-models' surfaced here (a reference to the iconography of Claremont). The protesters' apostolic succession was eclectic. These people saw themselves as the inheritors of a tradition that included Jesus (a former carpenter), Gaia, the Celts, the Earth, the red Indians, the Diggers, the Levellers, Kropotkin, William Morris, Martin Luther King, Gandhi, the Women of Greenham Common and David Icke (a former sports commentator, high-profile Green Party member and recently revealed prophet).

What did emerge from interviews held here was the mingling of philosophies: Romanticism, paganism, New Age mysticism with a touch of millenarianism and *fin de siècle* spirit. The vision, like that of the Wanstead residents, was global in terms of 'ecological vision', but betrayed a hankering for some pastoral or at least pre-industrial 'tradition'. Even the concept of resurrecting the 'Olde Englande' tribes contains elements of a nationalist agenda. Party politics was treated with disdain; some described themselves as 'apolitical' with their motivations based upon 'connecting with nature'. As I left the space I glanced across at more manicured parts of Epping Forest. I wondered how this vision of protest registered with the surrounding urban populace of London's East End? Driving here on a hot Sunday afternoon to feed the ducks was quite another vision of the landscape.

Transpositions

Rituals of resistance

> Epic drama is not very common in modern life. Modern life is mostly banal . . . An experience at the Claremont eviction reminds participants, and the public, that the issues are not just arcane matters for technocrats, they are dramatic choices for ordinary people.

> (McLeish, 1994: 41)

After many false alarms it began. The eviction commenced. The rituals of resistance thus accelerated; they become 'extra-ordinary'. The whole street transformed. Claremont Road was layer upon layer of material resistance. Phil McLeish, the last protester to be moved from the Claremont site, comments:

> Months of labour went into its preparation. Barricades, bunkers, towers, nets, tree houses, lock-ons, the tunnel . . . all energy stored and stockpiled for that final moment, everything tuned for maximum intensity during that one hundred hour explosion. I remember waiting on the tower for the police to arrive, dancing to 'The Prodigy' booming out at full volume. The moment there was a roar of anticipatory, adrenaline fuelled cheers.
>
> (McLeish, 1994: 41)

> The event, usually referred to in terms of a 'siege' or a 'battle', began at 2pm on Monday November 28th. It was announced by the arrival of both riot police and bailiffs. Dolly's home was the first to be destroyed. The art house was now the front line barricade; 'Its sacrifice as a gallery – the ground floor was filled with rubble and the feet of the Tower came through the roof – upset some people who wanted to leave it pristine to shame the bailiffs and demolition men'.
>
> (McLeish, 1994: 38)

Let us now be transported to the theatre of action. I will step back through space and time and watch the scene as I did on a (very) cold winter's day, the ultimate voyeur of the spectator of transformation. I will let those who have been my guides throughout the piece perform. To remember Claremont (the Art House), to take secret pathways of memory to link locates, to recreate identities, to recount history, to expound philosophy, to engage in remembrance. A finale?

'I sit and look out'

'Memories'

Bill, The Stables:

> We all joined together, the campaign was a series of occupations and evictions with different focal points; the Chestnut Tree with its tree-house declared an official dwelling, then Cambridge Park (which this time the declaration was as the Independent State of Wanstonia – we gave out passports!). Followed briefly by

Wanstonia Rising, then to Euphoria, Leytonstonia. The big one was Claremont. Strategically it was perfect. A whole street to defend, to keep as a unit and to barricade with art and sculpture.

Roger Geffen, Reclaim the Streets:

> At Claremont Road there was a tension between the art work and the real need to barricade. The sculptures were made from rubbish with no attempt to explain them; whole rooms, domestic interiors, were recreated in the middle of the street. I think it was about breaking down the barriers between private and communal space and the break-down of our society due to car culture. The idea of the segregation and seclusion of modern life where we all live in our separate boxes. The house as box, the car as box, the office as box, the coffin as box and the movement from one to the other. At Claremont and in the Reclaim the Streets project we have the idea of the road as a communal space not a place to hurtle down in your little box.

Sheila Freeman, Friends of the Earth:

> The Art House was interesting as it emphasized the devastating effect the Link Road would have. It was art with a message showing how peoples' lives have been disturbed. One of the objects in the Art House was a knife stuck into a wall; a kitchen knife with blood dripping down from it. Very symbolic when you remember the deaths . . . It was poignant, especially when you remember that several old ladies had died after the evictions because they found it so traumatic.

'Not meagre latent boughs alone'

John Garton, Wanstead 'resident':

> The Great Sweet Chestnut Tree had stood there since Sheridan lived at the top of the High Street and Tom Hood walked down to the House. It was part and parcel of Wanstead's history and to see it doomed was terrifying . . . The only comparison I can make is watching news reels of Nazis smashing down Jewish areas. I have never seen anything like it . . . It was a running fight, it was quite horrible, and from that moment on Moira and I thought – if this is what we have got, we are in 101 percent.

'Tears'

Moira Garton, Wanstead 'resident':

> Quite elderly residents were punched and kicked in the face [at the
> Sweet Chestnut Tree] or knocked to the ground and kicked, even-
> tually the local police were shouting at them [the bailiffs] to stop.
> In fact there is a story that the local police were sitting in a
> van down a side-street actually crying – because this is actually a
> peaceful area and this was messing things up completely for their
> relationship with the local people.

'A hand mirror'

Aileen Brown-lie, Wanstead 'resident':

> I saw the police in a very different light; [it was] brought home to
> me that these were not police – they were political armies really.

'I hear it was charged against me'

Andy, WEC:

> It [the CJA] has brought together more groups than ever before –
> in the last 30 to 40 years – maybe longer. Groups which would
> never have worked together; environmentalists, squatters, ravers,
> ramblers and people from different backgrounds. They can see that
> it includes issues such as access to land, peoples' rights to certain
> lifestyles, to ways of living, the right to protest in this so-called
> democracy and these are all being eroded.

'For you O democracy'

Moira:

> Thatcherian politics have taught people to keep their heads down –
> as the people near the gas-chambers did in the last war.

'Are you the new person drawn to me?'

John.

> You find something [an 'alternative life'] which is better than that
> you have got. Usually you spend a while between the two [lives] —
> when you are still in the old while visiting the new. For a while you
> struggle between the two. After a while you decide to go full-term
> in the alternative lifestyle and then you find out that the stuff you
> give up is given back to you and more . . . The main thing is guilt
> when you are first unemployed; the guilt of feeling inadequate, i.e.
> [you think] you should get a job and function in society. Then I
> found that I could still function, that I could still have a life, an even
> better life. You are free to use your skills and talents in these
> communities — for the benefit of that community. A community
> which is international. I was homeless for a time but now I have
> never had so many offers of a place to stay . . . I shall never be
> homeless again.

Green Dave, Green Man Camp:

> Ironically enough my trade is as a panel-beater and mechanic. So I
> was repairing cars and coming home and watching [environmental
> programmes] on TV; I'd turn it on and see all the destruction. I
> talked *to* another mechanic on my dinner break; he said, 'Look,
> don't just complain, do something about it'. I thought the only
> thing you could do was to get into party politics. I had no money
> and virtually no education; all the things you need to get into party
> politics . . . I went through two years of revelation. I could
> only describe it as revelation after revelation! Every day I would
> wake up discovering something else. Like a light bulb that lights
> up, and suddenly, everything makes sense. You can feel your
> head going click, click, click. Just about everyone I have talked to
> has been through the same thing. It's like an awakening, you get
> born again, it's like you were asleep. For some it is almost insanity
> when they realize how different the world is to what they thought
> *it* was.

'Gods'

Sheila:

> At Claremont there were many images of the Goddess and other
> Neo-Pagan icons. This was really icons of different belief-systems
> to tap into but is not a fixed one. It's not like everyone believes in
> it all — it's an idea of some kind of respect for the earth, an
> emotional attachment.

John:

> Spirituality is to do with life, the sacredness of life. It is not [really]
> religion but we have images of gooddesses and green men. It's
> about accepting life as sacred. It is about 'energy'.

'Faces'

Crow:

> I'm a shaman. We are all really one tribe — call them 'isms',
> shaman or road protesters, People of the Earth . . . We are one
> tribe. One tribe!

Charlie, Green Man Camp:

> Someone pointed out that I was the only woman on this camp. I
> hadn't really noticed. But women get the worst treatment from
> the Tactical Support Group.

'The prairie grass dividing'

Aileen:

> This road is not a typical community. It is a very Tory area around
> here as you can imagine. The street has some big houses and can be
> very insular. It is also a very divided place. Just as the miner's strike
> divided families, villages and streets, the [planned link] road has
> done the same thing with Wanstead residents.

'Halcyon days'

John:

> We have some role-models in the sense that modern society has lost its way and has lost a lot of the old communal, creative, arty things like the way in which a village people had culture . . . a lot of times this has gone by the wayside. We respect the way it was before, when the culture was really important. You know when festivals, gatherings, travelling, was really important. It's a freedom. It's about feeding yourself and expressing things about your culture. Also of visiting other groups. Cities are not really communal.

Crow:

> I would be happy if we could take our own land, our common land. I should be able to take this land and do what I want with it. We don't need people telling us how to do things. Things should just run naturally, on their own, we just want to be able to do it ourselves.

Aileen:

> Wanstead used to be a green oasis at the end of the East End . . . and people believe it will suddenly be like that again [with the M11 link].

'A Broadway pageant'

Bill:

> Sometimes the whole thing gets to be like theatre, especially at Claremont, where the art and sculptures were like props. We had puppet shows, parties and fancy dress . . . One day a film crew came with films of civil disobedience campaigns and projected them onto the wall. Excellent.

Aileen:

> [At Claremont] Some of the men would wear skirts. One wore outlandish, glittery short shirts; we found it funny and if people were laughing it is harder for the police to cope.

Bill:

> At the Siege of Claremont local people brought food but the police refused to let it through. People who lived in the surrounding area also had to have passes to get to their own home because they roped the area off.

'Outlines for a tomb'

John Garton:

> We had our call out for Claremont Road [the Gartons barricaded themselves into a second floor room]. It was pitch black day and night and all we had were night-lights and candles. For a while we had communication via a walkie-talkie; we only knew if it was day or night by looking through a few chinks in our armour-plated window. It was rather like being in a pyramid or something and being unearthed by an archaeologist. It was very funny when they [the bailiffs] did get through. A strange black face appeared through the chimney breast; probably he couldn't see a thing, yet we were fully used to the dark. An African Howard Carter! [laughs].

'O Captain! My Captain!'

John Garton:

> When Phil [McLeish, the last protester to leave Claremont] came down from the Tower [after 4 days] everyone was cheering at his bravery . . . he said to me, 'I fell asleep!' [laughs]. I have great respect for him and for all those who showed such courage.

Simon:

> The road-protest movement is not a culture of heroes.

'Recorders years hence'

Andy:

> The media was interested initially in human interest stories, the idea of the middle-class standing side-by-side with eco-warriors, e.g. so let's forget about the real issues! They talk about it [the campaign] in retrospect when it is safe for the media to use it. It's like being a painter [who] everyone ignores you until you are dead.

Mick:

> History shouldn't be kept in museums. Claremont is done with, over, finished; some things should be disposable so we can move on. There are new campaigns now.

Bill:

> We don't want commemoration or monuments, although it would be good to have our archives kept safe. We don't want to be seen as a case-study but as a working model.

'Spirit that form'd this scene'

John Garton:

> I am proud of this action and as long as it goes on I want to be involved.

Mick:

> It has given me a lot of faith in young people, their visions and in the modern, in the future.

Sheila:

> It was so empowering; when I think of the Tower and what we did! Wow! It's amazing! Even at the time we couldn't believe what we were doing!

'Songs of parting'

Simon:

> The campaign leaves a lasting impression on everyone involved or looking on. As long as you talk about it and people listen to each other, it gets bigger and bigger.

'Thou reader'

Crow:

> People who have seen all this can't forget it. It's impossible. And you are here aren't you, and you've listened to our stories? You'll tell other people about us won't you? That's a good thing, isn't it?

'World take good notice'

> 'We will not go away!'

Object in the Art House: Underwood typewriter. The sheet of paper in the carriage reads: 'Fillebrooke, Grove Green, Dyres Hall, Cambridge Gardens, Claremont, Colleville. Roads for living on, 350 strong homes for one hundred years, for one thousand people. They may go, but will never be forgotten. While we have hope, memory and truth, nothing can overcome us.' [Object: a single leaf in a glass case.]

'As I walk solitary'

Roots of resistance

The tree, the tower and the shaman offers an alternative collection and connection; the 'natural', the 'manufactured' and the 'human subject': situated, contextualized; an expression of an (albeit imperfect) pluralism of contact. A quest (never ending but constantly offering points of praxis) to make any subsequent 'manufacture' (written, oral, material, theatre, play) to connect landscape, spaces, people, things with a sense of time and of remembrance. Material culture as auto-critique has played its part.

Thinking back to my first contact with Claremont, my memory once again called up the image of the leaf in a glass cabinet. In this artefact I have been offered (at least) two competing visions (co-existent yet ambiguous) of possible futures; visions that crystallized into a dichotomy of despair and hope. In the first, the leaf represented a collector's Dodo-like 'specimen' of 'the past' – an absurd and redundant artefact. This vision functioned as a powerful moral comment insinuating how, in the wake of our contemporary culture's ambivalence to the environment, a future age may only be able to salvage small curiosities (a leaf) from the resultant destruction. The other possibility? A vision of the leaf as unicorn's horn; a reference to the search through time and space for the exotic, the mythical and the potentially transforming artefact. Here, in this 'inauthentic' parody of an inauthentic object of the 'irrational' past, we could at least place our hope in some 'magic' transcending current ambivalences and inspiring some belief in the power of the extraordinary to change our own everyday life.

Looking more closely still, I found the moment, like the visions and the object, had gone, had disappeared, was lost. I was left with the image of my own reflection in the glass. Yet the potential was there for more than simply holding a mirror to events. After listening to the voices of resistance (the oral history of my interviewees) I felt what needs to be transformed/sacrificed here is our uncritical notions of the pastoral (as the golden age/as utopia of the future) and of 'home' (to extend the category/to find alternatives; from all the points on the compass; north to south/from east to west). Trees can be home. Trees can grow in the urban as well as the rural. The potential to transform/to situate Claremont as a working (and replicable) model of *urban* resistance. To that end (or beginning) the leaf *is* (or can be) the 'journeyman [sic] of the stars' (Whitman, 1982: 57). And in this spirit, in this paper, in this resistance against historical amnesia it is taken/offered – shared – freely. . . . The rest, as they say . . . is myth.

'*Ages and ages returning at intervals*'

Myths of resistance

> Myths may both shape and be shaped by landscapes, not only localised and specific landscapes visible on the ground, but equally by archetypal landscapes imaginatively constituted from human experiences in the material world and represented in spoken and written words, poetry, painting, theatre or film.
>
> (Cosgrove, 1993: 297)

Crow, the Shaman told this to me as we sat by the camp-fire in the shadow of the Green Man:

> Long hundreds of years ago, before you or I were born, there was a small tribe living at the East End of a Great Town, at the Edge of a Great Forest. It was a fine clear day when the Big Tribe came armed with machines, to cut down the Ancient Great Sweet Chestnut Tree. People young and old wept as their 300-year-old friend was lost but continued to stand there in peace — amid the Violence of the Big Tribe — as the cold and the night came in. Declaring themselves a Republic and the naming of this place as Wanstonia only angered the Big Tribe, who then came in great numbers in strange livery to push the little people from their homes. The Big Tribe troubled the people no more moved out on to the neighbouring tribes settlement of Leytonstonia. Remembering their own fear and the injustice of the Big Tribe, the tribe of Wanstonia pledged their support. Thus the two small tribes met together. They then called up the magical peoples — the Dongas and the Dragons; tribes who came from nowhere and whose place was with nature. Even though they knew the Big Tribe would come — in celebration of what was and what could be — quickly and quietly the tribes dressed up the palace of Claremont in strange colours and decorated it with mystical symbols, splendid icons and mysterious idols. They created a sacred place of pilgrimage and made it loud with foreign drum beats, music and dance. Many came to visit and chose to stay. Even when the Big Tribe did come, the small tribes stayed to bear witness; they moved across rooftops, over great nets and through the air and secretly and silently under labyrinths in the earth. The small tribes — forced from their homes and barricades — built a Great Tower from which one could see for miles. As the Last Man was pulled down from this great height by the Big Tribe, he was suddenly blessed with vision, he saw why this had all happened. . . . It was The Coming of the Great Road — the straight line — by which the Big Tribe would complete their dominion over the whole land.

Crow then handed me a single leaf from the tree that he inhabited and defended — he then bade me take this to tell this story of the Tribes, the Trees and the Tower to the tribes of the New Ages that they may never forget the Time before the Great Road.

Acknowledgements

With many thanks to all those who agreed to be interviewed. To Sheila Freeman from Friends of the Earth for allowing me to use the 'M11 Archive' and to Margaret Glover for taking me to visit Claremont in the first place.

References

Adams, J.G.U. (1989) *London's Green Spaces: What are they Worth?* London: London Wildlife Trust/Friends of the Earth Publications.

Anon (1994) *Claremont Road E11: A Festival of Resistance.* A BE SEA – A Visual Paper, London: Sebastian Boyle Publishers.

Armstrong, M. (1994) 'The Art House Effect', *Guardian*, 25 June 1994: 28.

Bender, B. (ed.) (1993) *Landscape: Politics and Perspectives.* Providence, RI and Oxford: Berg.

Bray, J. *et al.* (1995) *Roadblock: How People Power is Wrecking the Roads Programme.* London: ALARM UK Publications.

Cosgrove, D. (1993) 'Landscapes and Myths, Gods and Humans', in B. Bender (ed.) *Landscape: Politics and Perspectives*, pp. 281–306. Providence, RI and Oxford: Berg.

Duncan, C. (1995) *Civilizing Rituals: Inside Public Art Museums.* London and New York: Routledge.

Harwood, R. and Hilborne, C. *et al.* (1992) *Ever Increasing Circles.* RSNC. London: The Wildlife Trusts Partnership.

Heller, A. (1984) *Everyday Life.* London: Verso.

Jordan, J. (1994) in *Claremont Road E11: A Festival of Resistance.* A BE SEA – A Visual Paper, 38. London: Sebastian Boyle Publishers.

Jukes, P. (1990) *A Shout in the Street.* London: Faber and Faber.

Lefevbre, H. (1991) *Critique of Everyday Life: Part 1.* London and New York: Routledge.

McLeish, P. (1994) in *Claremont Road E11: A Festival of Resistance.* A BE SEA – A Visual Paper. London: Sebastian Boyle Publishers.

Moore, S. (1994) 'Mooreover', *Guardian*, 20 May 1994: 15.

Parker, I. (1994) 'Lost in Ever-Increasing Circles', *Independent*, 13 March 1994: 5.

Pearce, S.M. (1992) *Museums, Objects and Collections: A Cultural Study.* Leicester: Leicester University Press.

Popham, P. (1994) 'Eviction By Any Means Necessary', *Independent*, 24 April 1994: 12.

Relph, E. (1976) *Place and Placelessness.* London: Pion.

Relph, E. (1987) *The Modern Urban Landscape.* London: Croom Helm.

Thomas, J. (1993) 'The Politics of Vision and the Archaeologies of Landscape', in B. Bender (ed.) *Landscape: Politics and Perspectives*, pp. 19–48. Providence, RI and Oxford: Berg.

Tilley, C. (1994) *The Phenomenology of Landscape: Places, Paths and Monuments*. Oxford: Berg.

Whitman, Walt (1982) *Song of Myself*. Oxford: Oxford Classics.

Wright, P. (1985) *On Living in an Old Country: The National Past in Contemporary Britain*. London: Verso.

Chapter 24

Robert J. Wallis

WAKING ANCESTOR SPIRITS
Neo-shamanic engagements with archaeology

[T]he Pagan renaissance is obvious. Bookstores are full of books on the ancient native religions. In Great Britain, you cannot avoid the Pagan network. They even have university professors who are openly Pagan. In Iceland, Paganism became an official religion in 1973. Everywhere in Europe . . . [w]itness the return of the Druids, the shamans and the priests of the Gods.

(Christopher Gerard, cited by Henry 1999: 3)

[W]e moderns have nothing whatsoever of our own; only by replenishing and cramming ourselves with the ages, customs, arts, philosophies, religions, discoveries of others do we become anything worthy of notice.

(Nietzsche 1983 [1874]: 79, cited by Jakobsen 1999: 147–8)

Introduction

THE SUBJECT OF THIS CHAPTER contrasts markedly with other contributions to this volume. Rather than exploring shamanisms of the past, I discuss contemporary – neo-shamanic – readings of those shamanisms. Neo-shamanism is a spiritual path among Westerners that utilises aspects of indigenous shamanism and representations of shamanism in the past, for personal and communal spiritual empowerment. This may sound like quite an *interesting* subject, but hardly *central* to the concerns of an 'archaeology of shamanism'. However, I seriously question the view that dismisses neo-shamanic interactions with archaeology as simply 'fringe' or 'eccentric'. Specific instances, from rituals and protests at archaeological sites to reconstructions of Viking and Celtic 'shamanism', require that archaeologists are aware of and involved with the political and ethical sensitivities of neo-shamanism. More than an afterthought, an 'add-on', supplemental to the main area of discussion, neo-shamanism must be taken seriously. And rather than beginning with shamanism in the past, an archaeology of shamanism necessarily begins with neo-shamanism, in the present.

Autoarchaeology

I came to this study as a trained archaeologist, but also with a personal involvement in neo-shamanism. This has created many tensions for me, tensions that I am forced to resolve on a day-to-day basis. Most of all, my 'coming out' as a so-called 'neo-shaman' is controversial. But where conventional anthropologists might promptly reject my ethnography based on my being 'native', recent movements in ethnography confront the fallacy of the insider–outsider dichotomy (see, for example, papers in Young and Goulet 1994). This fledgling 'experiential anthropology' challenges those anthropologists concerned with going native to alter their view. Their fear is a colonialist hangover, a fear of descent into 'savagery'. Experiential anthropology deconstructs the paralogism of absolute 'objectivity' and 'detachment', and replaces them with the nuanced understandings the 'insider's' view can bring. In challenging the impasse of going native, my theoretical and methodological considerations may be broadly characterised as 'post-modern', traversing specific concepts of alternative archaeologies (see, for example, Denning 1999), post-colonial discourse (see, for example, Ashcroft et al. 1998), queer theory (see, for example, Dowson 1998), and multi-sited ethnography (Marcus 1995). These ideas coalesce into what I call an 'autoarchaeology' in which self-reflexively considering and taking into account our own socio-political locations and motivations is crucial to understanding the past, to 'queering' archaeology (Wallis 2000).

As an autoarchaeologist I am being up-front about my own standpoint. If, as an archaeologist, I were to explore neo-shamanism without acknowledging my own involvement, or if, with an active role in neo-shamanism I downplayed my archaeological training, I would be compromising my integrity in both these 'worlds'. Autoarchaeology facilitates an ongoing addressing and redressing of my own partiality, my own perspective, in a politically explicit way that does not claim dubious credentials of objectivity and impartiality. Indeed, rather than threatening my academic credentials, I think they would be seriously open to question if I ignored or left unsaid my experiential, 'insider' approach for fear of ostracism. My intention is that such political explicitness actually promises a far more open-minded discussion. In making explicit my own positionality however, I in no way wish to imply that I have a moral high ground over other researchers, since my work is simply one way of telling. My aim is to get people who may currently think neo-shamanism has nothing to do with them, to think again, and to thereby open up dialogue between the disparate interest groups.

Neo-shamanism and contemporary Paganism

Archaeology has yet to recognise the implications neo-shamanism has for its ideas and subjects of study. Archaeologists tend to dismiss neo-shamanism as 'fringe' and regard the New Age, Paganism, and neo-shamanism – as with all alternative archaeology – negatively (but see Finn 1997; Denning 1999). This neglect of research is unprecedented and does not reflect an insignificant research area. Neo-shamanic engagement with the past is considerable and accelerating, thereby implicating and requiring the attentions of archaeologists. Neo-shamans approaching shamanisms in the past are most often contemporary Pagans, who fall into three categories (in order of popularity): Wicca (contemporary witchcraft), Druidry and Heathenry. Wicca (derived from the Anglo-Saxon *wicca*, possibly meaning witch) is an initiatory religion in which practitioners revere divinity in nature as manifest in the polarity of a goddess and god (with female often privileged over male). It has been considerably influenced by shamanism, for mention of it appears in many core texts (see, for example, Farrar and Farrar 1984; Starhawk 1989). Some Wiccans even term their religion 'Shamanic Wicca', 'Shamanic Craft' and 'Wiccan-shamanism' (see, for example, Adler 1986: 430–4; Luhrmann 1989: 134, 329). Practices such as inducing trance, working magic, divination, interacting with spirits and animal familiars, and healing via supernatural means, are certainly reminiscent of many shamanistic practices.[1] Of interest to archaeology is the way in which Wicca often claims descent from prehistoric European shamanisms. This idea was popularised in the first part of the last century by Margaret Murray whose first book *The Witch Cult in Western Europe* (1921) argued 'the victims of the early modern witch trials had been practitioners of a surviving pagan religion' (Hutton 1999: 194–5). Her second contribution, *The God of the Witches* (1933), 'asserted the doctrine that the horned god of the greenwood had been the oldest deity known to humans, and traced his worship across Europe and the Near East, from the Old Stone Age to the seventeenth century' (Hutton 1999: 196).

The more feminist and goddess-oriented branches of Wicca, by virtue of a common ancestry, in many ways resonate with the Goddess movement. Goddess spirituality has been heavily influenced by the work of Marija Gimbutas (see, for example, Gimbutas 1974), for whom the famous Turkish site of Catal Hüyük is a goddess site *par excellence* (see, for example, Jencson 1989; Meskell 1995: Hutton 1997). The current engagements between adherents to Goddess spirituality and archaeologists there are somewhat strained, due to conflicting approaches and interpretations. Despite Hodder's claims for a self-reflexive archaeological process at the site that accommodates both archaeological strategies and alternative goddess views (see, for example, Hodder's website: http://catal.arch.cam.ac.uk/ [accessed 17 August 2000]), other archaeologists see the practice being far removed from the ideal (see, for example, Hassan 1997).

Indeed, Meskell argues that the differences between Pagans and academics are so fundamental that there is little room for fruitful negotiation (Meskell 1999). Of course this realisation should not promote avoidance of the issues, and as I shall demonstrate, there are various instances where productive dialogues have flourished. It is interesting to note at this juncture that Gimbutas was not the first to suggest Goddess interpretations of archaeological data. Hutton suggests the most obvious precedents were Margaret Murray who, 'whole-heartedly endorsed the idea that the prehistoric European and Mediterranean world had worshipped a single supreme female deity' (Hutton 1999: 273), and Jacquetta Hawkes who portrayed Neolithic European communities as living in harmony with the earth and worshipping a single mother-goddess that personified nature (Hutton 1999: 278–9). Hutton (1999: 280) goes on to point out that such figure-heading archaeologists as O.G.S. Crawford, Vere Gordon Childe and Glyn Daniel declared 'their belief in the veneration of a single female deity by New Stone Age cultures' (see, for example, Crawford 1957; Childe 1958; Daniel 1958). Clearly, while some archaeologists today may do their best to forget it, their predecessors are strange but intimate bedfellows with neo-shamanic approaches to the past, a past that cannot be ignored because of its repercussions in the present.

Druidry is a case in point. It is perhaps, after Wicca, the second most popular branch of contemporary Paganism in Britain today. As is well known, Druids are inspired by the Iron Age druids and all things 'Celtic' that are perceived to relate to them, from medieval and romantic literature, to archaeology and the legacy of early antiquarians such as William Stukeley, a.k.a. 'Archdruid Chyndonax' (Sebastion 1990: 97–8). A number of authors consider the relations between druids past and Druids present (see, for example, Piggott 1968; Green 1997; Jones 1998), but while Modern Druids endure as an object of ridicule among most archaeologists, the negative stereotypes are transforming. The idea that Druids claim descent from ancient Iron Age orders, for instance, is increasingly being replaced – among both Druids and academics – by a recognition that Druidry is very much a tradition situated in the modern era (see, for example, Harvey 1997). Even so, its antiquity is at least as old as archaeology (Hutton 1997) and the two are indeed, 'blood brothers' (Sebastion 2000).

Like Wicca and Goddess spirituality, Druidry is markedly influenced by shamanism. This is particularly evident in the work of John Matthews who interprets the medieval Welsh manuscripts attributed to the Bard Taliesin according to shape-shifting and other 'Celtic' shamanistic metaphors (see, for example, Matthews 1991). These interpretations are controversial (see, for example, Jones 1998), since the poems' reliability and chronology is notoriously problematic (see, for example, Hutton 1991) and juxtaposition of the terms Celtic and Shaman appears anachronistic. It is neo-shamanic representations of the past such as this, however, that usurp academic publications in the popular realm. While Matthews claims scholarly objectivity, other Druids, such as Tim Sebastion of the Secular Order of Druids (SOD), are unashamedly romantic (see, for example, Sebastion 1990). He is a shield knight of the Loyal Arthurian Warband and is, like his liege King Arthur Pendragon, 'accepted as the reincarnation of one of the Knights of the Round Table' (Sebastion 2000). The aims of these Druids for the future of archaeological sites are often highly pragmatic, such as the Solstice Project's plans to reconstruct Avebury's Sanctuary and so employ the local unemployed and detract attention away from Stonehenge as a festival site (Sebastion 2000). Indeed where ancient sites, especially Stonehenge, are concerned, the Druids are increasingly being viewed as equals by archaeologists (and the heritage managers) (see, for example, Bender 1998).

The presence of neo-shamanism in Druidry is also made clear by my discussions with Philip 'Greywolf' Shallcrass (Joint-Chief of the British Druid Order). Not only does Greywolf claim to interact with spirits and a spirit world for healing and empowerment (as shamans do), and to have been 'chosen' by them (rather than he choosing to communicate with them, as is typical of most neo-shamans), but he also reconstructs 'native British' sweat lodges (for an archaeological reconstruction, see Barfield and Hodder 1987) and conducts rituals at ancient sites including Stonehenge and Avebury [. . .]. He is also heavily involved in negotiations with English Heritage over access to Stonehenge and, more controversially, the reburial of skeletal remains likely to be excavated during the Stonehenge Management Plan (Wallis 2000). Such issues may bring the alternative Other too close for comfort for many conservative archaeologists, but where such dialogue promotes positive compromise on both sides of the equation, rather than the violence of previous years (such as the 1985 summer solstice 'Battle of the Beanfield' near Stonehenge in which so-called 'New Age travellers' were forced into confrontations with police), the outcome can only point towards beneficial negotiations in the future. This sort of interaction contrasts markedly with the example of 'Kennewick Man' in the USA, where debates have recently raged over a 9,000-year-old skeleton found in Washington state (see, for example, Radford 1998). Under NAGPRA (Native American Graves Protection and Repatriation Act 1990), Native Americans demanded the ancestral remains be reburied with appropriate ritual. Some archaeologists believe that rather than being Native American, the bones may be ancient European in origin, and have requested time for further analysis. The 'Asatru Folk Assembly', a right-wing Heathen organisation, then argued that if the remains are European then as a traditional European religion, they should have exclusive rights to the bones. As a result, both Native Americans and the Asatru Folk Assembly were allowed to conduct ceremonies over the bones. This situation exemplifies how archaeologists cannot ignore neo-shamanism, cannot neglect the sensitive political outcomes of their 'objective' scientific research.

Case study 1

Speaking with the Viking dead – Heathen neo-shamanism

The Asatru Folk Assembly is part of – albeit an atypical right-wing aspect that does not typify the movement as a whole – the third popular branch of paganism known to its practitioners variously as Heathenism, Heathenry, Odinism, Asatru ('allegiance to the gods'), or more loosely the 'Northern' tradition. Contemporary Heathens utilise Norse and Icelandic literature and mythology, Viking and Anglo-Saxon Migration Period history and archaeological sources, and all things with a Germanic and Heathen theme, to revive and reconstruct a contemporary religion. In the same vein as other Pagan traditions, Heathenry takes many forms and there are a variety of functioning groups worldwide. Smaller localised groups known as 'Hearths' meet together and are comparable with a Wiccan 'Coven' or Druidic 'Grove'. Harvey's (1997) discussions mark the most comprehensive and erudite survey of Heathenism to date. He suggests practitioners are steadily growing in numbers and the practices are advancing in 'coherence' (Harvey 1997: 53). There is no need for me to replicate what Harvey details, but there is a great deal of room to explore the shamanistic elements in Heathenry. These, in similarity with Wicca and Druidry, are mostly only touched on by other ethnographers of the traditions and are of considerable significance to archaeologists.

Shamanism permeates Heathenry more than any other contemporary Pagan tradition, perhaps because more associations between the two have been suggested (whether correctly or not) in the historic and archaeological record (see, for example, Simek 1993). Numerous aspects of the god Odin and goddess Freyja for instance, may display aspects of shamanism, particularly their associations with 'seiðr'. Seiðr is an obscure practice of 'magic' in the sources that is often disreputable or related to sorcery, and various academics argue that seiðr was a shamanic technique (see, for example, Ellis Davidson 1993: 137). I have met numerous Heathen shamanistic and/or seiðr practitioners in the UK and USA; for instance 'Runic' John, from Lancashire, whose patron deity is Woden[2] and who gives 'rune readings' and 'shamanic healing'. When conducting runic divinations for clients, John says that he enters a trance in which Woden sits behind him and covers his right eye with his hand (in Norse mythology, Odin sacrifices an eye to gain wisdom). At this point, John knows he has the 'sight' to be able to read the runes. [. . .]

John is a highly idiosyncratic Heathen shaman, typical of the individualised and eclectic nature of neo-shamanism today. A more widely publicised and popular technique is that of *seiðr* (see, for example, Lindquist 1997) practised by among others, the Hrafnar community in San Francisco led by Diana Paxson. The best recorded ancient instance of *seiðr* is in the *Saga of Eiríkr the Red* (see, for example, Magnus Magnusson and Hermann Pálsson 1965) in which a seeress or *völva* performs a 'seance' for a Greenlandic community suffering a famine. Many features of this tale may, according to neo-shamans and academics alike, hint at shamanistic practices. The *völva* eats a strange porridge before the ritual, containing the hearts of various creatures. She wears unusual clothing such as a black lambskin hood lined with cat's fur and cat skin gloves. Furthermore, a pouch at her waist contains various (unstated) charms, perhaps similar to those found in a pouch at the Fyrkat site, Denmark including the bones of birds and small mammals, and enthogenic henbane seeds (Price, pers. comm.). She also holds a long staff topped with a brass knob that is studded with stones and she sits on a ritual platform with a cushion of hen-feathers beneath her. Viewed shamanistically, the items of dress may indicate the *völva*'s relationships to her spirit-helpers, and her character-istic staff may act as a connection with the earth, or it may symbolise the world tree Yggdrasil. However, this view is at variance with some academic (non-practitioner) interpretations (see Price in press). Thus attired, the seeress's *seiðr* proceeds: the verses that enable the spirits to be present are sung or chanted, and in communication with that realm, the *völva* prophesies a better future for the community and for each person who asks her questions. Con-temporary *seiðr*-workers use sources such as this to reconstruct and revive the *seiðr* seance.

The saga literature is also used by Heathens to reconstruct what may have been Nordic 'possession' practices. The impetus for this practice arose, Paxson told me, when a deity first possessed a *völva* during a *seiðr* session, an unexpected happening that required some explanation and contextualisation. Diana researched the historic sources and believes she has found examples of possession in the Norse texts, particularly the earlier material. A possible example is in the *Saga of King Óláfr Tryggvason* (*Flateyjarbók* 1, see Guðbrandur Vigfússon and Unger 1860–8) in which an idol of Freyr travels around the country in a wagon, accompanied by his 'wife', a priestess (*gyðja*). The hero of the tale, Gunnar, fights with the idol and takes its place, whereupon the Swedes are well pleased that the god can now feast and drink, and are even more pleased when his 'wife' becomes pregnant! The tale is written from the perspective of the Norwegians, and if read at face value is a gibe at the gullibility of the heathen Swedes who believe Gunnar's impersonation of Freyr to be real. If the saga is approached as a possible example of possession, however, as Paxson would suggest, then it may have been common practice among the Swedes for a person to take on the form of a deity and let the deity speak through them. In this case Gunnar is the 'shaman', or whoever else was accompanying the *gyðja*, before being usurped by him: Gunnar's struggle with Freyr would actually be a fight with the previous shaman.[3] Having come across this literature, Paxson also noticed that traditional shamanic societies often incorporated possession into their rites (see, for example, Lewis 1989). To build on the fragmentary Nordic evidence with contemporary possession techniques, Diana studied the increasingly popular practice of Umbanda, in Brazil. Essentially, she combined an ethnographic analogy with Old Norse sources to reconstruct a Heathen Possession technique. Whatever misgivings archaeologists and other academics with interests in the past may have – with a perceived 'inappropriate' 'appropriation' of ethnographic analogy and 'mis-reading' of the literary sources – these reconstructions of *seiðr* and possession are deeply empowering for the contemporary practitioners.

Case study 2

Waking prehistoric ancestors – neo-shamanism at ancient sites

Neo-shamanic engagements with the past are most direct at archaeological sites. In many ways these are explicitly shamanic. The goddess-oriented mega-lithic gazetteer to Britain by Julian Cope (1998) for instance, recommends that visitors to Avebury should 'always hold shamanic experiments' (Cope in Thompson 1998: 12). To give some bearing on why and how neoshamans are involved with archaeological sites, Greywolf told me:

> Druids like to make ritual at ancient stone circles since there is a strong feeling that they are places where communion with our ancestors may be made more readily than elsewhere . . . I am drawn to Avebury . . . because it is my heartland . . . the place where I feel most spiritually 'at home'.
>
> (Greywolf, pers. comm.)

At Avebury and similar sites, from other Later Neolithic stone circles to Iron Age Hillforts, Greywolf and his kind make ritual at the eight Pagan festivals that celebrate the wheel of the year.[4] At such events various rituals and festivities occur, including handfasting (marriage), and child-naming ceremonies (baptism). Increasing numbers of people like Greywolf make pil-grimages to ancient places each year. A Bournemouth University survey of Avebury's visitors recorded that 16 per cent of them expressed spiritual motivation as their reason for visiting (Calver 1998). This number surges to represent a clear majority around the Pagan festivals. Such intimate relationships with Neolithic remains have resulted in certain management, presentation and conservation issues for the site curators.

A good, recent example (besides the better-known problems at Stone-henge), concerns the events surrounding the excavation of 'Seahenge', a small Bronze Age timber circle discovered in 1999 at Holme-Next-The-Sea on the east coast of England. The expropriation of such monuments, ownership of and management of the past, and rights of access, involves many interest groups, from archaeologists (including academic archaeologists, field archaeologists, museum workers and site managers) and anthropologists, to students of religion and history, local groups, and even politicians and the police. Yet neo-shamans and their peers are not addressed seriously in site management strategies, and furthermore, the political nature of site presentation has not been adequately examined. The situation at the timber ring at Holme-Next-The-Sea is exemplary of the increasingly activist positions neo-shamans are assuming in relation to archaeological sites. It also shows how the aims of the interest groups can be successfully negotiated.

Perplexed by the 'meaning' of this idiosyncratic monument, a neo-shaman says she 'didn't feel any particular energy coming from it', and wonders, 'maybe it'll come to me in a dream?' (Brown 1998: 15). Meanwhile, the national archaeological agency English Heritage initially determined to record the circle and then allow it to be eroded by the sea; it was thought too expensive to be preserved. A campaign was co-ordinated by local people, archaeologists and neo-shamanic persons (including Clare Prout of the mostly Pagan organisation Save Our Sacred Sites) to excavate and remove the henge from the threats of the sea, preserve it, and then place it on display. Owing to destructive conditions and the close proximity of flocks of wading birds, the display could not be *in situ*; indeed, the original location of the monument would have been some 30 miles inland. Local people were also concerned the display would end up too far from Holme, with a subsequent loss of their heritage, and therefore tourism. English Heritage's dendrochronological tests then followed, involving use of a chainsaw a process that greatly upset the groups wanting to preserve the henge. *The Times* reported that protesters turned up to halt the excavations (documented by the popular British television programme *Time Team*); Druids claimed that the henge's location on a ley line meant that it should not be moved lest its spiritual essence be lost (Morrison 1999: 20). In the early hours of a June morning English Heritage came to finish the job – with bulldozers – in what was called a 'Dawn Raid' (*Sacred Hoop News* 1999 25: 8), only to face protesting Druids and others prepared to stand their ground. One sat on the central upturned tree (suggested by some to be a shamanic sky burial site) playing a didgeridu. This confrontation 'sent shock waves across the pagan and shamanic communities not only in Britain but also the US' (*Sacred Hoop News* 1999 25: 8). As with the example of Stonehenge, archaeologists are viewed very negatively at such times, 'as manifestations of imperialism' and 'an uncaring discipline, typical of a dominant elitist society' (Ucko 1990: xv). In the end, 'Seahenge' was excavated and 'preserved', and *Time Team* made a reconstruction of the monument. By and large, the *Time Team* programme demonstrated that the Druidic perspective was marginalised. Simply put, their claims on the monument were not taken seriously (cf. Plouviez 2000).

The happenings at this most recently discovered and probably highly sig-nificant ancient site – (interpretations range from shamanic sky burial site to fish trap) – exemplify the increasing tension that exists between site custodians and groups opposing their protocols, including local people and neo-shamans.[5] New situations seem to be emerging all the time: from the recent disagree-ments between Pagans, heritage managers and Christians over the erecting of a new monolith at Mayburgh stone circle in north-west England, to successful neo-shamanic and local objections to the planned removal of two standing stones in the Avebury region in Wiltshire (as discussed on the Stones and Nature Religions Scholars email discussion lists). Indeed, there appear to be increasing tensions amongst archaeologists too. A recent article in *British Archaeology*, by its editor Simon Denison, expresses discontent about the way 'Seahenge' was 'yanked out of the sands': 'The excavation . . . was destruction, nothing short of vandalism' (Denison 2000: 28. See also 'Letters' in *British Archaeology* 53: 24–5). Holme-Next-The-Sea compares with Stonehenge as a site of serious political contestation between heritage managers and alternative interest groups. However, the situation is most certainly not just doom and gloom, as I next discuss.

Seeing towards 'extra pay' for shamanisms, present and past

Neo-shamanic approaches to various aspects of the past, from Druidic and Viking reconstructions to engagements with archaeological sites, should clearly be of considerable interest to archaeologists and other academics with concerns over how the past is approached and represented. This interest should not only be of 'concern', however, since there are some distinctly positive neo-shamanic interactions with the past that give what Harvey (1997: chapter 7) calls 'extra pay'[6] to shamanisms past and present. A first example is where neo-shamans actively and positively engage in archaeological site man-agement processes. At 'Seahenge', Clare Prout joined David Miles (Chief Archaeologist, English Heritage), Druid protestors, archaeologists and other interest groups in a discussion on how to address the tense situation. She claims that through this dialogue 'we got a fabulous result' (pers. comm.),[7] though of course there will always be people who disagree: where Prout and English Heritage wanted to excavate and preserve the monument, other Druids demanded it be left *in situ*. Despite the conflicts, the example of 'Seahenge' shows how disputes *can*, largely, be resolved. For the most part, respectful and diplomatic negotiations between the interest groups appear to reap positive results 'perhaps to the extent that Seahenge will be the last disturbance of a sacred site without prior consultation and compromise' (Bannister 2000: 13). Interestingly, by the end of the dispute, many of the archaeologists who initially wrote off the Druids stated that in retrospect they wished they had got them on board. By getting involved in protest and negotiation, and by thereby challenging the negative stereotypes of themselves, neo-shamans are, I argue, giving 'extra pay' to shamanism, since it is used as a force for change and social critique, rather than a trendy word and bandwagon. In so doing, they are also giving extra pay to the archaeological sites they spiritually respect.

The issue of *seiðr* in Heathenism provides a second example of 'extra pay', when its practitioners undergo experiences that challenge Western worldviews. Some Heathen neo-shamans in Britain and North America, in contrast to being 'safe' and 'Westernised',[8] confront and challenge conservatism both in Heathenism and wider society. Heathenry writ large is a conservative new religion with moral, ethical and spiritual values adhering to 'middle' England and America. 'Traditional' family values are sacred and the issue of same-sex relations remains controversial. Associations with nationalism, racism and homophobia do not typify Heathenism,[9] but the unfortunate history of associations between Viking religions and Nazism this century is seized upon by contemporary groups motivated by far-right politics. They, in turn, are picked out by the tabloid press so that the liberal attitudes of others are eclipsed. *Seiðr* practices among liberal-minded Heathens are not always regarded favourably by the rest of the Heathen community because many of them find notions of 'spirits' and practices involving direct communications with deities and the ancestors to be extremely dubious, verging on the blasphemous (Blain pers. comm.; see also Blain and Wallis 2000). Nevertheless, Diana Paxson of the Hrafnar community told me that *seiðr* is becoming increasingly popular.

At the time of the Icelandic Sagas, *seiðr* was a disreputable practice (with an obvious knock-on effect today among the Heathens who use these Old Norse sources), and the working of magic was generally held to be antisocial behaviour. *Ergi* is an enigmatic term used in the myths and sagas to describe a male *seiðr*-worker or *seiðmaðr*. Loki the Trickster deity, for instance, calls Odin (a warrior god) *ergi* when he practices *seiðr* techniques he learned from the goddess Freyja (*Lokasenna* 24, in *The Poetic Edda* ed. and tr. Dronke 1997: 338). *Ergi* may refer to an 'effeminate man' or to being 'unmanly', and as widespread academic opinion has it, to passive male homosexuality, reflecting the pejorative sentiments surrounding a man or god who practises 'women's magic'. *Seiðr* and *ergi* contrast significantly to the sort of 'strong warrior' male role model deemed conventional and desirable during the unpredictable and uncertain times of Viking migration and conflict.

Their shamanic experiences have led many contemporary *seiðr*-workers to re-appraise the negative associations of *seiðr* and *ergi*. They suggest that in earlier times, certainly before Christian prejudice, *seiðr* may have been a more acceptable practice. Nordic society may have been more 'shamanistic' and the status of a *seiðmaðr* and his *ergi* might even compare with the shaman *berdache* in some Native American societies (for discussions of *berdache* see, for example, Roscoe 1991; Whitehead 1993). In similarity to *seiðr* and *ergi*, berdache is a loaded term, a colonial construction that imposed Eurocentric understandings of gender and sexual relations onto indigenous cultures. In contrast to Western values, berdache-type shamans (see, for example, Czaplicka 1914), gender-crossing priests such as some Hindu hijras (see, for example, Nanda 1993a, 1993b), multiple gender conceptions (see, for example, Herdt 1996), and same-sex relations (see, for example, Sparkes 1998), are cross-culturally consistent. This consistency deconstructs the simplistic Western conflation of gender and sex. Rather than the binary 'two-spirited people' (see, for example, papers in Jacobs et al. 1997), 'changing ones' (Roscoe 1998) may be the most applicable replacement for 'berdache'. As evidence for changing ones in ancient northern Europe, Heathens may cite Saxo Grammaticus who remarks on the berdache-type priests or 'wives' of Freyr (a male 'fertility' god) at Uppsala in Sweden. Saxo describes the hero Starkaðr as being 'disgusted with the womanish body movements' of the priests of Freyr, and the 'soft tinkling of bells' (Gesta Danorum, Book 6, tr. Ellis Davidson and Fisher 1998: 172). Elsewhere, Tacitus (Germania 43) describes Germanic priests dressed in women's clothing. Furthermore, some burial evidence may point towards changing ones in Anglo-Saxon society (Wilson 1992: 96–7; Clark-Mazo 1997: 11), although it is of course imperative that Western conceptions of gender are not imposed on artefact assemblages.

Simply by practising seiðr today then, neo-shamans engage in a dissonant act that receives prejudice from within their own spiritual community and from wider culture. Paxson suggested the 'opening up' of oneself psychically to be successful in seiðr can be regarded as a female ability rather than a male one, and only certain men generally want to be involved with seiðr because of this, these most often being gay men. The high proportion of gay men in the Hrafnar community is quite unrepresentative of Heathenry in general, so the combination of gay men and seiðr places Hrafnar further into a marginal category in Heathenry, perhaps reflective of its geographical location in liberal San Francisco. Being gay and practising seiðr presents a significant challenge to conventional Heathenry and the normative West. Not all men practising seiðr, however, are gay. Over time, Diana says more 'straights' have begun to practise seiðr. For heterosexual male seiðr-workers, experiences with seiðr also challenge conventional classifications of gender with a domino effect for other masculist Western attitudes. Bil is a seiðr-worker in New Mexico who works with the dying to ease their spiritual transition and has various 'ghosts' as spirit-helpers. He points out that:

> My sexuality is heterosexual. I was never approached by the ghosts who follow me to change that in any way. I was, however, severely 'lambasted' for carrying too much of a 'macho attitude' and was forced to make changes in that area – so much so, that folks often wonder, now, if I am homosexual or not. They usually figure it out soon enough when they meet my family and friends. My

eccentricity doesn't stem from sexuality or sexual preference but mainly from the fact that I have no emotional reactions any longer (I have emotions; I just don't demonstrate reaction with them, that's all).

(Blain and Wallis 2000)

And, Jordsvin has clearly been deeply affected by *seiðr* when he argues:

The concept of sexual orientation *per se* is a modern one. There do seem to be references in the lore connecting men who do *seiðr* with men who have sex with men, more specifically, men who are in the receptive role during such activities. Obviously, this should not be an excuse for bigotry against gay people today. Gay men and women seem often to show a knack for *seiðr*, but heterosexual men can and do learn it and do it quite well.

(Blain and Wallis 2000)

In a similar vein, 'James', a newcomer to *seiðr* practices living in Britain, has experiences that challenge various normative Western sensory and ideological perceptions. He says:

Ergi mainly fits with my rituals with Freyja, rituals of possession . . . I think many people (especially men) would find *seiðr* disturbing because of how it makes them feel (apart from the radical change into shamanic consciousness), going beyond stereotypes of male, female, gay, etc. For me, *seiðr* with Freyja allows an integrating understanding of what it is to be male, female and other multiple possibilities. That is empowering and affects how I live with my reality, world, local and spiritual communities. It changes who I am.

(Blain and Wallis 2000)

Harvey (1997: 122; see also 1998) asserts that working in environmental education comprises one example of how neo-shamanism embodies a postmodern critique of society and thereby gives 'extra pay'. I agree, and argue that *seiðr*-work and its subsequent disputing and altering of normative Western stereotypes similarly represents a significant disruption of, and protest to, modernity. Dowson argues 'the very practice of archaeology provides the foundations of social and epistemological privilege by authorizing a heterosexual history of humanity' (1998: 4). Conservative Heathens follow this line and cultivate their perceived closeness to their ancestors by assuming ancient Heathen communities consisted of heterosexual family units as we largely have them today. In direct contrast, the *seiðr*-workers I have discussed use their experiences to provide an alternative history of *seiðr* that challenges conventional understandings of the past. Where many archaeologists unconsciously underwrite homophobia in their reification of familial units and heterosexual relations, gay and straight *seiðr*-workers disrupt these biases, interpreting the past in ways beyond normative archaeology. They 'actively challenge the manner in which epistemological privilege is negotiated in archaeology' (Dowson 1998: 4). In their engagements with shamanic practice, they also challenge both the atheistic stance of contemporary society and the aversion to interactions with spirits in their Heathen communities.

These *seiðr*-workers are not simply going on shamanic trips for fun or profit, as the critics of neo-shamanism largely suggest, but are radically reorienting their worldviews. In terms of consciousness alterations, gender conceptions, sexual orientation and community interactions, these neo-shamans are more like some indigenous shamans. I argue rather than 'appropriating' aspects of indigenous shamanisms, or shamanism in the past, these neo-shamans give significant 'extra pay' to shamanisms past and present. They accord with Taussig's (1987) astute understanding of shamanism as being embedded in an intrinsically socio-political process that destroys any belief – neo-shamanic or academic – in shamanism solely as a safe or benevolent phenomenon. Taussig argues the shamanic career and its rituals are open-ended, there is always a tension in the air, an aura of unpredictability. Rather than there being a strictly followed narrative pattern and a cathartic shamanic 'healing', the nature of shamanism is consistently undermined and without certain or known outcomes, as Western observers would like to see. The ritual may be unsuccessful, disputes may not be resolved, the shaman's spirits may depart and the career end abruptly. This ongoing nature of unpredictability waxes and wanes alongside the desired catharsis and constancy all people and their societies want, just as shamans themselves often struggle with malevolent and benevolent spirits, sorcery and healing. Where shamanic vocations are culturally constituted, the shamanic world itself is also intrinsically political and in perpetual change. Recognising the uncertainty of the shamanic office allows Taussig to deconstruct the 'classic' Western model of shamanism in which shamans are perceived to be largely male, dominating figures who control social relations and charismatically master their communities. The intrinsic uncertainty of shamanism suggests this image is a fabrication by Western observers imposing their masculist ideals inappropriately. The same image is also reified by those neo-shamans who portray shamanism as being safe, controllable and desirable. *Seiðr* neo-shamanism, in sharp contrast, typifies Taussig's assertion that shamanism is a deeply political phenomenon, with the potential for 'dismantling all fixed notions of identity' (Taussig 1989: 57). As changing ones, *seiðr*-workers give extra pay to shamanism by permeating the perceived academic boundaries between 'shamanism' and 'neo-shamanism', by being more like indigenous shamans. They also positively give extra pay to neo-shamanism itself, empowering the term and associated practices in ways beyond the negative stereotypes critics impose on them.

Conclusion

Any discussions of neo-shamanism must inevitably consider issues of the invention of tradition and the authenticity of reconstructions of the past. In this chapter I have tried to demonstrate that neo-shamans are not somehow misinterpreting the past where archaeologists 'know best'. While some neo-shamans may be 'inventing' some rather outlandish interpretations, such as the Asatru Folk Assembly's claims on Kennewick Man, accusing these and other neo-shamans of 'inventing' tradition is deeply problematic. As Herzfeld states:

> such terms as the 'invention of tradition' . . . suggest the possibility of an ultimately knowable historic past. Although traditions are invented, the implicit argument suggests, there ought to be something else that represents the 'real' past. But if any history is invented, all history is invented. We should not view one kind of history as more invented than others, although its bearers may be more powerful and therefore more capable of enforcing its reproduction among disenfranchised classes.
>
> (Herzfeld 1991: 12)

Moreover, to assume these practitioners are merely 'pretending' when they reconstruct these religions would be naïve and would not take their beliefs seriously (see, for example, Salomonsen 1999). Re-enactors of the past are often very passionate about the authenticity of their reconstructions, but in contrast neo-shamans are reconstructing the past in and for the present, for personal and communal spiritual empowerment. The authenticity of the reconstruction is not the main issue, merely its relevance and pragmatism for the practitioners. Of course the question is inappropriate anyway: 'authentic in relation to what?' – archaeological interpretations, that are themselves ever-changing, transient, subject to fashions and fads?

Archaeologists may be custodians of the past, those most often with direct access to its remains and whose interpretations of it are perceived publicly to be scientific fact. But archaeologists are not owners of the past and do not have exclusivity to the market of ideas that interpret it. This is made blatantly clear by the multitude of books on Celtic shamanism, seiðr magic, and so on, that far outsell academic publications. As Hutton argues,

> It is a classic case of a situation in which the experts are feeding the public with information while leaving it free to make such imaginative reconstructions as it wishes . . . Druids [and other neo-shamans] are well placed to take advantage of it . . . indeed, it is almost a duty on their part to do so, for the more people who

are involved in the work, and the broader the range of plausible pictures imagined, the healthier the situation.

(Hutton 1996: 23)

If this bookish equation alone does not encourage archaeologists to engage with neo-shamans, then where neo-shamans are prominent in direct action at ancient sites, archaeologists are under an even greater obligation to engage with them. To quote Hutton again, where he specifically remarks on Tim Sebastion's SOD:

[W]hether or not outsiders may approve of the politics of SOD, God and Law, they have to be taken seriously. Their campaign has posed valid questions about the control and responsibility of the Nation's past, which eventually provoked a major debate among archaeologists. By 1992, 25 of the latter, many of them celebrities, were prepared to write a letter to the Guardian condemning the policy of English Heritage. . . . Between them they have made a distinctive contribution to the history of religion and magical culture in Britain, and another to the history of politics. It is an impressive dual achievement, in such a few years, for movements which so clearly address problems specific to modernity, yet do so in terms of images drawn from the remote past.

(Sebastion 2000)

Rather idiosyncratically, my role as an autoarchaeologist spans both these worlds of archaeology and neo-shamanism. I aim to have negotiated these worlds in this chapter, and promoted a dialogue between 'orthodox' and 'alternative' interest groups that is positive, tolerant and reciprocal. Only by pursuing an open-minded exploration of neo-shamanism is it possible to appreciate that beyond engaging with archaeology in an 'eccentric' and confrontational way, there are neo-shamans that are actively engaging in positive dialogues with archaeologists and heritage managers. There are others who, in contrast to many neo-shamans, avoid romanticising and appropriating indigenous shamanism, and who are well aware of the sensitivities of their practices, so embedding them in specific social relations. According to Dowson's 'elements of shamanism', they *are* shamans. These considerations of neo-shamanism are pertinent but controversial in current archaeology and anthropology. I hope this discussion makes plain to the various interest groups that neo-shamanism has very much to do with *us*. Such a strategy, alongside my advocating 'an archaeology of *neo-shamanism*', seems timely. If neo-shamanism continues to be side-lined as insignificant, then as archaeologists of shamanism we will be reifying academic exclusivity, ignoring the central role of neo-shamanism in influencing our understandings of shamanism. But most of all, we will be neglecting our responsibilities as autoarchaeologists. That is, being explicit about our own socio-political motivations for undertaking an archaeology of shamanism in the first place.

Notes

1   As an aside, in his definitive historical work on 'Modern Pagan Witchcraft' Hutton mentions a nineteenth-century Welsh cunning man who may have got the idea for his costume from accounts from 'Siberian tribal shamans' (Hutton 1999: 90).

2   Odin has linguistic variations including: ON Óðinn, OE Woden, OF Wodan OHG Wutan, Wuotan.

3   On the other hand, or in addition – for each interpretation is not mutually exclusive – Blain (pers. comm.) suggests the possibility that a 'spirit-marriage' is described, similar to the Siberian shamanic examples (Czaplicka 1914), with the wife as the 'shaman': she has a spirit-spouse, Freyr, and a human-spouse, Gunnar, which is customary for the Swedes but is incomprehensible to the Norwegians who assume Gunnar must be impersonating Freyr. And if Freyr is said to speak, this must 'really' be Gunnar speaking, rather that the gyðja relaying Freyr's messages.

4   The eight Pagan festivals mark and celebrate the seasonal changes seen in nature during the ever-turning 'wheel of the year'. There is an emphasis on the agricultural cycle and adherents use these times to connect with the land, reflect on how the changes in nature reflect changes in self and community, observe long-term patterns of stability and change, and to make ritual and celebration. The following dates are somewhat arbitrary since they may depend on planetary alignments, the proximity of sunrise and sunset, and the festivals tend to last for some days. In order: Samhain (Halloween) 31 October, Yule (Winter solstice) 21 December, Imbolc 2 February, Spring equinox 21 March, Beltane (May Day) 1 May, Summer solstice 21 June, Lammas 31 July, Autumnal equinox 21 September. For full discussion of their meanings, see Harvey 1997.

5   It is germane to note how the English Heritage view of the Holme-Next-The-Sea affair differs from that of neo-shamans. In *Heritage Today* (Issue 47, September 1999) the glossy magazine for English Heritage members, English Heritage are presented as having a common-sense approach (excavating the timbers as quickly as possible for preservation) in contrast to the rather hysterical responses of Druids and other neo-shamans. In their favour though, it is encouraging to see David Miles (English Heritage Chief Archaeologist) responding to the interests of alternative groups with an open mind. He was keen to put the point to me, when we met at the European Association of Archaeologists' annual meeting, that English Heritage's aim is not the museumification of the landscape. Rather, they have the difficult job of balancing the needs of preservation with the promotion of public interaction.

6   The term Harvey chooses to employ hints at a fiscal return from neo-shamans to indigenous shamans. In reality this is not solely the case, indeed there are many ways neo-shamans give extra pay to shamanism that have nothing to do with money. Despite the connotations of capitalism and a patronising 'pat on the back' of indigenous shamans that may be perceived in the term 'extra pay', I can think of no better way of describing the process in operation, so have chosen to continue using the term here. There are numerous ways neo-shamans can be seen to be returning

benefits to shamanism, such as using the term sensitively, raising awareness of the injustices faced by indigenous communities, and undergoing experiences that are acutely comparable to indigenous shamanism.

7   Similar 'fabulous results' have emerged at Stonehenge, which was open to all for the 2000 summer solstice.

8   Elsewhere I (Wallis in press), among others (see, for example, Harvey 1997; Jakobsen 1999), have pointed out certain problems with aspects of neo-shamanism, such as its universalising of shamanism in a fashion typical of occidental homogeneity, and reducing of shamanic experience to psychological archetypes, both of which avoid what Brown (1989) calls the 'dark side of the shaman'.

9   Certain groups, however, such as the Odinic Rite and Hammarens Ordens Sallskap in Britain, and the Asatru Folk Assembly in the USA, are ostensibly concerned with 'blood and soil' issues though they try to avoid being explicitly racist, nationalist (British and/or European) and homophobic.

References

Adler, M. (1986) *Drawing Down the Moon: Witches, Druids, Goddess-worshippers and Other Pagans in America Today*, Boston: Beacon Press.

Ashcroft, B., Griffiths, G. and Tiffin, H. (1998) *Key Concepts in Post-colonial Studies*, London: Routledge.

Bannister, V. (2000) 'A load of old rubbish', *Pagan Dawn: The Journal of the Pagan Federation* 135 (Beltane): 12–13.

Barfield, L. and Hodder, M. (1987) 'Burnt mounds as saunas, and the prehistory of bathing', *Antiquity* 61: 370–9.

Bender, B. (1998) *Stonehenge: Making Space*. Oxford: Berg.

Blain, J. and Wallis, R.J. (2000) 'The "ergi" seidman: contestations of gender, shamanism and sexuality in northern religion, past and present', *Journal of Contemporary Religion* 15(3): 395–411.

Brown, M. (1998) 'Henge of the sea', *Sacred Hoop* 24: 15.

Brown, M.F. (1989) 'Dark side of the shaman', *Natural History* (November): 8–10.

Calver, S. (1998) *Avebury Visitor Research 1996–1998*. Report on behalf of the National Trust, Bournemouth: Bournemouth University.

Childe, V.G. (1958) *The Prehistory of European Society*, Harmondsworth: Penguin.

Clark-Mazo, G. (1997) 'Shamanism or "bad bones"?: Comments on the International Medieval Conference', *Pagan Dawn: The Journal of the Pagan Federation* 125: 11.

Cope, J. (1998) *The Modern Antiquarian: a Pre-millennial Odyssey through Megalithic Britain*, London: Thorsons.

Crawford, O.G.S. (1957) *The Eye Goddess*, London: Phoenix House.

Czaplicka, M.A. (1914) *Aboriginal Siberia: A Study in Social Anthropology*, Oxford: Clarendon Press.

Daniel, G. (1958) *The Megalith Builders of Western Europe*, London: Hutchinson.

Denison, S. (2000) 'Issues: One step to the left, two steps back', *British Archaeology* 52: 28.

Denning, K. (1999) 'Archaeology and alterity', unpublished paper presented in the 'Method and theory 2000' session at the Society for American Archaeology 64th Annual Meeting, Chicago.

Dowson, T.A. (1998) 'Homosexualitat, teortia queer i arqueologia' ['Homosexuality, queer theory and archaeology'] *Cota Zero* 14: 81–7 (in Catalan with English translation).

Dronke, U. (ed. and tr.) (1997) *The Poetic Edda. vol. II Mythological Poems*, Oxford: Oxford University Press.

Ellis Davidson, H. (1993) *The Lost Beliefs of Northern Europe*, London: Routledge.

Ellis Davidson, H. and Fisher, P. (eds and tr.) (1998) *Saxo Grammaticus: The History of the Danes. Books I–IX*, Woodbridge: Brewer.

Farrar, J. and Farrar, S. (1984) *The Witches' Way: Principles, Rituals and Beliefs of Modern Witchcraft*, London: Robert Hale.

Finn, C. (1997) 'Leaving more than footprints: modern votive offerings at Chaco Canyon prehistoric site', *Antiquity* 71: 169–78.

Gimbutas, M. (1974) *The Goddesses and Gods of Old Europe: Myths and Cult Images*, London: Thames and Hudson.

Green, M. (1997) *Exploring the World of the Druids*, London: Thames and Hudson.

Guðbrandur Vigfússon and Unger, C.R. (eds) (1860–8). *Flateyjarbok: en samling of norske konge-sagaer med indskudte mindre fortællinger om begivenheder i og udanfor Norge samt Annaler 1–3*, Kristiania: no publisher.

Harvey, G. (1997) *Listening People, Speaking Earth: Contemporary Paganism*, London: Hurst and Co.

Harvey, G. (1998) 'Shamanism in Britain today', *Performance Research* 3(3): 16–24.

Hassan, F.A. (1997) 'Beyond the surface: comments on Hodder's "Reflexive excavation methodology"', *Antiquity* 71: 1020–5.

Henry, H. (1999) 'Trends: pagan powers in modern Europe', *Hinduism Today International* (July): 1–3.

Herdt, G. (1996) 'Mistaken sex: culture, biology and third sex in New Guinea', in G. Herdt (ed.) *Third Sex Third Gender: Beyond Sexual Dimorphism in Culture and History*, New York: Zone Books.

Herzfeld, M. (1991) *A Place in History: Social and Monumental Time in a Cretan Town*, Oxford: Princeton University Press.

Hutton, R. (1991) *The Pagan Religions of the Ancient British Isles: Their Nature and Legacy*, Oxford: Blackwell.

Hutton, R. (1996) 'Introduction – who possesses the past?', in P. Carr-Gomm (ed.) *The Druid Renaissance*, London: Thorsons.

Hutton, R. (1997) 'The Neolithic Great Goddess: a study in modern tradition', *Antiquity* 71: 91–9.

Hutton, R. (1999) *Triumph of the Moon: A History of Modern Pagan Witchcraft*, Oxford: Oxford University Press.

Jacobs, S., Thomas, W. and Lang, S. (1997) (eds) *Two-spirit People: Native American Gender, Sexuality, and Spirituality*, Illinois: University of Illinois Press.

Jakobsen, M.D. (1999) *Shamanism: Traditional and Contemporary Approaches to the Mastery of Spirits and Healing*, Oxford: Berghahn Books.

Jencson, L. (1989) 'Neopaganism and the Great Mother Goddess', *Anthropology Today* 5(2): 2–4.

Jones, L. (1998) *Druid, Shaman, Priest: Metaphors of Celtic Paganism*, Enfield Lock: Hisarlik Press.

Lewis, I.M. (1989) *Ecstatic Religion: A Study of Shamanism and Spirit Possession*, London: Routledge.

Lindquist, G. (1997) *Shamanic Performance on the Urban Scene: Neo-shamanism in Contemporary Sweden*, Stockholm Studies in Social Anthropology 39, Stockholm: University of Stockholm.

Luhrmann, T.M. (1989) *Persuasions of the Witches' Craft: Ritual Magic in Contemporary England*, Cambridge, Mass.: Harvard University Press.

Magnusson, Magnus and Pálsson, Hermann (1965) *The Vinland Sagas: The Norse Discovery of America*, London: Penguin.

Marcus, G.E. (1995) 'Ethnography in/of the World System: the emergence of a multi-sited ethnography', *Annual Review of Anthropology* 24: 95–117.

Matthews, J. (1991) *Taliesin: Shamanism and the Bardic Mysteries in Britain and Ireland*. London: Aquarian.

Meskell, L. (1995) 'Goddesses, Gimbutas and "New Age" archaeology', *Antiquity* 69: 74–86.

Meskell, L. (1999) 'Feminism, paganism, pluralism', in A. Gazin-Schwartz and C. Holtorf (eds) *Archaeology and Folklore*, London: Routledge.

Morrison, R. (1999) 'Mad dogs and Englishmen . . .'. *The Times* 22.06.99.

Murray, M.A. (1921) *The Witch Cult in Western Europe: A Study in Anthropology*, Oxford: Clarendon Press.

Murray, M.A. (1933) *The God of the Witches*, London: Sampson Low.

Nanda, S. (1993a) 'Hijras: an alternative sex and gender role in India', in G. Herdt (ed.) *Third Sex Third Gender: Beyond Sexual Dimorphism in Culture and History*, New York: Zone Books.

Nanda, S. (1993b) 'Hijras as neither man nor woman', in H. Abelove, M.A. Barde and D.M. Halperin (eds) *The Lesbian and Gay Studies Reader*, London: Routledge.

Nietzsche, F. (1983) [1874] 'On the uses and disadvantages of history for life', in F. Nietzshe *Untimely Meditations*, Cambridge: Cambridge University Press.

Piggott, S. (1968) *The Druids*, London: Pelican.

Plouviez, J. (2000) 'Debating Seahenge – archaeology and emotion', in *Rescue News* 81: 3.

Price, N.S. (in press) *The Viking Way: Religion and War in Late Iron Age Scandinavia*, Uppsala: Uppsala University Press.

Radford, T. (1998) *Equinox: Homicide in Kennewick*, London: Channel Four Television.

Roscoe, W. (1991) *The Zuni Man-woman*, Albuquerque: University of New Mexico Press.

Roscoe, W. (1998) *Changing Ones: Third and Fourth Genders in North America*, London: Macmillan.

Salomonsen, J. (1999) 'Methods of compassion or pretension? Anthropological fieldwork in modern magical communities', *The Pomegranate: A New Journal of Neo-pagan Thought* 8: 4–13.

Sebastion, T. (1990) 'Triad /I\: the Druid knowledge of Stonehenge', in C. Chippendale, P. Devereux, P. Fowler, R. Jones and T. Sebastian (eds) *Who Owns Stonehenge?*, Manchester: Batsford.

Sebastion, T. (2000) 'Alternative archaeology: has it happened?', in R.J. Wallis and K.J. Lymer (eds) *A Permeability of Boundaries?: New Approaches to the Archaeology of Art, Religion and Folklore*, Oxford: British Archaeological Reports.

Simek, R. (1993) *A Dictionary of Northern Mythology*, Bury St. Edmunds: St. Edmundsbury Press.

Sparkes, B.A. (1998) 'Sex in Classical Athens', in B.A. Sparkes (ed.) *Greek Civilisations: An Introduction*, Oxford: Blackwell.

Starhawk. (1989) *The Spiral Dance*, San Francisco: Harper & Row.

Taussig, M. (1987) *Shamanism, Colonialism and the Wild Man: A Study in Terror and Healing*, Chicago: University of Chicago Press.

Taussig, M. (1989) 'The nervous system: homesickness and Dada', *Stanford Humanities Review* 1(1): 44–81.

Thompson, B. (1998) 'Cliff Richard is a Pagan', *The Independent Weekend Review*, 24.10.98: p. 12.

Ucko, P.J. (1990) 'Foreword', in P. Gathercole and D. Lowenthal (eds) *The Politics of the Past*, London: Unwin Hyman.

Wallis, R.J. (2000) 'Queer shamans: autoarchaeology and neo-shamanism', *World Archaeology* 32(2): 251–61.

Wallis, R.J. (In press) 'Return to the source: neo-shamanism and shamanism in Central Asia and Siberia', in T.A. Dowson, M.M. Kośko and A. Rozwadowski (eds) *Rock Art, Shamanism and Central Asia: Discussions of Relations*, International Rock Art Monographs 2. Oxford: British Archaeological Reports.

Whitehead, H. (1993) 'The bow and the burden strap: a new look at institutionalised homosexuality in Native North America', in H. Abelove, M.A. Barde and D.M. Halperin (eds) *The Lesbian and Gay Studies Reader*, London: Routledge.

Wilson, D. (1992) *Anglo-Saxon Paganism*, London: Routledge.
Young, D.E. and Goulet, J.-G. (eds) (1994) *Being Changed: The Anthropology of Extraordinary Experience*, Peterborough, Ontario: Broadview Press.

Chapter 25

Terence McKenna

A BRIEF HISTORY OF
PSYCHEDELICS

PSYCHEDELIC PLANTS AND EXPERIENCE were first suppressed by European civilization, then ignored and forgotten. The fourth century witnessed the suppression of the mystery religions – the cults of Bacchus and Diana, of Attis and Cybele. The rich syncretism that was typical of the Hellenistic world had become a thing of the past. Christianity triumphed over the Gnostic sects – Valentinians, Marcionites, and others – which were the last bastions of paganism. These repressive episodes in the evolution of Western thought effectively closed the door on communication with the Gaian mind. Hierarchically imposed religion and, later, hierarchically dispensed scientific knowledge were substituted for any sort of direct experience of the mind behind nature.

The intoxicants of the Christian dominator culture, whether plants or synthetic drugs, were inevitably stimulants or narcotics – drugs of the workplace or drugs to dull care and pain. Drugs in the twentieth century serve only medical or recreational purposes. Yet even the West has retained the thin thread of remembrance of the Archaic, hierophantic, and ecstatic potential that certain plants hold.

The survival through long centuries in Europe of witchcraft and rites involving psychoactive plants attests that the gnosis of entering parallel dimensions by altering brain chemistry was never entirely lost. The plants of European witchcraft – thorn apple, mandrake, and nightshade – did not contain indole hallucinogens but were nevertheless capable of inducing intense altered states of consciousness. The Archaic connection of feminism to a magical dimension of risk and power was clearly perceived as a threat by the medieval church:

As late as the Middle Ages the witch was still the *hagazussa*, a being that sat on the *Hag*, the fence, which passed behind the gardens and separated the village from the wilderness. She was a being who participated in both worlds. As we might say today, she was semi-demonic. In time, however, she lost her double features and evolved more and more into a representation of what was being expelled from culture, only to return, distorted, in the night.[1]

That these plants were the basis for entry into other dimensions was the result of the relative paucity in Europe of hallucinogen-containing species.

The New World hallucinogens

Indole-containing plant hallucinogens, and their cults, cluster in the tropical New World. The New World subtropical and tropical zones are phenomenally rich in hallucinogenic plants. Similar eco-systems in the Southeast Asian and Indonesian tropics cannot compare in numbers of endemic species that contain psychoactive indoles. Why are the Old World tropics, the tropics of Africa and Indonesia, not equally rich in hallucinogenic flora? No one has been able to answer this question. But statistically speaking the New World seems to be the preferred home of the more powerful psychoactive plants. Psilocybin, while now known to occur in European species, of diminutive mushrooms of the genus *Psilocybe*, has never been convincingly shown to have been a part of European shamanism or ethnomedicine. Yet its shamanic use in Oaxacan Mexico is three millennia old. Similarly, the New World has the only living cults based on use of dimethyltryptamine (DMT), the beta-carboline group including harmine, and the ergotlike complex in morning glories.

A historical consequence of this clustering of hallucinogens in the New World was that Western science discovered their existence rather late. This may explain the absence of 'psychedelic' input into Western drugs for psychiatric uses. Meanwhile, because of the influence of hashish and opium on the Romantic imagination, the hashish reverie or opium dream became the paradigm of the action of the new 'mental drugs' that fascinated the Bohemian literati from the late eighteenth century on. Indeed, hallucinogens were seen as capable of mimicking psychoses in their early encounter with Western psychotherapy.

In the nineteenth century explorer-naturalists began to return with more or less accurate ethnographic reports of the activities of aboriginal peoples. Botanists Richard Spruce and Alfred Russel Wallace traveled in the Amazon drainage in the 1850s. On the upper reaches of the Rio Negro, Spruce observed a group of Indians prepare an unfamiliar hallucinogen. He further observed that the main ingredient for this intoxicant was a liana, a woody climbing vine, which he named *Banisteria caapi*. Several years later, while traveling in western Ecuador he saw the same plant being used to make a hallucinogen called *ayahuasca*.[2] [. . .]

Ayahuasca has continued to the present day to be a part of the spiritual life of many of the tribes in the montane rain forest of South America. Immigrants into the Amazon basin have also accepted *ayahuasca* and have created their own ethnobotanical-medical system for using the psychedelic visions it imparts to promote healing.

The word *ayahuasca* is a Quechua word that roughly translates as 'vine of the dead' or 'vine of souls.' This term refers not only to the prepared hallucinogenic beverage but also to one of its main ingredients, the woody liana. The tissues of this plant are rich in alkaloids of the beta-carboline type. The most important beta-carboline occurring in what is now called *Banisteriopsis caapi* is harmine. Harmine is an indole, but it is not overtly psychedelic unless taken in amounts that approach what is considered a toxic dose. However, well below that level, harmine is an effective short-acting monoamine oxidase inhibitor. Thus, a hallucinogen such as DMT, which would normally be inactive if taken orally, is rendered highly psychoactive if taken orally in combination with harmine. Native peoples of the Amazon region have brilliantly exploited these facts in their search for techniques to access the magical dimensions crucial to shamanism.[3] By combining, in *ayahuasca*, DMT-containing plants with plants that contain MAO inhibitors, they have long exploited a pharmacological mechanism, MAO inhibition, not described by Western science until the 1950s.

In the presence of harmine, DMT becomes a highly psychoactive compound that enters the bloodstream and eventually makes its way past the blood-brain barrier and into the brain. There it very effectively competes with serotonin for synaptic bonding sites. This experience of the slow release of DMT lasts four to six hours and is the basis of the magical and shamanic view of reality that characterizes the *ayahuasquero* and his or her circle of initiates. Uninvolved or so-called objective styles of anthropological reportage have tended to underemphasize the culture-shaping importance that these altered states have had for tribal Amazonian societies.

The experience of ingesting *ayahuasca* – organic DMT taken in combination with the *Banisteriopsis* vine – has a number of characteristics that set it apart from the experience of smoking DMT. *Ayahuasca* is gentler and of much greater duration. Its themes and hallucinations are oriented toward the organic and the natural world, in marked contrast to the titanic, alien, and off-planet motifs that characterize the DMT flash. Why such major differences should exist between compounds that appear to be so structurally similar is an uninvestigated problem. Indeed, the whole relationship of particular kinds of visions to the compounds that elicit them is not well understood. In the native areas of its use, *ayahuasca* is regarded as a general-purpose healing elixir and is called *la purga*, the purge. Its effectiveness in combating intestinal parasites has been proven. Its effectiveness in killing the malaria organism is now being investigated. And its long history of effective shamanic use in folk psychiatry has been documented by Naranjo, Dobkin de Rios, Luna, and others.[4]

Ayahuasca

The experience induced by *ayahuasca* includes extremely rich tapestries of visual hallucination that are particularly susceptible to being 'driven' and directed by sound, especially vocally produced sound. Consequently, one of the legacies of the *ayahuasca*-using cultures is a large repository of *icaros*, or magical songs [. . .] The effectiveness, sophistication, and dedication of an *ayahuasquero* are predicated upon how many magical songs he or she has effectively memorized. In the actual curing sessions, both patient and healer ingest *ayahuasca* and the singing of the magical songs is a shared experience that is largely visual.

The impact of long-term use of hallucinogenic indoles on mental and physical health is not yet well understood. My own experiences among the mestizo populations of Amazonas convince me that the long-term effect of *ayahuasca* use is an extraordinary state of health and integration. *Ayahuasqueros* use sound and suggestion to direct healing energy into parts of the body and unexamined aspects of an individual's personal history where psychic tension has come to rest. Often these methods exhibit startling parallels to the techniques of modern psychotherapy; at other times they seem to represent an understanding of possibilities and energies still unrecognized by Western theories of healing.

Most interesting from the point of view of the arguments made in this book are the persistent rumors of states of group-mind or telepathy that occur among the less acculturated tribal peoples. Our history of skepticism and empiricism would have us dismiss such claims as impossible, but we should think twice before doing so. The chief lesson to be learned from the psychedelic experience is the degree to which unexamined cultural values and limitations of language have made us the unwitting prisoners of our own assumptions. For it cannot be without reason that wherever in the world hallucinogenic indoles have been utilized, their use has been equated with magical self-healing and regeneration. The low incidence of serious mental illness among such populations is well documented.

The father of psychopharmacology

The modern era of psychopharmacology's interest in the aboriginal use of hallucinogenic plants has been extraordinarily brief. It dates to only a century ago, to German pharmacologist Lewis Lewin's tour of the United States.

On returning to Berlin in 1887, Lewin carried with him a quantity of peyote buttons, the vision-inducing cactus of the Sonoran Indians, that he had obtained from the Parke-Davis Company during his stay in Detroit. He set to work extracting, characterizing, and self-experimenting with the new compounds he discovered. Within a decade, peyote had attracted sufficient attention that in 1897 Philadelphia novelist and physician Silas Weir Mitchell became the first *gringo* to describe peyote intoxication:

> The display which for an enchanted two hours followed was such as I find it hopeless to describe in language which shall convey to others the beauty and splendor of what I saw. Stars . . . delicate floating films of color . . . then an abrupt rush of countless points of white light swept across the field of view, as if the unseen millions of the Milky Way were to flow a sparkling river before the eyes . . . zigzag lines of very bright colors . . . the wonderful loveliness of swelling colors of more vivid colors gone before I could name them. Then, for the first time, definite objects associated with colors appeared. A white spear of grey stone grew up to huge height, and became a tall, richly finished Gothic tower of very elaborate and definite design, with many rather worn statues standing in the doorways or on stone brackets. As I gazed every projecting angle, cornice, and even the faces of the stones at their joining were by degrees covered or hung with clusters of what seemed to be huge precious stones, but uncut, some being like masses of transparent fruit.[5]

The pleasures of mescaline

In 1897, Arthur Heffter, a rival of Lewin's, became the first human being to isolate and ingest pure mescaline. Mescaline is a powerful visionary amphetamine that occurs in the peyote cactus *Lophophora williamsii*. It has been used for at least several centuries by the Indians of Sonoran Mexico. Its use in Peru, where it is derived from species of cactus other than peyote, is at least several thousand years old.

The psychologist and pioneer sexologist Havelock Ellis, following the example of Weir Mitchell, soon offered his own account of mescaline's pleasures:

> The visions never resembled familiar objects; they were extremely definite, but yet always novel; they were constantly approaching, and yet constantly eluding, the semblance of known things. I would see thick, glorious fields of jewels, solitary or clustered, sometimes brilliant and sparkling, sometimes with a dull rich glow. Then they would spring up into flowerlike shapes beneath my gaze and then

seem to turn into gorgeous butterfly forms or endless folds of
glistening iridescent fibrous wings of wonderful insects. . . .
Monstrous forms, fabulous landscapes, etc., appear. . . . It seems
to us that any scheme which, in a detailed manner, assigns different
kinds of visions to successive stages of the mescal state must be
viewed as extremely arbitrary. The only thing that is typical with
regard to sequence is that very elementary visions are followed by
visions of a more complex character.[6]

Mescaline introduced experimenters to an agent of the *paradis artificiel* more
potent than either cannabis or opium. Descriptions of mescaline states could
hardly fail to attract the attention of the surrealists and psychologists who
also shared a fascination with the images hidden in the depths of the newly
defined unconscious. Dr. Kurt Beringer, Lewin's student and an acquaintance
of Hermann Hesse's and Carl Jung's, became the father of psychedelic
psychiatry. His phenomenological approach stressed reportage of the internal
vistas beheld. He conducted hundreds of experiments with mescaline in
human beings. The accounts given by his subjects are fascinating:

Then the dark room once more. The visions of fantastic architecture again took hold of me, endless passages in Moorish style
moving like waves alternated with astonishing pictures of curious
figures. A design in the form of a cross was very frequent and
present in unceasing variety. Incessantly the central lines of the
ornament emanated, creeping like serpents or shooting forth like
tongues toward the sides, but always in straight lines. Crystals
appeared again and again, changing form and color and in the
rapidity with which they came before my eyes. Then the pictures
grew more steady, and slowly two immense cosmic systems were
created, divided by a kind of line into an upper and a lower half.
Shining with their own light, they appeared in unlimited space.
From the interior new rays appeared in more luminescent colors,
and gradually becoming perfect, they assumed the form of oblong
prisms. At the same time they began to move. The systems
approaching each other were attracted and repelled.[7]

In 1927 Beringer published his magnum opus *Der Meskalinrausch*, translated into Spanish but never into English. It is an inspired work, and it set the
stage for the science of investigative pharmacology.

The following year saw the publication in English of Heinrich Klüver's
Mescal, the Divine Plant and Its Psychological Effects. Klüver, whose work built on
the observations of Weir Mitchell and Havelock Ellis, reintroduced the
English-speaking world to the notion of visionary pharmacology. Especially
important was the fact that Klüver took the hallucinogenic content of the

experiences he was observing seriously and became the first to attempt to give a phenomenological description of the psychedelic experience:

> Clouds from left to right through optical field. Tail of a pheasant (in centre of field) turns into bright yellow star; star into sparks. Moving scintillating screw; 'hundreds' of screws. A sequence of rapidly changing objects in agreeable colours. A rotating wheel (diameter about 1 cm.) in the centre of a silvery ground. Suddenly in the wheel a picture of God as represented in old Christian paintings. – Intention to see a homogeneous dark field of vision: red and green shoes appear. Most phenomena much nearer than reading distance.[8]

A modern renaissance

The investigation of hallucinogenic indoles also dates to the 1920s. A veritable Renaissance of psychopharmacology was taking place in Germany. In this atmosphere, Lewin and others became interested in harmine, an indole whose only source was thought to be *Banisteriopsis caapi*, the woody liana encountered by Richard Spruce nearly eighty years before. Indeed, Lewin's last published work reflected his new fascination with caapi; entitled *Banisteria Caapi, ein neues Rauschgift und Heilmittel*, it appeared in 1929. The excitement of Lewin and his colleagues was understandable: ethnographers such as the German Theodore Koch-Grünberg returned from Amazonas with accounts of tribes using telepathy-inducing plant drugs to direct the course of their societies. In 1927, the chemists E. Perrot and M. Raymond-Hamet isolated the active agent from *Banisteriopsis caapi* and named it telepathine. Years later, in 1957, researchers realized that telepathine was identical to the compound harmaline, extracted from *Peganum harmala*, and the name harmine was given official precedence over telepathine.

In the 1930s, the enthusiasm for the harmala alkaloids by and large vanished, as did much of the interest in ethnopharmacology. There were, however, notable exceptions. Among them was an Austrian expatriate living in Mexico.

Blas Pablo Reko, born Blasius Paul Reko, was a person of wide-ranging interests. His wandering life took him to the United States, to Ecuador, and finally to Oaxacan Mexico. There he became interested in ethnobotany and what is today called archaeo-astronomy, the study of ancient cultures' observations and attitudes toward the stars. Reko was an astute observer of the plant usages among the native people with whom he lived. In 1919, in rebuttal to an article by William Safford, Reko wrote that it was a hallucinogenic mushroom, and not peyote, that shamans of the Mixtec and Mazatecan people still used in a traditional way to induce visions.[9] In 1937, Reko sent Henry Wassén, an anthropologist and the curator of the ethnographical museum in Gothenburg, Sweden, a package containing collections of two plants that Reko had found particularly interesting. One of the samples was *piule* seed, the visionary morning glory seeds of *Ipomoea violacea*, which contain hallucinogenic indoles related to LSD.

Reko's other sample, unfortunately too decomposed to be identified to species, was a fragment of *teonanácatl*, the first specimen of a psilocybin-containing mushroom to be brought to scientific attention. Thus Reko initiated the study of the indole hallucinogens of Mexico and two chains of research and discovery, which would eventually be reunited when Albert Hofmann, the Swiss pharmaceutical chemist, characterized both compounds in his laboratory.

Whispers of a New World mushroom

Reko had obtained his mushroom sample from Roberto Weitlander, a European engineer working in Mexico. The following year, 1938, a small group including Weitlander's daughter and anthropologist Jean Basset Johnson became the first whites to attend a nightlong mushroom ceremony, or *velada*.

Wassén eventually forwarded Reko's samples to Harvard, where they came to the attention of the young ethnobotanist Richard Evans Schultes. Schultes had been a medical student until he had happened upon Klüver's work on mescaline. Schultes believed that Reko's mushroom might be the mysterious *teonanácatl* described by the Spanish chroniclers. He and an anthropology student from Yale, Weston La Barre, published a summation of the evidence for *teonanácatl* being a psychoactive mushroom.

The next year found Schultes accompanying Reko to the village of Huatla de Jiménez in the Sierra Mazatecan highlands. Specimens of psychoactive mushrooms were collected and forwarded to Harvard. But larger forces were afoot during the late thirties; like research in many other areas, ethnobotanical research slowed to a stop as the world slipped into world war. Reko retired, and as the Japanese solidified their hold on the rubber plantations of Malaya, Schultes accepted an assignment to the Amazon Basin to study rubber extraction for the U.S. government's wartime Office of Strategic Services. But, before this, in 1939, he published *The Identification of Teonanácatl, a Narcotic Basidiomycete of the Aztecs*.[10] Here he quietly announced his correct solution to an enigma that at that time seemed no more than a matter of scholarly debate among Mesoamericanists.

The invention of LSD

Yet, even as the lights were going out in Europe, a fundamental breakthrough occurred. In 1938 Albert Hofmann was engaged in routine pharmaceutical research at Sandoz Laboratories, in Basel, Switzerland. Hofmann hoped to produce new drugs that would ease labor and childbirth. While working with the vasoconstricting substances derived from ergot, Hofmann synthesized the first d-lysergic acid diethylamide tartrate – LSD-25. Hofmann, a modest man, merely noted the correct completion of the synthesis, and the untested compound was cataloged and placed into storage. There it remained, surrounded by Nazi Europe for the next five years, five of the most tumultuous years in human history. It is frightening to imagine some of the possible consequences had Hofmann's discovery been recognized for what it was even a moment earlier.

Alfred Jarry may have anticipated and allegorized the great event when he wrote 'The Passion Considered as an Uphill Bicycle Race'[11] in 1894. Indeed, the Dadaists and Surrealists and their forerunners grouped around Jarry and his *Ecole du Pataphysique* did much to explore the use of hashish and mescaline as augmentations to creative expression. They set the cultural stage for the truly surreal emergence of society's awareness of LSD. Every LSD enthusiast knows the story of how on April 16, 1943, feeling a touch of the Friday blahs, and unaware that he had absorbed a dose of LSD through handling the chemical without gloves, chemist, and soon-to-be counterculture hero, Albert Hofmann left work early and set off on his bicycle through the streets of Basel:

> I was forced to interrupt my work in the laboratory in the middle of the afternoon and proceed home, being affected by a remarkable restlessness, combined with a slight dizziness. At home I lay down and sank into a not unpleasant intoxicated dreamlike condition, characterized by an extremely stimulated imagination. In a dreamlike state, with eyes closed (I found the daylight to be unpleasantly glaring), I perceived an uninterrupted stream of fantastic pictures, extraordinary shapes with intense, kaleidoscopic play of colors. After some two hours this condition faded away.[12]

Pandora's box flung open

Finally, in 1947, the news of Hofmann's extraordinary discovery, a megahallucinogen active in the microgram range, surfaced in the scientific literature. As events in the 1950s made clear, Pandora's box had been flung open.

In 1954, Aldous Huxley wrote *The Doors of Perception*, a brilliant literary snapshot of the male European intellectual grappling with and agape at the realization of the true dimensions of consciousness and the cosmos:

> What the rest of us see only under the influence of mescaline, the artist is congenitally equipped to see all the time. His perception is not limited to what is biologically or socially useful. A little of the knowledge belonging to Mind at Large oozes past the reducing valve of brain and ego, into his consciousness. It is a knowledge of the intrinsic significance of every existent. For the artist, as for the mescaline taker, draperies are living hieroglyphs that stand in some peculiarly expressive way for the unfathomable mystery of our being. More even than the chair, though less perhaps than those wholly supernatural flowers, the folds of my gray flannel trousers were charged with 'is-ness.' To what they owed this privileged status, I cannot say.[13]

In 1956 the Czech chemist Steven Szara synthesized dimethyl-tryptamine, DMT. DMT remains the most powerful of all hallucinogens and one of the most short acting of these compounds known. When DMT is smoked, the intoxication reaches a peak in about two minutes and then abates over about ten minutes. Injections are typically more prolonged in their effect. Here is the discoverer's account:

> On the third or fourth minute after the injection vegetative symptoms appeared, such as tingling sensations, trembling, slight nausea, mydriasis, elevation of the blood pressure and increase of the pulse rate. At the same time eidetic phenomena, optical illusions, pseudo-hallucinations, and later real hallucinations appeared. The hallucinations consisted of moving, brilliantly colored oriental motifs, and later I saw wonderful scenes altering very rapidly.[14]

A year later, in May 1957, Valentina and Gordon Wasson published their now famous article in *Life* magazine announcing the discovery of the psilocybin mushroom complex. This article, as much as any other single piece of writing published on the subject, introduced into mass consciousness the notion that plants could cause exotic, perhaps even paranormal, visions. A New York investment banker, Wasson was well acquainted with the movers and shakers of the Establishment. Therefore, it was natural that he should turn to his friend Henry Luce, publisher of *Life*, when he needed a public forum in which to announce his discoveries. The tone of the *Life* article contrasts sharply with the hysteria and distortion that the American media would later fan. The article is both fair and detailed, both open-minded and scientific.

The chemical loose ends of the Wassons' discoveries were tidied up by Albert Hofmann, who made a second starring appearance in the history of psychedelic pharmacology by chemically isolating psilocybin and determining its structure in 1958.

In the short space of a dozen years in the recent past, from 1947 until 1960, the major indole hallucinogens were characterized, purified, and investigated. It is no coincidence that the subsequent decade was the most turbulent decade in America in a hundred years.

LSD and the psychedelic sixties

To understand the role of psychedelics in the 1960s, we must recall the lessons of prehistory and the importance to early human beings of the dissolution of boundaries in group ritual based on ingestion of hallucinogenic plants. The effect of these compounds is largely psychological and is only partially culturally conditioned; in fact, the compounds act to dissolve cultural conditioning of any sort. They force the corrosive process of reform of community values. Such compounds should be recognized as deconditioning agents; by revealing the relativity of conventional values, they become powerful forces in the political struggle to control the evolution of social images.

The sudden introduction of a powerful deconditioning agent such as LSD had the effect of creating a mass defection from community values, especially values based on a dominator hierarchy accustomed to suppressing consciousness and awareness.

LSD is unique among drugs in the power of its dose range. LSD is detectable in human beings at a dose of 50 micrograms, or 5/100,000 of a gram. Compounds that can elicit effects from amounts smaller than this are unheard of. This means that ten thousand doses of 100 micrograms each could in theory be obtained from one pure gram. More than any other aspect, this staggering ratio of physical mass to market value explains the meteoric rise of LSD use and its subsequent suppression. LSD is odorless and colorless, and it can be mixed in liquids; hundreds of doses could be concealed under a postage stamp. Prison walls were no barrier to LSD, nor were national borders. It could be manufactured in any location with the necessary technology and immediately transported anywhere. Millions of doses of LSD could be and were manufactured by a very few people. Pyramidal markets formed around these sources of supply; criminal syndicalism, a precondition to fascism, quickly followed.

But LSD is more than a commodity – it is a commodity that dissolves the social machinery through which it moves. This effect has bedeviled all the factions that have sought to use LSD to advance a political agenda.

A psychological deconditioning agent is inherently counter-agenda. Once the various parties attempting to gain control of the situation recognized this, they were able to agree on one thing – that LSD be stopped. How and by whom this was done is a lively story that has been well told, most notably by

Jay Stevens in *Storming Heaven* and Martin Lee and Bruce Shlain in *Acid Dreams*.[15] These authors make clear that when the methods that worked for colonial empires peddling opium in the nineteenth century were applied by the CIA to the internal management of the American state of mind during the Vietnam War they damn near blew up the whole psychosocial shithouse.

Lee and Shlain write:

> The use of LSD among young people in the US reached a peak in the late 1960s, shortly after the CIA initiated a series of covert operations designed to disrupt, discredit, and neutralize the New Left. Was this merely a historical coincidence, or did the Agency actually take steps to promote the illicit acid trade? Not surprisingly, CIA spokesmen dismiss such a notion out of hand. 'We do not target American citizens,' former CIA director Richard Helms told the American Society of Newspaper Editors in 1971. 'The nation must to a degree take it on faith that we who lead the CIA are honorable men, devoted to the nation's service.'
>
> Helms's reassurances are hardly comforting in light of his own role as the prime instigator of Operation MK-ULTRA, TRA, which utilized unwitting Americans as guinea pigs for testing LSD and other mind-altering substances.
>
> As it turns out, nearly every drug that appeared on the black market during the 1960s – marijuana, cocaine, heroin, PCP, amyl nitrate, mushrooms, DMT, barbiturates, laughing gas, speed, and many others – had previously been scrutinized, tested, and in some cases refined by CIA and army scientists. But of all the techniques explored by the Agency in its multimillion-dollar twenty-five-year quest to conquer the human mind, none received as much attention or was embraced with such enthusiasm as LSD-25. For a time CIA personnel were completely infatuated with the hallucinogen. Those who first tested LSD in the early 1950s were convinced that it would revolutionize the cloak and dagger trade. During Helms's tenure as CIA director, the Agency conducted a massive illegal domestic campaign against the antiwar movement and other dissident elements in the US.[16]

As a result of Helms' successful campaign, the New Left was in a shambles when Helms retired from the CIA in 1973. Most of the official records pertaining to the CIA's drug and mind control projects were summarily destroyed on orders from Helms shortly before his departure. The files were shredded, according to Dr. Sidney Gottlieb, chief of the CIA's Technical Services Staff, because of 'a burgeoning paper problem.' Lost in the process were numerous documents concerning the operational employment of hallucinogenic drugs, including all existing copies of a classified CIA manual titled 'LSD: Some Un-Psychedelic Implications.'[17]

The times were extraordinary, made only more so by the fantasies of those who sought to control them. The 1960s can almost be seen as a time when two pharmacological mind-sets clashed in an atmosphere close to that of war. On the one hand, international heroin syndicates sought to narcotize America's black ghettos, while hoodwinking the middle class into supporting military adventurism. On the other, self-organized criminal syndicates manufactured and distributed tens of millions of doses of LSD while waging a highly visible underground campaign for their own brand of psychedelic cryptoanarchy.

The result of this encounter can be seen as something of a stand-off. The war in Southeast Asia was a catastrophic defeat for the American Establishment, yet paradoxically barely a shred of psychedelic utopianism survived the encounter. All psychedelic drugs, even such unknowns as ibogaine and bufotinin, were made illegal. A relentless restructuring of values was begun in the West; throughout the seventies and eighties the need to deny the impact of the sixties took on something of the flavor of a mass obsession. As the seventies progressed, the new management agenda became clear; while heroin had lost some of its glamour, now there was to be television for the poor and cocaine for the rich.

By the end of the 1960s psychedelic research had been hounded out of existence – not only in the United States, but around the world. And this happened despite the enormous excitement these discoveries had created among psychologists and students of human behavior, an excitement analogous to the feelings that swept the physics community at the news of the splitting of the atom. But whereas the power of the atom, convertible into weapons of mass destruction, was fascinating to the dominator Establishment, the psychedelic experience loomed ultimately as an abyss.

The new era of repression came despite the fact that a number of researchers were using LSD to cure conditions previously considered untreatable. Canadian psychiatrists Abram Hoffer and Humphrey Osmond tabulated the results of eleven separate studies of alcoholism and concluded that 45 percent of the patients treated with LSD improved.[18] Promising results were obtained in attempts to treat schizophrenics, autistic children, and the severely depressed. Many of these findings were attacked after LSD became illegal, but better experiments were never designed and the work could not be repeated because of its illegality. Psychiatry's promising new uses of LSD to treat pain, addiction, alcoholism, and depression during terminal illness were put on indefinite hold.[19] It fell to the humble science of botany to advance our understanding of hallucinogenic plants.

Richard Schultes and the plant hallucinogens

At the center of this quiet revolution in botany was a single man, Richard Evans Schultes – the same Schultes who had seen his Mexican research interrupted by World War II. Schultes spent more than fifteen years in the Amazon Basin; he filed reports with the OSS on the natural rubber crop until the invention of synthetic rubber made that task unnecessary; and he studied and collected the orchids of the rain forest and the *alti plano*. As Schultes traveled, it became clear that his interest in Klüver's experiments with mescaline, and his fascination with the psychoactive plants of Mexico, would not be wasted in South America.

Years later, he would write of his work among the shamans of the Sibundoy Valley of southern Colombia: 'The shamanism of this valley may well represent the most highly evolved narcotic consciousness on earth.' What was true of the Sibundoy was nearly as true of the Upper Amazon generally, and over the next several decades it was Schultes and his graduate students who practiced and spread the gospel of modern ethnobotany.

Schultes focused on psychoactive plants from the beginning of his work. He correctly recognized that aboriginal people who had painstakingly composed an armamentorium of healing and medicinal plants were likely to most clearly understand their mental effects. After his early work on peyote and mushrooms, Schultes turned his attention to the several species of vision-inducing morning glories used in Oaxaca. In 1954 he published on the snuffs of the Amazon and thus announced to the world the existence of traditional shamanic usage of plant-produced DMT.

Throughout the next thirty-five years the Harvard group meticulously investigated and published all instances of psychoactive plant usage that came to their attention. This body of now continuously expanding work – an integrated body of taxonomic, ethnographic, pharmacological, and medical information – constitutes the core of the data base currently in global use.

The birth of ethnopsychopharmacology took place at Harvard under Schultes's watchful eye, much of it during the turbulent years when Timothy Leary was also at Harvard and attracting a very different sort of reputation through his own effort to place the psychedelic experience on the social agenda.

Leary at Harvard

It is doubtful that either Leary or Schultes saw much to like in the other. They could hardly have been more different – Schultes the reticent Brahmin, scholar, and botanist/scientist, Leary the shamanic trickster and social scientist. Leary's earliest psychedelic experience had been with mushrooms; he would later recall that he was recruited for what he called 'my planetary mission' by that first psilocybin encounter in Mexico. But the politics of expediency were forced on the Harvard Psilocybin Project; LSD was more accessible and less expensive than psilocybin. Michael Hollingshead was the person most responsible for making LSD the drug of choice in Harvard's psychedelic circles:

> [Leary] latched onto Hollingshead as his guru. Leary followed him around for days on end. . . . Richard Alpert and Ralph Metzner, two of Leary's closest associates, were vexed to see him in such a helpless state. They thought he had really blown his mind and they blamed Hollingshead. But it was only a matter of time before they too sampled the contents of the mayonnaise jar. Hollingshead gave the drug to the members of the psilocybin project and from then on LSD was part of their research repertoire.[20]

Psilocybin: psychedelics in the seventies

After the suppression of the psychedelic subculture that began with the illegalization of LSD in October 1966, the evolution of substance sophistication seemed to lose momentum. The most significant development during the 1970s from the point of view of those alerted to the psychedelic potential by earlier experiences with LSD and mescaline was the appearance, beginning in late 1975, of techniques and manuals for the home cultivation of psilocybin mushrooms. Several such manuals appeared, the earliest being *Psilocybin: The Magic Mushroom Grower's Guide* written by my brother and me and published pseudonymously under the names O. T. Oss and O. N. Oeric. The book sold over a hundred thousand copies over the next five years, and several imitators also did very well. Hence psilocybin, long sought and long familiar to the psychedelic community through the effusive prose of Wasson and Leary, became available at last to large numbers of people, who no longer needed to travel to Oaxaca to obtain the experience.

The ambience of psilocybin is different from that of LSD. Hallucinations come easier, and so does a sense that this is not merely a lens for the inspection of the personal psyche, but a communication device for getting in touch with the world of the high shamanism of Archaic antiquity. A community of therapists and astronauts of inner space has evolved around the use of the mushrooms. To this day these quiet groups of professionals and inner pioneers constitute the core of the community of people who have admitted the fact of the psychedelic experience into their lives and professions and who continue to grapple with it and learn from it.

And there we will leave the history of human involvement with plants that intoxicate or bring visions or consuming frenzy. We now know no more really than was known by our remote ancestors. Perhaps less. Indeed, we cannot even be certain whether science, the epistemic tool upon which we have come to depend most heavily, is up to this task. For we can begin our quest for understanding in the cool domains of archaeology or botany or neuropharmacology, but what is troubling and miraculous is the fact that all these approaches, when seen with psychedelic eyes, seem to lead to the internal nexus of self and world that we experience as the deepest levels of our own being.

Psychedelic implications

What does it mean that pharmacology's effort to reduce the mind to molecular machinery confined within the brain has handed back to us a vision of mind that argues for its almost cosmic proportions? Drugs seem the potential agents of both our devolution back into the animal and our metamorphosis into a shining dream of possible perfection. 'Man to man is like unto an errant beast,' wrote the English social philosopher Thomas Hobbes, 'and man to man is like unto a god.' To this we might add 'and never more so than when using drugs.'

The 1980s were an era unusually empty of developments in the area of psychedelics. Synthetic amphetamines such as MDA were sporadically available from the early 1970s on, and during the 1980s MDMA (Ecstasy) appeared in significant amounts. MDMA in particular showed promise when used with directed psychotherapy,[21] but these drugs were quickly made illegal and forced underground before they achieved any general impact on society. MDMA was simply the most recent echo of the search for inner balance that drives ever-shifting styles of drug use and inner exploration. The drug terror of the 1980s was crack cocaine, a drug whose economic profile and high risk for addiction made it ideal in the eyes of the already established infrastructure for supplying the ordinary cocaine market.

The costs of drug education and drug treatment are small relative to routine military expenditures and could be contained. What cannot be contained are the effects that psychedelics would have in shaping the cultural self-image if all drugs were legal and available. This is the hidden issue that makes governments unwilling to consider legalization: the unmanaged shift of consciousness that legal and available drugs, including plant psychedelics, would bring is extremely threatening to a dominator, ego-oriented culture.

Public awareness of the problem

To this point public awareness of issues concerning drugs has been lacking and public opinion easily manipulated. The situation must change. We must prepare to master the problem of our relationship to psychoactive substances.

This cannot be done by an appeal to some antihuman standard of behavior that spells more suppression of the mass psyche by dominator metaphors. There can be no 'Saying No' to drugs; nothing so asinine or preposterous will do. Nor can we be led down the primrose path by feel-good philosophies that see unbridled hedonism as the Holy Grail of social organization. Our only reasonable course is decriminalization of drugs, mass education, and shamanism as an interdisciplinary and professional approach to these realities. It is our souls that have become ill when we abuse drugs, and the shaman is a healer of souls. Such measures will not immediately solve the general drug problem, but they will preserve the sorely needed pipeline to the spirit that we must have if we expect to restructure society's attitude toward plant and substance use and abuse.

An interrupted psychophysical symbiosis between ourselves and the visionary plants is the unrecognized cause of the alienation of modernity and the cultural mind-set of planetary civilization. A worldwide attitude of fear toward drugs is being fostered and manipulated by the dominator culture and its propaganda organs. Vast illicit fortunes continue to be made; government continues to wring its hands. This is but the most recent effort to profiteer from and frustrate our species' deeply instinctual need to make contact with the Gaian mind of the living planet.

Notes

1   Hans Peter Duerr, *Dreamtime: Concerning the Boundary Between Wilderness and Civilization* (Oxford: Basil Blackwell, 1985).

2   Richard Spruce, *Notes of a Botanist on the Amazon and Rio Negro*, A. R. Wallace, ed. (London: Macmillan, 1980).

3   Richard Evans Schultes, 'The Beta-Carboline Hallucinogens of South America,' *Journal of Psychoactive Drugs* 14, no. 3 (1982): 205–20.

4   Claudio Naranjo, *The Healing Journey: New Approaches to Consciousness* (New York: Ballantine, 1973); Marlene Dobkin de Rios, *Visionary Vine: Psychedelic Healing in the Peruvian Amazon* (San Francisco: Chandler, 1972); Luis Eduardo Luna, *Vegetalismo: Shamanism among the Mestizo Population of the Peruvian Amazon* (Stockholm: Alquist & Wiksell, 1986).

5   Quoted in A. Hoffer and H. Osmond, *The Hallucinogens* (New York: Academic Press, 1967), p. 8.

6   Ibid., p. 9.

7   Ibid., p. 7.

8   Heinrich Klüver, *Mescal, the Divine Plant and Its Psychological Effects* (London: Kegan Paul, 1928), p. 28.

9   Cf. Victor A. Reko, *Magische Gifte, Rausch-und Betäubungsmittel der neuen Welt* (Berlin: Express Edition, 1987).

10   Richard Evans Schultes, *Plantae Mexicanae, II: The Identification of Teonanácatl, a Narcotic Basidiomycete of the Aztecs*, Botanical Museum Leaflets of Harvard University (1939) 7: 37–54.

11 Alfred Jarry, *Selected Works of Alfred Jarry*, Roger Shattuck and Simon Watson Taylor, eds (New York: Grove Press, 1965).

12 Albert Hofmann, *LSD: My Problem Child* (Los Angeles: Tarcher, 1983), p. 15.

13 Aldous Huxley, *The Doors of Perception* (New York: Harper, 1954), p. 35.

14 Steven Szara in *Psychotropic Drugs*, S. Garattini and V. Ghetti, eds (Amsterdam: Elsevier, 1957), p. 460.

15 Jay Stevens, *Storming Heaven: LSD and the American Dream* (New York: Atlantic Monthly Press, 1987); Martin A. Lee and Bruce Shlain, *Acid Dreams: The CIA, LSD, and the Sixties Rebellion* (New York: Grove Press, 1985).

16 Lee and Shlain, *Acid Dreams*, p. xxi.

17 Ibid., p. 286.

18 A. Hoffer and H. Osmond, *New Hope for Alcoholics* (New York: University Books, 1968).

19 Lester Grinspoon and James B. Bakalar, *Psychedelic Drugs Reconsidered* (New York: Basic Books, 1979), p. 216.

20 Lee and Shlain, *Acid Dreams*, p. 84.

21 Sophia Adamson, *Through the Gateway of the Heart* (San Francisco: Four Trees Press, 1985).

Further Study

THERE ARE VARIOUS WAYS to continue studying the topics introduced and debated in these Readings. First, most chapters come from larger works that are devoted to similar topics. Second, each chapter refers to other works of importance and each reference will probably lead to yet more sources, discussions and information. This is not entirely advice to work back from this book to earlier texts. It is an encouragement to enter the debates more fully. Close reading of the sources and contexts from which particular chapters have been extracted will almost certainly enrich understanding of what is presented here. To work forward is also possible. Material included here is rarely the only thing each author has written about shamans or their pursuits. Searches in library catalogues and databases may provide significant leads. Remember that most university library catalogues are available on-line through the Internet, as are those of various national libraries (e.g. the British Library and the Library of Congress). The Internet provides further possibilities. For example, a search for 'Harner bibliography' is likely to generate not only on-line works by Harner himself, but also citations of Harner's writings and of similar publications. It will also provide links to Internet bookshops, some of which list books under topics like 'shamanism'. It may be worth noting that an Internet search for 'shaman' or 'shamanism' is likely to lead to thousands of websites (even 'shaman bibliography' generates over 6,000 results). Narrowing the search by including either particular places, peoples or themes is more helpful. Interesting possibilities can also result from seeing what is available in the websites of particular academics or academic institutions: for example, those of the UK's Social

Sciences Information Gateway (http://www.sosig.ac.uk) and the American Academy of Religion (http://www.aar_site.org) provide links to a number of interesting syllabi and other sites.

Most introductions to those academic disciplines interested in shamans (especially Religious Studies and Anthropology) contain suggestions for guidance on the state of knowledge now and advice on further reading. One very good example is Fiona Bowie's *The Anthropology of Religion* (Oxford: Blackwell, 2000). Based on the expectation that readers will follow the above suggestions about finding further sources, what follows does not pretend to be an exhaustive bibliography – that would demand another large book, at least. My intention here is to suggest a few expert or exemplary texts.

Piers Vitebsky's *The Shaman* (London: Macmillan/Boston: Little, Brown and Co., 1995) remains the best single volume on the topic currently available. It provides insightful and powerful discussions of a remarkable array of issues, and an exceptionally helpful 'documentary reference' section.

Jane Atkinson's article 'Shamanisms Today' (*Annual Review of Anthropology* 21 (1992): 307–30) is invaluable as a guide to what has been of interest and what was becoming of interest. Similarly, Daniel C. Noel's *The Soul of Shamanism: Western Fantasies, Imaginal Realities* (New York: Continuum, 1997) engages powerfully with 'shamanism as Western scholars, storyteller, and seekers have imagined it – and as we in the West today might reimagine it into the future'. By challenging particular constructions and uses of 'shamanism', it clarifies significant issues, but also encourages positive consideration of 'imaginal' and creative interactions. While Noel helpfully focuses on only a few popularisers of 'shamanism', Jeremy Narby and Francis Huxley's *Shamans Through Time* (London: Thames and Hudson, 2001) provide a wider survey of Western writing about shamans. It should provoke readers to question whether they are seeing shamans or what they wish shamans were.

If shamanism is still largely seen as techniques and experiences of trance and/or altered states of consciousness, the forefront of academic interest is illustrated by references in Mark C. Taylor's important edited book, *Critical Terms for Religious Studies* (Chicago: University of Chicago Press, 1999). Shamans are mentioned once in relation to 'trance journeys' here, but only in discussing 'alien abductions' in a debate about religious experience. Shamans are also noted in a consideration of the history of the classification of religions, and in essays about embodiment, transformation, and transgression. This latter essay (by Michael Taussig) includes reference to secrecy and violence. In other words, shamans are now becoming interesting not for what they demonstrate about consciousness but for what they do. A turn to studying shamanic performance is not a return to either functionalism or structuralism, especially because it is not reductionist, but is an attempt to engage far more holistically with all that shamans do in rituals, relationships, daily life and much more. Two aspects of these recent developments are worth following further: performance and knowledge.

Performance Studies has generated a considerable body of valuable literature recently. Some of it is included and discussed in my edited *Readings in Indigenous Religions* (London: Continuum, 2002). The study of 'ritual' by scholars of religion and anthropology has been reinvigorated by encounter with studies of theatre and performance. Victor Turner's dialogue with Richard Schechner has been particularly valuable (e.g. Turner's *The Ritual Process: Structure and Anti-Structure*, Ithaca, NY: Cornell University Press, 1991; and Schechner's *Performance Theory*, London: Routledge, 1994). The journal *Ritual Studies* demonstrates the vitality of this sub-discipline. Once again, any decent introduction to the study of religions or anthropology will include relevant discussions, and it may be interesting to consider the choice of labelling such material 'ritual', 'performance' or the potentially more inclusive 'praxis: religious action'. These are strategies employed respectively by Fiona Bowie (*The Anthropology of Religion*, Oxford: Blackwell, 2000), Catherine Bell (in Mark Taylor (ed.), *Critical Terms for Religious Studies*, University of Chicago Press, 1998) and Michael Lambek (*A Reader in the Anthropology of Religion*, Oxford: Blackwell, 2002). Tae-gon Kim and Mihály Hoppál have edited a valuable collection entitled *Shamanism in Performing Arts* (Budapest: Akadémiai Kiadó, 1995) that illustrates some of what is possible when particular kinds of shamanic performance are considered in the light of these recent trends in Performance Studies.

Further intriguing possibilities are suggested by applying insights from carnivalesque approaches arising from Mikhail Bakhtin's *Rabelais and his World* (Cambridge, MA: MIT Press, 1968) – especially as debated in Peter Stallybrass and Allon White's *The Politics and Poetics of Transgression* (Ithaca, NY: Cornell University Press, 1986). Perhaps a consideration of technoshamanism (or cyberian shamanism) would be the most obvious focus for such a study. If so, it may well be helpful to approach it in dialogue with contributions to John Wood's edited *The Virtual Embodied: presence/practice/technology* (London: Routledge, 1998).

Meanwhile, knowledge has also been generative of both a large body of excellent research and writing and also of a section in my edited *Readings in Indigenous Religions*. Discussions in the journal *Anthropology of Consciousness* and various Internet lists and newsgroups exemplify trends of central importance here. Geoffrey Samuel's *Mind, Body and Culture* (Cambridge: Cambridge University Press, 1990) is a good example of what is possible here. There are obvious applications of knowledge about shamans and/or shamanic knowledges to the various debates about nature or ecology. Vitebsky's article in this book might well be complemented by consideration of debates in ecopsychology and environmentalism.

Recognition of the rights of indigenous owners of traditional knowledges has combined with strong indigenous interventions into academic domains that coincide with post- and anti-colonial trajectories. A brilliant and authoritative exemplar of the possibility of challenging Western assumptions with particular indigenous knowledge is provided by Eduardo Viveiros de Castro's 'Cosmological Deixis and Amerindian Perspectivism' (*Journal of the Royal Anthropological Institute* n.s. 4(3): 469–88). This may help readers change perceptions that indigenous peoples repeat untenable myths (perhaps until they receive the benefits of Western religions or sciences) and clarify some powerful aspects of the world experienced by shamans and their neighbours. Key here is a challenge to the assumption which underpins academia and its disciplines that there are many diverse cultures embedded in a singular common nature (illustrated in the distinction between 'natural' and 'social' sciences). Amazonian Amerindian perspectives critique that foundational position. If Amerindians are correct, there are many natures masking the singular culture of all who live – and that includes jaguars and vultures as well as humans. If we allow ourselves to be challenged, rather than marginalizing this perspective as a quaint or romantic enchantment or a mystifying illusion, we may find that shamans (those who train to see past the different natures to the cultural realities) have much to teach the West. It is arguable that, generally speaking, shamans have functioned in Western discourses as peculiar aliens or as parts of the scenery. Descriptions (whether ethnographically rich or naïvely appropriative) are collected and decorate displays in various media about more-or-less distant 'others'. Sometimes they may have been allowed to say something about 'alternative therapies' or privatised and internal spiritualities. Here, however, is a perspective that may encourage considerable expansion and enriching of human knowledge.

Some other areas may be worth following up for those interested in what is happening at the forefront of academic engagement with shamans. It is important to avoid separating shamans (and perhaps shamanists) from other indigenous peoples. Thus, a broader reading of discussions about indigenous cultures and religions will enrich understanding. In addition to the *Readings in Indigenous Religions* (Harvey 2002) cited above, I have edited a collection of important essays entitled, *Indigenous Religions: A Companion* (London: Continuum, 2000). Other general works cited above will be helpful as leads to broader debates.

Ethnobotany (the study of plants known and utilised by particular peoples) has devoted considerable attention to the plants and other natural derivatives that aid shamans and other healers and knowers. Michael Harner's early contribution to the genre is 'The Sound of Rushing Water' (*Natural History* 77(6) (1968): 28–33). Plants and derivatives that have been of particular interest include *ayahuasca*, psilocybin, peyote, fly agaric, and DMT. McKenna's chapter in this book introduces these and the names of experimenters and scholars. What to call experiences caused by the substances of interest here should not be mistaken for mere pedantry. The label 'hallucination' indicates a false vision or illusion, and suggests irrationality, sickness and 'drug abuse'. Similarly, 'psychedelics' and 'psycho-actives' carry connotations that might be alien to the understanding of those to whom particular plants or derivatives are helpful. In fact, 'visionary' might not be any less helpful if it suggests that what is seen is either not real or transcends mundane reality. If shamans are correct, what they see is what is there, it is not them but others who are misled by reliance on unaided sight. The term 'entheogens' is now becoming popular, implying that particular plants might help someone 'become divine within'. Useful discussions of these issues include R. E. Schultes and A. Hofman's *Plants of the Gods* (Rochester: Healing Arts, 1992), M. Ripinsky-Naxon's *The Nature of Shamanism* (New York: SUNY, 1993), Jonathan Ott's *Pharmacotheon* (Kennewick: Natural Products, 1996), Chas Clifton's 'If Witches No Longer Fly . . . ' (in *The Pomegranate: The Journal of Pagan Studies* 16 (2001): 17–23) and Robert Wallis's *Shamans/Neo-Shamans* (London: Routledge, 2002).

Not entirely disconnected from discussion of the use of stimulants of various kinds is the continuing debate about similarities and differences between shamanic experiences, trance and possession. Another Internet or library search for 'possession' or 'trance' will provide plenty of possible avenues for further discussion. Rather than entering or even surveying that debate, I want to suggest a trajectory arising from yet another debate. It is common (in academic discussions at least) to wonder whether 'shamanism' is specific to Siberia or whether it is really found in other places. Thus a consideration of the literature about 'possession' in the religions that evolved in the African diasporas may be exciting. Margarite Fernández Olmos and Lizabeth Paravisini-Gebert's edited *Sacred Possessions* (New Brunswick: Rutgers University Press, 1999) is a good starting point for that discussion. Its subtitle is helpful: *Vodou, Santería, Obeah and the Caribbean*. Paul Johnson's *Gossip and Gods: Brazilian Candomblé and the Transformation of a Secret Slave Society into a Public Religion* (New York: Oxford University Press, 2002) adds another important element for consideration: the continuing evolution of indigenous traditions entangled with the realities of a changing world.

Music is significant to most shamanic performance. The construction of shamanism as 'techniques for achieving ecstasy' or other 'altered states of consciousness' should lead swiftly to interest in the study of shamanic musics. Keith Howard's article 'Sacred and Profane: Music in Korean Shaman Rituals' (in Karen Ralls MacLeod and Graham Harvey (eds) *Indigenous Religious Musics*, Aldershot: Ashgate, 2001: 56–83) is exceptionally helpful here. Not only does it explore the distinctive pursuits of shamans in Korea, it questions the assumption that 'sacred' and 'profane' are separate domains, and does so with skilful reference to musics of various kinds. The article (and the rest of the book) establish some helpful orientations to ethnomusicology (the study of musics performed by particular peoples). David Turner's article in that book, 'From Here into Eternity: Power and Transcendence in Australian Aboriginal Music' (pp. 35–55) offers similar potential in relation to musics as Olmos and Paravisini's book does in relation to 'possession'. That is, although there is debate about whether 'shaman' should be applied to practitioners of Vodou or to Aboriginal Australians, the study of shamans and shamanisms might well benefit from seeing what happens in neighbouring contexts.

Sometimes (if not always) novels convey the creativity and playfulness of people's passionate concerns – whether entangled in everyday life or exalted in ecstatic visions – better than academic texts replete with footnotes and distance. Although there is an increasing library of excellent indigenous writing, little of it is concerned with shamans. Neo-shamans and techno-shamans are, however, highly visible in works that might be labelled 'fantasy' or 'cyberpunk'. Among the most famous of the former are Brian Bates' *The Way of Wyrd* (London: Arrow, 1983) and Marion Bradley's *Mists of Avalon* (London: Sphere, 1984). Robert Holdstock's works, beginning with *Mythago Wood* (London: Grafton, 1984), might convey a darker and more disturbing side of Western understanding of shamanry. The most famous of the books featuring technoshamans is William Gibson's *Neuromancer* (London: HarperCollins, 1995). Again, this genre now proliferates. Technoshamans are, arguably, better encountered in cyberspace than in imaginative litera-ture. Among the most useful Internet newsgroup and discussion list is alt.techno-shamanism newsgroup.

Gender issues are also important in recent developments. The chapters by Saladin d'Anglure and Balzer in this volume provide excellent foundations and useful pointers to further discussions. An interesting location for new thinking about shamans and gender is in relation to North European traditions. Jenny Blain and Robert J. Wallis offer a valuable orientation in 'The "ergi" seidman: contestations of gender, shamanism and sexuality in northern religion, past and present' (in the *Journal of Contemporary Religion* 15(3) (2000): 395–411). Blain's *Nine Worlds of Seid-Magic: Ecstasy and Neo-shamanism in North European Paganism* (London: Routledge, 2002) and Wallis' forthcoming *Shamans/Neo-Shamans: An Autoarchaeology of Heathen and Druidic Ecstasies, 'Wannabe Indians' and 'Plastic' Medicine Men* (London: Routledge, 2003) extend and enrich the debate considerably.

There are additional benefits of these works to the student of shamans. Blain's discussion arises from the application of recent anthropological methodologies to the study of Heathens. Much of the writing by or about neo-shamanisms has focused on traditions that are labelled 'Celtic' – among the best of these are the various works of John and Caitlin Matthews (John Matthews, *The Celtic Shaman*, Rider, 2001; Caitlin Matthews, *Singing the Soul Back Home*, Element Books, 1995; John and Caitlin Matthews, *Taliesin: The Last Celtic Shaman*, Inner Traditions, 2002). Blain's work offers new and exciting insights rooted in encounters with those who claim another ancient heritage. Finally, Wallis' work draws attention to another growing area of important debate: the archaeology of shamanisms. Unlike the work of Eliade (which dismissed contemporary shamans as corrupt exemplars of a once more noble spirituality), archaeology now debates the utility of contemporary shamanic (and neo-shamanic) perspectives in understanding rock art and other archaeological sources of data.

In these brief notes I have attempted to suggest a few key texts indicative of some recent trends in the study of shamanism without replicating too much of what is referred to earlier in this book.

Index